Reflections upon a Family

Reflections upon a Family

Teddy Gosden & Boston Sturgess – a perfect match!

Keith Gosden

Privately published 2025
Text © Keith Gosden 2025
ISBN 978-1-3999-9805-5
All photographs © Keith Gosden and members of the Gosden family,
Except where specified as a footnote to the image.

Design and layout by Kaarin Wall, Wiz Graphics, Norfolk
Image reprographics by Kevin Parker, Norfolk
Printed and bound in the UK by Page Bros (Norwich) Ltd, Norfolk

Dedicated to

Kate, the wider Gosden family as it is in 2025 and for all future generations.

Contents

Introduction	9
Prologue	12

Part One

Chapter 1 Arriving & Living in Kent 1955 – 1960	19
Chapter 2 School, Scouting & Eaton Village 1960 – 1973	35
Chapter 3 Work, Marriage & Children 1972 – 1990	90

Part Two

Chapter 4 A Fresh start, JP & Move to Bodham 1991 – 1993	137
Chapter 5 Married life, Extensions & Exams 1993 – 1999	174
Chapter 6 Ground up with Flints & Blocks 1999 – 2014	245

Part Three

Chapter 7 Life in Retirement 2014 – 2025	407
Chapter 8 The Gosden Mystery	622

Endnote	626
Acknowledgements	629

Appendices

Keith meaning: Outdoorsy	633
Family Tree	634
Synopsis of Recent Relatives	636

Introduction

Why a memoir and not an autobiography? My understanding is that there are key differences. One definition of an autobiography describes it as being a factual and historical account of one's entire life, from beginning to end. Clearly my life has not concluded yet, so if this definition is correct, thankfully, this title is not appropriate.

A memoir is an accurate narrative by which I, as the author, can shine a torch into the dark and sometimes distant memories, to record and share these times of growing up in Kent, moving to Norfolk, through to living in Holt. So, to me, this latter description most aptly defines this book of my life and experiences to date. It has been divided into three distinct parts: 1955-1990, 1991-2014 and 2014-2025, all accompanied by relevant photographs and documents. The rationale for dividing this memoir into three distinguishing parts is explained at the commencement of each of these sections. Within the appendices I have given some additional information, via a family tree and a brief summary of key members of my paternal relations where details are known. I hope that this will enrich your understanding of where my background and possibly some of my personality has derived.

At this point, I should like to say that the memories contained in the narrative, especially through my early years, reflect a period when the society and its attitudes were very different and do not necessarily conform to what we now refer to as 'political correctness'. In my early years my parents, like many other friends' parents, were very happy for me to be 'out and about' all day, only returning home when I was hungry. It didn't mean they were less protective towards me, it was simply that society was very different to how it is today. Some would say safer but that's a matter of personal opinion. It is for you, the reader, to make a judgement on the development of these principles, just as it is my role simply to record my memories of the time. Therefore, I have recalled times, incidences, situations and language which I grew up with, that today may be questionable, but as I have said times and attitudes change. That's progress, so please don't be offended.

There are family issues within this memoir that some, I am sure, will have a contrary view to mine. These, of course, will be their own memories of events and life in general. The narrative in this book though, recounts my memories be they right or wrong and from Part Two onwards they are supported by our contemporaneous diary entries. Time will be the judge but for me, at the time of writing, they are a correct reflection of my thoughts, recounted as accurately as I can, in an honest attempt to share them without bias or malice.

I know that there are some elements of my life that for various reasons don't necessarily need to be recorded or recounted. I feel a memoir allows for this discretion and if appropriate to be carefully and discreetly used.

So why, you may well ask, write anything at all? Well, I have been fascinated over the years whilst listening to the stories of my family's life, as related to me by my parents and other family members. I would like to think that these narratives and my own exploits are interesting enough to those who follow me in this world, to warrant them being recorded for future generations. Also, current and future family readers of this memoir-*cum*-scrapbook may wish to understand from where they themselves originate and why certain traits are held deep within their own psyche.

Out of courtesy both my sisters Judy and Sarah, along with our children Emily, Oliver and Sophie, have each been given a printed draft copy of this memoir and invited to identify any suggested corrections. Where these suggestions have been accepted they have been included within the text.

If this book helps the current and ultimately future generations to understand my own personal *Reflections upon a Family*, and is interesting enough for the reader to 'enjoy the read' then my aim has been achieved. Moreover, whilst writing this memoir I have discovered that for me it has been a greatly rewarding and cathartic process. I hope, therefore, that you enjoy reading the contents as much as I have enjoyed researching, composing and writing them.

Postscript

Having read the printed draft of this memoir I am immensely pleased and proud of my finished work. However, I am also very conscious that this has 'exposed' my lack of understanding of both the English language and its grammar. This has been primarily due to my lack of concentration and effort whilst I was at school.

As a result, I accept there are paragraphs and sentences that could have been written in a more succinct and fluent way had I, of course, been more attentive during my English lessons! Some of these syntax errors have been brought to my attention by both my wife and others who have read the drafts.

Whilst I have conceded that some 'adjustments' needed to be made, I have stood steadfast and dug my heels in, in order that this should remain a true reflection of me, my life, including my level of education. As such, I have resisted changing certain sections to avoid the text appearing to have been drafted by someone else. So, when you read this please be aware and understand that this memoir truly reflects me, my personality, warts and all. Therefore, some sentences or sections may appear 'clunky' or 'longwinded' but they do portray the true me, not someone pretending to be an English scholar.

Thank you.

Prologue

I have included a prologue to add some more in-depth context to the main text. Whilst this is useful, it is not necessary to understand the memoir.

Post World War II England in the 1950s, the decade of my birth, was a very different place to the one in which I write this memoir. The currency of pounds, shillings and pence (£/s/d), referred to as LSD was the main method of paying for items. However, the association to the 1960s and 1970s recreational use of the drug Lysergic acid diethylamide or LSD for short, was yet to be inferred.

Unlike today, the household finances were often managed by the 'man of the house' who was of course the husband, as unmarried couples living together was not commonplace. As such the 'lady of the house' was often given from the husband's salary, a set sum each week for 'housekeeping'. She probably wasn't in employment, as job opportunities for ladies were very limited and unlike today regrettably few aspired to higher levels of responsibility.

High Street banks were used for large purchases, such as cars and housing deposits etc., whilst cash (£/s/d) was mainly used to pay for household items and daily shopping. The idea of credit cards had only just been thought of by Frank McNamara, in 1950, in New York. He pursued this concept with his business partner, Ralph Schneider and together they developed the Diners Card. This is comparable in function to today's credit card, but it wasn't until 1966/1967 that a UK credit card was launched by Barclaycard, for the wider public. Other banks were soon to follow, working together to launch the Interbank Card Association (ICA), which was subsequently renamed to Mastercard, in 1979. This was followed in 1996, by Europay, Mastercard and Visa[1] developing the first international standard for contactless payment by bank cards. All these financial developments were to lead to a permanent change in how society conducted its transactions.

At the time of my birth there were neither computers nor the internet, although I can claim to have been born in the same year as Sir Timothy John Berners-Lee, the inventor of the World Wide Web (WWW) and who was born on 8 June 1955.

---

1 Credit to https://banks.am>news>fintech

The future development of both the WWW and the internet, coupled with the use of credit and debit cards for financial transactions, regrettably, was to open up opportunities for the increase of fraudulent behaviour.

In Parliament led by the UK's Second World War leader, Winston S. Churchill, it was recorded in Hansard, in April 1955, that the actual average weekly earnings for men, aged 21 and over, was £10/17/5[2], which in 2025 is equivalent to circa £362.00. In 2024 the average weekly wage has risen to £678. This shows that over the intervening years the value of wages has almost doubled.

Televisions were a luxury item so most people, including my parents, obtained their news through newspapers and the radio. In the late 1940s and early 1950s, the two main national newspapers were the *Daily Express* and the *Daily Mirror*, with circulation figures of 3.8m and 3.7m respectively. Some were more focused e.g. *The Financial Times* which specialised on the financial sector of society, whilst others concentrated on regional news, such as the *Manchester Guardian*. As expected, both the *Manchester Guardian* and *The Financial Times* each had a much lower circulation of around 200,000. Then, due to the myriad of other sources and methods of circulating the news around the world, mainly using the internet or television, the popularity of newspapers dwindled, and in 2024 the circulation of the *Daily Mirror* was recorded as 240,799 and the *Daily Express* at 152,699. A clear indication that during my lifetime our society was moving into a digital age.

Figure 1

In the 1950s / 60s private telephones were around but not everyone had a landline connected and even if you did it may have been a 'party line'. By that I mean one shared with another subscriber. If this was the case you could actually pick up the handset and hear their conversation, so you then had to wait until it was concluded before you could make your own telephone call. The alternative was to use a public telephone located in a tall, red, 'walk in' kiosk – this was always assuming that to pay for your call you had enough pennies to insert into the machine. The first boxes to appear on the streets, in 1921, were of a concrete construction and these were designated by the Post Office as K1

---

2   Hansard – 21 February 1956 – Commons Sitting – NATIONAL FINANCE

(Kiosk No 1). The more familiar style K6 (Fig. 1)[3], resulted from a winning entry by Sir Giles Gilbert Scott, in a competition to design a modern replacement for the K1. Scott's winning entry was put into service from 1926, and they and their successors were normally found at railway stations, close to local shops or other areas where there was a congregation of the public. I can recall seeing and using these when I was a young lad. Today, most of these telephone kiosks have been removed and either sold as ornaments for gardens, converted to house a defibrillator, or providing space for small libraries.

Mobile telephones were years away. It wasn't until 3 April 1973 that Martin Cooper, a company engineer at Motorola, made a step towards modernity with a 'mobile' call to another telecommunications company. He told them that he was using a mobile phone that was one not using a fixed landline, and this particular call was the very first communication in the world that wasn't linked directly to a cord or cable.[4] These large and bulky devices, something I can personally vouch for, could only make telephone calls. So there was no facility, as there is in 2025, to search on your mobile for any kind of information. We had to wait until 1999 for that privilege.[5]

Whilst the ownership of cars was rising from around two million in the mid-1930s, the start of Britain's motor revolution was yet to kick in. Car ownership grew from four million in 1950, to over 31 million in 2007.[6] Therefore, in the 1950s, travel by train, public transport, motorbike or foot was the order of the day, for most people.

As I have outlined earlier, this brief summary has described life in the 1950s and compared that era to how it is whilst writing this memoir in 2024/25, our society back then was certainly very different. What is more significant though, is that due to the increased levels of technology and ingenuity, the demands by our modern society have correspondingly increased.

For many people, in 1950 most of these changes were inconceivable. In 2025 we take these for granted and the advances in technology seem no longer to astound us. For example, in 1977 the USA launched Voyager 1 an un-manned spacecraft which by 2024 had travelled some 15 billion miles from Earth, further than any other man-made object. This was still in direct communication with

---

3 Example of a K6 model photographed in London 2012. Credit Wikipedia.org
4 https://www.uswitch.com/mobiles/guides/history-of-mobile-phone
5 https://www.pingdom.com/blog/15-fantastic-firsts-on-the-internet
6 Transport Statistics Great Britain 2011: Vehicles summary – GOV.UK

the National Aeronautics and Space Administration (NASA) in Washington, USA. It was not even the main news story, so it seems that we should just expect these achievements and to take them in our stride. I guess our expectations and beliefs in what man can achieve have simply moved on to a point where nothing seems impossible.

Now to the reality of my immediate relations. I was born in 1955 into a close, supportive and loving family unit that whilst being numerous was not extensive in its depth. It only extended, on my father's side, to three living generations, as can be seen by the photograph overleaf.

The oldest generation which included my parents and their siblings, had a wide and extensive knowledge of hardship, having either lived through or, in some cases, served in World War Two (WWII). This wreaked extensive destruction by the enemy on the UK's infrastructure, and the means of obtaining merchandise necessitated rationing for the wider population.

Everyone, man, woman and child had their own book that had to be taken to a specific shop, where the retailer had had their name and address stamped inside the front cover. My father's ration book is shown here (Fig. 2). Once the purchase had been made that particular retailer would stamp the book and remove the counterfoil for that week's ration. Fortunately, only a year prior to my birth this 'hardship' ceased in 1954, with meat being the last commodity to be de-rationed.

Figure 2

I think that these hardships gave my parents' generation a very different outlook on the world, than those of succeeding generations. My parents were grateful and content with their life, and whilst they didn't lack ambition, they knew that to achieve their goals they needed to work hard, save well and be satisfied when they reached the limits of their achievements. My personal view, of many members of their subsequent generations, is that they rather expect success and the bounty of life, but not the hard work required to accomplish these rewards. This is not a criticism, but more an observation of the change in how society has developed.

Overleaf (Fig. 3) is the earliest 'formal' family photograph that I have. It was taken in 1987, in Chaldon, Kent, in the back garden, on the occasion of my Uncle Cyril and Aunt Mabel Gosden's fiftieth wedding anniversary.

Figure 3

Standing left to right – Raquel Gosden (David's wife), David Gosden (Cyril's son), Jeannette Gosden (Keith's wife), Keith Gosden, Judith [Judy] Riddington (my elder sister), Roger Wiltshire (Sarah's husband), Tara Riddington (Judy's eldest daughter), David Riddington (Judy's husband), Win Horton (Cyril's sister), Len Gosden (Cyril's brother and my father), Ruth Mason (Cyril's daughter), Joyce Bennie (Mabel's niece), Peter Mason (Ruth's husband), Robert Hall (Mabel's nephew), Ann Hall, Nellie Hall, Fred Hall (Mabel's brother)

Seated middle left to right – Christopher Gosden (David's son – holding Raquel's hand), Sarah Wiltshire (my younger sister – holding her son David Wiltshire), Christine Horton (Win's daughter), Daphne Gosden (Len's wife and my mother), Mabel Gosden (Cyril's wife), Cyril Gosden (first name Thomas, Len's elder brother)

Seated front left to right – Rebecca Wiltshire (Sarah's daughter), Sophie Gosden (my daughter), Katy Riddington (Judy's younger daughter), Stuart Riddington (Judy's son), Oliver Gosden (my son), Philip Mason (Ruth's son), John Mason, Alan Hall (Robert's son)

PART ONE

In the first chapter of this book, whilst I am recalling times that are embedded in my memory, some of the details have either been passed down to me, or 'gleaned' over the years, from other family members.

From Chapter 2 onwards the recollections are very much my own thoughts and views. As I have already indicated, I can appreciate that other family members may have differing reminiscences of the same times and events but as this book contains my memoirs, I trust that you will understand that it is written from my perspective and recollections.

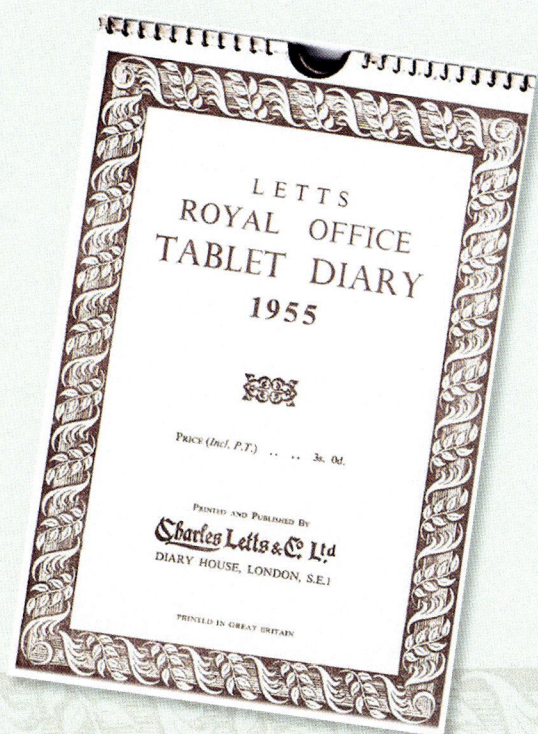

CHAPTER 1

Arriving & Living in Kent 1955 – 1960

Now, turning to my arrival: 26 February 1955 was a cold and slightly foggy Saturday morning. In a period when Great Britain was being affected by the worst winter storms, for many years, which caused road and rail disruptions and problems with food and medical supplies. My mother, Daphne Barbara Gosden, was in the Sidcup Ward of Farnborough Hospital, in Kent, awaiting the imminent arrival of her second child. The first being Judith Linda Gosden, who was born just two years previously, on 21 February.

All was well and Daphne had finished a light breakfast. It became clear that baby was on its way and sure enough at 07.45 I was delivered without issue, in what was described on my hospital tag (Fig. 4), as a 'spontaneous' birth. Weighing a healthy 7lb 5½oz and 20" (inches) in length, I was given to my exhausted and delighted mother. My father Leonard (Len) Montague Gosden was equally proud, as I was his first and only son, thus the male line was secured for the next generation. But what would my generation experience and bring to bear on the wider population?

Figure 4

It was around this time that I first met Teddy Gosden, a wonderful and loyal teddy bear that was almost as big as me and has remained with me through thick and thin! One day I was sure that like me, he was to find a soulmate.

After a short stay in hospital I, with my mother, went home. I know the stay was short, as all but one of the 'New Baby' cards and letters sent to my parents, were addressed to our home at 20 Allington Road, Orpington, Kent (Fig. 5).[7]

---

7   2012 Google image

Figure 5

Figure 6

Number 20 is on the left, with a small car in the drive. This was where my parents would be to receive the congratulatory post. The one exception to these cards was a lovely letter from my great-grandmother Alice Killick, who lived at 10 Church Road, Bromley, Kent. Her letter was posted on 2 March to 'Mrs Gosden, Sidcup Ward, Maternity Department, Farnborough Hospital, Kent. It arrived at the hospital and was then duly taken home with me. Whilst I did meet Great-Grandmother Alice, when I was a little older, I can't in all honesty recall much about her. However, later there will be more on her and the influence she had on me. At the age of six months, I was an archetypal bouncing baby (Fig. 6).

My home was a lovely but small, three bedroomed, semi-detached bungalow built in 1938. Of the three bedrooms, two were at the front and the left-hand side one had a bay window. From the age of five Judy and I shared the right-hand bedroom, with my bed being the furthest from the window and against the wall of the dining/living room. My parents had the left-hand bedroom. I recall that when you entered the bungalow through the front door there was a central hall that led to a small kitchen on the left, which overlooked the back garden. This was accessed from the kitchen back door, located to the left of the pantry. From the kitchen door you could go down two or three concrete steps, turn right and walk past the coal bunker. I remember that in the spring, this area was full of lily of the valley. It was glorious and something to this day that I am unable to replicate in my current garden. More's the pity. The Orpington garden was long and narrow, with a low hedge to the left side. To the right there was a wooden fence. The two earliest photographs I have of me are taken in our back garden. The christening photograph (Fig. 7), taken after the service on 21 August 1955 at St. Paul's, Crofton, presumably by my father as he is not included, shows on the far left, George Mars one of my godfathers, next to my mother who is holding me, my other godfather Ron Sewell and his wife Sheila my godmother, holding their

Chapter 1 Arriving & Living in Kent 1955 – 1960

Figure 7

Figure 8

daughter Hilary. To her left is Judy, my sister, seated with her doll, clearly not at all interested in the gathering!

The other photograph (Fig. 8) was also in the garden on the same occasion and shows far left, my grandmother (Nanny Randall), centre her sister, my Auntie Bobby, and of course my mother, with her left hand raised.

This is the only photograph I have found of all three of them together.

Figure 9

In the photograph (Fig. 9), taken a few months later, I am seen presumably holding the handle of a walking aid, of some sort, whilst Judy is holding her doll and looking much more interested in what is going on.

In another later incident, I was told, as I have no recollection of this event, that as a very young toddler but old enough to be in the garden on my own, I returned rushing into the kitchen and went straight to my room in some distress. When questioned by my mum, all I could say was that *'I have been sent in by...'* [Auntie Nellie, the next door neighbour.] Apparently, it transpired that I had been rude to her and as a punishment she sent me inside, but no one ever found out, or if they did they never revealed what was said to upset her. Happy days!

This didn't prevent me or Judy from enjoying ourselves, either on the stepladders in the front garden or on the swing in the back garden, as these

Figure 10

two photographs (Fig. 10) demonstrate. Why we were allowed to play on step ladders is a complete mystery other than I guess we were close to Dad who was also in the garden. Given our ages at the time and the Health & Safety concerns of today, playing on step ladders isn't something that would be recommended!

Whilst living at Allington Road I can recall many more lovely times for fun and laughter. One such time was at Christmas when I found that Father Christmas had left some parcels in a pillowcase on my bed, and within this was a large, yellow, plastic cricket bat. My Nanny and Grandad seemed to know all about it as, apparently, they had spoken to Father Christmas!

Figure 11

Bedtimes were always accompanied by Mum reading the next section of my favourite book, *The Magic Faraway Tree* by Enid Blyton. This magical story described how three young children, Jo, Bessie and Fanny found a tree in the Enchanted Wood, which they climbed to the very top. Whilst on the way they met the fairy-folk who lived inside it (Fig. 11)[8].

The children 'entered' their world and on their adventures met other friendly characters including Moon-Face, Silky, Mr Watzisname and my favourite

---

8   Image credited to and copyright of The Enid Blyton Society

The Saucepan Man, who always had a saucepan as a hat!

Whilst I snuggled down inside my bed, all warm and cosy, Mum would beautifully read the many adventures had by these children. I recall that they would have many exciting experiences with their new friends, like eating Pop Biscuits and sliding down the Slippery Slip, which was inside the trunk of the tree and took the children right back down to the ground. At the very top of the tree though, they entered different lands such as the Land of Take-What-You-Want and the Land of Topsy and Turvy.

All these different stories were such fun to listen to and not at all scary. At the conclusion of each one though, I was left wanting more but had to wait for the next bedtime. I guess this was a very subtle way of Mum getting me into bed, which certainly worked!

The book also had some wonderful illustrations that she and I both enjoyed looking at and chatting about, before I was tucked in, given a good night kiss and drifted into a deep sleep. The perfect way to end a day.

However, despite the bedtime story there was at least one occasion when I was not happy about the outcome of waking up one morning. Early each day the milkman came up the road with his faithful steed and horse-drawn milk float and stopped outside our house. I would be taken outside in order that I could both stroke his horse and probably give it something to munch upon. On this specific day though, to my horror he arrived with neither his horse nor float but instead he had a float that was electric, with a built-in driver's cab! Apparently, I was mortified but I guess that's progress. However, I can still recall the disappointment, which I probably expressed in no uncertain terms to both my mother and the poor unsuspecting milkman!

I have to admit that I could certainly cause a fuss but not as much as the noise that woke me up on 15 June 1960.

There was something going on that was not normal and calling out to my dad he came into my bedroom to explain. Lifting me from my warm and safe bed, he took me across the hall and into his and Mum's bedroom. There I saw my mother cradling my new baby sister, Sarah. Clearly, now I had competition on the 'fuss' front! Judy and I both look very pleased though, when the photograph (Fig. 12) was taken in the back garden.

Figure 12

With Sarah, we all settled into number 20 which, with your back to Oregon Square, was about halfway down Allington Road, on the righthand side. At the far end was where Judy and I went to Nursery School, but more on that later. On the left-hand side of Allington Road and opposite our house, were a line of prefabs. These hastily built temporary homes had been built during or just after WWII, as an exploding bomb had destroyed the previous houses. Judy and I would often go across the road to be with an old gentleman who lived in one of the prefabs. Although he was blind, he seemed to know who we were, and from memory he was very kind. Anyway, all three of us seemed to enjoy each other's company.

Enjoying 'other people's company' was certainly something that was paramount at our Nursery School, run by Mr and Mrs Upsdell. The school was located at the bottom of our road, in a semi-detached bungalow and comprised of just seven or eight children. From my recollection we seemed to do nothing but either played in the garden or in the air-raid shelter, which was great fun; learnt how to tell the time; listened to the steam trains on the railway, making their way to and from London; sang songs whilst Mr Upsdell played the piano; or simply drank orange squash. It was a wonderful introduction to education and it's just a pity that the curriculum in the next few schools wasn't the same!

For a short time during the day, Mr and Mrs Upsdell were both lovely substitute parents but then I guess I knew in my heart that I was always going back home, so I wasn't concerned by the change of location.

We all knew them as Auntie Dora and Uncle Wal, for back in the late 50s everyone outside the immediate family, no matter what their actual relationship was to you, was either an uncle or an aunt. By coincidence, my parents before they moved up the road to number 20, had lived in the adjacent semi-detached bungalow, number 134 (Fig. 13) which was next door to the school. This property was later to be occupied by Wal and Dora's daughter and son-in-law, who will appear in my life a little later on. I don't recall much about Dora, although we did keep in contact, and years later she came to Hingham to visit us. Wal, on the other hand, was much better known to us all, as

Figure 13

he was an accomplished pianist and had been a fireman in London, during WWII. Regrettably he lived with Parkinson's disease, and I was led to believe this was a result of unexpected explosions, in the area of London where he was firefighting. At my tender years his condition was not obvious, but as we grew up and visited he slowly deteriorated, to a point where he became bedbound.

One of the many 'treats' from Mum or Dad was to walk up Allington Road to the Kelvin Parade of shops in Oregon Square. Whilst I was not in the least bit interested in the main shops that needed to be visited to obtain essential groceries, I knew that if I behaved myself, there was a chance I would be allowed to visit the shop at the far end of the parade. The importance of this venue was that it was a newsagent, and not only did it sell comics but far more importantly it sold sweets and 1^d (one old penny) ice lollies. So, behaving myself was well worth it!

During these very early years, my sisters and I were able to visit our maternal grandparents, Nanny (Mabel Randall née Killick) and Grandad Randall, as they lived quite close by, in a small house called 'The Croft', located at the top of Footbury Hill Road in Orpington. Indeed, they had lived at 'The Croft' for many years and our mother was brought up there. See photograph (Fig. 14) with my grandmother [Nanny] outside. Also, a more modern photograph (Fig. 15) which puts the house into context with the more recent properties around it. I have been told that Grandad designed The Croft and had it built, but this I have been unable to independently verify. Nanny was really kind and whilst I recall getting on famously with Grandad, he was, according to others in the family, an indifferent and reserved man. I do recall him as a man of habit, sitting in the same chair in the lounge, next to the fireplace, smoking a pipe, reading

Figure 14

Figure 15

the paper or listening to 'The Archers'. This is still a popular radio series, based on the fictitious UK farming family, the Archers and their neighbours, which I still avidly listen to today.

Grandad was an engineer by trade and worked for Creeds in Croydon, who were famous for inventing and manufacturing the Teleprinter. Due to Grandad's electrical expertise, he was fortunate and capable enough to be able to build his own wireless (Fig. 16) and have one of the early wireless licences! He was often to be found in his garage, at the back of the house, tinkering with his motorbike or making something for use in the house or garden. My mother was an only child and conceived whilst they were on honeymoon, so was very close and special to her parents. That parental bond had a very dramatic influence on my life.

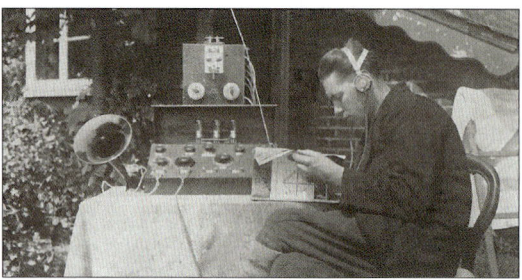

Figure 16

It's important to explain here that my sisters and I grew up with just one set of grandparents, my mother's parents. My father's father had died a few months prior to my parents' wedding, and was tragically followed, the next year, by the death of our paternal grandmother. Further details are provided in the appendices.

Before I elaborate on how our maternal grandmother's influence played an important part in my upbringing, it is important to put some context around the world's events at the time. In the immediate aftermath of WWII, Australia and New Zealand needed to increase their population, to enable them to rebuild defences and further their economic development. To achieve this a large-scale immigration programme was launched to attract mainly UK citizens, through the promises of a better life, a warmer climate, good jobs and a well subsidised outward journey ticket, by ship, for only £10!

During the period 1947-1971,[9] in total 76,673 immigrants, who were mostly from the UK, accepted this offer to emigrate to New Zealand.

Those who emigrated from the UK were known colloquially, in New Zealand, as 'pommies', hence the name '£10 Poms'. Whilst I am not sure of the

---

9   https://nzhistory.govt.nz/

exact timings, it was very probably around 1956-57 that both my parents saw this exciting, fresh start in New Zealand as a wonderful opportunity and were keen to investigate further.

My elder sister and I were young children growing up in the era of the '£10 Pom'. We all went off to London and the picture (Fig. 17) shows us in Trafalgar Square, presumably either on our way to apply or maybe even sign up to emigrate. However, my maternal grandmother wasn't prepared to see her only daughter and two grandchildren whisked off to the other side of the world, leaving her in the UK. I can only wonder and speculate on the conversations, and needless to say we didn't emigrate! Her influence kept my future life in the UK, for which I am most grateful. So, thankfully, that was where we all remained and continued to build our lives in Kent. Not for long though, as Dad's employment was to take us all to Norfolk, but I will outline these details later.

Figure 17

Figure 18

Another maternal influencer was my great-grandmother Alice (née Mayne), seen here (Fig. 18) circa 1895, on her engagement to George Killick, my great grandad. Alice, as you recall, was the lady who wrote to my mother in hospital. Her influence came when she lived at 10 Church Road, Bromley, Kent which was where we would often visit. Her property was a large Victorian end terrace, rented from the local church. The property was entered via the side gate that led you up a cinder path, edged with scallop shells. The back door led into a room, and below this, which was known as 'below stairs', we could go into the kitchen. Whilst this was a dark room, as it was lit by just one main electric light, supplemented by the sunlight that came from the sash window, albeit below ground, with a metal grille above at ground level, it was warm, cosy and often smelt of freshly baked cakes etc. Clearly the hub of the house. It is within this room that I became fixated with a wooden plaque that hung above, what was to me, a huge range/fireplace. It probably wasn't that big but being under five, it certainly seemed enormous. The plaque was inscribed with the words '*North, South, East or West, Home is Best*'. I loved that plaque so much that following my great-grandmother's subsequent death, my mother endeavoured to retrieve it for me when she learnt that the properties in Church Road were being demolished. Regrettably, she was unsuccessful, but those words and the image have stayed with me to this day.

Figure 19

I should say here that there was another relation on my maternal side who was also influential on my early upbringing. This was my Nanny Randall's sister, Auntie Florence Killick, known as 'Bobby' (Fig. 19). In the 1920s she was the first female in Bromley to have the new 'Bob' haircut. It was named the 'Bob' because that was how much it cost to have this particular style. A 'bob' is slang for one shilling. Afterwards, she was known as Bobby by everyone in the family and I suspect by her friends and colleagues, as well.

She lived on Widmore Road, Bromley and for all her working life worked as the Office Manager at a Bromley undertakers. She remained a spinster and used to knit wonderful cardigans and jackets for us. She also sent us celebratory Crown Coins, as and when they were minted. In the currency of the time these were worth five shillings, in 2024 this equates to 25p. These coins were very special to me and motivated me for a short while after she died to continue to collect them. Regrettably, finances stopped this luxury from being pursued. She can also be seen in the photograph taken on the day of my christening.

Holidays for us were usually spent in a static caravan, near to the coast. Bracklesham Bay in West Sussex was one such location but there were others including Woolacombe Bay in North Devon and Burton Bradstock in Dorset.

Chapter 1 Arriving & Living in Kent 1955 – 1960

It was on one of these visits that I found myself being chased by some geese which, apparently, I was insistent upon both playing with and feeding – lesson learnt!

The photographs (Figs. 20 – 24) of Judy and myself with Mum and Dad on holiday, mainly taken at Bracklesham Bay, give a really good insight into those very happy and idyllic holidays.

As I have indicated, not all our seaside visits were close by, as shown in figures 23 and 24 taken of us in Norfolk.

Figure 20

Figure 21

Figure 22

Figure 23

Figure 24

This 'professional' one (Fig. 25) was taken whilst in Great Yarmouth. Possibly captured whilst the three of us were on a recce to see what the town was like, as school blazers are not normally holiday attire and Dad, who is not in the picture, could have been at work. During the holiday season hopeful photographers, in this case a company called Barkers, would take random photographs of people, walking down the street and give them a ticket with a number on. In this case our number was 12079. If you wished to view the image, you could then present your ticket at their street booth the next day. If you liked it, as was our case, you could then purchase the photograph.

Whilst it's clear from the photograph (Fig. 25) and indeed the one shown earlier, taken in Trafalgar Square, we didn't always have a camera with us. Like many families we did own one which was brought out for use on 'high days' and holidays. Ours was a Box Brownie, a large black box covered in leather that you held at waist height and looked down through the small viewfinder in the corner. A click of the side button took a black and white image on the 120-size roll film, which could take around a dozen photographs. It's a far cry from today's cameras, housed within mobile phones capable of taking endless colour images and/or videos, with sound and special effects included. All of which can then be instantly sent around the world via the internet. By comparison, we had to firstly finish the film, then take it to the chemist to have it sent away for developing, only to receive, about ten days later, small black and white photographs and a set of negatives! This is yet another advancement that has taken place within one short lifetime. This time in photography, to say nothing of the scientific and medical advances also using photographic images over the same period!

Figure 25

Why, you may ask, were we on a recce in Norfolk and eventually to move in 1960, from a comfortable life, near our grandparents, aunts and uncles, to live in a county some 100+ miles away? As previously mentioned, this was made necessary due to my father's change of employment. It's a long story, as there is some mystery around Dad's employment, shortly before he joined The Solicitors' Law Stationery Society Ltd. We do know that after the war he had been working in the family business, E. C. Porter, in London, as an apprentice bookbinder, with both his father and his brother, my uncle Cyril

We also know that in May 1951 he was called up by the Territorial Army, for training in Thetford Forest, Norfolk. I presume this was some form of National Service, as men of his age were required to undertake this activity due to the threat from the Korean War (1950-53). However, father's military papers only show that he attended training from May – July in 1951, there is no mention of any actual military service.

We do know that E. C. Porter was trading in March 1952, as Dad received letters of condolence, sent there regarding the death of his mother. E. C. Porter ceased trading and was wound up, as per the London Gazette announcement of 4 March 1955. As a result, Dad had to seek new employment. He presumably had an inkling as to E. C. Porter's fate, as he was certainly employed by Hogben and Perrett, from December 1954 through to 10 June 1955. A 'reference letter' confirms that regrettably he was made redundant, by Hogben and Perrett in June, and from then on through to April 1958, his employment is unclear.

In another letter to my dad, dated 11 December 1957, from Dixon and Co., who had previously traded with Porters, there was also enclosed a copy of their character reference that he had requested to support a job application, made to Brown Knight and Truscott Ltd. in Tunbridge Wells. There is no evidence that Dad secured any employment with them, but he was obviously actively seeking a new job at the time. Finally, we do have a letter, from The Solicitors'

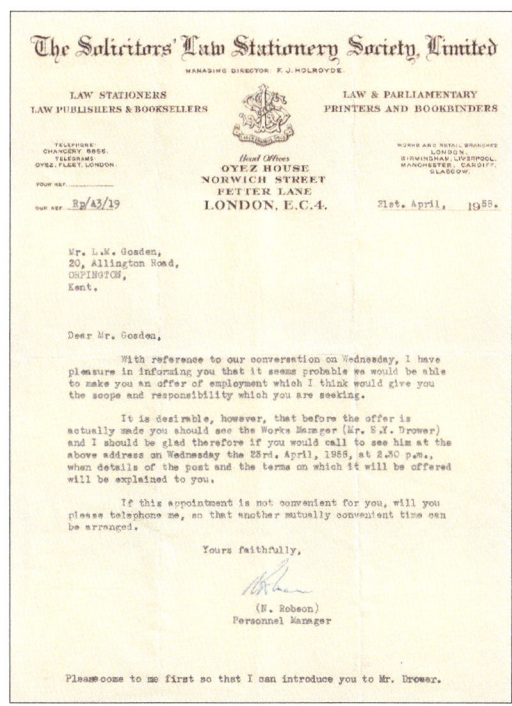

Figure 26

Law Stationery Society Ltd, dated 21 April 1958, with an offer of 'probable employment' (Fig. 26). Dad was duly offered and accepted this role which, on the face of it, appears to be one within the offices rather than as a salesman.

The salesman position was to follow on 5 October 1960, when he was appointed as the Society's representative in the East Coast area that was the Norfolk / Suffolk region. This came with a salary of £1,000 per annum and of course a move to Norfolk, which answers the question of, why we moved. The Solicitors' Law Stationery Society Ltd. was to become my father's employer for the next thirteen years.

With a move to Norfolk, 20 Allington Road was put on the market with R. W. Inniss and Co. for £3,650. The Particulars of Property (Fig. 27) are very flattering in their description of our bungalow, which in my opinion was just as it should have been.

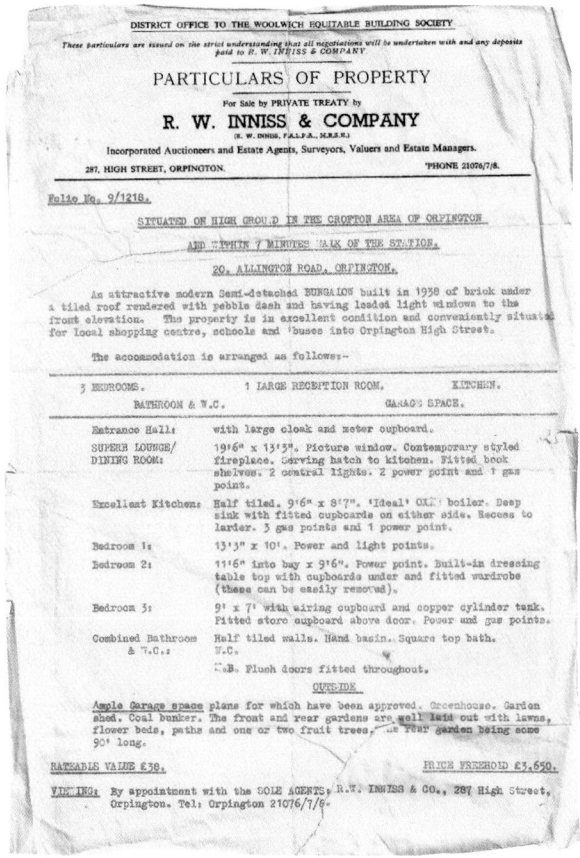

Figure 27

As such it wasn't much of a surprise and to my parents' great relief, it sold quickly, enabling them to move to Norfolk, ready for father's new job. Our possible new address was to be 28 The Avenues, Norwich, NOR 27G.

You may think that the postcode for our new house is incorrect but at the time Norwich was trialling a new system, as recorded on Google.

> *'In January 1959 the Post Office analysed the results of a survey on public attitudes towards the use of postal codes, choosing a town in which to experiment with codes. The envisaged format was a six-character alphanumeric code with three letters designating the geographical area and three numbers [and or letters] to identify the individual address. On 28 July Ernest Marples, the Postmaster General, announced that Norwich had been selected, and that each of the 150,000 private and business addresses would receive a code by October. Norwich had been selected as it already had eight automatic mail sorting machines in use. The original Norwich format consisted of 'NOR', followed by a space, then a two-digit number (which, unlike the current format, could include a leading zero), and finally a single letter (instead of the two final letters in the current format).*
>
> *In October 1965, Tony Benn as Postmaster General announced that postal coding was to be extended to the rest of the country in the next few years'.*

So, 28 The Avenues, Norwich, as seen in the two photographs (Figs. 28 & 29) was surveyed by O. A. Chapman, on 13 December 1960, who whilst noting that some work would be required in the next couple of years, confirmed that the house was…

> *'…sound, reasonably well constructed and unlikely to depreciate in value through any defects in the building'.*

Figure 28

Figure 29

That was music to my parents' ears, so with that in mind, coupled with the fact that Christmas was now fast approaching, it was full steam ahead for purchasing and occupation. Not an easy task, given that the family now had a six-month-old baby, as well as me and Judy.

With all the legal matters concluded and according to my sister the packing was completed, the move was undertaken on 31 December 1960. This does seem to be a very fast completion and regrettably there is no paperwork to support this date. I am indebted to the memory of Judy regarding this date.

'28 The Avenues' is no longer standing, following the murder by Alex Kelly, on 25 February 2015, of Pauline, Mr. and Mrs. King's daughter. Alex Kelly was sentenced, at Ipswich Crown Court,[10] to 25 years imprisonment. Mr. and Mrs. King had purchased the property from my mother and father. Number 28 has now been replaced by a very modern house.

---

10 https://www.edp24.co.uk/news/crime/20887461.norwich-man-alex-kerry-jailed-life-vile-murder-pauline-king/

CHAPTER 2

School, Scouting & Eaton Village 1960 – 1973

Before we moved north, I had in 1959 just started attending 'big school', which took the name of Crofton Infant School, Orpington. As suspected it wasn't like Auntie Dora's, but it was close to home. Judy, who had already started there, escorted me to school with Mum at my side. I really don't recall much about the school, probably due to the brief time I was there. I am reliably told though, that I vocally demonstrated in no uncertain way, my displeasure of attending. Enough said!

At five years old, I was certainly growing up and becoming more confident, at least enough to just about ride my bicycle without stabilisers. I clearly had to concentrate though, as my expression (Fig. 30) confirms. Bicycle safety was to feature more seriously in a couple of year's time.

Having now moved successfully to The Avenues, we had to find both a dentist and doctor. The former was a relatively easy task, as we were to use a recommended dental practice on Prince of Wales Road in Norwich. The choice of doctors though, was limited as you had to find one within a defined catchment area. My mother, who seemed to take the lead in medical matters, chose a practice on Dereham Road, which wasn't that far away. The family were allocated to Dr. Cowan, who owned the practice.

Now, I have nothing against doctors, but as far back as I can remember I have always hated injections and still do! I think this stems from an incident, when I was about six or seven, when I attended the surgery to have a standard booster but whilst there decided this was not welcome. Consequently, I was literally chased around

Figure 30

the consulting room, by a doctor with hypodermic in hand, followed by my frustrated mother who was also endeavouring, not very successfully, to comfort me. The injection was finally administered and that confirmed, for years to come, my negative thoughts regarding injections.

Going to the local school, Avenue Road Infants in Norwich, was quite a different experience to that in Orpington. Now I could walk to school, along a tree-lined road, next to a park, rather than along streets lined with houses and then across an open field farm track. In both scenarios though, I was with Mum and Judy and now we had a dog to accompany us as well. He was called Lucky and was a black and white collie, who was very special to me and rarely seen without a six-year-old boy close by.

During my first school summer holidays I had to say a sad farewell to Judith Evely, one of my new best friends. Judith was the same age as me and lived in a lovely house on the corner of Christchurch Road and Earlham Road. We went to each other's birthday parties, played in each other's gardens etc. and it was whilst we were living in The Avenues that we became good friends. Like us though, her family were having to move, as her father was to take up a new job in Hull and I recall us all saying a sad farewell to her and her parents, outside the City Hall in Norwich.

Figure 31

Avenue Road School, where I was destined to remain for the next few years, was attached to a larger Junior School. The entrance for the Infants was around the back of the complex, adjacent but not attached to a more recently built dining room.

Avenue Road Infants was a traditional, old-style school, built around the 1920s which, although now being a mixed school, still had the words 'Boys' and 'Girls' embossed in the brickwork above the separate entrances. These originated from a time when children were segregated by their gender.

During my time there, we all had the traditional school photograph taken, which was then given to our parents. Mine (Fig. 31) was taken with me attempting to read a book in the office of Miss Catton, the Headteacher of the Infants. As you can see there was no formal uniform, as this was only required in the Junior School.

At school we had the usual Christmas nativity play to which our parents came. The inevitable photo shoot then took place, and copies were made available for the family album. No memoir would be complete without the inclusion of one of these images (Fig. 32). I think I am one of the kings immediately beside the manger, on the left.

Figure 32

In the winter of 1963, there was a particularly heavy snowfall and having made my way to school through thick and deep snow, which in those days was something of a novelty to me, I said goodbye to Lucky who went home with Mum.

The school was located on a steep hill with the junior playground adjacent to

Avenue Road, and due to the extreme slope this had been split into two levels with steps in the middle. The infant playground was at right angles to the upper section of the junior one, with the refectory at its far end. Given that the recent heavy snowfall had made this area too dangerous, all the year groups were concentrated in the two linked junior playgrounds. Being seven coming up to eight I was allowed by the big boys to watch them build an igloo, in the corner of the playground, underneath one of the horse chestnut trees which lined the playground.

I have to say that whilst this took some time to build, the result was remarkably good. It replicated the perfect shape of a traditional igloo and was tall enough for us smaller boys to crawl into and stand up. There were obvious clear advantages to being short and going to school during a massive snowfall!

My infant schooling seemed to have progressed without any major incidents so at around the age of eleven I moved up to Avenue Junior School. The headmaster of which was Mr Allen whose office, from the playground entrance, was at the top of the stairs and adjacent to the cloakroom. Here, on your named peg you hung your school bag, containing a change of shoes and any papers for the teacher etc., along with your homework book. From the cloakroom you made your way into the main hall which had classrooms on three sides. This layout was replicated in an adjacent hall, on a back-to-back basis. This second hall, mainly used by the infants, also doubled up as a gym for the juniors with all its equipment, climbing ropes and bars etc.

Sport though, was not my forte but I was particularly keen on the art lessons. These were led by a teacher who was an artist himself and lived locally in Judges Walk, just off Newmarket Road. I know this as I had several private lessons with him at his house. My parents paid for these, and he taught me the rudiments of composition. This interest in art has always remained with me and allowed me to create several watercolours – one or two good enough to be hung in my current home for our family and friends to enjoy.

Moving up to the Junior school meant you had to wear a uniform, which included a school cap. I was now old enough to walk home by myself which, of course, left me 'vulnerable' to the big boys. About halfway home, I had to cross College Road, where there was a post box. Recollecting this now, it's obvious that big boys, post boxes and caps belonging to younger boys do not mix. This was to prove the case for me, as my cap seemed to end up being 'posted'!

Once back home, despite my incessant protestations to my mother that I was totally innocent and it really was the big boys, I was made to return to the post box, await the postal collection and ask the postman for my cap back. This procedure was duly carried out and I arrived home with cap in hand, and from then on I went home from school with my cap in my pocket!

One thing I do recall at the school, was the thrill at being asked to ring the bell at the end of each class, for the whole of that day. This involved walking around the two halls, whilst ringing the hand bell to let everyone know it was the end of that lesson. This responsibility, I must add, was only given to children who behaved themselves!

I can't give the impression that I was a perfectly well-behaved child at school, as I do recall once getting the 'slipper', in front of the entire class. I really don't remember why. Unfortunately for me though, Mr Cryer the teacher who was to administer the punishment, happened to know that in addition to my parents I had an elder sister. That meant I had three wallops, one for each parent and one for my sister. So, it's just as well he didn't yet know, due to the age gap, that I did in fact have a younger sibling, Sarah.

Despite this incident, I have to say that whilst the school was not as fun as that run by Auntie Dora, it wasn't that bad either. The teachers were, however, struggling to gain my attention and my reports confirmed my progress was poor.

The summary of my first-year report, dated July 1963 stated that:

'Drawings good, but written work often disappointing, due to poor spelling. Keith's work is neat. He does not always exert himself enough. Arithmetic and spelling need his special attention.'

In all probability, this was at that time a very accurate assessment of me. Regrettably though, in most aspects it could still easily be a valid modern-day summary, although I am not proud of the comment or its longevity. My overall marks for the six subjects in the report were 247 out of 600.

For me, my worst and dreaded lesson was French, with Miss Mann. Those who know me now will testify to my struggle with English, so to be confronted with having to learn a foreign language, at the time, was a step too far. French wasn't the only awkward learning experience. There were music lessons too, where I was to be taught the recorder, thankfully within a group. I say thankfully, as I never quite got the right fingering, so to avoid embarrassment I simply didn't blow and tried to mimic the fingering of the more competent musicians. The teacher never knew, of course, or so I believed!

When the time came for my July 1965 report, I was back with Mr Cryer but this time he was my class teacher. My marks hadn't improved, in fact they went down to a mere 205 out of 600. Mr Cryer did compliment me on my topic work though, with the comment *'V. Neat. Good sketches'*, which was pleasing for my parents until they read the overall remarks which were, *'These marks are disappointing. Keith seems to have been trying hard lately. His reading is still poor. Orally he is very good.'*

It is disconcerting that one's character is formed and embedded so early in life, and if not consciously challenged it remains almost constant throughout your lifetime. In many respects this is the case for me. At almost seventy I still enjoy Art, in all its many forms, I don't read very often and can only spell with the use of a 'spell checker' or by asking other people in the room. However, I am able to converse well, can chair committees and have held down senior roles both at work and in society. Food for thought!

I had one more year left to prove myself, before I was off to my Secondary School, in September 1966. My efforts are outlined later but unbeknown to me, following the 11+ examination, my parents had already been told my destination, in the letter (Fig. 33), sent on 6 May. I was to find this out nearer the end of term.

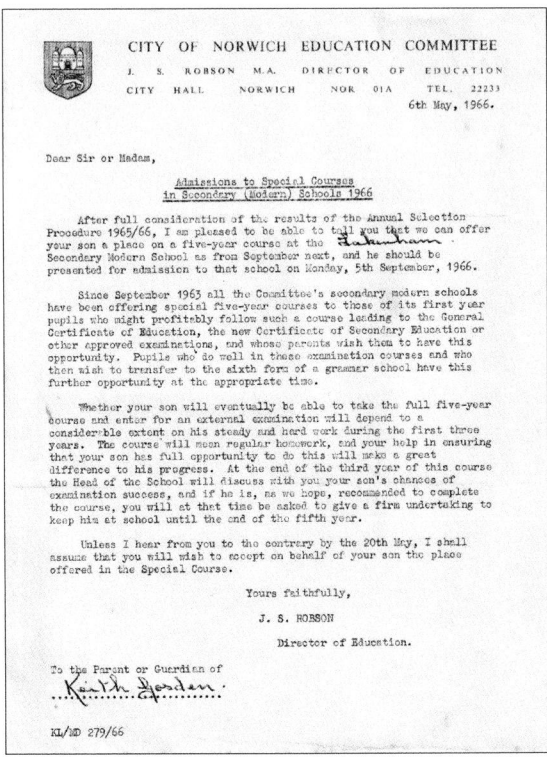

Figure 33

Chapter 2 School, Scouting & Eaton Village 1960 – 1973

Back at home and away from school, I would often be asked to help Dad in the garden, which I really enjoyed. I think all youngsters, especially boys, like being a dad's little helper, as it made you feel grown up and special and I was no exception. The back garden at 28 The Avenues was a good size and was described, by S. F. Upson and Co., in their Order to View, as being a *'Secluded laid-out rear garden with a large lawn fitted with a child's swing, fishpond and dry-stone wall with herbaceous borders. Kitchen garden with fruit trees.'*

The front garden was smaller but still a good size with a lawn, some standard roses and two large lilac trees, one each side of the front boundary wall that was between the drive on the left and a footpath on the right.

I remember the vegetable plot being at the end of the back garden, behind a trellis which was covered with scented roses. This made for an attractive divide between the play and the working areas, especially as it had a large flowering cherry tree to the right. As a family we all had great fun collecting its fruit. There were elements of the back garden though, that were not 'child-proof', as my parents were to find out later.

I recall that there was one very important job that required the expertise of men, who were, of course, Dad and me, which was to clean out the fishpond. Now, this was no ordinary garden pond. It was a large, oval, concrete one some 6' by 8', which you can just see on the extreme right of this photograph (Fig. 34), with the three of us sitting beside it and looking very angelic. Some care and expert handling were required. I was certainly up for this!

The only thing was that I didn't fully appreciate when I stretched over the edge to catch the fish just how deep it would be, coupled with the fact that there were frogs.

In my excitement to point out one of these to Dad, I managed to fall headfirst into the muddy pond – luckily, I didn't harm either the fish, the frogs or myself. But all hell broke out, with grown-ups rushing about, pulling me out and

Figure 34

squirting water at me to remove the thick, slimy mud. It was pandemonium. I survived though, and in an amusing way the 'event' was often recalled within the family.

This wasn't the first time I had caused chaos. For when we lived in Allington Road, Judy and I managed to lock ourselves inside the greenhouse, but to our horror discovered we couldn't get out. Once again pandemonium ensued but this time from two scared and very confused children, rather than the adults, with both of us shouting for all we were worth. This worked and after a short space of time, which to us seemed an eternity, we were reunited with our mum.

Back in Orpington, at the age of five, as it is for any young child, life was very much a time of learning, not only at school and home but also in my case, at church. With my parents' Christian beliefs and upbringing – my mum was Church of England and Dad was Baptist – it meant that each week I was taken to Sunday School. Whilst we lived in Kent, I managed to attend the Sunday School so regularly that on two consecutive years I was given for my excellent attendance, either a Bible story book or some other age-appropriate religious study book. These were affixed on the inside cover with a colourful bookplate, extolling my 'Good Attendance' for that particular year (Fig. 35). When we moved to Norwich, in order for this Sunday School education to continue, I was taken to St. Thomas Church on Earlham Road, which wasn't far from 28 The Avenues, so we could easily walk.

Figure 35

It was here that I first displayed my ability, in a well-meant way, to say the wrong thing at the wrong time. One Sunday, as we left church and were saying goodbye to the vicar, I noticed outside on the pavement a lady of advanced years. She was kind enough to chat to me and that was when, as any young, inquisitive child may do, I said *'you're very old'*, but unlike any other curious, young infant, I followed this up with *'when are you going to die?'* You could almost see the earth opening up around my mother, ready to swallow her up with her embarrassment!

I had to apologise, which I did, and I assume that this was accepted, as I don't recall any ongoing issues. I'm not sure that this was what Mr Cryer meant, in my school report, when he wrote *'Orally he is very good'*! I did continue to attend Sunday School, but I don't recall being presented with another book for 'good attendance'! Perhaps Norfolk churches were different to those in Kent – anyway, that's my rationale.

Holidays at this time, were still very much based around staying in a static caravan, but now this would be much closer to home, near the sea, in Sheringham (Fig. 36). Left to right are myself, Mum, Judy and Sarah. Holiday entertainment was playing in the sea, building sandcastles, sunbathing, eating ice creams, playing in the caravan site's children's play area and of course walking the dog in the local woods.

Figure 36

If it rained at night, which usually made a lot of noise on the caravan's roof, Dad would comfort us all by telling us that it was just the fairies playing football, whilst wearing their football boots. This seemed to work and allowed us to gently slumber.

Alas, our caravan site which was situated in Holway Road, Sheringham, which from the main A148 heads down a steep hill towards the town centre, has long since disappeared and been replaced by a housing estate.

Figure 37

At the time of our holidays though, we would usually select a caravan in the same part of the site, as we had in previous years and frequently had one next to the Turley family, who came from Sheffield. They too had young children, a little younger than us but we all enjoyed the same pleasures.

Seen on the slide is Roy Turley with his daughter Jackie (Fig. 37). Jackie, her brother Jon, sister Rosie and her parents all became regular holiday friends. Jackie had leg splints, I think due to either having part of her legs amputated or having contracted polio. These certainly didn't impede her ability to play and run around like the rest of us and was of no concern to anyone.

When their father, Roy, a previous Sheffield Wednesday Wing Half, had retired in the late 50s from professional football he then trained to be a teacher. Later he became a highly successful headmaster of Stalham School in Norfolk and was awarded an OBE. He was a wonderful artist and painted many Disney characters on the bedroom walls for his children. I was most impressed, especially as he showed me how to draw Donald Duck!

I have previously written that we had a black and white collie dog named Lucky, who was my best friend. Even at my tender age of seven or eight I used to take him out for walks on my own. In the 1960s there weren't the high levels of concern, as society was quite different and perceived to be considerably safer than today. It wasn't unusual for young children to be out on their own or with their siblings. However, I was to give my family the fright of their lives and have my first brush with the law!

I had taken Lucky out for his normal early evening walk and I thought it would be a good idea to walk down to the park, approximately ten minutes down the road, have a stroll around and then return home for tea.

I was sure that that would be fine, so I duly set off. When I arrived at the park I found that a bowls match was in progress and this, to a young boy, was so fascinating that it deserved me to sit down on the seat to watch, along with my trusty dog. Time must have ticked by, because I fell asleep and, unbeknown to me, back home I had two very anxious parents who were getting rather worried about my longer than expected walk. Back at the park, I woke up just in time to see the very end of the match and without a care in the world made my way home.

The greeting I received upon walking down our drive was very unusual, with Mum and Dad rushing out to hug me, saying *'where have you been?'* etc. Well, that was easy, I'd been out for a walk and fallen asleep. What I had failed to realise was that quite a few hours had passed, since I had set out on the 'short' walk, and as a result the Police had been called and they were still busy looking for me, out in the local area. When told this, I remember thinking that this was an overreaction on my parents' part, which now writing as a parent myself, probably wasn't true. My opinion then quickly changed when a policeman came into the house and gently teased the details of events from me. I'm happy to say that all was well and much more importantly for me, I was still allowed to take Lucky out, on my own.

It was around this time, early to mid-1960s, that Judy, Sarah and I started to receive a regular delivery of a new magazine called 'Knowledge'. This was a weekly children's magazine that built into a full encyclopaedia. When we had collected sufficient editions, Dad had them bound into volumes which made them look really good. Not sure they enhanced my educational prowess, as attested by my school reports but I still looked forward to its delivery, each week.

I don't know why but as time moved on, Mum and Dad had itchy feet at The Avenues and started to look around for a new home and on 13 February 1963, 28 The Avenues was put on the market, with S. F. Upson and Co., at a price of £4,250. It would appear from the correspondence (Fig. 38) that in March 1963 they were looking at a bungalow

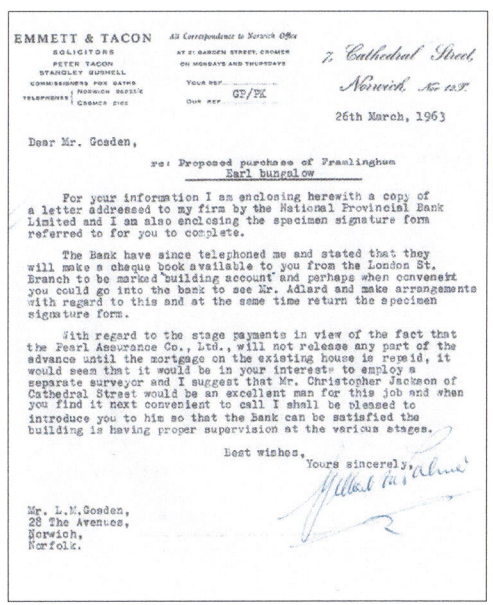

Figure 38

in Framlingham Earl. For whatever reason though, this clearly did not proceed as our family never ended up living in that village.

The sale of The Avenues wasn't a drawn-out affair, for on 28 April Dad received a written offer of £3,750 from Mr King, who was the Deputy Chief Constable of Norfolk, at the time. This was £500 below the asking price. However, according to the completion documents the actual sale price was finally agreed at £4,100, plus £5/10s for fixtures.

During this time both Mum and Dad had seen a possible site for a new house, in Eaton Village. On 21 May 1963, they received a letter from Francis Horner and Son, (Fig. 39) the agents on behalf of the developers of Eaton Village, which confirmed their reservation of Plot 169. The purchase price was £3,500 and the developer was James Miller and Partners. On 1 June, Emmett and Tacon Solicitors, confirmed that contracts were ready for this desired location.

TELEGRAMS: CONTINUITY, NORWICH.
TELEPHONE 24101/2/3

FRANCIS HORNOR & SON.
CHARTERED SURVEYORS.
LAND AGENTS, VALUERS & AUCTIONEERS
ESTABLISHED 1784

OLD BANK OF ENGLAND COURT,
QUEEN STREET,
NORWICH, NOR 07J

OUR REF. GM/JW/G.
YOUR REF.

21st May, 1963.

Dear Mr. Gosden,

Eaton Village Estate.

We write to confirm that we are reserving the detached house on Plot 169 for you until Saturday of this week 25th instant.

The price is £3,500. There are no road charges, the land is freehold and there are no outgoings. The rateable value under the new assessment is £94 per annum, the rates in the £ we understand being 11/- for the current year.

If you would like to inspect during the evening when the painter is not on the site we should be pleased to let you have a key if you will telephone and let us know.

We are finding a demand for these houses are now becoming much brisker and we should be most grateful if you could let us know the decision at your end by Saturday of this week. If you require any further extension to enable you to complete your enquiries should be pleased to help you in any way we can providing of course we have not somebody willing to write out a cheque in payment straight away.

Yours sincerely,

Mr. Gosden,
28, The Avenues,
Norwich.

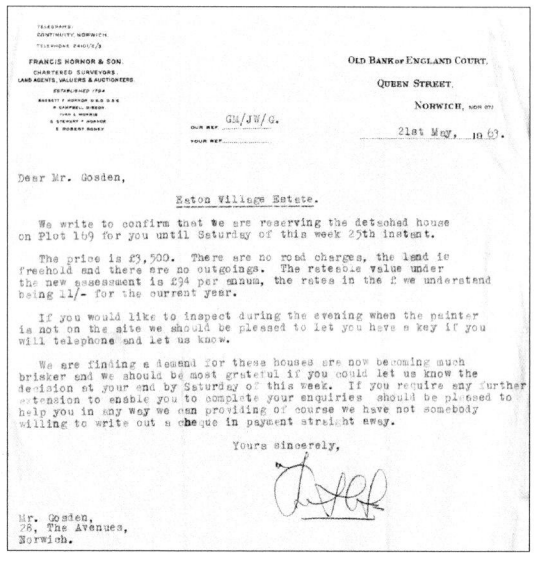

Figure 39

It was soon to be ours and our new address was to be 24 Cranleigh Rise, Eaton Village, Norwich. Indeed, a letter from Norwich Building Society, dated 24 June, confirmed an advance was available of £2,800, subject to the current mortgage on 28 The Avenues being redeemed.

EMMETT & TACON
SOLICITORS
PETER TACON
STANDLEY BUSHELL
COMMISSIONERS FOR OATHS
TELEPHONES { NORWICH 23355/6, CROMER 2195

All Correspondence to Norwich Office
AT 21 GARDEN STREET, CROMER
ON MONDAYS AND THURSDAYS
YOUR REF.
OUR REF. GMP/MRH.

7, Cathedral Street,
Norwich, Nor 12P.

20th August, 1963.

Dear Mr. Gosden,

Re: Your Sale and Purchase.

We have now prepared accounts relative to the above transactions, and have pleasure in enclosing herewith a copy from which you will see that after deducting all charges and expenses and taking into account the £500 paid to you on account, there is a balance in our hands of £89. 16.10d., and our cheque for this amount is enclosed.

We also enclose Messrs. Upsons receipted account relating to the sale of the Avenues property, and our own receipted Bills of Charges, and so far as the abhortive purchases of the Framlingham Earl and other properties are concerned, we do not propose to make any charge to you in respect of these matters.

With our thanks to you and your instructions, and all best wishes for the happiness of your wife and yourself and family in your new home.

We are,

Yours sincerely,

Emmett & Tacon

L.M. Gosden, Esq.,
24 Cranleigh Rise,
Eaton Village Estate,
NORWICH.

Encls.

Figure 40

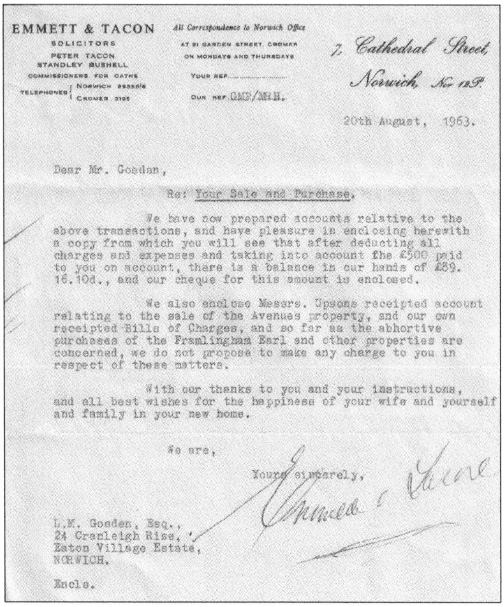

Given the extended dates of these various documents and that all correspondence was still being sent to 28 The Avenues, my assumption is that Mr and Mrs King, who had had their offer accepted on 28 The Avenues, back in April, had exchanged contracts with

an extended date for completion and moving-in, in-line with the expected successful conclusion of all the building works, on our new home.

Thus, the end result of this sale and purchase was that, on 21 July 1963, Dad received a request from J. F. Upson and Co. for their commission in selling 28 The Avenues. The transaction was completed on 12 August 1963 when Mum, Dad, myself and my two sisters all moved into 24 Cranleigh Rise, Eaton.

The date of this move has been verified by a letter (Fig. 40) from Emmett and Tacon which was sent to our new address in Eaton, dated 20 August 1963. The enclosures, not shown here, included a large spreadsheet outlining the financial transactions that culminated in Mum and Dad receiving a sizeable profit, of £589/16/10d. Given that Dad was now earning around £1,100 per annum, from Solicitors' Law Stationery Society, this profit was quite significant!

A year later, some of this was used to build a small conservatory/boot room and to convert the car port into a garage. All this additional work was undertaken by Dad and his now 'experienced' helper, me!

Living in 24 Cranleigh Rise, Eaton, on the left in the picture (Fig. 41), which was taken in the mid 1960s, was a very new experience for all the family. For both adults and children, it was the very first time that any of us had ever lived in a brand-new house. It was a joy, with central heating, no draughts, a television, a large garden with trees to climb and I remember Dad made a gate at the back, so we could walk out to the Newmarket Road. At the age of 8½ what more could I ask for?

Our new neighbours, in the chalet to our right (Fig. 41), were the Oelrichs. They owned a bakery and delicious cake shop on Colman Road. To the left (out of the picture) was another house like ours, owned initially by a couple from the services but later was sold to Mr and Mrs Judson, who had a son about my age and also called Keith.

As you can see in figure 41, we had a car which was thanks to Dad's job, and every three years he was able to change it. There was always excitement

Figure 41

when the time came to have a new vehicle, as we all had an input into the colour that we would like. When the time arrived for the actual changeover, the old car would be washed and then Dad and I, often accompanied by the family, would drive to Delves Garage in Norwich, to exchange 'old for new'. This was always a Vauxhall but later his employer decided that it was to become a Ford which was much larger. This didn't please Dad at all, due to the personal tax implications and the increased cost of personal mileage, as a larger engine gave fewer miles to a gallon of petrol. As children we didn't understand this. For us it was just a lovely, new, shiny car.

1966 was to be my final year at Avenue Road Junior School, and as such all my year group had to sit the 11+ examination, which I dreaded! As I have already outlined, my progress was not conducive to a highflying student and the 11+ result was to determine which school, Grammar or Secondary Modern, you were to finish your formal education. I remember the day of the announcement very clearly. We all had to sit, in rows, cross-legged on the floor of the Assembly Hall. The head, Mr Allen, then called out your name, and depending upon your allocated school you either went through the left or the right door. You were never actually told your grade, just which school you would be attending as from the following September. As per my previous comment, my parents were already aware of this allocation and had agreed to this decision.

I was now told that I would be attending Lakenham Boys and Girls School, which was the only Secondary Modern in Norwich. The buildings for both the Boys and the Girls were located on the same site and having been built in the 1950s were relatively modern. The two Grammar Schools in the area were The Hewett School, built in 1958 and next door to Lakenham School, and the City of Norwich School, which was just off Newmarket Road.

Ironically, with the introduction in 1970 of comprehensive education, Lakenham Boys and Girls School combined with the Hewett School, which was under the direction of headteacher Walter Roy, and together they formed a new Comprehensive School. So, the standard of education received by us all was the same no matter whether you had passed or failed your 11+. Then in the early 1970s, when there was a move away from selective state-funded Grammar Schools to non-selective Comprehensive Schools, the 11+ was no longer compulsory.[11]

However, I did have two successes before actually leaving Avenue Road.

---

11 https://www.google.com/

Chapter 2 School, Scouting & Eaton Village 1960 – 1973

Firstly, I managed to pass my National Cycling Proficiency test (Fig. 42)! This involved cycling around the playground, avoiding the obstacles laid out by the local examiner, demonstrating that you understood the highway code and finally you knew how to look after your bicycle. Secondly, it was passing my 'ability to swim twenty-five yards' (Fig. 43).

I am delighted to say that I was awarded a certificate for each of these achievements and still have these as evidence of my rather limited successes. So, at least I left Avenue Road School on a high, of sorts.

I am sure it was a short-lived disappointment for my parents that I wasn't going to a Grammar School. So now, following the summer holidays, I was off to Lakenham Boys School. This made life much easier for Mum and Dad, as my sister Judy was already at Lakenham Girls School.

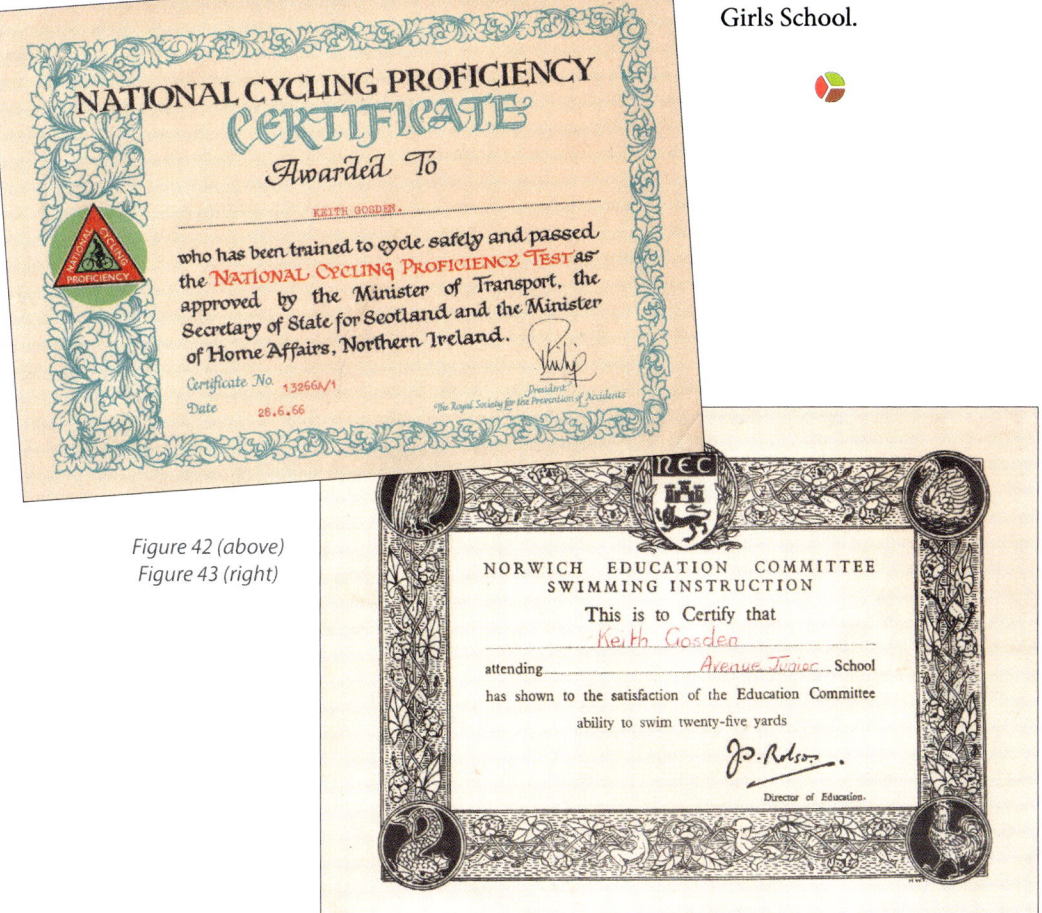

Figure 42 (above)
Figure 43 (right)

My time in The Scouting Movement

St. Thomas Church on Earlham Road, where earlier I was to continue my Sunday School education, also had its own Community Hall. Here, a Wolf Cub Pack was held and at the age of almost eight, I was encouraged to join this, which I was very happy to do. Having completed my Tenderpad which entailed learning the Cub Law, Promise, Salute and the Grand Howl, I was enrolled into the wider Scout Movement, on 22 January 1963.

For those unfamiliar with the terminology of Grand Howl, this is held at the beginning of each Pack Meeting and is shown pictorially on my 'Wolf Cub Tenderpad Test Card' (Fig. 44).

The Scouts for me and my father, and the Guides in the case of my mother and sisters, were to have a great influence on both my life and theirs. My mother was to start the Brownie Pack in Eaton, whilst my father would, in time, become a Scout Leader. Both my sisters also went right the way through the Girl Guide movement.

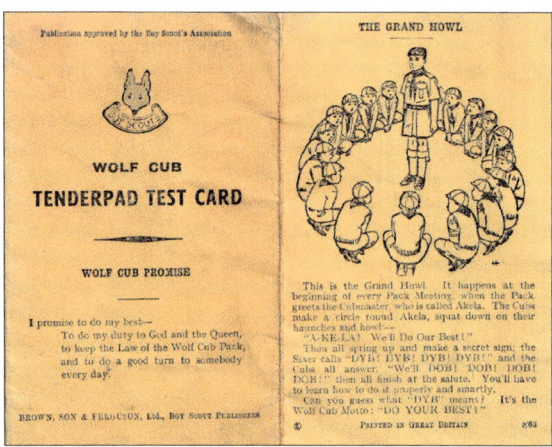

Figure 44

Unbeknown to me, as I have only recently discovered this fact, Scouts had run in the family, at least on my mother's side, for a number of years.

The photograph (Fig. 45) is of my Grandad Randall, third from left, in his Scout uniform and looking around 11 or 12 years old. Given he was born in 1902 that would indicate the photograph was taken around 1913/14. As the movement was started by Lord Baden-Powell in 1907/8, my grandad was probably one of the second generation of early Scouts.

Today's society is not so segregated by gender, so both young boys and girls can now join together to enjoy the whole

Figure 45

Chapter 2 School, Scouting & Eaton Village 1960 – 1973

scouting movement. I am delighted to say that, to this day, Scouts continue 'in the family', through my grandson, Ben Bedford. Having been a Wolf Cub, in his home pack in Tadley, he then became a Scout in 2023.

Now that we lived in Eaton Village, a suburb of Norwich, it meant that I had to move from St. Thomas Wolf Cub Pack to a brand-new Cub Pack in Eaton – the 34th Norwich. This had been set up by The Reverend Canon Hurd, who was the local vicar and The Reverend Jonathan Boston his new and very young curate. In 1963 their very first meetings were held in the Vicarage front garden, and now having moved to Cranleigh Rise I joined the Pack, in June 1963. Before our move though in August, I distinctly recall the walk with my mother from The Avenues down Unthank Road, to attend the first few meetings. Thanks to my previous time at St. Thomas, I found out that I was indeed the very first enrolled Cub in this new pack.

In 1970, I produced a history of Eaton Village, in which I drew this map (Fig. 46) which, hopefully, will help to explain where roads and key buildings were located. I have included references to the map in the following text.

The Vicarage was located at the point where Unthank Road joined Newmarket

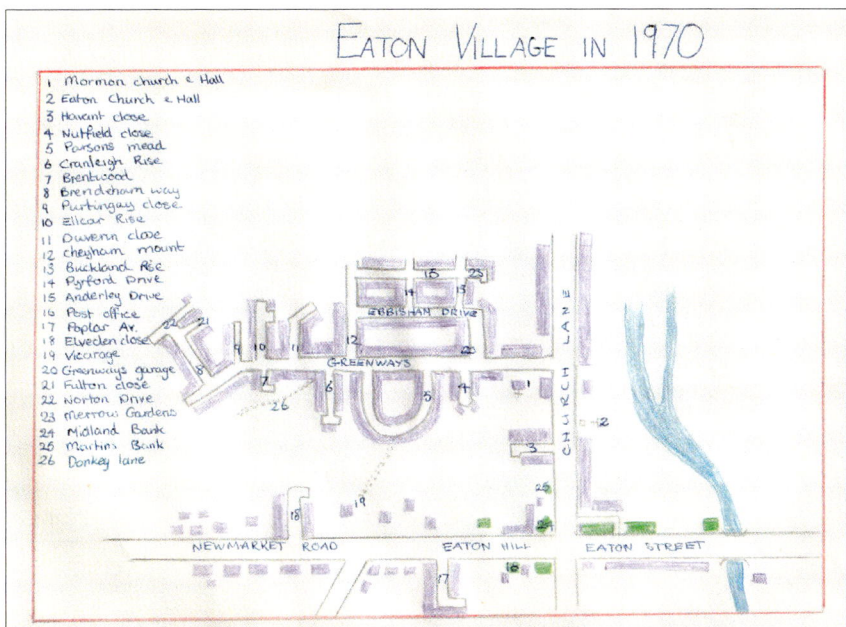

Figure 46

Road, off which was Eaton Village. For those of us who lived in Eaton, walking to the Cub meetings was made easier through being able to use a small footpath which ran between two bungalows in Parsons Mead (map ref. 5), which was next to Cranleigh Rise (map ref. 6), and gave access to the back garden of the Vicarage (map ref. 19).

Wolf Cubs, the name by which we were officially known, had meetings run by Mrs Brown our Akela/Cub Scout Leader, who made every meeting great fun. The meetings were made even better by the fact that Canon Hurd's housekeeper was a fantastic cook, and always came out at the end of the meetings with an array of homemade cakes and drinks, which were quickly devoured. All three, the vicar, his cook and Akela, clearly knew how to please us young Cubs!

The actual vicarage was a very large Victorian building, with the main vehicular access off the Newmarket Road and as you came up the drive the main front door was ahead of you. To your left, through a permanently open gate in a high wall, was a cobbled courtyard. On the left-hand side of this was a standalone stable block, above which there was a loft and at a later date this was to become our pack meeting room. Opposite the stables, across the courtyard, you could see the back door and kitchen window, from which pervaded the many delicious smells of homemade baking. The cobbled area also contained a water pump, next to the back door, and an enormous monkey puzzle tree. It was the first time I had ever seen such a tree and it really fascinated me, being all spiky and obviously very difficult, if not impossible, to climb. The gardens were extensive and included a large vegetable plot through which you walked if using the footpath entrance, as described earlier. To the right-hand side of the main house and adjacent to Newmarket Road was a huge horse chestnut tree, from which, as Cubs, we all gathered our autumnal supplies of conkers. This was fronted by an immaculately kept lawn leading to the vicarage, which was used in the summer for the church fête etc., as well as our Cub meetings.

Canon Hurd was the Vicar of Eaton and lived in the vicarage from 1949-1970. He was a wonderful character, very good with children, despite his obvious advanced years, and being without family himself.

In the parish of Eaton, he looked after two churches, St. Andrew's and Christchurch, the latter was in fact a mile or so down the Newmarket Road, towards Norwich. Both Judy and I joined the choir at St. Andrew's and can be seen here (Fig. 47), outside the

Figure 47

church in our full church robes, with Canon Hurd in his vestments.

I can't recall if Sarah ever joined us in the choir but at the time the choirmaster was the curate, The Reverend Jonathan Boston, and of course he was our Cub and Scout Leader. He was very keen to help and progress the scouting side of the church, which will become apparent later on. At the time he lodged with Mrs Craske and her son Colin, at 43 Muriel Road, Norwich, near to Christchurch Eaton. In time Colin was to become a close friend of Judy's.

As the Pack grew with new cubs joining not only did the pack require an assistant to Akela, but its meetings were moved from the vicarage stables to the relatively new Village Hall in Church Lane, Eaton. Unfortunately, the home-made cakes did not follow us, alas!

Throughout my time as either a Wolf Cub or Boy Scout, we seemed to be driven by working towards the passing of 'badges'. Then, when the certificate had been signed by the examiner and passed by the Cub or Scout Leaders, you proudly took it to the Scout Shop. This was located in an old church, in Elm Hill, Norwich, where upon production of your signed certificate you proudly collected your badge. For all of us youngsters these were seen as big and important 'events'.

Figure 48

The photograph (Fig. 48) of the 34th Norwich Wolf Cub Pack shows me on the extreme right, not only looking the wrong way but without my cap! I seem to remember commenting on lost caps before – so it was probably in my pocket for safety!

Whilst living in Cranleigh Rise, both my parents spent time creating a garden and then maintaining it. Judy and I were lucky enough to each have our own small garden plot, situated at the top of the garden and about the size of a kitchen table. Here we created miniature replicas of the main garden, and mine had grass, a pond and flower beds. In July 1965, this enabled me to gain my cub scout Gardener's Badge, but not until I had convinced the examiner, Mrs Richardson, that I knew my flowers and could explain the features of my mini garden.

Living in Eaton Village meant that we, as children, had the advantage of the farmers' fields, at the top of Ellcar Rise, where we could play, pick blackberries, and generally enjoy our childhood, in what we all thought was a relatively safe environment. Regrettably, today this area is now part of a housing estate and as such this luxury is lost to the more recent generations of youngsters.

I have used the words 'relatively safe environment' because what I am going to explain proved that this was not always the case, either for me or for a young woman who lived in Church Lane. On 18 January 1968, this young married lady having alighted from the number 90 bus, on Newmarket Road, was stabbed whilst walking down Donkey Lane. Fortunately, she was able to stagger to a house in Greenways, where the occupier called the Police and Ambulance Services.

Donkey Lane (map ref. 26) was located just at the end of our road and, at that time, was a very convenient and well used shortcut, from Eaton Village through to the junction of Newmarket Road and Judges Walk. Whilst it was just a rough and sometimes muddy track, for us children it saved considerable time as we used it on our way to and from school, to either catch or alight the local bus at Judges Walk.

The consequence of this attack was not only very distressing for the victim, who fortunately recovered but resulted in us schoolchildren, including me, being very nervous about walking down the lane. Whilst it was open to the skies at the Newmarket Road end, from the middle, where there was a large chalk pit to the side, through to Eaton Village it was covered by trees and very dark in winter.

Due to the risk that another attack might take place, in September 1968 the council, with some financial assistance from the developers of Eaton Village, eventually tarmacked the lane and erected several lamp posts. In fact, it wouldn't be too long before further housing developments were to be created at both ends of the lane, which removed the worries of many people.

Also, in the September the *Eastern Daily Press* reported that the developers had proposed to the council that Donkey Lane should be renamed Aldeburgh Walk, as this 'tied up with other street names on the estate, which have been chosen to commemorate famous golf courses'. However, I don't think this was ever implemented, for whilst I lived there the locals still called it Donkey Lane.

As mentioned before, there was a chalk pit about halfway down the lane and on the opposite side to this was a small opening into a wooded area. If on the way home from school and without getting your uniform dirty, you could scramble up a small bank and access the Civil Service Recreation Ground. We children often played on this, but our love of 'adventure' certainly waned following this really unpleasant incident. I never knew exactly what had taken place, as our parents didn't want us to be scared. However, following the council's work I don't believe any more incidents were recorded.

Now, as regards the second incident I have had to think long and hard about it. Firstly, should I say anything at all about an occurrence that took place years ago and secondly, if I do how detailed should this explanation be? I have concluded that I will simply mention it and then move on. At the time, which I recall was when we were living in Cranleigh Rise, I said nothing at all to anyone and whilst I have mentioned it to my wife to my knowledge no-one else is aware of what happened.

It occurred one day whilst accompanied by my sister Sarah, we were playing on the farmer's fields, enjoying a game of hide and seek. We were aware that we were being watched by an older man, who was sitting on a mound of grass, and he started to become part of our game. When it came to the time for Sarah to hide he suggested that I sat with him, whilst she found a good hiding place.

We sat awaiting the 'ready' call from Sarah, indicating that I could commence my search. Whilst waiting though, to my surprise the man enquired if I liked being tickled, and I replied that I didn't mind. He proceeded to tickle me under my arms and on my tummy. He then went further, and with his hand down the front of my trousers asked if I liked being tickled there. For a short while, he 'played' with me until thankfully the word 'ready' was shouted by Sarah. Having done up my trousers, I shot off to successfully find her. Afterwards, we returned to the mound of grass but by this time the man had disappeared. Whilst I had an inkling that what he had done was wrong, I kept quiet just in case I was at fault and with that thought in my mind I with Sarah, who was oblivious to what had taken place, returned to the security of our home.

It wasn't until years later I realised that what I had experienced was in fact child sexual abuse and, as such, was highly embarrassed and never spoke of the incident. Even now, years later, whenever I hear of someone, especially a child, being abused I recall that incident. Whilst what happened to me was very minor and cannot reasonably be compared with the child abuse that is sometimes prevalent in today's society, it is still buried deep in my memory. Should I have included it here? Well, this is my way of seeking closure, so now I will happily move on.

In September of 1965, having passed both my First and Second Cub Stars, which were proudly worn on my cap either side of my cloth Wolf Cub Badge, I was entitled to join the main Scout Troop. I was interviewed by The Reverend Jonathan Boston, now the 34th Norwich Scout Master, and by November I had passed my Tenderfoot and was enrolled as a Boy Scout.

The Scout movement would not only take me on a hugely enjoyable journey but would also bring my father under its wing. Having been a parent helper he progressed to become an Adult Leader. Then, in April 1970, after training, he became Group Scout Leader of the 34th Norwich, Eaton St. Andrew's. Eventually he became District Chairman for all of Norwich South. As a result, in 1993 in recognition of his 'distinguished service to Scouting', the Chief Scout awarded him with both the Silver Acorn, a very special brooch with the Scout insignia, along with an associated certificate. As I have previously mentioned, during this time, both my sisters also progressed through the ranks of the Girl Guide movement to become Queen Guides.

Being a Scout in the 34th Norwich was slightly different compared to most other troops, in that it had more of a military theme and feeling. For instance, it would undertake activities that others then, and certainly today, would never dream of organising.

I think this was mainly down to some of the personalities and backgrounds of its three leaders (Fig. 49). Jonathan Boston, centre, my father, left, and to a lesser extent Howard Kimber, to the right, whose son was also in our troop.

What I go on to describe next, stems from the fact that Jonathan was a keen member of the Territorial Army, and my father had been through WWII, as an army tank driver/engineer. These qualities combined to deliver camps and general outdoor activities that we, as boys, loved. I'm not sure that our mothers knew quite what we were doing or were aware of the perceived dangers that we faced. We thrived on it though!

Figure 49

From recollection, the troop offered the opportunity to go on two or three camps a year. The main one being 10-14 days, under canvas and in another county – in 1966 it was in Clapham, in Yorkshire. The photograph (Fig. 50) is

Chapter 2 School, Scouting & Eaton Village 1960 – 1973

of a typical Scout camp. Another time, I remember it was in the Midlands on land owned by a local, rather rotund and eccentric vicar, who was known to Jonathan.

By all accounts this vicar was the character upon whom 'The Fat Controller' was based, in the renowned 'Thomas the Tank Engine' books. The author of these books, first published in May 1945, was The Reverend Wilbert Awdry. We discovered later that the portly and rather unconventional landowner was, in fact, Jonathan's actual uncle and knew the Reverend Awdry well. This is totally plausible as they were both in the same profession, and his uncle certainly had a love of everything and anything to do with trains.

Actually, to say he loved trains was an understatement – he was totally besotted by them! In his vicarage garden, near to where we were camping, was a ¾ scale working steam railway on which we all thoroughly enjoyed having rides. It was, of course, driven by its owner who was dressed accordingly, not as a cleric but as a spectacular and very realistic train driver! When you went into the house it was packed full of train memorabilia and trinkets. These included train mugs, tea towels, pictures and even notices in the loo asking you not to flush the toilet whilst in the station! To us young scouts and also our leaders, it was paradise!

These camps, an example is shown here (Fig. 50), were supplemented with shorter ones nearer to home, some of which were on land owned by Jonathan's mother in Buxton Lamas, Norfolk. Another favourite location was Beetley again in Norfolk, and both of these sites had a river nearby. A river was most definitely an essential element for a successful camp.

A typical day would start with a kit inspection, by the scout leaders. This entailed the occupants of each tent laying out on a groundsheet their key items of clothing and equipment, ready for scrutinisation! As you can see (Fig. 51),

Figure 50

Figure 51

57

the overall standard/style of presentation differed somewhat from person to person!

Afterwards, once you had put your kit away, breakfast was cooked and served by the group of scouts allocated to that day's rota. Again, the quality varied from day to day but we were assured each evening of one substantial and nourishing meal, as this was always prepared and cooked by the adult helpers whilst we scouts were out and about.

'Out and about' could be interpreted in a number of ways, e.g. improving our map reading skills, visiting local villages or towns to experience how people lived and worked in the area, playing football on the campsite, or building obstacle courses through the trees. There were also opportunities to understand some more extreme challenges, and I can clearly remember one such challenge which was learning how to jump out of the back of a moving vehicle, which was invariably the scout van being driven slowly round the campsite. The key thing to remember was to roll when you hit the ground, otherwise it hurt! Whilst this was exciting, demanding and difficult, I never quite understood why the development of this skill was important.

But the *pièce de résistance* was the game of 'Attack and Defend'. Basically, the scouts were split into two groups, Attackers and Defenders. Each member of the group was given a particular-coloured sash so they could be identified as either attackers or defenders. If you either lost it or had this taken by an opposing team, you were rendered dead and therefore out of the game. As a result, you then had to follow your team members, to ensure your safe return to camp but were not allowed to participate. Each group would be given a map plus a map reference of the location that they were either defending or attacking. Nine times out of ten the location being defended would be a small river bridge, usually on an obscure country lane where there was very little traffic. Hence the importance of rivers being nearby the camp sites.

Once the attackers had been driven to their allocated location, a couple of miles away, they were also handed some matches and several 'bangers' which were small fireworks. These were to be used to 'blow up' their target. Clearly it was vital that you first identified exactly where you were on the map and where you were attacking, for if either of these were incorrectly identified your group was in trouble. So, the scout leaders would, of course, check your map reading skills before you were left to your own devices to navigate your way to the bridge.

In order to effect a successful ambush, finding the location being defended obviously had to be carried out without being seen, by any of the defending team. Once ownership of the bridge had been claimed, the defenders were eliminated by taking their sash(es). Then, with the bangers you could 'blow up' the bridge! This was achieved by setting off an agreed number of fireworks, either under the bridge or very close to it. Whilst all this activity was taking place the adjudicators, aka the scout leaders, looked on as judges. Their decision regarding the extent and success of the bridge being captured was always final!

As a member of the 'defenders', after having verified your map reference with the scout leader, you made your way by foot as unobtrusively and secretly as possible, from the camp to the bridge which normally wasn't that far away. Once there you had to try and establish which route any attackers might take and see if they could be eliminated, by removing their sash(es). Of course, you had to leave behind a sufficient 'force' to defend the bridge, just in case your assumption was incorrect as to which direction the attack might come. However, on the way, if any of the defenders were captured they had to return to the bridge but not take an active role going forward.

I have to say that it was good fun but with hindsight and with an understanding of the concern that today's society has for Health and Safety, it was most unsafe and dangerous. Nowadays, we certainly would not give nine to 15-year-olds fireworks to throw at each other! But we all survived, and I certainly don't recall any accidents. As I have said, our scout activities were certainly different and very loosely based on military training.

Years later, in 2024, whilst driving along a small country road (B1110) out of North Elmham, which was close to the scout camp site in Beetley, I had a 'light bulb' moment when I recognised one of the bridges that as a scout, all those years ago, I had had to either blow-up or defend. I can't recall which. Having stopped the car, I took this photograph (Fig. 52) of the bridge now very overgrown with greenery. Still all in good condition though, despite our 'explosive' attack!

Figure 52

REFLECTIONS UPON A FAMILY

Back home in Eaton Village, there were a number of children of our age some were Scouts or Guides whilst others were not, but we were all friends and played together. Both my and their parents were good friends and looked after us all when we were around their homes or in their gardens. Sometimes, we all just participated in the simple pleasures of going blackberry picking on the farmland that was adjacent to the estate, and we were able to do this so long as it hadn't just been sprayed. Later on, this land was to disappear under the new houses that were built, and in 2025 Eaton is three or four times the size it was in the 1960s. As a child, it was such a lovely environment and culture in which to grow up.

There was one process, mentioned above, which was connected to the farmers' crop management that has now, thankfully, been outlawed. This was aerial crop spraying and one activity that the adults, who lived on the periphery of the village, adjacent to the farmland, were not happy with and for good reasons. I shall now explain how it took place.

As the farmer's small light aircraft came swooping down to treat the field its sprays, located on the wings, were activated and gallons of weedkiller or other 'essential' chemicals like DDT (dichlorodiphenyltrichloroethane, a synthetic insecticide) would be sprayed all over the field. We children loved to watch this spectacle and were totally oblivious to the environmental damage, and the risk to ourselves should we be accidently sprayed. I must say that fortunately this never happened, as we were never close enough. However, the pilot whilst taking the aircraft into a steep climb to avoid the houses, was not always quick enough to turn off the spray and therefore gardens and areas of grass in its path were accidentally treated. This was not good, as invariably the error also killed many precious and lovingly tended garden plants. Luckily, our house was in an area that wasn't close enough to the fields and therefore not affected by this 'inaccuracy'. With Cranleigh Rise though, being at the top of a small hill, we did have an advantageous location from which to view the acrobatics. As I have said aerial crop spraying was to be banned and this came into force in Britain, in 1986, so all gardens and wildlife were now safe from its effects.

At this time, I had already shown a keen interest in becoming a farmer. What sort I didn't know and probably didn't fully appreciate what was entailed, but I had decided that farming was to be my vocation. To help me understand more about my possible career my parents, with the help of Wal and Dora my nursery teachers from Kent, arranged for me to have a 'working holiday'. This was to be with Wal and Dora's daughter and son-in-law, Brenda and Colin Hennah and their son, Rupert, who was around eight or nine years old. Arrangements were accordingly put in place and during one summer holiday I duly stayed with them on their mixed farm.

I thoroughly enjoyed this time 'being a farmer', working on the harvest, and for a while this was to be my dream occupation. Even today I wonder what would have happened had this ambition materialised. But regrettably, or maybe fortunately, it never did!

Years later in 1997 though, it was still in the back of my mind when Oliver my son, also showed an interest in agriculture and as a teenager he worked on a local farm, helping to deliver lambs. It was during this lambing season, in January, on one long cold night, when I was so fortunate to be able to be with him, and I too was able to deliver a newborn lamb. These times were wonderful and supported the father/son bonding. My successful efforts were also recorded for posterity by Kate, as you can see (Fig. 53).

Alas, farming would not become either of our professions, but it was a close thing for me at least!

Figure 53

As I have previously indicated, my dad and I always kept ourselves busy, not only in the garden but also in altering and improving the home. At Cranleigh Rise we or should I say Dad and a friendly builder, plus me as a general 'gofer' helper and cement mixer, converted a carport into a proper garage. There was also a small but useful enclosed conservatory/boot room with a door to the rear of the garage. From the garden you entered the boot room to go into the kitchen. As I have said this was used for boots and shoes etc. but on one occasion, when Dad wasn't around, we found an uninvited guest in there. The guest was a mouse, which Mum set about catching with the aim of returning it to the garden. The mouse, having found a comfortable and warm home, was having none of this and scampered off to hide in the adjoining empty garage. Mum followed with the inevitable 'cat and mouse' chase but, in this case, it turned out to be a 'mum and mouse' chase! The result was that the mouse was caught under a cloth, picked up and secured ready to be transported outside. But Mr Mouse had the last throw of the dice, when before being released back into the garden, he bit my mother's finger! That made it an even score!

Despite this incident, we did have frequent and very welcome visitors to Cranleigh Rise, among them were Rosemary and her first husband Mike Stone. Rosemary (née Horton) is my cousin and was a bridesmaid at my parents' wedding on 9 June 1951. As our garden was still in its infancy, during their short visit, Mike and I played with some of my toy cars, on a pile of sand that Dad was still using. I remember Mike showing me how to create roads etc. using my fingertips and soon we had made a really good track. It's strange how these little but generous interactions stick in your memory. I sometimes wonder, when my grandchildren reach my age, what they will recall about their times they have had with me.

Anyway, Dad's pile of sand was heaped there, as he was laying a 'crazy paving' patio. In those days, crazy paving was readily available at a very low cost from the local council and delivered to your door. It was created by the council taking up and replacing broken pavements and it made ideal and more importantly cheap garden patio slabs.

Whilst 'landscaping' the garden at the back, Dad made a large fishpond and beside it was a small, but evidently fast-growing, willow tree. For some reason I was kept at arm's length where this pond was concerned. I wonder why! In the front garden he also planted two small silver birch trees, either side of a rockery. Silver birch trees were all the rage, at the time, and ours were obtained late one evening, not from a garden centre but from a natural wood in Ringland Hills! Not sure that this was legal, but once planted in our garden they did look rather attractive.

Another advantage of living on a slight hill was that we could cycle down the road at some speed, without having to pedal hard. Of course, the return journey wasn't such fun but having endured the uphill slope we were able to make a further descent! One day though, whilst cycling up and down, a police motorcyclist came up the road. Now, Lucky our dog, who was always around us children, had an extreme aversion to motorbikes. Why, we never knew, but he was soon chasing the policeman back down the hill. 'Lucky by name and lucky by nature', it resulted in no action being taken and Lucky returned to us, out of breath and satisfied that he had 'seen off' the interloper. I recall that this was the last escapade for Lucky, who nevertheless lived a long and wonderful life before he died naturally of old age, a few years later. R.I.P. my faithful friend.

Cycling was definitely an activity that all of us children enjoyed, and it was certainly encouraged by our parents. There was, however, one time that cycling led to a catastrophic incident for me. One day, whilst out and about on my bicycle, presumably going to the shops, as that is the only rationale for being where I was, when I had an accident.

I was gaily cycling past the Methodist Chapel, on Church Lane, Eaton (Fig. 54 & map ref. 3), when I fell off having tried, totally unsuccessfully, to negotiate my bicycle down a kerb, at too fast a pace. The inevitable result was that I went headfirst over my handlebars, and the brake handle somehow cut the right side of my chin, causing not only a lot of pain but also, to my very obvious distress, a lot of blood!

Figure 54

I recall that some people around me rushed to help, and I know I was asked about where I lived. All I wanted to do though, was to return to the safety of my home but just how this was to be achieved is now a little hazy. I seem to remember walking along Greenways, pushing my bicycle. But also, I can't believe that those kind people who came to my rescue, would have allowed me, a small and badly injured boy of around ten or 11 years old, to simply walk home. But arrive home I did, and cloths, fresh bandages and stinging ointment were duly applied. The cut was still bleeding, and it was decided that I needed to go to the local hospital.

Luckily, the local dedicated children's hospital, the Jenny Lind, was not far away, so we arrived after a short drive. By this time, as it was 'out of hours', there was a short wait for the medical staff to come to my aid. When they did, the inevitable words were spoken – *'we will have to numb the area with a small injection and then just put in some little stitches'*. If I thought that an injection in my arm by Dr. Cowan was bad, this was to be considerably worse – I had to get out of there! The result was yet another ensuing struggle with the medics, but this time my father rather than my mother was supporting them. I lost that battle, and because of my constant fidgeting the stitching was not as neat as it could have been. It was successful though in closing the wound, but it has left me with a permanent 3" scar. A reminder to this day as to why I should not struggle!

There was, of course, a 'round two', when the stitches came out, but I don't recall that being too bad. As I have just said, the evidence has remained a personal facial feature, and in senior school my nickname was '*Gillie*', a reference to fish gills! My retort was always '*I'm ok, but you should have seen the other boy!*' Not sure if that actually helped, but it made me feel less self-conscious and appear really strong.

Following a summer of camping, seaside holidays and of course, on 30 July, the infamous 1966 England's Football World Cup win, the prospect loomed of joining my new school. The one thing that always happens when you move from Junior to Senior School is that in the '*pecking order*', you have to start all over again at the lowest point. In regard to this, Lakenham School was no different to any other senior school and from what I can recall it certainly wasn't that bad.

My first day was on Monday 5 September 1966 and was spent familiarising myself with the school and where everything was situated, as it was a much larger set of buildings to those of Avenue Road. Friends at school were easy to make, as some had followed me from The Avenues, others I knew as they also lived in Eaton Village. My best friends were Graham Nunn and our neighbour Keith Judson, who both seemed to have the same approach to education as me which was to do the very best you could and hope it was enough to get you through.

The timetable seemed to have very recognisable lessons, other than three new subjects. One being science, which took place in a laboratory, and I'd never been in one of those before. The other two were woodwork and metalwork when we always had to wear aprons, and sometimes goggles but those were only required for some specific activities. Still, all those subjects were enjoyable, and I got on well with the teachers.

The metalwork teacher was Mr Williamson, who, as I was to learn, was multi-skilled. Not only did he teach but he was building his own fibreglass cruising boat in his front garden, and during the school lunch break he played and built guitars. I enjoyed both woodwork and metalwork and by my reckoning seemed to be fairly good at each subject. So, when there was an opportunity, I plucked up courage and asked Mr Williamson if he would help me to make a guitar. To my great surprise and relief he agreed, and after many months of steaming, bending, planing and gluing of wood, I had a recognisable instrument ready for completion. Now I just needed the extra items that I couldn't make myself, in order to be able to finish my guitar.

My dad, who seemed to know everywhere in Norfolk and Suffolk where you could buy just what you needed, took me to numerous shops where we eventually purchased lengths of various wooden inlays in different colours,

Chapter 2 School, Scouting & Eaton Village 1960 – 1973

pegs/tuners, strings, frets and a bridge. All of which I fitted to my new instrument (Fig. 55). Alas though, despite following the instructions in the BBC book '*Hold down a Cord – Folk Guitar for Beginners*', I was unable to master the actual playing of my guitar.

At 13 though, perhaps I simply didn't have the determination. Something that now, in retrospect, I regret but other activities have now taken priority, so whilst it would be possible to learn, I doubt this will be achieved.

The closest I ever came to being involved in classical music was in December 1967, when I joined my sister Judy in the first production of Benjamin Britten's War Requiem. This was held at Norwich Cathedral, with the Norwich Philharmonic singers and orchestra, a range of choirs that included The University Choir, The Cathedral Choristers and some of the City Schools, Lakenham being one of them. To quote from the lavish programme, Britten was…

Figure 55

> *…particularly active in encouraging young people's interest in music, and much of his work reflects this.*

It was certainly an honour and a privilege to be involved. But apart from my singing in the local Church Choir, the War Requiem was to be my one and only public performance.

To our neighbour's horror, I did take up playing the cornet – if you can say the sounds that I produced was playing? But that too didn't last for long. I guess it was just like the recorder at The Avenues, and it was becoming clear that the playing of instruments simply wasn't my forte.

From my perspective, at school I generally seemed to be progressing well at most subjects. I recall, at the time being more skilled at the practical lessons, which were to be reflected later in life when renovating houses and landscaping gardens. In the academic subjects I enjoyed both geography and history, which

65

was endorsed by winning several 'Year Group' achievement awards. These two particular subjects have continued to appeal to me, for much later on I became an adult student studying 'The Landscape and Environment' and have also researched our family tree.

At the age of 14, in 1969, I began, like so many of my generation, to become more interested in world events. This was enhanced by the Space Race between the United States of America (USA) and the Union of Soviet Socialist Republics (USSR, now Russia). Although, in the 50s and 60s the USSR appeared to be ahead in this race, the ultimate prize went to the USA in 1969, when Neil Armstrong and Buzz Aldrin landed on the moon and returned safely back to earth. Many, including me, remember those immortal words from Armstrong: *'One small step for man. One giant leap for mankind'*. However, he later maintained that he had said *'One small step for **a** man, one giant leap for mankind.* He later annotated the official transcript accordingly.[12]

By this time, we had moved from Cranleigh Rise to 24 Ebbisham Drive, and I was of an age when I was allowed to stay up and watch this unforgettable 'Moon Landing'. On this momentous day, in July 1971, James Burke, Cliff Mitchelmore and Patrick Moore were hosting the BBC coverage.

It was an incredibly tense and a wonderful feat to watch. Just being able to see what was actually happening on the moon was mind-blowing, let alone the fact that they were real astronauts, risking their lives, thousands of miles away and determined to be the first humans to step foot on the moon!

My interest in space exploration continued, for in 1971, my fourth year at The Hewett School, I was awarded both Geography and Art awards. For my prize I chose a copy of Patrick Moore's 'Moon Flight Atlas', which can be seen (Fig. 56) along with the award certificates.

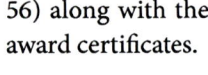

Figure 56

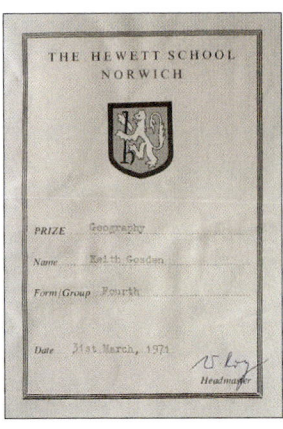
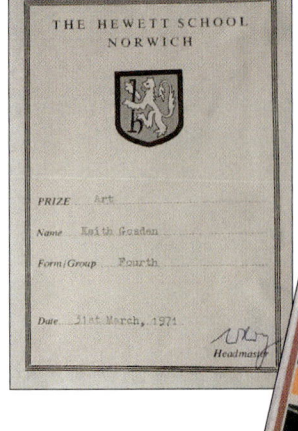

---

12   The American Philosophical Society 2023 / amphilsov.org

Chapter 2 School, Scouting & Eaton Village 1960 – 1973

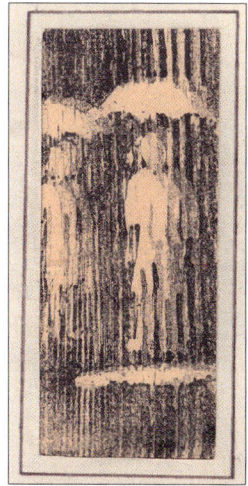

Figure 57   Figure 58

My winning artwork was a linocut entitled '*A Walk in the Rain*', (Fig. 57) and a scraperboard image of a flower (Fig. 58).

It is perhaps significant that my educational achievement awards were generally few and far between, and as they didn't take up much room in our house, I was able to save all of them, over my entire school career! But there is more to studying and education than collecting awards. Learning and acquiring social skills are just as important, as I was to demonstrate, later in life.

Returning to a few years earlier, in 1965, when I was almost ten, the world lost one of its greatest statesmen, orator, writer and Prime Minister, Sir Winston Spencer Churchill, who died, aged 90, on 24 January that year. Following a full state funeral, which was a huge honour for someone who was not royalty, he was buried in St. Martin's Church, Bladon, alongside other family members and within sight of his birthplace, Blenheim Palace. Like thousands of other parents and children, our family not only watched the funeral on television but also, later in the year, went to visit his resting place.

Back at Cranleigh Rise which, as its name suggests, was on a hill and at the top where we lived, there were several other families with children, who included the Kingstons opposite us, and the Judsons and Oelrichs either side of us, so there was plenty of fun to be had. This included football in the Kingstons' back garden, until the ball went over the fence, into Mrs Rogers's garden. Then it was a toss-up as to who would be brave enough to ask this formidable, elderly lady

67

if we could collect our ball. However, once or twice a year, she would astound us by coming out of her bungalow with a huge plate, covered with slices of pink and white coconut ice, for all of us children to share. Perhaps we had misjudged her?

For some reason, our end of the road seemed to be populated with young individuals and families, whilst in the middle section there were a few bungalows, including Mrs Rogers, that were mainly occupied by elderly people. Then towards the bottom, where the road joined Greenways, there were newer houses built much later, by a different developer, and like our end, those were occupied by younger families.

Eaton, at that time, was to be home for a number of newly transferred players/staff from the Norwich City Football Club. I believed the club owned some of the properties and rented them out, whilst the transferees and new staff looked for permanent homes. One such occupier was ex Rotherham United footballer Laurence (Lol) Morgan and his family. At this point in his career, however, he was the manager of Norwich City Football Club (NCFC), from June 1966-May 1969, and Judy and I were very fortunate as we would often earn a little pocket money by babysitting their children. As you can imagine, this was much appreciated by all sides.

One of the Cranleigh Rise middle bungalows was home to a lovely lady, Mrs Marion Taylor, and her Scottish companion and housekeeper, Agnes. Mrs Taylor was an elderly, 'well to do' lady, who spent much of her day sitting in her chair, with a cat on her lap. I became friends with both her and Agnes, as the cat was indeed ours, and being a typical cat she just seemed to enjoy everyone's company, living in both our house and their bungalow. I suspect she also received double the quantity of meals. As the saying goes *'as cunning as a cat'*.

Whilst both Mrs Taylor and Agnes kept themselves to themselves, everyone in the locality knew them, and would certainly pass the time of day with Agnes if she was in the front garden. I was a regular visitor though, and was treated to cake and squash, which seemed to happen to me every time I visited somewhere, not that I ever complained or refused!

My parents though, were insistent that I should not disturb either Agnes or Mrs Taylor when 'the family' were there. We knew when they had arrived because a large cream-coloured Austin A70 Countryman would be in the drive, and this was our signal to keep away and not to disturb 'the family'. Their actual car can be seen, in the contemporary

Figure 59

photograph (Fig. 59), parked outside their home and family's dental surgery practice, in Unthank Road, Norwich.

We, of course, duly kept away but unbeknown to me and everyone else at the time, one member of this 'family', when I was older, was to turn my entire life upside down and inside out. But that's a story for later in the memoir.

For a while, 24 Cranleigh Rise was also to house a large vehicle in its drive but certainly not one as smart as the Countryman! Ours was to be the large Bedford Scout van which we as keen Scouts were to repaint, whilst it sat in our drive. With 'wet and dry' paper in hand, prior to us repainting it, we all set about rubbing down the paintwork. Before the work commenced though, my parents had well justified concerns about the state of our lovely drive, so had wisely parked the van on protective sheeting. A very sensible move, as in the end after much work on the van and a little on the drive, the latter still looked clean and fit for use. Strangely enough though, my dad never again 'volunteered' our drive for Scout use!

From my perspective life in Cranleigh Rise was good, as I had friends, a large garden, scouts and was near to school. I was to learn from my mother though, many years later that she wasn't totally happy living there, as according to her some of the newer residents had become a little 'snooty'.

This was to be rectified by a short move to 24 Ebbisham Drive. Whilst the actual date is unknown to me, I have recently inherited an 'Air Mail' letter that I sent home, dated 8 March 1968, from the Nevasa cruise ship, which was addressed to Ebbisham Drive. So that would indicate a move around the end of 1967. I shall elaborate on this cruise ship, shortly.

The move, whilst being only a few minute's walk away, was too much for our cat, so she was 'adopted' by Mrs Taylor and Agnes. We did miss her, but other new pets were to replace our loss, including a budgerigar named Joey and another dog called Sheba, not the one in the photograph of our new home (Fig. 60).

Figure 60

There was one other secret advantage to the move that pleased me and that was the address. I couldn't spell 'Cranleigh' but there again 'Ebbisham' was only marginally easier – but nevertheless I welcomed this minor benefit.

The introduction of Joey to our family of pets was not well received by my sister Judy. She was fine with our budgerigar just so long as it stayed in its cage. Joey, on the other hand, liked to fly around the living room, always returning to his cage where he would normally find food. Judy was not amused by this and usually left the room. On the odd occasion, if she stayed for a short while, you could be assured that Joey would land on her shoulder or even her head, causing hysterical actions to ensure his removal. As a younger and probably an annoying brother, I was very aware of this aversion to budgerigars and kept this knowledge in my head, for future occasions!

Around this time, every Saturday at the Norwich City Library, I undertook some voluntary work as part of my scout awards, and I worked in the children's section on the upper floor of the main library. Here I checked-out and date stamped the various books that the children had chosen whilst also receiving back their returned books that when time allowed, I had to return to the correct shelves. This was interesting work, and from memory, it lasted for well over a year or so. I undertook all this, a couple of years before the library was unfortunately razed to the ground which I will refer to later.

My mother now clearly wanted some different work that was more stimulating than running the Brownies, that she had started some time earlier, and helping with the Eaton Nursery School, run by Mrs Barnett and held in the Village Hall.

At the time, Norfolk's largest employer was Norwich Union Insurance and in April 1969 she applied and was successful in gaining part-time employment, as shown in her appointment letter (Fig. 61), giving details of her hours of work and pay.

This not only brought additional income to the family but also gave my mother new interests and challenges, as prior to her marriage she had worked in the publishing business with the magazine 'Field', which was more demanding than her current work in Eaton village.

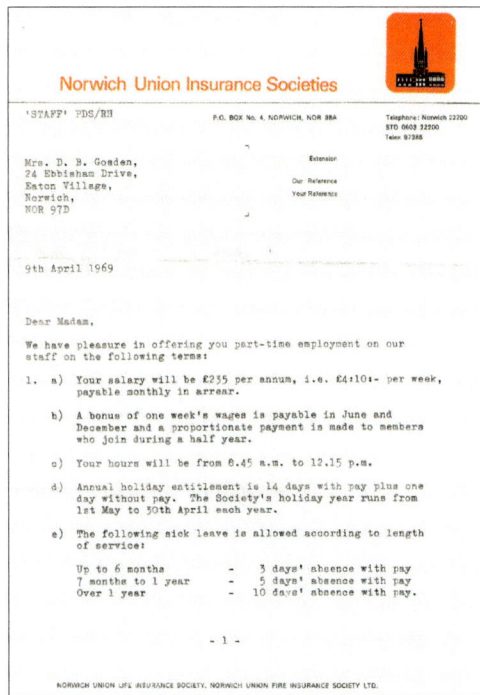

Figure 61

Chapter 2 School, Scouting & Eaton Village 1960 – 1973

Out of interest, at the time of writing, I can confirm that Mum was the first of our family to join Norwich Union. She was, in time, followed by all three of her children, both of her sons-in-law and one of her grandsons. Not sure on the collective length of service but it must be over 100 years!

There was one very important bonus to being employed by Norwich Union and that was a car parking space, in the centre of Norwich. This was to prove an absolute 'godsend' later on, when I was old enough to take a driving test. I will explain more a little further on.

Having spent a few years with Norwich Union, during which the family joined her on several staff social trips, including one to Rüdesheim in Germany, Mum decided to change her employment. She moved to Garlands of Norwich, a high-end departmental store, where she worked in the Royal Worcester department, which she thoroughly enjoyed.

This was after the infamous Garlands fire, (Fig. 62)[13], on 1 August 1970 which totally destroyed the original building and necessitated a complete rebuild. This was the largest fire in Norwich since WWII. That 'honour', however, was taken over by Norwich Central Library, which by coincidence burnt down on 1 August 1994, 24 years later. This latter fire was to become one of the biggest in Norwich and in their own ways both these redevelopments were to reshape and modernise the City centre.

Figure 62

Both Mum and Dad, in whatever they gave us and whenever they allowed us the freedom to do what we wished, were always scrupulously fair to all three of us siblings. A trait throughout my life that I have endeavoured to carry out, so I understand and respect the difficulties and sacrifices they must have endured.

That said, from my perspective, when my sister Judy was to go on a Mediterranean cruise with the school, I knew that at some point, I too would have the same opportunity.

---

13 (Image: Archant) https://www.edp24.co.uk/lifestyle/20751965.august-1-date-tragedy-years-norwich/

REFLECTIONS UPON A FAMILY

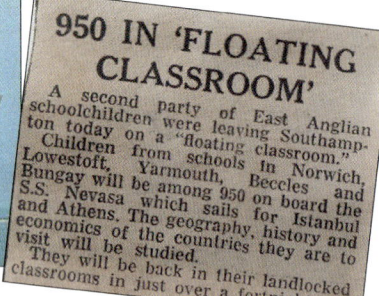

Figure 63 (above) and Figure 64 (right)

This was to materialise on 4 March 1968, when I set sail, from Southampton, on SS *Nevasa* (Fig. 63)[14]. The total cost of my cruise was £52.00, which was quite a sum in those days – by comparison the garage Dad and I built in Cranleigh Rise, just a couple of years earlier, cost around one hundred pounds.

We set sail and my dormitory was Collingwood where away from the port hole I had a bottom bunk. The local *Eastern Evening News* carried this short report about the cruise. As the cutting states (Fig. 64) we were due to visit both Istanbul and Athens but before this we actually docked at Ceuta, next to Morocco, on the north coast of Africa. From there we sailed, for a day, to Heraklion. This was followed by a day in Istanbul, then on to Piraeus and Athens, before cruising to Venice. Here we caught the flight back to the UK, where, with presents in hand, we met up with our waiting parents and then we all drove back home.

The whole experience was great fun and very interesting but as it was an 'educational' cruise there were lessons to attend and daily written logs to keep up to date. My letter home (Fig. 65) makes interesting reading, along with some unusual spelling. Even I can see that!

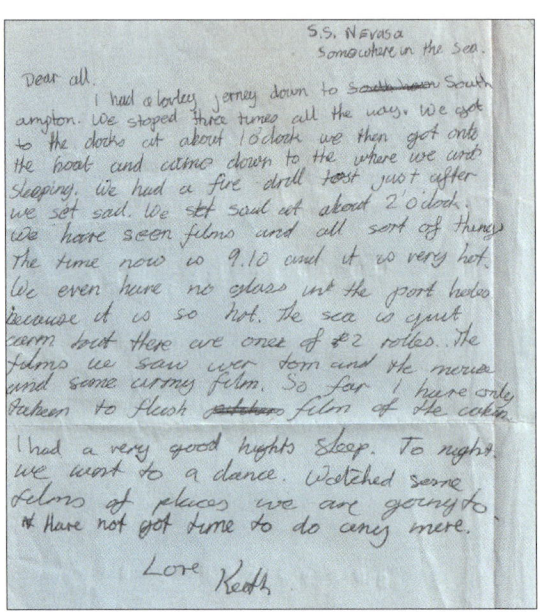

Figure 65

---

14 Image of SS *Nevasa* courtesy of SS Uganda Trust website

Chapter 2 School, Scouting & Eaton Village 1960 – 1973

It was around this time, 1967-69, that Grandad and Nanny (Randall) moved from The Croft in Orpington to Drayton, just outside Norwich. This followed Grandad's retirement from Creeds, as he had reached the mandatory age when a State Pension could be claimed. They moved to a bungalow called 'Woods End', situated in Pond Lane. In some way or other the property had previously been connected, not physically though, to the farm next door, for at the end of a large back garden, there were two or three very large farm chicken houses. One of my early memories is of helping both my dad and grandad to knock down and burn all but one of these sheds. What great fun that was, climbing on the pitch rooves and breaking up the structure with a sledgehammer.

Grandad was more than satisfied, once he had established and set up the remaining shed to his liking, for instance with a wood stove, bench with vices, tool racks etc. It turned out to be an almost exact replica of his shed/garage at The Croft.

In fact, when not either creating some mechanical gadget to put in the car or the garden, he would often be found sitting by the fire, in the work shed reading Swiss Family Robinson. He read this time and time again, and upon his death, in October 1980, the copy was literally falling apart through excessive use. It obviously gave him much pleasure and I suspect, more importantly, kept him out of Nanny's way.

Nanny was very careful with her belongings, and I recall that none of us grandchildren, unless we sat down and took great care, were allowed to have any ginger beer in her precious glasses. When clearing her bungalow, following her move to Norwich, Mum asked if I would like anything. Guess what I chose? So that I could remember her, there were just two items that I wished to inherit, and they were two of the ginger beer glasses in her kitchen (Fig. 66). They are just as safe now, as they were back then. I don't recall who had the others!

Figure 66

Grandad was always keen to help us or simply make something that he thought would be useful. For instance, over time, we would all be given our own Bird Table, elaborately and carefully made to his own design. He also made me a simple 'T' shaped tool, the handle of which helped with opening a water stopcock cover, whilst the long arm had a shaped end that fitted over the tap, this allowed the user to turn the tap without having to kneel down to reach it. Should I ever need it I still have this in my garage! Grandad had thought of everything!

It was in the late 1960s and like many youngsters of my age, I was looking to earn some pocket money. My choice was to become a paper boy, for the local newsagents 'Ottaways' situated on a parade of old shops, at the top of Church Lane.

Leaving home at about 06.00, each weekday I would first go to the back of the shop, where there was a small row of cottages of which only one was inhabited. This one was on the end, nearest the road and occupied by Mr Fiddy, a very elderly gentleman, who with his two goats all lived here together in the cottage! He was a real character and seemed to enjoy both the company and interaction with us paper boys. All these cottages were very old and dilapidated 'one up, one down' properties and due to their condition Mr Fiddy was the only human occupant! One of these cottages in the short terrace, housed all the bicycles and I would select my trade bike and make my way to the rear of the shop, to collect my newspaper round.

After announcing my arrival, I would collect my papers and magazines, already in order and numbered for me, and put them into my bicycle basket. This trade bike was the same type as that used by butchers, in that it had a small front wheel, above which in front of the handlebars was a large wicker basket, if you were lucky. If you were slightly too late you had a cardboard box instead. This definitely had to be avoided in inclement weather, which meant an even earlier start to the day!

Having been given all the papers etc. and a list of streets and house numbers, I commenced my delivery, setting off very carefully in order that I didn't disturb the order of the papers, and dutifully followed the route that I had been allocated. The actual delivery was reasonably easy and took an hour or so, meaning that I could be home around eight o'clock, in time to change for school. For six mornings of work, Monday – Saturday, I received about 12 shillings which in today's money equates to just over £12. Not a fortune but enough to make a difference.

As time went on and I became more familiar with the 'round', I would take on not only more 'rounds' but would turn up at the shop early, in time to bring in the bundles of papers, from the John Menzies delivery lorry. First these had to be 'marked up', which involved putting the newspapers and magazines into individual piles. Then, with the aid of a board which held small address slips, with the names of the papers etc. for each address, all placed in the order of the paper round, the day's papers and journals were 'marked up'. It was my job to take the appropriate papers off the piles, mark them up by putting the house name/number in the corner of the newspaper to create the 'round', resulting in a large pile of newspapers and magazines for the paper boy to collect. The shop owner and I, plus a couple of others, would usually set up around 10 – 12 rounds each morning. It was hard and fast work and as the shop was so small you couldn't have more than three maybe four people in it, all rushing to take various newspapers and magazines off different piles. Needless to say, this additional work meant extra income for me, which was gratefully accepted.

On days when it was raining etc. my dad, if he was able to, would join me and together we would deliver the round, sometimes on foot but more often from the back of his car. I was not only very appreciative of this help but also very aware that this was great father and son bonding.

Dad would sometimes tell me about his work and where he was going later that day. Other times he would confide in me and not only relate some of the events that occurred to him as a soldier during WWII but would also share some of his more harrowing experiences.

There was one occasion, and I was told not to say anything to my mother, as it would upset her, when he told me how he had stopped his tank and he and his fellow soldiers got out to 'deal' with several cattle. These were clearly suffering from shrapnel wounds, and as there was no farmer around, the only kind and humane action for them to carry out was to shoot them. Whilst I listened to this story, Dad was clearly very upset at this experience. He was not one for sharing his war-time stories so I felt very privileged, and it meant so much to me that he was prepared to confide in me, with these very personal accounts that happened to him during the war.

On a lighter note, the best time of the year, when under no circumstances you would ever hand over your round, to another paper boy, were the deliveries leading up to Christmas. Two of my rounds, Church Lane and Colney Lane, contained some very large houses, whose occupants always 'tipped' us paper boys, very well. Ten 'bob' notes (circa £10 at the time of writing) were frequently given to me, as a Christmas Box. This certainly made the extra hard work very worthwhile, as I was now undertaking Sunday deliveries, in addition to the weekdays. Sundays were more arduous due to the number of supplements and often one house had two or more papers. How could anyone read all those in just one day?

There was one incident during my rounds that infuriated my father, to a point that I had never seen before or since. In the early days of being a paper boy I was delivering, as usual, the morning papers along Ebbisham Drive, when I was stopped by a resident, Mr Woolley, who I instantly recognised as a teacher at Lakenham School. Obviously, he knew me and that I was underage and had clearly been monitoring my deliveries. Unlike me though, he was aware that to be a paper boy you had to be at least 13. Now to continue with this episode, I was then asked to get into the car of a council worker, who had obviously been observing me as well, and had presumably been tipped off by Mr Woolley, and I was taken to the shop where the shop keeper and I were told that I did not qualify for paid employment!

Figure 67

My father was summoned and heated discussions were held. Whilst all accepted that I was underage – by only a few months – my dad was incandescent with the council worker for taking me away in his car. Sensibly, I was taken home and was not involved in the ensuing actions. A month or so later, in order to collect my Employment Badge, (Fig. 67) which was issued by the Norwich Education Committee, I was allowed to go to the City Hall, in Norwich with my father, along with some form of identification. The badge bore a personalised number and came in the form of a small, round metal buttonhole badge which whilst on my 'rounds' I was to wear on my jacket. My number, as you can see, was 926. Paper rounds could now resume!

Of course, once the newspapers and magazines had been read, they had little use, other than for fire lighting or drying out wet shoes, so this is where the Scouts came to the rescue. Once a month, with the aid of our newly painted van, as well as a number of parents, lots of combined muscle power and the co-operation from many of the residents, we collected pile after pile of wastepaper, left out by the gate of numerous houses. It was now that I found out that being a paper boy was really advantageous, as I knew where the best quantities would be found. Everything collected was then loaded into either our van or car trailers and taken off to the Village Hall, where it was all neatly stacked at the back of the building. Dry paper definitely commanded a better price than wet, so to keep out the moisture a tarpaulin was put over the stack, which by now was huge, about 15 feet tall and 6-8 feet square. Warmingers, who were Norwich's pioneering waste disposal company and based in Ber Street, were then duly notified, and arrived once a month, with an enormous lorry to collect the pile. My dad, as Assistant Scout Leader and wastepaper collection organiser, would then wait a few days, until the lorry had been weighed and unloaded, before going to their office to collect the payment. These proceeds all went into the scout funds and were used to support both the Cubs and Scouts, a movement that Alf Warminger very much supported. These payments and the resulting funds were not insignificant.

Chapter 2 School, Scouting & Eaton Village 1960 – 1973

Another two huge vans which regularly made weekly trips around Eaton Village were the fishmonger and the greengrocer. The 'fish man', as we all called him, had a hand bell, similar to the one at the Avenue Road School, that he would ring to alert everyone that he was around. The greengrocer probably did the same, but he must have timed his rounds for when we children were at school, as I don't recall seeing him very often. Mum would go out to the fish man with her tin to collect the fish, usually smoked haddock but sometimes, if we were lucky, some other white fish. I can't say that I looked forward to the haddock as this was poached in milk, butter and a little pepper, all in a deep cream tin with a lid with recessed dimples across the top. You knew though, that it was going to be served for supper that night as its smell permeated all through the house, and for me that put a dampener on the whole evening. The greengrocer though, was ok, as his merchandise was acceptable – apart from the cabbage!

Other regular meals would be roasts on a Sunday, shepherd's pie on the Monday, liver and bacon during the week, along with a selection of the upcoming convenience meals. Often these were fish fingers, or a curry of something in a 'Birds Eye' box. Puddings might be 'Angel Delight', a kind of mousse or 'Arctic Roll', ice cream with a sponge covering. The choice wasn't wide and often you knew exactly what to expect by the day of the week. However, we all grew up fit and well, so we can't grumble.

There were times when Dad would certainly make us all laugh or simply 'lighten' the atmosphere, by doing something daft. This was not a recent phenomenon, as the family have photographs of both my father and mother, in the late 1940s early 1950s, before they were married, 'cross dressing' at a Pontins Holiday Camp in Paignton.

Every time was intended to be great fun, and it was. I can remember a few incidents, for example whilst in the car on a long journey, we played 'eye spy' or Dad would challenge us all to see who could spot the next car of a certain colour or make. I have to say that I recall repeating this activity with our four children and more recently with some of our grandchildren, but this by now has probably progressed to counting Eddie Stobart lorries.

He would also, on a twisty road where overtaking was difficult, slow down to well under the maximum speed limit to see how many cars backed up behind us. We had to count them out of the rear window, and during our journeys I think 15 was most probably the maximum number counted! There were also times when he would skip around or pull funny faces – all designed to entertain us children. Which it did. A small collection of Dad's 'entertaining' photographs is included (Figs. 68-70). The upside-down dog is Sam, who clearly had an affinity with my father. The frightening aspect of this for me, is that I can quite see myself lying down on the grass in exactly the same way with one of my own dogs!

The green car in the photograph was Dad's work car. Mum's car, on the other hand, was a Ford Anglia, seen in the photograph with Judy leaning against it, eating an ice cream and in which I was later to learn to drive.

Returning to Dad's antics, on one particular occasion, after a meal out with Jonathan Boston, we were in two separate vehicles and on our way home, when Jonathan made Dad stop on the side of Newmarket Road. This was in order that he could throw down a challenge to see which way was the quickest to our house, in Cranleigh Rise, either down the road or via Donkey Lane. As Dad had a company car and Jonathan a Land Rover, the choice of route for each was really obvious. Dad set off down the road, whilst Jonathan negotiated the alternative suggestion down Donkey Lane. At the time we must have had the Scout walkie talkies as there was commentary between the two drivers. I would like to say that it was a dead heat, but Jonathan was waiting for us at home when we arrived!

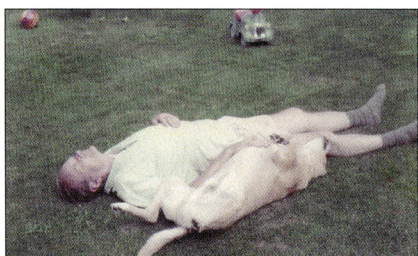

Figure 68

Figure 69

Figure 70

Chapter 2 School, Scouting & Eaton Village 1960 – 1973

Later in my life I was to spend a number of years working alongside Dad. But as a youngster I do recall 'working' with him in Ebbisham Drive. When he returned from a day's work, he would go upstairs to write out his orders from the various customers he had seen that day. Each order had to be signed but as Dad's signature was almost illegible, the company gave him a rubber stamp, with his initials on, so that this could be used instead. My 'important' job was to stamp each order with these initials. Not a huge role but one that meant a lot to me at the time and still does today.

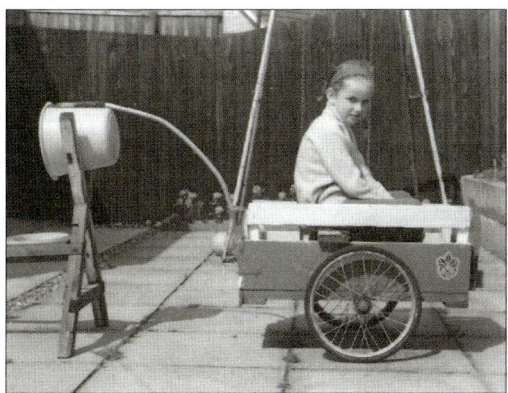

Figure 71

Whilst living at Ebbisham Drive I would often go out for long cycle rides to collect 'things'. Some of which were scouting related, others just items that would be 'useful' at some point or another. To help with the transporting of these 'things' I built a trailer (Fig. 71) that connected to my bicycle by means of a curved bar, from the trailer to a point just under my saddle. To secure this a six-inch nail was put through a hole in the saddle, from there it went down the bicycle frame and was fixed into the saddle post. All Health & Safety compliant, in my eyes! For in those days, health and safety was certainly not at the forefront of everyone's lives, nor was the society so increasingly litigious, as it is in 2025! So, by my calculation, my contraption was 'as safe as houses'. In fact, I don't ever recall any accidents, and it was obviously safe enough for my sister Sarah to be taken out and about. Perhaps, it was the engineering influence of my grandfather coming to the fore, and I hasten to add that Sarah was not a 'thing' for me to transport! But the trailer was both useful and great fun to use.

I normally cycled to school, but I frequently preferred to walk and catch the bus. This was good for my health, but it also meant I could catch the bus home from outside the Norwich High School for Girls. Now wasn't that fortunate! A group of attractive young girls regularly caught the same bus as me. I was never bold or confident enough though, to strike up a conversation with any of them, more's the pity! This was despite having been in the sixth form with a fellow student, Mandy Revell, who had transferred from the High School to the Hewett, to take A-Level Art. In my own environment, for some reason, I had no qualms in chatting and working with Mandy. I would like to think that was reciprocated and in time, with renewed confidence, my shyness would be overcome, later on in life.

As I progressed through Senior school, I took on more responsibilities. First becoming a sub-prefect, before being elevated to a prefect, and for both positions I had a badge to wear on my blazer. The latter role meant that I joined a group of other prefects who undertook marshalling duties, in the lower school. This wasn't difficult but it certainly alerted me to just how cheeky and awkward 11-13 years olds could be. Was I really like that at their age – I dare not ask!

In my final school photograph (Fig. 72) before I was to join the sixth form, I can be seen wearing my prefect badge (far left, first row of boys, behind the girls).

It was now June 1972, and my compulsory formal education had come to an end. As a result, I could leave school with five CSEs (English [2], Geography [2], History [3], Mathematics [4], Physics with Chemistry [2]). In addition, I gained two GCEs, one in Geometric and Mechanical Drawing, the other in Art.

Figure 72

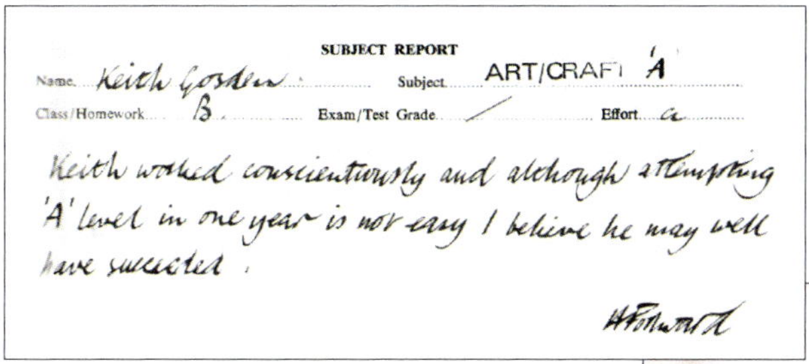

Chapter 2 School, Scouting & Eaton Village 1960 – 1973

Figure 73 (left)
Figure 74 (below)

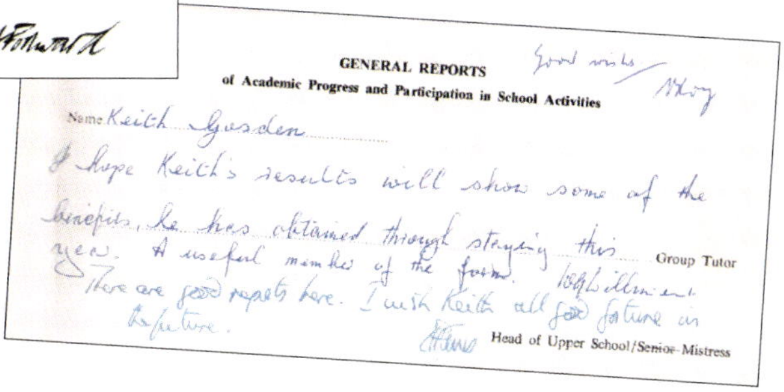

However, I took up the opportunity to stay on for a further year in the Sixth Form, to see if I could add to my collection and gain an A-Level in Art. I am pleased and proud to say that I managed to cram a two-year course into one year and successfully gained my one and only A-Level!

My very final school report, in 1972, I am pleased to say, was far more positive than my earlier ones, especially the one that accompanied my exit from Avenue Road Junior School. However, I have to accept that my Secondary School reports did start from a very low base!

The report for my A-Level Art course (Fig. 73), where I did indeed succeed in achieving my goal, was most encouraging! Alongside this, is the final, overall general summing up report (Fig. 74) which given this low starting point, reads quite well.

Now that I had left school, I still continued with my scouting and having been awarded the Chief Scouts Award, on 4 February 1970, aged almost 15 – my birthday was on 26 February – I moved from being a Scout to becoming a Venture Scout.

I was now able to work towards becoming a Queen's Scout and I did this alongside John Hunter, one of my fellow scouts and a really good friend. To gain the Queen's Scouts award we had to undertake, over a two/three-year period, a number of tasks that were split into four main groups, Responsibility, Self-Reliance, Activity and finally Exploration. Most of these tasks were designed to show that we, as Venture Scouts, could show leadership skills along with being able to demonstrate that we could undertake some recognised Community Service.

Figure 75

John and I decided for our final element, Exploration, that we would organise ourselves with Martin Rose, one of our fellow Venture Scouts, to walk across England, following the route of Hadrian's Wall. This was easy to agree but as we were to find out later, not so easy to achieve. However, as the last element of the award this simply had to be successfully completed.

The three of us agreed to take on the challenge and commenced all the planning which, as we discovered was more detailed and complex than we initially thought. This was, as I have said, to be the final part towards our Queen's Scout Award. As such, without any adult assistance, we had to research all aspects of the trip, organise and undertake it. For our expedition to be acceptable to the examiner, we had to prove that we were totally self-sufficient, so we agreed that photographic evidence was necessary. Photographs such as this one of me (Fig. 75) cooking one of our suppers, were to be added to our evidence log throughout the expedition. These would enhance the record of the walk which was to contain information not only about the physical side of it but also the history of the wall, its significance, the environment in which it stood and how it was constructed. In my research for this memoir, I found the original log which made for fascinating reading.

I was 17 at the time and John was 18. But more importantly John had a driving licence and the use of his mother's car to drive us to Newcastle, where our expedition would commence.

Suffice to say that for 12 days, commencing on Sunday 6 August 1972, we undertook and completed the challenge. This was not helped by some atrocious weather and, very early on, a trip to the local hospital A&E, as Martin was suffering from severe toothache. But despite these early setbacks the challenge was achieved. On Thursday 16 August 1972, our log records that we caught the bus, at 09.45, from Carlisle back to Newcastle, arriving at 12.00, to collect John's car and make our way home to Norwich.

Once back in Norfolk, we had to draft our log, gather all the evidence that was required and submit these for the ensuing one-to-one interview, with the District Commissioner (DC). With our paperwork all submitted, John and I attended our interviews on 22 January 1973 and our records were duly signed, by Eric Greenfield the DC and submitted to the scouting authorities for processing. This was the concluding element towards our Queen's Scout Awards, which we received at Windsor Castle, later in 1973.

We were the first Venture Scouts, in the 34th Norwich Scout Group, to be awarded this honour. Given that my surname begins with 'G' and therefore precedes John's which begins with 'H', I can say that I was not only the first 34th Norwich Cub to be enrolled but also, their first Venture Scout to receive this prestigious award (Fig. 76).[15]

Little did I know that years later I was to repeat the experience of walking Hadrian's Wall but more on that in Part Two.

My next challenge was to pass my driving test. As older Venture Scouts, in the 34th Norwich Troop, we all had, as you might have expected, driven the troop van, off road, around the campsites. So, for me to learn to drive correctly on the road, whilst being much more of a risk, was relatively straightforward.

Figure 76

After some professional lessons and 'L' plate drives with Mum or Dad, I was set to take my test. Unlike today, it was a 'one day' driving test which lasted around three quarters of an hour, followed by the examiner asking you a series of questions, to gauge your understanding and knowledge of the Highway Code. If you were successful, you were given a test certificate that you took to the City Council Offices, along with your red Driving Licence Book (Fig. 77), which following the payment of £1.00, was updated to a 'full' licence, by virtue of a new page being stuck into the book. However, my challenge on the day was twofold, not only to pass the test but also to actually arrive at the Test Centre venue. The latter was to prove a challenge in itself!

On the day of the test, it was normal practice to have a pre-test lesson, based on the route that your driving instructor thought you might be taken by the examiner. I was sitting at home awaiting the arrival of my instructor when the telephone rang. Upon answering, he very apologetically informed me that his car wasn't working, so could I get myself to the test centre and by the way, just in case, could I find a car for the test, as well! Whilst I endeavoured to stay cool, calm, and collected, it didn't work. I panicked! My mother's car, as mentioned was a Ford Anglia, registration LNG 199E, which I had driven in preparation for this day, was in the Norwich Union car park and my dad was out on his calls for work. A telephone call to Norwich Union and a conversation with Mum ensued and a plan was hatched.

---

15 Photo credit Eastern Daily Press Ltd

I was to see if our neighbour could drive me, in her car, to the Norwich Union car park, where Mum would meet us, with her car keys. I, under the supervision of our neighbour, was to drive my mum's car to the Test Centre, to meet my instructor. I could, if necessary, take the test in my mum's car, whilst my neighbour waited for the result. We would then drive back to meet Mum, again at the car park, so after work she had transport to drive home.

A plan that seemed to work and as if by luck, when we arrived at the Test Centre, the instructor's car was working again. My test commenced on time, starting with an eyesight test to prove that I could read a car's number plate from a specific distance away. I passed that without any problem! During the actual driving test my manoeuvres went well, and I recall that I was pleased that both my three-point turn and reversing round a corner were successful. As was the emergency stop when the examiner banged on the dashboard with his clipboard, indicating I had to stop immediately. All this without a pre-test lesson. Now, just the Highway Code questions remained between me and a full licence.

After a few questions on different types of signs and some more pertaining to the Highway Code etc., I was handed my pass certificate. Yes, I had done it! So, this time with me driving, my neighbour and I took my mother's car back to Norwich Union and handed the keys back to a delighted Mum. I then transferred into our neighbour's car and was driven home. My red licence book was updated on my eighteenth birthday, as shown (Fig. 77) – Job done! I was now able to proudly drive my friends around.

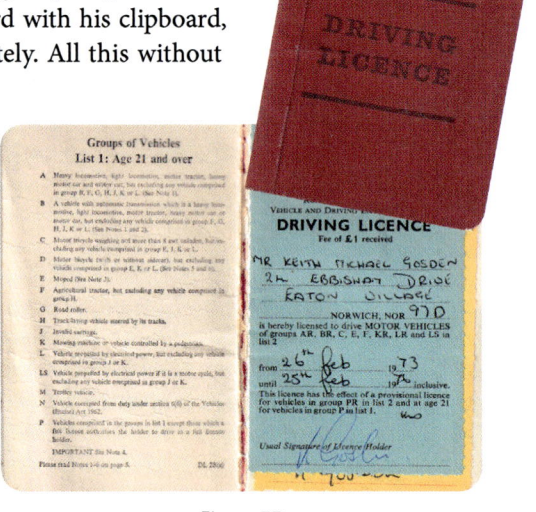

Figure 77

During my friendship with Martin Rose I had also taken a shine to his sister Linda (Fig. 78). We were both about the same age and slowly this friendship developed into a relationship. For a couple of years we went out together, mainly to undertake babysitting sessions for one of her neighbours, and this enabled us to have time together, which was important. Other times Linda was 'allowed' to join our boys' group, at the pub. This group consisted of myself, her brother Martin, John Hunter, Phil Kingston and Julian Kite. All of us, except Linda

Chapter 2 School, Scouting & Eaton Village 1960 – 1973

Figure 78

of course, were scouts. Julian lived in Hethersett, where we would often go out to the pub to have a drink and play darts. I am not quite sure now why my relationship with Linda ended, but after a while we certainly drifted apart.

Having given up my paper rounds and reached the age of 18 I could now legally go into some form of part-time Saturday employment. So, I sought work at Dixons, in Norwich, the UK-wide retail chain of photographic and home entertainment goods.

My interest in photography had been growing since we had moved to Ebbisham Drive. Partly because I had a camera myself and was keen to take, develop and print my own photographs, and also because we lived opposite the Green family, for whom I babysat. Budge Green, the father of the two children I looked after, was a very keen amateur photographer and helped me enormously.

Budge, as he was always known, took photographs of myself (Fig. 79) and my sisters and had a very professional home processing studio. This sparked and drove my interest further, to a point where I too built a small darkroom in a cupboard, off my sister's bedroom, that led to an area under the eaves of the roof.

Therefore, working at Dixons appealed to me, brought in an income and I could purchase equipment cheaper, by virtue of my staff discount. After I left school, this was to become my first full-time employment.

For some time though, I had seriously considered becoming a Police Cadet, as I had been shown around the Police HQ, by the Deputy Chief Constable who was the husband of the local Girl Guide Commissioner, who Mum knew well, and they lived close by. Whilst this was of great interest and a very positive step, I felt it

Figure 79

85

wasn't for me – mainly due to the rigorous academic entry requirements.

Whilst Dixons didn't require me to have any academic prowess, it was still very competitive. I remember going on a training/induction course in their London Head Office and being asked who was '*the best salesman in the shop?*'. The course leader went round the room seeking answers and, like me, most were naming a long-standing employee or someone who appeared to always be selling items. He stopped asking, when someone said, '*I am*'! That was the answer he sought and that summed up the entire session. It was all about finding and developing that self-confidence.

I did enjoy my time at Dixons, although it didn't last longer than about a year. Whilst there though, I learnt a lot about photography and how to act in an adult environment, and being the youngest and newest member of staff, I was teased quite a lot but took this all in good faith. We had fun as well, looking through and checking the people's photographs before they were collected – just to inspect the quality, you understand!

I do remember once, coming downstairs to the staff room/storeroom and was complaining about a particular customer. One of my colleagues, having a well-earned coffee break, was aware of the identity of the person in question and said, '*oh is he that tall, slim man with a beard*?' or words to that effect. As his description was of course correct, I said '*yes*' and continued with my character assassination. '*Oh, that's my uncle*', my colleague said. I was crestfallen but after a short pregnant pause he smiled and put me at my ease. I put this experience down to a learning exercise and it has remained with me to this day. As I have said, we did have some fun and, in the end, I was sad to leave, but I clearly was not cut out to be a salesman.

Having achieved my Queen's Scout award, I was now quietly looking around for something else to do, within the wider society. One of my father's friends, Don Hartley, who lived close by in Greenways, sought my father's views as to whether I might be interested in joining the Rotaract Club, which his Norwich South Rotary Club was in the process of setting up. An explanation of the aims of Rotaract is aptly given here from their website.

> '*Rotaract clubs bring together people ages 18 and older to exchange ideas with leaders in the community, develop leadership and professional skills, and have fun through service.*' [16]

---

16 https://www.rotary.org/en/get-involved/rotaract-clubs

Dad mentioned this conversation to me and said that now I was 18 this would be well worth joining. It sounded good fun, and I certainly agreed with him. Whilst I have never joined Rotary, my membership of Rotaract opened up for me many other opportunities for working in the community, which I will cover later. I am forever indebted to Rotaract for this introduction to community support, coupled with fellowship.

Having joined the club, I made a number of new friends and had the opportunity to use the skills I had acquired, to the benefit of the less fortunate. At the time there was a long-standing crisis in Vietnam, which resulted in an influx of refugees endeavouring to escape the war zones and who as a result required housing. By way of background information, the following professional synopsis from the internet outlines the Vietnam conflict.

> 'The Vietnam War was a conflict in Vietnam, Laos, and Cambodia, from 1 November 1955 to the fall of Saigon on 30 April 1975. It was the second of the Indochina Wars and was officially fought between North Vietnam and South Vietnam. The north was supported by the Soviet Union, China, and other communist states, while the south was supported by the United States and other anti-communist allies. The war is widely considered to be a Cold War-era proxy war. It lasted almost 20 years, with direct U.S. involvement ending in 1973. The conflict also spilled over into neighbouring states, exacerbating the Laotian Civil War and the Cambodian Civil War, which ended with all three countries becoming communist states by 1975.'[17]

The Rotaract group, in conjunction with the Rotary Club, managed to source a property, in Norwich and with some TLC (tender, loving, care), which comprised of a few minor repairs, redecoration, furnishings and fittings, was to make a very welcome home for a Vietnamese family. I and other members of the Rotaract Club carried out this work and it wasn't long before it was ready for occupation.

Personally, I found this approach to community service not only enjoyable but also very rewarding. To know that I was actually giving a family a new home, who through no fault of their own had found themselves in a new and strange country, was a very satisfying feeling. Something that I wished to repeat and as a way to achieve this I was soon to move on and join Round Table, where I undertook similar voluntary service.

---

17   https://en.wikipedia.org/wiki/Vietnam_War

Given that Mum was still working at Norwich Union and was a member of Pinebanks, the company Social Club, it meant that I was able to use these facilities as a 'guest'. I can recall two key events that occurred around this time, one with annoyance, the other with happy memories of a great evening. Coincidentally, they both took place at Christmas functions.

The first was at Pinebanks and was simply a Christmas dance with a live band. It was cold when I arrived, but I had suitable clothing in the form of a ¾ length sheepskin coat. This had been purchased from my mum's Freemans catalogue and was being paid weekly out of my salary from Dixons. I was very pleased and proud of this coat but for me, unfortunately, somebody else was somewhat envious, for when the time came to go home my coat had disappeared from the cloakroom! The security team were activated as were the local constabulary, but to no avail. If my memory serves me well, I think I was able to make an insurance claim – slightly ironic as it was taken from the premises of an Insurance Company! But this, at least, allowed me to replace my loss but not with a sheepskin coat this time.

The second occasion, which took place in December 1973, was altogether different, in that it was another Norwich Union Christmas dance but this time at the Norwood Rooms in Norwich. I remember having something to eat and then the band started to play. They were a well-known group having had a few successes, including some number 1 chart hits, which they performed to perfection. Their level of fame though, was about to change to one of enduring Christmas popularity. One of their songs, released for that Christmas, had that night made it to No 1 in the hit parade.

The group was SLADE and the song 'Merry Christmas Everyone' was to become a Christmas classic for years to come. I remember the excitement when Noddy Holder, the lead vocalist and writer of many of their songs, made the No 1 announcement which he was advised about during the evening performance. It was, without doubt, a very merry Christmas that night for them, and all of us attending the dance.

Having been through both my compulsory and the subsequent additional year of formal education, passed my driving test and reached the conclusion of my scouting days, I was ready to move forward to the next phase of my life – work, marriage and hopefully children. Before I continue though, I have included both my official pass and a photograph of me outside Windsor Castle (Fig. 80), following the Queen's Scout service, which took place on 29 April 1973.

Chapter 2 School, Scouting & Eaton Village 1960 – 1973

Figure 80

89

CHAPTER 3

Work, Marriage & Children 1972 – 1990

Coleman Wines 1972 – 1973
as an Assistant in the Marketing Department

This is not to be confused with Colmans Foods, of mustard fame, who were also trading in Norwich and had previously bought Coleman Wines and retained the name. The Colemans with whom I worked had an 'e' in the middle so, fortunately, its company name was pronounced differently. It too was based in Norwich, in Westwick Street at the bottom of Grapes Hill/Barn Road. My first position working with them was in the Marketing department and the firm had a very sociable and friendly staff, from the Managing Director, Gilbert Aikens, his son Kevin who was the buyer, right through to me as the 'new boy'.

The office where I worked was in the middle of a large site, from which on one side we overlooked the main offices and in the other direction we could see the production and bottling plant, and although this was not important, we had a good idea of all the comings and goings. Out of interest the site was finally sold, in 1988, to 'Toys R Us', cleared completely and a car park with shops were built in their place.

Colemans Wines had been trading since the late 1800s, with its main product being a fortified tonic wine called Wincarnis, which sold around the world – see the old advertising board (Fig. 81). When I was working there, the claim to fame was its deliveries of Wincarnis to Harold Wilson, at 10 Downing Street, during his time as Prime Minister (1964-1970 and 1974-1976). As the company's name suggests, there were other products too which obviously included wines. These included a large range from Franz Reh & Sohn in Leiwen, located on the banks of the river Moselle, in Germany. Also, sherry from Spain and

Figure 81

Delaforce Port from Portugal. But an odd, additional product was 'Punch and Judy' toothpaste! I never found out how or why this was included.

Whilst I worked in the Marketing Department, the actual advertising was all handled by a London-based advertising agency. So, most of my work and that of my colleagues was focused on supporting the UK sales force, with literature and other sale promotional material.

At first, the department was headed by Bryan Smith who was supported by Eric, along with Joyce who was the administrative person and kept us all in place, as well as making sure we were fed and watered. Being the youngest member of the team, she did tend to 'mother' me which I didn't mind. I worked with Joyce, looking after the budgets and helping when and wherever required. After a while an additional Head of Marketing was employed and joined us as a young executive. He was called Chris Eyers, and his wife worked for Elton John, the upcoming international pop star, which at the time was a great claim to have. Given his age and contacts through his wife we all had some great parties in his house, on the Norfolk coast – not with Elton John though!

Back at Colemans, as part of the Norwich Inner Link Road, the area around our site had been radically changed. Barn Road, which was directly outside the offices, had recently been converted to a dual carriageway and what many of the drivers didn't know, as they were heading towards Grapes Hill, was that they were actually driving over our extensive cellars, which contained thousands of bottles of wine!

The bottling plant (Fig. 82)[18] was at the back of the site and was incredibly noisy.

Figure 82

---

18 Photograph courtesy of EDP Newspapers, Norwich

As a rule, this was not somewhere we tended to go, unless they ran out of the little publicity tassels/cards that were only attached to the Franz Reh bottles. If that occurred, then it was my job to bravely go and deliver them. I say bravely for during my delivery, being a young lad, I was the subject of all sorts of friendly banter. Today we are all very conscious not to use repartee that could offend others. However, in the 1970s, I can assure you that this clearly didn't apply to the female staff on the production line, who gave me a friendly 'hard time' whenever I entered their domain. In those days it was called 'character building', today it's seen as verbal abuse. How our society and times have changed. It did me no harm and was indeed 'character building'.

Away from work, in March 1972, I had the great pleasure of shopping with my cousin, Christine, whom I greatly admired, and in my mind was going to marry – I even remember checking the list of permitted marriages, in the back of the church prayer book, to see if someone could actually marry their cousin, and sure enough, you could! Be that as it may, she had just qualified as a nurse and as a result her father, Frank Horton, had offered to pay for a silver buckle to go on the belt of her uniform. This appeared to be rather a special tradition for newly qualified nurses. We went around several antique shops in Norwich and ended up finding just what Chris wanted, in a small antique shop, opposite

Figure 83

Chapter 3 Work, Marriage & Children 1972 – 1990

Bonds, on All Saints Green. It was a lovely time together, only dampened by the fact that my Uncle Frank, her father, died the next month. I had briefly looked after him in hospital, whilst undertaking some of my community work, as part of my Queen's Scout Award.

He was a butcher, seen here on the right in his shop (Fig. 83), and following his death in 1972 I was given one of his carving knives, which I still use to this day.

Returning to Colemans, when in 1973 I reached the grand age of 18, I was presented with a handmade card, about one foot square, all edged with tassels and signed not only by all the administrative staff but all the directors as well. Of course, this had all secretly been contrived by Joyce, and it certainly gave an indication and 'flavour' of the family atmosphere that was so important to the company.

Later that year, I was invited to talk to Chris Eyres and his director Vernon Sankey who worked for Colman Foods. Given the style of management, a meeting such as this wasn't that unusual, but I did begin to wonder what I had done to warrant such a 'formal' conversation. When I arrived and we started chatting it seemed a little like an interview, in that they wanted to know my aspirations, what I liked doing, did I like the work etc. Then came the real reason – I was asked if I was interested in moving to Colman Foods, to join their Marketing Department. Even I could see that this was a huge opportunity, so my answer was, of course, *'yes please'*.

Back home, when my parents heard this news they were very pleased and to this day I am not sure if they had a hand in the planning of this move. I say that because I remember during a conversation with Kevin Aikens, he mentioned to me that *'he was going to set up his own business, just like your father'*. Now, how did he know this fact about my dad, as I hadn't said anything to him at all, and shortly after this revelation, Kevin left to set up a Wine Consultancy Business. His father, Gilbert, then retired and soon Colemans Wines became an integral part of Colman Foods.

Kevin, of course, was correct about my father. For unbeknown to me, the new owner of Solicitors' Law Stationery Society, Robert Maxwell, had made Dad redundant. This had never been discussed at home and I only found out many years later, after Dad had died. So, with his severance pay in the bank he was able to set himself up in business, basically doing the same as he had in the preceding years, this time though, under his own terms. More about this will follow later.

Colman Foods 1973 – 1975 as Assistant Product Manager

By moving to Colman Foods, I was entering a very different culture as it was part of Reckitt and Colman, a multi-million-pound, international company. The first thing I realised was that all my colleagues in the department, whilst being very friendly, were all university educated. My single A-Level in Art just didn't cut it! However, I was to work alongside Roy Mantle, as his assistant. He was the Product Manager for Robinsons Baby Foods and Gales Honey, and we not only worked really well together but became good friends, as well.

My new role reflected my previous one, in that I was an Assistant Manager but this time for the marketing of two very well-known products – Robinsons Baby Food and Gales Honey. The key difference between the two companies was in the scale of the role and the facilities available. In comparison to Coleman Wines, the offices were huge and the one I shared with Roy was on the penultimate floor, of a relatively new building. We overlooked the production complex which strangely was very similar to my previous outlook.

However, as I have said the scale and facilities were very different, as Colman Foods had its own power station, printing works, legal department, a laboratory which undertook research into new products, and it even had its own fire station. I was able to look around all these departments and was introduced to key members of staff with whom I would be having a working relationship. The exception was the manager of the power station as I really didn't need to know how the power was generated, just so long as it kept functioning. Later, I learnt that he lived very close to me in Eaton Village, and I got to know him well. To the point that he often gave me a lift to work, in his Triumph TR6 Sports Car. How could I refuse that privilege!

I had a good working relationship with the company printing staff, as I had picked up some knowledge of the processes etc. from Coleman Wines. My father had now set up his own company, L. M. Gosden Management Services, and as he needed stationery designed, I was able to help him by using the expertise of the design staff, who quickly gave me several options from which Dad chose his preferred one.

Gales Honey was one of the brands for which I had some responsibility and as this was an integral element of the Colman Foods extensive stable of products it needed to understand its competition. Thus, to further my understanding, I was given a 'pool car', for a week, and was sent off to Yorkshire, to spend time with one of the salesmen. My aim was to find out how a certain competitor, only based in this area, was received by the supermarkets' buyers, to gather some samples from the shops and return to Norwich. There was a thought that either

Colman Foods might wish to buy the company or, at the very least, understand how its various flavours of honey were being received, and decide if Gales could adopt this marketing advantage. Suffice to say that neither of these options were taken up by Colman Foods! However, my return journey brought me into my second brush with the law.

Driving back along the A47, on 4 October 1975, I was to lose control of the company car and end up crashing into a fence. This caused sufficient damage to both car and fence to warrant my father having to come to rescue me. Before the car could be transported back to Colman Foods though, I had to be interviewed by the traffic police, who obviously had been alerted to the incident. The cause of the accident was put down, quite rightly, to driving without due care and attention and a court summons was duly issued. For my misdemeanour I received a fine of £20 and my licence was endorsed with a seven-day suspension. This lenient outcome was due in part to my solicitor explaining that the car had hit the kerb, and this had caused the loss of control. Whilst I did not argue with this at the time, I did point out to him, after the case, that there was no kerb. To which he simply replied, *'they didn't know that'*!

To my surprise and relief none of my honey samples were damaged and when I returned to the office on the Monday, I was somewhat surprised by the reaction I received. It seemed that my bosses already knew of the accident and given that I wasn't injured they thought the whole saga was a good lesson learnt and so no action was taken.

During my time at Colman Foods, I joined the staff sailing club. Sailing was an important part of the culture of Colman Foods, as the original founder's family were not only very keen sailors, but the current Colman generation also supported the Norfolk Wherry Trust. One of my memories is of me and several other club members crewing a Thames Barge, *Kitty* (Fig. 84),[19] around the Thames estuary. This was undertaken over a weekend and was a great experience.

Figure 84

---

19 https://www.nationalhistoricships.org.uk/register/209/kitty

At the time, *Kitty* had no power other than its sails, so the professional helmsmen, who came with us, had to know exactly what to do in all kinds of different weather conditions. We stayed overnight in a pub, at the halfway point, which was certainly one of the highlights of the whole weekend, and then on the Sunday we sailed *Kitty* back and returned her to her moorings. We had all acted as the helmsman's crew which was good fun but jolly hard work!

Strangely enough, I knew the Chairman of the sailing club, as I used to deliver his newspapers! It is so strange just how 'small' Norwich and indeed Norfolk is, when it comes to people you know and then meet again in a completely different context.

I continued working at Colman Foods, but Roy and I were moved to oversee the marketing of Robinsons drinks. We still worked well together, and I recall a time when we asked our London-based marketing consultants if they could find a pop group, who not only identified with the younger generation but were willing to promote Robinsons drinks and that wouldn't cost us a fortune. Up until now the advertising for these drinks had been focused on their beneficial advantages through sport connections, for example by sponsoring the Wimbledon Tennis Championship fortnight. Now we wanted to keep this advantage, but also create some drive from the younger generation who, we hoped, would ask their parents to buy the drinks. For this we needed a marketing plan that appealed to this generation, hence our request to the London agency.

Figure 85

They came back to us with the name of a Scottish group, who were beginning to build a 'following' south of the border. This was good news but at the time no one seemed to have heard or recognised their name – The Bay City Rollers (Fig. 85).[20] However, they were signed up and within a few weeks they had had their first UK chart hits, with 'Remember' followed by 'Shang-a-Lang' and many more. This was fantastic for the 'Robinson' brand, as the publicity was jointly run with promoting the band's squeaky-clean image and how that was enhanced by Robinsons drinks, resulting in a very successful campaign for us.

Roy and I as good friends would go out in the evenings and meet up with some of his other friends. It was during one of these occasions, I think at the Woolpack pub in Norwich, that I was introduced to one of his female friends, who was out with her friend, Jeannette Halliday.

---

20 Picture credit to Michael Putland and Getty Images

Chapter 3 Work, Marriage & Children 1972 – 1990

We all seemed to get on well and met up regularly in the evenings. After a few months Jeannette and I became close and in the mornings I would drive round to her house she was sharing with Roy's friend, and take her to work at Ford and Slater, on the outskirts of Norwich. The car was essential for me to get to work and now it had additional importance! Our relationship blossomed and it wasn't long before people referred to us as 'a couple', and we were both comfortable with this.

However, one morning this status was to be severely challenged, and it very nearly fell apart. As I pulled up outside Jeannette's lodgings and went to the front door, I was to be met by a man who was obviously just leaving, and it was definitely someone who I didn't know. So, whilst driving Jeannette to work I enquired as to who he was, and it transpired that he had been a 'one night stand' with my girlfriend! Having never experienced anything like this before, I was devastated. My recollection of this event is that Jeannette just dismissed the occurrence, saying that it just happened after having been out with her house mate. For me it was more serious, and I took a long time to put it out of my mind. I spoke to my parents about this, and they too were shocked and gave me words of wisdom and advice. Some of which I heeded and some that I didn't, but despite this incident Jeannette and I continued to be a couple.

In early 1975 I thought I should try to find a house of my own. I was earning a reasonable salary, in a job that I hoped was secure, so I enquired about mortgages and started to look around at properties. Mum and Dad were very supportive of my intention and in February with their help, I found an ideal two bedroomed cottage, in Wymondham, that appeared to meet my requirements.

Our neighbour in Ebbisham Drive, Frank Smithson, worked in the finance department, for South Norfolk Council who controlled the area including Wymondham. Dad and I talked to him about how I might go about obtaining a 100% mortgage from them. His advice was most encouraging which made me feel very positive. So, after negotiations with the council, on 18 February, subject to me gaining a mortgage which matched the asking price, I put in an offer of £5,000 which was accepted. Following this I formally applied to the council and whilst I met all the conditions, I needed to show evidence that a recognised Building Society had refused to give me a mortgage, this I secured from the Norwich Building Society. Three days after my offer was accepted (Fig. 86), I was able to confirm to my solicitors, the same ones that defended me on the traffic issue, that I had the necessary refusal letter and therefore was able to formally apply to South Norfolk District Council for a 100% mortgage.

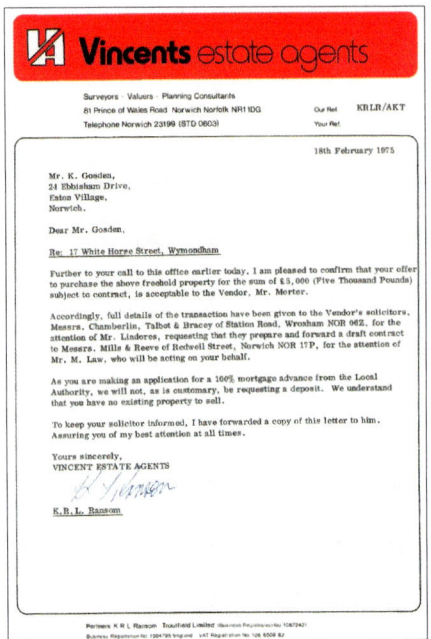

Figure 86

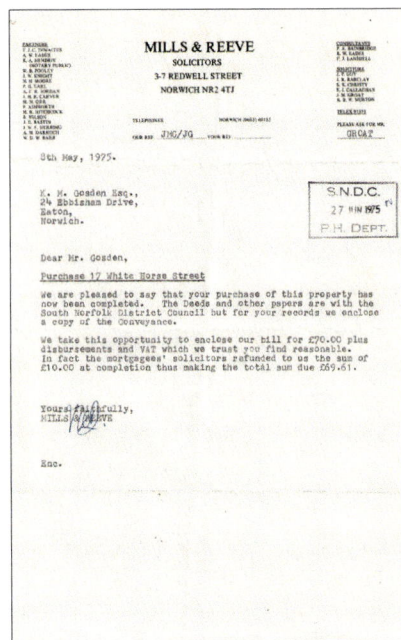

Figure 87

This application was successful and as from June 1975 the monthly payment was to be £31.36 per month. With the requirement in place and agreed, I was able to proceed with the purchase of my first home. Consequently, on 8 May 1975, I became the proud owner of my own house, as outlined in the letter from Mills and Reeve (Fig. 87).

I was aware that there were some minor works that would require attention, so I had already applied for an Improvement Grant. Fortunately, this was granted so the day after completion I agreed a schedule of works that covered a damp proof course, repointing where necessary, insulation of the roof and overhaul of the guttering etc. The following month, Norman Gooch commenced work, for a cost of £748.92 and all this was being undertaken before I was to move in, sometime in the autumn.

But what about Jeannette? She was aware of elements of my house purchase and certainly towards the conclusion was involved in the decisions. This was totally necessary, as after long and sometimes difficult conversations with my parents, I decided to propose to Jeannette, who accepted so we were now engaged (Fig. 88) and planning a wedding for the autumn of 1976. My mother was sceptical about this but accepted that it was my decision.

I was still working at Colman Foods at this point and had built up an interest in the artefacts that showed the development of the company and its products. These had been found in an old warehouse that was in the process of being converted to a storeroom for marketing material. I worked with the proposed manager of this refurbished facility and came up with an idea that the company should have a museum.

We mentioned this to our bosses, and it was acknowledged as a possible idea. Believe it or not, this suggestion then developed into the Mustard Shop, situated in Bridewell Alley in Norwich and was opened in 1973, as part of the 150th celebrations of the founding of Colman Foods, in 1823.

I felt very pleased to have been a small part of this museum-come-shop, as there needed to be a commercially viable element for it to

Figure 88

be approved and for funding to be released by the Board. Equally delighted was the new shop manager who was the previous manager of the marketing storeroom. Together we had saved the artefacts, secured his employment and given Norwich its Mustard Shop.

Despite being very happy at Colman Foods, with the prospect of getting married and now being a houseowner I needed to earn a little more. Having put together a list of my achievements and qualifications, I started to look around for a possible new job. Today that list would constitute as a curriculum vitae, but that was a little grand for my record of accomplishments! Anyway, I had experience in the wine industry, in the world of marketing and to a lesser extent in sales through my work at Dixons. These responsibilities, I hoped, would stand me in good stead for a new role. So, if I could find a position that matched my skills and had a company car, that would be ideal!

Fortune shone on me, as on 1 March 1973, the Driver and Vehicle Licensing Agency (DVLA) introduced a new green driving licence, which didn't show my conviction. Had this not happened there may well have been issues in me finding employment which warranted me having a company car.

Norwich Brewery 7 April 1975 – 1978 as a Trainee then Assistant District Manager

In response to an advert for a trainee, I applied to Watney Innkeepers – East Anglia. If I fulfilled expectations, this could lead-on to me becoming an Assistant District Manager, which would require me to oversee a number of 'tied' pubs, within a specified area of East Anglia. I would be responsible for selecting and appointing tenants; attending courts for the changeover of licences; monitoring wet sales; promoting the sales through local initiatives, for instance darts tournaments etc.; checking that no products were being purchased outside of the tenancy agreement; ensuring that all payments for rent etc. were made on time and with the assistance of the surveyors department reviewing the structure and fabric of the pubs, to ensure they were in good condition. A full-on role and of course one that necessitated a car!

First though, I would have to pass a six-month probationary period. To do this I had to work in the administrative department, as well as understanding how other areas of the business operated, e.g. sign writers and pub accounts etc.

One of my jobs, during this time, was to work out, through the introduction of a five-year turnover lease, the proposed new rents on a pub. In short this gave the publican/lessee a five-year lease guarantee. The rent would be based on a percentage of the expected turnover, as determined and set out by Watney Innkeepers.

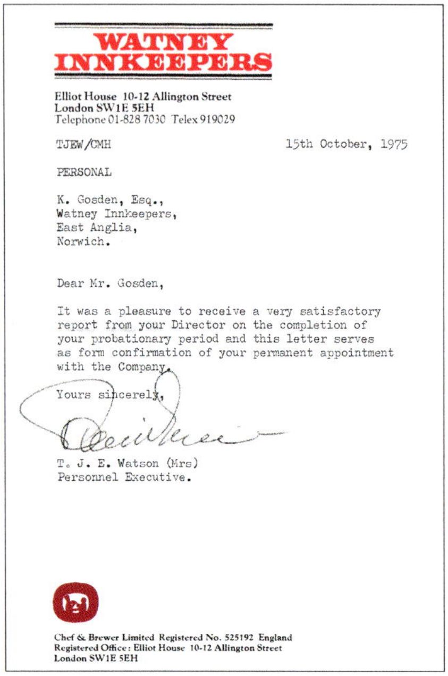
WATNEY INNKEEPERS

Elliot House 10-12 Allington Street
London SW1E 5EH
Telephone 01-828 7030 Telex 919029

TJEW/CMH 15th October, 1975

PERSONAL

K. Gosden, Esq.,
Watney Innkeepers,
East Anglia,
Norwich.

Dear Mr. Gosden,

It was a pleasure to receive a very satisfactory report from your Director on the completion of your probationary period and this letter serves as form confirmation of your permanent appointment with the Company.

Yours sincerely,

T. J. E. Watson (Mrs)
Personnel Executive.

Chef & Brewer Limited Registered No. 525192 England
Registered Office: Elliot House 10-12 Allington Street
London SW1E 5EH

Figure 89

To me this seemed very shortsighted, as any incentive for the lessee to increase sales would, for them, be met with a corresponding increase in the rent. Therefore, it would or could be very advantageous for the lessee, to simply purchase spirits from the local supermarkets, unbeknown to Watneys, which were often cheaper and would thus increase their turnover and profit, without a corresponding increase in rent. I put these thoughts to both my manager and his manager, and they were duly given some thought, with the result that future leases were amended.

Anyway, on 15 October 1975, almost six months to the day when I had been appointed, I received a letter (Fig. 89) confirming my permanent appointment and therefore I

Chapter 3 Work, Marriage & Children 1972 – 1990

joined the team of Assistant District Managers, for some 'on the job' training.

At first, I worked with the managers for Norwich, North Norfolk and West Norfolk, before being given my own permanent area to cover, which took me from Thetford right through to Ely.

I thoroughly enjoyed this opportunity and worked very hard to build up the sales in my region and improve the quality and reputation of the company. This was reflected in my salary, which upon my appointment in 1975 was £1,400 p.a. and rose to just shy of £4,000 in 1977. Plus, I had my own company car!

1976 was a momentous year. Not only had I started working in my own territory, but I was to be married to Jeannette, at the Salvation Army Citadel in Norwich. Jeannette's family were salvationists, and both her parents worked full time at the Norwich Citadel, managing their outreach centre. My mother now had a deeper understanding of Jeannette and fully supported us in our marriage.

The wedding was a wonderful service, after which we were driven by Rolls-Royce to a reception in the Castle Hotel, Norwich. Our order of service is shown (Fig. 90) along with one of the official photographs (Fig. 91) taken in the grounds of Norwich Castle. Jeannette, whilst being a member of the Salvation Army and leader of the Timbrel group, didn't conform to the Salvation Army's 'no alcohol' regime. I was never quite sure how my new role of promoting the sale and consumption of alcohol was received by my parents-in-law. But it certainly didn't stop Jeannette's father, Captain Halliday, supported by Reverend Jonathan Boston, who gave an address, from marrying us both on 2 October 1976. Just four days before my father's 51st birthday.

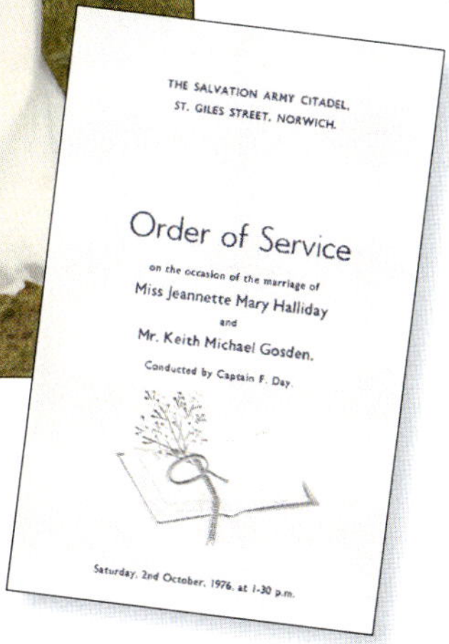

Figure 90 (right)
Figure 91 (above)

101

Figure 92

The significance of this observation will become clearer later.

Our wedding was followed by a honeymoon in Devon and upon our return to Norfolk we took up residence in 17 White Horse Street in Wymondham (Fig. 92), which thankfully was now free of builders. Moving in as a married couple was to begin, and all we needed to do was to make it into our home.

The first job was to transfer all the furniture we each owned and put it all together. Our bed, with which we had both fallen in love and purchased whilst at an antiques fair, was no ordinary divan. It was an antique, mahogany half tester which had a canopy over the top half of the bed with curtains either side. Luckily it all came to bits which we carried up the winding stairs piece by piece. Unfortunately, the chest of drawers that came with it was too large to follow the route upstairs so that was placed in the corner of the living room.

Number 17 was in the centre of a small terrace of four houses, with the front door straight onto the street and rear access was through a communal yard. Each cottage had a couple of steps down from its kitchen back door into a section of this shared concrete yard. At the far edge of which were buildings that once housed the lavatory and a washroom. Many years before we moved in, these had been turned into sheds and general storage. Whilst we liked our neighbours, we needed a little more privacy, so with their permission we erected a low fence down each side of our yard and built a couple of raised flower beds. In time these would contain an array of flowers including a large passionflower that grew up the outside of the kitchen wall. We needed the 'security' for we had now acquired a cat, which was to be joined later by a slightly larger friend.

This 'friend' Winston was none other than a pedigree St. Bernard puppy, who was born on 16 August 1978. After the payment of £125 he was to come and live in our two bedroomed cottage, alongside our cat! Now it's well known that cats and dogs don't always see eye to eye. We had been assured though, that Winston was very placid and therefore the best thing to do was to leave them both in the same room, and go out for an hour or so, during which time the 'pecking order'

Chapter 3 Work, Marriage & Children 1972 – 1990

Figure 93   *Figure 94*

would be established. Well, whilst this worked, the result was not what we had expected. Neither damage nor injury was inflicted upon either animal or the house, and it was very clear that the cat was now the boss – sitting on the back of the sofa looking very content with life! In fact, she would groom Winston, and both would happily curl up together.

Winston's full pedigree name was Firey Snowking and his great, great-grandfather was Champion Cornagarth Stroller and was a past Crufts champion of the breed. Winston soon made himself at home and was frequently found either sitting comfortably in 'his' chair (Fig. 93) or waiting patiently for our return (Fig. 94)

As my work now required me to leave early in the mornings, to drive to the pubs for which I was responsible, Jeannette moved from Ford and Slater in Norwich to being a Dental Nurse in Wymondham. As such, she was able not only to walk to work but also come home at lunchtime to check on Winston and the cat.

Whilst life in Wymondham was good, it was becoming very clear that two adults, a rapidly growing St. Bernard plus a cat was not an ideal mix for a four roomed terrace house. So, the decision was made to put the cottage up for sale and move to a more appropriate property.

Selling the house was not a huge challenge so we decided to market it ourselves and Jeannette used her skills to create the property details (Fig. 95). We had carefully considered the process of moving and had already found a small, modern estate of houses that were being built in Hingham, which is not far from Wymondham.

We soon found a buyer, Miss Duder, for a price of £7,800, however, this did not proceed very far, nor did the second potential buyer, Mr Snelling, who offered us £7,950. These two lost sales cost us in legal fees £27 and £10 respectively, which we could ill afford.

103

REFLECTIONS UPON A FAMILY

Figure 95   Figure 96

Winston, as you can see, was becoming a large but very gentle dog. Even happy to 'dance' with John Hunter, my best man and scouting friend (Fig. 96). So, a move was most certainly a necessity!

Finally, we successfully sold Whitehorse Street, to Mr Smith and Miss Platford, in the summer of 1978, for the grand sum of £7,950. The deal included a six-month extended completion date, which enabled us to select a plot of land in Hingham, number 89, and to put down a deposit. This was only made possible by my parents offering a guarantee of £1,553.50, to Norwich Building Society, which if required was to come from my father's pension fund. This was never required. So, coupled with our mortgage offer of £9,750 it gave us the required funds of £11,303.50 to complete our future purchase. This amount included the holding deposit of £100 and once this was paid, plot 89 in Hingham was reserved, with an anticipated completion date of 25 January 1979.

Chapter 3 Work, Marriage & Children 1972 – 1990

By September 1978 though, non-existent building progress was becoming an issue, as we would soon need to move out of Whitehorse Street. All the normal excuses from the developer had been used over the months including bad weather, the number of houses needing to be built, the lack of materials and builders, plus the unreliability of sub-contractors. As a result, on 12 September, as there was still no activity on site, I wrote a stern letter to the agents of the developer, explaining that we had exchanged contracts three months earlier, paid a 10% deposit and according to their letter dated 11 July, work was due to commence immediately. The reply dated 19 September confirmed that work had now commenced, and the completion date for Hingham, of 25 January 1979, would be met.

Finally, we were able to complete the sale of Whitehorse Street. Our sale costs from Hansells Solicitors were £127.44, a reduced rate as Dad knew the company and they were customers of his now expanding business. The profit from the sale also enabled us to dispense with the guarantee that had kindly been given by my father.

However, the sale wasn't to be the conclusion of the purchasing saga, as on 26 November I wrote another letter of complaint to the agents, again about the lack of work.

The opening paragraph of the agent's reply, three days later, contained the following words, '*We are surprised to hear that little work has been done on your house and are immediately checking the position with the builder...*' It was clear to us that as we now needed to vacate our house in Wymondham, but had nowhere to go, we needed to devise a twin plan of action. Firstly, to find somewhere to live until the house was finished and secondly to speed up the build.

By late December our house (Fig. 97) was at least starting to be constructed. Our wider family knew the problems we were encountering, and my Auntie Win took great pity on us. She very kindly offered us a room in her house in Hethersett, so long as Winston didn't poo on the flower beds! This seemed very fair, and a deal was struck that allowed us to move out of Wymondham on the agreed deferred date. I regret to say that at the time of writing I am unable to recall what happened about our cat.

The second stage of the plan was to enact some more persuasive action on the developer. Our solicitor was

Figure 97

called upon to apply this pressure and on 20 February, the month after we were originally due to move in, he wrote to the National House Building Council setting out all the facts. After a general introduction the letter read:

> '...... *My clients signed an NHBC agreement on 25 September 1978 between the NHBC and the builder G. P. Hall and Sons Ltd.*
>
> *They first registered their interest in June 1978 and contracts were approved and formally exchanged on 21 August 1978 with a completion date within six months (February 1979).*
>
> *Chase up letters had been exchanged in September with a commitment to start building operations immediately.*
>
> *By 8 January the property was at roof plate level and on the seventeenth, they were informed that it would be ready for occupation by 25 February'.*

Finally, the letter informed the NHBC *'that in pursuance of the promises made by your member my clients exchanged contracts on the sale of their existing property with a deferred completion date of not more than 6 months'*. This six-month period expired at the end of February 1979. He asked them to intercede, *'as the 'tardiness' of their member* [our builder] *could adversely affect the reputation of the Council'*.

That single, professional letter ultimately proved to be successful and that's why we use solicitors! Suffice to say that in June 1979, four months late, we eventually, and I suspect much to Auntie Win's relief, moved into our new house. It was an enormous relief for us as well and the end result was just what we wanted. However, since then I have never been tempted to buy another 'new build' property!

Figure 98

The photograph (Fig. 98)[21] is dated 15 July 2015 and shows the house with a small extension to the front and another at the rear, unseen, to provide an additional bedroom. It sold in 1998 for £68,000 and again in 2014 for £245,000.

It was really good living in Hingham as it had an array of excellent shops, and we soon made friends with other residents.

---

21   https://www.rightmove.co.uk/house-prices/

Chapter 3 Work, Marriage & Children 1972 – 1990

I was now coming to the end of my term as President of Rotaract, so it wasn't long before I progressed to joining the illustrious organisation, Round Table. Jeannette also joined its 'sister association' Ladies Circle.

Round Table was first set up in Norwich in 1927 by Louis Marchesi. The membership of 66 active members and ten honorary members comprised of local businessmen. The actual membership requirements, as set out in 1927, read as, *'[Gentlemen] not less than eighteen years or more than forty years of age, actually engaged in a business or profession in Norwich, as principal or in an executive capacity, or articled to a profession or serving a properly indentured term of apprenticeship, shall be eligible for election as active member'.*

In my collection I have Louis Marchesi's own original, 1927 signed handbook (Fig. 99), with its title, objects and rules laid out. This was given to me by one of the founder members.

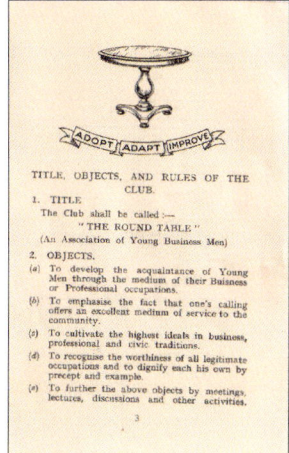

Figure 99

I joined No.1 Round Table at the age of 24 and being the youngest my first responsibility was to organise a weekly rota for its members, to drive elderly/disabled people to a community centre in Norwich. Each year this role was allocated to the newest entrant as it ensured that you were given the opportunity to meet and get to know all your other No.1 colleagues. It was a great 'introduction' to a very worthwhile and an extremely sociable organisation, which by 1979 had a world-wide membership.

No.1 being the very first Round Table was not only able to help other Round Table groups to set up around the country but also invite their members to its meetings and other social events. These, like most of our gatherings, were rowdy but great fun. Our 'Table' also joined up for an annual, European, No.1 meeting, which was also open to wives. Jeannette and I had three or four visits overseas, staying in members' houses and this was reciprocated, with us having them to stay in Norfolk. All of which were most enjoyable. There will be more memories later.

I think here is an appropriate place to include a second photograph, taken in the summer of 1979, and showing a much smaller family compared to the one shown earlier, at the commencement of this memoir. This family photograph (Fig. 100) includes both my maternal grandparents, and you will notice that at the time neither Oliver nor Sophie had been born.

Figure 100

Back – Roger Wiltshire, Sarah Wiltshire (my sister), Jeannette, me
Middle – Nanny Randall holding Katy Riddington, Mum, Grandad Randall
Front – David Riddington holding Stuart Riddington, Judy Riddington (my sister) holding Tara Riddington, Dad with Sam to his right and Winston to his left.

It was around this time (1979/80) that Judy, now married to David and living in Mulbarton just outside Norwich, started studying hard towards becoming a Lay Reader, for their local church. She was successful and I recall attending the official ceremony in Norwich Cathedral, with our parents along with friends and family.

To everyone's surprise, a few years into her ministry there was an 'incident' with a Mulbarton parishioner, which led to Judy being asked to leave her office. This was a huge shock and disappointment for my parents and the matter was never to be discussed again, within the family. Judy is a devout Christian, like my parents, my sister Sarah, both my brothers-in-law and their respective families. I, on the other hand, do not hold such a strong faith. Given their beliefs, the manner in which this incident was handled, was a surprise to me.

Now that Jeannette and I had settled well into our new abode in Hingham we had without any success been trying for a family. This caused us great concern, as it would any young couple, therefore a joint visit was undertaken to the Hingham GP Surgery.

The doctor was most understanding and gave us some practical advice that would hopefully assist us. I have to say that adhering to the advice made the act of intercourse very regimental as there were certain conditions that we had to check, like temperature, establish the point of the month when ovulation was at its best, all of which took the spontaneity out of the act of making babies. However, we adhered to the advice, and it worked, twice over!

Oliver was born on 3 April 1980 and Sophie followed on 1 July 1981! Two perfect children who were adored by us and Winston. Looking back now, I can see that it could have been very scary for any child to be that close to a dog of Winston's size. But both Oliver and Sophie just accepted Winston as part of the family and vice versa, as can be seen here on Oliver's first Christmas (Fig. 101), with Winston, an inquisitive gentle giant, looking on.

Figure 101

Life changed for us, now that we had two children, as it does for all young families. It was a dream come true and without doubt one of the happiest times in our marriage. Oliver's birthday coincided fortuitously with my mother's 48th birthday and as he was born early in the morning, on my way home from the maternity ward I was able to see her, wish her a happy birthday and deliver a card. I recall saying that '*I wasn't sure what to give as a present so would a grandson be ok*'! Both Mum and Dad were absolutely delighted.

Following Oliver's first birthday, Sophie had a summer christening in Hingham (Fig.102) which was very similar to that of Oliver's. The only difference was that for his we were joined by my playgroup teacher 'Auntie' Dora. Regrettably by this time her husband Wal had passed away. It was a delight to meet her again and we had some long conversations regarding both schooling and farming.

Figure 102

Both Jeannette and I had worked extremely hard to create a lovely 'sunken' garden – excavated by a friendly JCB driver who was working on the building site next door! We built a patio next to the house, then a sunken lawn with raised beds either side which led to a raised vegetable plot at the far end. We were very proud of our first proper garden.

However, the changes in our lives were not confined to gardens and babies, for in 1978 I joined my father in the family business L. M. Gosden Management Services Ltd. I will expand more on this in due course, but for now I will just say that this was a huge opportunity for all of us.

For a short while, whilst in Hingham, I helped at the local Cub pack meetings that were held in an old church hall building, adjacent to one of the two greens in the town. Whilst enjoyable this began to take over, so I pulled back and eventually withdrew altogether. This did, however, open my eyes to just how much time and work my father must have committed to his role at 34th Norwich. I was in awe of his commitment.

Like many families at the time, we often went out for car rides and dog walks with, in our case, Winston. Two occasions come to mind when thinking about these and they both involved Winston. First was when we were driving out of Norwich towards my parents' house in Cringleford. We had just pulled away from the Daniels roundabout on the A11, one of the main exits from Norwich, when I noticed the car boot sprung open on our estate car. To my horror, Winston who had been sitting up contentedly looking out of the back window, was now exposed to the elements. But worst of all as we were increasing speed he slid, still in a sitting position, out of the back of the car and landed in the road. He looked most indignant but thankfully there was no one behind us at the time. Whilst he was very surprised, he was totally unharmed and once we had quickly pulled over to the roadside he jumped back into the boot.

The second was far more serious. We were out walking Winston with the children through a wood when he decided to just sit down. Nothing peculiar about that, but he wouldn't get up and given his size, if Winston wanted to stay sitting down there really wasn't much you could do, other than wait! Therefore, we waited and after a while he did get up but was clearly not happy to continue with the walk, so we returned home.

Figure 103

We took Winston to the vet who gave him a thorough check and concluded that his heart was not in great health and was clearly giving him problems. To cut a long and distressing story short, a few years later, given that he was still struggling with his health, I took him to the vet again, who advised me that Winston was, in his opinion, suffering and the kindest thing would be to put him to sleep. I reluctantly agreed as I didn't want to inflict any more suffering, so this was carried out in the back of the car, due to his size and weight. I was inconsolable and even now writing this some 40 years later my eyes are filled with tears. Winston (Fig. 103) came home with me, and I buried him in his favourite spot in the garden. R.I.P. We still have the model of his great, great-grandfather Champion Cornagarth Stroller which is, of course, Winston in my eyes.

REFLECTIONS UPON A FAMILY

On a happier note, our family was growing up and we had some wonderful holidays and walks as shown in this montage of photographs. Family play time in the woods (Fig. 104). Winston checking that Oliver is ok, much to the amusement of Sophie (Fig. 105). Or maybe it's Winston looking after both of them.

Figures 106 to 108 stem from holidays in Spain. Oliver lapped up the

Figure 104

Figure 105

Figure 106

Figure 107

112

Chapter 3 Work, Marriage & Children 1972 – 1990

Spanish sun and Sophie was clearly determined to copy him (Fig. 106), she succeeded and looked very pleased with herself (Fig. 107).

Due to his fair hair, Oliver was an instant hit with the Spanish locals. So much so that he was given permission to climb a tree and select any one of the oranges that he chose. Needless to say, he was up the tree in seconds and was successful as this photograph (Fig. 108) shows!

Figure 108

In France, Sophie, Oliver and I enjoyed the Mediterranean sun on the veranda of our gîte (Fig. 109). Jeannette was the photographer.

Not all holidays were abroad as we also had the option to use the 'family caravan' in West Runton, Norfolk, which Mum had purchased from her inheritance following the death of her parents. This was often used and certainly reminded me of my childhood holidays – although the

Figure 109

caravan facilities had improved somewhat, since then! No more gas lighting for a start.

Schooling and out of school activities for both children were important and for all its qualities Hingham, in our view, lacked these essentials. As a consequence, we felt that a move into Norwich should be seriously considered. But where to go, and when, was a big decision.

As I mentioned earlier, in 1978 I had joined my father's company, so this was to have a bearing on where we were to live. We needed to be close to work but in an area that had the longer-term facilities that we, as a family, required.

Jeannette and I put our house on the market and very soon found a buyer, so we started to look around to see what areas of Norwich were best for us. Our key requirements were to be close to work, good schools, a safe environment plus a secure garden. Having worked on the renovation of 17 Whitehorse Street,

113

we were quite happy to take on a project but were mindful that now we had two very young children.

A 'project' is precisely what we found! 133 Christchurch Road, Norwich was on the market with Eric S. Bush and we both thought this was an ideal property. Built in 1942, its location in Norwich's 'Golden Triangle' was perfect and one that I knew very well, as it was literally, just around the corner from 28 The Avenues! In addition, there were good schools close by, so what could go wrong.

Well, the fact that the details said, *'A handsome traditional detached house thoroughly deserving modernisation and general improvement to revitalise its appeal'*, gave us a clue to the work required (Fig. 110). Also, it was up for sale by auction, a house purchase process that we knew nothing about. So, help was required and sought.

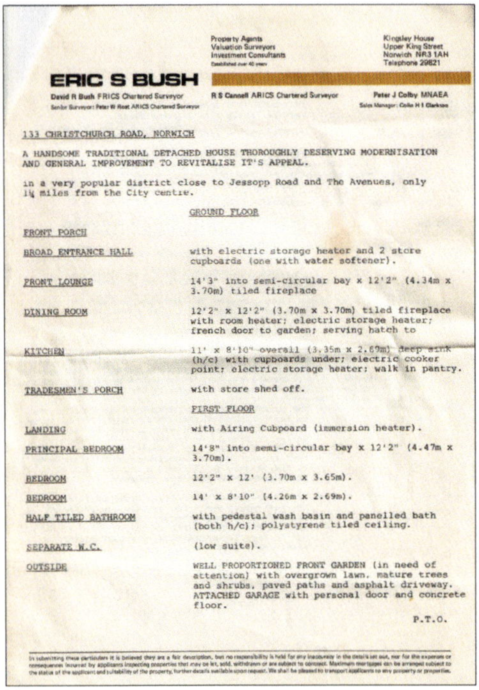

Property Agents
Valuation Surveyors
Investment Consultants
Established over 40 years

Kingsley House
Upper King Street
Norwich NR3 1AH
Telephone 29821

ERIC S BUSH

David R Bush FRICS Chartered Surveyor
Senior Surveyor: Peter W Rost ARICS Chartered Surveyor
R S Cannell ARICS Chartered Surveyor
Peter J Colby MNAEA
Sales Manager: Colin H I Clarkson

133 CHRISTCHURCH ROAD, NORWICH

A HANDSOME TRADITIONAL DETACHED HOUSE THOROUGHLY DESERVING MODERNISATION AND GENERAL IMPROVEMENT TO REVITALISE IT'S APPEAL.

in a very popular district close to Jessopp Road and The Avenues, only 1¼ miles from the City centre.

GROUND FLOOR

FRONT PORCH	
BROAD ENTRANCE HALL	with electric storage heater and 2 store cupboards (one with water softener).
FRONT LOUNGE	14'3" into semi-circular bay x 12'2" (4.34m x 3.70m) tiled fireplace
DINING ROOM	12'2" x 12'2" (3.70m x 3.70m) tiled fireplace with room heater; electric storage heater; french door to garden; serving hatch to
KITCHEN	11' x 8'10" overall (3.35m x 2.69m) deep sink (h/c) with cupboards under; electric cooker point; electric storage heater; walk in pantry.
TRADESMEN'S PORCH	with store shed off.

FIRST FLOOR

LANDING	with Airing Cupboard (immersion heater).
PRINCIPAL BEDROOM	14'8" into semi-circular bay x 12'2" (4.47m x 3.70m).
BEDROOM	12'2" x 12' (3.70m x 3.65m).
BEDROOM	14' x 8'10" (4.26m x 2.69m).
HALF TILED BATHROOM	with pedestal wash basin and panelled bath (both h/c); polystyrene tiled ceiling.
SEPARATE W.C.	(low suite).
OUTSIDE	WELL PROPORTIONED FRONT GARDEN (in need of attention) with overgrown lawn, mature trees and shrubs, paved paths and asphalt driveway. ATTACHED GARAGE with personal door and concrete floor.

P.T.O.

In submitting these particulars it is believed they are a fair description, but no responsibility is held for any inaccuracy in the details set out, nor for the expense or consequences incurred by applicants inspecting properties that may be let, sold, withdrawn or are subject to contract. Maximum mortgages can be arranged subject to the status of the applicant and suitability of the property, further details available upon request. We shall be pleased to transport applicants to any property or properties.

Figure 110

I had got to know a local Estate Agent, Keith Cross, at Spelmans Estate Agents, who not only looked after pub changes of tenancy when I worked at Norwich Brewery, but also undertook property auctions. Keith, who was also a member of No.1 Round Table, was approached and agreed to not only give me advice but would also bid at the auction, on our behalf. That was music to our ears, as his experience was very necessary. But we asked, '*what if we lost the auction*?' – '*you won't*', he assured us. Confidence like that was most impressive.

The auction day came, and having put all the necessary prerequisites in place, I sat next to Keith towards the back of the room. There were a few other properties before 133 came up. The auctioneer, who was also in Round Table with Keith and me, started by seeking some opening bids from around the room. It was clear that the auctioneer also knew many of the people in front of us as the camaraderie of the process was very evident. From memory there were a few people interested, who seemed to be builders, and as such had a very fixed view on what they would spend, if a profit was to be made.

Keith sat still and waited and waited. He made no indication as to his interest and from my inexperienced eyes we looked like losing without even making a

Chapter 3 Work, Marriage & Children 1972 – 1990

single bid. *'Why aren't we bidding?'* I whispered. It's too early to show our hand was the reply. Easy to say, I thought, but if we didn't win, we had nowhere to live!

It really looked as if we had lost it, *'any more bids'* was called, and then Keith raised his hand. Phew! Now we had a fighting chance as we were 'in the game'. A couple more bids between us and one other bidder raised the price closer to our limit. The auctioneer asked for any more bids, for the second and final time. Then, 'Bang', the gavel had come down. Sold! We were the proud owners of 133 Christchurch Road, Norwich! (Fig. 111).

To say we were relieved was a total and utter understatement. We now had until 29 September 1982 to put everything in order and complete the purchase to which we were legally bound. I have to say that whilst I don't recall all that happened, including how much we paid, we were so relieved that all went according to plan. Having met all the necessary deadlines, we packed up Hingham and we moved into 133, without a hitch.

We pretty much knew what we wanted to do which was to keep the layout much the same but update the electrics, install central heating, remove a large chimney in the kitchen along with a larder, decorate and then look at the garden. Easy, we thought – the naivety of youth! Well, easy to a point. I was helped enormously by both my dad and his best man, Ron Sewell who now lived just outside Norwich. All went well until we came to the chimney seen in the photograph (Fig. 111).

That certainly required a 'proper' builder with scaffolding and skips, but down it came and what a difference it made. Along with a huge mess!

Back inside, when we came to clear the larder, we discovered one very strange thing inside, numerous packets of Force breakfast cereal which were all filled with coal. There were also a number in the garage which led us to believe that the previous owner who was an elderly and reclusive spinster, according to our neighbours, took these one at a time to fuel her coal fire. Just the right amount for an evening fire, not too much and no need for a heavy coal skuttle.

Figure 111

115

REFLECTIONS UPON A FAMILY

Ron's wife Sheila Sewell, who was my godmother, was a Royal Academy Miniature Artist and asked us if she could submit a miniature of Oliver for the 1983 Exhibition. Obviously, we had no objections, and this was duly painted and submitted. To all our delights it was selected and exhibited in the Academy Exhibition of that year (Fig. 112). Normally Sheila kept all her exhibited miniatures but, on this occasion, she kindly gave this one to me which has been proudly hung in all of my homes ever since.

In their new abode in Christchurch Road, which was now fully renovated, both Oliver and Sophie made friends easily through nursery and great fun was had playing with water in the back garden – suitably clad (Fig. 113)!

After a few months, of settling in, life was back to normal, and we set about the front garden. Oliver and Sophie by this time were attending a private nursery school in Albemarle Road, owned by Yvonne Barnett, who my mum had worked with when Yvonne first set up a nursery in Eaton Village. The nursery school was opposite the side entrance to the High School for Girls, so not very far away from 133.

Figure 112

Figure 113

Chapter 3 Work, Marriage & Children 1972 – 1990

Figure 114

Playing in the sun with friends in the garden, during the summer holidays was a frequent occurrence.

Following nursery, Oliver and Sophie both moved to Cringleford Infant and Junior schools, which were close to where my mother and father lived, as well as Ron and Sheila. An early photograph of both of them (Fig. 114) in the early years of Infant school. How grand Oliver looked in his uniform and Sophie was just about to go off to ballet.

Oliver and Sophie were always 'helping' me in child friendly ways, with both building and gardening soil clearance – a family trait.

Oliver loved his AA car with its trailer which I recall having to constantly fill up with soil and, in his eyes, other 'useful' things (Fig. 115)!

However, both Sophie and Oliver certainly knew how to stop work and gain attention as they would simply sit on the roller, in the front garden (Fig. 116). This prevented me from continuing the rolling of the soil ready for seeding, until they decided the time was right. Still all help was welcome, and a short rest was often called for, so no complaints from me.

Whilst working on the garden it was very clear that the children both wanted a playhouse of their own. To grant this wish, I built a children's den in the shrubbery at the bottom of the garden, so they could play and hide whenever they wanted. The structure was large enough for even the adults to stand up in and although I say it myself, it was a great success.

Figure 115

Figure 116

REFLECTIONS UPON A FAMILY

Living in the city, rather than out in the country, did bring you closer to anti-social behaviour and it was at this time that I heard a noise in the front garden early one morning. Looking out of the window I saw, to my horror, our car being driven out of the driveway. Jeannette rang the police, who just happened to have a patrol car in the area, whilst I ran off to see where it was being taken. Alas, I didn't see, other than it turned left, up The Avenues and the police also had no success. The car and its contents were gone!

An insurance claim was made a few days later, but before this was fully processed I had a call from the police, to say that it had been found in a lock-up garage at the other end of The Avenues. Apparently, the police were looking into something else in the area and had cause to ask the owner to open his garage. Lo and behold, there was my car, so the police had one more solved crime, and I had my car back, undamaged.

At the beginning of this memoir, there is a professional photograph of the 'Wider Family' taken in 1987. The finished photograph portrayed a very well organised setting, with the photographer in total control of the situation. I recall though, that the lead up to the final image didn't totally support that appearance, as my image (Fig. 117) was that particular scene a short while before we were all settled!

Figure 117

Someone or something had certainly riled my sister Sarah, in the blue dress, on the left, with fists clenched looking very annoyed – sorry Sarah!

As you can also see, Oliver with a ball was growing up fast and hobbies were certainly taking over his and our lives, but funnily enough not ball games.

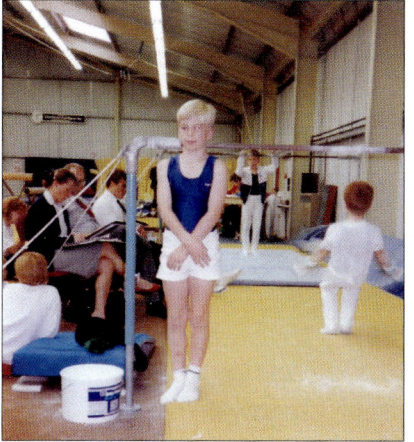

Figure 118

Despite the football, Oliver was not a great soccer fan. He was though, very keen on some sporting events which usually required much more family co-ordination.

These included gymnastics, at which he certainly became very proficient. He joined a local Gym club in Norwich, which was popular, very well organised and supervised by several staff. We travelled all over the place taking him to many different events. Hence the requirement for the family to be very co-ordinated. One such event is shown here (Fig. 118).

Sophie too had her sport of horse riding. I must say, she was also very proficient, hence the frequent rosettes (Fig. 119) and she still is today. It gave both her and me as her father, much pleasure. However, I have to confess that whilst being a lover of horses, I am certainly not a horseman. Neither am I a gymnast, so I am very proud of both children for excelling at their chosen sports. Rosettes, certificates and cups seemed to arrive home on a frequent basis. In the case of Oliver this sometimes entailed driving over to the Midlands and back in a single day, in order for him to attend a particular event. That's where the family co-ordination came in.

For Sophie, horse riding was normally held at the local riding stables in Cringleford, very near to us and almost next-door to my parents, so nice and convenient. It also meant that if a cup of tea, with a slice of cake, was required by the driver during the lesson or, indeed, post the lesson by the pupil and the driver, there wasn't far to go, to find just the place to fulfil this often vital necessity.

Figure 119

Figure 120

Sophie also joined the Brownies and is seen (Fig. 120) proudly wearing her uniform, in the hallway at Christchurch Road next to the front door. A door that I recall spending hours sanding down and varnishing.

The rather 'loud' wallpaper was a young person's choice befitting mine and Jeannette's ages at the time.

Our first couple of years at Christchurch Road, whilst being very busy were also great fun until, one sad day we couldn't find one of our two cats 'Gin' and 'Tonic'. We hunted around their normal haunts to no avail, whilst also letting our neighbours know that one was missing. A few days later the neighbour opposite came across to say that they had found a cat under the bushes, in their front garden. It was indeed Gin, who we thought had been hit whilst crossing the road and died, so she was duly buried in the garden. That was a dampener at the time, but we did recover and, of course, we still had Tonic.

I recall that at one point we offered to adopt a Red Setter from Jim and Jo Deacon and his family who lived a short distance away. Jim was also a member of No.1 Round Table and Jo was in Ladies Circle with Jeannette. He was a lovely dog, but he could certainly run! Despite having good fences and gates, they simply gave him the opportunity to demonstrate both his ability to run and his ingenuity at finding ways to 'escape'. After a few weeks we simply had to admit that he was really too much for us, so regrettably he had to be returned. We met up with Jo and Jim again in October 1987, the day after the Great Storm of that year.

A hurricane had swept through the UK causing millions of trees to be blown over, inflicting millions of pounds worth of damage. Generally, this storm is remembered by most people for the devastation caused overnight. However, the night before, the television weather presenter, Michael Fish had said: *'Earlier on today, apparently, a woman rang the BBC and said she heard there was a hurricane on the way. Well, if you're watching, don't worry, there isn't.'* It was this unfortunate narrative that made both the storm, and indeed Michael Fish himself, so memorable by most of us. As a few hours later that night, following this statement, hurricane-force winds hit the UK, mainly in the south, and East

Anglia including Norwich, with gusts reaching over 120 mph. As I have said, this caused enormous devastation including 19 fatalities, £2 billion of damage and an estimated 15 million trees were felled. Whilst, thankfully, our house was undamaged, Jo and Jim Deacon, who lived on Unthank Road in a lovely Georgian terrace, set back off the road with lovely gardens, had two enormous beech trees blown down, which just missed their house. Like thousands of others across Norfolk, in the morning after the storm we ventured out both to check our houses but also to see what local damage had been caused.

That's when we went to Unthank Road and saw the damage outside the Deacon's home. We did, like many others, offer to help where we could but all was in hand and thankfully no one was injured. It was a close thing though, as the photograph of Jim and Jo's front garden shows. This was taken the day after the storm (Fig. 121) by a young lady, Katharine Hutchison-Brown who, coincidently, was also there and could have been standing beside us. This was the second coincidence of being in the same place at the same time, which I will explain later.

Figure 121

We were advised at the time that storms of this magnitude were one-in-200-year events. The meteorological office had clearly not foreseen this storm, so to avoid a repetition of its errors, urgent work was undertaken to upgrade its forecasting technology.

However, less than three years later, on 24 January 1990, the UK was hit with another larger and more devastating storm. This caused over £3 billion (in 1990 values) of damage and 47 deaths. Lessons had clearly been learnt as the Meteorological Office gave advanced warning which certainly helped to lessen the consequences, but it was still very devastating. The storm hit a large area of England and Wales at around midday, which meant more people were up and going about their business, than they were in 1987 which, unfortunately, probably accounted for the increase in casualties.

It is rather surprising that despite 1990 causing more damage than 1987, most people only remember the 1987 storm. It has been suggested that this could be because of a four-letter word starting with 'F' – Michael FISH, the TV weather forecaster. But that is a little harsh, in my opinion, as the technology in 1987 was not as effective as that used in 1990. Anyway, throughout both storms our family and our home escaped unharmed.

Figure 122

As I mentioned earlier, I joined my father's business in 1978, to run the now ever evolving printing side of the company. The impressive progression of the business, in just a few years, from working at home in 1973 to being at The Tudor Barn in Old Costessey, where I joined him, was impressive and a tribute to Dad's business acumen and his reputation. In the photograph (Fig. 122), taken in 1980 whilst we were still living in Hingham, you can see that both Sam, Dad's Labrador and Winston our dog were very much part of the business.

The publicity feature (Fig. 123) drafted by Dad, was published in the Wiggins Teape Group magazine 'Gateway' in April 1980. It outlines firstly why they are publishing the article but more importantly the development of Dad's business.

My experience in the printing industry, however, paled into insignificance when compared to my dad, so I had a huge learning curve. To help with this, Dad asked a friend, who was a lecturer at the printing school in the Norwich City College, to come in during the evenings, to give me a 'crash course' on what was required. This, coupled with working with my dad, enabled me to at least master the basics.

Law & Orders

Seven years ago Len Gosden started a one-man business in his front room. Today the business is based in a 17th Century barn on the outskirts of Norwich and has a turnover of well over £300,000 a year. L.M. Gosden Management Services is one of the leading law stationers in East Anglia and has become an important customer of WT Paper's Norwich branch for Goatskin Parchment, Conqueror and other high quality papers.

Len Gosden was a field sales manager for a major London-based law stationer when he decided to go it alone. His initial idea was to act as a part-time office manager for a number of solicitors in the Norwich area, where he lived. He started by spending one day a week in each of three solicitors' offices, and soon had others ringing up for help.

"At first I was tidying up their administration and sorting out their stationery requirements. Apart from normal office stationery, solicitors use all sorts of special stationery, including over 600 different official forms dealing with everything from divorce to land registry."

Before long Len was supplying his customers with stationery, using a shed in the back garden for storage until the roof blew off in a gale. Within a year he had moved into small premises in the centre of Norwich, and taken on a partner, [illegible] a colleague from his previous company.

Len says: "We set out to provide a good service taking on a lot of the odd jobs that other people didn't want to do, and it seems to have paid off. Solicitors were giving us more and more of their business and we soon outgrew our premises. At the same time we wanted to set up a printing department to print forms, letterheads, account pads etc."

Their search for premises ended on the outskirts of Norwich in a thatched barn, which had been partly converted as a craft workshop. After further conversion they moved in, setting up the darkroom, studio and printing equipment in the pig pens, and offices in the hay-loft. The finishing department was established in one end of the barn which had been an abattoir until a few years before. The main body of the barn is used for storage, and it was encouraging to see plenty of Wiggins Teape qualities on the shelves.

When the business moved, Len Gosden and [illegible] felt that they would need to keep some premises in the centre of Norwich to provide an on the spot service for their legal customers; so they opened "The Stationery Shop" run by Len's wife Daphne. Their reputation for good service soon spread to the public, and the company reorganised again to meet the demand. The shop concentrated on general stationery, while a showroom over the shop was opened to specialise in legal stationery and provide a typing and copying service.

Altogether L. M. Gosden Management Services now employs 18 people and is attracting customers from all over Norfolk, Suffolk, Cambridgeshire and the East Midlands. They are building up the commercial printing side of the business, and Len's son Keith has joined the company to look after the works.

Since they moved into printing they have been buying almost all their paper from WT's Norwich branch, and envelopes from Chadwell Heath. Len Gosden explains: "We aim to provide a good service so we need a paper merchant who can provide a quick delivery on a wide range of papers. We do not want to tie our capital up in large stocks; like many small printers, we would rather spend our money on equipment."

WT representative Peter Campbell added: "Gosdens has become one of our larger accounts for fine papers, such as Goatskin Parchment and Conqueror, as well as taking a wide range of other WT Paper items. With overnight trunking from Stratford we can provide a fast reliable service for almost any item."

Photographs opposite show: (Centre) Len Gosden, and his son Keith, outside the 17th Century barn which houses his thriving law stationer's business. (Top left) The company also runs this showroom and a stationery shop. (Top right) The printing department. (Bottom left) Part of the paper store. (Bottom right) Over 600 different legal forms are kept in stock.

page 3

Figure 123

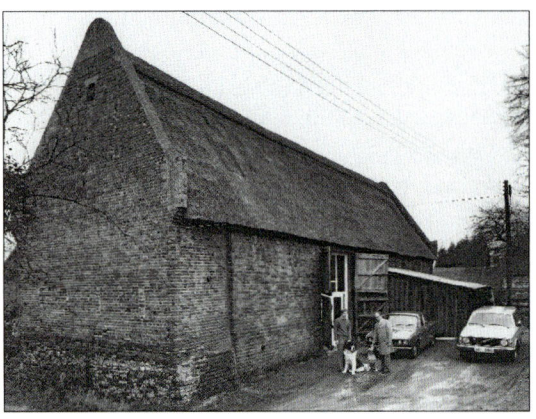

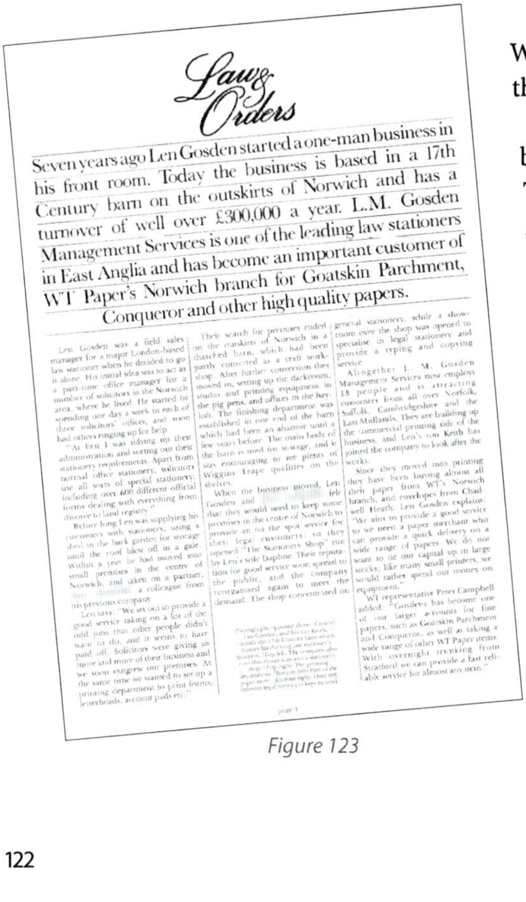

Chapter 3 Work, Marriage & Children 1972 – 1990

We were printing mainly letterheadings, forms and legal papers for wills and conveyancing, so not particularly difficult items, but there were standards that had been set in the past, that both customers and my dad expected to be met.

This was all fine until one of our salesmen convinced Barratt Builders that we could print their conveyancing papers for a new estate, just outside Costessey. All would have been routine had it not been for their logo.

This was a full colour oak tree that necessitated skills that I simply didn't possess to make the required printing plates. But having had the plates produced externally we commenced work. It did take some time to master, but I am happy to say that Barratts were very happy, and we received repeat orders.

As the printing side of the business expanded, we employed more experienced qualified printers. As a result, my role progressed to one of management rather than production.

Along with two more new printing presses and other essential plant, we also had a camera and darkroom (Fig. 124) which with my previous experience back at Ebbisham Drive, I felt very comfortable about using. There was also a large Herold guillotine which Oliver loved to help operate, under the supervision of either myself or his grandad, I must add. The guillotine had a button on each side that had to be depressed meaning that your hands were fully stretched, and clear of the moving parts. This was followed by a bar that swung out and ensured that the operator wasn't too close before the slicing action of the blade was activated. Tim one of our printing staff, is seen operating the guillotine to cut 500 sheets [a ream] of paper, in one slicing action (Fig. 125). When I used

Figure 124

Figure 125

the machine Oliver's job was to push one of these buttons, something that he thoroughly enjoyed. It's another example of Dad's and son's bonding as I did with my own dad when building garages or garden walls.

Looking back now, on the processes we used and comparing this to the progress made in desk top office technology, I can see that virtually all the work we undertook can be, and probably is now, created on an office computer. How times have changed through the rapid advances in technology.

I do recall that my dad, probably through his work in his father's bookbinding business, had the knack of twisting the corner of a pile of paper in such a way that the corners fanned out. He could then count out the required sheets five at a time. Despite all my efforts I never managed to replicate this. Clearly there are some things that dads are always better at!

Working in the Barn was most enjoyable as all the staff got on well and were very professional. In addition, a number lived locally so knew each other. There was one young lad, Nick Ajosie, who worked in the order collation area where orders taken by the salesmen were packed ready for delivery. He had a great love of dogs so got on fine with both Winston and Sam. However, he also liked his packed lunch, as did Winston. Therefore, to avoid a St. Bernard eating his sandwiches, Nick would climb up the Dexion racking and sit at the very top eating his lunch. Below was Winston sitting patiently for the odd crumb to be dropped. It was comical but no one minded.

By 1986 the business was performing very well and had not only the Stationery Shop in Norwich, run by my mother, but also branches in Northampton and Colchester. We had turned the partnership between my father and Andrew Richard Smallman (not his real name) into a limited company, with me as company secretary. We also had an early Olivette computer which was huge and produced our invoices and managed our stock control. Again, these are processes that now, at the time of writing, can be simply undertaken on a handheld mobile phone! That's progress and I just wonder what technology advancements will be produced for our great-grandchildren, should the family extend to that generation.

At this time Dad wanted to update the company stationery, with a new logo that reflected the locations of the three branches, Norfolk, Essex and Northamptonshire. He commissioned a graphic designer to carry out the work and briefed him accordingly. He was a customer of our Stationery shop in Queen Street, Norwich and I have used this image as a glyph to separate sections within the chapters of this book.

Dad was rightly very proud of his war record with the 4th/7th Dragoon Guard Tank Regiment, whose military colours were Brown, Red, and Green. I was told that at the time of the war, the colours symbolised the battle conditions which

Chapter 3 Work, Marriage & Children 1972 – 1990

the soldiers and their tanks went through, to achieve their objectives. There was a mantra for remembering the colours, which was '*Through Mud,* (Brown) *the Blood,* (Red) *to the Fields Beyond*' (Green). These colours were used for our new logo (Fig. 126).

My dad adapted this interpretation into the red brick fields of Northamptonshire, the green fields of Norfolk and the brown mud flats of Essex. The new logo was circular and denoted the geographical shape and the location of the three counties in East Anglia, where we traded.

The last time this logo was publicly used was at Dad's funeral on the order of service. It went with him to the end.

Turning back to the new company structure, Andrew, Dad's original partner and now like Dad a director, had previously worked as the local representative for Solicitors' Law Stationery Society. He was initially taught

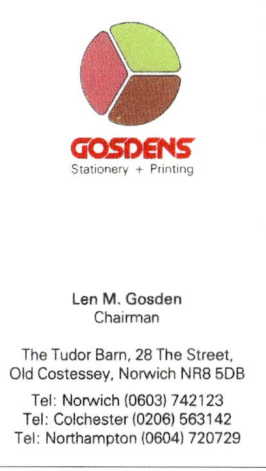

Figure 126

by my father whilst both were employed by the Society. With my father being Andrew's line manager for a number of years, as a result, they knew each other very well and Andrew was treated very much like a family member. I, on the other hand, was a 'new boy' and I think he didn't take to my appointment and viewed me as a threat to his assumed eventual control of the business, post my father's retirement.

However, in 1986 Andrew had an horrendous traffic accident. A van, belonging to British Rail, pulled out to overtake another car, and presumably didn't see Andrew in his Volvo coming in the opposite direction. They collided head on, and Andrew was very seriously injured. Indeed, he was lucky to be alive. Had he not been in a Volvo it was said that he would have been tragically killed, as was the other driver.

Andrew spent many months in hospital, followed by six months at home undergoing physiotherapy, which resulted in him being off work for well over a year. During this time, Dad agreed with me that we should pay him a full salary, in order that there was no additional stress on his family, as he had young children at the time. Dad was working very hard, and he decided that the responsibility was too much and now being 61 he made the decision to reduce his hours.

After Andrew had returned to work, it was clear that he was not happy with me being company secretary. This was compounded by me when I stupidly paid myself early one month due to needing the advance salary. Andrew became aware of this, and our accountants undertook an audit which confirmed that no criminal or fraudulent activity had been undertaken. They did though, suggest that all cheque payments should, in future, be signed by an authorised person as well as me. This was duly enacted.

I suspected that Andrew had realised that when Dad eventually fully retired there would need to be a redistribution of the shares. Given that he wasn't a family member, he probably realised that he would not become the major shareholder, as he had previously expected.

A few weeks after his return to work, I happened to need to go into Norwich and as my car wasn't available, asked Andrew if I could borrow his. This was agreed and I set off to Norwich. I collected the items I required and was putting these into the boot when I discovered some planning papers belonging to Andrew, outlining a possible new business. This was a total shock, so I had these copied, put the originals back and returned to the office. Unbeknown to us, whilst Andrew was at home he had been working on a scheme to form his own business, Anglia Law Stationers. This was to be funded using his compensation from British Rail. Andrew, along with colleagues who he would eventually poach from our business, would now be in direct competition to Gosdens. He was doing this with the full support of one of our salesmen who worked in the Norfolk area.

That evening, I met my father and the Director of our Colchester branch, Ken Oakley, and shared my findings. We were all shocked and realised that we had to suspend Andrew and dismiss the salesman he was working with. These two actions were undertaken the next day and Andrew now knew, that as far as we were concerned, the 'cat was out of the bag'.

I have to say that my father was deeply upset by these events and the way in which Andrew, whom he had treated like a son, was undermining our trust in him. Especially as we had been financially very generous during his time off work. I too was upset, as to this day I believe, rightly or not, that my shareholding had been the rationale for Andrew creating his new business. Possibly, due extensively to me probably taking over from my father and becoming the major shareholder as opposed to Andrew. Should I have resigned and handed back my shareholding? Who knows?

Writing these events is still very painful so I will just say that, after negotiations through solicitors Andrew left Gosdens and started his own business. However, things didn't stop there as over the next few years he systematically poached most of our staff, including Dad's next door neighbour Frank Smithson, who had been our in-house accountant, when we lived in Ebbisham Drive. Vengeance for Andrew was sweet but it caused much upset to Dad.

A few months before he turned 63, Dad made a huge and very generous decision. On 6 August 1987 he gave me a handwritten letter (Fig. 127). The crux of this was that he transferred at no cost, 80% of his shares to me. The other 20%

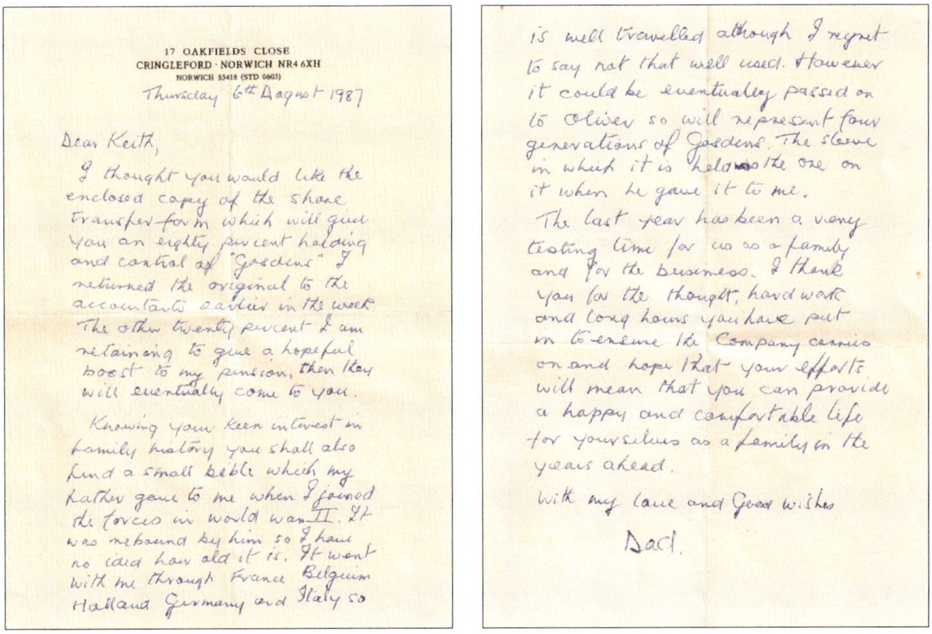

Chapter 3 Work, Marriage & Children 1972 – 1990

Figure 127

would follow as my inheritance. Whilst not in the letter, he explained that his Will would be changed to 'compensate' Judy and Sarah, through each having 50% of the house should Mum predecease him. I was and still am deeply moved by this and the faith that he had in me. As you will find later this was almost the same inheritance as Dad received from his mother, not that I knew that at the time. These similarities were to become even closer, as time went on.

It was clear at the time, the 'fight' and 'drive' that had for so long been the hallmark of Dad's success, had been shattered. He trusted people, looked after their futures and treated everyone with respect. The actions of Andrew and our local salesman in particular had a profoundly negative effect on him, from that day onwards.

I started 1988 as the majority shareholder of Gosdens who now faced a formidable competitor who, in my opinion, had a wish to cause me as much grief as possible. With hindsight what I should have done was to sell out to another competitor and move on. But I just couldn't do that as it would destroy my father's faith in me and cause him so much heartache. Instead, I battled on, to my detriment as it turned out.

At our expense Andrew's business grew through the poaching of our experienced staff, and to cut short a very long and upsetting part of my life, on 4 August 1989 an Administrative Receiver was appointed, who eventually in 1992 sold the company, as a going concern to Shaw and Sons for a mere £100,000. A fraction of its value, in my opinion. One positive was that all staff, including myself and Jeannette, who by this time was working with us as a salesperson, were kept on and transferred to Shaws. However, our personal employment with them was short-lived, for within a few months once they knew how everything worked, we were both made redundant and simply told to *'go and talk to your solicitor'*. But Andew's vendetta against me, along with that of his compatriots, continued as I explain later.

During this turbulent time, one of the decisions that I and my dad made together, just before the Receiver was appointed, was to move the printing part of Gosdens out of the company and into its own business called ABC Printers. Having been made redundant, this at least, gave me an income. Jeannette, on the other hand, sought and was successful in gaining a position with Norfolk County Council.

Given all the upheaval it was very clear to us that we had to downsize, so with reluctance we decided to put 133 Christchurch Road on the market (Fig. 128).

This was a big decision but in order not to cause more upheaval to either Oliver or Sophie, we limited our search for a new house to the local area, thus avoiding a change of schools and/or loss of friendships. With the house on the market and due to its condition and location, we expected it to sell quickly, so we started to look around.

We soon found a suitable property at 136 Lincoln Street which was not far away and on the market at £78,000 and our offer of £75,000 was soon accepted. However, whilst this property was acceptable it wasn't ideal. So, we kept looking and found a more 'acceptable' house – I can't call either of them homes though, as neither were our ideal choice. But the alternative house in George Borrow Road, was larger, more suitable and also cheaper at just £69,950. Clearly the sale of our home in Christchurch Road at £117,000 and the purchase of a different house at a much lower price would reduce our outgoings, whilst keeping a roof over our heads. At the time and in those particular circumstances, these actions were considered by us as the most appropriate way forward.

The sale and purchase, as expected, went smoothly and quickly. There was some negotiation with the seller of George Borrow Road, but that was soon sorted through the offer of printing, at no cost to her, some new business stationery. ABC Printers were indeed some help!

In 1990, I can't recall the actual month, we moved into 86 George Borrow Road. It was exciting for the children as it had two old caravans in the garden.

Chapter 3 Work, Marriage & Children 1972 – 1990

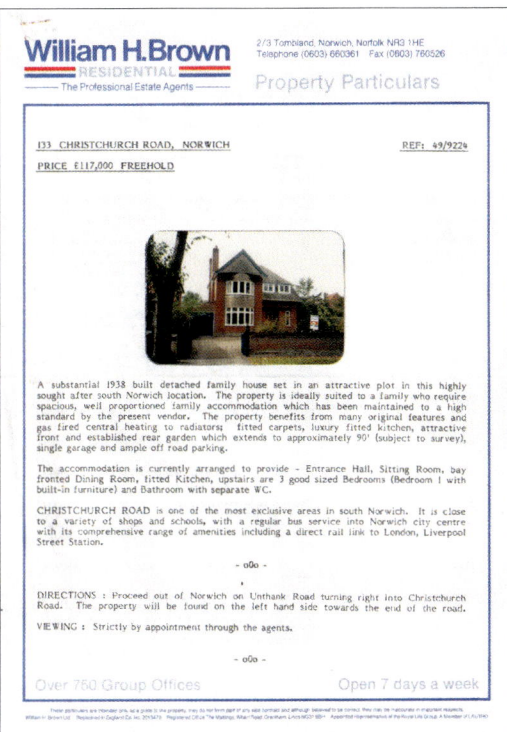

Figure 128

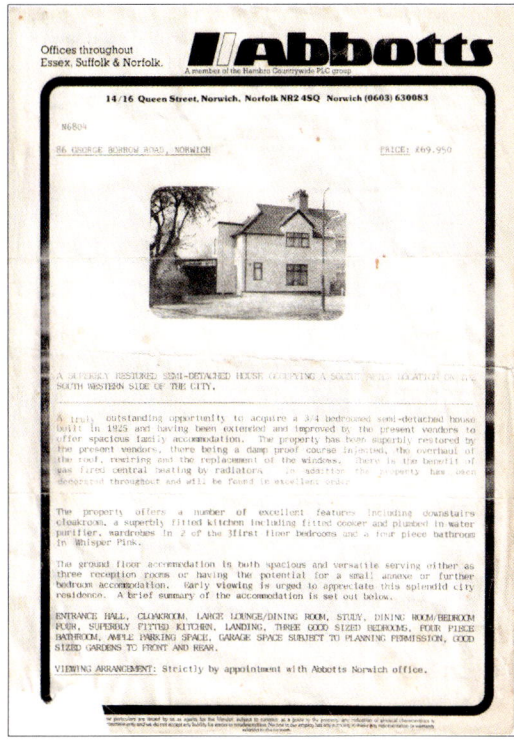

Figure 129

One was almost habitable and offered the potential of being a playhouse, whilst the other certainly wasn't and was soon to be removed.

The house, as described on the order to view (Fig. 129) was in good condition and had been previously well cared for. With our own belongings and with some minor decoration we soon made it our own. The important element in all of this was that our children were happy and as far as possible were unaffected by any of our own trauma. This we achieved but we still needed to deal with the caravans.

To our amazement we had a knock on the door one day asking if we would consider selling one of the caravans. Heaven sent, and of course we would. Taking the gentleman outside and towards the best of the two, he said, '*no not that one but the one over there*', indicating the worst and most dilapidated one, half buried in the hedge, at the bottom of the garden. A deal was soon struck, and arrangements were made for its removal. This was not easy but with a 4x4 Land Rover, coupled with a chain and winch, it was 'persuaded' and guided onto a trailer and taken away. Out of interest, I asked what he intended to do with it. '*Oh, that's easy*', came the reply, '*we are going to blow it up!*' Apparently, it was to feature in some sort of film or television programme that needed an old caravan to be blown up!

The remaining hole in the hedge spurred us all on to deal with the garden which definitely required attention. With shears, strimmers, spades and forks we set to and after a week or so we had made a significant impact. We also made a significant pile of weeds, hedge cuttings and other unwanted remnants of the previous garden. Now, like many people I love a good bonfire, and this opportunity was clearly staring me in the face. After a glorious three or four hours of bonfire, almost all of the waste had been consumed and turned to ash. This I moved to one side of the garden, near the 'not too bad caravan' so that it was away from the children and could just smoulder away.

We slept at the back of the house and had gone to bed quite late but also exhausted after our day's work. Just after midnight I was awoken by a knock on the front door. Whilst making my way downstairs I could still smell the bonfire but when I opened the door our neighbour said that our caravan was alight in the back garden! The fire brigade was called, and children awoken just in case we needed to flee. After a short while, the fire crew arrived and very quickly extinguished the flames. Comments were made by the firemen about how some people have unattended bonfires in their gardens, near combustible items like caravans, so I needed to be careful that I didn't make the same mistake! I made no comment, and we paid for the caravan which by then was a right-off, to be taken away.

By this time, I had been in Norwich No.1 Round Table for a number of years and held most of the key posts. I had stood for Chairman in 1987 but was beaten by Melvyn Bowen-Jones who only had a limited number of years before he reached the mandatory retirement age of 40.

I accepted this and we all moved on, but then a couple of years later I thought I would try again and I stood for Vice Chairman. This time I was successful. As a result, from June 1990 through to the end of May 1991 I was to be Chairman of Norwich No.1 Round Table. I thoroughly enjoyed this opportunity, and Jeannette had enjoyed her time in Ladies Circle, the affiliated organisation. There were lots of social events some local, others further away, as well as some overseas, as I have outlined.

At the conclusion of my year in office I was presented with my Past Chairman's medal, something that each exiting UK chairman receives. However, the No.1 medal is very different from the standard Round Table one, as it is the same design as the very first one crafted in 1927. Produced in silver by Tilletts

Chapter 3 Work, Marriage & Children 1972 – 1990

jewellers of Norwich. James Tillett, known as Jimmy, was also a previous member and chairman of Round Table. I am not sure that these medals are still produced, as Jimmy is no longer with us and his business in Tombland, Norwich, has long since gone. My medal of which I am proud is shown (Fig. 130).

Locally in Norwich, there were at the time, three Tables: ours No.1, being the founders table, No.892 Wensum and Yare, and finally No.1101 Norwich Castle. Whilst there was a friendly rivalry, we had many joint functions and of course the same Aims and Objectives. In the photograph (Fig. 131) taken in 1986 of the No.1 Annual Dinner which also had representatives from the other two tables, I have highlighted myself on the left hand side, indicated with an arrow.

Being the Founder Table, No.1 members were invited to many other tables to celebrate Charter Anniversaries and the presentation of Charters to new tables.

It was customary to give the Table you were visiting a gift, normally something ludicrous that had usually been given to us by a visiting table. There was one such visit that stands out in my memory and that was to Stornoway in Scotland. This was a dinner to celebrate their Round Table Charter Anniversary. Not only was this a long way to travel but it was also somewhere I had never been.

Figure 130

Figure 131

As I have said it was customary to take a gift, on this occasion ours was now becoming an issue, as it was taking up valuable space in the landlord's pub where it was being stored. The said gift was an upright piano! Luckily, a member of our Table, Chris Courtney, was the owner of a number of Vauxhall car dealerships and had access to a fast car and suitable trailer. On the due day we set off with four of us in the car, with the piano strapped on to his large trailer that was to be towed to Stornoway.

Chris was known for his fast driving and a short time after setting off, it became clear that towing an upright piano wasn't going to slow the journey time. We had, thankfully, decided to travel overnight in order to catch the early ferry from Ullapool to Stornoway. The crossing was about 2½ hours, so we certainly didn't want to be late. Of course, the inevitable happened. We were travelling up the A1 when there was an almighty crash from behind us and sure enough the piano was now scattered all over the verge. Having stopped and cleared the carriageway we continued with a trailer now full of the remnants of a piano.

On arrival at the ferry, we regaled our story to some other tablers, and word soon spread. On board the ferry there was plenty of banter and whisky and it seemed that the entire list of passengers not only knew of our journey, but they and a few members of the crew were also all going to the Charter weekend event. I'll just say that the hospitality was warm, very generous and alcoholic.

The event itself was, as you might expect, a wonderful affair with most people in Scottish dress, a flaming haggis being piped in followed by a huge meal, plenty of wine and spirits. I think we went to bed, but I can't be sure. I can recall the next day that we were taken around the island and then we caught the ferry back to Ullapool. This crossing was very sombre compared to the previous one! Norwich was reached, following a more sedate drive home. The tales of this particular and memorable Charter Night were to be recalled many times. I can't remember what happened to the remnants of the piano, but I rather assume we left them behind!

There were plenty of other visits including West Tynedale, York, a Regional 50th dinner in Cambridge, Doncaster, some European visits and a 75th dinner in Norwich at which I was a guest, as I had already left Round Table.

In 1986 Norfolk's Round Tables had the honour of hosting the National Conference. I joined the organising committee as Publicity Convener and worked alongside a dozen or so other Tablers from around Norfolk. It's a little ironic that I don't have any publicity material that I can share, but it was a huge success both for the attendees and the local economy.

One of the highlights of any Chairman's year was inducting new members and in my term of office I had the privilege of inducting a number of gentlemen. For one of them we made his occasion into a very special day, with the help of our local MP. We travelled down to London and had a guided tour with him round the Houses of Parliament, followed by lunch in one of the private dining rooms. It was here during our meal that I welcomed Les Brown into Round Table (Fig. 132).

Whilst we certainly enjoyed our social activities, we also raised money for many worthy causes, especially with our Christmas Float, which was a regular sight on the roads around Norwich. I would like to say that it was loved by everyone who saw it. However, whilst this was certainly the case for the children, I often wondered if the mums and dads were donating money in hope that we would move on quickly!

Figure 132

Figure 133[22] is a photograph taken in 1990, of three of us collecting outside one of the city's supermarkets, for Children in Need. Something that we frequently undertook and from memory I think this one was undertaken at the ASDA supermarket in Norwich.

Figure 133

In the photograph I am on the left, Peter Thouless centre, dressed as Santa, and Ian Shelton on the right.

Saturday 6 October 1990 was my dad's 65th birthday and to celebrate this, Mum and Dad had organised a family supper at The Old Rectory, Bawdeswell. Whilst this wasn't a 'formal' supper, we all dressed up for the occasion. The meal was lovely, and Dad had a wonderful time. Given the events in the previous few years, it was lovely to see both Mum and especially Dad, so happy and with the prospect of a long and happy retirement ahead.

After the meal we were all generally discussing who would host Christmas that year. At this time, we all lived in Norfolk and tended to share the responsibility for ensuring we all met up for key celebrations. I could sense that Jeannette was

---

22 Photograph credit to Eastern Counties Newspapers

anxious to go, so we soon left in the car, with both Oliver and Sophie. Jeannette commented that she couldn't understand why we all had to discuss Christmas in October. Little did I know that there was an ulterior motive to her wanting to get away and return home.

When we finally arrived and had put Oliver and Sophie to bed, Jeannette asked me to sit down as she had something to say. She then coolly told me that she was leaving me for another man called Dale, someone whom she had met at work. I was stunned and speechless. I telephoned my parents and agreed that they would come round the next morning to help with telling the children. The next day Jeannette and I sat them down on the sofa and explained the situation. Apparently, Jeannette had pre-warned our friends, Ian and Lin of her decision and agreed, if necessary and if it would be of help, that I and the children could go and stay with them over the weekend. We did indeed take up their offer but it was a very difficult period.

Later I was to realise that for some time Jeannette had been removing personal and sentimental items from the house, in order that she could have a clean break as quickly as possible. From memory, after both of us had explained the situation to Oliver and Sophie, she left and was driven away in a pre-booked taxi. Clearly this exit had been meticulously planned in advance. I packed some essentials and the three of us drove to Ian and Lin's.

During that time Ian did say that he thought something was wrong, as when we were both laying slabs in the front garden of George Borrow Road a week or so earlier, Jeannette came out and said that she was just off to do some shopping. Nothing odd about that but Ian, being sharp eyed, noticed that when she returned some time later there was no evidence of any shopping!

Following the 'announcement' there was obviously a great deal to sort out which our solicitors helped with. Suffice to say that, following an 'invitation' to divorce Jeannette on the grounds of her adultery, my solicitor recommended that this was accepted, and we were divorced in 1991. As part of that settlement the house was sold. As a result, I was again looking for a new home for myself, Oliver and Sophie who were going to live with me and visit their mother at agreed times.

I was in some ways fortunate as I certainly had the love of my family and children, coupled with the determination to make a better life for Oliver, Sophie and myself. But I concur with my father when he wrote in a Christmas card that year, that it had been *'a very testing time for us all as a family'*.

And for me it was challenging as well as testing. How was I to find a new home, keep the children happy, educated and well fed, whilst trying to run a printing business at the same time?

PART TWO

I need to explain, that from this point onwards my memory has been 'assisted' by our family diaries, especially from Chapter 5 onwards. I will explain more regarding the significance of the diaries within the text.

Suffice to say here, that due to the support of the contents of these diaries, going forward there will be more use of actual dates and perhaps additional detailed narrative of events. To assist the reader the chapters have been subdivided into years. Some may question why elements of the text are worth recording, but my rationale is that future generations may be assisted by the minutiae of the text which gives some overall context to life at that time.

As a result, the following text is more akin to an autobiography than a memoir. However, I do feel that the change in style, not only reflects my own change of lifestyle and circumstances, but also conveys more detail for you, the reader.

So, please accept these changes at this juncture of my memoir.

CHAPTER 4

A Fresh Start, JP & Moving 1991 – 1993

1991

During the final years of my marriage, Jeannette and I had been attending on a regular basis, the Holy Trinity Church in Norwich with both of my parents. Indeed, both Mum and Dad were very committed to the church, with Mum working in the Church Office for a while and Dad supporting other parishioners through his work as a Gideon. I know that Jeannette, with her religious background in the Salvation Army, found these church attendances helpful. On the other hand, I was not so keen but still attended after the divorce.

House hunting began, and this time I was the only adult but of course, was assisted by two very able assistants, Oliver and Sophie. Unlike me, both assistants seemed to know exactly what they required. We were a team and worked well together under somewhat difficult and, for us, unusual circumstances.

The financial settlement coupled with the fact that there were only three of us meant that a smaller house was a necessity. To find a suitable property, which also provided both children with appropriate schools and access to their hobbies, we reluctantly started to look outside of Norwich.

After a while and with some viewings behind us, we came across a sweet little end of terrace cottage in Swannington (Fig. 134). As the details stated it had two bedrooms and was in good condition. At just shy of £53,000, it was affordable, so a viewing was arranged.

All three of us looked around downstairs and then upstairs and out into the garden. On first viewing it looked good to me. We returned to the lounge and met the owner, Miss Mead. I was facing her whilst Oliver and Sophie were both behind her looking at me when, the inevitable question came – '*are you interested?*' I could see both Oliver and Sophie smiling broadly and nodding furiously. I had to answer so I said we were, but needed to sort a few things out first, like surveys, in the hope that this would buy me a little time. En route to Norwich, I had a quick lesson on house purchasing with the children and

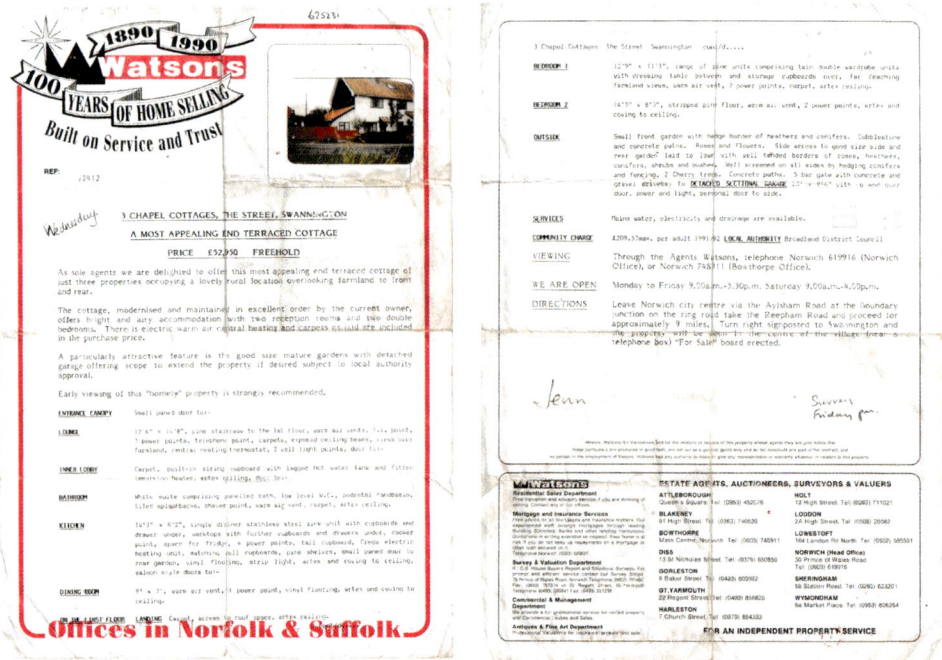

Figure 134 *Figure 134*

explained that I needed to make sure it was built correctly, whilst also making sure that I had the right amount of money to buy it. I'm not convinced that, at their ages, they fully understood, but they seemed happy with my explanation.

Just to make sure that I was making the correct decision I spoke to my friend Ian Malton, a local architect. We looked at how I might possibly extend the property on the side, to give a larger kitchen. He and I agreed a simple scheme that would achieve my aim, hopefully without any planning issues and within budget. Following our initial viewing and now having received the assurances from Ian, I put in an offer of £52,000, which was accepted.

Knowing my circumstances Miss Mead kindly offered me a number of useful fixtures and fittings at a price of £700, to which I again agreed.

The deal was sealed, and with my two very excited assistants we had a small celebration at home. An offer, of an advance of £46,800 from Nationwide Building Society, was confirmed on 12 September and contracts were duly exchanged on 30 September, with a completion date set for 4 October 1991. Why couldn't all purchases be that easy?

Although I can't recall all the details, I was recently reminded by Oliver that for a couple of weeks before we actually moved into Swannington, he, I and Sophie spent a couple of weeks living in my parents caravan in West Runton.

Whilst I think this was very probable, I have no recollection of this and just wonder what happened to the furniture during this time. Still, I am sure Oliver's memory was correct, hence my inclusion here.

We certainly moved into 3 Chapel Cottages in Swannington on 4 October, which was soon to be renamed Primitive Cottage. By November, Ian had drawn up plans for a two-storey side extension, not the single storey we envisaged, as my budget had expanded following the mortgage offer, which was much better than I had initially anticipated. These plans were quickly submitted to Broadland Council for planning approval and were passed on 2 January 1992. Work duly commenced.

My parents were hugely supportive and as I was still joining them at Holy Trinity Church on Sundays, were secretly pleased that everything was progressing well. It also meant that they could drop into any conversation we were having, information regarding single ladies who also went to the church! Whilst this was well meaning I really wasn't interested at this point. My mind was still full of grief and concern for Oliver and Sophie, to say nothing about the building work I was undertaking. But I found this difficult to explain to my parents who, thankfully, hadn't experienced this situation before. Consequently, I simply left the subject alone, and when at church I was 'introduced' to a single lady, called Karina, I was courteous but noncommittal.

It had been a very difficult couple of years with the business sale, followed by my separation and the eventual move to Swannington. This must have been very disconcerting and worrying for both Oliver and Sophie. I was so proud of them both, as they supported me and their mother which could not, due to their age have been easy, as I am sure it was very difficult for them to understand all that had happened.

Their lives thus far had been fun, with holidays abroad, large spacious homes and school friends close by. The environment they were about to enter was one of living in a small house in an area that they didn't know, without a mother at home, and a new school. I needed to be very aware and mindful of how these extensive changes could, and probably would, affect their behaviours.

Behind all this, of course, I too was affected by the changes taking place that I was only just about able to control. So, a very delicate and potentially sensitive position for all three of us.

1992

However, despite my ambivalence, Karina was determined to follow up the introduction and invited me to a party at her house in Lincoln Street, just a few doors down from the house I had looked at previously. Out of politeness I agreed to attend and, on 26 January 1992, found myself, for the first time since the divorce, knocking on a door to join a party. Not an easy position – what do you say when you introduce yourself?

This was to lead to the third coincidental meeting of Katharine Hutchison-Brown. The first one, being many years ago when I lived in Cranleigh Rise and Katharine, with her family, were visiting her grandmother, who lived a few doors down the road from us. The second, as I explained previously in Chapter 3, was outside Jim Deacon's house, whilst looking at the damage following the 1987 storm, where she was busy taking photographs. Whilst neither of these resulted in a physical meeting, it is evident just how close in previous situations, we came to talking to each other. The third encounter was us both being invited independently to the same party at Karina's. Now whilst drafting this memoir, Kate and I have found yet another twist of fate – when first married Katie, as she was known then, lived in The Cathedral Close and her telephone number was Norwich 54318. When I moved to Norfolk our telephone number was Norwich 53418, same digits but in a slightly different order – how bizarre!

Anyway, back to the party, the door opened so I was committed to joining the throng. I was given a drink and shown where to find the food and top-up drinks. So far so good, then Karina introduced me to a young lady, called Katie who was there with her gentleman friend Richard. By chance or design, I know not which, I found myself talking to her in one room whilst Richard was in another. Conversation was easy and I learnt that they weren't a permanent 'couple' and were about to have a mutual three-month break from each other, to assess their feelings. I really liked Katie. She was about my age, very attractive and made me feel very comfortable in her company. Something that I hadn't felt for some considerable time – was this love at first sight and if so, what do I do? I hadn't courted anyone in years – HELP!

Later in the evening I thanked Karina for the invitation, said goodbye to Katie and Richard and made my way home. I had a smile on my face and a lovely feeling in my heart. But I had to be realistic, I was living in a very mixed-up state with financial constraints, in a half-built house. Not an attractive prospect for anyone. Still, I arrived back at our cottage and later that weekend, Oliver and Sophie also returned home having been with their mother. Life returned to normal with any prospect of romance being put to one side.

Chapter 4 A Fresh Start, JP & Moving 1991 – 1993

The building work was progressing well at home and ABC Printers seemed to be holding its own and even had some orders from Shaw and Sons, probably thanks to the support of some of my previous employees.

Whilst this photograph (Fig. 135) looks a little messy, the structure of our cottage was really taking shape. Oliver was acting as a 'builder's mate' which was lovely to see and reminded me of how I did the same at his age.

I had some very good neighbours who were not only understanding of the work and in the case of my immediate next-door neighbours, they also had three children. One of whom, Matthew, was a similar age to Oliver and the middle daughter, Rachael, whilst being older than Sophie was happy to be friends. Ruth their eldest daughter was studying for exams. All the children got on well together.

As can be seen from the photograph (Fig. 136), the scaffolding made an excellent opportunity for Oliver to practise his gymnastics.

Figure 135

Figure 136

I have to say, that from my perspective both Oliver and Sophie had settled well into life in Swannington and at their new school, which was reassuring.

Not knowing anybody other than our neighbours, we did start to go to the local church which was very different to Holy Trinity. In Swannington there was a congregation of around 10, whilst before, we were used to seeing 50-60. Still, they were all very welcoming and friendly.

In between going to work, collecting the children from school, cooking meals and putting both of them to bed, I reflected about Katie and wondered if anything could have developed had I played my hand differently. I didn't even know how to contact her, without asking Karina which wasn't really very fair. During my conversation with Katie, she had revealed that she was in a very similar position to me, in that she was divorced and was bringing up two children, Emily and Angus. Therefore, it appeared that we had a lot in common, including both of us being 'unattached'. Still, I had a home to build and children to care for.

Then on 3 February 1992, I received a telephone call in the evening which went something like this:

> Caller –' Hi is that Keith, you may not remember me but I'm Katie and we met at Karina's party a couple of weeks ago.'

I quietly thought – you must be joking, remember you – I've done nothing but think about you ever since. But I mustn't seem too keen, so the answer was:

> 'Yes, I do remember you…..,' followed by some polite chat.
> Katie – 'I'm having a small dinner party, at mine with Karina, on Saturday 22nd at 19.30 for 20.00 and wondered if you would like to join us?'

Well, I don't think I have to write what my thoughts were but luckily, I was sensible enough to take her address and contact details. Now what should I do? First double check that Oliver and Sophie weren't with me that weekend. Phew, they weren't, so no problems!

22 February came very quickly. I didn't know any of Katie's guests other than Karina or what sort of party this was to be. Do I take flowers, wine or both? It was years since I had been to a party as a single man and now, I was invited to a second party, in as many weeks. I don't know what I took but I suspect it was both, just to be sure.

I picked up Karina en route as agreed and we arrived together, on time, as they only lived in the next street to each other. Karina knocked on the door and someone opened it, and I saw Katie coming down the stairs, in what I would describe as a 'flirty skirt'. She looked a million dollars! We were greeted warmly and whatever it was that I took was graciously accepted.

Karina and I were introduced to the rest of the party who were Sonny Vascalles, Stephen Hinde and Nan Ellis. The meal was lovely, and I sat opposite Katie. After much convivial conversation it was time to tidy up.

I duly collected some plates and dishes and stacked them in the kitchen.

Stephen and I shared the washing up and we were soon back in the sitting room. After a while Karina said that it was time she went home and as I had brought her, she expected me to take her back. That wasn't the plan that I had in my head. Whilst I can't recall what was agreed, I do remember that Stephen took her on his way home, leaving me at Katie's with some of the other guests.

Later that evening, having thanked Katie I left and whilst driving home I realised, probably for the first time in my life, that I was really in love. I had never felt so gloriously happy.

On the Thursday of the following week, I phoned Katie and having thanked her again took a deep breath and with a huge leap of faith, asked if she would like to meet up for a drink. I suggested the following evening at the Parson Woodford pub which was close to Swannington. To my utter surprise and great relief, there was no hesitation, rather a yes please. Was this to evolve into the relationship I dreamt of?

The evening at the pub went well and we exchanged many calls over the coming days. Some led to us meeting up, others were simply friendly chats, which in some cases extended to an hour or so!

Not having 'dated' in many years and this only being my third relationship, I was not sure how I could judge its progress. I did though, help with a car boot sale at the Hewett School at which Katie was sharing a pitch with a friend. Then on Sunday just two weeks since Katie's party, she joined me for supper, which I took as a good positive sign. Later the next week, it was Katie's birthday, we met up and had a walk over Alderford Common, just along the road from Swannington. There was light snow on the ground and a nip in the air, but we thoroughly enjoyed the time together. Katie rang me later that evening for a chat. To me this seemed to be getting serious, whilst I welcomed this I was very aware that Katie was on a trial three-month separation from Richard, whom she had been dating for some time. Was I just a good friend I wondered? I speculated privately, about what her feelings towards me might have been. I was to find out soon enough.

Figure 137

But before this, Sophie, Oliver and I had some family time together at How Hill, where we had an enjoyable time pond dipping (Fig. 137). I don't recall finding anything worthy of mention, but we did have a lovely day together, sorting through trays of mud, looking for creepy crawlies.

The meetings and telephone calls with Katie continued during the week ahead, and at the same time, I was aware that she was receiving bunches of red roses, not from me, so what should I make of this?

On the Friday, we met up and had a lovely meal at the Chequers Pub, Hainford, where we talked for a long time, before I dropped her off home in the early hours. I was feeling confused. I knew she was in communication with Richard and that probably the roses were from him, but for all this, we seemed to have a deep understanding of each other and clearly very much enjoyed each other's company. Just how was this all going to pan out?

On the Sunday we had lunch together. Then on Monday 23 March we agreed to meet up at the Eagle Pub on Newmarket Road, close to where Katie's work was based. She was a Teaching Assistant at the Norwich High School for Girls, which had also been the school that she and her siblings had attended years earlier. Many years ago, perhaps she had been one of the 'pretty girls' at the bus stop, who I was too shy to talk to!

I think it's fair to say that the conversation at the Eagle was not one that I wanted to hear. It clearly indicated that I was losing the love of my life, and it was clear that whilst Katie was going down a path towards Richard, she was still looking over her shoulder in my direction. Looking back, with hindsight, it was clear that both Katie and I were very confused and emotional. As I have already said – her path was leading her to Richard, so where did that leave me? I think the answer was obvious, but I couldn't bring myself to admit it.

Katie rang me on 26 March 1992 and the following day we met up again at the Chequers Hainford and went for a romantic walk along Waxham beach. It was there that I plucked up my courage and showed Katie my love, through our first kiss. It was gorgeous.

Then, on 2 April we met up at the Briton Arms for lunch where Katie's path was finally confirmed. In the conversation I was to learn that three days later on Sunday, she was flying off to St. Lucia with Richard. My heart sank further than I thought was ever possible. Was this the final goodbye, should I either throw in the towel and shut the door, or keep it open and just be friends? No matter how difficult the latter was, I decided, in my own mind, that the route was clear, and a friendship was the right thing.

Obviously, for just over a week Katie was not around and the heartache that this void created in me was to confirm my thoughts. If reciprocal love was not possible then we should, at least, stay friends. I felt more positive but now I had to convince both Katie and Richard. That opportunity came quicker than I expected, as I received an invitation to meet her at the Chequers Hainford on Wednesday 22 April.

We sat at a small table in the bar and Katie, obviously tanned, looked even more lovely than before, if that was possible. How was I to cope with just being friends when my heart was pounding and telling me differently? The niceties flowed and all I wanted to do was to give her a huge hug. Then the 'decision' was revealed.

Whilst away in St. Lucia, she had become engaged to Richard and they were to be married. Not only that, but Richard had also decided that Katie and I were not to see each other going forward. My world just collapsed. I remember the meeting so clearly even now, and to make matters worse we were both upset. It was clear that whilst this was Richard's plan, it wasn't one that Katie fully supported. The evening concluded with me agreeing to meet them both two days later in the Parson Woodforde. Was that good? – I simply didn't know as I was so distraught. Swannington, Oliver and Sophie and building work were to be my refuge.

I must admit that my memory of that meeting in the Parson Woodforde is scant, other than I do recall Richard behaving like a cat who had stolen the cream! What should I do? My upbringing was telling me to respect the decision and concentrate on bringing up Oliver and Sophie, whilst my heart was saying keep close and show your love to Katie – after all, they weren't married yet! The last telephone call that I had with Katie was at the end of April. To my regret there were no more calls which for both of us was unusual.

May passed with a deafening silence from Katie, but the building work progressed at a pace which, along with ABC Printers, both kept me fully occupied. I was hoping that the work would be completed by the end of the summer/early autumn, and this was looking realistic. I thought June was to pass without any contact as well, so I was resigning myself to not seeing Katie again. But then came a glimmer of hope. On 6 June 1992, as Richard was away on business, I agreed to meet her with Emily and Angus, for a barbecue at the Parson Woodforde pub, and I took Sophie and Oliver with me. Not only did we meet on the Saturday but the next day we all went off to the Odeon to see the film 'Hook', followed by a pizza. Matthew and Rachael from next door, along with Ben and Thomas who were staying with Katie also joined us for the film and pizza. So, two adults and six children!

Upon Richard's return on the Monday, I had a call from Katie asking if Richard could meet me. The intrigue made me accept and we agreed to meet for lunch, on the Tuesday at the Maids Head Hotel in Norwich.

The meeting was the most bizarre one I had ever had. We met in the lounge just off the reception area. Quiet, with only three or four other people around. Richard, in a loud voice, in order that all the people around could hear, was explaining to anyone who cared to listen, that I had 'stolen' his fiancée and as such he challenged me to a duel. Richard, having been in the army, clearly thought this is what you did! At that point, I simply declined his offer and left. So, I never did find out if there was another more serious point to the meeting.

Katie and I hardly talked over the next week or so, but as Richard was again away on business, as he gave guided tours of WWI sites in Europe, we agreed to meet up on Friday morning. Somehow, the conversation turned to us having a holiday together in Malta! I can't recall how on earth that developed but at 16.00 we were in Cooks Travel Agents checking availability! On the next day, Saturday, after I had taken Oliver and Sophie over to Neatishead where their mother was living with Dale, Katie joined me at Swannington for supper. It was becoming very clear to each of us that our relationship, whilst fraught with issues around Richard, had become loving, serious, and meaningful.

However, despite having supper together at Swannington, neither of us admitted this to each other. This 'closeness' became very evident the next day, as she returned to Swannington and took me to Barton to meet her mother, who had only recently lost her husband in August the year before. We also collected Oliver and Sophie and returned to Swannington, meaning that Jeannette was now aware of our potential relationship.

At this time there was a beautiful pop song, by Bryan Adams, called *Everything I Do, I Do It for Yo*u, which we both loved. It was the theme tune to the film *Robin Hood: Prince of Thieves* and was also number 1 in the charts. This became 'our song'. I happened to notice that Bryan Adams was giving a concert in Ipswich, on 14 July, so hastily purchased two tickets, in the hope that Katie would accompany me.

Success! So, we both travelled together to Ipswich. But en route the song was played on the radio, forcing me to stop in a lay-by, so we could listen. We then continued our journey and joined the audience. Like everyone there, we thoroughly enjoyed the concert.

We met again, at my house in Swannington late evening the next day, this time Katie was joined by Richard. The conversation was dominated by him who continued with the old-fashioned, chauvinistic language used at the Maids Head. He informed me, in front of Katie who by now was becoming increasingly embarrassed and emotional that she, Katie, would do her duty and provide him with children etc. She walked out of the living room into my half-finished kitchen and dissolved into tears. I endeavoured to console her but to no avail, so with that I suggested they both went home. I never knew or understood the rationale behind this visit.

Chapter 4 A Fresh Start, JP & Moving 1991 – 1993

As I have alluded to, for the past couple of weeks, Katie and I had been planning a holiday away, surprisingly with Richard's blessing. Katie was exhausted at work being the end of term and I too needed a break from the builders. We had agreed that we would go to Malta, on the strict condition that we had separate rooms. Richard was content with these arrangements and as he was very busy with his tours, consented to our trip.

We went back to Cooks Travel agents in St. Stephens, where we had been some weeks earlier, and before all the uproar regarding the engagement. This time when we came to check availability and book rooms, we found that there were no single ones available, but we could have a twin bedded one, if that was acceptable. I don't know what the assistant thought of us, but we both looked at each other waiting for the other to say yes or no. We had not crossed the threshold into an intimate relationship, so the question was a difficult one, but we agreed that if that was all they had, we would take it.

On leaving the travel agents in Norwich and walking excitedly up St. Stephens Street, we discussed how and what Katie would tell Richard. The decision in our opinion was that we wouldn't actually say anything about the sleeping arrangements, as the less he knew, the less he had to worry about. But I was keen not to cause any embarrassment for Katie or make any inappropriate assumptions, so I took her to a small but upmarket ladies outfitters that specialised in lingerie, in order that she could select some appropriate nightwear.

Then on 16 July 1992, the balloon went up and burst during a visit Richard made to Katie's, in Warwick Street. Despite having previously agreed to the holiday he now clearly had changed his mind, and during the meeting tore her engagement ring from her finger, really aggressively (her words not mine) and he then just departed. Katie was scared and inconsolable but luckily Emily was at home at the time and had the sense to telephone me and she explained the situation.

I obviously went to the house but as Emily didn't want her mother to know that a) she had witnessed the event and b) that she had telephoned me for help, I simply said I was *'just passing'*. In case Richard returned, Katie packed bags for Emily, Angus and herself and went to stay with her mother in Barton. Clearly, the engagement was over as far as Katie was concerned and given his actions the assumption was that Richard was also of the same mind.

I have often wondered just what was going through the heads of both Katie and Richard at that time. As I write this, I can say that in many ways Kate possesses a very private and reserved character, so at the time despite us having agreed to a holiday in Malta, I really didn't know just what her actual thoughts were towards me. I simply had to take each day as it came and hoped that my deep love would be reciprocated.

Back in 1992, I understand that Katie tried to ring Richard on a couple of occasions but to no avail, but he did respond later on the Sunday and again on Monday, though I have no knowledge of the content of these conversations.

The holiday in Malta now seemed even more appropriate than ever and was going ahead. On Thursday 23 July 1992, with the schools now closed for the summer, we travelled down to Luton and stayed in a small B&B so we could catch our 06.00 flight to Malta International Airport, Luga.

This was the first time we had been together as a 'couple', and we were both a little nervous which manifested itself that evening into the giggles. To the extent that the owner of the B&B had to knock on our door and ask us to keep the noise down, which of course caused us to giggle even more through embarrassment. Still, she did give us breakfast at around 05.00 the next morning, by which time we had control of our emotions.

Malta was simply wonderful, sunny and warm and just what we both needed. The hotel was a perfect choice, homely and the food was delicious. The views from our hotel were of a typical Maltese scene, looking out over the harbour, as shown (Fig. 138).

Were we really on holiday together or was this all simply a dream? The reality hit home, and I had to pinch myself to accept that we were actually on holiday together. A perfect location with loving and caring thoughts between us. But as we had agreed, not sexual. It was at this time that Katie's thoughts towards me began to reveal themselves. I hoped that they were just as loving to me, as mine were towards her. They seemed to be, and maybe I wasn't living in a dream world after all, but in one of reality, filled by two people in love with each other.

Perfect!

We had booked a small open top jeep so we could explore the island, which as you can see (Fig. 139) was great fun.

So much so that my time behind the steering wheel was somewhat limited, but I had no problem with this. Katie was just loving the driving, with the wind in her hair and the smiles

Figure 138

Chapter 4 A Fresh Start, JP & Moving 1991 – 1993

said it all. This experience in Malta was just the tonic we both needed at such a fraught time.

This photograph (Fig. 140) is one of my favourite of Katie, smiling, clearly happy and possibly in love with me. I certainly knew what my feelings were, and I hoped that the holiday was going to finally confirm that they aligned with Katie's. Who could ask for anything more?

Figure 139

Figure 140

During the first evening into the very early hours of the next day, we talked openly and extensively on the balcony of the hotel, about how our lives should or could progress if we both wanted to be together. This conversation was incredibly open and frank and covered all aspects of our lives and those of our children. As adults, we owed our children this honesty.

The discussions were very deep, as for instance, we both agreed that it wouldn't be wise to extend our family. But where would or could we live and what about schooling etc. From this you can tell the depth of the topics and why they extended well into the early hours. It was absolutely uncanny that we both had so much common ground, in fact I can't recall any areas in which we differed. By the time we went to bed everything had been sorted, and Malta was awakening and awaiting our presence, as a couple deeply in love with each other. Oh, how perfect life was going to be if these feelings developed and lasted a lifetime.

The photographs opposite give an insight into the happy and exciting time we had – at least until the last three or four days.

Whilst previously exploring the local area, we had found en route to 'our' beach, a lovely traditional ice cream parlour where we regularly purchased ice creams. This day was no different so we stopped as usual, and I think on this occasion Kate decided that she would try a pineapple variety. I say Kate because the previous evening we had both decided that that was what she would like to be now called. So, with a new start and a new name, we could put the past behind us.

That particular flavour of ice cream was not a great idea as later that day she became very ill, with what we assumed was some form of food poisoning. Back at the hotel her health deteriorated to the point where the concierge phoned for a doctor. He duly arrived and luckily, like most of the population, spoke perfect English. After an in-depth consultation and with Kate hyperventilating, he diagnosed severe gastro enteritis. Kate stayed in bed, whilst the staff who were so helpful and kind, rearranged the room booking, as ours was about to expire. The doctor returned twice every day to check Kate's condition and after three days warned me that she may need to go to hospital.

With that news I started to telephone around and make the necessary arrangements. The children's other parent was advised, as was the insurance company. Luckily, the entire holiday had been paid for on my American Express card and as this was a Gold Card we had more than adequate cover. I even telephoned Richard whose first reaction was to come out and take control '*as Katie is my fiancée*'. I think he had conveniently forgotten what had gone on before. Kate certainly hadn't though, and on hearing the conversation, insisted that he remained in Norwich, which he did!

Over the next 24 hours Kate improved significantly enough for the doctor to pass her fit to fly home on Thursday 6 August, six days after our original departure date.

Following a call back to American Express to confirm the insurance claim, we were given the choice of some first-class flights. We settled on one that gave us a connection in Rome, as we both thought that would be a good place to stop. But of course, come the time we weren't allowed to leave the airport! Neither of us being 'frequent flyers', we clearly didn't understand the airport process. Still, we arrived home in Swannington safely, albeit at midnight on 7 August. But more importantly, Kate was feeling much better. Despite all the worries of the final few days, the holiday was for us, a momentous success, it cemented our

Chapter 4 A Fresh Start, JP & Moving 1991 – 1993

Figure 141

Figure 142

Figure 143

Figure 144

Figure 145

Fig. 141 – One of many lovely restaurant meals we enjoyed together.
Fig. 142 – A totally relaxed, content and happy Katie.
Fig. 143 – Katie enjoying the warm sun at our secluded spot on the local beach.
Fig. 144 – Me in the traditional fishing village of Marsaxlokk.
Fig. 145 – Both of us taken in Marsaxlokk by a kind local.

151

relationship and left us with so many wonderful memories, despite the need for medical care. Or so I thought.

On the Saturday we collected the children and had a lovely walk around Barton Turf staithe. Sunday, we went to church in Attlebridge, the next village to Swannington, where I read the lesson and then we drove over to Barton again, and had lunch with Kate's mother.

Despite all that had been said and agreed between us, Kate then decided on the following Saturday evening to meet up with Richard to explain the position. However, to my horror and total disbelief she arrived back having been convinced by Richard that they should try another three-month trial!! Was my life yet again collapsing around me, I dared not think, but if so, I would challenge this arrangement, as now I was very sure of Kate's views and thoughts, unlike the previous time.

On the Monday, Kate had agreed to take her mother to King's Lynn to meet up with Olive, who lived in Fulbeck, near RAF Cranwell. Olive was Kate's father's niece and she with Kate's mother would then make the journey back to Fulbeck for a short break.

Later in the week, Kate and I went up to Fulbeck to meet Olive and collect Kate's mother for the return journey home. I got on with Olive famously and after a full supper was ushered to my room, at around the same time that Kate's mother also called it a day. Kate and Olive stayed downstairs and from all accounts there was a very deep 'heart to heart' conversation about relationships which unsurprisingly focused on ours, in particular. We returned to Norfolk without comment on the conversation between Olive and Kate. But there was plenty of other things to chat about en route whilst Kate and I returned to Norfolk.

On the Sunday Kate met up with Richard at Sprowston Hall Hotel and all I know is that in Kate's diary in capital letters and underlined is written, <u>RELATIONSHIP FINISHED COMPLETELY</u>! As I say, I don't know the conversation details between Kate and Olive, nor should I, but the result was to change our lives, for which we are both eternally grateful.

Kate didn't see Richard for many years until, whilst shopping in Holt, she saw him in the High Street. Whilst Kate acknowledged him, the compliment was not reciprocated.

Chapter 4 A Fresh Start, JP & Moving 1991 – 1993

Now a new, very loving and exciting new chapter in our lives commenced. Kate had been divorced for a number of years, from Alex Hutchison-Brown who was father to both Emily and Angus. I was estranged from Jeannette but not divorced. So, if our relationship was to progress, as I certainly wanted it to, and was now certain that this was a view equally shared by us both, then plans had to be put in place.

Shortly after Jeannette and I separated, on 6 October 1990 I had received a letter from her solicitors 'inviting' me to seek a divorce, on the grounds of adultery.

Clearly, Jeannette and Dale intended to marry and as there were no grounds upon which she could divorce me, an application from me was the only option that would allow their marriage to proceed, without incurring a long delay. The life cards being dealt to me were now looking very favourable indeed.

After some thought, it was clearly time to face the reality of life and accept that my marriage was over, the family business had gone, I had a limited income from ABC Printers and a house which was being practically rebuilt! This was a sobering state to be in. However, on the plus side, and it was a huge plus, I had Oliver and Sophie living with me and I had met and fallen hopelessly in love with Kate.

I agreed to the divorce and on 25 November 1991, this was granted and six weeks later, on 10 January 1992 I was sent the final Decree Absolute.

Some of the very serious decisions, that were spinning through my head, now needed to be made and quickly. I had received an offer to buy the goodwill and stock of ABC Printers from one of the employees. Whilst this didn't include any of the trading debts, it would allow me to repay my father, who was now retired but still had a vested financial interest in the business. I talked this through with him and we agreed that perhaps the best course of action was to accept the terms of the deal.

On the Friday I formally accepted the offer, on condition that all the monies due to my father were cleared and that I was given an acceptable role in the future business. The income from which would help me to pay off some of my debts.

On the Monday of the next week the deal was concluded. Prior to this, two of my staff whom I had known for a number of years, had been 'poached' by Andrew Stephen Smallman. Neither of whom had had the courtesy to be honest about their future, one saying that he was retiring which could have been true, the other said he was to become a milkman! I was not that naive and knew, full well, that his future did not include milk deliveries.

A few weeks later, following their exit, my suspicions were confirmed. Whilst it hurt at the time, upon reflection it was a good move to sell the business, even though this wasn't financially to my advantage. I had ensured that my father received the return of his investment which was a key driver for me.

More reflection was required by me, on where my life was heading. I now had some employment, but I wasn't sure for how long, and my financial status was a mess with almost £5,500 of debts. After some hard and at times, depressing soul searching I concluded that a 'clearing of the decks' was required. This would enable me to build the relationship with Kate, which I so desperately wanted. That was assuming she still wanted one with me, now that she understood my full circumstances. I would then be able to put behind me all the negative thoughts and activities of the past, that I had been experiencing.

Having now dealt with ABC Printers, ensured that my father's investment had been repaid, and following the receipt from the courts confirming that I was divorced (Fig. 146) subject to there being no objections, I needed to think seriously about my relationship with Kate. From my perspective, our relationship was going extremely well, and I was certainly deeply in love with her. I believed this was reciprocated, but there was only one way to confirm this – to propose to Kate that we were married.

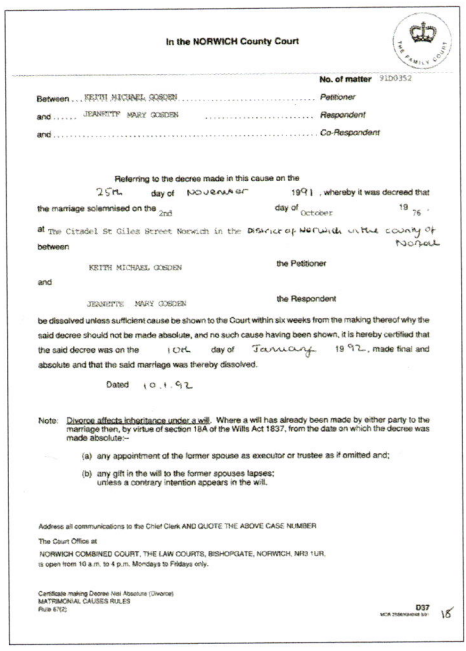

Figure 146

However, this was a decision that, from my side, involved not just me but also Oliver and Sophie. I wanted to seek their thoughts about Kate possibly becoming their stepmother, so when the time was right, and I can't honestly say when this happened, all three of us had a friendly conversation. To my surprise and relief, this was short and very positive – they were very happy and wanted me to marry her. The ball was now well and truly in my court.

On 18 August, Kate and I met my parents at West Runton, where they had a static caravan that was used by members of the family. We had a lovely walk through the woods, followed by supper. My parents were very supportive of my relationship with Kate as were both of my sisters Judy and Sarah.

I recall, at a later date, Judy saying that as they were of a similar age, she and Kate could go clothes shopping together, in London. However, this has never actually happened to my knowledge. Judy also told me, privately, that '*I shouldn't try out the goods before the purchase*', or words to that effect. Meaning no sex before marriage. Unbeknown to her, Kate and I had already agreed this, before we went to Malta and had upheld that commitment.

On Friday 21 August 1992, I tentatively asked Kate to marry me and had received a positive response but as old fashioned as I am, it had to be done correctly, so the approval of Kate's mother was essential.

I had met Kate's mother a number of times, but not her sisters. This was all to change when I was introduced to them on Monday 24 August whilst they were staying with Kate's mother at Barton.

It was almost a year since Kate's father had died (31 August 1991) and his family had decided to gift his many sailing books to the Royal Yachting Association (RYA). Her father was a well-known and respected sailor, the author of many of the rule books on competitive international sailing, thus resulting in him being asked to judge various competitions, including three Olympic Games. He was therefore well known to the RYA and his collection of books were gratefully received. However, they all needed to have a bookplate affixed to the inside cover, denoting the gift and from whom. This was being undertaken by Kate and her sisters.

I had the opportunity, whilst helping to prepare lunch, to privately talk to Kate's mother about my desire to marry her youngest daughter. I tentatively asked if she was happy to give us both her blessing. After a very short pause, her face lit up with a smile and that was the confirmation I sought. The offer of a proposal was emphatically endorsed. We talked and it was very clear that Kate's mother was way ahead of Kate and me! Not only was she expecting us to announce an engagement, but she had secretly been wondering why it was all taking so long!

Following this I found myself being nominated to carve the joint – ostensibly because I was the only male in the room! Or was this a challenge of my suitability to become a son-in-law? I was obviously nervous but accepted the carving challenge and suffice to say, we all had a delicious meal.

I appreciated that at this juncture, my status was not particularly attractive, as I have already outlined, but marriage is based on love not status, and I certainly had the former in bucketfuls. Also, I was soon to have an opportunity to talk to her older brother Peter, about our marriage plans.

Peter lived in Farnham, in Surrey, and we had been invited to stay with him and his family on the weekend of 28 – 30 August.

The day before we drove to Peter's, Kate and I went to Dipples to purchase an engagement ring. My receipt is seen here (Fig. 147).

This was very successful, and we were both very happy and delighted. However, I also distinctly recall Kate's words to me, whilst we walked down London Street away from Dipples. They were, *'just because you've bought an engagement ring, it doesn't mean I am going to marry you'*. This was said whilst we walked hand in hand, both of us with huge 'Cheshire grins' on our faces. As such I took the comment as it was meant, as both frivolous and flippant. Time has proved this to be correct!

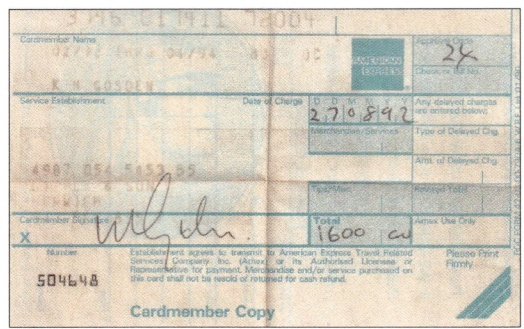

Figure 147

To recap; I had both sought and had confirmed the positive opinion of the children, had 'unofficially' asked Kate to marry me, sought and received the blessing of Kate's mother and had purchased an engagement ring. Finally, Kate had flippantly indicated that marriage was not a certainty! Not the best order of events. If you as a reader are confused, just imagine what I was thinking. But in our hearts, both Kate and I absolutely knew what our destiny was to be and were so thrilled and excited. This was true love at its best, but nothing could officially be said until we had the blessing of Kate's brother and had announced it properly.

On 28 August 1992, we drove down to see Peter and Jane in Farnham. On arrival Kate suddenly realised that she was wearing her engagement ring, so had to discreetly take it off, or at least turn it round, as Peter and Jane were unaware of the engagement. We went out on the Saturday to the theatre and then, on the Sunday, we walked through Frencham Heights.

On the evening of our arrival, I spoke privately to Peter and explained my wish to marry his sister. To which Peter gently and graciously said that he was neither his sister's keeper nor was any permission required from him, despite being the male head of the family, following his father's death. I took that as a positive! Having enjoyed the rest of the weekend, Kate put her ring back on and we left for home, feeling very pleased that we had received the endorsement from Peter, and we could now plan the formal announcement, once all four of the children had been told.

After arriving home, we told our children of our engagement which was greeted with much delight by all of them. A new blended family was on the horizon!

Chapter 4 A Fresh Start, JP & Moving 1991 – 1993

I had become rather renowned, from the children's perspective, for doing 'odd' things that demonstrated my love for Kate or what they would say were 'embarrassing acts'. We often went out in separate cars as we were not able to safely get all four children in the back of one car. On one such occasion, we had stopped at the traffic lights on Unthank Road, with Kate in front of us, when I jumped out of my car and gave Kate a huge kiss, through her open driver's window. I will let you imagine the reaction of all four children!

Another is lodged in my memory and is recorded in Kate's diary on 22 September 1992. This time, I surprised Kate on a school visit, whilst she was taking a group of young ten-year-old pupils from Norwich High School, back to school. In a pre-planned 'ambush' I presented her with a bunch of roses in the middle of St. Stephens, a central shopping street in Norwich. This time, the children and Kate were totally surprised and highly amused, and I am sure it was the topic of conversation for the rest of the day. Love makes you do some strange things at times, and I just wish that our children had understood this, rather than just being embarrassed.

At the end of September, we were again staying with Kate's family but this time in Wandsworth with Henrietta, Kate's niece, and James her husband. This allowed us to easily take our place at the Chris de Burgh concert, later that evening at Earls Court. It was a great concert and was followed on the Sunday by lunch with Abigail, Henrietta's sister.

When we returned to Norfolk, I happened to be upstairs in Kate's house when I passed a bedroom, and I noticed a Teddy Bear (Fig. 148) sitting on the windowsill. I asked Kate, who it belonged to and what was it called? Kate confirmed that it belonged to her and his name was Boston. I took this all in and then it occurred to me that following our marriage, Kate's Boston was to be the perfect soul mate to Teddy, who

Figure 148

belonged to me. The hope that I had had all those years ago, when I lived in Kent, was to be fulfilled. Teddy Gosden was to meet up with Boston Sturgess – a perfect match and one that was a very gender-neutral partnership, for our modern society.

October was to be a very special month, as I had booked a meal for both Kate and I at Brasted's Restaurant. At the time, this was one of the best and most intimate restaurants in Norwich. The stage was now set.

157

Figure 149

It was here on 22 October that I formally proposed to Kate, on one knee, in front of the other restauranteurs and staff. I presented a single red rose and a ring, much to the delight of the other customers, and received back a formal acceptance – phew! Now Kate could wear her ring proudly in public and we could announce our engagement to friends and family.

So, on 23 October 1992 the *Eastern Evening News* carried our announcement. This was followed on the 24th by the *Eastern Daily Press*, on the 26th by the *Daily Telegraph* (Fig. 149) and finally on the 28th by *The Times*.

Also included in the Court Circular, on 26 October is an announcement that Prince Edward was at a performance of 'The Ragged Child', on the previous evening. By coincidence, Kate and I, along with Peter, Jane and other members of their family were also at this performance, as James Sturgess, Peter and Jane's son, was taking part in the play. I found myself standing next to Prince Edward but had no idea until Kate told me later in the evening. He probably didn't know he was standing next to me, either!

Going back to my need to reflect on my situation, I needed to seriously think about this, especially with Kate. Having been for a long walk together we agreed that the best course of action regarding my finances, was to seek professional advice. Therefore, I made an appointment, for 5 November, to talk to Cork Gully who had worked with Gosdens on the sale to Shaw and Sons. I outlined my position, which included 40 unsecured creditors amounting to £5,394, a debt to Customs and Excise for ABC printers of £4,494.00, along with two County Court judgements. One of these was from W.H. Brown for the sale of George Borrow Rd, amounting to £2,888.52, the other from a Trade printer, for £569.09. In addition to these debts, I had the Nationwide mortgage on Swannington of

£49,119.00. Not a good position. The advice reflected that and was blunt and crystal clear.

The best and probably only option I had was to declare myself bankrupt. That was what I was expecting but it still came as a shock. The consequences could be enormous, would this impact upon my potential marriage to Kate, who had already received and accepted two proposals of marriage in one year? Would I lose the family home in Swannington, how would I look after my family, etc., etc?

Having recovered from the initial shock, I left and thought this through at length. I met Kate and we talked through the likely consequences if I went ahead with bankruptcy. We agreed that it would be in the best interest of us both if I took the advice given. Kate's view was that this would give us a clean start to our married life, so clearly, Kate was happy to see that position maintained. Also, hopefully, as the house was not in a fit state to sell, due to the alterations, that were partly being funded by Kate, we would be able to keep this as our new family home, as its value was lessened by its current condition, with only part of the alterations having been completed.

On 12 November 1992 I attended the County Court in Norwich and swore my Affidavit. Seven days later at 09.45 in the morning I was declared bankrupt for a period of three years. I am not proud of this but am confident that I did the right thing for my family and creditors who could now claim some of their losses against potential tax returns. In 1995 I was discharged as per the letter (Fig. 150).

There was a residual matter to this, in that the Official Receiver forgot to remove their claim to the title deeds of Swannington, meaning that we couldn't remortgage, when

Figure 150

we enquired some four years later. However, this was swiftly sorted out and we received a letter on 23 February 1999, confirming that the Official Receiver had no interest in the property. All was agreed and the remortgage, with Kate's name being added to the title deeds, was concluded.

Strangely enough, being bankrupt but still working at ABC printers, whilst not a desirable status, did remove considerable pressure. This allowed Kate and me to concentrate on both our personal relationship and future marriage, along with building a cohesive family. But first we had some practical matters which required attention.

We were now a family of six, split between two locations. Me at Swannington with Oliver and Sophie, whilst Kate was in Norwich with Emily and Angus. The only 'transport' we had was Kate's Ford Escort, as my role with ABC Printers didn't come with a car. So, having looked around, considered our financial status and borrowed some funds, we purchased a second-hand Peugeot 505 family estate, for £4,425 from Norwich Car Centre. This certainly made life easier and was also large enough to carry building materials to and from the house, an extra and welcome bonus.

1993

Knowing that once married, we would set up home in Swannington, we worked with our architect friend, Ian Malton, to design a conversion of the roof space which would provide two more bedrooms, one for Emily, known as Em, and the other for Angus. Having agreed the plans with both of them, we applied for planning approval.

This was given, and we commenced work using the same builders who were still finishing off the extension to the kitchen etc.

We could now turn our attention to our marriage for which we wanted a traditional church wedding, but legally this wasn't possible as the Church of England would not marry divorcees. Therefore, we had no option but to marry at the Norwich Registry Office and the day was booked for 22 July 1993. On viewing the registry office, we found it was well designed and much more friendly than we had imagined, but it still wasn't a church! We came away and decided that whilst legally this would be our wedding date, we would keep this civil ceremony very small and would have on 24 July 1993 what we considered to be a 'proper' wedding.

Despite all the upheaval we successfully endeavoured to keep life 'normal'. With joint suppers, which were often spent together at Warwick Street (Fig. 151). Although, in this case, I am not quite sure why Angus and Oliver were looking rather 'odd'!

Figure 151

Chapter 4 A Fresh Start, JP & Moving 1991 – 1993

We spent most of the first few months of 1993 going through all the arrangements for the church wedding and the honeymoon. But this was interrupted on 26 May by Kate's car being stolen from outside her house. Unlike mine, hers wasn't found, so Chris Courtney, still a good friend, helped out with a loan car.

Back to the wedding, early on we had agreed that as we both knew The Reverend Keith White as he was vicar at Holy Trinity Church, where I had attended with my parents and was close to where Kate lived, we asked if he would conduct the service at Barton Turf. All four children were to be totally involved, with Angus walking his mother down the aisle, Oliver as an usher, and Em and Sophie as bridesmaids. In addition, Angus drafted and read his own speech at the reception. This was to be held at The Petersfield House Hotel in Horning, which was close to Barton Turf church, where the blessing was to take place. As I have outlined previously, Barton church has a special place in the lives of Kate's family.

Keith White was delighted to be asked and made the arrangements with the Barton Turf incumbent vicar. He also agreed that to make the service special he would be happy to include a short Holy Communion, as the final part of the service. I was to produce and print at ABC Printers, the necessary orders of Service. The invitations, on behalf of Kate's mother, were produced by CCA Stationery, a wedding printer used by ABC Printers.

Both Kate and I had long discussions on where we would like or indeed could afford to go for a honeymoon. We finally whittled down our ideas to those where there would be some guarantee of sun and a good beach. Having been through the brochures, yet again, Greece was chosen and in particular the Skiathos Palace Hotel, as this not only looked ideal but also overlooked the Bay of Koudounaris.

With that decision made, we booked our honeymoon on 9 January 1993 (Fig. 152). It was a day of drizzle in Swannington, but we now had some sunshine to look forward to.

January was to be the month for booking the key requirements of the wedding. Kate's bridal gown was to be made by Maureen Jennings, the lady from whom I had

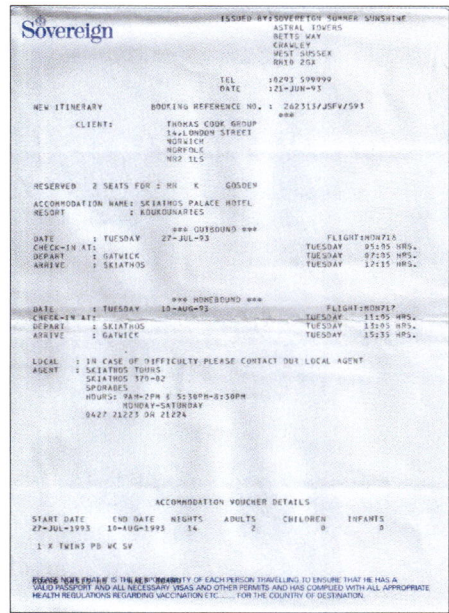

Figure 152

REFLECTIONS UPON A FAMILY

purchased the house in George Borrow Road. There was some rationale to this as she owned a reputable wedding gown business, Buttercup Brides in Norwich, and she was delighted to be able to help. Whilst I only saw the end result on the day, I can say that the gown was absolutely wonderful but more on that later. For now, it's back to 'preparations', so a wedding cake was ordered from Sally Spelman and on the same day we met up with a photographer, John West, who was subsequently booked on 28 January. All these arrangements though, were only for the blessing. For us, this was to be THE wedding day, rather than the civil ceremony that was, of course, still the 'legal' marriage. With all these plans in place we were both extremely happy and excited.

For my first birthday with Kate, 26 February 1993, I received a copy of Emily Post's Etiquette with the following beautiful inscription: *Darling Keith, my first birthday present to you honeypie. Given with <u>all</u> my love to the most wonderful, kind, caring, loving, trustworthy, understanding gentleman in my life. Happy Birthday forever yours Kate.*

This was a most appropriate present as Kate and I, along with the children, were often having discussions on etiquette and the correct meaning of various words. For the latter we would turn to the 'Red dictionary' being a large red 1968 Chambers version, that I had inherited from my grandfather who frequently thumbed through this when endeavouring to solve a crossword clue. Both books became 'go to' references for a number of years promoting many family conversations on their accuracy and validity.

Unbeknown to Kate, the day after my birthday I booked the first two nights of our honeymoon which was to be a surprise for her on the day (Fig.153). I had found a lovely hotel in Southwold, The Swan, which wasn't too far to travel. Here we could

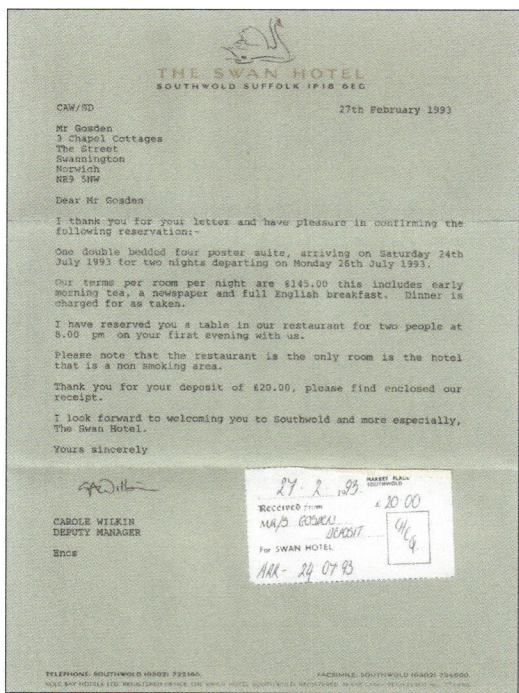

Figure 153

Chapter 4 A Fresh Start, JP & Moving 1991 – 1993

Figure 154

have a four-poster bed suite. Figure 154 is taken from their leaflet at the time. I thought this hotel would be very special, plus their reputation was excellent, so meals and service should be very good.

However, on the practical front there was still Kate's house to sell and alterations to finish at Primitive Cottage in Swannington. So, no time to sit back and rest! But in my opinion, both of us needed a short time away from all the hurley burley of wedding arrangements.

To that end, I booked a surprise romantic weekend away for both of us in Herefordshire. We were to stay in Weobley, at the 500 year old, Ye Olde Salutation Inn (Fig. 155). The children were staying with their other parent that weekend, so the coast was clear.

At 09.00 on Saturday 27 February 1993 we set off, having previously enjoyed, as a family the evening before, a surprise birthday supper for me. The weather was kind with bright blue sky, but it was cold. On the Sunday, there was actually a flurry of snow. This wasn't a hinderance and it made the five-hour journey home even more fun. But not before we had visited Pembridge and had a good walk around, looking at all the timber framed houses. We left for home at 17.30 arriving back in time for Kate to prepare for Norwich High School parents' evenings, which were to run all the next week!

Figure 155

Schooling was to be a significant part of our life over the next few years, with Em taking nine GCSEs, all during the summer, Angus choosing his GCSE options and in trepidation, Oliver and Sophie were looking on, as to what they would face in the coming years. But before we could celebrate or commiserate any examination results, we had a wedding to enjoy.

I recall that despite not yet being a resident of Swannington, Kate was often able to join us at the church, where Oliver and Sophie were in the choir, and I frequently read the lesson. Something that in the future would be shared with Kate. Neither of us declare to be devout Christians, but we still

163

attended our local church and found this of comfort when life seemed to be overwhelming us.

One thing I do remember about our relationship that indeed continues to this day, was that we would leave each other little notes, saying where we were etc., and always signed off with an expression of our love at the end.

It's small things like this that remind us both of our deep loving relationship.

Obviously, residing in different homes before our wedding, leaving notes for each other wasn't always possible. Kate, like her mother, kept a diary into which appointments and key memories/reminders were recorded. So, I was able to write little messages, like the one shown, dated 19 February 1993, as a substitute for a note. These diary entries may have been on the current day or in the future when I knew that we wouldn't be together. As can be seen I was in King's Lynn on the particular day mentioned (Fig. 156).

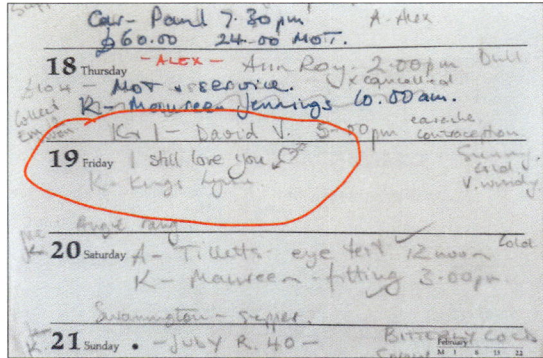

Figure 156

Figure 157

The big day was approaching, and towards the end of March, it was time to visit Moss Bros. in Norwich to have morning suits fitted and ordered.

As the wedding day was a significant celebration, the wedding party were to wear multicoloured ties, whilst the bridesmaids would complement this with colourful hats and waistcoats. But for now, it was the Top Hat and Tails fitting for the men – the ladies would follow later, assisted by Kate.

Throughout all of this turmoil, poor Em was fervently revising for her GCSEs, and I have to say that we were both so impressed with her diligent and painstaking efforts (Fig. 157). April Fools' Day was her first exam, English Oral, but Em was no fool and she came back very pleased with her progress. A great start and a boost to her

Chapter 4 A Fresh Start, JP & Moving 1991 – 1993

confidence. We would know this was justified with the results due in August.

The building adaptations to the cottage were progressing well, but regrettably some additional plans, to the previously agreed main ones, for the work in the loft, were declined by the planners and thus required minor alterations. These were undertaken by Ian Malton and re-submitted in early May, this time with a positive outcome. Work would commence with the same builders, whilst Kate and I had already started redecorating downstairs.

Mid-April was the time for the bridesmaids to go shopping. I recall this went well, other than one outfit had to be sent to Norwich from Ipswich, as it was the only store that had that particular size. Still, we were almost ready. Kate had her second fitting, us men and boys were all sorted, and now the ladies too, were ready.

Throughout all these wedding plans both Kate and I found time to attend events, some together and some individually, that gave us some respite from wedding plans, building works or exams. A couple of our 'events' were to exhibitions of artists that we both admired. One was Jason Partner, who had exhibited some lovely small watercolours in Picturecraft in Holt. So much so that one ended up being purchased by us! Quite where this was to hang was a mystery, as together we had a vast collection of paintings to hang in a relatively small cottage. But that didn't stop us as we also purchased a couple of Hugh Brandon Cox paintings, whilst at his exhibition in Blakeney.

These were, of course, of little interest to the children. So, to even up the events I took all four of them up to Alton Towers on 1 July. Great fun was had by us all, especially on the Log Flume (Fig. 158). Clearly both Em and Oliver were enjoying the experience, as I am sure we all were, but not showing it quite so obviously.

Upon our return, Kate and I had conversations about the honeymoon arrangements, just to check that all was in order. I was hoping that Kate would not ask the obvious question, *'where are we staying between the wedding on the 24th and the flight'*. The

Figure 158

question was probably thought about but, thankfully, was never asked!

By mid-July, the wedding preparations had almost been completed to the point that on the 14th we were to have a rehearsal with the vicar, Keith White. Earlier, on the same day, Kate had her final fitting with Buttercup Brides and Em had a hairdresser rehearsal. Clearly, I was not involved in these, but Kate and I had a successful rehearsal with Keith White and Ian Malton, my best man.

Two days later, Kate and I went to see Mr Podolski, a jeweller who had a shop in Norwich, just a few yards away from Brasteds, where we had become officially engaged. Mr Podolski was making a wedding ring for me with the design based on two very special rings. One was a ring (Fig. 159) which originally belonged to my maternal grandmother and was given to my mother who used to wear it. This is now in my possession and is hallmarked Chester 1894 and based on a barley twist. The other was a ring which Kate has worn for a number of years, and again is a weave/flat twist of two gold bands. My wedding ring, based on a combination of these two designs, was now ready and available for hallmarking. However, given the proximity of the wedding and civil ceremony, being only a few days away, we decided not to risk having the ring sent away for a hallmark. We already had Kate's wedding ring, having collected this from Dipples some weeks back. In our eyes, we were now ready to be married.

Figure 159

There was just one thing left to do, and that was to be put in place when a Round Table friend, Bryan Baxter, came to see us both at 87 Warwick Street. Wearing his Estate Agent's hat, he valued Kate's house at around £69,000 but we weren't quite ready to market this at the time, so we put the sale on hold.

Two days later at 11.30 on 22 July we officially became married. The ceremony in Churchman House was kept very low key. Kate's mother and my parents were in attendance and the 'official' witnesses were Em, Angus, Oliver, and Sophie along with Ian Malton. The ceremony was followed by a tea at The Maids Head Hotel which was very good and just what we all needed! This time I wasn't challenged to a duel! The day was legally very important and hugely significant as it resulted in both our families becoming 'blended' into one. However, we still found time later that day, to view the progress made on our wedding cake.

The pictures (Figs. 160-163) taken in the office and gardens of Churchman House by Ian Malton, give a 'flavour' of the day. With the huge support of our parents and children we were now legally married. The ceremony, whilst small and intimate, was wonderful.

Chapter 4 A Fresh Start, JP & Moving 1991 – 1993

Figure 160

Figure 161

Figure 162

Figure 163

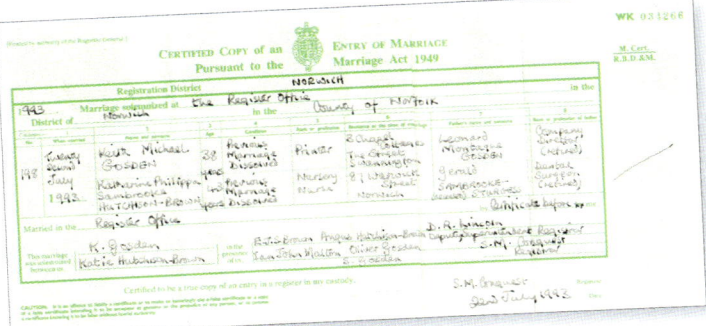

Fig. 160 – Myself and Kate
Fig. 161 – Emily, Oliver, Me, Kate, Angus, Sophie
Fig. 162 – Emily, Me, Kate, Sophie
Fig. 163 – Kate's mother (Betty Sturgess), Me, Kate, my father and mother
Figure 164 – The legal piece of paper that means so much to both of us (left).

Figure 164

167

REFLECTIONS UPON A FAMILY

The day of the Blessing service (Fig. 165) arrived and what a day it was. The sun was shining, the wedding party looked fantastic, as did the church. The bride looked a picture of pure perfection being walked up the aisle with a very proud Angus by her side. It was a 'million dollar' moment that has lived with me ever since. Even now some 30+ years later, my eyes are tearful as I recall the day.

It wasn't just Angus who was proud. But both bride and groom had to be careful, as Angus almost stole the show when he gave a speech, in place of his grandfather. As it can be seen in the selection of photographs, he was to deliver such an eloquent and wise speech. All the family and friends made the day so very special for us both. For the rest of my memories of the day I will allow the following photographs to tell the story.

Figure 165

Chapter 4 A Fresh Start, JP & Moving 1991 – 1993

These photos were all at Barton Church, with the below including Leticia, Kate's great niece and Tia Kate's niece, both as bridesmaids. Figure 166 is Kate laying her bouquet at the graves of her father (left) and brother (right).

Figure 166

169

REFLECTIONS UPON A FAMILY

The others are at the reception with William, Kate's nephew who was an usher, sitting on the steps, the final one is of us both leaving under a veil of confetti.

Chapter 4 A Fresh Start, JP & Moving 1991 – 1993

Kate's diary for the day just has the words, '*FABULOUS DAY from beginning to end*'. Words that I did and still do, fully endorse. My respect for Kate and our family which we had 'blended' will endure for as long as I live. As will my unabating love for them all.

Having changed and with the celebrations coming to an end we were off, but Kate knew not where! Our transport was a Nova, which Chris Courtney had kindly lent us back in May, following Kate's car being stolen. However, to avoid any 'interference' with our luggage etc. we had packed my car and hidden it, so we could simply swop cars en route.

With all the children, from the now truly 'blended' family with their respective other parent, we made our way to Norwich. Kate, as I have said, didn't know our destination for our first night as a married couple, so the guessing started as to our venue.

Having thought all the celebrations were in the past, when we stopped at the traffic lights on the Norwich ring road, we found ourselves queuing next to some of our guests, also making their way home! Still, we carried on, waved goodbye and continued our journey to Southwold. Kate guessed the location about halfway there as the town started to appear on the signposts – but not the hotel which was a wonderful surprise.

We were booked into the Swan Hotel for one night only. Then we were to continue our journey, ultimately to Skiathos, with a further one-night stay at Goffs Park, in Crawley, a Jacobean Hall built around circa 1450. We were to leave our car here whilst a taxi took us early in the morning to Gatwick for our flight to Greece. All these arrangements went according to plan and on 27 July, we booked into the Skiathos Palace Hotel.

Figure 167

We had the most relaxing two weeks enjoying each other's company, swimming, waterskiing, jet-skiing and generally doing all the things we wouldn't normally be able to afford. This included paragliding as seen here as evidence! (Figs. 167 & 168).

Our hotel is the building on the clifftop, in the background, of the photograph (Fig. 168).

Our meals were taken on the terrace beside the pool, on a beautiful table, located under a large oleander, (Fig. 169). This table was reserved for us, by the staff who clearly wanted to please their guests. They did look after us extremely well.

During our stay we met up with a young couple, Wellie and Adam who were also on their honeymoon and had been married the day prior to us. We became and have remained good friends, and they still live in Wheathampstead.

Chapter 4 A Fresh Start, JP & Moving 1991 – 1993

Figure 168

Figure 169

We returned to the UK and the family home on 10 August 1993, only to return to London the next day, to see Em and Vicki a friend fly off to the USA for a short holiday. They departed on the 07.10 flight from Heathrow. Em was to be away for ten days during which time she was expecting her GCSE results!

CHAPTER 5

Married Life, Extensions & Exams
1993 – 1999

1993 continued

Having returned home from Skiathos, we commenced the daunting task of moving furniture around at Swannington, in readiness for Kate's furniture and chattels from Warwick Street. It was like moving two houses at once, with frequent trips to and fro transporting furniture in the back of the car. I remember Kate commenting that it was amazing how much you can accumulate and re-discover. This equally applied to both of us! By the time we had all the main furniture in place, we were left with just 60 paintings to hang and three sofas to fit in – and we managed it, somehow.

While all this was going on, we also had a carpet laid in Angus's bedroom, so that he could be the first to feel at home when he returned from his father's. Oliver and Sophie already had their rooms which just needed redecorating, so now it was time for us to work on Em's.

As Em was still in America, this provided the opportunity and time for me to build a new double wardrobe for her, before her carpet was laid. Once finished, Kate and I unpacked her clothes etc. and put away as much as we could, ready for her return, and yes, her room was all finished before she arrived back.

Her plane landed in the UK on 26 August at 08.30. She had had a wonderful time, but during her final few days there, her thoughts were focused on what the dreaded slip of paper would reveal. We picked up her GCSE results from Warwick Street and made our way home to Swannington with a very healthy air of satisfaction and relief. Two years of hard work had paid off, achieving 4As, 4Bs, and 1C. We were both so proud of her and I chauffeured a delighted mother and a relieved and overjoyed daughter back home.

I recall that in September, whilst clearing Kate's house, we decided that the front door in which Kate had designed a beautiful stained-glass window, would look lovely at Swannington and be an appropriate 'link' back to her previous home. To this end we asked Eddie, who was a carpenter working at Swannington, if he could remove it, store it for us and install a new one at Warwick Street. This he

Chapter 5 Married Life, Extensions & Exams 1993 – 1999

did and in October Kate's door was duly installed and was a great enhancement to our cottage.

One of my 'wish list' items was achieved on 11 September, when we both went to Earls Court to see Paul McCartney play with his band, Wings. He was brilliant and well worth the effort of getting there. His repertoire included songs both from his Beatles time and, of course, with his current band 'Wings'. One of my favourite songs was *Mull of Kintyre* which when I worked for Norwich Brewery, I recall was played almost constantly in one of my pubs in Thetford, whilst it was being renovated. The landlord and I got on very well, and on one of my visits to check progress we ended up having a few whiskies whilst we talked and listened to the music. It was a very long and enjoyable visit!

Whilst we were at Earls Court, Sophie was away for the weekend at a Guide Camp at Patterson Lodge, so we had to be back from the concert in order to pick her up the next day. But the Peugeot then decided to 'die' in the middle of Kensington High Street! Luckily, the AA recovered both us and the car and we were relayed home, arriving at 03.00 in the morning! All was well and using the Nova instead, we were able to pick up Sophie on time. Apparently, she enjoyed the experience of camping which pleased all three of us – I don't think she had to do a kit inspection or blow up a bridge, so that was a relief! Homework was next on the agenda for all of them, so a little quiet time for us both.

By the end of October, we had had two Estate Agent valuations for Warwick Street, Bryan Baxter and Ken Shipman. Ken gave a suggested value of £69,950, which Kate accepted and 87 Warwick Street was finally put on the market. I recall that there was some interest, but I think this was more curiosity rather than serious viewing, as no offers were received.

By mid-January 1994, Kate had on Ken's advice reduced the price to £67,950 and it was actually sold a month later for £56,500, whilst this was a significant reduction, Kate was very happy with the deal, especially as she had purchased it in 1984 for £24,800. Following a weekend 'blitz' by all of us to clean the house from top to bottom, completion took place on 22 April.

Back at Swannington, at the end of October we managed to spend a weekend hanging 14 of our pictures, which cleared a little more space and certainly enriched the rooms. This exercise was carried out again with 17 paintings hung in the Snug and was all completed a week or so before our very first Christmas together, as a family.

1993 was a momentous year for all of us as change is not always easy. Both I and Kate were so proud of how the children supported us and dealt with all the changes in the creation of their new home. There were difficult times and some things, like the decoration of the bathroom, that didn't meet their tastes. Overall though, it was hard work but great fun. This was reflected (Fig. 170) in the last page of a letter we circulated to family and friends, in October of that year. To my knowledge this is the only paper that we have all signed as a family. Hence, it's special and included here as a valued memoir.

Our memories of "The Day" are filled with happiness as we hope yours are too.

It was wonderful to see so many family and friends and perhaps our only regret was that we did not have long enough to be able to sit and chat to everyone.

However, our policy of having an "open house" still remains and therefore we will be delighted to see you at any time should you find yourselves in the vicinity of Swannington.

Love from

Keith, Kate, Emily, Angus, [illegible] and Sophie.

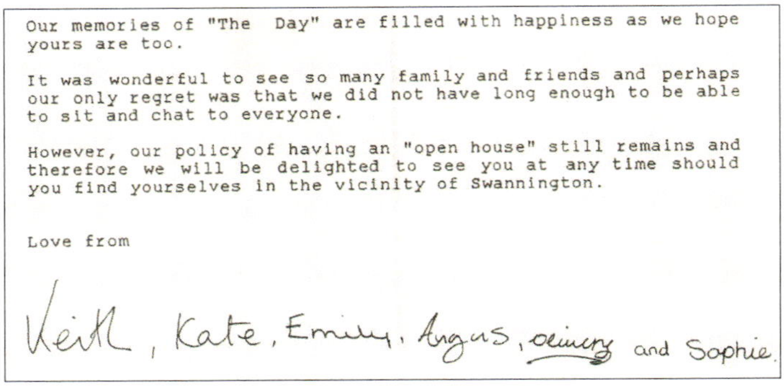

Figure 170

The photographs (Figs. 171-175) are of work being undertaken at Swannington, and how it looked for our first family Christmas.

There was still much to do, especially in the front and back gardens, to say nothing of the need for a new garage. That was to follow in the year to come. For now though, we were happy to simply enjoy living there and going to three different schools, actually four if you included Kate's work. Life was certainly busy, along with decorating!

Figure 171

Before you strip a wall, you can always draw something on it first, without being told off (Fig. 172)!

Our new front door was now installed in the fully decorated hall/snug, with just a couple of boxes still to be emptied, nestling under the church pew (Fig. 173)!

Figure 174 shows our first Christmas in Swannington, with 'Tonic' our contented cat, asleep in the Drawing Room.

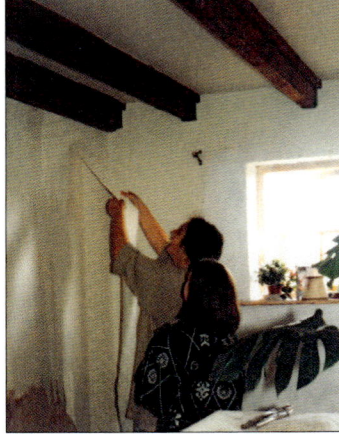

Kate and I, whilst aware that life was changing for all of us, were equally aware that the new situation had to reflect and acknowledge the past lives that we had had. Small reminders, such as the door, were in our opinion important to ease this transition. The window in the front door (Fig. 175), designed by Kate, acted as a gentle reminder of where she, Em and Angus had spent many happy years together.

Chapter 5 Married Life, Extensions & Exams 1993 – 1999

Figure 172

Figure 173

Figure 174

Figure 175

REFLECTIONS UPON A FAMILY

Figure 175

Chapter 5 Married Life, Extensions & Exams 1993 – 1999

1994

Living in Swannington didn't impact on my continued enjoyment of Round Table, whilst Kate and I still supported the social functions, and I went to most of the meetings. However, with finances as they were, I did feel that the time was approaching where I would need to resign, prior to my actual leaving date of February 1995, the point at which I reached the compulsory leaving age of 40. I was saddened to have to leave but knew, in my heart, that this was the right decision.

On 26 April 1994, we started our final alterations when the kitchen and our bedroom were both extended, a twin chimney for the Aga and a fire in our bedroom were built. This concluded with a conservatory which was erected linking the space between the kitchen extension and the property next door. The montage (Fig. 175) shows the kitchen floor being laid and the walls being built, which provided us with a good size kitchen that housed the Aga. The chimney is shown along with the conservatory.

A new home brought with it a desire to not only redesign the interior, but also the front and back gardens. With spades, forks, buckets and wheelbarrows at the ready, we all took to digging up the front garden, laying a new brick and flint path, combined with a new tree and flower beds, which were far more in keeping with our style (Fig. 176). New turf was to be next, and this was purchased and loaded into the back of the estate car. However, our trusty car was not happy again, so some friends who lived close by, came to our rescue. Our family and turf were duly transported home and laid to finish the front garden.

Figure 176

One evening, Kate suggested that as we both liked art, we should think about organising some Art Courses, where professional artists could give tuition, whilst we managed the publicity and organisation. This seemed to be a good idea, and after some research we decided to explore the possibilities further. We spoke with two local artists, Jason Partner and Adrian Taunton, along with Bryan Thatcher who lived further away, to gauge their reaction and thoughts. We then took the idea to Picturecraft, in Holt, as we knew the owner, to also seek his views. All the feedback was positive, with Adrian even suggesting that he would happily offer a trial for us and one guest at his home studio.

Adrian was known to Kate and her family, so we accepted his offer and asked a friend in Swannington to join us. The day was a resounding success and convinced us that there was a future in proceeding with our idea.

Figure 177

We successfully ran summer courses, for a couple of years, under the name of The Sambrooke Art Foundation and these were located in a building in Attlebridge.

Regrettably, we had to close them when due to the recession, demand tailed off. Whilst in operation we had a wide selection of local and international artists including the three I have already mentioned, plus Ron Ranson, Elizabeth Hartley and Martin Sexton.

The photograph (Fig. 177) is of a course tutored by Bryan Thatcher. Overall, the courses which covered a variety of styles and mediums, were great fun and we enjoyed running them, as well as learning how to improve our own artistic skills. Martin, in particular, conducted many of the tutorials, as he was a very popular local watercolourist and had a very easy teaching style.

Em, being the eldest of our children, was now of an age where she wanted to learn to drive. So, on 6 February with a provisional licence in hand, she had her first lesson with Kate. Due to this success and her determination she progressed to regular professional lessons. However, after a number of these and a couple of unsuccessful tests, Em decided to take a break.

In early February, Angus flew from Gatwick to join a well-earned educational cruise, which was to visit Greece, Egypt, Israel, Turkey and finally Crete. It reminded me of my Navassa cruise some years earlier and like me he thoroughly enjoyed the experience. He returned on the 19th and slept for almost the entire day!

Later in February, my 39th birthday was slightly marred, by having been given the day before, one month's notice of redundancy from ABC Printers. I say 'slightly' as I had been expecting this to happen.

Neil, the new owner, was doing his level best to move the business forward, in his own style. It's always difficult though, working alongside the previous owner as I had experienced whilst working with Shaw and Sons, who had purchased Gosdens. So, I perfectly understood and empathised with his rationale for wanting me to move on.

All this was put behind us on my birthday and we had a lovely family day, followed by an equally lovely meal of roast turkey with all the trimmings and trifle to finish, perfect!

Kate and I decided that due to the continuing work on the cottage, as previously mentioned, I would take time out of job hunting, to finish this off 'jointly' with the builders. During this time, I also took the opportunity to consider my work options.

This new joint arrangement didn't start straight away as we had booked a short family holiday in the two weeks of half-term. On the Saturday we set off from Portsmouth to St. Malo. We were to stay in a cottage (Fig. 178) in Quimper, owned by one of the partners at Hansells Solicitors. Although this was nice, the weather was not so good and after 12 wet but relaxing days, we all returned home as planned.

Figure 178

On 11 May further changes to our family were proposed. This time by Jeannette and Dale, who during a meeting at Swannington proposed that Oliver and Sophie moved to live with them, rather than with Kate and myself. Clearly this suggestion was upsetting for us, but we agreed to seek the views of both the children, who were both very clear that they wished to stay at Swannington, with us.

REFLECTIONS UPON A FAMILY

By the end of May 1994, the main roof of the second and final extension was completed. Steel RSJs were in place, allowing us to remove some of the internal walls and create the new rooms that were required. With all this happening at home, we decided to go over to Wroxham with just Oliver and Sophie to have a practice sail, as Kate was to crew for Stephen Hinde, a friend, in the Three Rivers Race, at the end of the month. Em was at a 'Levellers' concert and Angus was with his father. It was such a good sail and as Monday was a bank holiday, we decided we would return, but this time to Hickling Broad.

Come the weekend, Kate and Stephen set sail in the race, from Horning. It was very cold, with heavy rain, no wind and as a consequence little progress was made. Suffice to say that at midnight the race was cancelled, so they retired and motored back to Horning, where I met up with them both. Whilst disappointing for all the participants, given the conditions it was an accepted outcome.

The next few days saw electricians hard at work both in the house and outside, where new supply cables had to be laid.

June was to be a milestone for Sophie, as she started school at Taverham having decided that school life at Reepham was not to her liking. She now joined Oliver who was already there but in the year above. This made school journeys a little easier for all of us.

The month continued with the oak beams being put into the kitchen. As the Aga had already been installed, it was waiting to be commissioned so that would have to follow later. The kitchen floor was laid, following the completion of the central heating. Now we were finally able to see an end to the building works. Finally, the Aga was commissioned, and we were given a demonstration on how to use it, which for some reason Oliver was the only one to join us. Perhaps this sowed the seed in later life, for him to cook his family meals, but not on an Aga!

Although taken later in the year, the photograph of the kitchen (Fig. 179) gives an indication as to how it looked, albeit without curtains!

Figure 179

Chapter 5 Married Life, Extensions & Exams 1993 – 1999

Over the past few weeks, Em had been considering universities and had been to Nottingham, and others would follow. This was a sobering thought, in that after only a year together as a family, Em now a young adult was considering where she would go to spend the next three years. This was hard, but just as it should be and in time the others would also 'fly the nest' – but would they return, would they be happy?

As parents we knew that we could neither stop them nor interfere, just offer support and guidance when appropriate, in other words, when asked for!

On a more upbeat note, 24 July was our very first wedding anniversary. With all four children safely being looked after with friends or walking, as I will outline later, we set off for a long weekend at Combe Grove Manor Hotel (Fig. 180) in Monkton near Bath. To say it was relaxing was an understatement. Just think about the upheaval I have previously described, at home in Swannington and compare that with staying in a luxury hotel with all the usual wellbeing facilities, these being a jacuzzi, massages and swimming pools. All on offer and preceded by breakfast in bed, and you will understand just why it was so relaxing! We did though, find time to visit Bath and found a lovely reclamation centre where we purchased a stone sink, as you do! We also visited Castle Combe, where Kate enjoyed her ice cream whilst sitting next to the 14th century Market Cross (Fig. 181). The village had recently become famous as an important location for the film *War Horse*. Our final piece of extravagance was supper on the second and final night, which was complemented with champagne. On the Monday we walked around the extensive grounds and bid a farewell, before making our way home.

Figure 180

Figure 181

Whilst we enjoyed the height of luxury, Angus was out on a 20-mile hike with a 100-litre backpack, as part of his Duke of Edinburgh Silver Award. The walk, with some friends, was successful but like all boys he questioned why he needed all the clothes, a couple of boxers and T-shirts would have been fine!

With Oliver's bedroom re-decorated, we started painting Sophie's. Fortunately, there wasn't much to do, so after the re-decoration we moved her furniture out of Oliver's room, where they had been sharing, and into hers which she appreciated.

On a warm July Sunday, I started work landscaping our back garden, alongside a local farmer Richard, who arrived with his huge digger (Fig. 182). The aim was to level the area, take out the leylandii trees, including the roots, and build a new wall with a fence on top, between us and our neighbours, who I must add were fully supportive and very happy with the final outcome. After just a few days, the trees were dug out with some being cut up for logs, and a large bonfire removed the leftovers from the site. Our 'reward' for all this was our first meal cooked on the Aga, which was now fully installed and working. The children were away with their other parent and by coincidence all four were in Scotland, but not in the same location.

Figure 182

Chapter 5 Married Life, Extensions & Exams 1993 – 1999

Figure 183

Figure 184

When the children returned, they too were to help with the landscaping. Our team of support workers provided not only muscle, but also encouragement and sustenance. By 24 October 1994, the outside at the rear of the cottage, was beginning to look more like a garden as seen here (Fig. 183), as opposed to the previous mud bath.

On the same day, but looking the other way, Kate and I were still laying the slabs before working on the pile of bricks to create the path edges (Fig. 184). Together we were able to create a wonderful garden.

In some ways the work was very beneficial, as I was effectively 'on the dole' at the time, which was now well spent finishing off our new home. But I realised that whilst this was very enjoyable, being outside and working with my hands, it wouldn't pay all the bills.

I decided that I would investigate a career in landscape management and signed up for a short Farm and Estate Management course, to see if this suited me. I was still actively looking for work but without success, despite having had some interviews. To supplement my course, I also volunteered to work for the National Trust, at Blickling Hall in the Forestry Department.

Here I did have some success. I cycled the 18 miles there and back each day and found myself planting tree whips, checking/repairing gates and fences, helping to cut grass and fell trees – I had yet to be trained on some of the machinery, so was not allowed to work the large equipment, but it felt really positive, and I enjoyed every day. On one autumn day, I helped to build a very complex Chinese bridge, which I now sometimes walk past and recall how I helped to put that in place.

Kate could see my love of this and suggested that we both went on a hurdle making course at Easton College. Having been presented with a six-foot-high tree trunk, we were after some tuition in the use of traditional tools, able to split, cleft and hew this, into what looked like a pair of miniature five bar gates.

REFLECTIONS UPON A FAMILY

Figure 185

But being smaller, were in fact, a pair of Suffolk sheep hurdles. We proudly took them home and they were put to use as a small fence in the front garden.

Later I remember making the gate (Fig. 185), whilst on another course at Easton. Regrettably, I have no knowledge of what happened to it, but it was a very good gate. I am on the far left of the photograph.

Oliver at the age of 14 was thinking about what career he may carve out for himself, and Kate and I had some long discussions with him about this. At the time, his initial idea was to go into farming. The local pig farm in Swannington was owned by the chair of the Parish Council, whom I knew well through being its clerk. So, we approached her to see if Oliver could gain some work experience. Both parties agreed and Oliver started some weekend working.

Once again, November and most of December (1994) were taken up with Mock Exams. This time it was three A-Levels for Em, and Angus's GCSEs. A quick look back at our calendar for the week of 5 December, revealed the extent of these mocks! Angus was taking Maths, English Literature, English Language, Double Science, French, Geography, German and something called Tech! Em's A-Levels were Psychology, History and French. The work involved in preparing for these was very extensive and their positive aptitude and dedication was most impressive.

Chapter 5 Married Life, Extensions & Exams 1993 – 1999

With the house completed we were able to enjoy another Christmas and even entertained my parents, both my sisters and their husbands, for tea on 28 December.

Two small occurrences that have stuck in my memory about living in Swannington were firstly, the 'friendly banter' that went on, when all four children wanted to watch a very small television. There was one 'key' chair beside it, which was a premium place and much coveted. As such, there would be a rush to claim this location. The losers would have to either sit on the arms of the chair, or on the floor, and as both these seemed to have a priority sequence, speed and determination were the order of the day. To protect one's claim to the seat, or their alternative location, cries of '*I'm still sitting there*' would be uttered, despite the fact that that person had actually left the room for whatever reason. Eruptions would occur if upon their return 'their' seat was not vacant!

Secondly, was of the four of them washing up, drying, and putting the items away. As they all agreed, the two girls worked together, as did the boys, alternating each session between either washing or drying. There weren't many 'house rules' but the one or two that we did have, we expected to be respected and in truth so did the four of them. I should say here that if it was a large meal, then the dishwasher took pride of place, and the jobs were to stack and then clear the machine. But come the end of a small meal or breakfast, the crockery, cutlery and the utensils were gathered, and the sink filled with, hopefully, soapy water. To describe a typical session the boys would wash an item and then pass this to the girls to dry. Oliver and Angus famously named their session as '*soak and scrape*', or words to that effect. Invariably, this removed the grime, and all was well with the said item being handed to the girls. But the drying process seemed to morph into a quality check and there were frequent cries of '*reject!*', with the item being returned to the boys. A further inspection then ensued, and an agreement on, firstly, where the reject material manifested itself and secondly, whether this 'reject' call was indeed justified. It was, I must say, all conducted in a light-hearted manner, with much laughter and noise. When the washing up was completed then of course the 'friendly banter' commenced again, as this time the television viewing rites would take over.

Children! Who would have them? We do love them dearly though, and they have created some lovely memories, and they continue to do so for both Kate and me. So, as written in our annual 'round robin' letter to family and friends, that stated with a pinch of sarcasm, '*we've extended the house, been on holiday and had a very relaxing year*'. But whatever took place in reality, we had thoroughly enjoyed our first year of married life with all our children.

Today, 10 September 2023, I write these memories in a sun filled garden, where the temperature is 32° C, making it the hottest day for quite a while.

It's therefore difficult to recall that at the end of September 1994 the first snow of that winter was falling. Would that continue through to 1995? Well, the answer to that was no. However, inclement weather continued in various forms and by 4 January 1995 the snow had been replaced by heavy rain.

1995

My immediate recollection of the next couple of years, is one of children maturing and leaving home, to seek further education or training for future careers. In some ways this is heartening for parents in that they can support and see their offspring growing up, but certainly for me, and I suspected Kate as well, it was a time when we started to see our family unit disintegrating, in a positive way though.

The start of 1995 reflected 1994 with work progressing on Swannington, both internally and externally, with Kate and I both working together to create a loving home. Oliver continued to keep the NHS busy with minor and not so minor injuries and me looking for jobs. I recall that Oliver kicked the year off very early on, by hurting his middle finger of his right hand. Not something that you would expect to remember well, but this happened on Friday and by Sunday he was in A&E having it looked at, and on the Monday was in the fracture clinic having it bandaged up. Apparently, he had 'chipped' the bone, so the NHS attention was well justified. All ended well and he was soon back to normal.

Em was still looking at universities and had a number of visits lined up. The first being to Essex on 18 January, which if we could have foreseen the future could have been the only one that was necessary, as that's where she eventually studied. But obviously we didn't know this at the time. On the other hand, I was still at Easton College and volunteering at Blickling. My time at the latter was spent planting hundreds of hedging whips which I am pleased to say have now, some 30 years later matured into some mighty fine hedges, which I drive past with a sense of pride and satisfaction.

Something else that gave me satisfaction, was accompanying my father on a damp February morning, bird watching on the North Norfolk Coast. This was something we hadn't done for a long time.

One of our earlier excursions, when I was much younger can be seen in (Fig. 186). Whilst Dad was a very proficient ornithologist and had gained a

Chapter 5 Married Life, Extensions & Exams 1993 – 1999

Figure 186

superb knowledge over the years, as a mere amateur I hadn't progressed to that standard. But that didn't matter, it was the time together that was important for both of us.

For my 40th birthday all the family went for a lovely walk around Sheringham Park followed by a delicious meal cooked by Kate. Having digested this, I was treated to a massage with some exotic oil. Around this time, my attention was drawn to a job advertisement for a number of positions, including one for an Office Services Manager at Wherry Housing, a local Housing Association (Fig. 187).

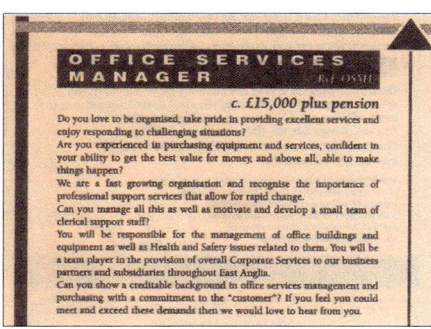

Figure 187

Whilst this wasn't my ideal career, I thought, 'I could do that!' This assumption was based on the experience I had acquired whilst working both with my father and, more latterly at ABC Printers. My application was duly drafted and delivered.

189

On 6 March, I attended their offices in Norwich and had an interview with Peter Lewis, the Chief Executive, and Jenny Manser, the Personnel Manager. I thought the interview went well and they assured me that I would hear back soon. Soon was to be the next day's postal delivery, so the letter must have been written almost immediately I had left and posted that afternoon!

As you can read, in the extract of a three-page letter (Fig. 188), I was offered the position and subsequently agreed a commencement date of 20 March 1995. I was employed again, not perhaps the role that I thought I would hold, but I had an income and a purpose. However, there was to be a sting in the tail when my nemesis returned once again.

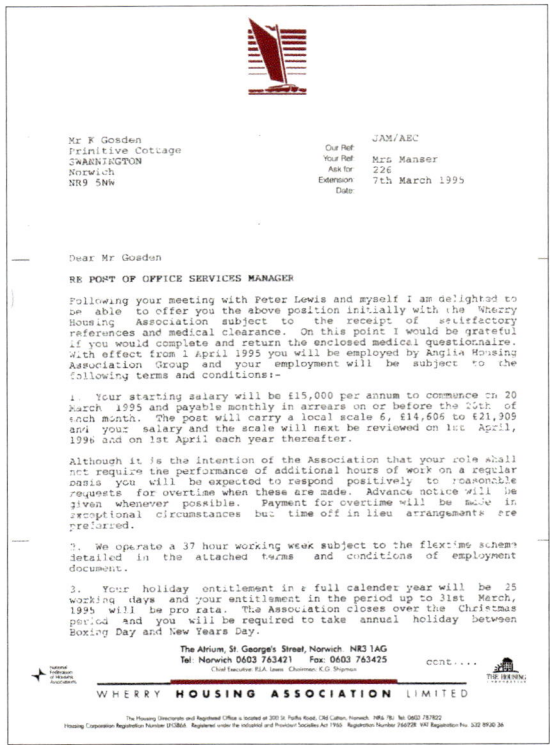

Figure 188

But before I explain, another 'historical' event took place, and this one had a very amusing and interesting theme. First, I need to explain that Kate grew up mainly in 'The Old Vicarage' in Barton Turf. But soon after all their family reached adulthood and left home, her parents moved to a more modest and modern house called Shepherds Loke, located in the centre of the village (Fig. 189). The Vicarage, now in other hands, was converted into two properties and sold on.

Figure 189

To Kate's surprise one of these was now on the market and she simply

Chapter 5 Married Life, Extensions & Exams 1993 – 1999

couldn't resist taking a look inside and I was to accompany her. We duly arrived and were shown around by the current owner. There were elements that Kate instantly recalled whilst mourning others that had been lost. Once back in the kitchen the owner, who we didn't know, started to tell us about the property's history. We listened intently but didn't let on who we were.

We were told that, apparently, the house was owned by an elderly gentleman and his wife who was rather eccentric. The explanation carried on with, '*the story goes that she used to keep animals in the house and was known to have put newly born piglets into the Aga to keep them warm*'!

This simply had to be relayed to Kate's mother, who now lived just down the road. The story however, had some elements of truth in that there certainly was a pig farm the other side of the church but nothing to do with Kate's family. Also, if there were abandoned eggs from Kate's family's flock of bantams and chickens that roamed the vicarage orchard, Kate's mother would often put these in a warm place to hatch, sometimes the coolest Aga oven. But that was a far cry from piglets in the Aga.

Needless to say, both Kate and her mother found the story very amusing. It's so strange how simple and innocent actions can develop into very different stories! We didn't make an offer on the house but much later both properties were reunited into the once grand house it was, much to Kate's and her family's delight. This now meant it reverted back to the large Victorian house with extensive gardens that Kate grew up in, as shown in figures 190 & 191, when Kate's family lived there. Both were taken around 1981, one in black and white from the church tower next door, the other in colour with the snow on the ground, from the rear lawn.

Figure 190

Figure 191

REFLECTIONS UPON A FAMILY

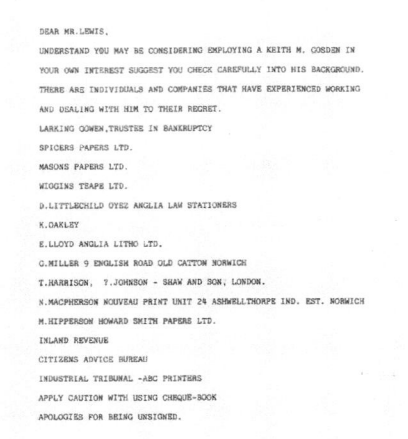

Figure 192

Back to my nemesis, in the guise of a disgruntled previous Gosden's employee who simply wanted revenge, no matter how inappropriate. The tactic this time was to type the obnoxious and anonymous letter (Fig. 192), to the Chief Executive of Wherry Housing, some three months after my appointment.

The letter caused some minor concern and, in my opinion, could have only been written with knowledge gained through working with me at a high level, as some of the comments related to matters that were not in the public domain. I suspected that my appointment came to light through an order I had placed with Anglia Law Stationers, owned by my father's former business partner, for some legal forms as part of my work at Wherry Housing. Whilst being sickened by this letter, I am happy to include it

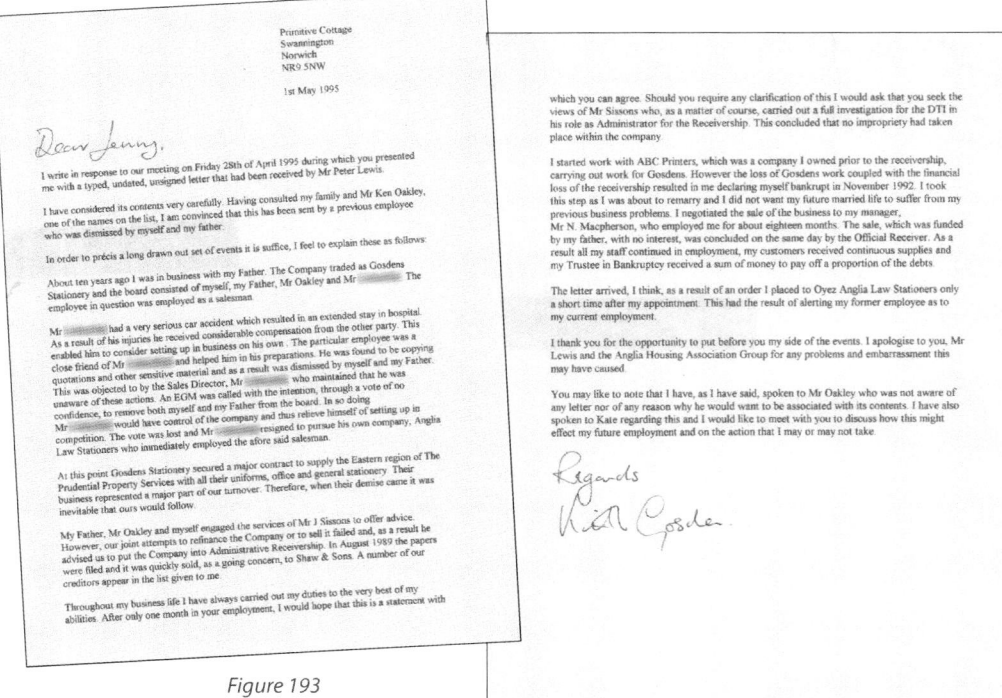

Figure 193

Chapter 5 Married Life, Extensions & Exams 1993 – 1999

in my memoir to demonstrate that it was not and would not be effective.

I met with Jenny Manser to explain the content and followed this up with a full and frank explanation as, in my opinion, I had nothing to hide, the matters were historic and contained nothing that I was ashamed about. I include a copy of my letter (Fig. 193) followed by the response from Jenny Manser just three days later (Fig. 194).

As far as I am concerned, including this in my memoir has finally concluded the matter for me. Kate was very aware of the letter, understood its content and possible outcome but supported me then and now. Suffice to say, that at the time I quickly received the response from Jenny which I feel speaks for itself. There haven't been any further incidents.

Figure 194

As I was now working a full five-day week, I had to give up my voluntary work at the Blickling Hall estate which allowed me time to spend some of the weekends at home.

One expensive and annoying memory I have of not only this year but previous years, was the precarious state of our Peugeot 505 estate car. It was very helpful when it was working, in that it could transport not only our family but also, as an estate, could accommodate building and gardening materials. Kate and I started to look around for a replacement, so were test driving other cars at various times. Nothing was found but in time my new employment was to solve the issue.

Over the next couple of months, I recall working very hard at Wherry Housing, which as you can see from the letterheading, was now rapidly expanding into Anglia Housing Association Group. As such I was supporting the integration into the Anglia Housing Group, of Stort Valley Housing in Bishop's Stortford,

Blackwater Housing in Braintree, along with Wherry Housing in Norwich. This would involve many visits to each one, mostly with Jenny. As part of my role was the management of the fleet of vehicles, I was able to use from time to time, a 'pool' Renault Espace vehicle. In the months to come I made a successful case for this being permanently allocated to me as a company vehicle. The Peugeot was then gracefully retired.

In May 1995 the round of school examinations commenced again but now with Sophie doing Key stage 3 SATs, Oliver Year 10 exams and Angus taking 7 GCSEs. Not an easy time for any of them. For Angus, August the dreaded month for the results was yet to come.

To complement this, I applied to the University of East Anglia (UEA), unsuccessfully as it happened, to study for a Master of Business Administration degree (MBA). Not put off, I slightly lowered my expectations and was successful in joining the City College two-year course for a Diploma in Management Studies (DMS).

By the latter part of June, the examinations were over, and Angus was to join the Sixth Form after the summer holidays. What next? Well, Angus along with Gordon, a friend and accompanied by me, Kate, Em, Oliver and Sophie, all piled into the Espace and we headed off to Hadrian's Wall, in order that Angus and Gordon could walk from end-to-end, camping en route. More on that later.

Em and Angus now wanted some more freedom so decided to take driving lessons, or in Em's case pick up where she left off, in the hope that once they had passed their tests they could venture further afield under their own steam.

Oliver though, whilst a competent tractor driver, was still having difficulty in staying on his bike. This time he came a cropper in Swannington, seriously injuring his back, elbows and knees. Mostly caused through not wearing a shirt, as it was a hot sunny day. Once again NHS casualty was the next point of call. Luckily, no long-term damage was physically done, though credibility and ego were a little damaged, but he was allowed home with appropriate dressings that would need changing regularly.

We were able to keep an appointment to visit Oaklands College at St. Albans where Oliver was hoping to study a full time Agricultural Course. We were all impressed and thought, exam results permitting, this would be an ideal next step.

Sophie was also still keen on outdoor pursuits such as regularly going out on hacks, which I am pleased to say she still does to this day. She also attended Guides each week and was able to join their camping weekends. In mid-July

1995 she was off with them again for a short camp at Eaton Vale, which by all accounts was a great success.

The past couple of months had been a strenuous time for all of us but perhaps even worse for Kate, as she was 'picking up' the issues stemming from examinations, giving encouragement where needed and mopping brows when necessary. It was time for her to have some time away.

One Friday I came home early from work and with all children staying with their other parent, surprised Kate with a weekend at the Swan Hotel in Lavenham. We had a lovely relaxing time, visiting antique shops in Long Melford, and a long walk concluding with lunch at The Bull Inn. We always looked forward to having tea and cake in various tea shops and had some wonderful meals at the Swan. Just what the doctor ordered.

In August, Wellie and Adam our honeymoon friends, came to stay for a short break with their first child Polly. We all had a very lazy time, with an evening BBQ on the Saturday, followed by a walk along Waxham beach on the Sunday, before they returned to Wheathampstead Monday lunchtime. It was good to catch up and recount memories of our wedding days.

Figure 195

As I mentioned before, on 4 June, Angus set off with his friend Gordon to walk Hadrian's Wall as part of their Duke of Edinburgh's Silver Award (Fig. 195). Having driven them both to the start, they set off whilst Kate, Em, Oliver Sophie and I all went to find accommodation in Haydon Bridge.

Regrettably, after about 30 miles, Angus's knee was causing such pain that the walk had to be abandoned. We all stayed the night at Haydon Bridge and before returning home in the morning, we drove the route to see the sites of the intended walk.

The June 1995 A-Level results were upon us and Em was a little disappointed with a B in Psychology, C in French and a D in History, so this meant she had to swiftly send off her UCAS form to ensure her university place. It all worked out in her favour though, as she was allocated a place in Essex University which was her preferred choice.

Angus also had his GCSE results. These were: one A* for Maths; one A for French; Bs for both Music and Geography; 2 BBs – one for Double Science, the other for English Literature and Grammar; and finally one C for German. All of which he was very content with. He now knew that he had more than sufficient grades to enable his return to school in the Sixth Form, for his A-Levels.

Before any of our family moved away on a permanent basis, we asked my father to take a photograph of us all. In the back garden he lined us all up one behind the other with the shortest at the front and tallest at the back and then asked us to lean alternately left or right (Fig. 196). From top to bottom are, Angus, Em, Me, Kate, Sophie and Oliver in the front.

It certainly reminded me of the Von Trapp family in the film of *The Sound of Music*. But we did as we were asked, and the photograph was taken. Whilst the end result was reasonable, I don't think any of us actually thought it was great, and it became a talking point for years to come.

Figure 196

On 3 September Em was due to move out of Swannington to start a 'year out' working in a Children's Hospital in Tadworth. This would be a complete break from educational studies before returning to them at university. Whilst no parents want to see their children leave home, we were hopeful that Em's break would do her good and that it would provide the respite she needed.

The 1 September though, was an important date as it brought success for Em when after starting her driving test at 09.30, she was finally rewarded with a positive result. Able now to drive herself, in the evening she packed her things for Tadworth and drove over to see her dad in Brooke and then made her way to Tadworth with him.

Em phoned the next day to say she had arrived safely and was settled in her room which was number 42. All was well and we arranged to go and see her at the weekend. But first we went shopping with Sophie for a pair of walking boots, as she was off for three days to Hope, in the Peak District, at the end of the next week.

Chapter 5 Married Life, Extensions & Exams 1993 – 1999

As Angus started his A-Levels at the Hewett School, I started my DMS at City College. My course was one day a week, for two years with appropriate 'assignments' throughout each year. It was a long time since I had been anywhere near formal education for myself, and it took a few sessions to acclimatise.

Kate had for some time been looking to move from the Norwich High School as she really didn't feel that she was appreciated. Coupled with the fact that she had been there both as an infant aged four, through to the sixth form and was now a member of staff as a Teaching Assistant. The only break being her training to become a qualified Nursery Nurse, followed by starting up a state school nursery class and a short time in one other school, all prior to her current appointment at the High School. Given this, she commenced some active job hunting.

Oliver's hard work was rewarded with a conditional place at Oaklands, commencing next summer but dependent upon his exam results next year. Now he had something to aim for, which was much understood and appreciated by him.

In October, Sophie was fortunate to have been included in a German exchange at Taverham School. She or we, were to host Miriam Roggendorf who lived in Mechernich in the south of Germany, about 35 miles from Cologne. The exchange week commenced on the sixth of October extending to the 14th.

I remember Miriam being reasonably fluent in English and a very nice polite child. Her time with us was a little limited as the school had organised a tour around Norwich and a day visit to London. But the week started with both of them going to school and then Girl Guides in the evening. Tuesday was Norwich and Wednesday they both went roller skating in Bury St. Edmunds. On the Thursday it was London and on Friday a half day back at school. Saturday was Miriam's return home, and she left from Taverham school early in the morning. A very packed, 'whistle stop' introduction to the UK.

Miriam was the first foreign guest we had hosted in Swannington, but she wasn't to be the last.

At the end of the month, I returned to working on the garden – why do I seem to always do this in the damp, autumn weather? Anyway, I cleared the area around the french doors, continued this from the kitchen back door to the rear of the house, and then along past the kitchen window to the door of the conservatory. When this was finished it was measured, and sufficient slabs were purchased for laying later. This didn't take too long, and the end result can be seen on the far left of the aerial photograph (Fig. 197). This was taken in 1996 of all three

Figure 197

cottages, ours being the one on the left.

Oliver had taken his mocks and whilst the results were close, if they were repeated in the finals then we were reasonably confident about his place at Oaklands. That was a really good result for him and another good result took place on 24 November, this time for all our family but especially me, when I was discharged from being bankrupt.

December 1995 was uneventful with most of us at Swannington, however, I do recall attending a dinner dance with Anglia Housing, at the Norwich City Football Club (NCFC) Executive Suite. Fairly uninspiring but at least I was there.

Christmas Day was enjoyed with just Kate and I at home as the children spent time with their other parent. But by Boxing Day, relaxation was put aside as I was working hard on my first DMS assignment. This was followed by the second one over the New Year weekend. Now I knew how the children felt throughout their recent examinations!

Throughout the year, I recall seeing a slow but steady decline in my relationship with Sophie. I say mine as I can't write for others but looking back and discussing my thoughts with them later there is a synergy. I appreciated that as a young lady of 15, there were hormonal changes and I was very aware that these were in evidence, but to me these did not explain some of the outbursts and moronic conversations. This concerned both me and Kate, so much so that we wrote down the changes in her behaviour and our own thoughts. Below is that narrative.

Those written in italics are our observations or Sophie's actual comments. These are accompanied in normal text, by the private thoughts Kate and I had at the time.

- *Not bothered whether we come to say goodnight or not* – She's rejecting our love and affection.
- *Not interested in other people* – No time to listen, if she even bothers to ask.
- *Homework, we spent at least 2 hours researching with her* – When asked how the presentation went, which was given at school the following day, a curt reply – *How should I know. You should know I only did it on Monday.*
- Generally, very rarely any thanks given to anybody re. help with homework, lifts, suggestions or shopping expeditions.
- ADAMANTLY INDEPENDENT. Has told us vehemently – *does NOT want help.*

Sophie seemed to feel that no-one was interested in her life, what she had done, where she had been or whom she had seen. She seemed to feel that we had no respect for her and treated her with contempt. From our perspective, this simply was not an accurate assessment, but how were we to convey this to her? This was clearly a major headache which would take a long time to resolve.

We tried reminding her of a wish that she had previously voiced, in that she wanted us to be close again, and so we sought her opinion as to how she had recently shown that desire, in her affections. There was little response and no remorse for hurting the feelings of others, which was not helpful.

At this point we endeavoured to outline a couple of examples of her actions, to see if this would help to open up a conversation. We used one example in the home and one external in public. But again, we drew a blank. So, we also reminded her of the many conversations we had had about her 'feelings' and how we desperately wanted to help but again this didn't seem to be reciprocated.

We were at a loss as to what we could do to help and support her, but agreed between ourselves, that we would do whatever we could to bring back the Sophie that we loved and knew in the past.

Regrettably, this worsening issue was to ebb and flow frequently over the next 20+ years, and still causes much upset for Kate and myself and has had an impact on our relationship. The immediate family have also been affected.

1996

January 1996 had arrived and of course so had the 'January Sales'. Whilst Oliver worked on the farm, Kate and I took Em and Sophie shopping and from memory, Top Shop seemed to be the favourite, with shoes and trousers being the main purchases.

We all returned to work including Em who went back to Tadworth on the Sunday, ready for a Monday start. Apart from Angus deciding, after many years, to give up piano lessons, the start of the year was uneventful.

Kate was however, studying French holiday brochures in great detail, as we had a wish to have a foreign summer holiday. I do recall that when we attended the Year 10 Parents' Evening at Taverham School, we did have a very positive and pleasing report about Oliver's progress. This, coupled with his mock results, all boded well for his future aspirations.

The month, as I recall, was getting cooler by the day and in the last week the snow arrived, only to be cleared a couple of days later by rain. However, the snow did allow for some good sledging for Oliver, Sophie and Angus, on Alderford Common which was adjacent to Swannington.

At work – now that's an expression I hadn't used for a long time – Anglia Housing was fast filling the space it had in the city centre, so a small group of us, led by the Chief Executive, went out looking for alternative locations. Having seen some terrible offices in various places it was decided, over a pub lunch, that a new build was the obvious choice.

After some searching, a suitable location was found, and negotiations opened with the Council and the developer involved in a new build at St. Andrews Business Park, just outside Norwich. I and the Property Director were to lead these and present the terms to the Board for approval. Agreement all round was reached, and the next nine months was taken up with ensuring that everything we had signed up for, was achieved.

Back home we started what was to become an annual ritual by making about 14lbs of marmalade. After much cutting up of seville oranges, adding copious amounts of water and sugar, the Aga came into its own, with jam jars in one oven and a huge, full preserving pan on one of the plates, bubbling its contents to setting point. The resulting mixture was then poured into the now warmed jam jars and left to cool. The end result was perfect and went down a treat with all who sampled it.

I note that on 9 February, our diary told me that *'All the snow has gone'* but it

Chapter 5 Married Life, Extensions & Exams 1993 – 1999

was still cold and dull, so not much fun for Oliver who was working weekends on the farm.

Not being in the garden, due to the inclement weather, allowed Kate and I to agree on a destination for our summer holiday in France. The conclusion was a large house on the outskirts of Regusse and a deposit cheque was sent to secure the deal. With six of us in the Espace, four of whom could drive, going by car on the 915-mile journey was definitely the preferred option, so tickets were booked for the Channel Tunnel crossing. We had agreed a date in mid-August but were very much aware that this clashed with Oliver's results, so that had to be factored into the itinerary.

Each year for Christmas I purchased, on behalf of one of our pets, a Letts desk diary for Kate – we had very considerate and intelligent pets! This was then populated with annual key dates and activities in order that they were not forgotten. This tradition was also undertaken by her mother and upon her death Kate inherited all her diaries, so we can look back to the 1950s and know what her family were doing! We were both born under the zodiac Pisces sign, so our birthdays are marked on the calendar with a suitable symbol denoting our enduring love. Both examples are seen here.

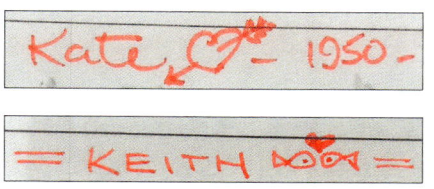

Anyway, that year after my birthday, I had a two-day course in London on Health and Safety (H&S) as I was now to assume the H&S lead role at work. This is easy to write but given the number of staff spread over four offices in different counties and hundreds of houses and care homes, again located all over East Anglia, it was quite a large responsibility. Luckily the training was comprehensive and did continue covering more aspects as time went on.

Whilst I have already mentioned, Oliver was forever cycling, be it on the road or over the rough ground and through the woods, very often with Mathew from next door. So, it came as no surprise when he wanted to upgrade his bike. We took it to Free Wheel, a bicycle shop in Norwich where they were to comprehensively customise all aspects of his bicycle.

My time at Anglia Housing was becoming very demanding since the decision was made to move offices. I was endeavouring to keep a watchful eye on the progress of the new office, whilst also working out the internal layout that would be acceptable to as many of the employees as possible.

I was also keen to have the front reception, which was a glass atrium with stairs to the first floor, looking as professional and welcoming as possible. I floated the idea of a large watercolour painting, made up of a montage of key buildings in each of our three locations, Norwich, Bishops Stortford, and Braintree. This was accepted by the Board, and I commissioned Martin Sexton to paint this for us. On the opening day Martin unveiled it with Peter Lewis the Chief Executive, and it looked very good and not at all ostentatious – we were after all, a social housing provider, not an art gallery.

Having been 'holiday shopping' on Saturday to purchase a bikini and swimming trunks, Kate and I in the evening went off to see Hugh Grant and Emma Thompson in the film *Sense and Sensibility*, which was excellent. Time to ourselves, perfect.

Back with the family 19 March was to be a most eventful day. I was to sit an exam at college, Kate went on a school trip to Thrigby and whilst there held an 18-month-old alligator, and Sophie was on a geography field trip. It was then that Oliver had another visit to the hospital, this time with a fractured vertebra and a pulled ligament! After treatment and rest at home, all appeared to be ok, thank goodness. He was fully discharged on 2 April, the day before his 16th birthday.

On the 3rd Oliver received two cards from his mother, one for his birthday, the other a good luck one, which sparked the following conversation between him and Sophie which we noted on our calendar at the time.

Sophie – *Why has she sent **you** some cards?*
Oliver – *What are a lot of people doing at school at the moment?*
Sophie – *Taking Exams*
Oliver – *That's why Mum sent me a card.*
Sophie – *So*
Oliver – *To wish me good luck and to congratulate me on my interviews.*

Life was not easy, and the next day Sophie was in a foul mood. Kate took time to chat to her and established that there were rumours being spread about her around school, but she declined any help from us, as in her words, she '*would sort it out herself*'.

The following day after supper, Kate and I were due to meet up with our financial adviser, so we wanted to wash up quickly. Sophie suddenly had a 'injury' and came into the kitchen. I explained that I would take a look after the washing up, as it didn't appear to be urgent. With that, Sophie responded with '*It's nice to know my father isn't even sympathetic*'. Ten minutes later I had finished washing up and asked how she was. The reply: '*It's all sorted out. I told*

Chapter 5 Married Life, Extensions & Exams 1993 – 1999

you I was going to do it. You don't have to worry about me'. Clearly, I just could not win!

For Oliver's birthday, Kate and I paid for a tractor driving test in order that Oliver could work more extensively on the local farm. We had previously all spoken about this with Janet Mutimer, the farm owner, who was very supportive.

Later that day, Em arrived back home from Tadworth and was accompanied by a young man, Björn, a work colleague she was seeing regularly. Being Easter, they were able to stay with us for a few days, which was wonderful. I recall all of us packing in numerous visits and activities, which included visiting both the top, the battlements, and the bottom, the dungeons, of Norwich Castle. To say nothing of the 'Buddy Holly Story' at the Theatre Royal and a showing of the film 'Toy Story' at the Odeon, a day later!

On 19 April 1996, Angus was 17 and wasted no time in having his first driving lesson with Brian, who had also taught Em and was in time to teach both Oliver and Sophie. However, I seem to remember that having had his first 'professional' lesson he then went out for a family lesson in the Espace. In fact, over the next few days, he drove to his work at the library, around Norwich and over to his grandmother's in Barton. He was clearly keen to practice, take and pass his test quickly!

Back at school, Oliver was to start his GCSE exams with French Oral – not an easy start for anyone, in my view. Whilst we wished him good luck, Sophie simply ignored the subject. She had no interest and later in the day didn't even ask how it went.

Later in the week, Kate and I visited the school with Sophie as it was her Parents' Evening, and we came away most impressed with the excellent feedback on her progress. She was though, still undecided what she wanted to do. The time with Sophie in the car back home, allowed us to chat with her about her own feelings. She admitted to being two people and had 'other things' on her mind. I explained that I felt 'hurt' during the parents' evening, as I simply didn't recognise the daughter they were talking about and questioned if she treated her mother and Dale in the same way as Kate and me. There was no feedback from Sophie at all – no conversation or any kind of emotion. We were very concerned as whilst she was doing well and was popular, we felt that she wasn't happy. We were very conscious that once she was home from school, she wouldn't discuss the day and seemed to just forget all about school.

On one particular day, I was about to go into Norwich with Kate, so explained to Sophie where we were going, what time we would be back, and that Oliver and Angus were playing basketball. Her response was *'I know. There's no need to tell me all that I know already'.* We left it there as we knew that the next week, she would again attend a Parents' Evening but this time with her mother and

Dale and we didn't want to cause any problems. Also, Em and Björn were off for a short holiday to Ireland and Em needed to go to the dentist before leaving, so time was tight.

Em and Björn were away for around a week, arriving back at Tadworth on Friday, having had a good time. It was Sophie's turn to go away, but not on a holiday as such. Hers was to be a Duke of Edinburgh's Award practice walk and camp, just outside Dereham. But this was only for the weekend, and after we picked her up everyone in the car was keen to know how she'd got on and what it was like. I asked what she had been doing and how it all went. The reply was *'walked'* followed by *'don't be such an idiot, Dad. You know perfectly well what I've been doing'*. We drove home as planned.

Towards the end of May, Sophie had her Year 10 exams and Oliver had a week's study leave so it was heads down for both of them. The weekend saw all three away at their other parent, so Kate and I took the opportunity to go and watch the Wherry *Albion* delivering some Caen stone, to Norwich Cathedral via the River Wensum. We followed that excitement with supper at the Buckinghamshire Arms in Blickling.

Next week was half term and Angus, being still keen to drive us all everywhere and anywhere, acted as chauffeur. But regrettably his driving test date was changed, again by the Driving Agency – he was most disappointed.

The start of June saw a similar pattern of examinations and I was studying as well, for I had another DMS assignment to finish.

There was to be a change for Sophie, as on Monday 10 June she commenced her work experience with the RSPCA in Norwich. I don't recall any negative feedback, so I assumed that all went well. The week ended with a call from Em to say that she and Björn were enjoying time on the Isle of Wight, so that was good to hear.

A key June date for Oliver was the 24th as this was his Tractor Test. As expected, given all the practice and experience he had built up, he passed with ease. I don't have a photograph of that day but figure 198 is of Oliver driving whilst on work experience.

The end of June was also the conclusion for both Em and Björn's time at Tadworth. They were both collected by Em's father and brought back to Norfolk. On the Sunday, we

Figure 198

took both of them plus three suitcases and a bicycle down to Harwich, where Björn was to catch a ferry home. Was that to be the end of their relationship, I wondered?

July 1 was of course Sophie's 15th birthday and an appropriate tea with presents was served before she went off to Guides. As she was now a young lady, Kate and I had made an appointment for her to have her ears pierced, so she could wear the earrings we had given her. We were hoping that this would give her more confidence, as well as appearing more grown up to her peers.

On the same day Angus passed his driving theory test, so now was on his way to a full licence with just the practical test to go.

Our summer holiday in Regusse, set for mid-August, was fast approaching and we paid the final balance and subsequently received directions on how to find the property.

Matters pertaining to Em and university were now coming to the forefront of all our minds. Forms were being completed and sent back, whilst thoughts were focusing on what was needed for the commencement of the course. Angus, on the other hand, was just starting this journey by visiting Reading University and others were to follow before an application was made.

Em answered one of our private thoughts by visiting Björn in Hamburg – but she arrived two hours later than expected! Oliver also made a step forward by starting to attend Easton College on a 'Farm Start' course. He now needed to review the standard and status of his bicycle again, so time and money was spent at two bicycle shops, this time Free Wheel and Apple Pie.

In between these visits it was our wedding anniversary, and I was to meet Kate for a lunch at the Playhouse just down the road from my work office. However, I was late, but that didn't spoil our lunch, it just meant we had to eat a little quicker!

Having had a long chat/interview with the owners of Youngs Farm, this was to be the future workplace for Oliver. He was already known to them as it was here that he had helped with some of the night-time lambing shifts. He could cycle there, as it was only just outside Aylsham which wasn't far away. So, the bike had to be ready, and it was now with a third company, Aerographs in Horsford, for painting, but his deadline was still achieved!

Early August witnessed the arrival of the Anglia Housing painting by Martin Sexton. Somehow, I really don't know how, but I had managed to rope in my family in assisting with elements of the preparations of the move, from the existing office in St. Georges in Norwich, to the new offices in St. Andrews.

As I say, quite how this came about I don't recall but I was extremely grateful, nonetheless. The actual move was carried out by professionals on 8 August. I had written a welcome note for each member of staff and left it along with some chocolates on their desk, for them to find the next day. I had previously agreed this with Jenny and Peter Lewis.

On 15 August we were on our way to a very well deserved and much needed holiday in Regusse. We set off in the Espace at 21.30 and caught the 03.00 shuttle arriving in a very foggy Calais at 03.30, where we commenced our journey through France. Given the night-time start we parked up at around 06.00 and all had a good snooze. We stopped for breakfast in Chalòns sur Marne, then in Vouécourt for lunch, well just sandwiches and an ice cream, concluding with an overnight stop in a hotel in Varennes. Whilst the hotel had a lovely swimming pool, the actual bedrooms were dire, with Em and Angus having to sleep on the floor, coupled with the fact there was no vegetarian food for Em, so not a great start!!

We left heading for Lyon but wasted time trying to find our way out from Varennes, – no sat nav in those days, but Em was superb in asking for directions. En route we stopped for a group photograph (Fig. 199) before arriving in Regusse at 19.00.

The gîte was well worth the drive and the first thing Oliver did, on arrival, was to jump in the pool!

As the montage of photographs opposite indicates, the weather was glorious, and the accommodation was perfect with its outdoor private pool. All this made for a very relaxing time either in the pool, taking a snooze in the sun or just at the poolside with a good book in hand.

Figure 199

Chapter 5 Married Life, Extensions & Exams 1993 – 1999

207

But some daily chores still needed to be undertaken whilst still enjoying the sun! As can be seen (Fig. 200).

On the Monday four of us went into Draguignan looking for a hyper-market whilst Sophie and Em prepared breakfast as it was their turn on the rota. The rest of the day was spent exploring Regusse, followed by a barbecue before Angus went out to take some night-time photographs and then regaled several scary ghost stories.

Bright and early the next day we all travelled to Lac de Sainte Croix where we found a great place to hire pedalos and canoes (Fig. 201). Oliver almost succeeded in deliberately capsizing one of the latter and had to be 'rescued' by a French family in a pedalo. Later we drove to Sainte Croix du Verdon where some of us had a swim before making our way back for our family favourite, a barbecue.

Figure 200

By mid-week, the weather having been sunny and very warm, was on the change so we ventured out to Marseille, but I recall Kate and I were not impressed! It was a typical large city with its red-light area and fish market being the only areas that made us curious. So, once we'd all met up again, we decided to drive back through the mountains and stopped to watch a wonderful thunderstorm in the distance.

Figure 201

Figure 202

Thursday 22 1996 was a special day as Oliver was to receive his exam results – would they allow him to take up his place at Oaklands College? We all went with him to the public telephone box in Regusse where he phoned the school. The results were good but tight, with 3 Cs, 2 Ds, 3 Es and 1 F, ironically the latter in French! But he had passed!

A call, from a local telephone box, was then made to Oaklands to seek their views. After a tense wait his place was confirmed and a well deserved celebratory meal was enjoyed by us all that evening, in Les Pins in Sillans-la-Cascade (Fig. 202).

The next morning the weather was hot, so the day started beside the pool. Whilst for some even this wasn't cool enough, so a long dip was necessary, and this was followed by lunch.

The afternoon was cooler and found us boulder climbing, up to a beautiful waterfall and large pool. Oliver swam but I recall Em was not so adventurous, especially on the climb up and down again. However, we all arrived safely back at the gîte.

On the Saturday we drove to Castellane, a town high up in the mountains where we climbed up to the church. From here we had a fantastic view over the town (Fig. 203). Later we were to enjoy a wonderful sunset en route back to Regusse (Fig. 204) but only after a supper at a creperie in Aiguines.

Figure 203

Figure 204

REFLECTIONS UPON A FAMILY

Figure 205

Traditionally Sunday is a day of rest and relaxation, and we observed this tradition, which was great. My relaxation was to sit in a local field sketching a windmill similar to the one depicted (Fig. 205). The rest of the family, when not checking my progress, enjoyed the pool and their books.

Towards the end of the day, we all visited another local windmill where the locals were seen all dressed in traditional costume. Back at the gîte, Oliver at his own expense was to cause an outbreak of laughter, when he mistook a salad dryer for a deep fryer! In years to come he was to become a very competent chef, but he had to accept the jibes on this occasion.

You cannot go to the south of France without a visit to St. Tropez, just to see how the other half live, or in the case of Oliver and Angus to take note as to what they drive. Our visit was on the Monday and extended to looking at all the yachts in the harbour, luxury cars on the roads followed by a little shopping, and once we had found Pampelonne beach a couple of miles away, we settled down and enjoyed the sun, sea and sand.

On our penultimate day we all, with the exception of Oliver, went to explore the cave at La Grotte de Saint Cézaire, where we saw stalactites and stalagmites that were over 150,000 years old (Fig. 206). Oliver decided to stay and help the owner pump out the gîte's cesspit, as you do! In the evening, Kate and I had a lovely meal together at Les Pins.

On our way back on the shuttle there was a poker game between Oliver, Angus and Kate. Kate was losing hands down but then beat both of them with three kings. Let that be a lesson!

We arrived back on 1 September 1996, safe, well, relaxed but exhausted after the long journey.

Figure 206

Chapter 5 Married Life, Extensions & Exams 1993 – 1999

September was the start of the academic year, and this was certainly the case for Kate and Sophie as well. Angus had viewings of universities to organise, whilst Em sorted her accommodation at Essex University. Sophie was to start back at Taverham but unfortunately had a fall at the local Aqua Park, went to casualty and ended up having her arm in a half cast and sling. It transpired that she had fractured her arm and torn some ligaments.

On the Monday, 16 September, Oliver started a block release course at Easton College. My DMS course wasn't due to start again until the next week, so I was able to spend two days in Cambridge at the British Institute of Facilities Management Conference.

Angus and Em both went down to Guildford University by train to see if that was to be added to the list of possibles for Angus. For Kate and me, it was business as usual back home, where we finished clearing the garage at the weekend, ready for us to commence dismantling it and having a new one built. A very busy time for all of us!

Before the month was out, Angus re-took his driving test but regrettably was unsuccessful, so more lessons were on the cards. The final day of the month was Em's packing day before starting Freshers Week on 2 October, at the University of Essex. We took her there and were able to meet up with her again on the next Sunday, just to make sure all was well and of course it was!

For some months, Kate had been awaiting an NHS operation and 10 October was the due date. She was admitted to Rockland Ward and underwent her Burch Culposuspension operation at 10.00. All went well and by 12.05, Kate was in the recovery ward where she stayed for a couple of hours, before going onto the ward. Luckily, progress was good, and she was discharged just four days later.

It was more good news for Angus on the 17th when he passed his driving test. Two down with two, Oliver and Sophie, to go! That night Angus drove into Norwich, in the Espace to pick up his friend Gordon and they both went to Megazone, a favourite indoor UV laser tag game venue.

On the Friday, Kate and I renewed our acquaintance with Keys Auction House, where we had purchased a number of paintings before, and ended up buying another couple by two Norwich School artists. One was by John Paul (Fig. 207)

Figure 207

211

which we took to Fairhurst Gallery in Norwich as it needed to be cleaned, and the frame repaired.

Our builder, Malcolm, who was almost a resident, arrived on Monday to start the work on the new garage. This was in fact not a garage at all, instead it was an open cart shed/oil tank area with a workshop to the left, all under a pantile roof. I am seen here (Fig. 208) dismantling the old garage, and the replacement can also be seen (Fig. 209).

Figure 208

Figure 209

By early November the replacement workshop and cart shed were well on their way to being completed, just in time for the winter delivery of heating oil.

This also coincided with torrential rain and strong winds which meant that Malcolm was patching up other properties, rather than being with us. He was to rejoin us in around a week's time.

Figure 209 is the new workshop on the right and the open cart shed on the far left where the oil tank was located.

In the corner of the garden, we placed a bird table which was originally built by my grandfather, and it was very popular with the wildlife and indeed the whole family. We proudly stocked this each day with bird seed and as is always the way, some fell on the ground and started to grow. We allowed some of these to stay in place, as whilst we didn't know exactly what the plants were, they were pretty. That was until one day a friend, who knew more about wildflowers than we did, was admiring the garden and commented that we were actually growing cannabis and did we know! No, we didn't, so this 'pretty' plant was quickly removed!

Now returning to the dreaded exams. Sophie could not avoid her upcoming mock examinations, all eight of them, which were to last for a couple of weeks. At the end she joined Kate and I to look around Norwich City College with a view to studying her A-Levels there. Her results were encouraging with Cs, Ds and D/Es across the board, so we hoped that this would be repeated in the actual GCSE exams.

The 25 November saw the official opening of Anglia House and with all the staff settled in, the invited dignitaries were able to see the building at its best. Everyone was most impressed which brought a huge sigh of relief from me.

December brought mock A-Levels for Angus, commencing with Philosophy followed by Maths both Further and Applied. This was then topped off with Statistics! Whilst I didn't understand the Maths, I was sure that Angus knew exactly what he was doing. Meanwhile, I concentrated on my DMS course instead. Em returned home from university and was very happy with her Psychology course and accommodation.

The normal round of Christmas carol services, school events and parties preceded our family Christmas. On the day there was snow in Norwich but none, regrettably, in Swannington. However, that was fine with us, as Angus and Em were off to collect Björn on Boxing Day, and we didn't have snow until the day after Björn arrived – perfect timing! Then on 31 December Oliver and Sophie joined their mother and Dale for New Year.

Before I outline my memories of 1997, I would like to give a few examples of family phrases that were being used extensively at the time, along with some interesting but somewhat amusing conversations. This gives a clue to the friendly banter that all four children had with each other. Some were logical, and some totally illogical!

Phrases:
Chill/Chill out,
Slap head,
Dog breath,
Dog Duff,
Dogs from Hell and finally,
If you don't eat it, you wear it!

It is worth noting that at that time we didn't even have a dog!

Conversations:
Oliver – Most adamant *'there's no hot water'.*
Keith – *'Are you running the hot tap?'* Oliver – *'No. It's the cold tap!'*

Sophie – when requesting Em to keep the large bottle of orange her side of the chair rather than next to hers – *'The floor is closer to Em her side of the chair than to mine!'*

As I have said before, children, who would have them? We certainly would, for if nothing else they bring a big smile to your face, most of the time!

Back to life in Swannington, universities and colleges had and continued to enter our lives, thus curtailing that personal bond, and Kate and I missed these lively exchanges.

1997

1997 commenced with some very cold weather, which was evident when walking through Blickling Park, as we found the lake had frozen over. The weather also caused Björn's return ferry crossing to be delayed by four hours, but he did arrive back in Germany safe and well at around 16.00.

The first full week of January saw us all, apart from Em who had an extra week at home, returning to our normal weekly schedules. I was at college on Tuesdays and at Anglia Housing the rest of the working week, Oliver was on the farm every day of the week, Sophie was at Taverham School and Angus at the Hewett School. Kate was still recovering from her operation so was on sick leave from Norwich High School. From my perspective, the person who was working the longest hours was certainly Oliver. It was lambing season, and his hours were 06.00 – 18.00 during the day and when on nights it was 18.00 through to 06.00 the next morning.

Figure 210

As I explained previously in Chapter 2, I was able to be with him on a few of his night shifts which were most enjoyable but hard work. Lambs were being born very frequently and it was his role to make sure all was well, that they were breathing ok and bonding with their mothers. There were a few moments though, when we could be together (Fig. 210) and it seemed that Oliver was very good at delegation, as I fed the lambs, whilst he sat and relaxed! The photograph was taken by Kate who frequently joined us both at this time.

Oliver was getting on well with the farm owners and they suggested that to save him the cycle ride, he might like to stay on the farm, in a small flat they had on site. This was gratefully received and at the weekend we transported food, clothes and bedding.

At the weekend, Em was also to return to her accommodation at Essex University in Colchester, and Angus joined her on the journey in support. Her summer semester started the next day, 13 January so not much time to 'settle in'. She was to commence her examinations on the Tuesday and had been revising hard over the Christmas break, so she was reasonably confident. This proved to be justified with a pass mark of 85%!

Later that day, Angus went to the Open Day at Nottingham University and concluded that, if possible, this was probably his first choice and the next week he started his A-Level exams. By now it was the end of January and Kate was fit enough to return to The High School but still needed to be careful.

During February, Kate and I turned our attention to the final push in the back garden. With roses from Peter Beales planted along with other flowers from Taverham Garden Centre, we were hopeful and dare I say confident, that by the summer the garden would be looking really good. We set up bird feeding stations in the apple tree along with nest boxes, in the hope that both would be used. But this time we made sure that no cannabis plants were accidentally grown!

Through working at Anglia Housing, I had got to know a small local company that not only tended office plants which they did for our offices but also landscaped gardens. I agreed with the owner that they would deliver five trees to us at Swannington at a cost of £133. The trees, two birch, a rowan, an acacia and a eucalyptus duly arrived on 20 February and were planted over the half term week.

By mid-February Oliver's long working hours caught up with him when he had an accident in the tractor, hitting a support for one of the open cart sheds. Luckily no one was hurt and the damage, whilst being fairly serious, was repairable on site.

Sophie having previously had an interview for the Sixth Form, at the Hewett School and had been unsuccessful, had a similar one with the City College. This time she was successful so with luck would be able to start in September.

My birthday was celebrated with a lovely meal with Kate and the children, except Em of course who was at university. Presents included a number of useful garden implements, books and from Oliver and Sophie a DVD of *All Creatures*

Great and Small. This is one of my favourite television programmes so was ideal to watch either after a hard day at work or being outside gardening.

The first weekend of March was set aside to build a pond in the top corner of our back garden. Following much digging and measuring, the liner was fitted on the Saturday, followed on Sunday by the water, plants and a good sense of satisfaction. According to the calendar, I also apparently cut the back grass for the first time!

Whilst I had left Round Table as explained earlier, I was still in touch with many Tablers, and I was able to join them for a 70th anniversary Dinner at Dunston Hall. This was a really good experience and enabled me to catch up with several past members that I hadn't seen for some years. The following day was Kate's birthday. Angus and Em were at home, so having collected Kate's mother we all had a lovely tea together at Swannington, followed by a delicious supper. The next day we took Em back to Colchester followed by a visit to the Parson Woodforde pub for a drink, and this was the first opportunity for Kate to wear her new, pearl lapis lazuli and aventurine necklace, that I had given her as a birthday present. Sophie also gave her some matching earrings.

March was the month for Angus to finally sort out his university choices. So, his form for the Universities and Colleges Admission Service (UCAS) was sent in, with Nottingham as his preferred choice and a grant form was to follow. On the other hand, I had a re-run of moving offices, this time it was for Wherry Housing, also based in Norwich, who were moving into a second purpose-built office next to ours in St. Andrews. All went according to plan over the weekend move, with staff back at their desks on the Monday, ready for business.

With the Easter holidays upon us, Em took the opportunity to fly to Hamburg to visit Björn. Whilst they were together, they decided to travel eight hours on the train to visit Prague. We just hoped that it was worth it. I also took a holiday at home and managed to fall into my new pond! That was after I had been telling everyone else to be very careful, so you can imagine the comments that followed. Luckily no harm was done to either me or the plants!

Oliver turned 17 on 3 April 1997, so now his car driving lessons could commence. But first he had a drive out in the Espace that all went well despite it being very different from that of a tractor. When would he take his test, and would it be a first-time pass? We would wait and see. He certainly didn't wait long for his first professional lesson, with Brian the family instructor, in fact it was just five days after his birthday!

There was a small group of us at Anglia Housing who liked walking. We were convinced by my colleague Mark, an ex-military man, whom I had recently appointed, that we should undertake some long-distance trails. To kickstart this and to gauge how this idea would be received, he organised for staff members and partners, a practice walk through Thetford Forest. This took place on the Sunday and was around 20 miles which I managed to complete. Kate managed 10 miles which we were both impressed with, given her recent operation. The outcome, back at the office, was that we would all walk the 'Three Peaks' in July. Did I really agree to that?

Driving lessons, studying, university tutoring, assignments and examinations kept all of us, with the exception of Kate, very busy. Personally, I was really pleased with my latest assignment as I had received a distinction. Now I just had to finish my dissertation.

The UK was about to change politically, as on the first of May, Labour under Tony Blair, won the General Election, by a landslide. This followed on from the Tories, led by Sir John Major, who had been in government for 18 years. How was this going to impact all our lives? It was a question that many were asking.

Following the success of the Thetford walk we undertook a second in Southwold. This time it was restricted to Anglia Housing staff, so whilst Kate came with me, she met up with a friend in Walberswick for the day. By the end of the walk there were a few of us who wished that we had joined her!

GCSEs commenced in May for Sophie, so it was head down if she was to take up her place at Norwich City College. The same pressure was to fall on Angus when his A-Levels started in June. I had a two-day residential at Barnham Broom for my DMS, so with Em at university it was only Kate and Oliver who were free of examinations, other than Oliver's upcoming driving test. He took his theory test at 09.00 on 21 June and passed, now he just had the driving test to take. Em's results in her psychology, sociology and statistics were very good, so the next year beckoned for her.

June ended on a high with Angus and the family going to Brands Hatch. This was a belated 18th birthday present, and he was to try his hand at driving a racing car. We travelled down and met Em there, as she had come straight from university to support him as well.

Figure 211

Figure 212

Figure 213

After a very professional safety briefing, he emerged from the offices looking for all the world like a Formula 1 driver. A lap around the circuit, with a professional driver, in a performance saloon (Fig. 211) gave him the feel of the circuit and more importantly where to brake, or in some cases where to accelerate!

This was followed by a couple of laps in a single seater racing car (Fig. 212), which was thoroughly enjoyed by all concerned, and I suspected his mother was very glad to see him back at the starting grid, safe and sound. Figure 213 is a celebratory picture of Em and her racing driver brother!

On the Sunday I had another practice walk, this time in Derbyshire. This was the final one before the main challenge at the end of July. So, we all needed to make sure we were happy and comfortable with our kit, especially our boots. All went well with none of us admitting afterwards to any aches or pains, and certainly not to dropping out of the main challenge.

Sophie's birthday, on 1 July 1997, coincided with an open day at Norwich City College, which she attended. But more importantly, the day concluded with her and four friends having a 'sleepover' at Swannington. Clearly the news of her pierced ears had spread as she had earrings for presents from Em, my parents, as well as us. Luckily there were plenty of other alternative presents.

The next weekend and the preceding few days were focused on the Three Peaks Walk. The challenge was to climb the three highest mountains in the UK – Ben Nevis, Scafell Pike and Snowdon, all within a time limit of 24 hours. The key to this was the travel time between the three locations in Scotland, England and Wales respectively. Over the time allocated we would actually walk around 22 miles. If we slept at all, this would either be travelling in the car or staying at a youth hostel. It was certainly a challenge, but I have to say great fun and very well organised by Mark. His army training was a great benefit to us all. Needless to say, that following all the practice walks, we completed the challenge within the time limit and on the Monday celebrated at the top of Snowdon, where I

Chapter 5 Married Life, Extensions & Exams 1993 – 1999

Figure 214

Figure 215

phoned Kate at 10.35. We were all worn out but very happy and looked forward to the journey home. A selection of photographs from the walk shows us about to leave (Fig. 214), en route with Linda, Mark and myself all looking relaxed (Fig. 215), sitting on top of Peak 1, Ben Nevis, with me second left (Fig. 216), On Peak 2, Scafell Pike (Fig. 217) I am on the far left. But for some reason, I don't have or can't find a photograph from the top of Snowdon. I can assure you though, that we did all make it to the summit!

It was very misty at the top of all three peaks, especially Ben Nevis, and we were all very proud of our success.

Figure 216

Figure 217

219

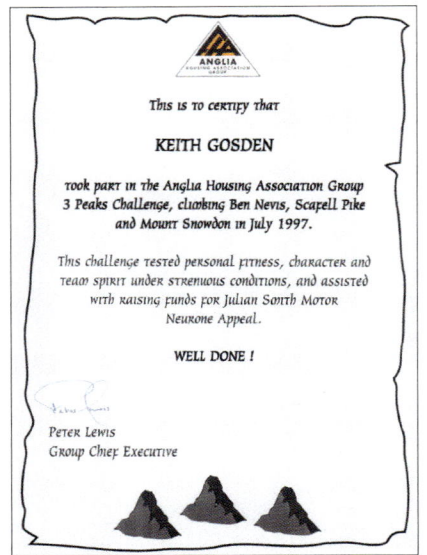

Figure 218

Quite rightly that success was recognised by Anglia Housing (Fig. 218) as a perfect team building exercise. Not that we saw it like that. We just wanted to have fun, be part of a challenge and support Julian Smith (now in a wheelchair) in his quest to raise funds for his Motor Neurone appeal, which we did.

The next day I went with Kate to collect my final DMS papers from the City College. Was it good enough for me to graduate? Time would tell.

The rest of July was quite subdued and normal by comparison to the first couple of weeks. However, August was to kick off with a celebration, as Oliver passed his car driving test, and despite the rain, Em went to the Radio One beach party, whilst Kate and I went to the Status Quo concert. The following day, Kate and I had a much quieter afternoon enjoying tea with Kate's mother at Barton.

Sophie was still working on a regular basis for the RSPCA. Her love of animals, along with their welfare, was clearly something close to her heart. Could this develop into a vocation perhaps?

I took a week off work which was spent 'pottering' around the house and gardening with Kate, which I must say was most relaxing and certainly boosted by Angus's A-Level results: Pure Maths A; Further Maths B; and Philosophy B. We were confident of his place at Nottingham but awaited the official confirmation. Results were also good for Sophie at GCSE level with two Bs, six Cs and three Ds and, as a result, her place at City College was also safe. All four of the children had worked very hard, through what was a challenging time, given my divorce, marriage to Kate, living as a 'blended' family, in a house which seemed to be constantly being expanded by builders. We were very proud of all of them and very happy, so we all went out to the Ratcatchers pub for a celebratory meal.

September was ushered in with the funeral of Diana, Princess of Wales, having been tragically killed the week before, in a car accident in France. The month though, was to see Oliver start at Oaklands College, Sophie to start at City College doing A-Levels in Psychology and Geography, whilst she still lived at home, Angus off to Nottingham University and Em back to studying in Essex. The cottage just had Kate, Sophie and me, which seemed very strange and quiet.

On 13 September 1997, Sophie was then to drop her bombshell. She announced that she too was leaving home, to go and live in Cromer with her mother and Dale whom she seemed to hold in high regard. This was devastating as we were unaware of any rationale for this decision. When we enquired why, Sophie couldn't give a reason other than, *'because I want to'*.

Both Kate and I were shocked at what appeared to be a sudden decision and just wondered who or what had influenced it. Was it due to the other three siblings now living away at college or university, leaving her on her own? We dismissed this as she would obviously be on her own when living at Cromer. We were perplexed and this move was to have a devastating effect on her in the future and one that to this day, I feel still probably impacts on her wellbeing.

Kate and I decided to join a course we had seen at Cambridge University on Biological Monitoring and Wildlife Conservation. This meant that every Thursday we travelled over to Cambridge, which whilst being a huge commitment the course was most rewarding, especially the site visits that were to follow. Wicken Fen being the first on 19 October.

Oliver had met up with a young lady called Emma and we met her for the first time when they came home on Friday 3 October, for the weekend. My father had a small dinghy moored on the Broads, so we all went out sailing in her. Having had a good time, they then met up with Matthew Farrow, a previous school friend of Oliver's, before we took them both back to Oaklands on the Sunday.

Also in early October, Kate was looking very seriously at possibly training to become a qualified Massage Therapist. Having carried out some research, she found that there was a very good tutor in Norwich, so she made contact. This was to develop into a parallel career to her teaching but more on this later.

Life carried on as usual during the rest of October, until 1 November 1997, as that was the day of my DMS graduation in Norwich Cathedral (Fig. 219).

Figure 219

All the hard work over the past couple of years had paid off. It was a lovely occasion as all our family joined me and Kate to witness my graduation. Then with the help of other family members they all duly returned to their various homes, colleges and universities.

It was Kate's mother's 88th birthday and we managed to see her at Barton, with Kate's brother Peter and Jane his wife, who had come up from Farnham for the day. We all had a lovely tea to mark the occasion.

Whilst at Oaklands, Oliver had taken a fancy to playing rugby. I'm not sure if this was a result of working on the Youngs's farm, that belonged to Nick who had once been capped by England, or the influence of his two sons Tom and Ben who also gained England caps, or whether it was simply to enjoy the game, whilst at college. Whatever the reason, it led to a fairly significant injury to start with, which was followed, in comparison, by some that were more minor. The most serious was in late November when he suffered a ruptured kidney. He went over to stay with his mum to recover, but at 02.00 on the morning of 23 November we were telephoned, to say that he had been admitted to the Queen Elizabeth Hospital (QEH) in King's Lynn. We went over to see him in the hope that a surprise visit would boost his morale. I think it did but not as much as being discharged on the Tuesday, after a two-night stay.

Kate had been experiencing problems with talking and constantly losing her voice, so had been visiting the Ear, Nose and Throat (ENT) department at the Norfolk and Norwich Hospital, but after a second visit a few days later after Oliver's accident, she too was given the 'all clear', along with some daily vocal exercises to carry out.

Oliver though, not satisfied with seeing the QEH once, was back there again this time with a broken hand!

As for the rest of December, our time was filled with the normal Christmas activities, carol services, drinks parties, annual letter and card writing and of course shopping! Whilst we spent Christmas Day on our own, which was both enjoyable and relaxing, I do recall though, that on Boxing Day we both stained the attic staircase – as it was probably raining, therefore a walk was not possible! For New Year, Oliver came over with some friends and they all stayed, along with Em, Angus and Sophie, and we all celebrated the turn of the year together, which was lovely.

1998

At the start of the New Year, Oliver took Sophie back to her mother's in Cromer, and then made his way to Oaklands, whilst Angus travelled up to Nottingham. As far as I can recall, Em stayed on at Swannington.

Angus had been giving further thought to his original choice of degree, and it was no surprise to us when upon returning to Nottingham, he switched courses from Philosophy to Computer Science. A change that suited him much better and aligned with both his interests and skill base. Due to this change of course, he had to leave Nottingham and return there in the October semester. So, he came home and soon found a job on 16 February at Norwich Winterthur. Being in the city it was ideal for him to stay at Brooke with his father, as his office was close to Angus's work, so he could then have a lift to and from Norwich.

Back in Swannington, we continued the final finishing touches with some carpets being laid and 17 more paintings being hung. I was still supporting the Parish Council as clerk, a role that I quite enjoyed, as it enabled me to do something constructive but not particularly challenging. When the opportunity arose, I volunteered to be the village's Tree Warden and went on a day's training at the UEA. This suited me down to the ground, anything to do with nature and working outside was ideal.

After all the work we had both been doing on the house, to say nothing of the stresses related to all things educational, I took Kate on a surprise visit to Paris for a few days over half-term. It was wonderful and again just what we needed. Flying from Stansted was easy but was slightly delayed around an hour later than expected, with us touching down early evening on St. Valentine's Day. Our hotel was fine and there was still time for a meal out to celebrate the day. This was in a restaurant opposite the Gare du Nord station. Not a particularly romantic location, but nonetheless it had a lovely French atmosphere and good food.

During our limited four-day visit, we packed in as many of the tourist attractions as we could, starting with a climb up the Eiffel Tower, where we had a sumptuous meal. Followed by an illuminated river cruise along the Seine, and on our last day a lovely walk around Montmartre. All this before we left on the Tuesday, arriving home around midnight.

As it was February half-term, Kate was able to follow up her interest in Massage Therapy, by visiting Alison Rostron's massage centre. This was just what Kate wanted, and it exceeded all her expectations. As a surprise birthday present from me, a place was booked without hesitation, for her to attend a Swedish Massage Course.

We celebrated Kate's actual birthday with a delicious meal at The Flags in

Marsham. Whilst nothing was said, at the time, I was very aware that no contact came from Sophie on the day which upset both of us, particularly me. But there was a shared present from both her and Oliver that did help a little.

In April, as I was away working, Oliver and his new young lady Maria were collected by Kate from college, and they came home for his 18th birthday. They stayed for a few days which enabled them to witness one of my roles as a tree warden, whilst an oak tree was planted on the village green, in memory of Princess Diana. At Easter, Em, Oliver and Maria were able to come to stay, and as usual we had an adult Easter Egg Hunt, with clues that they had to solve. Today we still do this but for our grandchildren instead, who are given support by their parents. I guess it's now become one of our family traditions which is rather lovely.

For Angus's birthday, on 19 April, we all had a home cooked roast followed by trifle with, of course, a 'proper' birthday cake with candles. Afterwards we all had a walk around Pretty Corner – not quite as sensational as Brands Hatch but we all enjoyed the day. When we got back Sophie had to pack for a geography field trip in the Lake District, so we dropped her off in Cromer at her mum's.

In the latter part of April, I was signed up for a few weeks, to attend a Tree Warden course at the UEA. Professor Tom Williamson, a landscape historian was the principal tutor and was brilliant. I got to know him reasonably well, as Kate and I were to attend one of his other courses, coupled with the fact that he, like me, was very supportive of Blickling Hall and its countryside management.

On April 27 1998, Marcus, Kate's nephew was to marry Sam, in Hastings, Kent. I arranged with a supplier of car finance to Anglia Housing, that we could test drive a new BMW Z3 for the trip to Kent. It was collected on the Saturday and returned on the Tuesday, having given us a lot of pleasure. On the way to Hastings, we stopped off for tea at Tunbridge Wells, and then joined 25 other family members for supper at the Priory Court Hotel. It was a wonderful wedding and a lovely relaxing weekend. At the time, Marcus was working with Sir Cameron Mackintosh, who was also at the wedding and after the reception Marcus and Sam flew off in Cameron's helicopter to his Scottish estate, for their honeymoon.

I was brought down to earth with a bump the next week when I received a telephone call from St. Albans police station. They politely advised me that Oliver was 'helping them with their inquiries', regarding a firearms incident at Oaklands College. Kate and I picked up his mother from Cromer and all three of us went to find out the details.

Having arrived at 09.20 we were advised that Oliver was involved, with another student, in a minor incident involving an air rifle where an adult had been shot, but luckily not seriously and didn't wish to press charges. From

Chapter 5 Married Life, Extensions & Exams 1993 – 1999

memory, I think the person who was injured was a member of staff, hence they knew from where the rifle had been fired, and probably by whom. Although it wasn't Oliver's rifle, they probably knew the name of the other student involved. After talking to the police and suggesting to them that this was clearly an accident, and simply being taken to the station and interviewed was probably sufficient punishment, Oliver was issued with a formal caution and released. I don't know what happened to the other student or the rifle. Oliver's girlfriend Maria was also at the station but not involved with the incident. Afterwards, we all had lunch, including Oliver and Maria and then made our way back to Norfolk. They then returned to Oaklands, and we returned to collect him on the Wednesday and brought him home. In between these times, he and Maria regrettably had split up. Eventually, on the Wednesday of the following week, Oliver returned to Oaklands and was cautioned by the college. There was no further action taken by any party and Oliver abided by his caution. Lessons were learnt and remembered! I feel that this well-known phrase is most apt here: *'The past is history, the future is a mystery, now is a gift, which is why it is called the present'*. So, we all moved on.

The rest of the month was uneventful in Swannington, but in Colchester Em was sitting exams, most of which were apparently ok, but not her statistics exam which she described, in a telephone call home, as being awful!

Summer was due to start in June, but in Swannington we were greeted with torrential rain, which caused some minor flooding. This inclement weather was to continue for the next couple of weeks, only turning to sunshine on Father's Day. I hardly dare comment on this, but in fact it was 29°!

During the 'rainy season' we went to hear a fabulous talk by Paul Heiney at Waterstone's in Norwich. The talk was all about his new book *Home Farm* (Fig. 220) in which he described home farming and the fulfilment of farming your own land. Kate's mother joined us, and it was a lovely event – and we came home with a signed copy.

Figure 220

The Anglia Housing walking group had now set their sights at the end of July on walking Hadrian's Wall. So, practice walks were happening on a regular basis. The next one, on 7 June, was a walk from Thetford to Brandon followed by lunch in a pub. Partners and other staff members were invited and we all started at 09.00. After about ten miles though, the numbers on the walk had dropped a little but as a result the pub was getting more customers.

The rest of us joined them later for a drink. To walk Hadrian's Wall always assuming I was fit enough, of course, would be the second time for me. The first being way back when I was a scout.

Oliver received his exam results from Oaklands and passed, so he was rightly very pleased, and the great news continued with Em receiving really good results for all her exams, including the dreaded Stats.

As part of her course, Em was given the exciting opportunity to study in Italy at Padova University, where she stayed through to the end of August. She had met Pete a fellow university student and whilst she was there, he joined her for a few weekends. On the other hand, we had to wait until the school holidays in August before we could go to see her, but in the meantime, we had had very regular telephone calls from her.

For the first, and I have to say the only time, Kate and I were invited to an evening at Newmarket Races (Fig. 221). We, plus others, were guests of Gilbert Offrex, a company which I dealt with for Anglia Housing. Having never been to the races I was unsure what to expect, but as a corporate event all the stops were pulled out, and it was excellent.

I can't recall how much we won but am assured by Kate that we left richer than when we arrived. The hospitality experience was wonderful. I have not returned to the races since, as I am sure that just being an everyday 'punter' would take the shine off my memories of being a corporate guest.

Figure 221

Figure 222

The Hadrian's Wall walk started on 23 July 1998 and this time we had a support group led by Kate. We all drove up to the start point, on the east coast at Wallsend and prepared for an early start the next day. The terrain of the walk can be seen in the photograph of part of the wall (Fig. 222).[23]

---

23 Image courtesy of drainswallholidays.co.uk

Chapter 5 Married Life, Extensions & Exams 1993 – 1999

*Top left –
Setting off.
Top right –
Reality hits home!
Above –
Our support crew led by Kate.
Above right –
The easy stretch.
Bottom –
Lunch break.*

227

REFLECTIONS UPON A FAMILY

Figure 223

The walk was relatively uneventful, given that there were thirteen of us negotiating a comparatively unknown terrain. We had set ourselves a target of five days to complete the 84 miles, which when you consider it took two days of driving there and back, this equates to walking around 28 miles per day. So, for us amateur walkers that was a good stretch.

We did make it without any major incidents, other than sore legs and the odd blister here and there. I was older this time and not so fit, as shown in one of the pictures entitled 'Reality hits home!'

We arrived at our destination, Bowness-on-Solway on the west coast, at 12.30, exhausted but delighted to be able to say we had completed the full walk (Fig. 223). I am third from the left, in the middle row.

We had a late lunch at the parent's home of one of the walkers, followed by a sleep before setting off south, back to the office. In total Kate and her support team of two had clocked up 1,124 miles – thank goodness we didn't walk that far!

This was just as well because Kate and I were off to Italy to meet up with Em and Pete, for a ten-day holiday and we were lucky enough to be able to stay with Em.

Chapter 5 Married Life, Extensions & Exams 1993 – 1999

Figure 224

Figure 225

Whilst we were there, we visited the Piazza delle Erbe in Padova (Fig. 224), St. Mark's Square in Venice (Fig. 225), along with other beautiful places and we also had a day at the seaside (Fig. 226).

Whilst in Italy we took the opportunity to retrace some of the routes that my father had taken during WWII and just after it had ended. In particular, the town of Montegalda, in the province of Vicenza, Veneto Italy, where he was billeted in the church hall. We also managed to find some locations in Padova (Padua), where there had been an enormous tank park and Dad had parked his tank there.

Prior to our tour to Montegalda, we had both sat down with my dad and looked through his original photographs, in the hope that when we returned from our trip, we could show him the current views and compare them side by side. Some locations and scenes were easy to establish, but others had over time changed due to new buildings or road changes. Dad was thrilled to see the pictures and was able to recount some of the exploits that he and his fellow comrades had been up to, at the time.

Figure 226

229

REFLECTIONS UPON A FAMILY

Montegalda

Chapter 5 Married Life, Extensions & Exams 1993 – 1999

Padova

Five of the closest comparison images are shown, with Dad's being the black and white ones. He was delighted.

After a lovely time, we arrived home mid-morning on Friday 14th and went to pick up Oliver from the farm. The next day we had tickets to go to Blickling Hall in Aylsham, for an evening, outdoor music concert by Il Divo, coupled with a laser and fireworks show. Both of which were excellent, and we were joined by my boss Jenny, her husband, sister and mother, all of whom lived in Aylsham.

231

REFLECTIONS UPON A FAMILY

The following day was Angus's last at Norwich Winterthur and at the end of the month he was to return to Nottingham to commence his new degree course.

Living at Swannington in 1998 was almost like being in an airport transfer lounge, as no sooner had one of the four come home, another one departed. This time Angus was off to the Dominican Republic for a holiday, before university started in earnest. Kate had now started her International Therapy Examination Council (ITEC) Massage course, which extended over the next five weekends. Fortunately for me, if I was feeling stressed at any time, I could always turn to her, as she needed to practise and develop her massage skills, and I was to be the beneficiary of these sessions!

Angus was due to arrive back in the UK on 22 September, but his flight was cancelled due to the hurricane that had hit the country. Thankfully, he and Matt his friend who had travelled with him, arrived back at Gatwick, three days later on Friday 25th. They then had to catch a Jet Link coach to Norwich, and arrived at 16.30, exhausted but relieved. Apart from the hurricane, they had had a great time. Unfortunately though, he only had a short time at home, as his new course at Nottingham started on 28 September!

Em was to return to Colchester at the weekend, so again it was the transfer lounge situation. Oh, and in between all this Oliver bought himself a car. So, his many hours working on the farm, some of which were very unsociable, had had a positive outcome.

Not to be 'outdone' by the younger generation, Kate and I enrolled at the UEA on a Landscape Studies course led by Tom Williamson. We took the option not to take any exams, rather just develop and enhance our understanding of the landscape. As such there was a mixture of students like us, and others who were studying hard to qualify and develop their credentials. It was a great course that kept us busy for an evening a week plus a few weekend site visits. The first one was at West Runton to study the coastal retreat issues and how this had both revealed hidden fossils but also destroyed some coastal habitats.

On 23 October 1998, I was in Court. Not, I hasten to add, due to a misdemeanour, but for an interview. Some months earlier I had, with the support of Kate, my boss Jenny and our friend Roger from Hansells Solicitors, sent in an application to become a Magistrate. This interview was the second stage of the process. The first was an 'in house' review of my application to ensure that I met the criteria. In this the second stage, I was interviewed by two ladies and a gentleman who all sat on the Norwich Bench, the gentleman was the Bench Chairman, the other two Lay Magistrates. I recall that the interview was not easy as some of

Chapter 5 Married Life, Extensions & Exams 1993 – 1999

the questions were quite difficult to answer but I felt positive at the end of it. I was then informed that my application would proceed but I wouldn't hear any final decision for some considerable time. Whilst I was disappointed that I had to wait, at least I knew I was moving towards my goal.

Over the half-term, Kate was studying hard for her ITEC qualification in Swedish Massage with physiology and anatomy, during which she was also covering subjects like reflexology, Indian Head massage and lymphatic massage. There was also an assignment to write which entailed a lot of research and reading, plus practical case studies that had to be recorded in great detail.

Talking of anatomy, over the weekend Oliver had been up to his old tricks again doing 'wheelies' on his bicycle, falling off and in the process injuring himself. This time the Norfolk and Norwich Hospital dealt with a cracked wrist, which necessitated in him attending the fracture clinic the following day. Thank goodness it was on his bike and not his car which had been taken to a local garage for a re-spray.

In preparation for Kate's final examinations, she undertook a number of mock exams in both the theory and the practical aspect. Although the former was 'very hard' she passed both with credit which gave her a great boost for the finals. Having taken her final practical exam on the Friday, Kate spent most of the weekend and the following weeks revising for the theory exam which was due in mid-December. She did this with her fellow student and friend Karen. All this was undertaken whilst still holding down a demanding role at Norwich High School! I was in awe of her knowledge and dedication which certainly confirmed just how serious she was in wanting to pursue this as a career.

Figure 227

A week or so later after his accident, Oliver collected his Vauxhall Nova (Fig. 227) which looked really good, and he was justifiably very proud of his purchase. Over the weekend he fitted speakers into the rear parcel shelf, before he drove himself back to Oaklands.

On Sunday 13 December, thank goodness it wasn't Friday the 13th, Kate sat her final theory exam at 09.30. She now had a few weeks to wait for the results and despite realising, after the examination, that she had missed out a question, there was a definite air of confidence and both she and Karen were both well pleased with their revision.

Unfortunately, our car, the Peugeot 505 was not behaving itself but that was nothing new, for a number of months it had been having all sorts of issues.

So, we looked around for a replacement that we could afford. We test drove several cars, but none seemed to fit the bill, so we kept looking and on 21 December, we finally purchased an Escort, H964 FJF for £2,695.00, which met all our requirements.

Christmas was now almost upon us, the cards had been written and posted, the decorations had been hung and our family were slowly filling the house. We all had stockings to open on Christmas Day and it was lovely that all four of our children sat on our bed whilst they opened them. It was a super Christmas, despite Kate's description of the weather on the calendar being recorded as being '*Dull and boring*'!

Boxing Day was a day of rest and a grand tea for all of us before they all went their own ways. Unfortunately, Sophie and her friend Ian had had a minor car accident and required hospital checks, fortunately they weren't seriously hurt, so were discharged the same day. So, apart from returning Angus and Em to university, that was 1998 and we looked forward to 1999.

1999

Living in Swannington was an almost ideal location, as it was close to Norwich for work for both Kate and me, close to schools for the children, and as a home was large enough to provide all the accommodation we required. However, circumstances had changed since its purchase. I was very aware that it wasn't 'our' home, that being Kate's and mine, simply because 'we' hadn't chosen it together. I was not sure how Kate felt about this, but I was certainly aware that she may have felt that the house had simply been changed to accommodate the extended family.

Now with three children away in further education and Sophie choosing to live with her mother in Cromer, it was therefore, in my view, time to review where we resided. As with most major decisions, Kate and I were of one mind on this and as such we started to think about what sort of a home we wanted, and where this could be located.

Once Kate had gained her qualifications, she was keen to start a Massage Therapy practice, so that was a serious consideration which led us to look closer at North Norfolk. We carried out a recce and concluded that the best area for us was around Sheringham or Holt. We had a look around and, to cut a long story short, decided that a converted barn would meet all our expectations. But these were in high demand and costly, so it would be necessary for us to find a barn that needed restoration.

Chapter 5 Married Life, Extensions & Exams 1993 – 1999

Kate was very diligent and regularly checked the properties for sale, to see if any were appropriate. As this was such a huge decision, the next chapter will expand further and give the details. But for now, I will simply reflect upon 1999 in Swannington.

As an update on where we all were, I was still working for Anglia Housing as a Facilities Manager, Kate remained at the Norwich High School for Girls, Em was in her final year at Essex University, Oliver in his final year at Oaklands, whilst Sophie was in her final year at Norwich City College and as I have said, living with her mother. Angus had resumed his university studies in Nottingham but this time on a Computer Science course. So, life was certainly different and would change again, during the year, with the conclusion of so many 'final' years.

In February, we managed to sell the now redundant Peugeot for £50, to a gentleman who took the car away. We thought that would be the last we saw of it but that wasn't to be quite the end, as a few weeks later we had a call from the Norwich Police to say that the Peugeot had been abandoned and found parked in a Tesco car park. After a short discussion, it was agreed that we had submitted all the correct paperwork regarding the sale, but the purchaser had not! Not only that but when we contacted him, he denied he had even bought it despite giving us £50. The end result was that the car was removed and scrapped, at no cost to us.

The next 'communication' was Kate contacting ITEC for her results, which she received. What a result: she had passed her theory with 82%, that's the one she thought was the hardest, her practical with 73% and an A (87 – 90%) for her assignment in 'Infant Massage'.

All of us were delighted. Karen her friend and fellow student had also passed with similar results which was fantastic, as they had both worked so hard. That evening a celebratory meal was enjoyed at the Ratcatchers Inn.

In February, during the half-term, Kate and I went up to the Derbyshire Dales for a break and to spend some quality time together, whilst staying at the Woodroffe Arms in Hope. We did have some quality time but the weather, from memory, was cold and wet, so not ideal. It did though, give us time to think about how and where Kate could start her business, how it could be promoted, and we considered how to combine her requirements into our house search. All of which was really helpful. The weather eased a little, so we took the opportunity to brave a visit to some of the local sights, one of which was going down the Blue John mine, which fortunately, wasn't weather dependent! All in all, not a bad few days.

We returned home refreshed and ready to set up Kate's Massage Therapy clinic. Having found a suitable room located in a large private house in

Aylsham, leaflets and brochures were designed and printed. Couches and other vital appliances were purchased and installed, and the business was soon up and running, with her very first professional fee-paying massage, given on 18 March 1999.

We were still keen to move and now we had a much clearer understanding of what Kate needed for the running of her business, which was to operate alongside her full-time work at the High School. Our attention was now focused not only on Kate's business and where we could live, but also on preparing Primitive Cottage for a potential sale. To this end the conservatory was transformed into a more habitable area rather than a 'dumping' ground full of boots, shoes and jackets.

May was to witness the start of the university and college examination period, and whilst all exams are important, to paraphrase from *Animal Farm*, some are more important than others. This was certainly the case that year, as for Oliver, Em and Sophie these were final examinations. There were stressful times and luckily the children felt able to talk to us and seek some valuable reassurance that all would be fine. Both Kate and I appreciated this small peep into their now adult life.

From our searches, perspective new homes were beginning to surface, and we visited a small, but growing number of old houses and small farmsteads in North Norfolk. It was becoming clear that whilst our desired location was around the Sheringham and Holt area, they too were very popular with many other buyers. As a result, 'ideal' properties either didn't make it onto the market being sold privately or were sold within days of being advertised. This presented a problem as viewing for us could only be done in the evenings or at weekends. Still, we decided to have Swannington valued, in order that we could gain a realistic view of just what we could afford. Arnolds Estate Agents came to view on 6 June and gave us a valuation of between £110k and £130k which, from our perspective, we thought was very good.

We accepted the advice from Arnolds and agreed an asking price of £128,500 and details were agreed as shown (Fig. 228).

Figure 228

Chapter 5 Married Life, Extensions & Exams 1993 – 1999

Without any formal advertising we agreed a viewing by Mr and Mrs Philips, on 15 June at 18.00. They made us an offer of the asking price, which was accepted there and then, and completion took place on 27 August, so the hunt for a new home was now urgent.

The next couple of weeks were very hectic indeed. Em received her final results from Essex University and had passed with a 2:1. A very credible and well-deserved result and she was to have her graduation ceremony on 16 July. At the end of June, Angus had the results of his first-year exams which were equally impressive and if repeated in his finals would, with just a 2% increase, result in a First. He was obviously very pleased, as we all were, and it certainly justified his change of course.

Kate continued our house search and found a Norfolk Barn called Walnut Farm Barns for sale in Bodham, (Fig. 229) which seemed to fit what we were looking for and met our specifications. So, despite it being a weekday evening we decided to drive up to Bodham and have a look.

I recall it was dark, and we weren't sure where the barn was actually situated, but we eventually found a barn and it certainly looked ideal. Whilst being unused and ready for conversion to a home, it had all the character and charm we wanted, and we could see on the order to view, how this matched the artist's impression. At offers around £55k it was perfect.

It was advertised with architect's drawings for conversion to a four bedroomed house along with a workshop – ideal for Kate – a garage and gardens. From our perspective there was no time to lose. The next day we contacted the agents and registered our interest, subject to a survey and just to be sure, that afternoon we went up in daylight, to view the barn. It was then that we found that it wasn't the traditional barn we had seen the night before, but one on the opposite side of the road and very different indeed.

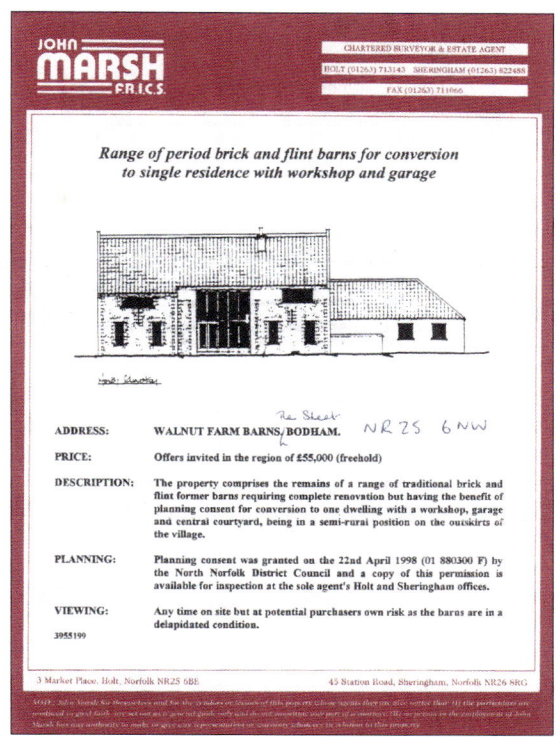

Figure 229

In fact, what we had registered an interest in was utterly dissimilar from the barn that we viewed that evening, in that it was completely dilapidated and barely recognisable as a barn. So just what had we let ourselves in for? Now, of course, we knew why it was only on sale for 'offers invited in the region of £55,000'.

Figure 230

Figure 231

These two photographs, of the front of the barn (Figs. 230 & 231), give a clear view of its condition. At the back there were two caravans, and an old Volvo car included in the price! These can be seen clearly later (Fig. 242). This recollection is continued in the next chapter, but I must say here that we did have a survey carried out which was reasonable, and we eventually had an offer accepted for £50,000. But were we actually capable of restoring this to an acceptable home, with a clinic for Kate? Yes we were and we changed its name to Walnut Barn but it was always known as 'The Barn'.

The children came to see the new family home and were surprised to say the least. Privately, I am sure they thought the two of us had lost our marbles! I think there were similar thoughts along that line from both Kate and me as well! But neither of us admitted these feelings to each other.

Figure 232

In the photograph (Fig. 232), Em and Pete are making their way from the front hall, through the drawing room, to the rear barn doors as shown on the architect's sketch (Fig. 229). This is obvious if you have a very, very good imagination!

Chapter 5 Married Life, Extensions & Exams 1993 – 1999

July sixteenth was very much Em's Day, as she graduated. The ceremony in the Lecture Hall was excellent and was followed with ten of us all going to a local Mill, for a luxurious meal. The official photograph (Fig. 233) is shown with one of Kate, Em and me (Fig. 234). A wonderful day and an excellent result that reflected all the hard work that Em had put into her degree course over the past years.

Figure 233 *Figure 234*

Two days later, Kate and I met up with Sophie at the Red Lion in Stiffkey, where she informed us that she was moving to High Wycombe to live with her mother and Dale. This was a surprise as they both worked for Norfolk County Council, but we had no choice but to accept the situation and thanked her for letting us know.

After eight months of waiting and unbeknown to me at the time, on 4 July, on behalf of Her Majesty The Queen, The Lord Chancellor had approved my appointment to sit on the Norfolk Bench, as a Justice of the Peace (JP) or as we are commonly known, a Magistrate. However, due to the administration delays, I wasn't informed of this until a letter finally arrived, on 19 July. Despite the delay I was thrilled and very honoured. I had to wait though, until 15 October, almost a year after my final interview, to receive my official certificate of appointment (Fig. 235) at the swearing in ceremony in Norfolk's County Hall in Norwich,

REFLECTIONS UPON A FAMILY

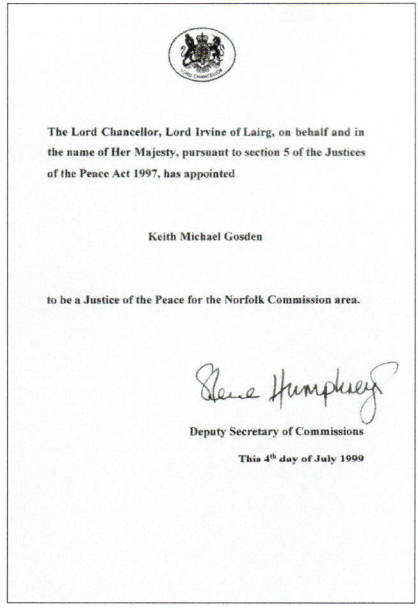

Figure 235

when according to Kate I had to make sure I wore my best clothes. Kate does look after me very well!

Having taken the Judicial Oath and been officially sworn in, a photograph (Fig. 236) was taken of all the newly appointed magistrates in Norfolk, along with the Judge and Norfolk's Lord Lieutenant. I am third from right on the back row.

Over the next few weeks, extensive and rigorous training then ensued, leading up to my first sitting in the Norwich Magistrates Court, on January 7, 2000.

Other than the observations required prior to my application, this was only my second time in court. The first being as a defendant, following my car accident whilst working at Colman Foods. So, it was good that this time, I was delivering justice rather than receiving it!

I was very proud of my appointment and was sharing this news with my sister Judy, when one of her children asked what a JP was. In reply Judy was totally dismissive of the role and appointment saying,

Figure 236

240

Chapter 5 Married Life, Extensions & Exams 1993 – 1999

'*oh that's what so and so wanted me to be, but I said no*', or words to that effect.

Given the lengths that I and all the other Magistrates have to go through to be appointed, coupled with the responsibilities that come with the role, that dismissive attitude was very hurtful and has been very clearly remembered by me for the last 25+ years.

The Anglia Housing walking group were off again, but this time without the benefit of a support group as we were walking through the Brecon Beacons. It was another resounding success story, and we were able to raise some more money for charity.

Back at work we were all involved in checking that the date change in six months' time to the year 2000, wouldn't cause a melt down with IT and other systems, that were driven by dates. This meant that our IT department was having to carry out tests and practise mock change of dates. As Head of Facilities, I had to run similar tests on heating clocks and other date driven and controlled devices. The overall worry, at the time, was that moving from 1999 to 2000 would not be recognised by the technology, as the date had a series of zeros. Luckly there was no impact, and all was well on the day.

Kate decided to sign up and join me on one of my UEA modules entitled 'Landscape Painting and the Artists of East Anglia'. This was most interesting to us as we had a number of paintings, some of which were by renowned East Anglian artists, so it was very appropriate and gave us both a much wider appreciation of the artworks.

Despite all the activity we did remember the date of our wedding anniversary, 24 July, which we celebrated in style. We took time out to travel down to Southwold where we enjoyed a meal in the Swan Hotel. This was a lovely quiet day. There are times when you simply have to step back in life, take a deep breath and remind yourself of where you have progressed from, and where life is leading you now. That day was one such time for us, as well as being a very suitable reminder of our lovely wedding. Unbeknown to us, this was to be the lull before the storm, and what a storm that was to be.

It was also time for A-Level results for Sophie. She passed Psychology with an E. This, whilst being a pass, was disappointing to her, but as she wasn't intending to progress to university, it didn't affect her future prospects, though it was nevertheless a dent to her pride.

As we wrote in our Christmas letter that year, '*August was stressful to say the least. Every single member of the family was on the move. Keith and Kate to North Norfolk, Oliver and his young lady, Jenny, to Hitchen, Sophie to High Wycombe,*

REFLECTIONS UPON A FAMILY

Angus organising a house-move for his second university year and Emily, job and flat hunting in London'.

August concluded with us selling and moving out of Primitive Cottage and into a mobile home in Bodham. The contents of our home had to be packed and stored whilst we undertook the building work. Luckily, Kate's mother was very generous with her support by allowing us to completely fill her double garage to the ceiling and one of her large bedrooms. Without this I am not sure how we would have managed.

We finally exchanged on the Cottage in Swannington on 5 August and followed this on 11 August by exchanging on the Barn at Bodham. With completion on both properties on the 27th of the same month, there was no going back!

We were relieved and high with emotions but not as high as Angus. As on 16 August he undertook a tandem parachute jump at Old Buckenham airfield. This was a birthday present from Kate and me and after an exhilarating descent he regrettably had to return to Nottingham.

This jump ignited a love of parachute jumping, sky diving and BASE jumping (Buildings, Antennae, Spans [bridges] and Earth [cliffs]), all of which he excelled at and thoroughly enjoyed (Fig. 237).

Figure 237

Work was to start on the Barn but given that the next chapter is focused on this, I will outline the work carried out within that chapter. Suffice to say here, on 27 August 1999 our new abode in the form of a caravan was delivered to the site. So, with change of address cards sent, we moved in!

Em was delighted to telephone us to say that she had accepted a job, with Hays Management Consultancy as a Diagnostic Analyst, with a start date of 1 October. So, in September, in preparation for the big day she moved into her new home at 25 Lawn Gardens, Hanwell, London. A great start to her birthday on 7 October. By contrast, Angus was back studying at Nottingham University whilst he also had part-time employment as a fishmonger, in Sainsburys supermarket.

At the commencement of November, we were treated to gale force winds and torrential rain. Living as we were, in a caravan, this was not only 'interesting' but reminded me of being on holiday in Sheringham with my parents many years earlier. However, the only difference now was that I knew it wasn't fairies playing football on the roof!

Chapter 5 Married Life, Extensions & Exams 1993 – 1999

Our cat Tonic (Fig. 238) had come with us from Swannington and seemed oblivious to the change in her living standards, from a warm Aga kitchen to a cold caravan. As can be seen here, she soon found the alternative sunny spots. That was to be her final move before passing away a few years later.

Figure 238

Having now moved to High Wycombe, in December Sophie was successful in landing her first full-time employment with the Association of Accounting Technicians. She was to commence this work on 20 January.

During all the activity over the past few months, Kate had still found time to develop her art of Indian Head Massage, which proved to be a valuable asset to her massage repertoire.

Having sent out our change of address card (Fig. 239) we had a number of friends and family come to see just what we had bought. I distinctly remember that the one phrase that Kate and I were constantly using was, '*it will be lovely when it's finished!*' The retort from our family and friends was normally '*are you completely mad*?' and whilst the answer to that was '*probably*', we also knew that with a lot of hard work, sweat and tears we would eventually be able to say, '*we told you it would be lovely, and no, we weren't mad.*'

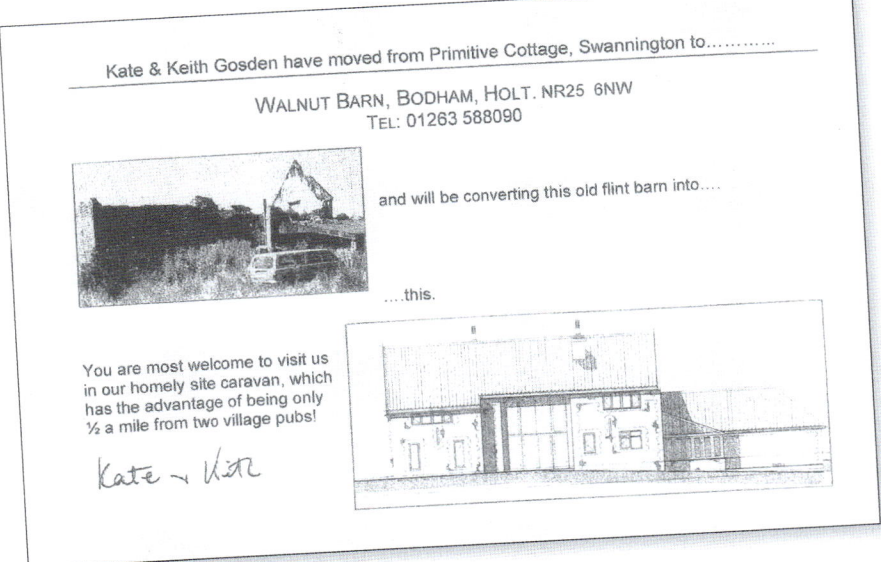

Figure 239

REFLECTIONS UPON A FAMILY

Just before we had our first Bodham Christmas, which was to be in the smallest and most cosy home we had ever lived in, a static caravan! We suddenly received a call from Gillian, Kate's sister, who asked us if whilst they were away, we would like to house and dog sit for them, in Rookes House, Elephant Green, Newport. An offer we simply could not refuse, so Tonic went to a cattery, and we drove to Newport. We stayed until 30 December and were joined for part of the time by Oliver and his girlfriend Jenny, along with Em and Pete. Gillian and Geoffrey's black Labrador called Rumba had his daily walks, and we had a comfortable home for Christmas. What more could we have asked for?

To assist when reading the next chapter, I have included the floor plan below which will assist the understanding of the final layout of Walnut Barn (The Barn) (Fig. 240).[24]

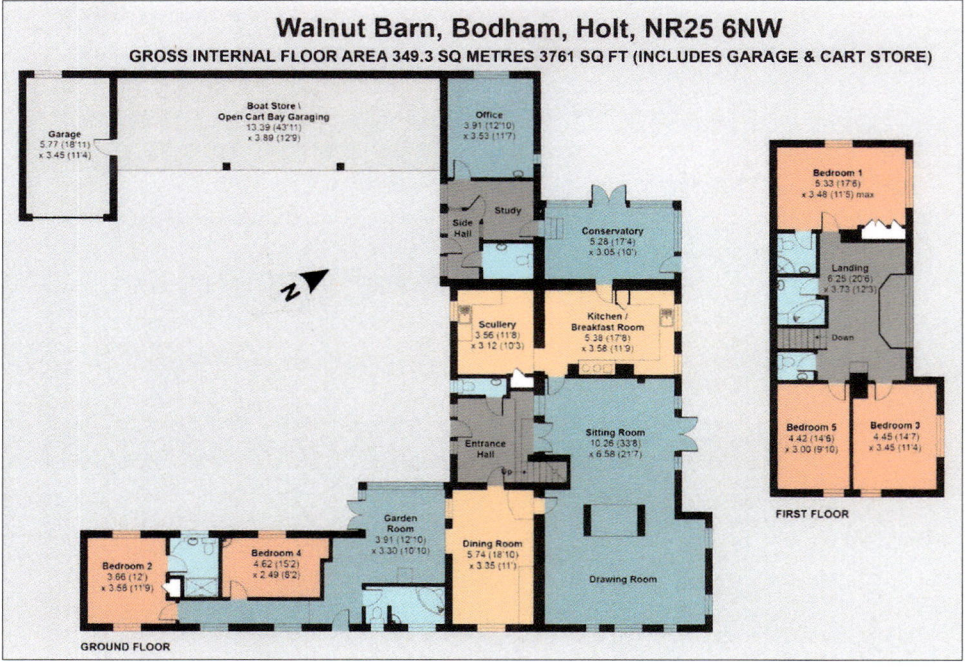

Figure 240

---

24 The Plan above is copyright of nichecom.co.uk for Strutt & Parker

CHAPTER 6

Ground up with Flints & Blocks 1999 – 2014

1999 continued...

Below and overleaf are three photographs of Walnut Barn. The first was taken in September 1971 (Fig. 241), the second was how it looked when we purchased it (Fig. 242) and finally the completed project, taken in 2010 (Fig. 243), where we happily lived, following all our hard work. The difference between all these three, demonstrates the work entailed to create our new home, and all this is outlined in this chapter.

Figure 241

Figure 242

To help, Fig. 241, is taken from the south. 'The Barn' is in the centre, with a large, corrugated shed to its left. In order that all three properties had shared access, later, the drive was moved to the right of the long barn, which were the original stables, and can be seen in the foreground of the picture.

In Fig. 242, also taken from the south, the remains of the barn can be seen along with three caravans. To the right and bottom of the image are the

Figure 243

farmhouse and the stables which had now been developed, prior to the builder being forced to sell the remaining barn at a low price, to us. The revised access drive can also be seen here.

Unbeknown to us at the time, the caravan with a green stripe mysteriously disappeared during our purchase of the barn. No one ever found out how or by whom!

The final image (Fig. 243)[25], taken from the north, features the rear of 'The Barn'. The large, corrugated shed in figure 241 has been removed and replaced with a new wing, mirroring the one on the left, which had been the old bullock sheds. The property on the far left is the original farmhouse, which had also been restored and extended, as can be seen in figure 243. The stables adjacent to the road, in both figures 241 and 242 are not visible in the final view.

Having now given the overview pictorially, I decided to start this chapter returning to 27 August 1999, the day of our completion. It was a busy day, and going forward that description was to sum up our lives for the next few years.

Having now established that the caravan with the green stripe, which was on site, had been removed, we hastily purchased a replacement and at 06.30 on

---

25 2010 Photograph by ScanAir, Devon

Chapter 6 Ground up with Flints & Blocks 1999 – 2014

27 August 1999 this was duly delivered (Fig. 244) to Walnut Barn, Bodham. Then at 10.30, British Telecom (BT) put in a connection for the telephone, and later in the day the electricity was fully connected, via a 'builders' supply, which was a safe but temporary solution.

At Swannington, the final task before handing over the keys, was for our Aga engineer to completely dismantle the Aga. He kindly put it into storage for us, in one of his barns, which by coincidence, were not far away from Bodham.

Figure 244

Supper on the Friday was kindly supplied by my sister Judy and her husband and was most welcome. Then on the Saturday the plumber arrived, to ensure we had a water supply, and by Sunday supper time we had everything sorted and a 'snug' and warm caravan. Figure 245 was taken a few weeks later and shows a typical scene, with a 'Gosden' notice board and pictures on the wall, as we wished to continue some of our traditions! We could now start work on the barn.

Figure 245

As I have said previously, the purchase included planning permission to convert 'The Barn' into a modern home, for without this nothing could be done.

We asked Ian Malton our friend, who was an architect, to draw up our own ideas and submit these for planning approval. We awaited the outcome of this which was ultimately passed, and in the meantime, we were given permission to start to clear the site, in advance.

During the next week a proper three-phase electrical supply was installed and connected, which allowed us to use heavy duty cutters and drills etc., on site. However, prior to this I had to drive a small digger and create a trench, 45' long by 4' deep, and now that the electricity cable had been lain, I had to fill it all in! So, by the first week of September, we had light and power, both in the barn as well as the caravan!

247

We now turned our attention to site clearance. Kate moved over 300 flints whilst with the mini JCB I set about removing earth and rubble, so we could actually see what we had purchased! It became clear though, that we really needed a full sized JCB and an expert driver. Luckily for us, there was just such a man called Russell, who owned a JCB and lived in the next village. He was incredibly helpful and ended up doing all sorts of work for us. But for now, he cleared the site, whilst Kate and I went off to Norwich to earn some money.

Below are two photographs before and after the clearance (Figs. 246 & 247) taken from the back of the barn. We had to remove the Volvo but the dilapidated caravan we kept for storage.

On Monday, before I had changed and set off to work, Russell had arrived with his JCB, and he and I discussed the clearing of the area for Kate's Consulting Room (Fig. 248).

Figure 246

Figure 247

Figure 248

It so happened that during that week, Russell called me at work, which I instantly thought was bad news, but luckily this was not the case. In fact, whilst he was clearing the inside of the barn, he had discovered an entire threshing floor (Fig. 249) and was most concerned that if it was left there, it might be targeted by thieves. So, unexpectantly our job over that weekend was to lift all the tiles and bricks, store them safely out of sight, so they could be used later in the conversion.

By November we had a clear site, a set of agreed plans and a delivery of building materials. Having spoken with a local company who were to supply our lime mortar, we had also agreed that work would start on the exterior walls, using two expert flint layers, who were used to working with flint and lime mortar, through their work on local churches.

Figure 249

Figure 250 – Front view taken whilst standing next to garage wall, on the righthand side.

Figure 251 – From the end of the back garden with 'storage' caravan.

Figure 252 – The only gable end still standing.

Figure 253 – The main area of 'The Barn'.

Figure 254 – View of front entrance and front garden with our temporary abode, the static caravan, in the background

But first we had to have some of the scaffolding erected. This was put in hand and by the time Peter, Kate's brother and Jane, his wife, came to see the work, on 20 November, the builders had commenced a small area, in what was to be our dining room. At the time, we didn't seek their opinion on the purchase of the barn, as we thought that they would think that we were completely crazy!

The agreed plan was to build the internal skin of the walls with concrete blocks and the external would be flint and brick. This had been agreed, as part of the formal planning approval, with both our structural engineer and building control at North Norfolk District Council (NNDC). The floors would be concrete with steel mesh which would extend under the external walls at regular intervals, to give them some support. Again, our structural engineer had worked with NNDC to agree this.

Figures 250 – 254 were taken by Peter. All these show the site having been cleared but before we started the building work in earnest. Some images were shot with a fish-eye lens hence the 'bent' walls!

During the October half-term, we worked extremely hard, preparing the site for the builders, having some of the scaffolding erected, ordering bricks and blocks along with sand and vast quantities of Bleaklow slaked lime putty. This came in very heavy 25 litre size tubs! I hate to think how many of these were used over the course of the build, but it must have been in the hundreds. Even now, years later, we still have a couple of empty ones that are incredibly useful in the garden.

The building work commenced in earnest on 3 November and would continue through to March 2000. In order of priority though, we had split this work into three phases. Phase 1 was the main living area of 'The Barn'. Phase 2 was slightly larger with Kate's Massage Clinic, the cart shed and garage. The final Phase 3, at the front of the barn, was the conversion of the old bullock sheds into a wing for a two bedroomed Bed and Breakfast accommodation.

Again, we were very fortuitous for we had found another local craftsman, Keith Reardon, who made all our oak roof trusses and internal beams. The oak was purchased from Hevingham sawmill who over several months got to know us quite well. Certainly, well enough that when the time came, they found us a wonderful curved oak trunk that when cut in half lengthways, made two perfect lintels that went over our double-sided fireplace. We were told that the oak had been in their yard for quite a number of years, just waiting for the right person and project to come along – that was us and Walnut Barn. Believe that if you will but it is a true story, from our perspective.

REFLECTIONS UPON A FAMILY

2000

The main beams were delivered early January, and to make them look authentic and to give them more character I set about hand chamfering the edges. This was harder than I thought and was a long but very rewarding task. These had to be finished quickly as the builders were just reaching the point where they needed us out of their way, in order that the flint work could be finished.

Figure 255

Figure 256

In the photograph taken on 8 January (Fig. 255) Andrew, a neighbouring farmer, along with Mark, one of the builders and I are manhandling one of the main beams into place, over the front door. Luckily for us, Andrew had brought his farm teleporter (Fig. 256), otherwise it would have been very difficult indeed. This was just one of two that we did that day, with many more still to be put in place.

Throughout the rest of January, work carried on at pace, and by the 20th the barn wall at the front, was at wall plate height and ready for the roof trusses to be put up, but there were three other walls to finish first, including the back wall (Fig. 257).

Figure 257

On Kate's 50th birthday we both went out for a quiet meal at The Red Lion in Upper Sheringham. At the weekend all the family came home and stayed in Rookery Farm opposite the barn, and we all celebrated her 'official' birthday with a fantastic meal at the Wheatsheaf pub in West Beckham.

Our joiner Keith, who was to make the trusses, came to measure up, to ensure they were all made to the correct size. Making these was a long job as each

Chapter 6 Ground up with Flints & Blocks 1999 – 2014

Figure 258

one was different and had to be individually crafted. They wouldn't be ready until April! However, that gave the builders time to finish the other walls, build the two chimneys and put the steel work in place, for the trusses to sit on. The back walls didn't take long as there were several window openings in them.

By the first week in April, we were not only greeted with some sun but with a trailer load of oak trusses (Fig. 258). Keith was going to move by hand, up onto the roof, each element of each truss and then assemble them in place. No glue or screws were being used, just oak pegs. He was a master craftsman and only the traditional methods would be acceptable.

His agility up on the roof, without netting or harnesses was both unnerving and scary, but he didn't seem to be aware of any of the potential dangers posed. He was moving huge oak timbers into place and hammering in wooden pegs, without a care in the world, or so it seemed. Although years later, we met up again and he recalled the installation of all these trusses and said that we would not catch him doing that again!

His work was masterful and gave us great confidence. It also meant that we were close to putting a roof on Phase 1. Still a huge amount of internal work to do but seeing the roof beginning to take shape was a significant milestone, nonetheless. This photograph (Fig. 259) shows the first six trusses in place by the end of April.

Figure 259

Once Keith had completed his trusses, the roofers, a father and son from Norwich, moved in to put up the rafters and lay the tiles. As with all the tradesmen we had been using, they too were very skilled, careful and determined to do a professional job.

The rafters were finished by 10 May, with the main front section of the roof, battened and felted ten days later. The front tiling was completed within eight days, with the entire roof tiled, lead flashing complete and scaffolding down by 15 July. This was a momentous day for us. The series of four photographs opposite show how the front roof progressed, and it was most impressive and gratifying. 'The Barn' was beginning to look like an actual habitable house. That was until you went inside which was, of course an empty shell!

Whilst we were concentrating on 'The Barn', our family went about their business as usual. Well, usual for them, for at the end of March, Angus decided to follow up his success at parachute jumping by attending a course at Langham, to learn how to sky dive. Having completed eight tandem jumps with his instructor, and a further ten solo ones he was given the necessary competence certificate. This enabled him to jump elsewhere and more importantly to be insured.

We, on the other hand, continued with our paid employment and in my case, sitting in court when time permitted. I was coming to terms with the 'authority' we had and the impact we could make on people's lives. This was brought home to me when I sat on a case that ended with, for me, the first custodial sentence. The defendant was an elderly gentleman and regrettably for everyone, his guilty plea meant that a short custodial sentence was the only one that could be passed, given that there was insufficient mitigating evidence, to avoid custody. Once this was read out in open court he then asked if he could go home, pack a case and collect his toothbrush. The answer from the bench was, of course, 'no', as the latter would be provided. I found that very sobering indeed and whenever I passed a similar sentence I thought about that gentleman, and the impact we had on his life.

Earlier in the month, Em had signed her new lease on a flat which was good news. Sophie was still working away but did, like her siblings, come to see us from time to time. It was difficult for all of them to visit for more than a day, as the caravan wasn't large enough. However, we did manage to squeeze them all in on rare occasions. Squeeze being the operative word.

When Sophie did visit, she would invariably find time to go for a good hack and had now been able to purchase some very smart riding gear. Angus was

still at Nottingham and had been taking exams for a few weeks. We were in regular contact to give encouragement, when necessary, and to receive feedback on how a particular examination had gone.

June 2000 was, on the whole, a good month with lovely weather. Indeed, on Sunday 18th it was, apparently, hotter in Cromer than on the Mediterranean. So, we were all able to enjoy some summer days. Kate was developing a strong client base for her Massage Therapy in Aylsham, and we started to think about Phase 2, which would give her both a reception area and a consulting room, at home instead of Aylsham.

At the end of July, Oliver and his young lady, Jenny, came to see us and helped with some of the work over the weekend. Our previous mini digging expertise was put to good use again, as we had to dig out the floors at ground level, ready for hardcore, followed by insulation. The latter was hard work on our knees, the tips of our fingers and bottoms and it was certainly a luxury to sit down in the caravan.

Figure 260

Back on site, the internal work was progressing well with both Kate and I taking it in turns to use the hired mini digger, to dig drainage trenches. One of which we didn't finish until 23.00 – clearly, we had very understanding neighbours as nothing was said about noise etc.

Exactly one year on from the exchange of contracts all the external work was completed on Phase 1. Windows were in and glazed, the back screen was completed. We really did think we were on the home straight.

We had decided that we would have electric underfloor heating throughout the barn complex and had found a company who installed this into churches, so were experts at laying them in large open spaces, such as our barn. But first Kate had to dig the trenches for the power supply (Fig. 260). The system chosen was made by De-Vi, who undertook all the installation, upstairs and down.

In August, once the insulation and heating elements had been laid on the ground floor, the concrete was delivered. This had to be laid all on the same day, so we had numerous concrete mixers arriving and delivering their loads of wet concrete, through the window (Fig. 261).

Inside, Kate and I were trudging through with wheelbarrow loads to try and give an even and level finish, which we achieved. Wading through wet concrete was no easy task, especially on a warm, sunny day in August. For those who understand measurements we laid 6m³ in the drawing room and 4m³ in the living room on one day and 6m³ in the dining room the next day. I don't think either of us have ever worked so hard and under such pressure, before or since.

Figure 261

On August 25, I was in for a huge surprise, if Kate could only get me away from 'The Barn' without telling me why. This she managed and we ended up going to Morston Hall for supper, followed by an overnight stay and breakfast. This was sheer heaven and as Kate had so correctly written on our calendar I was *'lost for words'*.

Early September, Em and Pete made us very envious as they flew off from Stansted to Rome for a short holiday. I was to have a change of scenery on Friday though, as I went to Snowdonia with colleagues from Anglia Housing, to do some leisure walking. It was lovely as the weather was very kind to us and I returned refreshed on Sunday evening.

The 'rest' days were over, and for both of us it was back to paid work during the day, followed by working in the barn during the evening.

My next task was to plasterboard the bedrooms and I must say once I saw the end result it made a huge difference to the look of the rooms. Obviously, I had to work following the electricians first-fixing (Fig. 262) in each area, but within ten days the upstairs was finished.

We were still attending our UEA Landscape Studies course which was due to finish next year. I found this a complete break from working either professionally or at the barn, and after my positive UEA feedback session at the end of the month, it was back to laying floors. Just to make a difficult job a tad more complicated, we dropped and broke the halogen light, so had to lay the scullery and

Figure 262

kitchen hoggin by torch light! We succeeded, and on the Saturday, we smoothed out 6m³ of concrete, starting at 07.30 in the morning and finishing at 09.00. Clearly, we were becoming very proficient.

Outside, in the September sunshine, we tentatively started to clear more of the area for Phase 2, which was to be Kate's Massage Clinic. Given it was just two ground floor rooms and a toilet, the construction work wasn't planned to take that long. However, the boundary wall to the left of the property, that formed an outside wall of her consulting room, was partly below ground level and had to be 'tanked'. This was a job for professional builders, and we sought guidance on how this was to be constructed. This would ensure that when the time came, probably in 2002, we knew what was required.

The next week seemed to be dedicated to Paul, one of our builders, who put up more plasterboard in just about all the rooms downstairs in the barn. Kate, in the meantime, was sanding and oiling beams and trusses upstairs. These were looking good after a couple of coats of Danish Oil which, whilst being hard and sticky work, made all the difference.

On Saturday 7 it was Em's 24th birthday, and on the Sunday, we met up with her and Pete, along with Angus at their new flat in Clapham Common. From there we all went out for lunch before returning home. It was a nice celebratory break.

After further insulation was laid, De-Vi came in on 20 October and laid the heating cables in all the remaining downstairs rooms, the kitchen, hall and scullery, ready for us to lay the final screed. Then over the next two weeks

Keith Reardon fitted all the window frames whilst Anglia Windows fitted the double glazing. By 3 November we were watertight. Ironically this was the week when Norfolk had the worst storms since 1947. With 100 mph gale force winds and much flooding recorded in the south and in York, with over 170 rivers in the country on flood alert. We, on the other hand, were dryish, but the rain continued in Bodham, and in fact it seemed to be getting worse, with the storm coming our way causing some severe local flooding, to the extent that it was only a couple of inches from the bottom of our caravan door! We seriously thought the water would enter the caravan, so everything on the floor that was moveable, was put up a level either on shelves or onto cupboards. We were also concerned that as the caravan was not anchored in any way, it might suddenly start drifting! To our great relief, thank goodness, the water subsided. Inside the Barn, as it was dry and watertight, I laid the base for the Aga to sit on.

Oliver and Jenny gave us a surprise visit, to see how we were progressing – a dangerous thing to do as there was always something that could be done. But on this occasion, they managed to just miss the staircase arriving on the Monday. This was eventually fitted in mid-November.

Towards the end of the month, Kate and I were thinking about what floor tiles we wanted. After viewing some, we brought home 10 samples and as is usually the case, both agreed on the first one we had seen at the shop. We also agreed that these would be laid in all three phases, throughout the ground floor. So, before we committed ourselves, we had to be assured that they would still be available. With that reassurance an order was placed. The first area I laid were the steps in the hall, as it was the smallest section, but it still needed to be in straight lines to marry up with the rest of the barn, when that was laid. With string and lasers to assist, they went down straight as a die, and by the end of November we had a tiled floor. Now, precision laying was required to ensure the rest of the floors matched the pattern.

This was followed in December, when I laid the threshing bricks in the hall and the larger pamment tiles in the dining room. These were the original tiles and bricks that Russell had found, in the first few days of our ownership, whilst he was clearing the site with his JCB. It was wonderful to see them back where they belonged, in the barn where they had originally been laid probably a few hundred years ago. In the case of the bricks these had been put down in a coursed pattern. The same precision was applied to the larger pamment tiles in the dining room, but these were laid in a more traditional floor tile pattern, with a square central area, within which the tiles were set diagonally and surrounded by two rows of tiles, laid at right angles to the walls.

REFLECTIONS UPON A FAMILY

During the year, I had been toying with the idea of moving to a new and better paid job. This had been prompted by the departure of Nick Frazer, a friend and walking colleague at Anglia Housing. On talking to him privately, he told me that he had managed to significantly increase his salary whilst undertaking a very similar role in the private sector. This made me think and in due course I had a couple of interviews, unfortunately though, these were unsuccessful, but the seed had been sown.

We took Christmas Day off, as we had been invited for tea over at Sarah's, my sister. This was most welcome. Just sitting on a sofa was wonderful, and we hoped that with luck by next Christmas, we would be able to do the same at 'The Barn'.

2001

There was to be a very 'bittersweet' start to the year for us both, as I will explain. First though, in January, we graduated from the UEA Centre of Continuing Education, both of us having achieved a certificate of Higher Education in Landscape Studies, which of course was good news. As was the news that on 5 February, Oliver had left the printing paper distributor Masons and started a new job with Manpower, a career change that was to take him much further, in later life.

Then on January 24, I received an email at work from Sophie asking about Angus's Christmas present and where he was at that time, as she wanted to send him an email. It was then that I noticed that the message was sent from Sophie Crowe, at AAT Org. UK (Association of Accounting Technicians) which was her work email. This was the first formal confirmation that I or Kate had received, indicating that Sophie had officially changed her surname from Gosden to Crowe. I had become aware of this possible change when we all attended a family wedding at the end of 2000 as her proposed new name appeared on the reception seating plan, so this had now clearly become 'officially' enacted.

We had a short but courteous exchange, during which she confirmed that she had changed her name a couple of months ago, as she, in her own words, *'wanted to have the same surname as the people I was living with'*. She also stressed that it was nothing to do with not wanting to be a 'Gosden'. In my response, I accepted that at her age, she was free to do what she wanted but that I was saddened that she didn't advise me, in advance. I also commented that we seemed to be growing apart, something that we had talked about when we met her in the Red Lion in Stiffkey, before she moved away. I don't recall receiving any reply to my response, which was really disappointing.

In an effort to close the developing void between us, on 1 February, I invited her to join me for lunch at the Villa D'Este restaurant in Marlow, to celebrate my birthday. She quickly replied to my email with a positive response. A great start, I thought.

We met up and having chatted and ordered our lunch, I commenced the conversation, and I thought at the time I tactfully commented that for a while we had been hearing rumours about her 'association' with her stepfather Dale, along with the change of her name. At that point, Sophie stormed out leaving me to pay the bill for meals we had ordered but that had not even been cooked. This transaction took a few minutes and when outside I found that during this time-gap she had disappeared, leaving me to make my way home. I was mortified and felt suicidal, but this action confirmed to me that there was more to the rumour than mere speculation.

Whilst I made my way home, Kate received two very abusive telephone calls, both ladened with expletives commencing with 'F'. The first from Jeannette at 16.30, and the other from Dale, eight minutes later. They had both slammed the telephone down on Kate, who took the initiative to write down both short conversations. When I arrived home, I read the transcripts from both calls which we have kept in our family papers, and sent Sophie the email (Fig. 263), in a vain attempt to rectify the situation. Again, I don't recall receiving a response. Over the next few months whilst there was communication on both sides, these

Keith Gosden

To: Sophie Crowe
Subject: RE: Meal on 25/2/01

Hi

Thank you for my birthday card which I opened this morning. It was one of three that I had so I expect the postman will bring some more today.

I am very sorry for the problems caused on Sunday. Can I please assure you, again, that I am in not accusing you of any thing. I have no reason to do so nor would I. My only concern was, and still is, to establish how I, as your father, can enjoy what I consider is a normal relationship with my daughter. By this I mean - being able to phone or write to ask how each of us are, to hear your news, to offer support and help when invited to do so etc. In fact exactly the same relationship I have with Emily, Angus and Oliver and of course my own parents.

From the abusive phone calls Kate received whilst I was driving home (she was told to 'F' off by Jeannette and you were called my 'F,ing daughter' by Dale) I guess I have hit a very raw nerve - for which I appologise unreservedly. It would seem that you miss understood what I was saying, or I did not make myself clear, as Jeannette seems to think that I have told a pack of lies. I have not. As I have said, I have not made any accusations so there can be no lies. I only asked questions - you can't lie when asking questions!

Please accept that the purpose of the meal was to try and clear the air and understand where I have failed you in order that I can put that right. What ever you decide to do in or with your life is your own business, you are an adult and I have always wanted you to be independent. All I ask is that I be involved. I don't want to interfere in any way. With your name change I accept that this is what YOU want and that's fine. I happen not to agree with it but that's my problem not yours. My upset was at the way I had to hear of it - not the actual decision.

I sincerely hope that this helps to explain yesterday and that this can be put down to a misunderstanding all round. Good luck with your applications and I hope you hear good news from them both.

I hope to hear from you in the future if you feel able.

All my love, as always

Dad

xxx

Figure 263

were strained, and from Sophie's side very 'to the point' and 'matter of fact'. We have never been given, to this day, an explanation of what was happening at the time. However, further on in the memoir I outline Sophie's explanation on how her circumstances changed, as a result of living with Dale, which I have assumed was the rationale for her actions at this particular time. But even this didn't confirm any of our suspicions or the rumours, around the time of our abortive meal.

On 23 March, whilst at work I received a distressed call from Kate, asking me to take her to Barton, as her mother had unexpectedly died at home the evening before, from a ruptured aorta. The following weekend she had been due to come over to 'The Barn' to celebrate Mothering Sunday with us. So, this news was devastating and bitterly upsetting for all the family. On 31 March, a beautiful funeral service was held for her in Barton Church, led by Jonathan Peel, a close family friend, after which she was laid to rest and united with Kate's father (Figs. 264 & 265).

Now the need to move our belongings out of Kate's mother's garage was to spur us on, to at least bring Phase 1 of the main barn, to a point where it was

Figure 264

Figure 265

actually habitable. In order that I could undertake the plastering, it was time for us both, but especially me, to learn how to render a wall, rather than wait for a professional. We had decided that we didn't want super smooth plaster, mainly because that was far too skilled for me, but also it wouldn't have been in keeping with a traditional barn. As it happened, Kate was on very good terms with the parents of one of her pupils and whose father was a local builder and plasterer. She explained to him what it was that we needed to learn, and he willingly came over to the barn and gave us both a crash course in rendering. Having expert tuition was so important, as personally I had no idea, for instance, that to allow the render to adhere to the flints they first had to have a layer of PVA glue applied. Without that kind of helpful advice and support, I don't think we would have managed.

Figure 266

As it was, I found I was hopeless at corners, so each corner had most of the plaster finishing in a nice wavy manner. It looked fine, as can be seen in the photograph (Fig. 266), and I actually received some nice comments as to how it looked.

With our tutoring concluded, Kate and I set about finishing the rendering with gusto. Kate with brush and PVA in hand, and me with a bucket of mortar and trowel. As we weren't having to create a smooth finish it was a lot quicker than we expected and we went through the barn, room by room. Figure 267 is me working in our bedroom. Not as much plaster fell on the floor as I had expected and given that this is dated July 2001 it was probably one of the last rooms that we tackled.

I did draw the line though, at trying to do the upstairs vaulted ceilings, so they were completed by a professional which allowed us time to collect the first four van loads of our chattels, from Barton and deposit them in 'The Barn'.

Figure 267

I commented a while back that I was considering a change of employment, from public sector to private sector, so I applied for a role as Service Manager with Norwich Union. This was before the company became Aviva. The interview, on 2 April, went well and I was offered the role later that month. As you can see from the extract from my offer letter (Fig. 268), there were conditions that I had to fulfil before I could commence my role. These coupled with my notice period at Anglia Housing, meant that I was to start at Norwich Union (NU) on 4 June 2001

I recall on my final day at Anglia Housing, 25 May, there was a fire alarm. Like all the other staff, I had to exit the building and be checked in by the fire marshals. Whilst outside I was standing next to Peter Lewis, the Chief Executive, who leant over and asked, with a smile on his face, if this was my doing. I apologised for the inconvenience but assured him that I knew nothing about what had happened. However, we all found out soon enough when Mark, my assistant and soon to become my replacement, announced that this was the only way he could have all the staff together, to witness my leaving presentation. I was suitably embarrassed but also very humbled.

My move to NU was a great step up financially and increased my annual salary by over £10,000 to £30,000. On top of this I had a company car, annual bonuses, and was part of the company Sharesave scheme. This was perfectly timed as it enabled Kate and I to put additional finances into the barn conversion and finish the work more speedily.

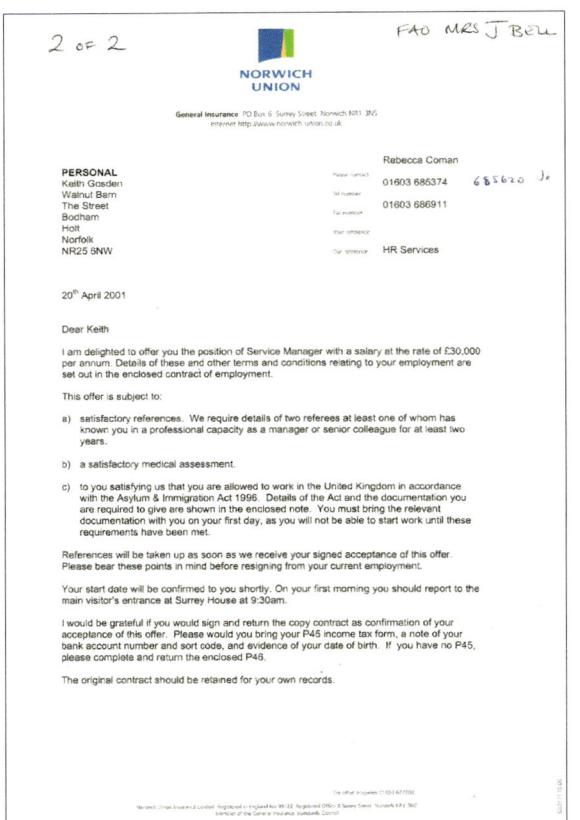

Figure 268

Chapter 6 Ground up with Flints & Blocks 1999 – 2014

Back at the barn, work was progressing at pace with more of the floor tiles being laid (Fig. 269). In the photograph you can also see the plastered walls which both Kate and I had now finished throughout Phase 1. Having successfully laid the tiles on the hall step, my confidence had built up, so I set out to lay the

Figure 269

first and the most important line of tiles, from one end of the barn to the other. As I have said previously, if these weren't laid straight, then the entire floor would be out of line. All went well and both Kate and I were very relieved that they had lined up beautifully, and we were both very happy with the outcome. Oliver and Jenny came for a weekend and whilst they helped with laying the floor, Kate cooked our first meal in 'The Barn' on the Aga! Over the next few weeks with long days in the barn, we both worked incredibly hard which eventually culminated on 29 June, to the laying and grouting of the very last floor tile.

With the floors completed, this now allowed us to collect more and more items from Kate's mother's garage. Following other visits to Barton though, Kate and her siblings Judy, Gillian and Peter had agreed how the inheritance was to be shared, which meant that there were now additional items of Kate's to be brought back to 'The Barn' as well!

In July 2001, Sophie started a new job in Moorgate with the Institute of Chartered Accountants in England and Wales. Whilst on 4 July, Angus was to graduate from Nottingham University with a 2:1 in Computer Science (Fig. 270). After a short break he was successful in securing a job, on a three-month probation period with Detica, in Guildford. Which in 2008 became part of BAE Systems, a British multinational aerospace, defence and information company.

Figure 270

265

REFLECTIONS UPON A FAMILY

For Kate and me, back at the barn when one big job concluded, another suddenly became important. As we had finished plastering and laying floor tiles this was to be, of course, decorating. With colours agreed and litres of paint purchased, walls and ceilings were painted and what a difference it made.

Having already had the Electricity Board on site, to connect a permanent power supply which, as you will recall, had replaced our temporary builder's supply we now needed this to be connected permanently to our fuse box and distribution boards. These had now been completed by our electrician and located in a cupboard within our scullery. At the conclusion of this work, we were hopeful that the sign-off from the Electricity Board, of all our installations would ensue. All was agreed and by 30 September at 08.00 we were to have the luxury of electricity. Well, for an hour or so as there were major issues. But after electricians galore worked both inside and out for two days, by 19.30 we finally had a stable supply on 1 August.

Regrettably, sparks also flew between Oliver and Jenny, but unlike our power supply, their relationship didn't heal and they parted company. Whilst Em and Pete travelled to Madrid, Kate and I went to York. Just another example of the younger generation being more carefree and adventurous than their parents. Still, it was good, but as I was working there for a few days we only had limited time. This didn't stop us from partaking in all the normal tourist attractions which included open top bus tours, walks around the city, visiting the Minster and having tea at Betty's Tea Rooms, a well-known traditional tearoom and restaurant in York for both residents and tourists alike.

The week of our wedding anniversary I took as holiday, and we worked hard to finish off as many of the jobs as we could. We did though, find time for an anniversary dinner at Morston Hall which was delightful. We were now almost ready to move into 'The Barn'. But first of all, Kate and her sisters were to spend a full 12 hours, spring cleaning Shepherds Loke, their mother's house, as it was due to go on the market that week.

Back in 1999 on 11 August, we had exchanged on the purchase of 'The Barn'. Two years to the day, we then moved into the Barn, albeit only into the main part, but it was indeed progress and a momentous day. I noticed on our calendar that it records us as having our first bath in the barn – such a luxury wasn't possible in the caravan, and that night we slept on a mattress on the landing. Not that we slept well at all, as we both had lain awake listening to all the unknown creaks and noises created by the beams etc. The caravan then received our attention and was cleared of our bits and pieces, ready for its disposal.

Chapter 6 Ground up with Flints & Blocks 1999 – 2014

On 11 September 2001, not long after I commenced work in the Norwich office of NU, we heard on the internet that two hijacked aeroplanes had been flown into the Twin Towers of the World Trade Centre in New York, killing almost 3,000 people. I remember being very worried, as were a number of staff. In Norwich, we too had two large office blocks that towered over St. Stephens, located around 100 feet away from where I was working. It would be quite a few days before all the staff were settled and less fearful.

Angus, as I have said, was now working for Detica in Surrey and he was also looking for a house to rent. He was successful and shared this news with us on 25 September. In the same conversation he warned us that following his successful probation period, we might receive a call from the Home Office, in connection with his appointment. Very strange but he would not say any more. Kate and I never knew what he did at Detica, but we understood it was connected to some kind of Governmental security, as we and he, had to not only be 'vetted' but also had to sign the Official Secrets Act. A few days later he rang to say that he had been cleared by the Home Office, so could now take up his new role as a permanent member of staff. Still all very confidential and he moved into his new address on 30 September and the next day collected a new car!

October was to witness Kate and I towing my father's Bosun dinghy, from Barton back to 'The Barn'. He had passed this onto us when he was no longer able to sail her. Not being a great driver when towing, we both undertook this manoeuvre one evening, when the roads were less congested. This was certainly a good idea, and we arrived safely back at the barn and the Bosun, named *Fizz Buzz*, was secured and berthed in our garden! The following day we met up with Kate's brother Peter, at Barton and loaded the very final items into our van, leaving Shepherds Loke completely empty and ready to go on the market. It was 20 October and a sad day for both Kate and Peter.

Due to the urgency of my new role with Norwich Union, as a condition of accepting the job, I had agreed to suspend my judicial duties for a few months. I was originally told that I would have to give up being a JP, but I pointed out that this was not something that they, as a responsible employer, could enforce. Luckily this was accepted, and an agreement was reached. In November 2001, I resumed my duties as a magistrate, and was sitting again, mainly on Saturdays. I was also on the Licensing Bench, so sat mid-week when required to deal with pub landlord changes etc. This sitting pattern, on a regular basis, was easier to accommodate around my paid employment.

During November, Kate and I hung pictures and paintings, in an effort to make sure that by Christmas, 'The Barn' would be looking like a welcoming home. I do recall also sanding the upstairs floors and then staining them, so given the dust I'm not sure how this impacted on the barn being ready for Christmas. Still, all must have been ok, as Kate sorted books onto shelves and brought logs indoors for the fire.

Back in October, Kate and I had gone to view some paintings and jewellery in Westcliffe Gallery in Sheringham. Where I saw a beautiful black pearl necklace from the Pearl Partnership, that I asked to have put aside for me. This was to be a Christmas present for Kate and was duly sent to me on 4 December. However, this didn't arrive when expected, and in a panic, I spoke to Penny Corah who owned the Pearl Partnership, to obtain full details. After an anxious two weeks the parcel turned up at Holt Post Office, so Christmas was safe and could be celebrated.

However, before all the celebrations could take place, there were important tasks to undertake, like having the Aga serviced, ordering a trailer load of logs, writing and posting cards, and of course purchasing and dressing our 15-foot Christmas tree (Fig. 271).

Finally, our annual round-robin letter which by necessity was a very truncated version, was written and circulated (Fig. 272). It conveyed a 'flavour' of a very hectic and bittersweet year and one full of changes.

We had set our sights on being in 'The Barn' by Christmas and we achieved it, with all the furniture in place. With underfloor heating and roaring log fires it was the perfect location to spend the festive season.

Figure 271

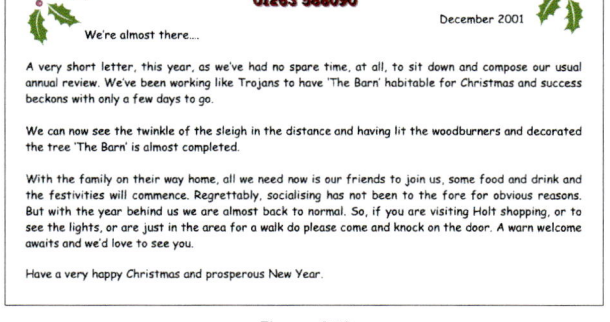

Figure 272

Chapter 6 Ground up with Flints & Blocks 1999 – 2014

2002

2002 started with blocks and flints being laid by Trevor our builder, to create Phase 2, which was to be Kate's Massage Clinic. The floor was ready to have the hoggin laid but regrettably this hadn't been delivered and it finally arrived on 16 January. By the end of January, whilst Kate and I had laid the concrete floor, Trevor had built all the walls, up to wall plate height, laid the hoggin and created a personal access for Kate, into what was to be her reception area, from the proposed conservatory. It looked for all the world like a proper room but without a roof or internal walls. Back in the barn, Kate and I had also been busy hanging curtains on the back screen which was not easy as they were incredibly long and heavy.

Come 2 February, we felt confident enough in our progress, to start work on the open cart shed (Fig. 273). This involved building

Figure 273

piers for two large oak supports for the roof which then had to be secured to the front roof cross- members. For this we required both more hands and the use of a hoist. So once again Andrew our local farmer, came to help. Each cross member slotted into a wedge-shaped bracket on top of the post and had to be secured with a number of long screws. Not easy when the structure moved but once all three were in place it was stable and ready for the rafters to be added.

Half-term week was, as our diary records, 'manic'. When Keith Reardon was working on our oak roof trusses for the cart shed, he happened to ask what we were going to do with our caravan. We hadn't thought about this at all, but we enquired further, and it transpired that he was to build his own house and needed a caravan. Well, that certainly solved a problem, so when it was ready, we agreed that he could take it off our hands. Kate set to, to 'blitz' it, which took almost the entire week, in readiness to hand it over to him. During this time, we had numerous deliveries of bricks, blocks and another cart load of logs for the wood burners. Whilst all this went on, Trevor carried on building. But the end of the week was to witness a monumental moment and another milestone.

The collection of the caravan was very early on 15 February and is shown in three images – Going, Going, Gone! (Figs. 274 – 276). It had served us well over the last year or so and we were confident Keith would find it just as serviceable during his own 'project'.

It took a while to 'drag' the caravan onto his trailer and given its two-year tenure, it had become fairly well established on the site. But with some brute force and persuasion the move commenced.

Figure 274 – GOING...

Figure 275 – GOING...

Figure 276 – GONE!

This was indeed a monumental milestone!

That weekend, 16-17 February, we had our first guests to stay. Wellie and Adam, who we befriended whilst on honeymoon, drove up from Wheathampstead. We all thoroughly enjoyed the weekend, visiting the seaside, travelling from Holt to Sheringham on the steam train, eating and just relaxing. It was really good to see them.

A local carpenter, Paul, had now joined our small group of tradesmen and set about cutting rafters to size for both Kate's massage rooms and the cart sheds. Plus, as Trevor had now moved to building the conservatory, the walls of which didn't take long, Paul was able to put the rafters on this as well.

Chapter 6 Ground up with Flints & Blocks 1999 – 2014

With the caravan gone and us now living in the barn we then turned our attention to the gardens. Whilst this was to be hard work, it was a change, and as the saying goes '*a change is as good as a rest*'. However, by the middle of the year, our 'change' of activity moved back to our previous hard work regime, as we were now faced with clearing out what was once a turnip shed. This was, in time, to become our garage. The original farmer was renowned for never throwing anything away, so we weren't at all surprised that from the contents of the shed we amassed a huge bonfire and disposed of over 100 plastic fertiliser bags. But it was soon cleared and ready to be converted. Next, we created an area in the centre of the front garden, ready for planting some multi-stemmed silver birch trees.

During the weekend, 2-3 March, Em and Pete moved into their new flat in Harwood Court on Upper Richmond Road, and this suited them well. For us it was a time to celebrate my birthday with a belated meal at the Saracens Head. Our first but certainly not the last visit as the food, ambience and company, were perfect.

Throughout March, the garden was to receive most of our attention as the building work was progressing well and didn't need our help. We had a desire to have a stream running from the house into the farm pond but first we had to clear this which was in a sad and sorry state.

On 16 March we – well, Russell and his JBC actually – commenced the pond clearance (Fig. 277). This was not a simple spade and wheelbarrow task, as the pond was the original clay-lined one, which would have been used for the farm horse and carts to be taken through, to clean them after a day in the fields. As such, it was very large and very silted up. It was also a shared pond with Bob our neighbour, who had some years earlier, bought the farm to convert it into three properties. Unfortunately, for him and luckily for us, he ran out of money and had to sell the barn at a reduced price, which we of course purchased. In time we would have to sort out how to secure the garden and pond, but for

Figure 277

Figure 278

Figure 279

now it was a matter of dredging. That could only be tackled by our experienced JCB driver, so enter our regular driver Russell, yet again.

How he managed to dredge the pond without either disrupting the clay lining or his machine getting stuck or toppling over, was beyond me. The photographs (Figs. 278 & 279) tell the story well.

We continued our work clearing the garden and endeavouring to create some sense of normality in what was in fact a large building site.

The next week, we were due to have nine large trees delivered so needed to have the ground ready to receive them. We had, of course, cleared the area for the four silver birches, so I was able to plant these. I also planted some hazel trees and a crab apple. Now that Russell had finished his pond work, there was a location ready beside the pond for the main tree, a large London Plane. However, the size of this required some mechanical help, again from Russell.

By the time he had finished working on the pond, which took just six hours, we could see the real shape of it. This had a low water level, but due to the natural water table, would in time fill up and resemble the original farm pond, once again.

Figure 280

The trees arrived and with Russell's assistance were planted (Fig. 280) with the London Plane beside the pond and the others closer to the barn. Hopefully, by the summer they would all be in leaf.

During the week commencing 18 March, Kate was to have a rest from the barn and gardening, as she was going to How Hill with a group of 'Year Six' High School Girls. To me that sounded much harder than gardening, but all went well and a good time was had by all. Returning on the Friday, she then went to see her sister Gillian in Suffolk, to meet up with her and her other sister Judy, to sort out their mother's jewellery. It was a year since she had died so was still hard to come to terms with, but meeting like this made the necessary task a little easier.

The end of March found us in London on a visit to meet up with Em and Sophie. After a lovely lunch at the Royal Festival Hall, we went shopping at Ikea, which was a new experience for us.

The following day, after staying with Em and Pete, Kate and I sought out the location of 90 Ederline Avenue, SW16. This was the end house, on the Avenue, named 'Homeleigh', and was once the home of my paternal grandparents, George William and Louisa Emma Gosden. It was the first time I had actually seen it and it appeared to be a lovely traditional 1920s style house, in a favoured position (Fig. 281).

Figure 281

The next day 30 March, we learnt that The Queen Mother had died aged 102. Very sad news but not altogether unexpected.

On the Sunday we finished levelling the area around the pond, created some flowerbeds and started to dig out the stream. Russell, who was still on site, helped by levelling out most of the back garden ready for us to landscape, at some point.

The first week in April I took as holiday. Given the ideal weather conditions, I worked hard on the stream and front garden. The stream had to be constructed using two different materials, as due to the natural water levels, part of it didn't require a liner.

Firstly, from the barn to the drive it was with a pond liner (Fig. 282). Then under the drive by way of a couple of large concrete

Figure 282

Figure 283   Figure 284

sewer pipes, followed by a natural water course to the pond (Fig. 283).

By July, the pond was slowly filling up and, in the photograph, (Fig. 284), you can just see the bridge over the drive, which was to enable the pumped water in the stream to flow back to the pond. But that was still two months away!

Oliver kindly came up by train to see us and as was usually the way, he became involved in the building works, this time to give me a hand demolishing a shed and finishing off some of the flower beds. But it was always good to see him and his siblings, whenever they joined us.

By mid-April the back of Kate's consulting rooms had been felted and battened ready for tiling. The front section whilst being ready had to wait until the cart shed was at the same point in the construction process. This was to be reached a week later, which resulted in the front of Kate's clinic and the cart shed both being felted and battened. By the end of April, the consulting room, conservatory and cart sheds were all tiled (Fig. 285). All that was left

Figure 285

were the internal walls which I helped build in early May.

With work progressing well, we decided that we could tentatively start to prepare Phase 3. This would become our Bed & Breakfast wing. I dug out the footings and these were checked and concreted. By early June we even had the block work up to DPC, damp proof course level. This allowed us to lay grass to the front and finish off the flower beds, as future building works wouldn't now interfere with the garden.

Having finished the internal walls in the consulting rooms, the first fixings of electrics and plumbing were completed by the end of May. On 1 May we were delighted to see our first baby moorhen on the pond which was a good sign that all was well. With some trepidation, that we might disturb our visitor, we put railway sleepers around the edge of the pond and finished off the landscaping by sowing 175g of wildflower seed. This activity didn't seem to concern the mother moorhen, who took it all in her stride.

At 04.30 on the morning of 13 June I had a very nasty reality check. I found out, the hard way, that you can't use a render mix to finish a ceiling. With an almighty crash, large sections of the kitchen ceiling came down. Given this, I had to set to and remove the ceilings throughout the ground floor (Fig. 286). Not something I was keen to do. But once down and the plasterboard cleaned, I had them replastered by a 'proper' plasterer. Lesson learnt. Meanwhile, I turned my attention to screeding the floor in Phase 3, something I knew I could do.

Figure 286

With my building repairs completed, I returned my attention back to the garden. We had decided that to secure our front garden pond, we would have a boardwalk built with a fence on top. Having found a tradesman with the appropriate expertise, he started work on 21 June. Seven days later and £1,200 better off, he had finished. Kate too had stained all the woodwork so all I had to do to finish it off, was to put up the rope handrail. With some pond planting

Figure 287

in place, the streams working and the wildflower mix beginning to be seen, the area was completed and ready for nature to work its magic (Fig. 287).

Much of July leading up to the end of the school term, was focused on our paid employments. But the weekends were spent finishing off the areas that the builders had vacated, these being around the front garden, the drive and in front of Kate's consulting rooms. These were now ready for plastering, which, apart from the ceilings, I undertook. The floors too were laid and by 15 September it was ready for the second fixing. I finished off the less important areas, for example finishing touches like the architraves, whilst Kate sanded and stained the woodwork.

It was now that we felt confident enough, to agree a possible opening date for Kate's therapy business, and to seek Angus's help in designing and launching our first website. We were both aghast at his computer skills and the fact that whilst we talked to him on the telephone, about possible changes etc. he could translate these into reality and then show us the resulting web page. This almost instantaneous process was very new to both Kate and me and most impressive. In 2025, of course, people take this for granted. Angus's hard work resulted in an impressive, multi-paged website, that proved a real benefit when the business was launched a few months later, in 2003.

However, having now finished both the driveway and the pond, we decided to take some time together to enjoy a short break in Burford, to celebrate our wedding anniversary. We stayed at the Bay Tree Hotel and wandered around the many antique shops and enjoyed numerous cream teas! We also managed to visit Blenheim Palace and gardens which were both superb. Whilst also visiting a nearby gallery selling John Piper prints, which was a dangerous thing to do given our love of paintings and John Piper in particular. Before we left, we threw down a challenge to them and also to another gallery, to find a particular signed John Piper print after which we then returned to Oxford. I will say more on those challenges later.

After visiting on foot, the old part of Oxford we drove to and wandered around Bourton-on-the-Water and the Upper and Lower Slaughters, staying that night at Meysey Hampton. The concluding surprise treat from Kate, was joining the Inspector Morse tour around Oxford. Being huge fans of the television series, this tour was absolutely fascinating, as were the 'behind the scenes' comments from the tour guide. Within our group there were clearly some very informed aficionados, who obviously knew the episodes inside and out. There were also clearly a number of deeply inquisitive people on our tour, judging by some of the questions asked, the answers to which were to enlighten the rest of us as well.

We left for home, arriving at 21.00 having driven over the weekend, some 463 miles. It was well worth the effort and just the break we both needed.

One aspect about living at 'The Barn' that I clearly recall is the abundance of wildlife. I've mentioned the moorhens, but we also had newts, dragonflies, and even some small fish in the pond. In the gardens we saw all the normal birds including house martins and any number of pheasants. One of which had a deformed foot and limped. Em named him Frank, why Frank I never knew, and despite his injury he got around without too much of a problem. Some of the birdlife was a little scary and I do recall having to catch a sparrow hawk which had inadvertently come in through one of the rear doors. It was big and very strong, and thankfully once covered, it calmed down. Later, I was to see a kingfisher on the boardwalk which I thought was brilliant and most encouraging. The closest we got to any wild birds, apart from the sparrow hawk, was when a couple of blue tits made a nest in a tiny gap next to our bedroom window. It was fascinating to watch them whilst we sat in bed.

On 19 September, we treated ourselves with a visit to the 25th anniversary, *End of Cromer Pier* show, which was not only very professional but also highly

REFLECTIONS UPON A FAMILY

Figure 288

entertaining. We were joined by Peter, Kate's brother and Jane his wife, who also stayed with us for the weekend. Then on the Saturday we all met up with Gillian, Kate's sister and Geoffrey her husband, at Womack Water in Neatishead.

Awaiting us was a Broads Steam Cruiser named *Amaryllis* (Fig. 288). It was a perfect replica of one built in 1830 and took us all on a short but most enjoyable cruise around the broad. The weekend ended with a meal at Morston Hall near Blakeney.

By mid-October all of Kate's consulting rooms had been painted, the woodwork stained, and the lintels oiled. Over the October half-term, the electrical second fixings were completed and apart from grouting the floor tiles, which I finished in early November, the rooms were ready for furniture, curtains etc.

Early November heralded the start of winter preparations, in that the logs for the two wood burners were delivered and stacked neatly in the cart shed. By the time that Holt had switched on its Christmas Lights on 27 November, Kate's consulting rooms were furnished.

In early December, one of the London galleries we had asked to find a John Piper signed print, of Blenheim Palace had risen to our challenge and come back to us with a positive result. The print was ready for collection, and should we be interested they had also acquired another John Piper signed print, of Babingley Church. So, on Saturday 7 December we caught the train from Norwich and made our way to the Marlborough Art Gallery. Prior to leaving London though, for the return 15.00 train, we treated ourselves, along with Em and Pete, to lunch at Brown's in Mayfair, London's oldest luxury hotel. As you may have guessed, we bought both prints and we didn't stop there, for on the Sunday we went to an exhibition in Holt and also bought a Sheree Valentine Daines signed print, entitled *Champagne on Ice*!

The build up to Christmas, our first in 'The Barn' without a huge rush beforehand, was well organised by Kate with cards sent on the 15th, parcels posted the next day, and spare beds prepared for the family, some who arrived just before the 25th, whilst others came just after. However, the Barn was to have its final display of contempt when on 23 December the cobbler's chest fell off the wall and I had to refix it with larger brackets! Luckily none of the ornaments on top were damaged!

Kate, Angus and I had a very pleasant Christmas lunch at The Pheasant Hotel in Kelling. Caroline his young lady joined us from Birmingham on Boxing Day, and Sophie who now seemed to be more amenable to us, arrived on 27 December, as did Em and Pete. Then to complete our family gathering I collected Oliver from Letchworth. We all enjoyed one of Kate's delicious meals, after which a complicated card game was played, which required Em to frequently check the rules (Fig. 289). The next day they all went off to visit their other parents, before returning to their homes.

Figure 289

That was 2002. A year of hard work and some lessons learnt on how not to plaster ceilings! But the year ended well, and we looked forward to 2003. But before the New Year was heralded in, we hung our newly acquired artwork, then sat down with a glass in hand, in front of the wood burner, where we somewhat self-indulgently, admired and wondered at just what we had achieved, both inside the barn and outside in the garden, and compared it all to our purchase back in 1999 (Fig. 242).

We were both suitably impressed and justifiably so, and greatly admired each other's handiwork!

2003

Much of January and February was spent tidying up in 'The Barn', preparing a business plan for Kate's Therapy business and clearing the garden. To support the latter, we had twenty tonnes of topsoil delivered on 23 February which was used to create the flower beds in the front garden. However, there was one good piece of news for Sophie, when she passed her driving test on 25 February. So now all members of our family had full driving licences.

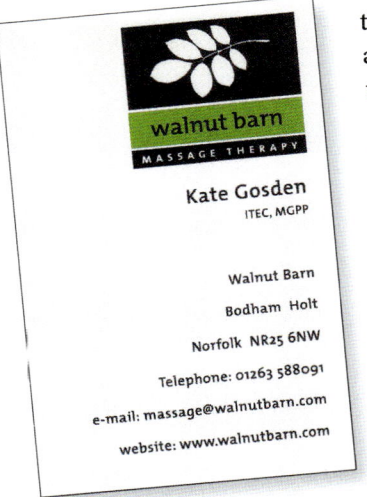
Figure 290

The first weekend in March was spent digging over the new flower beds and laying grass turf which was always pleasing, as it always made such a difference to the garden and this time was no exception.

Kate attended a couple of seminars on starting a new business that obviously were valuable. Stationery was printed and business cards (Fig. 290) distributed which were clearly working, for just before her birthday, she had her first client at her clinic on 13 March.

Her actual birthday was more like a *'Gardeners' World'* day rather than a relaxing time. Together we laid more turf, this time around the pond, planted some lavenders and roses in the flower beds and 50 'whips' which in a couple of years' time we hoped would form a good hedge alongside the driveway. Not very relaxing but it was very satisfying.

Over the last few months, in memory of Kate's mother, a number of kneelers for Barton Turf church had been made by some of the local parishioners, who all knew her well. On the Sunday 23 March, a service of Dedication to these kneelers, led by the Bishop of Thetford, was held at Barton church and attended by most of Kate's family, who after the service came to 'The Barn' for lunch. This was a very fitting memorial to their mother, who was an avid supporter of the church, as well as being in the choir.

Following all the hard work in the garden, Kate and I decided that we deserved a short break before Easter. To that end, on Saturday 11 April we set off for The Lake District, where we had a relaxing time and were able, over the following days, to visit Barnard Castle, Appleby Market, Caldbeck Fells and Cockermouth.

It can be very windy around the Lakes, as the photograph of the tree (Fig. 291) testifies, but for us it was warm and pleasant. In Cockermouth, we looked around Wordsworth's childhood home, but we found this was disappointing, as it was more of a museum of his later life and in our opinion didn't reflect the era of his childhood in Cockermouth.

Chapter 6 Ground up with Flints & Blocks 1999 – 2014

Figure 291

Figure 292

During our time away we stayed in a B&B on a working farm which was within easy reach of a number of other places that we also wanted to visit. So, we spent time at Beatrix Potter's Hill Top Farm and wandered around Loweswater, before we returned home on the 16th, via two more gardens en route. The photograph (Fig. 292) is of me at Loweswater. This was a lovely break and gave us several new ideas for landscaping at the barn. In fact, no time was wasted as we started gardening again the very next day after our arrival home!

For Easter and to celebrate Angus's 24th birthday, we had most of our family home and managed to have a birthday meal together. With all of them now driving and wanting to see friends whilst in Norfolk, 'The Barn' was very similar to a B&B, with children coming and going all the time. But that's what families develop into, so we weren't concerned and loved having them at home.

At work I was asked if I would be interested in joining a new team being set up that was to deliver key changes to the company. The team was very small with Stuart Smith as its Director and Colin Guthrie as Head of the Programme Office. I was to be interviewed by both Stuart and Colin and subsequently was invited to join them.

I readily accepted and was now part of the project entitled the UK Cost and Efficiency Programme. Over the coming weeks more colleagues were to join us. The programme was very confidential as it was to deliver, in just two years, annual ongoing savings of £250m per annum which included some 4,000 redundancies in the UK. The new role required me to move to a dedicated secure floor in Kings House, located in Surrey Street, Norwich, opposite the main NU offices.

During this time, I was going to London and York for work on a regular basis, as the programme was shaping up to be much larger than I expected. The programme, which was driven by a desire to reduce costs, had a degree of irony.

The need for our programme was driven by the fact that there was also a need to address the serious lack of investment in the office accommodation, over a number of previous years. This was brought into sharp focus back in April 2001, when a window fell from the fifth floor of an office block in Norwich and landed in St. Stephens. In October the BBC had the headline of *'Firm fined after window plunge'*, along with the photograph (Fig. 293). Luckily, no one was injured but the company were fined for a breach of Health and Safety and ordered to pay £30,000, plus £11,000 for costs. The solution for ensuring that nothing like this happened again was to be radical. Our programme commenced with almost all the NU offices across the UK, be they large or small, being sold, then leased back to Norwich Union with an agreement in conjunction with NU that they would be fully refurbished by the new owner. To avoid any future litigation over lack of maintenance the new owner would be responsible for their long term-upkeep. Hence the new multi-million-pound programme that I had recently joined.

Figure 293

I was Programme Office Manager and reported to Colin. The work to be carried out was to last for several years and required two new offices to be built on the outskirts of Norwich, thus enabling staff to be rotated into these whilst their particular offices were refurbished. Some years later one of the offices was sold for £7.1m, offsetting some of the refurbishment costs.

It was a complex and for obvious reasons a very confidential programme. It was also complicated by some of the offices being owned by the Norwich Union Pension funds. This required some careful internal negotiations to ensure that the pension fund didn't lose out financially, whilst also keeping our own programme finances within their strict budget.

One of the issues that arose, when talking to a number of potential purchasers of the property portfolio, was what was to happen to Marble Hall. This still forms the interior of Surrey House, a Grade 1 listed building (Fig. 294)[26] and was considered the 'home' of Norwich Union.

---

26 Marble Hall, Surrey House, Norwich. Norfolk-geograph-5673905-by-Adrian-S-Pye.jpg – Wikimedia Commons.

Chapter 6 Ground up with Flints & Blocks 1999 – 2014

It was built from marble which was originally destined for Westminster Cathedral but as there were financial concerns around the cost of the cathedral's work, it was purchased by George Skipper, the Norwich architect of Surrey House. Norwich Union was to benefit from this, and Surrey House with its Marble Hall interior, was built and opened in 1906 as their head office. Clearly, in 2003 this building was not suitable for modern offices, but to sell it was not an option. Equally,

Figure 294

the main purchasers didn't have a solution so it was suggested that it could be used as a museum. This idea stemmed from the Bank of England in London, who had created a similar use for one of their buildings. I went with the now retired previous NU Chief Executive, to be shown around their solution, in order that we could gauge if this could be a viable option for Surrey House. It was a successful visit, but within a few weeks one of the prospective bidders for the refurbishment contract, had come up with a solution. Their suggestion was to use the Marble Hall as a 'grand reception', whilst at the rear it was proposed to build a two-storey glass atrium. This could house a restaurant, and the finished complex would link all three of the surrounding office blocks. Thus, uniting all the accommodation together for ease of access. This was accepted by the Board of Directors and the Norwich City Council planning department and was subsequently incorporated

Figure 295

as part of the main contract. This can be seen (Fig. 295)[27] as a green/grey flat roof connected to the rear of Surrey House, with its stunning stone facia. On the other three sides, are the now linked and fully refurbished offices.

---

27 www.webbariation.co.uk 2015, Bild-Kunst Urhebernummer 221 16 27.

So, as you can imagine, my work was very hectic at Norwich Union, as well as at home with a somewhat smaller, miniscule building project, in comparison!

Em and Pete had been on an Italian holiday and returned on 13 May. We had also decided, as a family, that we would have a summer holiday, in Portugal in July. Kate had found a superb villa, so that and associated flights had to be booked and pre-paid, and all this gave us something to look forward to.

In the meantime, spring half-term was spent 'titivating' the garden, with an old wooden ladder positioned over the drive and climbers being planted to eventually trail across it. The final brickwork was being completed on the conservatory, and I began to look at Phase 3.

During this time, Em had been studying for an Italian AS exam, that comprised a matrix of examinations covering Italian listening, reading, oral, translation and written papers. Her final exams commenced on 2 June with listening and writing that apparently, all went well.

At the end of June, Sophie came home for the weekend and on the Saturday, we had our first barbecue at 'The Barn'. The following day all three of us went out for tea and a walk around Baconsthorpe Castle, which is in the next village to Bodham. Life was still difficult for Sophie and our general relationship seemed strained, but we were still meeting up and had time together, so that was a positive.

July 2003 seemed to be the month for clearing the old bullock shed for Phase 3, our B&B wing (Fig. 296). This began with a general clearance of weeds and the odd elder bush, followed by lifting the concrete floor, but only where I could do this by hand. There were areas that required the extra assistance of a mini digger which had to wait until the next weekend.

Figure 296

With this delivered, Kate and I set about lifting and breaking up the concrete. Figure 296 is prior to our work, and the grey block structure housed a previous builders' loo, which was totally removed early on.

Chapter 6 Ground up with Flints & Blocks 1999 – 2014

Working on the digger made life much easier and generally, Kate was using the machine whilst I broke up the larger pieces with a sledgehammer. We changed over when there were some very large areas of concrete that I attempted to move.

One particular area didn't want to budge and giving it one last go with the digger, whilst still in the cab I very nearly brought both the digger and me crashing down (Fig. 297). Luckily all was well, but I was a little less 'gung-ho' going forward. By the end of the weekend though, all the concrete had been lifted.

Figure 297

The next week, Russell came with his JCB and a friend's ten-tonne lorry to remove the concrete which took just two loads. It was a little depressing when you saw a pile of concrete, that had taken over two days to lift, just being swallowed up in a couple of hours by a JCB. It was made to look so easy! The end result though, was now ready for us to lay the hoggin (Fig. 298) and start the final build on the site.

Figure 298

Not quite so thrilling as nearly toppling over a mini digger, was Kate's visit on 25 July, to see me sitting with a judge, hearing appeal cases in Norwich Crown Court. This was my first sitting in the Crown Court, so she came to experience the day from the back of the court. Unfortunately, as often happens the cases didn't last long, so we had lunch and made our way home, but it was nice that Kate could see me in my official capacity.

Kate had decided to treat herself to a new car, a four-month-old ex-demo. So, I met her at the garage, and she took it for a test drive, which sealed the deal! The last time I had seen Kate so happy driving a car, was in Malta.

Figure 299

Now, her new car was a shiny blue Megane Cabriolet (Fig. 299), and by the look on her face when taking it for a test drive, it was just as thrilling as a Maltese 4x4.

Angus came home just for the weekend to see us before Kate and I caught a flight from Norwich to Faro in Portugal. Unfortunately, despite having left home at 18.25 and arriving on time, the take-off was delayed, and we arrived in Faro at 21.40, where three quarters of an hour later we met up with Oliver. We picked up our hire car, had some supper in Purgatório and went to meet the owners, who escorted us to our villa, Quinta da Promessa in Lentiscais (Figs. 300 & 301).

Figure 300

Figure 301

Figure 302

Chapter 6 Ground up with Flints & Blocks 1999 – 2014

To say that the villa was fantastic was a huge understatement, as can be seen in these two photographs of the front, and the rear with its pool. It was in a perfect location for a wonderful two weeks.

The villa was surrounded by an olive farm and having been there a very short time, we couldn't believe our eyes when the local farmer turned up in his tractor, (Fig. 302) bringing Ivone his wife to work, who was our housekeeper. This was to be a regular scene every day.

We were so well looked after, with Ivone cooking breakfast, and keeping the villa spotless.

The only minor issue, as I recall, was communication, which was not always easy, as Ivone spoke mainly Portuguese with some French. But we all managed, and were able to establish where the shops were to obtain the basics etc. The weather on arrival was 104°, and only dropped to 84° at night! It remained like this for most of our stay, which made the pool very welcome and well used!

Em and Pete arrived later having flown to Lisbon, where they caught the train to Albufeira where we met them, and we all returned to the villa. Like us, they were impressed with the accommodation. Unfortunately, Angus was unable to join us due to skydiving and BASE jumping commitments and Sophie also couldn't be with us.

During the fortnight we managed to undertake some touring and sightseeing. One excursion being to Paderne Castle, a 12th century building that was damaged by an earthquake in 1775. Kate, Em and Pete explored but both Oliver and I felt uncomfortable, so whilst we looked around the Water Mill close by, neither of us ventured up to the ruins.

Another excursion on Friday 1 August, was to Monchique via Alte and Silves. The views en route were stunning with beautiful red roofed houses all nestled on a steep slope, encircled by tree covered mountains. It took us half an hour to walk to the Convento de Nossa Senhora do Desterro (Monastery), one of the oldest Marian sanctuaries, which had a magnificent ceiling, with equally stunning views and surrounded by cork trees, so was well worth the effort.

Figure 303

As Oliver was only able to join us for the first week, we had to take him back to Faro for his flight home on Sunday 3 August 2003.

On the 8th, Kate and I went to explore the Praia Grande beach (Fig. 303). This is what I would call a typical Portuguese seashore.

REFLECTIONS UPON A FAMILY

Figure 304

Lots of sand and sunshades which, given it was 101° that day, were certainly needed.

Our penultimate day was spent on the coast in Portimão, in and around the harbour (Fig. 304). On Sunday we took Em and Pete to the station, then made our way to the airport, to return to a wet and dull UK. Back down to earth!

The twelfth of August was a big day for us but especially for Kate, who collected her new car from the garage. Unfortunately, the day was both very foggy and raining, so a drive home with the wind in your hair was not possible. But it was still good fun and so nice to have a mode of transport that didn't need constant garage attention.

That week, Em also received her Italian AS-level results which were excellent. She passed with an A grade which, given that in three of the exams she achieved 100%, was perfectly justified.

Figure 305

The next weekend was devoted to a grand tidy up in the back garden with a large bonfire, which included burning a small wooden trailer that was no longer needed. All the corrugated iron from the roof of a lean-to was put into the old 'storage' caravan, which was then hauled onto a trailer and destined for the scrap heap (Fig. 305).

Bonfires seemed to be the order of the day, as in September, having scythed the back garden, I had to have another one to remove all the grasses, nettles, and thistles. However, some of my time at the weekends was spent laying the membrane for the damp proof course, in Phase 3, ready for 30 tonnes of concrete that arrived on 27 September. This was all raked and levelled by hand in the course of one day (Fig. 306).

Chapter 6 Ground up with Flints & Blocks 1999 – 2014

Figure 306   *Figure 307*

This was hard work, so the next day I was pleased to go for a walk along Weybourne beach with Kate, in preference to manual work at the barn.

With all the attention on Phase 3, I need to say that whilst this was ongoing, two of our builders, Paul and Gary, were putting rafters up, battening and felting the roof of the cart shed, ready for tiling.

During the autumn half-term, Trevor our bricklayer, was working hard on Phase 3 and making excellent progress. The design for the front outside elevation of this area, was to have brickwork up to the bottom of the windows, and then wood cladding up to the roof. This was not only cheaper but also a lot quicker to build. This proved to be the case as on 3 November, Trevor had put in three windows (Fig. 307), before the scaffolding was erected to enable work on the wall plate, and subsequently the roof to follow on swiftly. Once at wall plate level on Phase 3, Trevor turned his attention to the cart shed floor, where he laid three tonnes of crushed concrete, which was screeded over at a later date. He then concentrated on Phase 3 again, to a point in early December, when the six roof trusses were installed. By mid-December the roof insulation was fitted, and it was battened and felted very soon afterwards. Our aim was to have this watertight by Christmas. Would this be achieved, we wondered?

Oliver would often come home to help with the work, but we hadn't seen him much recently. We discovered that this was for a very good reason, for on 10 October he advised us that he was taking Jude on holiday, to Drymen in Scotland. She was a young lady he had been dating for a year, and this was my first recollection of him and Jude being together. We were to meet her for the first time when they both came to stay and we celebrated my 48th birthday, at the end of February in 2004.

REFLECTIONS UPON A FAMILY

For a break from building and to give time to Sophie, Kate and I met her in London for a visit to the Horse of the Year show. Unlike Sophie, I wasn't a rider, and I thought it may not be particularly interesting for me. How wrong I was, the show and expertise of the competitors held all of my attention and was most enjoyable. The train journey home though, was a disaster due to the volume of passengers, and rather took the shine off the weekend.

Back at 'The Barn', despite the best efforts of Trevor and Paul, they were beaten by high winds, heavy rain and snow, which meant that our Christmas target was missed. We were close, but not totally watertight, so that now had to be our aim for early January. Christmas Day was spent at 'The Barn' with Em, Pete, Angus and Oliver all at home. We also had the pleasure of my mother and father, which was nice. The children were only with us for a couple of days and then one by one they returned to London, Guildford and Letchworth, and then back to work. My parents had already returned to Ashill, where they lived, late on Christmas Day and Sophie was to join us later. But she left on 30 December, for a short rendezvous at Snetterton, with her young man. She did return though, to celebrate New Year with us.

2004

2004 was to pick up quickly where 2003 had left off, with Trevor battening and felting with some help, or was that hinderance, from me. Having made the main Phase 3 structure almost watertight, attention was turned to building the internal walls. These would create two double bedrooms, one with an en suite, the other with a separate bathroom plus a communal guest sitting room, which overlooked the stream and front garden, and was to be known as the Garden Room. Whilst Trevor was building the walls, Paul worked on the trusses for the garden room. These were soon completed, and the final area battened and felted.

Unfortunately, the weather was very wet and windy, which resulted in Kate and I twice having to bail out the area. Other than not having glass in the windows it was completely watertight once more. By mid-January though, the bedroom walls were almost finished and with a corridor down one side, we were able to see the size of all the rooms. Then at the end of the month, we had snow instead which rendered some roads impassable, into and around Norwich! During this time, we obviously couldn't safely work outside, so Kate and I turned to making marmalade! We made and potted up 12lbs altogether, ready for use when the family came home.

By very early February, Trevor had finished as much of the internal wall as he could, given that Paul was still working on the roof. In between the rain showers I had been laying roof tiles over the end bedroom, and this was now ready for Trevor to start laying the ridge tiles. Unfortunately, Paul had an accident and fell off the roof and whilst not too serious he was off-site for a while, so we asked our previous roofers if they could finish the job, which both they and Trevor were more than happy about.

When Kate left school, at the age of 18, she had trained as a nursery nurse in Lowestoft. During this time, she had had a number of incredibly young babies in her care, either awaiting foster or adoptive parents. One young girl called Andie, having spent her first three years in Kate's care, was adopted by Patsy and Peter. They regularly kept in touch with Kate, and now we had been invited to stay with Andie and her own family, in Rochester, Kent. She was married to another Keith and had her own three children, so Kate was very excited to see both her and her parents, for the first time since they left Lowestoft all those years ago.

The weekend was a resounding success with much to talk about, some exchange of photographs, and a few tears of joy along the way. We stayed overnight and late on Sunday afternoon before we returned to Norfolk, we did a little shopping which included the purchase of an antique dressing table mirror.

Half-term week followed, and Kate had several massages booked whilst I worked in London and Norwich. The work continued on the rooves and the builders prepared the doors and windows in Phase 3. The glaziers followed and we were soon to be totally watertight. By March, the access from the main barn into the garden room had been created, which was much easier, as it didn't involve us having to go outside in the rain or the snow. We also booked the plumber and electrician to undertake the first fixings, so Jon the plumber, was the first to start on 20 March.

However, on Kate's birthday, 15 March 2004, we celebrated this together at home, with me cooking a birthday meal. There was also a second celebration that day, as all the work on the roof had finally been finished! Later in the week, Sophie took her stage 1 British Horse Society (BHS) examination in Surrey, which seemed to go well.

My father had decided that he would have an operation on his knee, so on the

Tuesday he had been admitted to the local BUPA hospital with the operation planned for the next day. All went well, and after a couple of weeks recovering and learning how to walk again, he was home.

Figure 308

The rest of March, leading up to Easter, saw a lot of 'hidden' work on the electrics, including the installation of underfloor heating, before the concreting of the floors (Fig. 308).

At Easter, the tradition still was to have an Easter egg hunt, and we have kept this custom despite all our children being grown up. But that Easter, we had also found four real eggs which our wildlife, in the form of a pair of moorhens, had laid in a nest which they had built in the reeds, on the edge of the pond. We just hoped that all the work on site hadn't disturbed them.

On Good Friday, Angus flew off to Switzerland, to join some friends for a few days skydiving. We, on the other hand, celebrated Easter, and prepared for our own short break in Jersey, staying at the Almorah Hotel in St. Helier. On our first day we wandered around the town, had tea outside at Henleys, followed in the evening by an Italian meal, at La Braca, in St. Aubin Bay. Whilst at the meal, I presented Kate with her mother's signet ring. The ring was engraved with the family crest – a cockerel above a sturgeon fish (Fig. 309). When Kate inherited this, from her mother, it was very difficult to see the engraving. So, one day in my lunch hour at work, I had redrawn the image on a large sheet of paper, much to the consternation of my colleagues, and had the image re-engraved by a jeweller at Winsor Bishop, in Norwich.

To me it looked really good and by the reaction of Kate, she too, agreed. Kate, like her mother did before her, wears it all day, every day. However, there was one time when I arrived home to find Kate in floods of tears, as she had been outside gardening and

Figure 309

the ring had fallen off, and she couldn't find it. I went out to where she thought she had lost it, and after a long and very meticulous search, by a stroke of luck, I found it. Tears of sorrow, turned to tears of joy.

Figure 310

Back in Jersey, we spent the next few days with the aid of a hire car, searching out the main sights and buildings. These included the botanic gardens at Samarès Manor in St. Clement, the beautiful town of Gorey, where we climbed up to Mont Orgueil Castle (Fig. 310[28]) and, of course, a visit to Jersey Goldsmiths. Here we saw some fabulous jewellery, some once owned by Marilyn Monroe, Elvis Presley, James Dean, and other celebrities. It is always 'dangerous' for either of us to go into a jeweller, so to go back to one for a second time was just too tempting, even though there was a genuine reason, which was to have Kate's mother's signet ring resized. We ended up purchasing a gold necklace, and a pair of pearl earrings. The necklace needed to be lengthened, so this was to be carried out on-site and then sent to us direct at Walnut Barn, Bodham.

Later in the day, we drove through some very narrow lanes to reach Plémont Bay, on the northwest coast. Despite it being a high tide it was lovely, very wild and dramatic, and a total contrast to the east coast. As the mist was rolling in, we decided to make our way to Jersey Pearl.

This was both very interesting and again ultimately expensive. At the shop, we once more met a really knowledgeable assistant, who helped us to select two different pearl necklaces, and some earrings. Kate, at the time, was wearing a black pearl necklace and earrings and she asked if they could be authenticated. It turned out, that the earrings were Tahitian, whilst the necklace was made of Japanese sea oyster pearls. When the assistant looked more closely at the necklace, she said that ideally it should be re-strung and showed us why. We agreed to this being carried out but explained that we were going home in a couple of days. This was not a problem, and the next day we collected it. It was then that we met the lady who had re-strung all the pearls and found out that she also had strung necklaces for the late Queen Mother!

On the Thursday we walked along the causeway to Elizabeth Castle, where we spent two hours looking around. The castle is located on a tidal island just off

---

28 Photograph copyright of jerseyheritage.org acknowledged.

REFLECTIONS UPON A FAMILY

Figure 311

Figure 312

St. Helier and was built in the 1600s. Our photograph (Fig. 311) was taken from the battlements which date to when Sir Walter Raleigh was Governor of Jersey. The island and castle were occupied by the Germans in WWII. The photograph (Fig. 312) is the Jersey Liberation sculpture and commemorates the liberation of Jersey on 9 May 1945. The statue was unveiled by Prince Charles in 1995, on the 50th anniversary.

After a lovely meal at Dorans Courtyard Bistro, in St. Helier, we packed and settled down for the night. Only to be awoken at 05.00 by the alarm clock!

We made our way to the airport and caught the 07.00 flight back to Stansted. On the way home we called into Newport in Essex to have coffee with Gillian, Kate's sister and subsequently arrived home at 13.30.

There was no real rest for Kate as on the very same day at 17.00 she had a new client for a massage, and on the Saturday, I helped both Steve and Lee install the conservatory window and door frames. Uni-glaze came on Monday 19 April, to measure up for the glass, which was also to be put in the roof.

Oliver and Jude came to see us for a weekend, at the end of April, and spent most of the time with me, installing insulation! We did manage a walk along Cromer beach though, which was glorious, as it was a nice sunny day.

On the Monday, Uni-glaze was installing the conservatory glass roof. At the end of the week, it was time to screed both Bedroom One and the corridor in Phase 3 and all this area was finished by the middle of May. By the end of the month, I had also finished screeding the conservatory, so all these rooms were now ready for tiling.

During the summer half term, 31 May – 6 June, most of my time was spent plaster boarding Phase 3, and having returned to work, the final area in the garden room was completed over the next weekend.

For the first time on the ninth of June, Kate and I went to the Hampton Court Palace Garden Festival in London and thoroughly enjoyed the day. We were so pleased we had travelled by car, as we had not only purchased two antique milk churns, along with a large selection of silk flowers, but en route home, we picked up Em from Putney and all three of us travelled back to Norfolk. Three days later, Em was to return by train to her home.

By Sunday 18 July, we recorded on the calendar that Phase 3 was all ready to plaster, and then on 30 July we recorded that all ceilings had been completed. This didn't take as long as the plasterer originally thought, so the cost was reduced by £700!

My turn to plaster was next, and on 8 August, I started to render the walls, commencing with the furthest bedroom and its en suite. This was a long job, as following a day's work I had to do it in the evenings, but by the next weekend I had finished both rooms. With still lots to do, I took a week's holiday at the end of August and worked like a trojan, until Kate finally recorded and underlined in red on the calendar, 'FINISHED ALL PLASTERING IN PHASE THREE'.

My next task was to commence laying the floor tiles throughout the area. As with the ones in the main barn it took some time to ensure that they would all line up and look professional. Once this was complete, I could start laying, followed by the grouting, some of which Kate did whilst I was away for work in Bournemouth. Both of which were long, hard and tedious jobs, but the final result was certainly worth the effort.

As each room was completed, Bob our electrician, would come in and complete the second fixing, so we had to keep going at pace to ensure he wasn't standing around with nothing to do.

The 18 September was a momentous day, but nothing to do with the barn. Firstly, Kate and I went to a Lacy Scott and Knight auction, in Bury St. Edmunds and were successful in bidding for two clocks and a table. The main one was a long case clock made by Francis Dusgate of Holt. We didn't know it at the time but to be successful we had to outbid Mike Darley, a clock restorer, from whom we had already purchased two clocks and for many years he looked after all our time pieces.

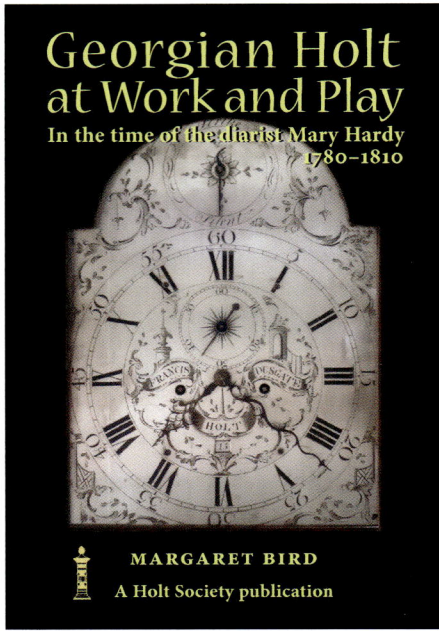

Figure 313

He congratulated us after the auction and confirmed that it was indeed a very good purchase. The clock face was later to appear on the front of a booklet (Fig. 313) which was published by the Holt Society, during the time that I was the Chairman.

Secondly, on the same day of the auction Angus moved to Gloucester, and finally and most importantly, Em and Pete announced their engagement. We were surprised but delighted. What a day!

During October, Angus was working abroad for three weeks, so we had no idea where he was, or what he was doing! But were very pleased to know on 1 November, that he had arrived back in the UK, safe and well.

On the 18th, Pete commenced a new job with the BBC. On the same day, Kate and I went with a friend from Norwich Union and her daughter to the Apollo in Hammersmith, to an evening show with Billy Connolly. Kate and I had afternoon tea at Claridge's, before we all met up at the theatre. I have to say that I haven't laughed so much for many a year, both prior and since. How anyone can bring an audience to the point of crying with laughter, just by talking about the colour 'beige', I will never know. But I guess that's the professionalism of Billy Connolly.

By the end of October, Kate and I had finished decorating all the rooms in Phase 3, now referred to as the B&B. Aldiss, in Fakenham, delivered all the necessary beds, linen, towels etc. So, much of Kate's half-term holiday was spent cleaning and making the B&B habitable.

There was also a wedding to think about with Em, who sought our help in the basics for example who should be invited and when, along with where it would or could be held.

On 10 November the B&B came to life, as Bob had finished his electrical work, and the lights were on! However, it was short lived, for when we connected the underfloor heating to the circuit, we had a power cut, in the early hours of the next day, followed by another one the day after at 06.45, and yet another one at 22.20 on the Friday. Finally, the electricity board came out and decided that a new fuse was required in the substation. This seemed to work, much to our and Bob's relief.

Chapter 6 Ground up with Flints & Blocks 1999 – 2014

Towards the end of November, we met up with Angus in Cheltenham and had a delicious meal with him in the Prestbury House Hotel. The next day he took us to a warehouse where he climbed, followed by lunch, and then we journeyed home.

The first couple of weeks in December were spent carrying out a final clean in the B&B and deciding where furniture and ornaments would be best placed, to create the right atmosphere for our guests. I must say, that when this was all decided the whole place did look very welcoming and 'homely'.

On 13 December, Kate's business advertisement was processed and placed in the *Yellow Pages* – at the time this was the best way to advertise as very few people had access to the internet. This had only started to become popular in 1995, with Netscape Navigator. Google was to start three years later, on 4 September 1998. It's hard to believe now, given the rapid growth in the use of the internet, but in 2004 we were all quite content to look up the details of a company, in a volume of the Yellow Pages. In just a similar way that we found a particular telephone number, which necessitated a thumb-through a printed and very thick telephone directory. How times have changed – now you just ask 'Alexa' a question and she will tell you the answer verbally!

Returning to December, Christmas was delivered on the 23rd, in the form of a 16-foot-high Christmas tree, which was as tall as the back screen of 'The Barn', which itself extended to both floors! The tree was duly decorated, the meat was collected from the butchers in Holt, along with the vegetables etc., so we were all prepared.

Em, Pete and Sophie arrived on Christmas Eve, whilst Oliver came on Christmas morning. Angus wasn't able to join us, but we did have a long telephone call with him. Before lunch we all went to the Dun Cow in Salthouse where we enjoyed a festive drink, in front of a log fire. The tradition then, that has now regrettably stopped due to a change of ownership, was that the first round was free, with customers paying for any subsequent drinks ordered. Needless to say, on that Christmas morning the pub was packed and even more popular than usual.

Post Christmas and the leading up to New Year, was a little like a merry-go-round, with family coming and going, and the New Year was celebrated by Em and Pete in London, Sophie in Diss, and Oliver in Letchworth. Kate and I were in Coltishall, at a friend's party and we didn't return to 'The Barn' until about 03.00 on New Year's Day!

So overall, a good year and we looked forward to 2005, with its very special family gatherings.

2005

The 2005 New Year commenced with, just for a change, a lot of hard manual labour. Our first challenge in January was to start hard landscaping the back garden. With over a thousand flints piled up beside the piggeries, we decided to make use of some of them. This entailed me building four dry-flint walls about a metre high, in the style of seaside gabions, to create a formal path that led out to the field next door (Fig. 314). The finished work can be seen later in figure 456, in Part 3.

Figure 314

This was followed with the side driveway, to the B&B entrance, being dug up by BT in order to lay a cable. Never being a couple to miss an opportunity, once the trench was all filled in, Kate and I immediately weeded and levelled the drive in preparation for the final layer of shingle.

February took Kate to the great metropolis of London. A fun but exhausting few days helping Em and Pete taste various foods for their reception. This was followed by wedding dress hunting with Em, in which I wasn't involved, but understood from the feedback, that it wasn't as successful as had been hoped. Many dresses were apparently tried on, but none had the 'wow' factor.

With Kate having now returned to Norfolk, we planted lots of snowdrops that she had given to me for my 50th birthday, and I hasten to add here, she had also bought me a beautiful painting by Sheree Valentine Daines, entitled *Les Secrets*.

Then in March, I commenced making the internal doors for the Bed and Breakfast. These were wide panelled ledge and brace doors, and I had made a 'jig', in order that when all the pieces were put together, each door was identical. Each section of the door was hammered together using handmade nails that we had sourced on the internet. Although I say it myself, they did look extremely good and were subsequently replicated throughout 'The Barn'.

On 10 March, as frequently happened, Angus telephoned us from Heathrow Airport to say that this time he was just about to board a plane to Arizona! Was this work or skydiving, we were not told. I guess it was the former, as he clearly couldn't tell us why he was going. However, if it had been skydiving, he might not have said, as he was aware of our parental concerns and didn't want us to worry. Better not to know or ask, was our policy. We needn't have worried though, as all was well and he returned on the 25th, which was Good Friday.

By 12 March I had turned my attention to cladding the exterior top half of the B&B, with wood panelling. Being determined to have it completed and stained over a weekend, I managed to ward off the rain, until the final brush stroke when the wind blew, and the heavens opened. Within minutes though, Kate and I, despite getting soaking wet ourselves, had made the most efficient 'Heath Robinson' tarpaulin, with sheets, planks, and string. Not a drop of water landed on the stained woodwork!

At the end of March, the ceiling debacle was to return, this time in the dining room. It had been checked after the last occurrence in the kitchen and drawing room, but at the time it seemed to be ok. Clearly it wasn't, and down it fell just as we had almost finished decorating the whole room!

The mess was unbelievable, so drastic measures were taken. We had it professionally plastered, and we then re-decorated the whole room a completely different colour. Which meant new soft furnishings to match, different lights, and new pieces of furniture. This was a cost that we hadn't expected but it was totally necessary. Given that the room now looked so smart, we decided to complement it with a new canteen of cutlery, so our future guests would, hopefully, be impressed.

Later in the month, both Kate and I visited our local doctor, me for a minor concern regarding my toe, but Kate for a rather more serious concern regarding her groin. The doctor was very thorough with Kate and suggested that a couple of X-rays of her hip would be appropriate. These were taken on 12 April and the results indicated that there was indeed an issue with her right hip, and she was referred to an orthopaedic surgeon.

With spring on its way, we turned our attention to the garden once again. With the help of Russell and his trusty JCB the back garden had been cleared of rubble. So, we hired a lethal piece of machinery and rotovated it, cleared the weeds and had another huge bonfire, which was always satisfying. Following this, we carefully sculptured the 14 tons of topsoil that had been delivered, into raised flower beds and raked the rest level, ready for sowing grass seed.

With Em and Pete's wedding set for 17 September, time was becoming short to book the photographer and venue. Over the Easter holidays, Kate and Em met up in London again and the bookings were sorted. Then, having frequented with Em at least five more bridal outfitters, walked miles, run for buses, trains and tubes and Em having tried on well over 25 dresses, the last one was 'THE ONE'. The hassle and frenetic few days all disappeared, and on her wedding day she looked fantastic. So, this last visit was 100% successful and some of the 'stress' of planning a wedding, had been removed.

Returning home, Kate then prepared and gave a very successful PowerPoint presentation to the local WI, on 'The Benefits of Massage'. Is there no end to her talents?

Whilst Em and Kate were in London, I had taken the opportunity to sow the grass seed. Followed by planting some shrubs and a 20-foot whitebeam tree. The latter, being planted in one of the newly created flower beds, at the back.

At the end of April, we both met up with Oliver, who had bought a flat in Letchworth which overlooked the high street and required some re-decoration – enter Dad and Kate. We started with the kitchen and bathroom, both of which were retiled. New kitchen cupboards were then built, and some new lighting fitted. It all made an enormous difference and, thankfully, Oliver was very pleased, so to celebrate and by way of a 'thank you', he took us all out for a meal.

Back home the back garden, although nice and flat, was bereft of any grass. I gave it an ultimatum – grow or be turfed! In the end, I decided to meet it halfway, by giving it some more seed at the beginning of May, and a fortnight's extension. It took the hint and grew. Not quite as fast as the weeds though but was ready to have its first cut a month later. This was just in time, for on 28 May, Oliver, Jude, her sister and her boyfriend all came to see us, as they had all been to Sea Palling for the day.

Throughout my life, I have been a somewhat frustrated landscape artist, never having quite achieved a picture with which I was happy. I think my desire to paint was inherited from my dad, as I first remember him painting the view of our back garden in Cranleigh Rise, from my sister's bedroom. I watched, wide eyed with amazement, as the image of our garden slowly came to life, on a previous blank canvas. It seemed to be created just simply through what appeared to be flicks of a brush but clearly these were being administered by an expert hand.

This was possibly the first memory I have of seeing my father actually create something like this – I was certainly transfixed and in awe of his skill. It was a lovely painting and hung in my parent's homes for many years but, I regret that I don't know where it is today.

So that is how the artistic 'seed' was sown in me. Dad went on painting, especially during his retirement and one of my favourites, (Fig. 315) is in his distinctive naïve style. It is proudly hung in our bedroom, so I am delighted to wake up to it each and every day.

Chapter 6 Ground up with Flints & Blocks 1999 – 2014

In an effort to resolve my lack of expertise and whilst Kate was on a geography field trip, at How Hill with some school children, I enrolled on a two-day, weekend watercolour course, led by Ian King, in the vain hope that I could further develop my techniques and try and match my dad's expertise. I was hopeful that I would be inspired, acquire the skills that I craved and gain the self-confidence that I needed. I was very pleased with my modest efforts, which resulted in some very acceptable

Figure 315

paintings, one of which was of Cley Mill which was framed and proudly hung in 'The Barn' (Fig. 316). However, the inspiration didn't last but perhaps what was missing was the time, so I hoped that retirement would rectify this.

Later that month, Sophie like her brother decided to move flats, this time to Langley in Berkshire. Following the customary Luton van haulage, she was duly moved and installed into her third-floor flat. When seeking help though, she seemingly forgot to mention the three flights of stairs! Amazingly, the contents of her studio flat were transported and accommodated all in one day.

Figure 316

301

However, that day just happened to be one of the hottest days in May!

Regrettably, our Escort went to the car park in the sky and was duly depersonalised by the DVLA. So, in an effort to support the environment, we both decided to car share. This meant that the vintage sports car that I desired, still remained an ambition.

On 9 June, Kate and I went to BUPA to see Mr Nolan, an orthopaedic surgeon. This consultation was still under the NHS, as Kate had been on the waiting list regarding her hip, for too long. Mr Nolan was really helpful and agreed that despite Kate being younger than most of his patients, a full hip replacement was required. We both agreed to his decision, and she was duly added to his list. It was hoped that the operation would be within the next six months.

June was becoming hotter by the day, and on the weekend of 18/19 the temperature reached 32°. Most people would sit back and enjoy the sun, but that's not for me. Instead, I decided to finish the last flint gabion in the back garden. The theory was, that this would be a way of clearing the unused flints and support the raised beds that I had created. They were successful but it was very hard work indeed. Now, with all four gabions completed, they all looked really good, and we both planted some rock plants into the finished walls.

Since a young age, Oliver had always been very keen and quite successful at trampolining. He had now progressed to wanting to support a local club, by volunteering to teach the younger children. In June he successfully completed his trampolining examination, enabling him at the weekends, to further craft the skills of his young charges.

By comparison in June, Angus's skills were put to use again, when he extended our web design and ideas, into a different live internet site, now for both Kate's clinic and the B&B. The plunge was taken to hit the button on 15 July and for a second time, the site was opened to the world! The result of which proved to be very successful in attracting bookings, for within hours the telephone was ringing and the first of many guests were booked in. Over the years we received a huge number of congratulatory messages not only on our website, but numerous guests signed our visitors books as well (Fig. 317).

July started with a huge downpour of rain, this caused flooding in the village to such an extent that I rang Kate who was at a colleague's leaving event, with some friends from school, to suggest that she came home before the roads became impassable. She managed to drive home safely, as luckily it hadn't become any more treacherous. It did though, continue to rain for three or four more days. During this incident, we had a very similar thought like before, but this time

Chapter 6 Ground up with Flints & Blocks 1999 – 2014

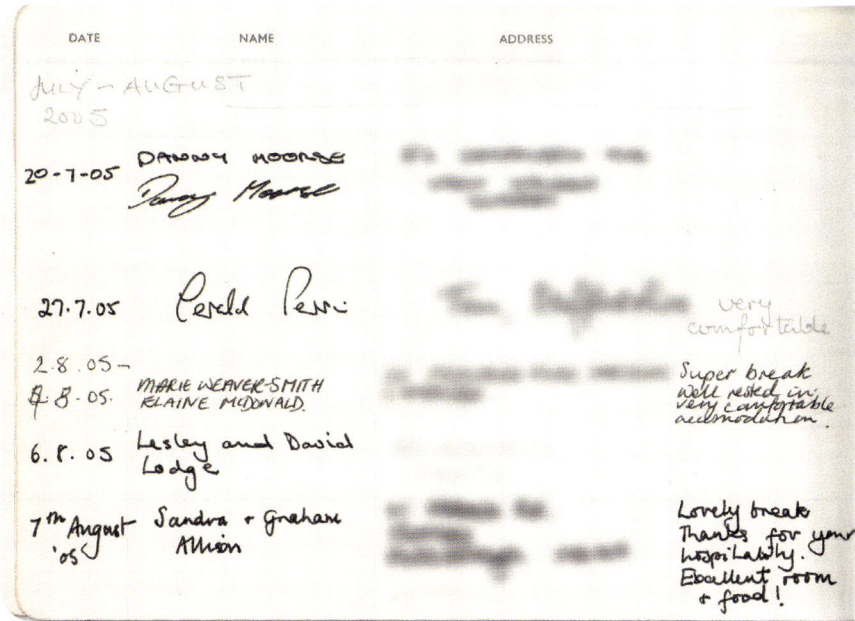

Figure 317

we had envisaged the barn being flooded instead! This was due to all the excess water that was streaming at great force, straight off the fields behind us, across the garden and down towards the back screen. Luckily, the barn remained dry!

In August, one of our guests arrived in her car, and despite not having had any alcohol, managed to drive her car over the edge of our bridge and partially into the stream below. Despite much embarrassment, both driver and car were undamaged. With many thanks to Andrew our ever-resourceful local farmer and his tractor, the car was duly pulled to safety. This prompted us to have some further cast iron signage made, in order that guests did not drive into the wrong area of the garden!

London was hit by six bomb explosions, on 7 July, all accredited to the Irish Republican Army (IRA) and we instantly thought about our four children who may well have been in the area. After some frantic telephone calls, thankfully our fears were allayed, as they were all safe.

With the grass now in full growing mood, I turned my attention to the laying of paths in the formal herb garden and the building of a pergola.

No pressure to finish the job, but a full family celebration was to take place on 28 August, to mark my 50th birthday, my father's 80th, Emily and Pete's wedding and various other notable events within the family.

303

Figure 318

Figure 319

Figure 318 is my father at his home, on 6 October 2005, enjoying his special birthday with my mother and the rest of the family. The photograph (Fig. 319) is my father and me, at 'The Barn', during our celebratory day together.

So, prior to this family celebration, all the landscaping of the garden had now been concluded, with the back garden also successfully prepared (Fig. 320), with garden furniture and parasols, kindly lent from friends. Now, should the weather become inclement at any time, we would be able to enjoy our festivities in comfort, both outside and in the barn itself.

Figure 320

Family from both Kate's side and of course from mine, along with friends, all arrived for the celebrations, and without any prompting, which I had suspected, apparently incorrectly at the time, they duly admired the grass and paths. With caterers taking over the kitchen, Kate was able to enjoy the day, sitting, chatting and relaxing for the first time in the back garden, whilst also soaking up the sun. I won't dwell on the wind though, which lifted up a parasol and nearly hit Kate's sister. However, despite that minor incident the weekend was a complete success.

September was Emily and Pete's month. With a glorious wedding at Chiswick House, on the 17th, followed by what seemed to be a never-ending honeymoon in Italy, they arrived back in the UK, on 8 October. Em and Pete's efforts to create a very special day, supported in the wings by the family, proved a match for any event organiser. All the guests enjoyed themselves and gave them a fitting start to married life.

The official photograph records the day (Fig. 321).

Signing the register (Fig. 322) made it all legal whilst Kate the mother of the bride, looked on with pride (Fig. 323).

Figure 321

Figure 322

Figure 323

Angus also went to Italy but not with his sister! Having flown there on a scheduled aircraft flight, he landed and then took the more unconventional route by skydiving to his destination, close to Lake Garda. His holiday enabled him to perfect his skydiving skills, which took his tally of jumps to well over 1,000!

My 'virtual' birthday present, from Em, Pete, Angus, Oliver and Sophie materialised in October, when fourteen bare root roses arrived from Peter Beales. Kate and I then ordered the remaining roses that were required to finish the rose bed, beside the stream. These were all duly planted and by the spring and summer of 2006, they all looked fantastic.

Kate spent many evenings updating and finalising her accounts, for preparation by her accountant. Her year of very hard work was duly rewarded, when her accountant advised her of the good news that she had doubled the previous year's turnover and increased the profitability.

With the rush of summer B&B guests slowing down, Kate was able to reflect on a very busy and profitable first season. The comments in the visitors' book, about the superb food and quality accommodation also paid tribute to the relaxing and stress-free atmosphere that Kate provided. This was justifiably a further highlight of the year, coupled with all the other family celebrations and it boded well for 2006, as Kate already had advance bookings for that year. She continued to have her regular massage clients, and many of the B&B guests had also enjoyed the use of her massage clinic.

Since becoming a JP, I had been sitting regularly, save for the period just after I joined Norwich Union. Some of my sittings were in the Licencing Court, and as this was now, due to a change in legislation, to be assigned to the Local Authority, the Norwich Licencing Court final sitting was scheduled for 8 November. In future the Magistrates Court would only hear appeals, from the relevant local councils or tenants. After the final sitting finished, all the magistrates met for a drink and a celebratory lunch, in the appropriately named 'Last Wine Bar', which was just down the road from the courts.

Figure 324

November preparations for entertaining seemed to be never ending and whilst Kate prepared Christmas lists for cards, food shopping, presents etc., and juggled family with bed and breakfast bookings, I was able to grant her a Christmas wish, and decorated the ceiling in our master bedroom.

The magical winter months arrived with gusto. The first snowfall fell, so the newlyweds and Sophie decided to make a miniature snowman (Fig. 324).

In mid-December the Christmas tree, which had spent many happy years growing on the local estate, was duly felled and delivered on the 18th. It was man handled into prime position and decorated ready for the festive season.

With the cards sent, presents wrapped, food ordered, and the tree decorated, we were ready and looking forward to our family arriving. They joined us for Christmas, but at different times – Sophie from the 24th, Angus from Boxing Day until he decided to leave! Oliver and Jude from the 24th to the 26th, and Em and Pete from the 27th until sometime, that was to be determined! Later in life, they were to learn just how difficult it was to organise meals etc., when you have no certainty about who would be there to eat them. But that's life, and secretly we love it that way!

It was a lovely Christmas and as I have said, we even had some Christmas snow, to round off a very full and enjoyable 2005.

2006

January greeted us with more snow falling for several days, which made the time even more magical. With three wood burners and the Aga, to say nothing of the underfloor heating, the barn was very warm and snug. But with snow on the ground, you can't just stay at home, so we went for a wonderful walk along the coastal path at Blakeney.

However, when the snow had melted, it exposed all the tidying up we needed to tackle in the garden. As a result, most of January and February was spent undertaking this task, with huge bonfires, clearing out the pond, making marmalade and preparing for our next B&B guests. But who would they be?

Following my parent's decision to move from Ashill to a bungalow in Necton which, whilst being relatively modern, required some updating and alterations, as did the garden. In the latter a pergola was dismantled, to make way for a huge shed. We all became adept removal men, repositioning all Mum and Dad's goods and chattels, in preparation for the influx of workmen arriving, to gut and transform their new property. The B&B was temporarily suspended, for the next day 16 January 2006, my parents came to stay as permanent B&B and supper guests. This was until such time as their new abode in Necton was completed and ready for occupation.

Not only was the family extended with my parents living with us, but we also found that a stray dog had taken up residence in our cart sheds. Mum and Dad stayed for seven weeks until 4 March, the dog was eventually caught and re-housed after 15 weeks which I shall outline later.

February 2006 saw us still busy creating different areas in the back garden. We had fifteen tonnes of topsoil delivered, along with four tonnes of sharp sand and 110 concrete slabs. With all this delivered we set about landscaping the area, ready for the planting of fruit trees, herbs, vegetables and dahlias. Later we had a number of round, nine-foot-tall wooden posts delivered. These were crafted into an arbour/gazebo at the top of the garden, where half the slabs were also to be laid. The remainder of these were put down outside the conservatory, to make our new courtyard and a path along the rear and side of the barn.

As I have commented on previously, living at 'The Barn' meant we were much closer to nature, than in our previous homes. In March 2006 we were delighted to be able to watch two barn owls hunting over the field behind us, whilst a hare and a number of pheasants looked on. Thankfully, one of these was not Frank, as he was in no fit state to defend himself. The wildlife that lived around our pond was also becoming more active, so we hoped to see another family of moorhens.

For Kate's birthday, Oliver and Jude came to stay for the weekend. On her actual birthday, a few days later, she and I had a lovely meal at The Victoria hotel, which is on the edge of the Holkham Hall estate. We still had our visiting dog who was just beginning to build enough confidence in us, to come up to the door. Soon he was to make the bold move of coming into the barn. This grand gesture of confidence happened on 3 April. The dog warden was alerted, two of them arrived and following sedation by a vet, he was carefully taken away to be permanently re-homed. He was a sweet dog, and we were sure that he would make someone very happy.

The Easter week was a holiday from paid employment for both of us, and I took the opportunity to not only finish the laying of the courtyard slabs, but also to build the arbour/gazebo at the top of the back garden. This was a major step forward, as it enabled us to plant numerous flowers and shrubs in the surrounding beds, along with a grape vine, which we hoped would one day cover the arbour. Which it did and it also produced some very tasty grapes as well!

The sun shone throughout the summer and the first harvest of home-grown fruit and vegetables, not eaten by the local wildlife, was enjoyed. We did record on 6 May the first sightings of swifts, swallows and house martins. Great fun was had, especially to the amazement of the general public, as a very smart new bike was transported from Halfords in Norwich to Bodham, on the back seat of Kate's convertible. My old bicycle tyres were pumped up and with the saddle cleaned both bicycles were instantly put into action, with many exhilarating rides taking place over the next few months.

As recommended by our dentist, a visit to the hospital by Kate on 16 May, for an oral check-up, suddenly became a very painful tongue biopsy. Once back home 'The Barn' was uncannily quiet without the Kate's voice being audible. All was well though, as the biopsy results were negative. But it was a worrying time as I recall.

Having had a short respite, it was time to set to work again. With rain clouds looming, 2.5m³ of concrete arrived and with the help of the driver it was piled into the turnip shed and levelled, hardening just before the raindrops fell. This was to form the floor of the new garage and workshop. Obviously, the floor had to be tested first to make quite sure that it would hold the weight of the car ok! With success!

Having eaten our own strawberries, we decided to spoil our B&B guests with not only homemade marmalade but jam as well. With strawberries and special jam sugar purchased, 25lb of jam was made. No problem! Until, upon opening the first jar it was discovered to be decidedly runny. Going for a second attempt it was re-boiled and reduced but setting point was still not achieved. Not to be defeated, additional pectin was added and hey presto, superb jam was duly served at breakfasts and thoroughly enjoyed by everyone who ate it. I don't recall this being repeated but certainly the homemade marmalade was constantly being made for a number of years.

On 3 June, Kate and I met up with Oliver and Jude, as he had recently received a compulsory purchase order, relating to his flat. This was an unknown field for all of us, and we all came to the same conclusion that as it was compulsory not much could be done. However, he was able to negotiate a deal that he and Jude were comfortable with, but they now needed to find somewhere else to live, so a search ensued.

Back at home in Norfolk, having sat late into the night, on one of the many warm balmy evenings, the weather suddenly changed from a heatwave to cool damp evenings. This was the very night that we planned to attend one of two outside concerts, in Blickling Park. The first on 21 July, to see 'Simply Red'. No longer were strappy tops and sandals the attire for the evening, but winter woollies and sensible shoes, but an excellent time was had by all. The second concert was the following night, and swimming costumes would have been more appropriate! Sitting in deckchairs, under an umbrella, in torrential rain was the ideal position to end up basically in a fully filled, cold bath. Never before had such a wet and bedraggled audience sat and appreciated superb singing and a brilliant concert by 'Il Divo'. No complaints and almost everyone was in good spirits, as hundreds of us strolled back into the fields, in the pitch dark, to find our modes of transport.

Only one disgruntled couple was heard, whilst we walked through the estate to our cars, with the husband giving directions over a mobile: *'Go down the path and you'll find it parked, on the right, under a tree. Have you found it yet?'* Wry smiles came over many faces within earshot of this conversation. All thinking, which path and however many trees are there on The Blickling Estate?

With no issues for us thankfully, as our car was duly found and soon the welcoming lights of Walnut Barn were greeted by us both with a sigh of relief and cheers. Once indoors we had lovely hot showers, dry clothes, followed by warm mulled wine, served beside a roaring log fire – in July! By the end of the month though, the weather had completely reversed and we were enjoying hot sunshine again, with only occasional showers.

However, one further torrential shower was to follow, on 2 August, which resulted in Sheringham being severely flooded, with over three feet of water in places. Fortunately, this did not prevent a drive by Kate to King's Lynn, to attend a two-day renewal Red Cross First Aid Course, required as part of her work at school. With only five attendees, the days were pretty intensive, but highly successful with 100% pass rate.

The last few days of August were spent in Gloucestershire where, on the 19th we met up with Angus and had a superb meal, in a seafood restaurant at the Old Passage Inn in Arlingham, which had beautiful views of the River Severn. Kate and I stayed at a wonderful brand-new farmhouse, built in a very contemporary style, with lots of glass and wood. These expanses of glass enabled us to enjoy the fantastic views across the River Severn and beyond to the Forest of Dean. The bed and breakfast and the farm were owned by Diana and Tim Merrett.

On the Friday, I took Kate on an unexpected visit to Frampton Court, where a birthday surprise present from Sophie awaited. The day was set aside for Kate to work one-to-one, with birds of prey (Fig. 325).

Kate's reaction confirmed that this was a perfect day for her, and the birds certainly seemed to like being fed! It was just tremendous watching them swooping down so gracefully to perch on Kate's hand and

Figure 325

Chapter 6 Ground up with Flints & Blocks 1999 – 2014

Figure 326

receive their due reward – a small piece of raw meat. My reward was the smile on Kate's face.

However, not all the birds had the correct landing for eating their prey or perhaps, just weren't hungry. So, instead they just wanted a perch from where they could admire someone's hat (Fig. 326)!

Falconry along with being spoilt by a wonderful couple at Putchers, their B&B, visiting Slimbridge, looking around antique shops in Tetbury, going out for superb meals and discovering the area, was the best medicine that anyone could prescribe for both of us. It was indeed a most relaxing time!

However, there was one surprise and somewhat of a shock to us, which manifested itself on a visit to Abbey Gardens in Malmsbury. To our surprise, upon arriving, we were informed that the day was a *'clothes optional'* day and yes, a number of visitors had taken up this opportunity to walk around with nothing on, along with the owners who just carried on with their gardening chores! Along with several others, we declined the invitation to join them, but we were still able to wander around the gardens. I have to say that after a very short time, the environment felt very natural, and your attention was drawn to the wonderful and immaculate array of flowers etc. The gardens were, some years later, featured on *Gardeners' World* but the camera shots were tasteful, thankfully just like my photograph (Fig. 327).

Figure 327

311

REFLECTIONS UPON A FAMILY

Back home at 'The Barn', serious considerations were being given to the installation in the back garden, of a 12-metre-tall wind turbine. But having investigated this in more detail we decided not to pursue the idea. However, we were keen to find a way of supporting the environment by reducing our carbon footprint, so we continued to review our options in this quest, and to our delight these were to be realised in 2012.

Late August and early September 2006 was to be a monumental time for Sophie. My recollection and understanding of events were that Sophie, who was now living with us at 'The Barn' rather than near High Wycombe, was in severe financial difficulties. She described to us that during her time in Cromer and High Wycombe, some years earlier, she had become involved with Dale her stepfather, and from her description of events we concluded that this was probably a coercive and controlling relationship which Sophie had now confirmed and had extricated herself successfully from this behaviour. Apparently, during this time he had been certainly using Sophie's financial income and possibly her mother's as well, all for his own ends. As a result, she had fallen deeply into debt. What happened to trigger Sophie's realisation of her situation, I don't know, but luckily, she did recognise the severity and vulnerability of her position and came back to Norfolk to live with us at 'The Barn'.

Whilst this was indeed a shock to both Kate and I and the rest of the family, it did confirm and, in some ways, answer the questions I had endeavoured to ask Sophie back in 2001. However, that aside, when requested we gave advice which led her to declare herself bankrupt and seek employment in a new career in the welfare of animals, something that was very suited to her. At first, she applied to the RSPCA, having some understanding of their work, but was unsuccessful. She then decided to explore the possibility of training to become a veterinary nurse. This was to be successful and led her into a very promising and rewarding career.

Throughout 2006, Angus travelled for short holidays, several times to Spain, Switzerland and Italy, all to pursue his passion of either skydiving or BASE jumping. The latter was now his new extreme sport and in between times he was rock climbing or bouldering in England and overseas in Europe too. On 12 September, having returned safely from Italy, he telephoned us to confirm his return which was much appreciated but perhaps not at 05.00 in the morning!

On 15 September, Sophie endorsed her return to the family, by officially changing by Deed Poll, her current surname Crowe, back to Gosden. Having done this and updated her passport details, she secured an interview at one of the stables in Newmarket. This was followed by an offer of a job as a groom in the USA, which she accepted and on 2 October we took her to Heathrow, where she flew on the 11.50 flight, bound for Washington.

Figure 328

At around the same time, I was considering volunteering with the Prince's Trust and went along to several meetings at Bethel Street Police Station, as the current chairman was a serving Police Officer. Due to the commitment required though, I decided not to pursue it any further, as I felt it was too much, given my time that was already committed to the Magistracy. Kate and I though, did support a number of their fundraising events over the coming years, as seen in (Fig. 328).

In September, Kate and I had a lovely day out at the Ingworth Trosh, where we watched vintage farm machinery harvesting fields, along with a ploughing match (Figs. 329 & 330). I must confess that I am addicted to the old traditional ways of farming, and firmly believe that some of the old ways with horses etc. will at some point make a return. Not necessarily in everyday farming but in perhaps other more supportive roles, like they are in the world of forestry work. Their future use does support the current and growing environmental agenda. I know also that some members of our family pour scorn on this, but I am happy to accept that.

Whilst still in the USA and having undertaken a number of weeks working on a stud farm, Sophie then flew to Florida to work on another one, and having had a very successful time she returned to the UK, on 31 October.

Figure 329

Figure 330

The end of October also saw BUPA as the temporary home for Kate, where she had a total hip replacement on the 27th.

Whilst the operation concluded well, Kate was in the operating theatre from 14.10 through to 16.50, which I thought was a long time. I was told that there was some concern about her low blood pressure, and she had also remained in the recovery room longer than expected. Much to my relief, thankfully all was well. She was discharged on 3 November and given several exercises to undertake. Despite having had 29 staples removed on 7 November, three days later Kate was up and walking, with the aid of two crutches which over time were replaced by two sticks. She was still having to sleep on her back for 6 weeks – not something she found easy but clearly was making a strong recovery.

Now that Sophie had more experience she re-applied to the RSPCA, and then flew off to Edinburgh for a short break with Tim, her young man. They returned on Saturday 18 November, the same day that Kate managed to walk downstairs, for the first time since being discharged. The calendar records a number of days as being a 'Good Day' and by the end of November one stick had successfully been abandoned.

Sophie, having not been successful on the second occasion with the RSPCA, was still seeking employment and applied and had an interview with Blue Cross in Felixstowe. Blue Cross provided veterinary care in their own hospitals and clinics. Unfortunately, she wasn't successful, but the process confirmed to her that veterinary nursing was to be her vocation. However, for this she needed professional qualifications and to gain these she required funding. Kate and I assisted with this, and to her credit Sophie took a job as a groom at Emblems Farm in Essex, that enabled her to save some money.

At the beginning of December, we had some furry visitors, in the form of several mice, which we caught and released at the top of the field behind us. Having commented to local farmers, they advised us to take them further away, as according to them *'they will simply turn around and come back to the barn.'* How right they were and upon catching them when they duly returned, this advice was enacted and, on my drive to work I took our little visitors to Aylsham and released them in a field there instead. I just hoped that they liked Aylsham!

On Saturday 16 December, I was sitting in the Norwich Court and as Oliver, Jude and Sophie were all staying at 'The Barn', they decided to come and see what being a magistrate was all about. The court sitting was short, as they often are on Saturdays and consisted mainly of remand cases, so all four of us were able to have lunch in Norwich before returning home.

During the year Em and Pete moved again, this time to Surbiton where they celebrated their first wedding anniversary. Em also had a complete change of career, as having left Hays in November she was now working for two photographic libraries and thoroughly enjoyed the challenge.

With Christmas approaching, our tree which again was a 15-feet high Norway Spruce, was delivered and decorated, along with the rest of the barn. Em and Pete arrived on the 23rd, as did Angus and Sophie. Oliver followed the next day and with everyone home we had Christmas lunch at The Sea Marge in Overstrand, followed by a short walk along Cromer Pier. My Christmas present from Kate was to see her walk halfway upstairs, without any sticks – which was progress indeed and a wonderful present.

With Kate's determination, coupled with the superb progress that she had achieved since October, we were both reassured that not only was the operation a success but that it wouldn't be long before she was back to full health. A perfect way to start the new year.

2007

As there was very little construction work required on the barn, 2007 was very much a year of travel and in the case of Sophie it was a change in her job. The B&B was up and running and Kate's Massage Therapy was also operational, so both had to be considered when holidays were planned.

In January, Sophie was very keen to pursue her career as a veterinary nurse and to fulfil this ambition, she needed to find a practice that would take her on as a trainee, but this was proving difficult. On her part, the desire was certainly there and on 23 January, to seek a position she sent out letters to 15 local veterinary practices. Whilst awaiting replies she worked for May Gurney in Trowse, just outside of Norwich and this provided her with an income of sorts, for essentials.

The responses to her letters came back and unfortunately none of them had any vacancies, so all were negative. But undeterred she began researching a new list, with practices further away.

Figure 331

She also, with a little help from the bank of Dad and Kate, purchased via the internet, a lovely, three-year-old labrador, whose name was Barney. Whilst his pedigree was unknown, he was certainly a calm and very sociable dog. He is seen relaxing in the garden at 'The Barn' (Fig. 331).

Kate's hip was very much on the mend and the prescribed cycling exercise had certainly strengthened her muscles. It was also a most enjoyable pastime, and both of us could often be seen cycling along the lanes around Bodham and further afield. Those were the days!

On Monday 5 February, Kate and I exchanged the cold and damp UK climate, for a drier and hotter one, as we flew off to Madeira. Regrettably, due to some weather issues en route that had caused a delay in our take-off schedule, we eventually flew from Luton to La Palma in Spain. Here we had to sit on the aeroplane for one and a half hours before we could finish our journey to Madeira and Funchal Airport. It was a long and tiring journey but well worth the effort.

Our room, number 306, in the five-star Cliff Bay Hotel in Funchal, was even more sumptuous than we had hoped, plus the view over the sea (Fig. 332) was superb.

Our first full day was to be the ultimate test for me, as Kate wanted to travel by cable car, up to the top of the mountain to the town of Monte. I am not great with heights but even I had to admit that what I could see out of my almost closed eyes was fantastic. Not as good though, as the view from the top (Fig. 333) when standing on a solid rock base!

Figure 332

Figure 333

We walked around the Monte Palace Tropical gardens and then up a further 74 steps to the Church of Our Lady of the Mount (Igreja de Nossa Senhora do Monte). From here the views were as stunning as the internal decorations of the church.

Outside, we watched in awe and trepidation as large, wicker toboggan baskets, into which two or three people sat, were expertly guided at great speed by two very talented drivers, down the steep, twisty mountain road (Fig. 334).[29] We declined partaking as this could have caused problems with Kate's hip, and for me the cable car now seemed a much safer way to return.

---

29 https://www.thevagabondimperative.com/guides/how-to-hurtle-down-a-hill-in-madeira-in-a-wicker-basket/

Chapter 6 Ground up with Flints & Blocks 1999 – 2014

Figure 334

Back at street level we visited the Casa Oliveria Embroidery factory, where Kate purchased two small lace mats which were the same design as the ones she had inherited from her maternal grandparents. After a lovely meal we retired for the day.

Wednesday 7 February, we endeavoured to book a boat to go whale and/or dolphin spotting, but unfortunately there weren't enough passengers so regrettably the trip had to be cancelled. Instead, we took a taxi to Camara de Lobos where Winston Churchill often painted. Given this, and my appreciation of everything Churchillian, coffee in Churchill's Place which overlooked the harbour, was a must! Dinner was in Reid's Palace Hotel, one of the top, most luxurious hotels in the area. And here I received, to my utter surprise, an early birthday cake.

On day four, we decided to widen our visits. So, a hire car was required and for a very short journey I started on the wrong side of the road! Then having mastered the art of driving on the correct side of the road, I drove over to the east coast to a wicker factory in Camacha (Fig. 335). The craftsmen and women were remarkable. Their skill and speed of weaving was something to be admired, as was the end product. We managed to find a lovely traditional village restaurant, Mercado Velho in Machio, where we had a superb meal sitting in their courtyard, beside a lovely fountain (Fig. 336). Lunch here was so good and filling that come the time for supper we decided that we just couldn't manage another meal.

Figure 335

Figure 336

317

Figure 337

After lunch we drove to Casas de Santana where we saw the most unusual, thatched, triangular heritage properties (Fig. 337). These just had an attic to store agricultural products and on the ground floor a residential area for one family, that just had a kitchen and a bedroom. Being constructed of wood, which was cheap and easily available, the internal temperature was kept at a regular level. The rooves were thatched using wheat and rye which were again both readily available.

On Friday we ventured from Funchal to Ribeira Brava and then further north to Sao Vicente. Here we watched the pounding waves crashing against the huge boulders of the volcanic coastline. We then drove further on to Ponta Delgada with its old colonial style houses and then onto Sexial.

This was a very pretty village on the coast, where we sat beside a man-made pool, before paddling on Laje Beach, also known as Jamaica Beach because of all the palm trees planted for hundreds of metres. We saw many fish swimming in the lava pools, all awaiting another 'top up' of sea water from the incoming tide.

We continued our journey which then developed into a 'white knuckle' drive upwards (Fig. 338), to a point where we were above the clouds, before our route took us back down to the coast. Never again! Our evening meal was in a very popular and again a traditional restaurant, this time adjacent to the hotel. I can't recall what I had, but Kate had grilled limpets and some multi-coloured parrot fish which apparently were excellent. I took Kate's word on this.

Figure 338

Saturday was a lazy day, and it was cooler than the previous days, so we stayed locally. In the evening, we had another delicious meal at a family run Manisa Rest restaurant. I recall that the young waitress was learning English, so she was practising on us, whilst in return Kate complemented this by trying her Portuguese. It must have worked both ways as the food which we had ordered was both correct and delicious.

Figure 339

The Sunday was a day for a guided walk following some of the lavadas (Fig. 339)[30]. These were 16th century networks of irrigation channels and aqueducts, which distributed water from the mountains and slopes for agriculture and drinking. At the hotel, there was a slight misunderstanding as to where the walk was to start, but after talking to our booking agent, we were put in a taxi and driven, at speed, to catch up with our group, who were about to commence their walk. Having arrived just in time we had a wonderful two and a quarter hour walk. Our guide was very knowledgeable and pointed out the various plants en route, as well as explaining the history of the area. We returned to the hotel for a lazy afternoon, during which Kate had a hot stone massage – so good for her to receive a massage rather than giving one.

On the Monday we returned to the UK and arrived at Luton just after 17.00. Kate's diary says, *'Fantastic Holiday'*, and I would certainly endorse that sentiment.

Back in Bodham, Sophie was putting Barney through his paces with training. He was very good, intelligent, and seemed to enjoy these sessions. He did, however, have a couple of lapses, where he decided at his leisure to explore the surrounding countryside, but that was soon rectified, by some additional fencing.

Sophie was now wanting to change jobs again, as the travelling to Lynford Hall had become an issue, as it was an hour's drive away. So, on 5 March, she started work at Cawston Hall which was much closer. Her desire though, was still to find a veterinary practice that would take her on as a trainee, to this end, 94 more letters were sent out. She was thinking about planning ahead, so she and I looked around for a suitable car, in order that should a placement be found transport would not be an issue.

---

30 https://en.m.wikipedia.org/wiki/Levada_(Madeira)

With Easter looming, Oliver and Jude came home, and on 7 April 2007, we went out to Upchers restaurant to celebrate some wonderful news – Oliver and Jude were engaged. This wasn't a surprise for Kate and me, as on a previous occasion with Oliver he had asked our opinion as to whether or not he should propose to Jude. We were delighted that he had followed our advice and that she had accepted. Unfortunately, the next day was a day of hard work for both Oliver and me, as we attempted to dismantle part of the piggeries which, as we discovered, were very well built! Anyway, we succeeded in our endeavours before Oliver and Jude returned to Letchworth, on Easter Monday.

I had the Easter week off from work, so once ten tonnes of topsoil had been delivered, I was able to create some raised beds, which Kate duly bedded out with numerous plants from Taverham garden centre. The back garden was now beginning to look like a proper garden, rather than the original rough ground that we had purchased, which then became a builder's yard. This was great motivation to finish the work and at various times all our children had given a helping hand, which was so much appreciated.

However, a telephone call from David Corbett a Round Table friend, who also knew Alex, Kate's former husband and the father of Em and Angus, was to put a temporary stop to any work.

The call was devastating, as Kate was told that on 25 April, Alex hadn't turned up for work, and when investigations were carried out, he was found to have died in his London flat. Kate then had to break this news to both Em and Angus. Whilst this was due to natural causes, it was an enormous shock to Em, Angus and Kate, along with all who knew him. His private cremation was on 9 May, with Em, Pete and Angus in attendance, along with their stepmother, her two daughters and some close friends.

Following this, an open memorial service took place in Brooke, which Kate and I attended with a large number of friends and family, who were known to both of us. Some through Round Table and others through Kate's previous marriage to Alex. Em and Angus were very stoic and supportive to both their mother, stepmother and her two children. I found this experience really difficult. As the stepfather to both Em and Angus I wanted to comfort them but felt at the time that this was perhaps a little intrusive, as it could cause concerns and possible conflicts of loyalty for them both, so I abstained. Was my decision correct given the circumstances? Today I am still not sure.

The following day Pete returned to work at the BBC in London, whilst Em and Angus came back to 'The Barn'. I was in court on the Friday and both Kate and Em came to observe, and then we all had lunch before returning to the court for the final few cases.

Mid-May was traditionally the time when Kate was at How Hill, on a field study trip, again with a group of 'Year Six' girls from Norwich High School and that year was to be no different.

Moves were very much the theme of May, as having relinquished his flat in Letchworth, Oliver along with Jude had found a modern ground floor flat in Welwyn Garden City and wanted us to view it with them. It was certainly very nice and would suit them perfectly, so a swift purchase ensued. The month continued in a sombre mood for both Em and Angus, as would be expected. So, Angus decided that it was appropriate that he took some time away, so on the 28th he travelled to Lake Geneva for a long weekend.

This time Kate and I perfectly understood his rationale. However, as I have said before, we often never knew if these quick visits, or indeed the longer ones, were either to pursue his love of skydiving and BASE jumping or were for his work at Detica. We didn't ask and he never said but he always told us where and when he was going. We understood that if it was for the former activities then he didn't want to worry us about his safety, and if it was work related then his adherence to the Official Secrets Act forbade him from saying anything, anyway. Whilst both were sound but difficult reasons, we had great faith in his ability to keep himself safe and to return home.

May though would be very different for Sophie, as she had successfully applied for a position as a Trainee Veterinary Nurse, in a Hampshire practice. This necessitated a move into a friend's spare room in Church Crookham, with the help of her friend Darren.

At the start of June, I too was off to work in a different location. Not as glamorous as Angus, as my destination was Dublin. My director, Stuart, and I had been asked to give some advice and guidance on how to set up a cost saving project that was being considered by the Dublin branch of Aviva. We flew from Norwich and were regally wined and dined on the first night. I decided to choose a crocodile meat dish, as I had never eaten this before, but was violently ill overnight! Lesson learnt, in the future I will always be wary of different foods and maybe stick to those with which I am more familiar. After two days and evenings of hard work I flew back to London and returned to Norwich. Stuart stayed for an extra day to present our work to the Board before he returned to Norwich as well.

Working with other segments of the Aviva Group was to become a theme for the next year, as having successfully delivered our UK cost cutting programme, we were asked to assist other members of the Group, with the design and structure of similar projects. Indeed, in June alone we received two requests for assistance. One from Egypt, which my colleague Colin managed, and one from India which I was to assist with. Both were long term commitments and required travelling to their local offices. In my case this was Pune on the west coast of India and then Bengaluru, or as it's more commonly known, Bangalore.

On 11 June 2007 at 05.00 a company chauffeur arrived at 'The Barn' to take me to Heathrow airport, for an 11.00 flight. There I met Stuart, John the programme accountant and Lisa our programme office colleague. After a nine-hour flight, we arrived in Mumbai at 01.26 local time and from there we took an internal flight to Pune, arriving at 10.10.

Figure 340

When we had finished our work in Pune we then flew to Bangalore where we were based and stayed at The Lalit Ashok Hotel, (Fig. 340). The plan was to meet the director, and her team there and then move on to the local offices.

This was my first visit to India and the two extremes of the social classes was an eye-opening experience. We had been told that we were not to accept any rides locally and to always use the company transport. This was very reassuring until I saw the way that the local company chauffeurs drove. If a vehicle was in their way, they simply blasted their horn and drove around them no matter what traffic was approaching. If that necessitated you being driven on the wrong side of the road at length, then so be it! I found the best way to cope with this, was to close my eyes and hoped that I arrived at my destination, which we always did.

As I said, the extremes of the social scale were so clearly evident during my route from the luxurious hotel to our modern air-conditioned offices. This route involved a drive through the shanty townscape, where the local people were working out of tin shacks, on the side of the road. These led right up to our office grounds and in many cases their equally poor housing accommodation was located just at the rear of their tin shack. The contrast with our office accommodation was mind blowing. What struck me, was that some of those shanty town inhabitants had probably worked on our offices as building labourers, so they knew exactly how luxurious they were compared to their own homes. I wondered just how they felt, but they seemed to simply accept the situation and were happily engaged in their pursuits.

Our work went really well, and by the time we left, the local team was focused and able to drive the project forward. We did have time for some sightseeing and again it was the cultural differences that totally surprised me.

One of our outings involved a long journey, which we undertook in a company minibus. During the drive and having turned off the main highway onto a local almost dirt track road, we drove over piles of rice on the road being sorted by the locals. We asked the driver why he didn't stop, he explained that the rice was deliberately thrown onto the road, in order that the wheels of the vehicles would crush the rice husks, to reveal the rice grain inside. This obviously saved the locals having to purchase harvesting machinery. There was logic to this but no thought as to Health and Safety!

The second trip involved even less Health and Safety considerations. As we drove at some speed along a tarmacked highway, similar to our main roads, we found ourselves following a local bus. Nothing unusual in that, until we saw a couple of men climb out of the side window, then up a fixed ladder on the side, normally used to gain access to the roof to store luggage, and all whilst the bus was still being driven at a fair speed. Here they started to unfasten a spare wheel. Again, asking our driver what on earth was happening, we were calmly told that a couple of miles back the bus had had a puncture, and the men were getting the spare wheel ready to replace the punctured one. By preparing it in advance it saved a lot of time when the bus stopped. Thankfully, the vehicle was using double wheels at the back, so was still just about drivable. But the actions of these men were considered totally normal, and it was just what they did!

My time in India was so very different to my life in England and it left me with an impression that I will never forget. The work rate of employees was phenomenal, the security intense, no matter what your status, no one was allowed mobile phones in the offices, as these caused distractions and could be used to photograph secret papers. This coupled with the two extremes of the society living cheek by jowl in the same city or town, was a revelation. After eleven days away I returned home to Heathrow and via my chauffeur returned to Kate in Bodham.

At home I noticed that the tiling above the kitchen floor cupboards, which had been undertaken whilst I was away, had been finished very professionally, but that the grass needed cutting, so very much back to normal with a bang!

Sophie's birthday was on 1 July, the same date as a new law came into force throughout England, banning smoking in public places. There is no connection here as I am pleased to say that none of our children smoke or drink to excess.

The next week witnessed two firsts. On 4 July I had a fitting for my first hearing aid in my left ear, whilst on Friday 6th Oliver and Jude completed the purchase of their first flat together, in Sefton Court, Welwyn Garden City. They duly moved in the next day but without our assistance as I was attending a day's JP training.

Em, Pete and Angus came home to visit on the 21st, so we all had a lovely walk across the seashore before visiting an Art Exhibition in Salthouse Church. This was capped off by lunch and a drink at the Dun Cow, which was now becoming more of a local pub for us. Upon arriving back at the barn, we also noticed that our resident moorhen was now leading three chicks around the pond, and they looked very much 'at home'.

With all the comings and goings of the family and the fact that it was our wedding anniversary soon, Kate and I decided to go for a short break to Barcelona.

We flew out from Stansted on Friday 27 July and returned on the following Monday. A short visit but packed with interesting visits and outdoor cuisine. An open top bus tour helped us to understand the layout of the city and have significant landmarks explained, like the Antoni Gaudi architecture and the *Mirador de Colom* also known as the Columbus Monument. The temperature was around 30+ degrees so when the bus tour finished, we slowly took our time to seek out the sights not visible from the bus.

Figure 341

The walk along La Rambla was a 'must', with its tree-lined pedestrian street, its many colourful shops and the incredible human statues (Fig. 341) coupled with numerous street performers.

As was Palau Güell mansion, one of the most spectacular buildings by Gaudi and here we bought a resin reproduction of his lizard, located in Park Güell. Unfortunately, the Sagrada Familia was closed to the public, so instead we visited the open market, Mercat de la Boqueria, with its colourful fish, fruit and vegetables, which inevitably made us feel very hungry, so we found a lovely restaurant for a traditional Spanish lunch.

Later, after a long walk, we managed to visit the gothic Cathedral of the Holy Cross and St. Eulalia, and it was well worth the effort. The views of Barcelona from the top were spectacular, stretching out over the rooftops of the city to Montjuïc Hill, the sea and beyond. On the way out we found several geese in the cloisters and some huge fish in the pond, which had a statue of St. George on top of the fountain.

In the evening, we sought out a lovely restaurant in the porticoed Plaça Reial square which, with its waiters all touting for business, was fascinating.

Chapter 6 Ground up with Flints & Blocks 1999 – 2014

We selected a Catalonian restaurant and had a lovely paella. The square was full of street performers and had a wonderful atmosphere all of its own. The hustle and bustle was, without doubt, entertaining in itself. When we eventually left, we walked alongside the port, past the floodlit Columbus Monument (Fig. 342), before arriving back at the hotel around midnight.

Saturday was an equally busy day again, using the hop-on and hop-off bus to see some more sights that we would have never found, like the *Font màgica de Montjuïc* (Magic Fountain of Montjuïc). During the evening, after queuing for an hour for a table, we had a superb meal and then en route back to our hotel, whilst admiring the human statues, which were different from the previous ones, we came upon a puppeteer and were most impressed with his portrayal of Kermit, who was playing a grand piano.

Figure 342

Our penultimate day was mainly spent on the beach, where a couple of sun loungers cost us £10 to hire, and when we left, we managed to sell them on to an Italian couple. But not at a profit though!

We also had a stroll around Port Olympic before making our way back to the city centre. One thing that did amaze us were the number of parakeets in the trees, all making such a noise that you couldn't possibly miss them. After a pizza and drinks for a late lunch, we just sat outside as it was so hot and enjoyed watching the world go by. This incredible temperature continued from 17.30 in the afternoon and well into the evening! Back at the hotel we packed and then had our delicious tapas meal, with all sorts of wonderful food including steak, fish, quail, some chips and lots of different sauces. Followed by chocolate soup, melon and coffee ice cream!

On Monday we had an 11.30 flight, so it was a croissant and a cup of tea for breakfast before the taxi arrived to take us to the airport. After the normal delays, we endured a slightly turbulent flight to Stansted. Following a coffee stop at Birchanger service station, we arrived back at Bodham around 17.00. It was certainly a fantastic trip and one that we thoroughly deserved.

Whilst we were 'in the air', Angus was also on a plane, this time to Norway. I too was to be flying again, returning to India before the week was out. So, the same journey as before but this time it was just for a few days, to check that all was going to plan.

But before I left, Kate and I had the opportunity through Aviva, to be spectators at the Crystal Palace Athletics. Whilst not being an athlete I did find the experience great fun, but that may have been the convivial hospitality. We also attended the presentation of the awards by Kelly Holmes, and all in all it was a most interesting and enjoyable day.

Figure 343

Back in India, between my two visits, Lisa had opted to continue to remain there to assist the programme office. She had been so supportive that when I arrived, I was asked by the Project Director if she could stay on again, and with her blessing, Lisa and I agreed. In fact, she was to stay for a number of months and apparently thoroughly enjoyed her time, whilst also making a significant contribution to the performance of the programme office.

Angus called us from Norway and this time it was clear that his trip was for pleasure, as he commented that a tent for the night was £15.00, and a beer was £5.00 a pint. Clearly, he was paying, not the company! By 13 August 2007 he was on his way to Møre og Romsdal, a county in the northernmost part of Western Norway, 513 miles from Lysebotn. By the 24th he was ready to leave Norway and return to the UK, we thought. But the next telephone call from him, on the 29th originated from Italy! Was this to be another social expedition or perhaps now work related, we knew not?

September for me, was a return to normal 'Barn' life, as I mixed and laid the concrete in the first of three bays inside the cart shed. The last two were to follow over the next few weekends, and it was good to have these done so we could store the boat in the dry, over winter.

On the ninth with some superb weather, we took a day off for a lovely coastal walk along Holkham beach (Fig. 343).

Chapter 6 Ground up with Flints & Blocks 1999 – 2014

By 14 September, Angus was to telephone us again, this time from Lauterbrunnen in Switzerland. His travels were beginning to resemble a Victorian Grand Tour, but he was thoroughly enjoying both the experiences and the locations. Kate and I on the other hand drove five miles down the road to enjoy the 1940s steam train weekend, in Sheringham and Holt. The evening hog roast alone was worth the trip.

With autumn just around the corner, Kate and I drove the five hours over to Worcestershire, to wander round the Malvern Royal Horticultural Show (RHS). We had been to other RHS shows, but Malvern was more compact and overall, a more pleasant experience, due to there being less people. Also, the setting and the surrounding scenery was just perfect.

The show was good, and we managed to resist any purchases but did come away with some ideas for our own garden. Whilst in the area we drove to Lower Broadheath and visited the home of Elgar who is one of my favourite composers, something that I seem to have inherited from my maternal grandfather. At the time the house was under the care of local people and the Elgar Society and had been kept almost unaltered (Fig. 344). However, it was later to be taken over by the National Trust in 2018 on a five-year trial basis.

Figure 344

The first of October was to find Angus in Perpignan in the South of France but, according to the telephone message he was due to drive back to Italy the next week. His travels though, seemed to be coming to an end as I spoke to him on the 20th and he was back in the UK. For how long we didn't know and possibly he didn't either.

With Kate massaging all day on the 20th I finished putting up the concrete posts for the back fence, that was in the style of an open trellis and back filled the area behind with soil. Once completed I then turned my attention and prepared the area from outside the kitchen to the back screen of the barn, in order that I could lay some more of the slabs.

It was half term the next week, so Kate was able to spend some time at home, where she planted more than 200 bulbs, in a raised area that I had created along the edge of the back fence. We hoped that these would make a lovely spring show whilst also attracting some wildlife. That was on the assumption that the wildlife didn't dig them up over the winter!

The first week of November, I had to turn my attention to filling in a form for Aviva, as we had been advised that there was a possibility that within my area of work, some redundancies would be implemented. To avoid the possibility of this happening, we all had to fill in this form, outlining our responsibilities and qualifications, in the hope that we would be selected and be retained on the team. This was stressful for all of us, but I felt fairly secure, which proved to be correct.

When originally looking for somewhere to live in North Norfolk, we had considered places like Blakeney, as it was close to the sea. Blakeney was now on Flood Alert and overnight the sea breached the sea defences, flooding large parts of the village and surrounding areas. The tides were the worst for 50 years. We ventured down a day later and there were boats everywhere marooned on the land, having been tossed and upturned by the tide. Seaweed and flotsam were strewn all around, and the car park adjacent to the estuary was still flooded. It was awful and must have been heartbreaking for local residents, whose houses were flooded, and which would obviously take ages to dry out. It's interesting to see some 16 years later, just how many houses now have their own flood defences. Clearly, at the time our choice to live in Bodham rather than Blakeney was correct.

The end of November was the final push to finish the conversion of the old turnip shed into a garage. To this end a local builder put up the roof trusses, which were followed by battens and felting, in preparation for tiling. This really did indicate that our work on 'The Barn' conversion was almost at an end, after eight years of incredibly hard work. But what an achievement, it was just what we wanted, a house where all the children could come home and enjoy being one family.

I was still working for Aviva but now was part of the Life company so spent more time in York, rather than in Norwich. I didn't mind this, because on Monday mornings I could catch the train from Peterborough and return on the Thursday, having stayed in a hotel during the week. For Aviva, I wasn't sure that this made financial sense, but no one seemed to mind. Some of my first projects were based around the finance department and included the redesign and relaunching of Aviva's High Net Worth Management Offering, to some selected customers. These were individuals or couples with investments in excess of two million pounds, which had some historic long-term issues, that I can't outline here. Suffice to say, I was able to build a good working relationship with several of the top staff and directors, which was to prove very helpful in the future.

Talking of finance, Sophie having now been working as a trainee veterinary nurse for some months, was able to pay back the money we had lent her, to purchase Barney. She could now call him her dog. She had £550 of course fees to cover though, in order that she could pursue her dreams and we were happy to pay this as it was very plain to see that she had found her perfect occupation and was clearly excellent in the role. For once, studying became a desire for more understanding, rather than a chore to be endured.

Figure 345

So, with Christmas a week or so away, logs having been purchased (Fig. 345), 'The Barn' was ready for the traditional festive celebrations, and we were ready too, to enjoy a full Christmas with family popping in and out, just as it should be.

2008

The second half of 2008 was to prove to be very difficult for us all, but especially for Kate. But first I will outline what we were doing, in the first half of the year. On 4 January, Em flew to Florence for three months, as part of her employment with Scala Archives, an Italian photographic, image and audio library. On the other hand, I was still working in York for Aviva, with occasional visits to London, as well as supporting the Prince's Trust and sitting as a JP. Kate had three demanding jobs, teaching at Norwich High School, a massage practitioner at her clinic, and bed and breakfast, also at 'The Barn'.

Early January, started with me having to take the 'Blowers' grandmother clock to be repaired by 'Old Time', based in Wacton near Long Stratton. Whilst winding it up I had caught the pendulum, which was stabilised by a small, glass counterweight balance full of mercury. This broke and the mercury spilt, in small goblets all over the floor. I managed to salvage most of it, which the repairer was very pleased about, as replacement mercury was and still is extremely expensive. Anyway, the clock was duly repaired at a cost of £425 and returned on 14 March, just in time for Kate's birthday. Ever since, it has worked really well and keeps time accurately, despite it being made in 1727, which makes it nearly three hundred years old! I am now even more careful when I wind it up.

In early February, despite having a flurry of snow, we had a huge bonfire to clear rubbish from the garden. There is something quite satisfying about a bonfire, but now that they are environmentally frowned upon, I do miss not having one in the garden, especially with all the smoke and smells. The clearance allowed us to clear the last vestiges of the machinery from behind the back of the garden wall. In so doing, this allowed me access so that I could repair the wall over the next few weekends.

For my birthday, on 26 February, Kate and I had a lovely meal at the Walpole Arms. I think that one of the advantages of living in North Norfolk was the number of quality places to eat, be they pubs or restaurants and we were really spoilt for choice.

On the next weekend, we drove up to the Peak District, where we met up with Oliver and Jude. Kate had to do some research for a forthcoming Year Two topic, and went to visit Eyam, a small village with a population of just 800 which regrettably, became famous for having had 260 deaths due to the 1666 Great Plague, and she then went onto Hathersage, famous for its links to Charlotte Brontë, authoress of *Jane Eyre*. Whilst she was doing this, Oliver, Jude and I had a lovely 11-mile walk, through the undulating countryside, eventually meeting up with Kate, with all of us tired but very content with our achievements.

We also met up with Angus and all five of us had a meal together, before we made our way back to our respective homes. On the Sunday, Kate and I went for a walk, this time much shorter, around Pretty Corner in Sheringham, and then drove to Blakeney for a walk around the village and along the coastal path. This was very clear evidence, if any were needed, that Kate's hip operation had been a great success, and her strength was returning to normal.

Saturday 15 March was Kate's birthday and our treat that day was a trip to the Theatre Royal in Norwich, to see the performance of the musical *Shout!* This was set in the 1960s with all the appropriate fashions and music. It was brilliant and thoroughly enjoyed by both of us and the rest of the audience. We exited the theatre singing the songs, which we along with other members of the audience had all grown up with.

On the Sunday, we went to Cinema City in Norwich, a small independent cinema, to watch *The Other Boleyn Girl*, as Kate's nephew James (Jim) Sturgess was cast as Ann Boleyn's brother. Again, this was superb, and Jim has now gone on to star in numerous films around the world.

Easter was spent with Em in Italy. Having left home at 07.00, we flew from Gatwick arriving in Pisa at 16.30, local time. We then had a long wait from a delayed coach which took us to Florence, where we met our bed and breakfast host, who looked after us for the next couple of nights.

Figure 346

On the Saturday, we set off by bus to Ponte Santa Trinita, the oldest elliptic arch bridge in the world, where we walked down to meet Em on the Ponte Vecchio. Here we viewed the shops, as well as some others in the surrounding piazza. We had a fantastic day sightseeing, although the crowds did mean that we couldn't go into the Uffizi Gallery. We did, however, as tradition allows stroke for good luck, *Il Porcellino*, the bronze statue of a boar. After coffee/tea and cakes with Em, we all had an evening meal at Baccofino (Fig. 346), not far from Ponto Santa Trinita. On Easter Sunday, in the Piazza del Duomo, we attended a celebration entitled Scoppio del Carro or The Explosion of the Cart which dates back over 350 years.

This grand celebration (Figs. 347 & 348) is always officiated by the Archbishop of Florence. The streets were packed with spectators and security officers, but the photographs here give a fair reflection of the fireworks and the enthusiastic crowds that had all come to witness this annual spectacle. Tradition, no matter where you are, is important not only due to the heritage of an event but also, as in this case, to support tourism. As such, a visit to Florence would never

Figure 347

Figure 348

Figure 349   *Figure 350*

be complete without the half an hour climb of nearly 300 steps to the top of the Tower of Pisa (Fig. 349). Even with my vertigo I managed this and was so pleased that I did, but not as pleased as when I was back at ground level. We resisted the classic photograph of one of us holding up the tower, so our view, (Fig. 350) is more conventional!

Back in the UK, as Oliver and Jude were now engaged, we were invited to meet Jude's parents for lunch, in Newmarket at the Bedford Lodge. Whilst Jude was born and brought up in the UK, her family were originally from Hong Kong. Her father was far more confident in speaking English than her mother, and we managed to chat either in broken English, which was much better than our non-existent Chinese, or Jude interpreted for them. All in all, the lunch was a great success and gave us all an opportunity to meet up, and in our case, start to understand some of the cultural differences between Hong Kong and the UK.

Early April, I was working in York and as such was able to meet up with my brother-in-law, David Riddington, who was celebrating his retirement from Aviva. He had spent all his working life at Norwich Union/Aviva including stints in Australia and Dublin, so there were a good number of colleagues wishing him well.

The weekend of April 12/13 was set aside in order that I could go walking with my colleague Colin Guthrie. He and I had worked very closely on the Occupied

Chapter 6 Ground up with Flints & Blocks 1999 – 2014

Figure 351

Property Strategy, and as we both enjoyed walking had decided to go up to the Derbyshire Peak district, to walk Kinder Scout and then over to Jacob's Ladder.

This walk which started from Packhorse bridge (Fig. 351) took us through some beautiful landscapes and as it was only around eight miles in length it was easily accomplished in a day.

Kate with Anne, Colin's wife, joined us but rather than undertake the walk, they visited Bakewell and sampled the famous Bakewell pudding. Afterwards, we all met up for a cream tea and on the way back to Norfolk called in to wander around Haddon Hall, where Jim had filmed some of the scenes in the *The Other Boleyn Girl*.

For work, I was still commuting to York each week and by mid-April 2008, my role there was made permanent, which gave us both some security, but also raised the question as to whether we should relocate. This wasn't a difficult decision, and it will be no surprise that we decided to stay in Norfolk at 'The Barn'. It did mean that I had to commute by car to Peterborough and then train to York. This was a small inconvenience and the platform in Peterborough was frequently populated with a number of like-minded Aviva colleagues, all undertaking the same journey. So, our decision was not unusual.

Towards the conclusion of The Occupied Property Strategy, in which I was heavily involved, some of the team worked on the purchase and integration of the Royal Automobile Club (RAC) into Aviva before the entire team was disbanded following the successful conclusion of both programmes. Those of my colleagues, who were still in this team, were either re-integrated to other projects and joined me in York or they were made redundant. Fortunately for me, having been previously transferred to other programmes in York, my role was secure.

Its senior Director though and my previous boss Stuart Smith, chose to retire at this point. He was given a special evening in The Marble Hall, where invited guests including myself and Colin, had a beautiful meal. This was followed by a presentation to Stuart by Patrick Snowball, the previous Aviva plc Director, and the driving force behind those two major transformational programmes.

This meant that back at the barn, my work was curtailed to the weekends, whilst Kate's massage and B&B were very much a daily undertaking. However, with the major building work now completed, I could focus my efforts on my preferred activities of maintenance, gardening and general upkeep of the fabric of the building. I was also able to help Kate at the weekends with the B&B, which was now very busy and had received some very good reviews. Kate had also built up a number of regular guests who, in some cases, always planned their visit to the area around the B&B's availability! Which says a lot!

Figure 352

On 14 May 2008, Angus and two of his fellow BASE jumpers, Tim Emmett and Roger Holmes, were to make history by being the first people to climb and then BASE jump off the 450', Old Man of Hoy in Orkney (Fig. 352).

Tim, at the time, was a Bristol television presenter, and along with his wife they made a documentary film of the climb and jump. After three years of planning, seven hours climbing the stack, it took just ten seconds to return to ground level! Angus, who wasn't a trained climber, was so thrilled to have achieved their goal and their amazing feat was reported in many of the newspapers. A film of the event, at the time of writing, is still on YouTube, under timemmettmovies.

Two days later, I was to undertake, along with several Aviva colleagues, a more modest climb up the Yorkshire Three Peaks. This well-known challenge was to cover, in under 12 hours, the 24.5-mile route up Pen-y-Ghent (694 metres), Whernside (736 metres) and Ingleborough (723 metres), ideally in that order. If successful you had the honour of being a member of the Three Peaks of Yorkshire Club.

Having signed in at the base shop, we then had our start time recorded by the independent recorder, mine was 07.54, we then all set off on our challenge. We walked, climbed and in some cases ran the route. We all arrived safely back

Chapter 6 Ground up with Flints & Blocks 1999 – 2014

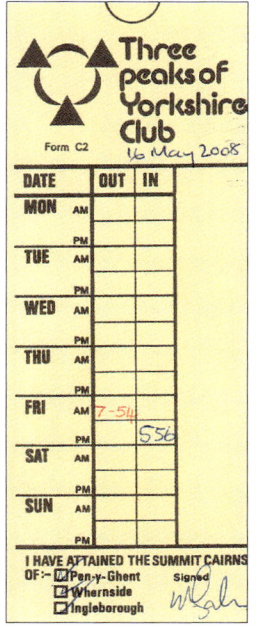

Figure 353

at the base, and I was clocked in at 17.56, having completed the challenge in 10 hours two minutes. The official verified my times, so I was now deemed a new club member (Fig. 353).

When I write this, it seems to appear on paper, to be an easy challenge. But I can assure you it certainly was not, as far as I was concerned anyway. It was competitive, not just to complete this within the 12 hours for the official judicator, but also within our small group of colleagues, some of whom, I regret to say didn't finish in the allotted time, but we still all enjoyed the day. Whilst not being in the first batch to complete the course, I was very happy to finish within the time limit and receive my mug and badge. Returning home triumphant, on the following day I had a well-earned cup of tea, obviously christening my new mug, (Fig. 354).

On the Sunday, Kate and I had a leisurely cycle ride around Kelling Heath which was most relaxing and enjoyable.

We rang Angus on the evening of 22 May, as we were aware that he was driving over to Grenoble in Switzerland, to BASE jump the Eiger and then meet up with friends to jump in one of his favourite and most visited locations. He was in good form and looking forward to new challenges.

Figure 354

What happened next was unbelievable and changed our family for ever. I have thought long and hard over many days, as to how I could write the next section in order that I both relay the facts accurately and help you, the reader, to understand the emotions that Kate, I and others felt at the time.

I have concluded that the best way is to firstly give the facts as they appeared in a press report (overleaf) written by Kate and myself, in conjunction with our friend Amanda Sandland-Taylor, who owned 'Newsmakers PR'. This was published by the *East Anglian Daily Times* amongst many others. I will then follow with my own personal thoughts and reactions.

335

EAST ANGLIAN
DAILY TIMES

BASE jumper killed in mountain crash.
25th June 2008

AN extreme sports fan died after crashing during a leap from a Swiss mountain, his grieving family has revealed.

BASE jumper Angus Hutchison-Brown suffered multiple injuries after deploying his parachute late to avoid power lines.

His mother, who lives at Bodham in north Norfolk, has paid tribute to the son who 'lived life to the full.'

Mr Hutchison-Brown, a 29-year-old computer consultant, had made more than 1,000 skydives and 500-plus BASE jumps from mountains and man-made structures in the pursuit of the ultimate adrenaline rush.

He was one of a party of five extreme sport enthusiasts making an early morning BASE jump at Meiringen in Switzerland on May 25.

After delaying his chute to miss the power lines, he did not have enough height to slow his descent to a safe landing speed, said a spokesman for the family.

Other jumpers and Swiss emergency services were unable to save him. An inquest opened and adjourned by Norwich coroner William Armstrong confirmed he died from multiple injuries.

Extreme sports fans, family and friends recently packed Holt parish church to celebrate Mr Hutchison-Brown's life.

Just days earlier he and two friends had become the first BASE jumpers to conquer the 450-foot Old Man of Hoy in the Orkneys – spending seven gruelling hours climbing to the top, all to experience the adrenaline rush of a 10-second flight back to the rocks below.

His mother Kate Gosden, a school teaching assistant and massage therapist, said: 'Wherever he was in the world, he delighted in telephoning us to let us know about his latest jump success and we were always very supportive of what he was doing.'

> 'He loved living life to the full, on the edge but not being fazed by anything. He was very kind, caring and considerate.'
>
> Her husband Keith paid tribute to the Swiss authorities and British officials who had Angus's body repatriated within three days of the accident.
>
> Born and brought up in Norwich, Angus attended Colman First, Avenue Middle and Hewett schools. He gained four A levels – becoming a Norfolk Scholar for his results – and went on to gain a 2:1 degree in computer science at Nottingham University.
>
> In his younger days, Angus was a chorister with the Wymondham Choir. He performed in a number of the nation's top cathedrals – and on Songs of Praise.
>
> On leaving university he took up a post with an IT consultancy company. His love affair with parachutes began when his family bought him an 18th birthday present of a tandem skydive at Old Buckenham, which kick started a hobby that took him to the USA, Norway, Italy, Spain, France and Switzerland.
>
> Mrs Gosden said Angus was always very methodical in his preparations and took extreme care – often phoning to say he had called off a jump and was facing a long climb back down a mountain.
>
> 'He would call and share his excitement with us – and later show us films he had recorded on his helmet camera. But at the same time, he was very modest about his achievements. Underneath it all he was a very private and quiet person.'

What follows is my recollection of what happened over the next few days and weeks.

On Sunday 25 May, Kate and I were in Clare, attending a celebratory lunchtime drinks party, hosted by her sister Gillian and husband Geoffrey. So, we were totally unaware that something catastrophic had happened. When we returned home our B&B guests advised us that the police had called round but as we weren't at home, they would try again on the Monday. We thought no more about this.

The Monday was the start of half-term and after breakfast having said goodbye to our guests, at mid-morning there was a knock on the B&B front door.

Kate opened the door to find two police officers, standing on the step, in full uniform wearing all the usual police regalia including handcuffs, pepper spray, batons etc., and who had parked their marked police car in the drive. Kate confirmed her name and then proceeded, to their dismay, to ask for their ID. Which of course they produced, and at the time, little did we know that probably they had had the hardest job to do that day, and one that all officers must dread.

They came indoors, sat down and proceeded to tell us both the dreadful news that Angus had died. I recall that we were both composed and were able to ask sensible questions like '*where is Angus now, who do we need to talk to in Switzerland, how do we bring him back to the UK?*' etc. Not all the questions were, or could be answered, but we were given the name of the contact at the British Embassy in Switzerland. The officers then left, and having closed the door, I turned to Kate who simply said, '*can I scream now,*' and she did. I often wonder what the police officers thought when they heard that scream whilst walking back to their car. We hugged and sat down, I simply can't recall the emotions that we shared, but I do recall that both of us were incredibly focused and within minutes were on the telephone to the British Embassy in Switzerland.

Doris Lourens, The Vice Consul to whom we spoke was so understanding and absolutely brilliant. Without her support and calm approach, I don't know how we would have coped. She put us in touch with the local police, who had attended the accident, and they confirmed that they had found and secured Angus's car, and with the help of his BASE jumping friends had sorted through his papers and found that he was fully insured. All this information was given to the Embassy, who then organised the repatriation of Angus back to the UK. First though, there had to be a Swiss autopsy which ruled out any possible issues and confirmed the assumption of accidental death. With the renowned efficiency of the Swiss authorities, Angus arrived back in the UK on Swissair flight LX324, at 16.25, on 28 May. Two days later his beautiful lead lined coffin arrived in Norfolk and was taken to the undertakers in Holt. Here the necessary preparations were made so our family could visit him.

The family all came home to 'The Barn' and before his cremation we were all able to see him, at the Chapel of Rest and say our goodbyes. We all agreed that following his cremation there would be a Service of Remembrance, at St. Andrew's Church in Holt, and to this end on 13 June we both met Father Howard, who was the priest to Holt Church. He kindly agreed to host the service and to allow The Reverend Jonathan Peel to officiate, as he was a close friend of Kate's family. The undertakers, Peter Taylor, could now commence work on an Order of Service.

Whilst Angus was in the Chapel of Rest, Kate and I had noticed that there were stained glass windows around the room featuring seals. By coincidence,

Chapter 6 Ground up with Flints & Blocks 1999 – 2014

we had both recently seen and liked a beautiful pair of ceramic seals, in Bircham Gallery, in Holt. Angus very rarely sat on a comfy chair, preferring to lie on the floor, in a similar laid-back way as real seals do on the sand. Now, having made that connection, we thought the ones in the gallery would make a wonderful remembrance gift for us and they are now kept as a reminder on our bookcase, out of harm's way (Fig. 355).

Whilst all these arrangements were being planned and slotted into place, there was a need for the local coroner, Willian Armstrong, to review the cause of death and if agreed, endorse the findings of the Swiss Authorities. We gave him all the details and paperwork that we had, which included the Swiss Death Certificate.

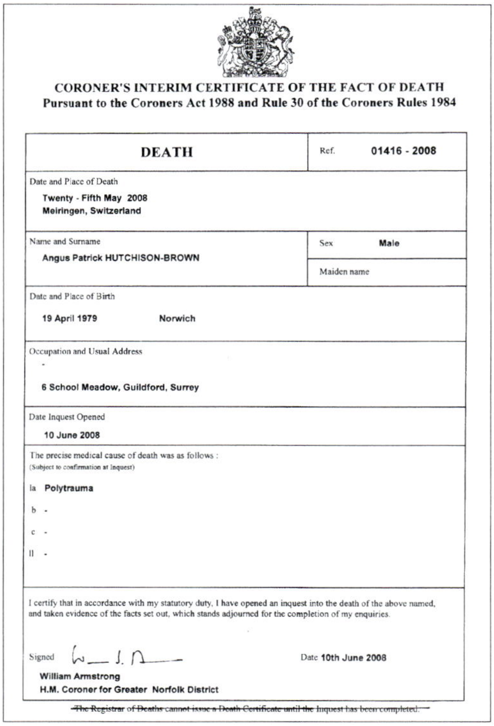

Figure 355

As had happened many times before, his group of friends had filmed the day's jumps in Meiringen, which included the one of Angus. This DVD was handed to the coroner, who having looked at all the evidence and the film, stated that his findings, of accidental death concurred with those set out by the Swiss authorities.

On 10 June, the film was returned to us along with the necessary paperwork (Fig. 356). But we were advised that a formal UK inquest would need to be held. The coroner's office had also inserted a warning on the film just prior to Angus's jump, in order that if we desired, we could stop the film at that point. This was most thoughtful of them, and we thanked William and his staff for their kind consideration.

Figure 356

339

At the cremation service, attended by just family, I was included in the pallbearers, and I recall just how heavy the coffin was and saying quietly to him, *'what on earth have you been eating'*. They were my very last words to Angus. The service went according to plan and his ashes were collected from the undertakers in a classical, wooden spherical urn.

This was to be carried at his memorial service, with such dignity by Kate, down the aisle of St. Andrew's Church. Not only did Kate carry him into the church but she also wrote and delivered a very moving eulogy, as the transcript below records.

To this day I simply don't know where Kate found the strength and composure to deliver these words, so eloquently.

> *Before I start, Keith and I would like to thank everyone here for all your love and support that you have given all our family over the last few weeks. We are all absolutely amazed and have taken so much comfort from this.*
>
> *A number of you have also agreed to talk about different aspects of Angus's life, as you will have seen in The Order of Service. We thank you so much for these and I'm sure we will all agree that they will add colour and depth to this service which celebrates Angus's Life and Achievements.*
>
> *Angus, and I know a lot of you know him as Gus, being an expert Consultant in IT, will on the one hand, be thoroughly impressed by all the modern technology that has been used in preparation of his service but on the other will be saying most definitely 'what on earth is all this fuss about'!*
>
> *Angus as we all know was not an impatient person.*
>
> *Nothing seemed to faze him, even in his teenage years we never saw an obstreperous or bolshie side of him.*
>
> *A determined side, yes most definitely and that was apparent even before he was born, for he had obviously decided in his own quiet and resolute way to start enjoying life as soon as possible.*
>
> *His godmother Jenny, who regrettably is unable to be here today, as she is in France, will verify that in true Angus style he arrived into this world, without any fuss or bother – but four weeks early and that we were all safely ensconced back home before he was even eight hours old.*
>
> *He was brought up with the love of fresh air and as a baby would go to sleep quite happily outside, in his pram, in all weathers – rain, sun, wind and snow. I really was a tough mother, and I can remember to this day, one winter, carrying him indoors on one arm, he was all toasty warm and on the other holding an armful of rock-solid frozen terry nappies! That's how cold it was but Angus was none the worse for wear!*
>
> *In the summer he would be out in the garden as much as possible and I have*

wonderful memories of him climbing up the scrambling net, up to the top of the wooden climbing frame, then jumping off from a great height with squeals of delight. Little did we know that these small pleasures would become the major challenges and exploits and the love of Angus's life. For his 18th birthday we gave him a tandem Sky Dive jump at Old Buckenham and the whoops of exhilaration could be heard by us on the ground below, long before he came through the clouds to land right beside us. I'm convinced those shouts of pure elation were still audible today on the clip of him landing on the airfield.

Back home, before and after he was born, whether he liked it or not, he was always surrounded by a diverse range of music.

From Chopin to The Cream. From Elgar to the Eagles and his own love of music became very apparent, early on, when he would quite happily lie in his cot and play his Fisher Price Activity Centre. I'm sure many parents will recall those wonderful toys. Angus's is still up in the attic! Later on, he would sit either on the kitchen floor, whilst a meal was being cooked or in the Drawing Room, whilst Top of the Pops was broadcast and would play along to the Top Ten Hits with his wooden spoons and an array of upturned saucepans and pudding basins.

Moving on to First School, his Music Teacher spotted his talent for singing and at the age of eight he auditioned and successfully became a chorister with The Wymondham Choir, becoming a Bishop's Chorister just before his voice broke.

Now I wonder how many of his friends knew of this talent. I bet he kept that well hidden under a bushel!

The Choir's Musical Director was Adrian Lucas who, like many of you, has had to travel long distances to be here today. His choir was an independent choir made up of about 40 boys and men all from the Norfolk area. Their repertoire was very varied, taking church music to choir-less churches, singing regularly in other Norfolk churches, both large and small. Performing at weddings; concerts, recitals. On the Radio, at The Royal Albert Hall and with Harry Secombe at Walsingham Abbey for television. The Choir also made annual visits to some of the country's great Cathedrals e.g. Salisbury, Gloucester, Ely, Beverley and York Minster to name but a few, and here they sang in place of the resident Choir. One year they visited Koblenz, in Germany, which Angus thoroughly enjoyed until the day before their return home when he ate a dodgy German sausage. He was so ill on the ferry back that he had to remain in the captain's cabin throughout the journey. Unfortunately, he had no recollection of this exciting and eventful voyage but I'm sure Adrian will be able to tell you more about it when we all meet at The Lawns.

The picture you saw earlier of Angus was taken at Norwich Cathedral, the night he sang the solo verse of 'Once in Royal David's City'.

My toes curl even now at the thought of it.

To be able to stand up and sing to a capacity audience of 600 people, still amazes me.

That's courage for you! And this, as we were to see, remained with him throughout his life.

The photograph does rather depict him as the stereotypical blond, blue-eyed, innocent, angelic chorister but having escorted the choirboys to many of their venues; I can reassure all present that that was certainly not the case. He was a typical young boy, constantly up to mischief and playing pranks and I'm convinced that this continued right up into adulthood.

Come to think of it, we do have recent photographic evidence from Ric and Amanda of Angus fooling around and obviously enjoying life to the full.

I know Oliver, his brother, and Emily and Sophie, his sisters, have some wonderful memories of Angus when they were all at home together and I'm sure Oliver will talk in more detail, shortly, about some of the escapades they got up to. Some of which I'm sure we as parents were never ever aware of!! Maybe even now we shall never find out!

There must be many of you here today thinking of some ridiculous activity that Angus initiated and that inevitably ended up in guffaws of infectious laughter with that wonderful smile and the famous lean back laugh!

Having outgrown the wooden spoons, he moved on to a mini guitar, given to him as a birthday present and would play the most unbelievably, excruciating, discordant chords. Which at the time he thought were brilliant? I'm not sure we did, but little did we appreciate that the sound would actually be far more pleasing to the ears than the screeching cat wail strings of the violin which he decided to learn to play at Middle School. The examiners of The Norfolk Music Festival though, were obviously duly impressed for with a group of friends making up a string Quartet, they achieved a Highly Commended performance. Ben, if you are here. Well done!

Whilst the choir was still very much part of his musical life, with Alex and Dave's influence, their passion for music and their own group The Kommotions, Angus's love of the guitar was rekindled, and he never looked back. Many happy hours were spent composing his own pieces of music for GCSE, which later progressed to reading and playing the scores of many bands, e.g. Eels, Counting Crows, Sheryl Crow and Nirvana.

We did not always have the same taste in music but as parents you very rarely do with your own children. I know my parents must have despaired, at times, when they had to endure my choice of records when I was in my teens. We did discover though, very recently indeed that our love of James Taylor music had obviously rubbed off on Angus, as he had taken one of his albums to Switzerland.

So maybe he did have some excellent choice in music, after all!

Hence the track that follows Oliver's tribute.

Throughout his life he was quiet, unassuming, unpretentious and always the mediator. His calming influence was always a positive factor within the family. However, when it came to philosophical debate around the supper table, Angus would always hold his own, sometimes to the point where continued debate would be utterly pointless.

Again, Oliver may enlighten you further.

We will all remember his wonderful, quick, dry sense of humour and as already mentioned his lean back laughs, appropriately captured on film for posterity.

Many of you will also have seen the serious side too, thoughtful of others in preference to himself, caring, kind, loving and loyal with a strong sense of right and wrong.

He became the sibling spokesman, at an early age, whether by choice or because his elder sister, Emily, would more often than not push him in front, when entering a room full of strangers, saying 'Go on, Angus, you go first. You can do all the talking' and before he knew it, he was in the front and leading the way. He did, though, rise to the occasions and we suspect that this may have been a good grounding for his leadership skills.

I'm going to end with those awesome hugs of his. They started when he was knee high to a grasshopper and would catch you completely unawares, hugging your knees with such a force that you were nearly knocked off balance. Through the years as he grew taller his hugs moved up your body and I shall never forget one of his visits home from University, when he had suddenly put on such a spurt that he was able to rest his chin on the top of my head and the hugs then became shoulder hugs. Still, he continued to grow but his hugs never diminished, if anything they became tighter and firmer and more full of love. If, like me, you wear glasses you may have had these squashed out of all alignment as I have frequently and we've certainly all experienced the air being squeezed out of your lungs.

He had so much love to share and today seeing you all here is testament to the tremendous friendships that have been built up over the years and the many hearts that he has touched. Thank you all so very much.

Angus's service was not the traditional sombre affair but was very much a celebration of his life. Following Kate's eulogy, Oliver gave a moving reflection of growing up with him, outlining some of the antics they both participated in during their teenage years, including an attempt to soak Kate, with a bucket of water propped on top of a half open door. Luckily, at the time, this was unsuccessful.

The remainder of the service was handed over to his school and university friends and fellow sky-diving and BASE jumpers, and from there on it certainly wasn't a normal service. For it also included the first showing of the momentous climb up the Old Man of Hoy, with Angus, Tim and Roger being filmed by Tim's wife, and the three of them had all been able to join us for the service. The film was lovely, and afterwards at the wake, a copy was presented to Kate.

In the following weeks it transpired that Angus, through his employment, had the benefit of a Death in Service agreement, and Kate had to explain to the Trustees how she thought this should be used and by whom. This was necessary as the mandate that Angus had signed made mention of his father who, of course, had predeceased him. Kate and I wrote a letter, as can be seen below, which in short suggested that she was to be the only beneficiary, and that the money was to be used for the benefit of his brother and sisters.

> *5 August 2008*
>
> *To The Trustees of Angus Hutchison-Brown Death in Service Funds*
>
> I understand from Sarah Dillingham that you are to make a decision upon the distribution of our son's Death in Service Benefit. This would, of course, normally be carried out in accordance with the mandate held by you. However, as you are aware. this has not been kept up to date as his father has predeceased him. As his mother and next of kin, I would like to explain to you Angus's family situation and how I feel the funds could be distributed in a fair and equitable way.
>
> Angus's father left when Angus was only 5 years old. For a number of years both he and his sister, Emily, lived with and were brought up by me and by mutual agreement they stayed with their father every other weekend.
>
> For the last 16 years Angus, along with Emily, have been part of a very happy and close family unit with Keith my husband, Oliver and Sophie.
>
> We have always collectively considered this to be our 'family' to the point following the death of his natural father Angus called Keith, 'Dad'.
>
> We all support each other in different ways. As parents we support through advice and where sought, financial assistance. Angus contributed to this support in a number of ways e.g. through his help with Oliver's GCSES, as outlined during The Service of Thanksgiving his frequent socialising with his sister and extended family and without fail he helped all of us with his IT expertise!
>
> As his mother, I would like to see the funds provide a long-term benefit that mirrors the care and support that Angus has shown for his brother and sisters. To this end, it is my intention to use a large proportion of his estate to purchase a holiday home in France. This will benefit all his extended family by providing

free holidays for them and their children, during my lifetime and will provide a lasting beneficial memory to Angus. Upon my death, I envisage all my children inheriting a share of the property.

In addition, an amount of money will be put aside for all our children to share and to borrow in times of need and to give them support at key times throughout their lives. This is something that we have done throughout our marriage and all our children have benefited. Most recently, Emily and her husband Peter were given a contribution to enable them to take a well-deserved break, in Greece. When they have each been in a position to be able to do so, the loan has been repaid. However, this is not a requirement by us.

I am aware that each one of our children is embarking upon Life Changing experiences and I would like to support them and their aspirations both emotionally and financially.

- *Emily and Peter are looking to purchase their first home.*
- *Oliver and his fiancée Jude are planning their wedding next year*
- *Sophie is in her first year of training, as a mature student, in Veterinary Nursing. She is looking to complete her second year and to extend her experience and further her qualifications.*

I understand that at your discretion you can distribute the funds in a number of ways. I am mindful that all three of our children see Angus as their brother and therefore, I hope to avoid any undue jealousy resulting from the distribution of his estate. Furthermore, I am clear in my own mind that I would like to see long term benefit derived from Angus's untimely death.

The scenario outlined above, which I have discussed with Keith who totally concurs, ensures that:

- *the funds are invested wisely to ensure that they provide long term benefit rather than short term gain, e.g. paying off Credit Cards*
- *a holiday home provides equal access to all family members, thus avoiding any possible jealousy from a purely cash distribution.*
- *the funds will be administered in accordance with family principles that have always been in existence.*
- *each individual member of the family will benefit from private gifts of lump sum payments when the time is right and most advantageous to them.*
- *they and their families can enjoy free holidays and the final distribution, upon my death, will pass Angus's legacy to the next generation.*

I would ask you as Trustees please to consider this approach and if you feel it is appropriate to allow me as Angus's mother and next of kin to distribute his funds from his estate as outlined.

Angus, I know, would have continued, throughout his life, to help his siblings in every way possible. Clearly, now, this is not feasible but his legacy if administered wisely will ensure that his name supports them and their families in the future.

In conclusion, I would like to express to you the gratitude of my family for the support and consideration that has been extended to us by Detica, and in particular Sarah Dillingham.

Thank you for taking the time to read and discuss this letter and I look forward to receiving your considered response.

Yours faithfully,
Kate Gosden (Mrs)

This suggested outcome was accepted by the trustees and in time each of his sisters and his brother benefited from a generous gift towards the purchase of their future family homes.

Angus pursuing his dream (Fig. 357).

Figure 357

Meanwhile, some of the Death in Service funds were also to be used to purchase a holiday property, which was to be available to the family, when not being used as a holiday let. This decision was followed by an extensive and, in most cases, a fruitless search looking for suitable properties in Europe that included France, Austria and Switzerland.

However, the closest contender, during this search, was this lovely half restored house in Jumilhac-Le-Grand, in France (Fig.

Figure 358

358). We didn't proceed though, as we felt the cost of completing the work was too uncertain at the time. So, the search continued.

Returning to 'The Barn', we were approached by Aga, who wanted to run a feature in their UK magazine, about our B&B. The rationale was that they knew we exclusively used an Aga, for cooking all our B&B guests' meals, and given this they wanted to promote how an Aga was the ideal cooking appliance. Kate and I agreed, and a photographer arrived to take some suitable photographs (Fig. 359). This took virtually the whole morning, but in our opinion the result was really good. Em though, thought her version, (Fig. 360) was much better! We weren't so sure, and a jovial conversation ensued.

Figure 359

Figure 360

Figure 361

Over the weekend of 27/28 September 2008, Angus's fellow BASE jumpers organised a memorial jump off the Swaffham Turbine (Fig. 361), which also raised money for charity. Kate and I drove over to watch and also climbed to the viewing point so Kate could release some of his ashes from the top, just so he could be part of the event. It was an emotional day, but it was fantastic and highly successful. It was also featured on the Monday, in the BBC's *Look East* news bulletin.

On the following Sunday, with life returning to a new normal, we accompanied Oliver and Jude to view Wolterton Hall, as a potential wedding venue. Having spoken to Lady Walpole the owner, Oliver and Jude were convinced that they had found their ideal location, particularly as it was within easy reach of our barn where we had already agreed to hold the reception, in our back garden.

Come October 2008, given the year that we had endured, we both felt the need to have a short holiday. So, a week's break to Ibiza was purchased, with a flight direct from Norwich, at 14.55 on 25 October. As a holiday, the visit was reasonable, in that we went sightseeing around the Ibiza town, and took a bus to St. Eulària des Riu, but everything, everywhere was closed! We also had a boat trip but everyone on board was so cold and damp that when we landed, no one wanted to stay, so the skipper turned the boat round and we all happily returned to Ibiza! The weather all week was mostly cloudy, wet, windy and very cold, with the warmest day on the Monday, and even then, the temperature struggled to reached 20°.

Still, we had a good laugh, relaxed and actually had some very good meals and plenty of coffee (Fig. 362). The sunsets were also a wonderful sight, but I don't think we will ever return!

Figure 362

Chapter 6 Ground up with Flints & Blocks 1999 – 2014

We arrived back on Sunday 1 November to a very cold Norwich Airport. Whilst we were away, Kate had been in contact with Sterling Helicopters, that were based at Norwich Airport, to book a flight in order that she, along with Em and Pete could fly over 'The Barn' and scatter Angus's ashes, which we had all thought was most appropriate.

Figure 363

The flight was booked for the weekend of 22/23 November and was obviously dependent on the weather. Despite there being snow on the ground, the flight still went ahead (Fig. 363) and it wasn't long before those of us at the barn, were outside looking for the helicopter.

In the photograph (Fig. 364) taken by Kate, you can just see me in the front garden (indicated by the arrow), standing between the two walls. His ashes were scattered and we all wished Angus well and bade him to 'Fly Free'.

Figure 364

349

The end of November was examination time for Sophie, and as she had worked so hard she was quietly confident as, in fact, we all were. December was upon us before we had time to think about it, but we did witness both the Holt and the Cromer Christmas lights being switched on.

With all our family at home for Christmas, we had to do something to make it just that little bit special. Knowing how we all liked mystery murders, we organised a Sherlock Holmes Murder Mystery Dinner, where each of us had to portray a particular character, along with suitable notes, that if asked we had to deliver at the appropriate time.

Fig. 365 – The cast in full costume.

Fig. 366 – Oliver learning his lines (above).
Fig. 367 – The cast whilst enjoying their meal, are seen acting out the 'Who Done It….' (right)

Chapter 6 Ground up with Flints & Blocks 1999 – 2014

A good time was had by all, although neither Kate nor I seem to recall who was murdered but we think Jude was the murderer? Figures 365 – 367 were taken on the day and are outlined with the accompanying descriptive captions.

This concluded a really difficult year for all of us, but a finale we were sure that Angus would have approved.

2009

As one might imagine, Kate and I started the year in a quiet and reflective mood, but with two key achievements on our minds. Firstly, to find a suitable property using Angus's legacy, that our family could use for holidays. Secondly, to ensure that Oliver and Jude's wedding reception, which was to be held in our garden, met their expectations and proceeded without any hitches.

The first achievement involved some long weekends abroad, as I have outlined previously, in countries that were familiar to Angus but not to us. The second was a matter of finishing all the landscaping and planting, which we had commenced but not quite had time to complete, and a certain wedding reception was the ideal motivation for this. So, it was unsurprising that when referring to our 2009 calendar, January 1 reads *'Bonfire, weeded bed in front of kitchen window. Finished all sanding today'*. The latter related to various internal and external beams that were being prepared for staining.

Before we commenced our gardening in earnest, we took the opportunity to visit Gillian and Geoffrey in Clare. They are both expert gardeners and regularly had their garden open to the public, including opening as part of the National Garden Scheme. Seeing their immaculate garden filled me with awe. If ours was to look anything like theirs, hard work would be required, but there was one significant advantage in our case, as much of our garden would be covered by a wedding marquee.

So, following our trip to Clare, during the next few months, most of the weekends but not all of them, were spent working in the garden.

Having travelled up to York as usual, I remained there on Saturday the 10th, in order that I could join Lisa Bolton and Mike Woodcock, both Aviva colleagues, on a walk in

Figure 368

the East Riding of Yorkshire. It was lovely but the weather, whilst not raining, was foggy and very cold, as can be seen (Fig. 368).

Over the past tumultuous months, Kate had been reviewing, in her own mind, her extraordinary workload and how she could manage this going forward. Both she and I were clear about what was important to her, and that was our family, living at 'The Barn', her Massage Therapy business and the B&B. Not necessarily in that order, apart from our family being uppermost in her thoughts. What was less enjoyable and now becoming a deflection to her other work, was working at Norwich High School.

In one capacity or other, Kate had been at the school as a five-year-old pupil, through to the sixth form. Then, after college and working as a teaching assistant for two state schools, she returned to the High School to become a member of staff where she taught six- and seven-year-olds.

Following a good deal of thought, Kate decided that ideally, she would like to concentrate her efforts away from the educational environment. A meeting with the head of the Infant School was held, where she gave advance warning that come July and the end of this academic year, she would leave her employment. This advance notice allowed plenty of time for the school to find a replacement, if that was their choice. Always putting others first, is a trait that Kate learnt from being a young girl and has been evident throughout her life, sometimes to her detriment. But this decision was to her total benefit and having made the choice we were both very happy.

The first week of February was mainly devoted to sorting out the papers pertaining to Angus. The previous week though, Kate had had an operation to remove a neuroma and have a toe reset, so some sedentary work was ideal. Whilst she recovered, this time had been used wisely, for when her foot was re-dressed, the view of the medic was that the healing process was all going according to plan. A week later the stitches were removed, and the wearing of a shoe support was no longer deemed necessary. That was music to her ears!

Oliver and Jude came home on 14 February, primarily to visit The Lawns, a small hotel in Holt, where Jude and some of her family planned to stay, during the wedding weekend. They also wanted to take a closer look and sample the food that was to be served at the reception, by an outside caterer. So, a visit was arranged, followed by lunch and the company passed the 'inspection' and was duly booked. That was one positive tick, on a very long list of wedding requirements.

Kate and I were busy visiting garden centres and nurseries, in a quest for shrubs and plants that would enhance the garden, in time for the wedding. Slow growing specimens were not on the list, no matter how lovely they would become 'in time'. Back in the garden, we then had a weekend's work, weeding beds, moving plants to more appropriate locations, and planting all the new purchases.

The first half of my 54th birthday, was spent on a train from York bound for Peterborough, then another one to Norwich, followed by a final train to Sheringham, where I met up with Kate. A long journey but one that we both knew well, as it now occurred each week. Due to court sittings and general time constraints, my birthday meal was celebrated later in the week, at The Walpole Arms, a favourite for both of us and a lovely venue in which to relax and unwind. It was just what we both needed – some time to ourselves.

Whilst all the fine details of Angus's accident had been agreed, therefore allowing the funeral to take place, we had been advised earlier that there was still the need for an official inquest to be held. In early March, we both met up again with the local coroner, William Armstrong, to establish what the process would be and how we would be involved. There was little for us to do, other than to be available, if required, and to receive the final findings, so a date was agreed for 17 April.

We had also decided that over Kate's birthday weekend, we would travel to the Austrian/Swiss borders to view several potential holiday properties, that Kate had found on-line. This required the booking of flights, setting up arrangements to meet the property agents, and sorting our accommodation. All of which Kate had in hand. Luckily, by 9 March, she was able to not only wear her normal shoes but could drive as well, so this was a big positive for the trip, in a week's time.

On 12 March, just three days prior to our flight and Kate's birthday, a visit to the doctors, regarding her neuroma, resulted in her being signed off, with a 'return to work date', agreed of the 18th. I was to spend all of Friday 13th in court, and on the following day we spent time titivating the garden, with a focus on the vegetable plot, outside the kitchen window.

Our flight, on Kate's birthday, flew from Luton, at 17.00. We were booked into the Geneva Ramada Hotel, where we had a lovely evening meal. The next day we took a train to Sion (Fig. 369) and before we met our agent Ludovic, we had the opportunity to wander around this town, which was

Figure 369

Figure 370

beautiful and as it met a number of our requirements was a clear possible location. Ludovic drove us to Les Collons, a small ski resort, not far from Verbier and our first viewings here were a selection of 2/3/4-bedroom apartments (Fig. 370). We were then driven further up the mountains to be shown some other properties, in Thyon. Here we discovered that very recently this area, had had six metres of snow, and apparently had been cleared. We could still see a metre or so on the rooves, but I guess that is 'cleared' in the eyes of the Swiss, as they as a nation are far more familiar with dealing with deep snow than we are!

Having returned to Les Collons, Kate and I had a gorgeous meal at La Maya restaurant. In order for us to gain the full experience of sleeping in a Swiss ski chalet, Ludovic had kindly arranged for us to stay overnight in one of the three bedroomed properties. This was certainly interesting, quite comfortable, and had everything you needed for a skiing holiday.

The next and final day at 10.00, we again met up with Ludovic, who drove us back to Sion, where we caught the train to Geneva, before being taken to the airport to catch our 13.00 flight, back to Luton. On landing, we were greeted by Oliver, who kindly returned us to our car, after which we made our way home, arriving in the early evening exhausted, a little confused and with an awful lot to think about.

One of the key features of both places we had visited was that they were primarily ski resorts and secondly, during other times of the year, were picturesque areas for trekking. As such, the property values reflected this and consequently the prices were high. Whilst this was expected, we had to consider that like us, none of our children to our knowledge, were either skiers or hikers.

Mothering Sunday fell on 22 March, and Gillian, Geoffrey, Peter, Jane and Judy, in other words all Kate's siblings and their partners, came to 'The Barn' for lunch after we had all attended the service in Barton Church, where Kate's parents and brother are buried. It was lovely to see them all, as this doesn't happen very often, due to the distances involved.

For Kate, the end of the Spring term loomed, with it ending in two days' time, as did the formal submission of her letter of resignation. This was handed over on 25 March 2009 and Kate's last day of paid employment was to be Friday 10 July 2009.

At the weekend, I undertook a long walk along the coastal path, starting at 09.30 from Morston Quay, through to Salthouse arriving at 12.15 and then onwards to finish at Sheringham, at 13.50. It was a damp and windy day so not ideal for walking, but it was enjoyable and kept me fit. Kate met me there and we both returned to a warm and cosy barn.

The last day of March was spent catching trains to York, with the first one being at 05.52! However, there was another house hunting trip at the weekend, this time to Austria, which Kate again sorted out. This was in-between her spraying weeds in both the front and back gardens, to ensure they looked well-kept for the forthcoming wedding!

On Friday, 3 April, we flew at 06.30, with Ryanair from Stansted to Salzburg. Given we were on a budget flight, I recall Ryanair not being the best choice of airline, but we did arrive safe and almost well. After collecting our hire car, we drove to Wagrain to meet Gunther our guide. We had one property to view there, another one in Flachau and two in Katschberg.

Figure 371

They were all good but not quite what we were looking for, as they weren't in an ideal location, given that we needed to ensure that traveling wasn't to be an issue. We then proceeded to Zell am See to find our hotel the Seehof (Fig. 371).[31] Overlooking the lake, it was stunning, and after a wander around the town, we enjoyed a delicious supper, reviewed the properties we had seen and prepared for day two.

The next day we had a three-hour drive to Zwieselstien, in the Tyrol. The scenery was fantastic and just as we had imagined, very *Sound of Music* and picturesque. The flats in the building (Fig. 372), were lovely but unfortunately a little too small for what we required, so we did not pursue this any further. The village was not particularly attractive either, so we proceeded to the next town, Sölden. This was lovely

Figure 372

---

31 Credit to www.tui.co.uk

Figure 373

during the day but very rowdy long into the evening, as we found out later whilst staying overnight at Gasthof Zwieselstien, (Fig. 373).[32]

After an uneventful but scenic three-hour drive back to Salzburg, we caught our delayed flight back to the UK and arrived home at 19.00. Had we found the perfect holiday home? No! Had we had a good time? Yes! The time wasn't wasted, but it did cause us to think about future options and locations, be they in the UK or in Europe.

At the weekend Oliver, Sophie, Barney and a friend from Aviva, Phil Churchman, undertook with me a different North Norfolk coastal path walk. This time further north from Burnham through to Cley. Unfortunately, due to an injury, Sophie was unable to finish it, so was driven back to the barn by Phil. Oliver and I did manage to complete it, and if my memory serves me correctly, I believe Barney stayed with us and thoroughly enjoyed the walk as well.

Back at 'The Barn' the annual Easter Day egg hunt was undertaken by the younger family members, but this year it hadn't taken them long, so in future we guessed the clues would need to be more cryptic.

In order that we could continue to 'blitz' the garden, I was on holiday for the week after the Easter celebrations and once we had said our goodbyes on Easter Monday, I resumed laying slabs around the back of the barn, whilst Kate finished the herb bed. It was a major job and took me until Thursday to finish laying them. But as all the wedding guests would need to use the area to access the marquee, it was essential work, and we were now a step closer to being ready.

On Friday 17 April 2009, we had the inquest into Angus's accident, so both Kate and I attended the coroner's office, to hear his findings. They were very much as we both expected, in that after reviewing the evidence from his fellow BASE jumpers, seeing the reports from the medical services and watching the film, he concluded that his death was an unfortunate accident. The inquest was now formally closed.

At this juncture, Kate and I would like to record how impressed we were by the

---

32 Credit to Booking.com

professionalism and the consideration of both the coroner, William Armstrong, and his staff who were all exemplary. As I have previously said, they were all so incredibly considerate.

Angus and his friends were cleared of any suspicion of not being professional on the day, meaning we could all, like Angus, now rest in peace through knowing that this was simply a tragic accident.

Oliver, Jude and Sophie all came home for the weekend, as it was Angus's birthday on the Sunday. Oliver and Jude had brought with them a chinese lantern along with a small card and gift. Adhering to a Chinese tradition, the card and present were ceremoniously ignited, as was the lantern which was then released and took their love and wishes up to Angus. This was repeated for years to come, and Sophie would set free a helium balloon from her garden as well. After the chinese ceremony, we then had afternoon tea and cake before they all returned to their homes. Regrettably, Em and Pete were unable to join us, as Em was working in Earls Court on that day.

Kate's last school term at Norwich High School commenced on 21 April, so to ensure her pension payments commenced on time, the advance letters were sent off to the Pension Trust. To be a pensioner was a sobering thought for Kate, until she realised just how active she was at home. She is certainly not a typical senior citizen!

The May Day Bank Holiday weekend started with Kate and I planting even more plants, whilst Sophie undertook a 14-mile sponsored walk, raising an impressive £130. On the Monday, I too had a walk planned with friends. Mine was a 24-mile walk around Suffolk, commencing at 08.00 at Framlingham College. I was home for tea at 17.15, exhausted but ready for the train journey to York, early the next day.

The following Saturday and Sunday saw even more planting, which seemed to be a frequent occupation at the time. That was until 23/24 May when Kate and I went to Yorkshire to view some holiday properties in Patrick Brompton, Middleham, Leyburn and Hawes.

We were particularly struck by the small town of Middleham, although the two cottages weren't of interest. We returned to Norfolk, and having considered the locations in Yorkshire, we decided that perhaps a cottage in the UK was a more sensible plan. With this in mind, the next weekend we left home at 05.00 and drove to the Yorkshire Dales, where we viewed some more cottages in Gunnerside and Muker. Neither location was appropriate, but it was a nice day out in the sunshine.

Whilst working in York, in early June I took the opportunity to borrow a friend's car and visit Middleham again. This time I found what I thought was a very acceptable cottage overlooking fields, many of which were used for training racehorses. Middleham was famous, at the time, for having one hundred and thirty racehorses stabled there, with thirteen professional trainers. The owners included a number of sheiks and other high-profile people, and in the industry, it was known as the 'Newmarket of the North'. In 2023 there were fifteen Horse Racing yards.

Figure 374

At home on the Friday, I spoke to Kate and on the Saturday we both drove to Middleham to view the cottage together. This was definitely the one for us (Fig. 374). It did require some minor work but its location, near the town centre and the fact it had off street parking outside the front, made it a perfect choice. Over the next few weeks negotiations ensued, culminating in our offer of £181,000, being accepted which included some furniture and other items.

The position of Vale Cottage, as it was known, was ideal. The views were superb and fantastic for future guests who either loved horses, the Yorkshire Dales or even better, both!

The photograph (Fig. 375) shows the view

Figure 375

Chapter 6 Ground up with Flints & Blocks 1999 – 2014

from the front bedroom window overlooking one of the racing stables.

A view of the street (Fig. 376) with Vale Cottage being on the righthand side, and adjacent to the left of the property with the railings.

Figure 376

On Saturday 20 June, Oliver and Jude came to 'The Barn' and met my cousin Rosemary, who was an excellent cake maker, to talk about their wedding cake. With just six weeks to go, the final arrangements were now being put in place. On the following weekend they returned, and this time were joined by Jude's sister, Lai Ming, with all three of them visiting Wolterton Hall, where the ceremony was to be held. For all of us, an evening meal at the Honey Bell pub, in Hunworth, rounded off a couple of positive weekends.

The barn was just about shipshape and ready for the wedding. There were just two final things to do. Firstly, the drive up to our B&B entrance needed to be levelled and re-dressed with shingle and secondly, thirty four bags of bark chip had to be laid around the slabs on the path, from the back screen up to the rear of the back garden. Both of these tasks were completed over the next few days. We were now ready for the professionals to erect the marquees, set out the tables and chairs etc. But that was to be undertaken much closer to the day.

Kate's 'Red Letter' day arrived on 10 July, when she finally left school! There was a suitable lunch at Stafford House, the location of the Infant School. However, the previous day she had made a speech during the school assembly and presented the head teacher with a silver salver, which was to be awarded annually to future pupils (Fig. 377). It was inscribed with:

Stafford House
The Infant Award
For
Progress and Perseverance
Presented by Mrs Kate Gosden
July 2009

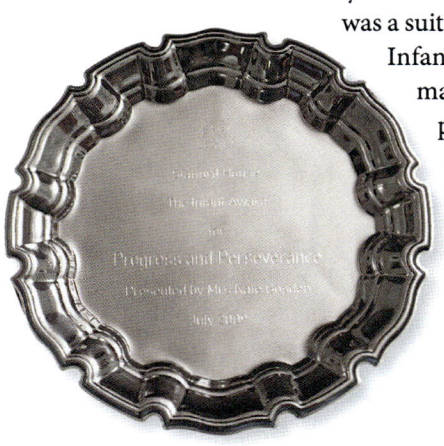

Figure 377

359

A very fitting leaving gift from someone who probably knew more about life at Norwich High School for Girls than anyone else in the room. We also held a leaving party at 'The Barn' where many of Kate's colleagues and friends were able to join us and bid her farewell, in a more relaxed environment.

Kate may have 'retired' but there was to be no rest. There was a wedding reception to host, a Massage Therapy business to run, as well as a B&B. Not to mention her ongoing support of our family.

The next day Jude was back in Norfolk, for a practice 'hair do', and asked Kate to accompany her. As far as I am aware all went well, although experience has taught me not to comment. Jude was preparing to leave her family nest and set up her own home with Oliver. However, she wasn't the only one taking a giant leap of faith, as we had a nest of swallows, who fledged on 18 July. We were to witness this whilst preparing the garden for the marquee, cutting the grass, clearing the pond, tying up hollyhocks and tidying other large plants. We were ready for the marquee. But in all honesty, we had no idea just what to expect.

The next morning was to reveal just what we had agreed to, with the marquee company. A Land Rover and trailer, along with four men 'arrived' on the 28th at 09.30, and by the evening that day, the contents of their trailer had been converted into a perfect wedding reception venue. The creation of this is best told in the series of photographs (Figs. 378 – 391).

When viewing these photographs, you should be aware that the workday was peppered with heavy showers, and that all this was undertaken by just four men.

Figure 378

Figure 379

Chapter 6 Ground up with Flints & Blocks 1999 – 2014

The section below (Figs. 380 – 381) was to house the 'Tea Ceremony', whilst the main seating area, photographs of which follow on (Figs. 382 – 389), was adjacent to this. However, there was access to both marquees that were linked, in order that on the day, their guests could see the happy couple, during the tea ceremony. This was to follow on with a meal, the cutting of the cake and the speeches.

Figure 380

Figure 381

Figure 382

Figure 383

Figure 384

Figure 385

361

Later into the evening, Jude, her sister and Oliver, set out their seating plan (Figs. 390 – 391). Em, Pete and Sophie arrived the day before the wedding. The sound system was installed, the tables were laid with cutlery, glasses, napkins and table lanterns etc., and we were all ready for supper, bed and the big day on 1 August (Figs. 392 – 395).

Figure 386

Figure 387

Figure 388

Figure 389

Figure 390

Figure 391

Figure 392

Figure 393

Figure 394

Figure 395

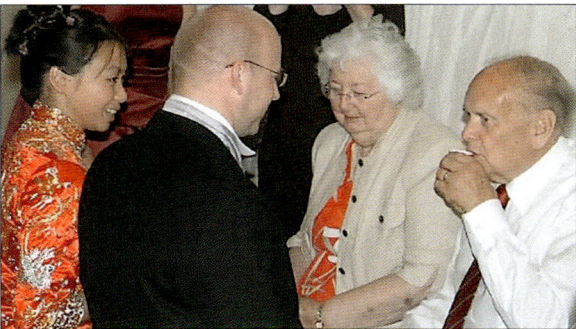

Figure 396

Above (Fig. 396) is Oliver and Jude joining my parents, in the traditional Chinese Tea Ceremony.

Oliver and Jude spent their first married night at Morston Hall, returning to 'The Barn' on the Sunday morning. Unbeknown to Kate and me, Jude's close family also arrived, so we suddenly found we had 17 guests for Sunday lunch. As always, Kate rose to the occasion and from somewhere, goodness knows where, she prepared and served a lunch that all of us thoroughly enjoyed.

Em and Pete left around 15.30, as did Jude's family. Oliver and Jude stayed a little longer and thanked us for all our work and support, that had made their day so special. They then returned to Morston Hall and Kate and I concluded the day with a meander around Blakeney followed by an ice-cream!

Monday 3 August was a tidying up day. Whilst Oliver and I returned the linen to Great Yarmouth, and the suits to Moss Bros. in Norwich, the chairs and tables were collected, the marquees taken down and everything was packed away. By the evening the garden resembled something like its pre-wedding reception status with just a few visible areas of flattened lawn. On the Tuesday, Oliver and Jude returned to Welwyn Garden City. Their honeymoon was to follow later, which was to be spent in the Maldives and was subject to flights and other arrangements and I was back at work in York, on the Wednesday.

By comparison to the previous ones the next few days were normal, that is until Thursday 13 August when Kate drove up to York to meet me. I had the Friday off, in order that we could both go over to Middleham, to take another look at Vale Cottage.

This time we were joined by two local builders, Steve Rowlett and his son, who happened to both live in Middleham and, by chance, had previously worked on the cottage. We looked around and described to Steve what we envisaged doing, to seek his views and thoughts around costs, which all seemed favourable. We also met up with Victoria, from Yorkshire Country Cottages, who was able to advise us as to how the company could support us with letting the cottage.

It was most important to us that the family were not limited to a specified number of bookings in any one year. After all, the cottage was for the family in the first place, with holiday lettings to the public being second. To our surprise, as our research with other letting agents was contrary to this, Victoria was perfectly happy with our proposed mix of bookings. All had gone well, so we made our way back to Bodham, pleased and assured that if we did purchase Vale Cottage it would work for us, as a family.

On the Monday, we signed up with Yorkshire Country Cottages, instructed Hansells our solicitors regarding the purchase and confirmed with Steve, the

Chapter 6 Ground up with Flints & Blocks 1999 – 2014

builder, what we wanted undertaken, in order that he could provide a quote and timeframe.

In mid-September, Sophie came home for the weekend, accompanied by a new young man, Leigh, having met him on 17 August. We had already decided to visit a Green Build event at Felbrigg Hall as we were thinking about having some sort of wind or solar power generation installed, so both Sophie and Leigh joined us. This gave us the opportunity and time to get to know him. I'm not sure how he felt about this 'introduction', for on the Sunday, Oliver and Jude also came home and we all went for a walk along Weybourne cliffs. For Leigh it must have seemed a daunting weekend.

The next few weeks were mainly focused on Vale Cottage, with Kate checking with her accountant the tax implications, opening bank accounts, seeking the guidance of the local authority on what we could and could not do, finding suppliers for the additional fixtures and fittings that were required and agreeing with our builder, what he needed from us by way of materials. However, nothing could proceed until we had completed the purchase. We were though, confident enough to pre-order a new toilet suite and a king size bed, as both had extended delivery times.

Aldiss, in Fakenham, delivered the bed to the barn, on 5 October 2009, whilst the bathroom fittings were also delivered there, on the 7th. Luckily on Friday 9 October we completed on the purchase of Vale Cottage, 6 East Witton Road, Middleham.

On the Saturday, we drove to the cottage in a hired van, which was full of sanitary ware, a bed and numerous other essentials. We met our neighbours, a lovely couple who insisted we join them for supper, which we did. We initially stayed at the cottage for a week, preparing it for the alterations we wanted to undertake.

No time was wasted in commencing these, as on Sunday 11 October, we took down the stud wall in the back bedroom, along with a small wall and a whole lot of tiles, ready for Steve to start work on the following Monday (Fig. 397). Our bed proved too big to be carried by the conventional internal route up the stairs,

Figure 397

REFLECTIONS UPON A FAMILY

Figure 398

so with Steve's help, the bedroom window was removed and the bed plus mattress was manhandled through the open space (Fig. 398).

We both decided to stay at the cottage for a second week in Middleham, so we could oversee the work, and clean and prepare the rest of the cottage, not affected by the building work. The cottage was compact, which meant any rubbish had to be removed, almost immediately, so that Steve and his son, who was now also working there, could carry out the building works without any hindrance. The hired van became very familiar with the route to the local tip, which saved precious time for Steve, and we didn't have to finance the hire of skips.

On 17 October, we had a surprise telephone call from an excited Sophie to say that Leigh had proposed and that she had accepted. Whilst surprised at the speed of this, we were happy for them both.

For a short while, we considered building a conservatory on the rear of the cottage but the objections from the other neighbours changed our minds. Which in the long term was the right decision given the restricted access.

Work at Vale Cottage progressed at pace, and it wasn't long before we could have it photographed for the Yorkshire Cottages website. We spent much of this time in Middleham, so for once it was good that my work for Aviva was located in York, which was just over an hour's drive away.

The list of things to do from the back of our calendar (Fig. 399), sets out the tasks to be completed in just 24 hours, and that included travel time!

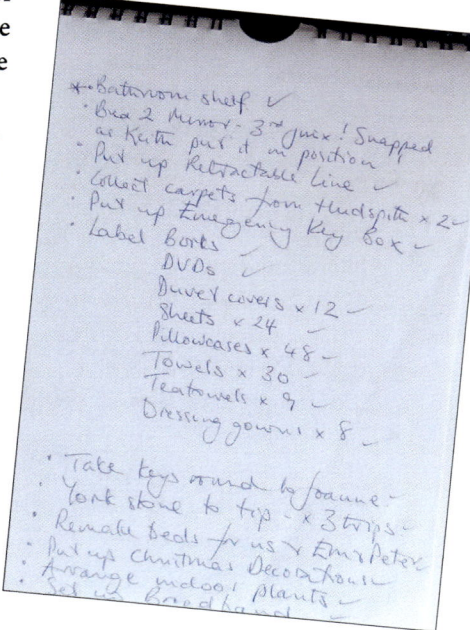

Figure 399

Chapter 6 Ground up with Flints & Blocks 1999 – 2014

Figure 400

All this was achieved, apart from the broadband connection which took quite a few attempts, with BT having to 'reset' it at the exchange. The final task was to replace the house sign next to the front door. In keeping with Walnut Barn, we had a Vale Cottage cast iron sign made (Fig. 400) and 'The Cottage' was now ready.

October 24 was another wedding day. This time we were there as guests, as Rebecca my niece, was to marry David Wyse. It was lovely to just enjoy the day without being concerned about all the arrangements. Unfortunately, Oliver and Jude weren't able to join us as it was the day they flew to the Maldives for their honeymoon.

After Sophie had sat her final theory exam, she and Leigh came home on 19 November. If she passed this, and her final practical exam, which was to take place on 12 December, in Nottingham, she would then be admitted to the Royal Veterinary College, as a registered veterinary nurse, with RVN as a post nominal. Given all the work she had put into the course, we were all convinced it was a 'given' and that she would become qualified.

With all the normal Christmas preparations in Norfolk completed, with cards written and posted, food and tree ordered, and newsletter written. It was time to go back to Vale Cottage for a day of Christmas preparations, before our first 'guests', Em and Pete arrived, to join us on 12 December. All four of us had a lovely weekend and we were also joined, just for the Sunday, by Sophie and Leigh. As we hoped, Sophie's examinations had gone well, but she now had an agonising wait for her final results.

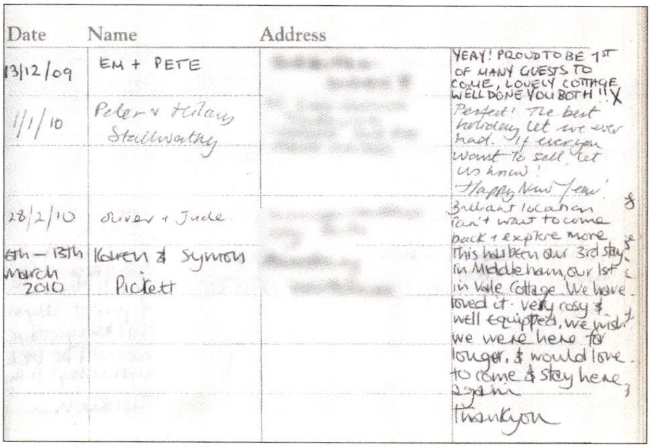

Our first entry in the Vale Cottage visitors book was signed by Em and Pete with a lovely comment (Fig. 401). Had it not been complimentary we could of course have removed the page! But that wasn't necessary and there were to be many more very positive comments over the years.

Figure 401

Returning to 'The Barn', Kate and I attended midnight Mass and on Christmas morning we were able to telephone all the family to wish them a Merry Christmas.

We had our customary drink at the Dun Cow, followed by a walk along the coast at Salthouse. Our evening Christmas meal was at home with just the two of us, and compared to previous years whilst quiet, it was lovely.

Oliver and Jude joined us on Sunday 27th, and after hearing all about the honeymoon in the Maldives, which made us very envious, we went for a circular walk around Bodham. On the Monday, Oliver cleaned his car – as he was very proud of his modes of transport and still is, cleaning and waxing his cars was a regular activity! Lunch was at Byfords in Holt, one of Jude's favourite places, and on the Tuesday and prior to Oliver and Jude making their way home, all four of us went over to Hickling for a walk followed by lunch.

2009 had been a very busy year, and one that was full of love and happy memories. Whilst it didn't have a white Christmas, 2010 was heralded in with a light snowfall which made it still feel very festive.

2010

The year commenced with further visits up to Middleham by Kate, where I joined her from York. I was still sitting as a JP in Norfolk, Oliver and Jude were living in their Welwyn Garden City flat, Sophie was awaiting her examination results, and Em and Pete were living in Surrey.

Early in the year, on 7 January, Sophie received some good news, in that she had passed her first set of final exams and I'm sure that she and Leigh would have celebrated.

Snow was still falling and settling, which made driving very hazardous. So, travelling up to Middleham was kept to an absolute minimum but we were very much aware that the cottage had bookings from the public. The first of which was on New Year's Day, so we had to keep abreast of any repairs etc.

One advantage to living where we did in Bodham, was that Holt with all its shops, art galleries and places to eat, was within easy reach, even in the snow. With both of us being lovers of John Piper artworks, we made a point of visiting an exhibition of his works in Bircham Gallery in Holt. On this occasion, we did manage to resist the temptation of purchasing any more, and it was lovely to see a large collection of his art that we had only seen in books, all exhibited in a very comprehensive and well supported exhibition.

Out of interest, on the day after the exhibition and with the roads now wet rather than icy, we decided to drive over to Babingley, near Sandringham in Norfolk. We wanted to find the church ruins which feature in one of our existing John Piper prints (Fig. 402), which was painted in 1989 and entitled

Babingley Church. We found it eventually and the scene was still very similar to the one he had painted, even after all these years. We lunched locally at The Crown in East Rudham and in spite of its excellent write-ups by various food critics we weren't all that impressed.

The 21st was a 'Red Letter' day for Sophie, as she received formal written confirmation that her hard work over the past two years had enabled her to pass both her practical and theory examinations, and thereby become fully qualified. Nothing less than she deserved. Sophie was duly presented with her certificate in due course (Fig. 403).

Figure 402

Figure 403

Kate drove up from Norfolk and met me in York, and as we had been invited to a Burns Night supper in Middleham we stayed at Vale Cottage. We met up with our neighbours again, who introduced us to several other local residents and a good time was had by all. A four-mile walk around Middleham and its hinterland on the Saturday, enabled us to explore and see our new surroundings and enjoy the fantastic scenery.

Back at the Barn, we spent a couple of weekends clearing out the stream, as we wanted to rebuild it and replace the existing pvc liner with some fibreglass stream liners. But first, over 200 flints had to be removed, along with the original liner and by doing this we were then able to create two different levels with a small waterfall in the middle.

The new liners came from a company, Water Gardening Direct near Peterborough, which I had noticed on my journeys up to catch the train to York. We chose our design of stream that came in three sections, it was delivered later that week, and we installed it over the next couple of weekends. It all looked very good, but we still had some work to do.

Sophie's last day, as a trainee veterinary nurse, at Nine Mile Vets was on 18 February, as she had secured a new position as a now fully qualified veterinary nurse, at Vets4Pets, a practice in Newbury. She was due to start there on 22 February. She came home first, and I suspect regretted the decision, as I found her a role helping me to take over eight barrowloads of soil from the farm opposite, which was then used to bring the stream to the correct level. Still, her help was much appreciated.

My birthday weekend was spent in Middleham and culminated with a surprise meal at The White Bear in Masham, with Oliver and Jude, which was excellent. On the Sunday, Kate and I walked along the river Ure and then back past Middleham Castle which, as it was warm and sunny, felt very spring-like.

Kate's diary reads, for her 60th birthday, on 15 March, '*Into Norwich John Lewis and lovely supper*'. I have to admit that I don't recall what came out of the visit to John Lewis or what we had for supper, but it seems that both hit the mark. Secretly I think Kate was a little disappointed. But unbeknown to her, the actual birthday surprise was to come the following weekend, when all our family came home, along with extended family members and many of her friends, some of whom she kept in regular contact but had not actually seen for years (Figs. 404 – 410).

The surprise party required Em to take her shopping in Norwich, followed by a Thai massage, whilst the rest of us prepared 'The Barn'. Banners were hung, balloons blown up, a cake delivered, and fifty guests from local locations and further afield, duly arrived. Oliver and I were now on lookout duty.

The waiting was tense, but Kate and Em duly returned and with all the cars parked in the farm opposite and with total silence observed, Kate had no idea into what she was about to walk, as can be seen on the look of surprise in figure 406.

Perfect reaction, well done Em!

Figure 404

Figure 405

Figure 406

Figure 407

Figure 408

Figure 409

Kate wrote in her calendar five days later, all in red capitals '*FANTASTIC SURPRISE LUNCHEON. BRILLIANT WEEKEND*"

The photograph (Fig. 410) is Olive talking to Gillian, Kate's sister. Without Olive's late evening talk with Kate, before we were engaged, we may never have been married at all, so she was a very special and important guest. It was wonderful that she had travelled down from Lincolnshire, for the celebration. As can be seen, it was an excellent birthday party and one that Kate will always remember.

On the Sunday a walk around Sheringham Park was enjoyed by all the close family, before they commenced their return journeys homeward.

Figure 410

Just prior to Kate's surprise party, Kestrel Kitchens had undertaken an update to our kitchen which basically meant having a new Corian worktop and sink. After a long wait for this to be cut to size, the installation took place on 17 March and was totally completed the next week. The kitchen now had a continuous worktop, and it did look really good and certainly enhanced the room.

2010 was the year for 'zero ending' birthdays, and with Oliver being 30, there was another surprise meal. This time, Jude had organised a celebratory meal at the China City restaurant, Russell Square in London. We travelled by train from King's Lynn and returned home very early the following morning at 02.00! In between times we had enjoyed a lovely meal with all our family.

The B&B was now becoming very busy, both with regular guests and one-off visitors. Some of the regulars had become friends and would only book with us. If we couldn't accommodate them then they changed their plans to suit us, which was really complementary.

One such gentleman was a Professor in the Department of Geography at University College London (UCL) and the leading expert on endangered crucian carp. He and his colleagues were undertaking a series of studies of pond habitats in the area, and they checked where the carp were known to exist, the health of the fish and the quality of the water etc. They also looked for the location of ponds where the fish could safely be introduced. They all came to stay regularly for a number of years and even put some carp into our farm pond. Some years after we moved from the barn, we met him again in a coffee shop and he not only recognised us but gave us a glowing report on our B&B, which they now no longer used.

By mid-May, we needed a holiday, so we booked a week in Vale Cottage and spent the days there being tourists. It was lovely. We visited Thirsk and walked along Sutton Bank, in hot sunshine under lovely blue skies. As a 'James Herriot' fan I could not have asked for a better walk.

Another day, we went to Harrogate and sampled 'the waters' in the Pump Room, which wasn't such a pleasant experience. It may be good for you, but it tasted terrible. By contrast, the tea at Bettys afterwards, was absolutely spot-on and definitely suited our tastebuds, whilst it also removed the previous unpleasant water. So, the day was a success. We also enjoyed the simple pleasure of having a picnic on the banks of the river Ure, just on the edge of Middleham and from there we went for a long walk over the hills and watched some of the racehorses being exercised on The Gallops, which was most interesting.

The break must have been just what we needed, for back home at the barn, on the Saturday we just had a lazy day at home, with 30° sunshine which continued into Sunday.

In June 2010, Em was to renew her acquaintance with the city of Florence. She flew from Stansted but this time it was for business and only for four days, during which time she had workshops to attend. She flew home from Pisa, on a midnight flight, arriving back in the UK in the early hours. We had visitors which was lovely as Wellie and Adam, the couple we had met on honeymoon, came to stay for a long weekend. We enjoyed breakfast outside each morning, but unfortunately not beside an oleander bush! We did, however, introduce them to a Byfords lunch, along with some of the Holt shops, that were very much to their liking.

Another 'zero ending' birthday was celebrated by Gillian, who was 70. She and Geoffrey hosted a lovely lunch, where we were able to meet up with members of the family and friends that we hadn't seen for some time. This was followed, a week later, by my sister Sarah celebrating her 50th birthday and, as with Gillian's, we had a lovely family party. I did say a few words, as everyone else seemed to be obeying Sarah's instructions not to make a speech. But in my opinion, they had gone to so much trouble to make the party a success, they deserved our thanks, and it was gratefully received by them both.

On our wedding anniversary 24 July, we went to see an exhibition of paintings by Rolf Harris, who was also in attendance. The exhibition which was held in Holt was very impressive and reminded me of the times I used to watch him on children's television, where he had a huge paintbrush in hand, and painted an incredibly quick picture, whilst talking to the camera and asking the audience *'Can you tell what it is?'*

Whilst Em and Pete had a short break in Vale Cottage with Sophie and Leigh joining them on 7 August, Oliver came home for the day to discuss his career prospects with me. It was clear that he was not content where he was, and having now brought Kate into the conversation, we both gave our thoughts which he took on board and we hoped, in time, that they would be used in his decision making.

Figure 411

We were able to 'lighten' the day, by going to see *The A-Team* film, in Cromer. It was appropriate as the television programme from which the film was adapted was one of Oliver's favourites. It was a ludicrous script but good fun.

A couple of weeks later, we again had an evening out, but this time watching one of my favourites in London (Fig. 411).[33] This wasn't a film, but a theatre production of the book about *The Railway Children*, performed on Waterloo Station and included a real steam train. This was an experience that has stayed with me ever since, it was just wonderful and so professional. We didn't arrive home until just before midnight, but it was worth every minute.

Following Sophie and Leigh's engagement, on 17 October last year, we took the opportunity and drove down to Hungerford on 28 August, where we met them at their flat. We all set out on a lovely walk around the town, followed by a meal at The Feathers. On the Sunday before returning home, we had another walk, this time over Watership Down on the Hampshire Downs and then lunch where we had the opportunity to meet Leigh's parents, which was really good.

The last week of September / first of October we had a break in Middleham. There were matters to attend to, but ostensibly this was a holiday not a working visit. Therefore, we dedicated the first day to completing all the 'we must do' jobs which included sorting the linen cupboard and many telephone calls about carpets, wood burners and heating. From then on, our focus was on ourselves and being tourists.

On the Tuesday we had booked a guided tour around the Black Sheep Brewery, which was very interesting, especially for me, having worked for a brewery many years ago. Lunch in their Bistro was also most enjoyable. The afternoon was spent in Leyburn, followed by a walk along the riverbank near Middleham and a drink in the White Swan. This all makes us both sound like mini alcoholics, but I can confirm that this is simply the wrong impression.

---

33 Credit to London-tourist-guide.com

Wednesday was a trip to Northallerton, not only to look around but also to view some wood burners. This was followed on Thursday with a visit to the 12th century Jervaulx Abbey, which was stunning, and just begs the question as to how someone, all those years ago in Henry VIII's time, could demolish so much of it? But they did what the King told them to do, I guess.

Having walked to Askrigg Falls and had tea in the village, we drove to Grassington and as is our want, purchased yet another painting, this time though, for Sophie and Leigh. At the weekend we were walking again, this time on a seven-and-a-half-mile walk, ending up in Reeth, where we had a Yorkshire tea. Gayle Mill was our next visit, on Sunday, which was fascinating, and the day concluded with supper again in the White Swan, back at Middleham.

Our second week gave us more opportunities to walk and explore the area. The highlight of this week was catching the Keighley and Worth Valley railway to Oxenhope, better known as Oakworth and used as a location in the adaptation of *The Railway Children*. As you can imagine I was in my element. Before we could return home though, we had one more important chore at the cottage which was to obtain a gas certificate. Just one of those pretty uninteresting jobs, but a necessity and a positive result was vital. Luckily everything was given the green light.

The return journey back to Norfolk had a short detour, as we needed to collect an owl sculpture, from Steve Blaylock, which we had commissioned on one of our previous trips. Steve was an artist who made metal sculptures, which either contained or were made entirely from the last Sheffield stainless steel ever manufactured in the UK.

His past work included the BBC *Blue Peter Ship* that now resides in the public garden at Media City. He had a huge metal owl on the side of his house which was how we found out about him. Our sculpture was unique, as we asked him to include the owl carrying a mouse and the finished result (Fig. 412) looked wonderful and has graced our gardens ever since.

Figure 412

The 16 October was a day that brought back some lovely memories of old England, for in the village there was a ploughing match. Not something that is seen very often these days, but it was so good to be taken back to the 1950s and 60s, when tractors were small machines driven mainly by men, who really knew the countryside and their fields in particular. The experience was enhanced through being able to pick en route, 4lbs of blackberries, which later was to be made into blackberry and apple crumble. What a wonderful sunny day was had by us all, and who cared about who won the match, as it was the 'taking part' that really counted.

Back at 'The Barn', the next weekend Oliver and Jude came to stay, and we had a wonderful walk through Pretty Corner and down to the coast at Sheringham. It was good to see them and hear all about their current news.

Just up from the courts in Norwich is the Great Hospital, a medieval hospital that has been serving the people of Norwich since it was founded in 1249, and which has now been converted into a sheltered housing complex and a retirement home.

Figure 413

For many years I had wondered what the oldest building looked like inside, and on 18 November, Kate and I had the opportunity to find out, as we attended a Magistrates Bench Christmas Dinner. The image (Fig. 413)[34] shows the main room set out for a wedding reception.

The final weekend of November was spent up at Middleham. Having had a very smart wood burner installed, and with a stack of logs it was ready for our winter guests to stay. Obviously, we had to try the wood burner out, just to make sure all was well, and I can confirm that it was excellent and made the room feel very warm and cosy.

On the Sunday, we decided to visit the Harrogate Showground that was hosting the 'Living North' Christmas event. To enhance the occasion, and make it even more of a Christmas theme, the snow arrived again, and it really did put everyone in a festive mood.

---

34 Image credit, The Great Hospital and Google Images

By Monday the snowfall had reached 3" deep but luckily the roads were passable, so life carried on as if nothing had happened. I guess if you live in the Yorkshire Dales, you expect snow just before Christmas, so it was no big deal!

Anyway, we stayed at the cottage for a few more days, during that time we dressed it for Christmas, and when we left we knew it would be in good hands because on 4 December, Sophie and Leigh were our next guests, up until the 7th.

At 'The Barn' we commenced festooning the B&B for the festive season. For us this was early, but we had to understand that for some of our guests their visit was part of the festive build up, and as such they appreciated seeing our decorations. Secretly, we were pleased to oblige, as both Kate and I love the Christmas period, especially when the weather obliges. And this year it certainly did as the snow started to fall during the week and by the weekend there was a good covering (Fig. 414), and it was still on the ground on Christmas morning.

The children arrived on Boxing Day for a few days, and with the snow still very evident, a great time was had by us all. It had been a good year all round and we looked forward to 2011, and yet again little did we know as to what that year was to bring.

Figure 414

2011

January commenced with 'Tidings of Great Joy' from Em and Pete, when they announced that later in the year they were to have our first grandchild. There was such excitement in the barn, but all tinged with a little apprehension, as the 'due date' was very close to another joyous occasion which was Sophie and Leigh's wedding. In fact, the entire year seemed to be dotted with family gatherings and celebrations, which was wonderful.

Nothing seemed to quite match our January news, and the next few months were very quiet and uneventful. I carried on with the garden structures, the latest being a fence at the side. Whilst Kate continued with her massage, the B&B and of course the booking and management of Vale Cottage in the Dales.

For my birthday, not only did we visit Em but also went to the London production of *The Mouse Trap*, a murder mystery by Agatha Christie. It was brilliant, and of course due to the tradition of people not revealing the outcome of the play, it prevents me from saying any more!

Figure 415

Whilst in London we visited Tate Britain, and 18 Stafford Street. The latter may seem a little odd, but it was the previous home of Edward Linley Sambourne (1844-1910) (Fig. 415).[35] He was a cartoonist, illustrator and photographer and was to become the senior cartoonist for *Punch* magazine. His first artwork was published by *Punch* in 1867. His London home was a museum to his work and was laid out just as it was when he was living there. It was fascinating and a very worthwhile visit.

Towards the end of March, we had decided that, in our effort to support the environment and save ourselves some heating/electricity costs, we would install photovoltaic (PV) solar panels at both Walnut Barn and Vale Cottage. We chose a company called Solar Essence for 'The Barn' and DDR Electrical for 'The Cottage'. Surveys were carried out, and on 25 March, we agreed a price of £13,680 for the barn, followed by £8,715 for the cottage. Whilst, at the time, this seemed a high price, the systems allowed us to generate sufficient electricity, at both locations, to not only offset our daily usage but also give us a worthwhile income from the electricity suppliers. In effect we had free electricity for the next 25 years, the lifetime of the agreement, but also an estimated payback period of just a few years.

---

35 Self Portrait (1891) – credit to Wikipedia and others

When we purchased the barn in 1999, it came with planning consent to convert it to a residential dwelling. A further condition though, stated that there should be a workshop included in the conversion, and that this workshop was to be used by the occupants of the barn. Whilst we adhered to this, because Kate wanted a massage clinic on-site, we were very aware that at a future date should we wish to sell the barn, the condition would restrict its possible sale. So, in June 2010 we applied to have this removed. Nine months later, on 17 March 2011, we had confirmation that should we request the removal of the condition, it was considered that there would not be any '*substantive planning grounds for objection*', as planning policy had changed since the original consent was given in 1988. With this information in writing, we had the condition removed. Whilst it made no difference to us at the time it would certainly help later should we decide to move.

Kate and I were now thinking seriously about having our own addition to the family, in the form of a puppy. We read up on the various breeds, to ensure that they would enhance, rather than dominate our now growing family, and thought about either a Hungarian Vizsla or a Labrador.

No matter which breed was chosen, we needed a kennel. So, to make room, two garden sheds were emptied, dismantled and burnt. Guy Fawkes would have been quaking in his grave, the heat was so intense that the concrete base cracked underneath! The contents of the sheds were sorted, recycled or taken to the tip. Now the site was all ready for a puppy kennel to be built later.

When spring arrived in April, we had the start of many 2011 family gatherings. The first was to celebrate my mother's 80th birthday. A wonderful quirky and unique venue, called Strattons, was found in Swaffham, where we all enjoyed a 'high tea' and great conversations. The venue and the opportunity to meet up was thoroughly enjoyed by everyone and Mum is seen here cutting her cake (Fig. 416). The white line left, is the string holding a birthday balloon!

By the middle of April, I was busy preparing the area for the kennel and dog run despite not having found any suitable occupant. However, there was

Figure 416

to be a man shed attached which I could certainly justify building.

By the end of April, with Oliver's help, the roof was on, and the kennel and dog run were complete (Fig. 417). But still empty!

With a growing family, Em and Pete decided that Pete needed to learn to drive. Living where they were, trains and buses were their main form of transport, but with the arrival of a baby, it would be easier to have two licensed drivers. Pete had his first lesson, one of many but unfortunately, he never progressed to the point of having a full driving licence.

Figure 417

The month of May found us all at our second family gathering, in Marylebone in London, to celebrate Jude's 30th birthday. We all had a superb meal in a great restaurant, with friends and relations who came from far and wide.

Figure 418

Later in the month we had the installation at both Walnut Barn and Vale Cottage, of the solar PV panels. The Barn was the biggest domestic installation the company had ever undertaken, in all their years of trading! Our photograph (Fig. 418) was taken beside the entrance of our B&B and shows the first line of panels fitted on the barn. Both installations happened in the same week, so as the scaffolding was being dismantled at Walnut Barn, we drove up to Yorkshire to oversee the work on 'The Cottage'!

The sun continued into the summer and even by our standards it heralded an incredibly hectic period! We joined family and friends, for the third family occasion, to celebrate my parent's Diamond Wedding Anniversary, hosted by Judy and David.

A duplicate photograph, but this time in colour (Fig. 419) was taken to mirror their original wedding photograph. In the colour image are their bridesmaids, back left Rosemary Tidaldi (née Horton), back centre Ruth Mason (née Gosden) and back right their best man, Ron Sewell. Seated front, Dad left and Mum right.

In the original black and white image (Fig. 420), back left Jeannie Morris, now

Chapter 6 Ground up with Flints & Blocks 1999 – 2014

Figure 419

Figure 420

deceased, Dad, Mum and Ron Sewell. Front left Ruth Gosden and front right Rosemary Horton.

Mum and Dad's anniversary was very special and appreciated by all the family who were able to join them on their day. Due to the imminent arrival of their firstborn, Em and Pete decided they didn't want to chance driving to Norfolk for the event, which was good thinking on their behalf, as three days later, in the very early hours we were off to Kingston, Surrey, to see our new granddaughter. Olivia Mae, known as Libby, was born at 02.45 on 14 June 2011. Seen here (Fig. 421), in the safe arms of her proud grandmother Kate, and (Fig. 422), a few months later at home with her mum.

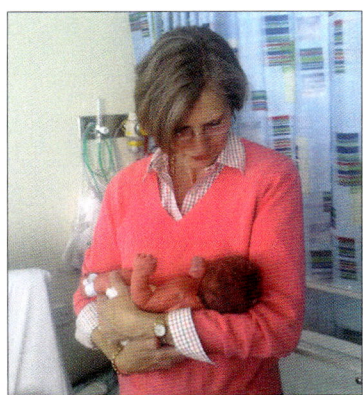

Figure 421

Figure 422

381

REFLECTIONS UPON A FAMILY

Just to make the journey even more exciting, on our way back we had to collect en route, Kate's hat for the next family gathering in three days' time!

So, three days after Olivia was born, we drove to Donnington Grove Hotel in Berkshire, to attend the wedding of Sophie and Leigh, hence the importance of the hat.

Sophie looked stunning, and I was so proud to be able to walk her up the aisle of the church. Afterwards, a horse and carriage (Fig. 423) took them to the reception just a short distance away. After a lovely meal, as the proud father

Figure 423

Figure 424

Figure 425

Chapter 6 Ground up with Flints & Blocks 1999 – 2014

of the bride I did my best to relay some of the more 'interesting' stories about Leigh's new wife (Fig. 424). It made them both smile and laugh, so I obviously didn't say anything too embarrassing!

Unfortunately, Em and Libby were still in hospital with Pete in attendance, so we texted them both with photographs and a running commentary throughout the day!

Several days later, Em and Pete were now delighted to have Libby safely at home, in Surbiton, and to ensure that our family records showed the new expanded family, the wedding party photographs were repeated (Fig. 425,) in November. This time with Em, Pete and Libby there as well. Everyone looked so resplendent again, in their wedding attire.

Later that week, we travelled again up to Yorkshire, this time to collect our new black Labrador puppy, which we had chosen whilst visiting Middleham a few weeks earlier. We came home though, with two instead! (Fig. 426). Well, they were inseparable brothers after all and I hasten to add that this was a joint decision, by us both. As was the naming of them, Dan, named by me and Archie by Kate. Yes, we are both fans of the Radio 4 serial, *The Archers*, whose main character, when the programme was first aired in the 1950s, was Dan Archer!

Figure 426

Returning home, they were introduced to their new 'home' in the garden that we had taken so long to build, but after a good sniff around, they simply exited it by walking between the railings! They were so small, and in my case I was so soft with both of them that they never actually lived in the dog run. Lying in front of the Aga or on a rug beside the wood burner was far more comfortable.

In July, we drove to London for our fifth family gathering, to celebrate Judy's, Kate's eldest sister, 75th birthday. Glorious weather and a sumptuous meal made it a most splendid occasion.

Figure 427

A lifelong ambition of mine was fulfilled in August when I took delivery of 'Lilibet', a 1952 MG TD classic car (Fig. 427). Many happy hours were spent driving her around the Norfolk countryside, and whilst I would have loved to have taken her to Yorkshire, I don't think she would have made the journey, even on a trailer.

It is often said that dog owners find that they have complete strangers coming up to them to admire and stroke their dogs. This happened to Kate and me on 5 August in a car park in Newark, where we had stopped whilst driving up to Middleham. However, this meeting was quite extraordinary, as during the conversation we found out that the couple had just returned from abroad and were off to Yorkshire to collect a puppy that they had reserved some months earlier. What a coincidence we said, and it was then that we found out that they were collecting one of Dan and Archie's brothers. How bizarre was that!

At the end of August, Kate and I were both ready for a holiday and had booked Vale Cottage out for our own use. It was a new experience visiting places with two puppies but also good fun. We went to the Wensleydale Show where we saw the Wensleydale Long Cross sheep and, of course, ended up ordering a jersey for Kate. We also visited the Redmire Steam train and had a glorious ride to Leyburn and back. This was a first for Dan and Archie who both loved all the attention. On the Sunday we met up with Dan and Archie's breeders and were introduced to one of their brothers called Storm, whom they had decided to keep. It was strange but there was no recognition of each other by any of the three dogs, despite them only being a few months old. I'm not quite sure what I expected – perhaps a shaking of paws or rubbing of noses? But still all three of them played really well with each other.

One of the best days whilst at the cottage, was spent visiting the now world-famous open-air Beamish Museum, which told the story of life in the North-East of England, from the 1820s through to the 1950s. We were there all day and could, if truth be known, have spent another day there as well. The museum was a large, life size, replica town with shops, houses, factories and a coal mine which were all open for visitors to walk around. Transport around the 'town' was

Chapter 6 Ground up with Flints & Blocks 1999 – 2014

either by a 1930s bus or tram (Fig. 428) [36] and an alternative transport could be used which in some cases was a steam train. For both children and adults, it was a fantastic way to learn about modern history and I just wished it had been available to me when I was at school. Dan and Archie were fantastic, probably due to all the attention which two young puppies would and did undoubtedly receive.

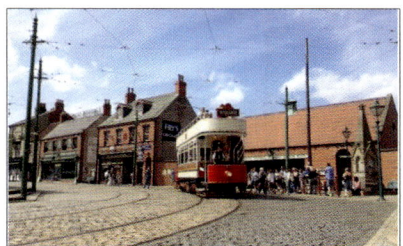

Figure 428

Our sixth and seventh family get-togethers took place in September when William, one of Kate's nephews, celebrated his wedding day, and then the following month, Kate's second sister and brother-in-law celebrated their Golden Wedding Anniversary. Both days were tremendous and executed with great style and panache.

On 16 September 2011, Leigh took a 'leap of faith' and decided to leave his paid employment, at a regional car dealership, and set up in business on his own. A huge step having only just become married, but I am pleased to say that at the time of writing, some 12 years later, his used car sale business has expanded and is keeping him fully occupied.

Early in October there was an eighth and final family get-together. Again, on Kate's side of the family, hosted in Farnham by her brother Peter and Jane his wife. Coming from a large family it was no surprise to find that there were 38 people attending. I don't recall there being any particular rationale for the gathering, other than for all the family to meet up, and it was lovely and very sociable.

Figure 429

On another sunny Sunday in October, we had a second opportunity in Holt, to meet and chat to Rolf Harris (Fig. 429), when he had come to promote his one-man art exhibition. The paintings were without doubt stunning and confirmed his very obvious talent. At that time, he was an admired artist and television personality who had been privileged to paint the portrait

---

36 Credit to https://www.beamish.org.uk/explore-discover/

of our late Queen Elizabeth II. But later he would fall out of favour, following a court case for indecent assault, for which after the trial he was sentenced to five years nine months in prison. However, putting the court case aside, his paintings were very good although also very expensive.

November brought the news that Sophie, at her employer's National Conference in Birmingham, had capped off a fantastic year by winning the 'Directors Choice Award for Outstanding Performance'. This I am sure was well deserved and was a great ending to a wonderful year.

For Kate, on a personal level, 2011 was also a good year, full of Vale Cottage bookings, combined with an equally very busy Bed and Breakfast and Massage Therapy clinic. In contrast, I had my work in York for Aviva and my magistrate sittings in Norfolk.

Christmas that year was with the whole family at Walnut Barn – ten adults which included my parents, one baby and three dogs, one of which was Sophie's Barney. It was busy but perfect!

2012

We commenced the year with Em needing a Magnetic Resonance Imaging (MRI) scan of her hip, which had been giving her a lot of discomfort, ever since Libby had been born, but nobody could give her any definitive answers as to what was causing it. At long last though, the result of a recent x-ray eventually confirmed that she had a fractured pelvis, and I understood that it could have occurred when Em was in labour, because afterwards she wasn't able to lift Libby up at all, without a lot of pain. Em was referred to a spinal unit in Tooting, so not a good start to the year for her. However, she did partially recover after a tough few months, and now lives with osteopenia.

Snow arrived in Norfolk during the first week of January, much to the consternation of both Dan and Archie, who had their first walk in this unknown, strange, cold white fluffy substance. It didn't take them long though, to become acclimatised to it, and within a short time they were charging along with their noses in the snow, trying to eat it and following various new scents.

Sophie and Leigh were house hunting around the Tadley area, whilst Em and Pete, despite her osteopenia, were also looking for a home of their own in Surrey. With all of them being first time buyers we hoped that this would give them an advantage in the housing market.

Sophie and Leigh viewed two properties and much to everyone's surprise, including theirs, their only offer on the second property was accepted straight

Chapter 6 Ground up with Flints & Blocks 1999 – 2014

away! Everything all went according to plan with very few hitches, and they completed and moved into their new four bedroomed house in March. The property was ideal for them and whilst requiring some redecoration to put their 'stamp' on it, it was in very good condition and with a secure garden for Barney. The back garden is shown in (Fig. 430), along with Sophie demonstrating her DIY skills (Fig. 431). The end result was very good, and they had made the house look very comfortable and homely.

Figure 430

Figure 431

Em and Pete were not so fortunate and had to view many more properties before they found 'The One'. Negotiations then started on 10 January before an offer was finally accepted on Valentine's Day. But the traumas continued right up to completion day. All the way through the transactions, we were convinced that they could lose it at any time, and you could most definitely feel the air move when later in the year, we all sighed with relief, as all the transactions had been completed.

My father, who was to be 87 in the October, was feeling his age and was thought to have the onset of dementia. As such, Mum was looking after him at their home in Necton, which she was finding very tiring. My sisters and I all had a chat and agreed that she would benefit from some respite, so we started to look for somewhere for my father to stay, in the short term.

My birthday was on a Sunday, so time was spent driving in our MG to Cley, with Kate and on the rear seat our two dogs. They were not that impressed due to the open top causing a rush of wind round their heads. However, all was forgiven when they realised that they had found the sea! Lunch was at the Dun Cow and in the evening, we went to see *War Horse* at the cinema. An excellent film but some scenes did upset me, for they made me recall previous conversations I had had with my father, whilst on my paper round, when he had to shoot some farm animals, who were suffering from shrapnel wounds.

The weekend following Kate's birthday, was Mothering Sunday and was spent with Em, Pete and Libby, not at their flat, but at the barn instead, which was a first for us all. I took them back to London on the Wednesday, as Em had an appointment at St. George's Hospital. There was also a further viewing of 2 Romney Close, the hope-to-be new home.

Easter was spent at 'The Barn' with all our children and for the first-time our granddaughter. The traditional Easter Egg hunt took place and was followed by drives out in Lilibet our MG. The excitement disappeared on Easter Monday when they all returned to their own homes, with the exception of Em and Libby who stayed on with us, so that Kate could help her with lifting Libby etc. It was sad to see them all go but the barn had allowed us all to be together which is precisely why it was purchased and converted. So, it certainly achieved our desired aims.

Figure 432

Figure 433

April 26 was the 'Red-Letter' Day for Em and Pete as they completed their house purchase (Fig. 432). I took Em and Libby down to London to meet up with Pete and they were given the keys to their new home (Fig. 433). I couldn't stay as the next day was a full day in court. However, after having had a look around to check all was as they had expected, I took them all back to their flat, where for them packing and moving in, was the order of the day.

In May, Dan and Archie were deep into their training with Kate. As you might have expected she was also training me, as I was far too soft with them. Dan and Archie continued to improve, and as we wanted them to go on some local shoots, we needed to know the etiquette that was expected, both from us and from Dan and Archie! So, Kate found a professional gun dog trainer, Roy Tomlinson, who was brilliant. He gave us some additional, invaluable help and guided us through what both we, their handlers, and our dogs should do on a shoot, when and how to retrieve, how to carry the birds etc. Apparently, I also responded well to his training with 9 out of 10 for most of my efforts! I hasten to add that this did not include picking-up dummy pheasants.

We hoped, once we were all fully trained, that both Dan and Archie and us humans, would be able to participate and they could 'pick up' on the local shoot, organised by our local friendly butcher.

Figure 434

May 11 was a first birthday for both Dan and Archie, now collectively known as 'The Boys'. They didn't expect much on their special day, just a lovely walk and they weren't disappointed! We did take a super photograph though (Fig. 434), with Dan looking very superior, on the left, and Archie on the right, looking just as important!

May went out with a flurry of activity. I was admitted to the Norfolk and Norwich Hospital Accident and Emergency (A&E), after a third dizzy spell in as many weeks, plus I had collapsed in the city, just outside the bus station and very close to Marble Hall! From the A&E, I was then transferred to the Acute Medical Unit. After many tests, I was subsequently discharged and told to rest and not to drive, so that scuppered both court work and going to the office in York.

Regrettably, we had to have both Archie and Dan neutered as Archie's second testicle had not descended, as it should have done. So, to keep the equilibrium between them we were advised to have both dogs operated on. Not a pleasant operation for them and thankfully they both recovered incredibly quickly. Then on the 26th, whilst out on a walk with Sophie, Leigh and Barney, 'the boys' were running around and managed to collide with Kate. As a result, she turned her ankle and as she couldn't put any weight on her foot, thought she might have either fractured it or torn her Achilles tendon. Luckly this wasn't the case, but it was really painful, none the less.

Then to cap it all, Archie managed to get a staple stuck in his cheek whilst we were at Sophie and Leigh's house. Luckily, I was able to remove it without too much trouble. We did manage to return home safely from Tadley on the Sunday, which was the same day that Oliver and Jude were undertaking a charity cycle ride, from London to Brighton. On the Monday, both Dan and Archie had their stitches out, I was allowed to go back to work and Kate's ankle was definitely on the mend. As I said, quite a flurry of activity in just one week!

Also in May, Oliver and Jude were following Em and Pete's example and sought advice on fertility treatment, when they attended the Oxford Clinic and talked to their experts.

Libby had her first birthday in June, which was celebrated in style, during August with a belated 'Garden Party', the first in her new home. Kate and I had been in Middleham during the week of her actual birthday so were really pleased that, like royalty, she was to have an 'official birthday' later.

Middleham was good, not sunny but fine and warm. We spent most days out walking but there was sad news on the Friday 15 June, when we learnt that Ian, Kate's eldest sister's husband, had suddenly died whilst sitting in his armchair. Whilst he was 84, some 22 years older than Kate, it was still a shock. We returned home as planned the next day and Kate had a long chat on the telephone, with her sister.

Over the summer, Jude and Oliver successfully competed in several charity fundraising events which raised much needed monies for a number of good causes. As I previously said, they had already taken part in the 56 mile long, London to Brighton Cycle Ride, and also planned to undertake the Yorkshire Three Peaks, on 16 June. Regrettably, this was cancelled due to poor weather conditions, however, Oliver did participate in a 10k run, around central London.

Later in the month, Kate and I drove down to Charterhouse School in Godalmimg, for the funeral of Ian which took place in the chapel. Following Ian's retirement from the army, as a Lieutenant Colonel, and being an old Carthusian himself of Charterhouse School, he then returned there to teach, hence the location for his funeral. During the service, which Kate attended with other members of her family, I and 'The boys' (Dan and Archie) who had just had their longest drive so far, went to watch the school cricket match, which was being played on the square, just outside the chapel. The sound of leather on willow was very relaxing and after the service I joined Kate for the wake, and both proved to be a perfect send off for Ian.

Chapter 6 Ground up with Flints & Blocks 1999 – 2014

Figure 435

In a fit of over confidence on 2 June, back at The Barn, I laid the foundations for a new brick and flint garden wall, which was to have a door in the middle! I had taken time off work to undertake this task and was hopeful that it was achievable by an amateur, just so long as it didn't need plastering! With the foundations in place, I returned to work in York, with the block and flint work confined to the weekends.

This was not just a straight wall but one with a lovely curve. It was also a two-person job, so whilst I mixed the lime mortar, Kate was chief transporter of approximately 2,000 flints. These were piled up beside the piggeries, so they first had to be brought across the field in a wheelbarrow and into the garden. I then laid them all in courses, as a facing to the breeze blocks which formed an internal wall (Figs. 435 & 436), so that the flint walls matched the walls of the barn. After three months of hard labour, a spectacular 17' x 6' curved brick and flint wall was created, with a feature door in the middle, which had been purchased from a local reclamation yard.

Figure 436

It made such a difference to the ambience of the garden and the dogs loved to lie beside it, and depending on the time of day they were either in the shade or the other side where the flints had been heated by the sun.

On 8 July, we were fortunate enough to find an antique long case clock that had been made by a local clockmaker in Bodham. Knowing our love for long case timepieces, our clock restorer Mike Darley, gave us first refusal, as he had just

REFLECTIONS UPON A FAMILY

reconditioned it, ready for sale. We didn't hesitate and secured the clock for £1,350. The clock can be seen in Fig. 437.

Our wedding anniversary 24 July was celebrated not once but twice. First with a surprise cream tea at Morston Hall organised by Kate, then followed with a formal supper at the Wiveton Bell. Both were superb and very enjoyable.

July was also the start of the London Olympics which was, for some of the time, compelling watching. As you may already remember though, I am not a great sportsman like Kate, who really does enjoy it.

Despite still having occasional dizzy spells I continued to work in the garden and in York, whilst Kate enjoyed some of the Olympic coverage. However, on one occasion when I had a dizzy spell at home, coupled with a panic attack, it caused Kate to be so concerned that she called the paramedics. After a thorough check over, which found everything normal, I was told again to rest, which I did. Later on, I was to have blood tests for my liver, kidneys, cholesterol, thyroid and a full blood count and all these came back normal as well! So, still no one had any idea why they were happening.

Figure 437

By the end of the month, I was feeling much better, and we enjoyed a night out in Cromer, watching the *End of The Pier* variety show with Colin, my previous Aviva colleague and his wife Ann. It was very well produced and most entertaining.

Libby's 'official birthday' was celebrated in style on 18 August, in the back garden of her home. The weather was superb, and family and friends all enjoyed a delicious luncheon, whilst Libby was clearly in her element, surrounded by all her relatives. She also thoroughly enjoyed her chocolate smartie birthday cake, as did most of the grown-ups!

With all the excitement of the summer and my dizzy spells, Kate suggested that it was time for a holiday. So, she and I along with Dan and Archie, travelled to Middleham and spent an enjoyable time at Vale Cottage. It was relaxing but as we are both always ready for a challenge, we decided to climb the 80m (262') Malham Cove.

This certainly proved a feat and a half, especially in the rain, and it seemed most unfair only having two legs, as we watched our four-legged friends leap like goats, up the 400 irregular stone steps, to the top. Well worth the effort though, for the view was fantastic, despite the drizzly rain, and great fun to think that not only were we walking on the limestone pavements which were over 300 million years old, but also in the footsteps of Harry Potter!

We also visited Richmond and then on to Hawes, where we sat for a while in the basement of our favourite antique shop. This sounds slightly crazy, so by way of explanation, the basement had a lovely old coal fired kitchen range, which was always lit, warm and very inviting. It was not unusual, or frowned upon, if people just took a while out from browsing the antiques and had a warming sit down in front of the fire. Something in which we both partook whenever we were in Hawes, and on that particular day it was cold with heavy rain, so it was most welcoming.

The autumn started with the tough decision that from 17 September, my dad would need to move into a permanent dementia care unit. This was very difficult for all concerned, but it would mean that my mum would have a much easier time at home. Whilst Dad, who had become more prone to be physically aggressive, was of course, going to be well cared for. As time progressed, he became much more withdrawn, didn't recognise family or friends, and almost regressed back to his childhood, with comfort coming from a large toy lion. I did and still do, find this so very upsetting. As I write this, my eyes are watering with the memories. Dementia is such a cruel and debilitating disease.

We spent the first weekend in October with Em and Pete, helping them to sort their house out, which wasn't easy with a young Libby, who by then was crawling and able to pull herself up, on any piece of furniture be it safe or not. The phrase '*Eyes in the back of one's head*', comes to mind and was most apt!

Lilibet, our 1952 MG TD, was sold, and I agreed to deliver her to Rugby, where her new, keen MG owner lived. But we wanted to replace her, so before she was taken to Warwickshire, we purchased a 1934 MG PA 4-seater Tourer, which arrived on 12 October!

Whilst we were sad to see Lilibet go, 'Gertie' (Fig. 438), her replacement, would be just as much fun. She did need some tender loving care (TLC) though, to bring her back to her former

Figure 438

glory, but more importantly with more room in the back we would be able to take Dan, Archie, children and grandchildren for rides. Obviously, taking it in turns though!

On 10 October, I had an appointment at the Norfolk and Norwich hospital, with an endocrinology consultant regarding my dizzy spells. Despite more tests being carried out, nothing could be found that gave cause for concern. Whilst in some ways that was disappointing, it was also comforting to know that there appeared to be nothing seriously wrong with me.

Good news was to follow, when Sophie and Leigh came home for the weekend and announced that she was 13 weeks pregnant. We were to become grandparents again and in April next year, 2013, Sophie and Leigh were to become proud parents. We privately asked ourselves, was this the same Sophie who was never going to marry or have children?

Before the year was out, we did manage to squeeze in one more weekend in Middleham, which whilst short, was most welcome. We also spent time with my dad, but as I have already said, he was deteriorating, and this was clearly visible each time we visited.

Libby was making great strides in every sense of the word, as she had now taken her first steps, small but progress indeed. This was followed a week or so later with her first six-word sentence, *Mummy, doctor, no more monkeys, sofa*. Make of that what you will!

In 2012, we went to Holt and have continued this every year since, to watch the Christmas lights switch-on and fireworks. Despite being in the middle of November it always seemed to set us up for Christmas and that year was no exception.

At the end of the month, as I had agreed I took Lilibet up to her new owner, on my trailer, but the weather was very wet. I recall there being really heavy floods and luckily, I was not forced to drive through any of them. However, I do remember seeing the fields either side of the road being underwater and wondered what the return journey would be like. It was all ok though, albeit a slow drive home.

Our final piece of news before Christmas was on 10 December, when Sophie's scan confirmed that our new grandchild was to be a baby boy and all was well, so one grandchild of each sex which was excellent news.

Gertie went to Wroxham to have some preparatory work carried out but was re-united with us a few days later, but only after I had paid a bill of nearly £900! That was an indication of things to come, although I didn't know it at the time!

Putting up the christmas tree and decorations was a welcome distraction and led on to another lovely Christmas period. As the children weren't coming home until the 27th, our Christmas lunch was another delicious meal in Byfords

Chapter 6 Ground up with Flints & Blocks 1999 – 2014

restaurant in Holt. No cooking or washing up. It was wonderful!

All our children and granddaughter came home for the New Year, so lots of lovely meals cooked by Kate and we had the inaugural Walnut Barn Trophy competition, which was repeated the following Easter.

The photograph (Fig. 439) shows the trophy, being held by the joint winners and is so small it can hardly be seen! In fact, I am not even sure that it exists now, all these years later. Though, Kate has just told me that it does and is in a safe place.

All we had to do now was to serve and enjoy the wonderful New Year's Eve supper, lovingly prepared by Kate. This was recorded for posterity by Jude (Fig. 440), hence her absence from the photograph. We all had a super time, before they all returned home on New Year's Day.

Figure 439

Figure 440

2013

With all the children and Libby now back at their homes safely, on 7 January, I was to say a fond au revoir to Gertie, as I took her over to David Wall in Hoveton, to be re-sprayed, black. This was to return her to the original colour when she left the factory on 15 May 1934. Having joined the MG car club, I was able to source copies of the car's records. These included details from the time when she was originally sold, along with information from the sales department sent to the MG service department (Fig. 441). Also contained in the documents was the returned guarantee form, from Gertie's first owner, Miss K. M. Chapman of Leicester, as shown in (Fig. 442).

FROM:- TO:-

Sales Department. Service Department.

TYPE......P......MODEL......

CHASSIS NO......ENGINE NO. 1163AP.

BODY COLOUR......STARTER NO......

UPHOLSTERY COLOUR......BODY NO......

WHEEL COLOUR......DELIVERED TO......

GEARBOX NO. 675......DATE DELIVERED. 15/5/34......

DYNAMO NO......MAIN AGENT......

REAR AXLE NO. 690......

SIGNED......

Despatch Department.

Figure 441

I was now hopeful that I could have my car re-conditioned and returned to its original colour scheme. David was a very experienced restorer of classic and vintage cars, so I knew Gertie was in safe hands.

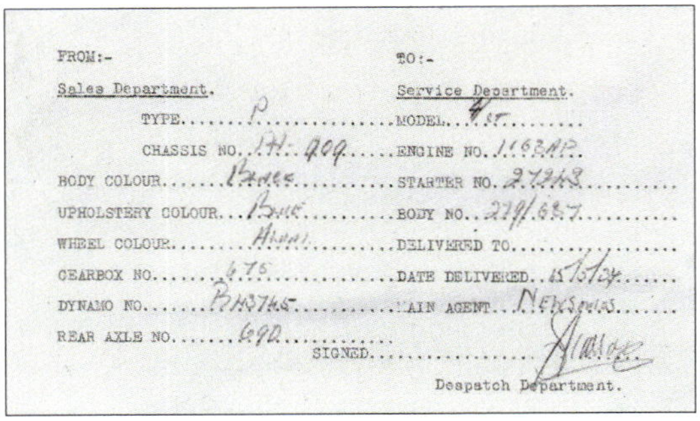

Completed 1-6-34

On receipt of this card, duly completed, we shall be pleased to forward a Certificate of Guarantee and Instruction Book.

(It is particularly requested that the name be inserted in block capitals, and your kind attention to this will be appreciated.)

Name K. M. CHAPMAN. (MISS.)
(State Rev., Mr., Mrs. or Miss)

Address YEW LODGE, KNIGHTON. LEICESTER.

Date of Purchase 12th May 1934.
(i.e. date on which you took delivery of car from the Dealer's Showrooms)

Name and Address of Dealer from whom car was actually purchased: H. A. Hamshaw Ltd. Humberstone Road, Leicester.

MAKE	MAKERS' CAR NUMBER	ENGINE NUMBER	MARK	MODEL
M.G. Midget	P.A – 0909	1163 A.P.	P.	
M.G. Magna				
M.G. Magnette				

The makers' car and engine number will be found on the plate which is fixed to the dash underneath the bonnet.

S.H. Newsome & Co. Guar: 6 months.

Figure 442

Oliver and Jude returned to the Oxford Clinic for a second round of IVF. Kate and I were very conscious that Em had already had a successful pregnancy and Sophie's was going in the same direction. Therefore, it would be very difficult for both Oliver and Jude if their IVF treatment wasn't successful. We just hoped that one day their dreams would be fulfilled.

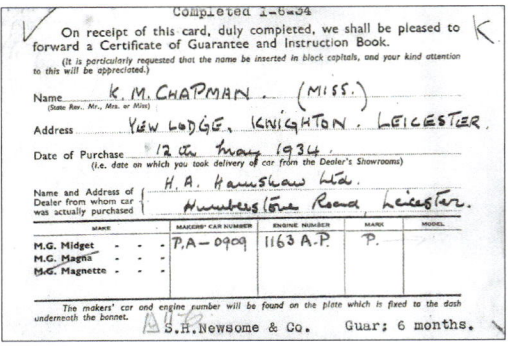

I too visited hospital, this time to see Dr. Gilbert a cardiologist, as we were still endeavouring to identify the reasons for my dizzy spells. I have to say that I don't recall the outcome of this, but at the time of writing, I haven't had any further incidences for a long while.

Dan and Archie were still receiving obedience training from Kate, which was working well. I knew that their pedigree was littered with previous gun dogs and Field Trial Champions, which meant that some skills were probably inherited, but nevertheless Kate's patience and training aptitude were really impressive.

Chapter 6 Ground up with Flints & Blocks 1999 – 2014

Having had our training last year, from Roy Tomlinson, we didn't want to actually be one of the 'guns', on the shoot, but we wanted to allow Dan and Archie to undertake the retrieval of game birds which was obviously a natural instinct for them both. So, we chatted to Paul, our local butcher and he said that we would be more than welcome to join him on a number of his shoots, later on in the year.

For my birthday weekend, we stayed with Sophie and Leigh, where we went again for some lovely walks, along with shopping in Mamas and Papas and Mothercare for their son-to-be. Given that it started to snow on the Sunday, we left after another circular walk and arrived home at 17.30, safe and sound.

Then in mid-March, a time when the MG Club have an International Show at Stoneleigh in Warwickshire, Kate and I decided that we would attend, just to see what the show was all about. Having put the dogs into kennels, we drove up to our hotel ready for the show on the Sunday. We spent all day there and agreed that elements were very interesting, especially the spare parts etc., but we didn't think we would return any time in the future.

In March 2013, I found there was a local car upholsterer in Aylsham called Paul Moore, and on my way back from work, called in to see him. His work on classic cars was most impressive and I agreed a time and price for him to perform his magic, on Gertie. I had already sourced from an accredited restorer some proper MG hide, so I was confident that this was the correct colour and texture. Unfortunately, that supplier was too busy to take on my work, hence the need to find an alternative upholster but I was able to give Paul the hides that I had purchased for him to use.

The month finished with snow and strong winds. These were strong enough to blow down the boardwalk fencing across the pond. So emergency repairs in the bitter cold had to be undertaken. When I had finished, I was very glad to be back in a warm barn and sitting next to the wood burner. However, by Easter, a few days later, the sun was warm, and whilst there was the odd snow flurry, the skies were blue. So, a lovely walk through Blickling Park and the woods was the order of the day for Kate, me and the dogs.

April started well with Gertie gleaming, and she was taken over to Aylsham to have her upholstery upgraded. But this was soon replaced by some very sad news for all of us. For after a night with all the immediate family being at my dad's bedside, and with his hand being held by my mother for comfort, he died peacefully at 19.00, on Sunday 14 April 2013, aged 87.

397

Over the next few days, arrangements were put in place for his funeral, which was to be held at Necton Church, on 8 May. It was a difficult time for all of us. I was though, and still am so pleased that within the memories, written by his grandchildren and great-grandchildren that were included in the order of service, Em was recognised as a granddaughter. This, for me, was confirmation that the 'blended' family that Kate and I had nurtured for so many years had been accepted as an integral part of the Gosden family.

Just five days later, on what would have been Angus's 34th birthday, Benjamin Michael Brett Bedford entered this world at 12.05, seven days early.

Figure 443

The next day, whilst our neighbour kindly greeted our B&B guests, we drove down to Basingstoke hospital to see a proud Mum and Dad with Ben, our first grandson (Fig. 443). At the reception I was told that we could not go in, as it wasn't visiting time, and we would have to come back that evening. Rather forcibly, I have to admit, I told the receptionist that we had just driven all the way there from North Norfolk, to see our first grandson and his parents, and that we would go and see them. The receptionist backtracked and we were told how to find the ward. All was well! Sophie and Ben were discharged and home on 22 April. Ben was a super little baby, and once his feeding pattern had settled down, there was no stopping him – it would be a full Christmas meal for him as well, that year!

Oliver and Jude were beginning to think about moving home, but due to their work locations they wanted to stay either in or around Welwyn Garden City. Therefore, when we said we were going to the Grand Designs Exhibition at Excel, on 6 May, they decided to join us.

It was a huge and very interesting exhibition with so much to see, and in spite of having arrived early we didn't actually leave until much later in the day. Then following a really good meal with Oliver and Jude, at the Red Lion in Old Welwyn, where after exchanging comments and ideas for new houses, we made our way home.

We were all to meet up again for my father's cremation which was followed by his Service of Thanksgiving in Necton. Em, Pete and Libby joined us, as did Oliver, Jude, Sophie, Leigh and Ben. The Service of Thanksgiving was very emotional for me, but I managed to give a tribute to Dad that I had written. It included references to his school days, along with the time when Frank, Win's husband, had died. He had asked Dad if he would support Win and her two children, Rosemary and Christine and Dad was very willing to undertake this role. Win was also very comfortable with his support. I had sought my cousins' consent before I wrote those final words and they both were more than happy to have them included in my eulogy. His Thanksgiving Order of Service can be seen at Figure 444. The service was very moving and a perfect tribute to a wonderful father and an inspirational friend to so many.

The week following the service, I took as holiday, and we went up to Middleham. As was normal, there were a few small jobs that had to be done first, but they didn't take long. The rest of the week we spent simply enjoying the countryside and walking with 'the boys'.

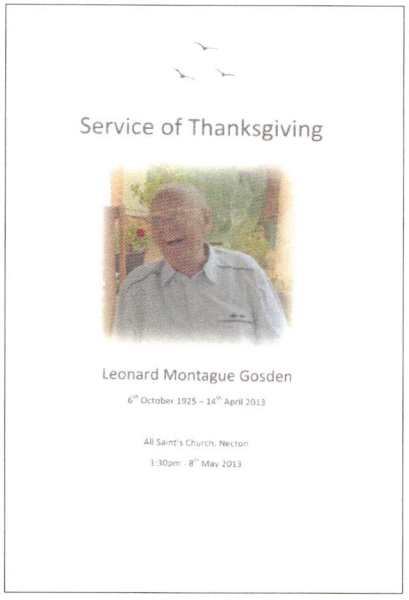

Figure 444

We returned home to 'The Barn' on the following Sunday and heard our first cuckoo of the year. My dad was a keen bird watcher, so was that cuckoo call significant?

The sun was strong now, and it was great to see the solar panels generating and recording some impressive volumes of kwh power. This certainly endorsed and, if it was needed, justified our decision for the installations. In fact, the amount of money being paid back to us meant that not only did we not have to pay any electricity bills, but we also had a steady, surplus income in repayments, which was just as we had hoped.

Oliver and Jude had progressed from thinking about moving, to going for a second viewing of a bungalow, that was on the market, following the death of its elderly owner. It did need some updating, to say the least, but they seemed to be keen, especially given its location by some woods and within walking distance of the shops. We were to hear their thoughts, later on.

Aviva had previously announced that there would be another round of redundancies and on the Friday 14th, my department received the news that some of us would definitely be made redundant, and that all of us had to go through a selection process.

On the Monday, like so many of us, I had a number of moderation meetings, and then it was a waiting game. It appeared that large companies, such as Aviva, frequently had purges on their staff numbers, as my time with them had indicated. For me, this begged the questions as to why and at what cost, both to the company and the distress it caused to its staff, to say nothing, in the first place, about the effectiveness of their staff selection. Was this all justified? But I guess that was how life was, at the time. Gone were the days of careers for life, with one single employer.

On the Saturday, Oliver and Jude invited us to view their potential new home. As the sales pitch said, '*it had lots of potential*', and this was to be in their favour, for if they were successful in their purchase, any changes would enable them to modernise it to their own design and taste.

Our calendar for the first week in July 2013 was headed '*Wimbledon men's final Murray v Djokovic*', followed by '*Murray Wimbledon Champion 6:4, 7:5, 6:4*'. I guess this was important to those who play tennis, but as I have said I am not a sportsman. Still though, it was good for British tennis I guess, and Kate, a keen tennis player, was very happy.

Whilst the final was actually being played, we were visiting Em and Pete, as Libby was having her second birthday party. With seventeen adults and children in attendance, the youngest being Ben, it was a very noisy and fun time being had by everyone. So, listening to a commentary on Wimbledon wasn't at all easy!

Em, along with Pete had also celebrated, for only a few days earlier, just before Libby's party, they had completely redecorated their sitting/dining room!

The glorious summer gave the opportunity for Libby to experience her first 'bucket and spade' visit to the beach – a great time was had by all, building sand piles (Fig. 445) – they should have been castles but that was a little ambitious! Pete also had a significant birthday when he reached 50 and celebrated with a number of festivities.

Early, on 13 July, Kate and I joined Mum, my sisters and their husbands to scatter some of Dad's ashes on the top of Grambrough Hill, a cliff on the coast at Salthouse.

Figure 445

Chapter 6 Ground up with Flints & Blocks 1999 – 2014

This was a place that both Mum and Dad visited many times when birdwatching, so it was a most appropriate choice of Dad's. We then had breakfast at home for ten of us, before we all left for Necton, for a 12.00 interment of the remains of his ashes, into a plot at the rear of Necton church. A moving day but we did have glorious bright blue skies, so someone was looking after us.

Four days later, my future at Aviva, if I was to have one, was outlined to me by my director. For many it wasn't good news but for me I was very pleased with the outcome.

I was given the role of Programme Office Manager which suited me perfectly. The icing on the cake was that again I would be based in Norwich, so no more extensive travelling to York.

Our Wedding Anniversary in July was celebrated in style, travelling for the first time on Eurostar, to Brussels for a two-day visit. We stayed at the fabulous Royal Windsor Hotel, in the centre of the old quarter of the city (Fig. 446), and only a ten-minute walk from the Grand Place.

Figure 446

Figure 447

We sampled the traditional waffles, ate delicious meals and did lots of sightseeing, which had to include the Grand Place (Fig. 447), a plaza in the centre of the city, where we had evening drinks at La Rose Blanche. We also took a bus tour around the city and saw the Atomium, a very modernistic building and found the famous 1619 *Manneken Pis*, a bronze sculpture of a little boy urinating. This all went to make a superb break, one that we would both definitely repeat.

However, the return train journey was a little concerning as there were armed guards with machine guns at the station! We didn't ask any questions but just made a discreet exit. We never did find out why they were there, but perhaps this was normal for Brussels, as the locals didn't seem at all phased by them being there!

401

At the weekend, we collected Gertie (Fig. 448), who by now had had a complete engine overhaul, a new black coat of paint, with a beautiful blue leather interior, along with new black carpets. She looked tremendous, and almost brand new, like she would have done in 1934. She drove really well and later we all set off in her, to the Holkham Country Fair, where she joined the car rally and received some glowing comments. It was a lovely day and a superb afternoon.

Figure 448

For a couple of years, we had been thinking about leaving Norfolk to find a property that was nearer to our children. This desire was enhanced following the arrival of Ben, so we began to actually view some properties rather than look at them online. Our search took us, in this instance, to Burford in the Cotswolds, where we stayed at the 'Inn for All Seasons'. We spent two days here looking around but without success. But we did have a fun day out though, in Didcot at the heritage railway. A good short break but we were no nearer to finding a suitable property.

Given the dogs were now outgrowing our cars, we put a deposit down on a Land Rover Freelander and tried to establish the sale price for Kate's Megane.

'*We Buy Any Car*', a company that advertised extensively in the UK, offered us £325 which was not at all acceptable. So, whilst noting this we didn't pursue it any further and looked at other options which, finally resulted in an acceptable result.

On the Thursday, 22 August, Sophie and Ben arrived for a long weekend and to her surprise we were joined on the Saturday by Leigh. He kindly looked at the Freelander with us, and in his opinion, it passed muster, so a deal was clinched on its purchase and Kate's convertible was traded in as part exchange.

September 25, 2013, was a milestone day for Oliver and Jude, as having sold their flat to their first prospective buyer, they completed the purchase on their bungalow, 131 Oakdale in Welwyn Garden City (Fig. 449).

Figure 449

Our long ambition as parents was to have all our children owning their own homes, with gardens and space to create their own lives, and this had now been achieved! Oliver and Jude seemed to want to replicate our own lifestyle, through embarking on a large building project, which entailed extending and improving their newly acquired property. We suspected that it might have been 'pay back' time for all the help they gave us on 'The Barn'!

Unbeknown to my sisters, I had been talking to the National Trust, who owned Grambrough Hill, about putting a memorial seat there to commemorate where some of our dad's ashes were scattered.

After some discussions with Keith Zealand, the warden who I knew from my work at Blickling Hall, a deal was struck. At a cost of £250 he would supply from the

Figure 450

Felbrigg Hall estate, a felled log or rather half a tree, as it was 1.5 tonnes of sweet chestnut, and bring it to Salthouse. There, he and his team would install it for us on Grambrough Hill.

On 28 October, the day arrived for the delivery and installation. Kate and I went with the dogs, to witness the 'event'. The tractor arrived and in no time the log, which was huge, was in place. My mother, Oliver, Sophie and Leigh (Fig. 450) all approved when they came to see it, on 14 December, and our descent down the hill was followed by a pub lunch.

The end of the year saw the biggest 'test' for Kate's dog training skills, when Dan and Archie along with us, were all invited to join our first local shoot! Figure 451, taken by Kate, shows me, Archie and Dan on this 'shoot', during a break for lunch.

Figure 451

The 'test' was passed with flying colours, or should that be 'feathers', when 'the boys' each successfully picked up and delivered correctly, both pheasants and partridges, to their handlers, who of course were their master and mistress.

In total 78 birds were bagged with both Dan and Archie contributing and certainly not looking out of place. The proof that they had made the grade was made clear when a second invitation was extended! What a great way to end a year of very mixed emotions and blessings.

Em, Pete and Libby arrived for Christmas on 23 December, closely followed the next day by Oliver and Jude, and then by Sophie, Leigh and Ben. We had a superb family Christmas, before they all went their separate ways to celebrate the New Year.

PART THREE

As you have reached Part Three of this memoir, you may perceive this as being, at the very least, the commencement of a time for a gentle and relaxing retirement.

Well, as you will discover, whilst I certainly write about life in retirement, our approach to life thus far, has demonstrated that our lifestyle is certainly not very gentle or relaxing. Instead, it is full of fun, excitement, adventure and sheer hard work. So, you probably won't be at all surprised by the activities that we have undertaken over the next few years!

Would we have it any other way? Well, frankly Kate and I simply do not see life like that. Life is, as far as we are concerned, for both living and enjoying, but this does require effort. So, as this memoir draws to a close, we still have plenty of hard work and fun to fit into the next few pages.

CHAPTER 7

Life in Retirement 2014 – 2025

We were in holiday mode when we were due to join Sophie, Leigh and Ben in Scotland, on 11 January. We left Bodham at 03.00 to meet up with them at the cottage, that was near Oban. Having made good progress, some 12 hours later we arrived just after three o'clock, in the afternoon! Whilst we were there, we did lots of walking and visited several places that were new to all of us and some that were very special to Sophie and Leigh. One of the places they showed us was where they became engaged and also during the holiday we all had a wonderful time visiting Tobermory on the Isle of Mull, as well as Glencoe, Ben Nevis, Ganavan Beach and Dustaffnage Castle.

Figure 452

One claim to fame, which I suspect thousands of others have made, was that we walked over the Atlantic! This was achieved by walking over the small Clachan Bridge that separates mainland Scotland from the island of Seil. By doing so, you walk over the Atlantic Sea, or a very small part of it. The bridge that enables this is shown in figure 452.

The holiday was great fun and very enjoyable with good weather and plenty of sightseeing, in some stunning countryside.

Upon returning home to Bodham from the West Highlands, whilst out walking very close to home, we were unexpectedly treated to a wonderful display of the Aurora Borealis – surely this should have happened in Scotland, not in North Norfolk!

I returned to work at Aviva, to be told that once again redundancy loomed for a number of staff. It did seem to be a very regular occurrence at Aviva, and I couldn't help thinking that it must put off potential employees pursuing an application for work. It was also beginning to annoy me, as it was causing too much stress by never knowing if or when the next round of redundancies would land. Given that I was 58 and 11 months old and therefore, only just over one year from Aviva's retirement age, I spoke to my director about taking early retirement, on the assumption that an acceptable financial deal could be agreed.

After some long conversations at work, and at home with Kate, and Dave Gill our financial adviser, an agreement was made which allowed me to work to the end of February, by which time I was 59, and I would be paid a final payment that amounted to well over a year's salary. However, from Aviva's perspective this had to be a redundancy rather than an early retirement. That was fine by Kate and me, so my last day with Aviva was on 28 February 2014.

When I finally retired from paid employment, I had been responsible for the Aviva General Insurance element of the Global Programme Office, which managed 14 individual projects, with an annual budget of £98.52m. Not too bad, for someone who started work at 18 behind the counter at Dixons, with just one A-Level and a few GCSEs and CSEs!

With the third phase of life in mind, Kate and I decided to join the local Ramblers Club and in addition, Kate took up pilates. Unfortunately though, due to Bed and Breakfast commitments, we weren't able to go along to either as often as we would have wished. But walking was still an activity and an integral part of our lives that we both enjoyed and took great pleasure in.

To celebrate Kate's birthday on 15 March, we had a lovely long walk across the beach at Holkham with the dogs. In the spring sunshine this walk was hard to beat and when it's followed, as ours was, by a lunch at The Victoria Pub on the Holkham estate, I would say it was almost impossible. Whilst we had to be home to greet our B&B guests, we managed a belated supper meal at the Wiveton Bell. It was a great day of walking, eating, playing with the dogs and generally relaxing. Clearly retirement had its positive elements, and quality time together was an important feature.

Given my retired status I was not only able to help Kate with the B&B, as well as the gardening, but I also had more time to devote to the magistracy. I was now sitting on average, two days a week which I found rewarding, and it also kept my brain active.

With both of us now retired from full-time paid employment and having two grandchildren, we again started to look with even more conviction for a new home, nearer to all our family as this is what we understood they wanted.

We were also seriously considering the purchase of a plot of land somewhere, upon which we could possibly construct a self-build Potton house. The scope was still wide and varied, as we searched in Gloucestershire, Oxfordshire, The Cotswolds, Wiltshire, Hertfordshire, Surrey, Berkshire, Hampshire and Suffolk, as our diary shows (Fig. 453).

We had lists of towns and villages which we methodically went through. However, our excursions away, thankfully, were not only confined to house hunting, as we were able to attend the MG car club weekend in Lincoln, where we also had a most relaxing day in Stamford.

Closer to home we took my mother and the dogs over to Blickling to see the magnificent carpet of bluebells, all growing in the Great Wood. This visit back to Blickling brought back happy memories of when I worked there in the Estate Management section, this prompted me to meet up again with David Brady, to see if there were any voluntary opportunities, perhaps giving guided walks around the park or wider estate. This was a silly question, as there were always possibilities, and it wasn't long before I was taking small groups of people up to the Mausoleum. When fully trained I would then be able to unlock the incredibly heavy doors and show visitors the inside.

But before that commenced, I decided to renew my acquaintance with amateur painting by joining an oil painting course at Castle Rising. I had never painted in oils before, always preferring pencil sketching or watercolours. So, it was therefore a new experience and medium, and I must be honest and say that it wasn't to my liking.

However, one thing I was certainly able to do was to support our children with garden maintenance. Whilst over the years I had spent time in all three of their gardens. On that occasion, it was to be with Oliver and Jude in their new location. With all manner of devices in my car, ranging from wire cutters to chainsaws, I arrived at Oliver's house on 14 April and didn't return home until the 17th. During that time, we had cut down a massive tree, had a huge bonfire and generally tidied up their garden. At least the builders, who were shortly due

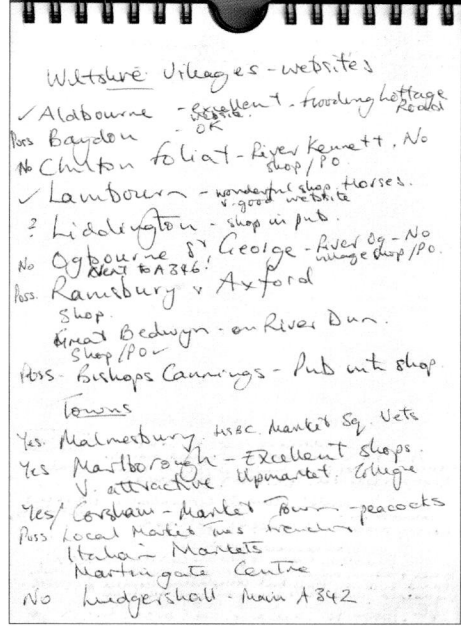

Figure 453

to carry out some alterations, would now have some space for their equipment.

In May, another holiday was spent at our cottage, where we had some glorious days walking and visiting our old favourite haunts, as well as new locations such as Barnard Castle and Robin Hood's Bay (Fig. 454), seen from the cliff top. An amazing local tulip festival gave us a chance to see what could be done at home – if only we had an 18th century parkland, with five acres of landscaped garden in which to display more than 6000 bulbs!

Figure 454

Another day, Dan tried out his retrieving skills, learnt last year. This time though, it was out of season, and he very proudly presented us with a most beautiful cock pheasant, which he had just found dead in the nearby woods – well, dogs don't understand diaries. This was despite my continued efforts to train them, even on the beach at Robin Hood's Bay (Fig. 455)! Well at least, Dan was sitting and looking at me, but Archie seemed not to care. This would never have happened with their mistress!

Whilst on our visit to Barnard Castle, we both managed to find several vintage 1940s/50s clothes and appropriate accessories – mine was a suit and yellow waistcoat, Kate's was a handbag, hat and jewellery which complemented a dress that she already had at home. The reasons will become apparent shortly.

We joined both Leigh and Ben on 17 May, at Beaulieu Motor Museum and Auto Jumble. These events were fascinating to wander round as you never quite knew what you would find next. They can, for this very reason, be a danger to the wallet! But luckily not on this occasion. A very hot and superb day was had and as we stayed with Sophie and Leigh afterwards, we were able to spend more time with them all, which was lovely.

Figure 455

Whilst not as grand as the Beaulieu gardens, ours at 'The Barn' were looking really good too. Having been created by two amateur gardeners, Kate and me,

Chapter 7 Life in Retirement 2014 – 2025

Figure 456   *Figure 457*

it had recovered well from the wedding reception last year, when the view (Fig. 456) had been incorporated into the marquee.

On 23 May, I and a fellow magistrate sat again in the Crown Court with a judge in his wig and gown, to hear and adjudicate appeals from the Magistrates Court. As magistrates we didn't often have the opportunity to sit in the Crown Court, so as on previous occasions I found it very interesting working alongside the judge. I continued to sit in the Crown Court until I decided to no longer work in the adult/criminal court, and I moved to Family sittings only. It was fascinating observing how the judges worked. Whilst it might be expected that if he or she so wished, a judge would simply overrule the two magistrates, but this was never the case. The judge was very aware that if the two magistrates, sitting with him on the bench, so desired they could make a joint majority and binding decision. However, I was never aware of this occurring, and all three of us always worked as a single, unified bench, just as it should be.

At the end of May, the vintage clothes we had bought in Barnard Castle, were given their first outing (Fig. 457), when we were invited and drove in Gertie, to the East Anglian Air Ambulance Vintage Garden Party. In the private grounds of Oxnead Hall, with the sun shining, we were treated to traditional games, music and refreshments. A flypast of the Air Ambulance reminded us all as to why we were there, and it was a very successful fundraising event!

A few days later in June, we drove, not in Gertie, to Chessington, where we assisted Em and Pete in the preparations for Libby's third birthday celebrations. An outdoor party for ten children was thoroughly enjoyed, and the numbers were increased when friends and more senior family members arrived for the birthday tea.

A more mature party had been held privately at the barn for Gertie, to celebrate 80 years since her first purchase, in May 1934. Unlike Libby, Gertie simply enjoyed a good wash, followed by a wax and polish! She did look really smart and would not have looked out of place at the Silverstone, MG90 show, that Oliver and I visited later on in June.

On that particular day, I left home at 05.30, drove to Welwyn Garden City to collect Oliver and then up the A1 to the show. The displays of vintage, historic and modern cars whetted the appetite of both of us. Even Oliver, a die-hard Mercedes driver, managed to agree that he could see the virtues of one particular modern MG, being put through its paces by a professional rally driver. It was certainly not for sale though, and after a worthwhile day, I eventually arrived home much later that night.

During the year, we continued to spend time every day, looking at possible properties on the internet. Viewings had been made on some, but nothing seemed to fit the criteria, which was, we admit, quite stretching! However, after a couple of visits to a thatched cottage in Monk's Eleigh, Suffolk, we made an offer and to our surprise it was accepted. All we had to do then was to sell Walnut Barn!

Having spoken to several agents we engaged Strutt & Parker and on 4 July the photographs, both inside and out were taken by a professional photographer. The main outside one, that was to be used on the cover (Fig. 458) was taken by me, as to catch the right light it had to be photographed at 06.00!

With prices and commission fees agreed, plans approved, and glossy brochures printed, we were ready to put our home on the market and move on to a new phase in our lives. We had agreed that a local representative for Strutt & Parker, Mary Cubitt, who also lived in Bodham, would show any prospective purchasers around to save us the work.

Walnut Barn officially went on the market on 11 July, with an asking price

Chapter 7 Life in Retirement 2014 – 2025

Figure 458

of £685,000. At first there was a trickle of people who obviously, just out of curiosity, wanted to take the opportunity to see inside 'The Barn', but there were one or two who seemed genuinely interested. So, the wait for an offer commenced.

Also in July, Norfolk always hosted the annual holiday for the Blues and Royals cavalry horses. They were always very popular equine visitors, especially if you were fortunate enough to see them in the early hours of the morning, being exercised on Holkham Beach. Regrettably, we haven't yet been able to witness this amazing spectacle. Every year though, during their summer camp in Norfolk, these magnificent horses were stabled in Bodney, just outside Thetford Forest. So, on one of their 'open days' we took Ben, Sophie and Leigh to see them,

Figure 459 is me with Ben, as I introduced him to one of the horses and he gave it some hay. It is one of my favourite early photographs of us together.

Around this time, I became involved in forming a Court Social Club where the magistrates from around Norfolk, both currently sitting and retired, could have a luncheon, listen to a speaker and catch up with colleagues that they may not have seen for a while. This proved to be very popular and attracted some very prominent speakers over the years, who included senior High Court Judges, Members of the Lords, the Secretary of State for Justice who was The Rt. Hon. Elizabeth Truss and who went on to become Prime Minister, as well as many other local dignitaries. During the year, these luncheons were generally held bi-monthly, and I also organised a grand Christmas evening dinner. It was all good fun, but as always, hard work.

Figure 459

413

Whilst helping at Walnut Barn, when we had been doing all our major building works, Oliver and Jude had gained a lot of knowledge, multiple skills and an understanding of what was involved in the construction of a house, so they had already decided to extend their new home. Having appointed a builder, their major extension commenced, and the foundations were started on 21 July. This turned out to be a complicated build, not due to the size of the extension but more to do with the high standard of workmanship that Oliver and Jude and their builders wanted to achieve. Oliver and Jude were extremely happy and pleased with all the hard work that had been undertaken.

Our wedding anniversary was celebrated on 24 July with a glorious evening meal, at the Kings Head in Letheringsett. We came home to see a tawny owl sitting on the roof of our barn. We were really excited, as we had heard it on many occasions, but this was the first time we had seen it.

Our 'grandparenting' skills were tested for the first time in July, when we had Ben home on his own for a week's holiday, whilst Sophie attended a course in Scotland and Leigh focused on his new business. With a 15-month-old grandson and two dogs to walk, outdoor activities were the order of the day. Suffice to say that we all had great fun with visits to the seaside (Fig. 460), various playgrounds and The North Norfolk Railway. We were really sad to see him return home and looked forward to a full family holiday in Norfolk, later in the year.

Figure 460

The theme of 'firsts' continued with Gertie winning 'First Place' twice, in the 'MG Pride of Ownership' competition, which took place at the MG events at Longham and then at Gayton. Our presentation was to take place later as part of the club's AGM meeting.

The 'first' offer was also received on Walnut Barn, which whilst not accepted was soon negotiated to match the professional valuation. We were still thinking whether to accept this, when the cottage in Monks Eleigh, Suffolk, which we had found and made an offer on, suddenly fell through. After frantic visits to the county, resulting in no success with the vendors, we declined the offer made to us for Walnut Barn and accepted that it was to be our family home, for a few more years.

As a distraction from the building works and house selling, Oliver and Jude joined us at Blickling Hall, on 9 August, for the Summer Proms, where the

Chapter 7 Life in Retirement 2014 – 2025

theme was linked to the two World Wars. We listened to the superb orchestra, watched a visit from 'Joey' from the film *War Horse* and an amazing aerobatic display by a Spitfire, called Grace, which was flown in synchronisation with the music. This display was to confirm that there was no doubt that Britain's pageantry was certainly world class.

With the sun still shining, the whole family joined us at Walnut Barn, and they all enjoyed an old fashioned 'bucket and spade' holiday. With visits to the beach, boat trips to see the seals, walks, picnics, swings and roundabouts, a great time was had by us all, especially at the ice cream shop!

In the photograph (Fig. 461) of us all awaiting the boat trip to see the seals, it was quite difficult, as Jude couldn't join us, and whilst Kate and I were aware of the genuine reason, the rest of our family had to be told a 'white lie', that she was not feeling too good.

Figure 461

However, by mid-September, Jude had her 12-week scan, that indicated all was well and Kate and I looked forward to our third grandchild arriving next year. This exciting news was formally 'announced' to our family, after her 20-week scan, on fireworks night, 5 November.

As often is the case, her natural pregnancy had followed a hospital assessment when Jude and Oliver had been advised that given her endometriosis, it was very unlikely that she would conceive. So, following this devastating news, she and Oliver took a holiday and lo and behold she became pregnant! We were all so pleased for them both.

The summer season was rounded off with another 'outing' for the vintage clothes. This time to the North Norfolk Railway 1940s weekend. We took Gertie, with Dan and Archie in the back and with so many people in period dress it really was a most impressive event.

One thing that I did need to do was to keep the garden looking well kempt. This obviously involved cutting the grass for which, sometimes, I needed the assistance of an expert, in the guise of Ben (Fig. 462).

Figure 462

Mid way through September, we had another very relaxing adult holiday in Middleham. However, unfortunately on the day we returned, Kate managed to twist her leg. After a very careful drive home, visits to the doctors and being advised to rest followed by a week on crutches, she was cleared of any permanent damage. Thankfully a week later she was walking without any aids!

4 October brought Emily, Pete and Libby to Anglesey Abbey, where we met up in the pouring rain – summer had just broken! We visited the house and mill and worked our way around the nature trail! The huge tree house was an instant hit with Libby, who thoroughly enjoyed the clattering of coins, as they went down the drainpipes to awaiting collection buckets – an ingenious way to raise funds!

Back home, I finally had my induction day with the National Trust, and started work as an estate guide at Blickling Hall. My course was very thorough and most informative and once I was fully trained, I was not only able to commence tours around the park, but also take visitors into the Mausoleum. Previously I had only been able to show them the outside. It is some 15 years since I had last worked there as a volunteer, but the draw of the estate has never waned.

The next day we prepared my father's Bosun dinghy for a nautical auction in Wroxham. We weren't able to sail her as often as we had hoped, so we felt the correct course of action was to sell her, in order that someone else could enjoy the fun and experience of taking her out on the water. She was sold for £240.

The run up to Christmas enabled Dan and Archie to go 'picking up' again on the local shoots – this time legally as it was within season, unlike Dan in Yorkshire! Once again, they both excelled and Dan can be seen waiting to give us, his 'handler', a pheasant that was nearly as big as himself (Fig. 463).

Over the next few weekends, we managed to go and see the progress being made on the second phase of Oliver and Jude's building works, which obviously now needed to be finished in time for

Figure 463

their new arrival. The work was looking really good and had made a huge difference to the layout of the bungalow. They had both spent a short break staying with Jude's sister, to give their builders more space, and as the builders departed, they moved back home.

Back in Bodham, with the presents purchased, the mince pies made and meals planned, we awaited the arrival of Father Christmas and looked forward to Christmas Day and the New Year when our family all returned to Walnut Barn.

Our Christmas present from Em and Pete was certainly different! We knew that Em was pregnant, as at various times we had taken her to have ultrasound scans etc. I recall one visit though, when I had taken both her and Pete to the hospital, that afterwards they were very secretive about the images. This was most unlike them and didn't reflect their attitude at all during Em's pregnancy with Libby. But on Christmas Day, we found out why, when we were presented with our present. It was an image from the scan, which was lovely, then a second image which we both thought was just as good but possibly from a different angle. We were then advised to read the headings of the two images – Baby 1 and Baby 2! Em was pregnant with TWINS!

Given what they had had to go through with IVF treatments, this was a complete and a very happy surprise for us, and we suspected that it had been the same for them, at the time when they had been told. What a brilliant Christmas present!

Later that evening, when all the excitement had settled down, Kate gave me my Christmas presents. Upon unwrapping one of them, I found a copy of Humphrey Pakington's *English Villages and Hamlets*, first published in 1934, by Batsford Books. My edition (Fig. 464) was a reprint of the 1949 edition.

Figure 464

The significance of this present was that we had both thoroughly enjoyed a BBC series called *Penelope Keith's Hidden Villages*. Armed with a copy of Batsford's book, the same one that Kate had found for me, Penelope Keith visited a number of villages seeking out stories and traditions from the 1930s and before. It was a lovely series, and I recall saying that it would be nice to explore some of the villages in Kent. So, my present not only took some detective work to find but was also gratefully received. Little did I know that this was only the first part of a much wider surprise.

2015

For Dan and Archie, the new year brought another opportunity to attend a shoot, to further demonstrate their expertise, at both finding and retrieving the game birds. They performed really well, and the excessive tail wagging was a clear sign, that they were very happy indeed. During the day there had been the odd flurry of snow but not very much at all. However, it was very cold, so the hot toddies provided halfway through the shoot were extremely welcome.

For the rest of us, the spring of 2015 started unassumingly, with Kate and I enjoying a glorious time at Walsingham Abbey. With bright blue sky and sunshine, we wandered around the gardens and woods, amongst the beautiful swathes of snowdrops – which from a distance you could have been mistaken for thinking that you were walking towards several massive snow drifts. They were quite spectacular.

February was to herald my 60th birthday and Kate had been secretly working on a celebration with all our family. She suggested that it would be a nice idea to take my Batsford book and to see if we could locate some of the villages in Kent, particularly those that had a connection to my family history. We initially stayed at the Powdermills Hotel, a converted Grade II, Georgian Country House near Battle. We spent several leisurely days in Kent and Sussex, visiting places that neither of us knew, whilst also trying to discover where my paternal great-grandfather (Randall), had worked as a chauffeur.

The family story says that he worked as a chauffeur for the Mitford family.

Figure 465   *Figure 466*

However, through my own research I discovered that for a short time, in their younger years, the Mitford sisters lived in Asthall Manor in the Cotswolds, followed by Rutland Gate in Knightsbridge. Whilst my great-grandfather's photograph (Fig. 465) was taken by a photographer, based in Brompton Road, Knightsbridge, London. I do wonder, if this is sufficient evidence to support the family's understanding, that whilst in London he was working for the Mitfords? I am not totally convinced.

To add more confusion, I have a photograph (Fig. 466) of the lychgate in Penshurst, in Kent. Penshurst Place, being the ancestral home of the Sidney family, where chauffeurs would have been required, at the time when my great-grandfather was in employment. This photograph was held in my mother's collection, so I can only assume that it had some importance, but I have found no references or connections with the Sidney family to the Mitfords, so I still have no idea of its precise significance. Is there a connection, I ask? – a perfect detective story that at some point in the future needs to be solved.

Whilst we were staying near Battle, Kate suggested that we drove down to Rye in East Sussex, where she had booked a room in The Mermaid Inn. Nothing unusual about this, as Kate often organised our short breaks, so I agreed and drove to Rye, parked the car and found the Inn. We entered and to my utter surprise I was to find all our family had gathered there. We had a fantastic celebratory meal, which included an amazing cake, in the shape of a classic MG (Fig. 467), which had been organised by Jude. I had well and truly been 'stitched up' from a Christmas present through to a birthday party. Credit and love to Kate!

The Mermaid Inn had an incredible history, having been built some 600 years ago. Its cellars date back to 1156, whilst the building above ground was rebuilt in 1420, following a disastrous fire in the town, which was started by some French Raiders. The history of this Inn and the town of Rye itself, all added that extra dimension to the weekend.

Figure 467

The next week at the MG club annual AGM we were presented with our 'Pride of Ownership Cup', along with two rosettes which are proudly displayed in the library. The trophy was only kept by us for the year. This followed our win in Gayton last year. As we were the first to receive this prestigious award (Fig 468) our names were engraved in pride of place at the top of the trophy.

Figure 468

Then on 14 March, we drove to Em and Pete's to have yet another double celebration, as it was not only Kate's birthday that weekend, but also Mothering Sunday. Having had a good weekend with Pete, Libby and Em, who was now 24 weeks pregnant with twins, we called in to see Oliver and Jude on our way back home. Jude was due to give birth on 25 March and all was well with them both, but exhaustion was setting in for Jude.

Easter was to be extra special, as Jude gave birth to Eve Mei-Bo on 7 April, at 02.16 in the Lister Hospital, the day after Easter Monday. A good-sized bundle of joy, at 9lb 3.5oz. Much to Kate's delight, Oliver and Jude unexpectedly asked her to go down to stay for several days, in order to give them all a helping hand.

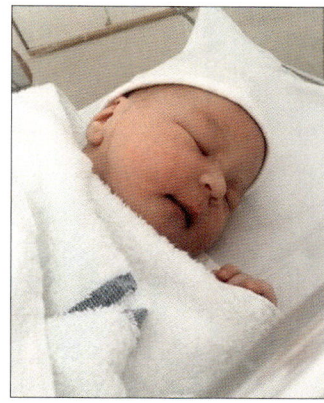

Eve's arrival (Fig. 469) meant that all three families had now granted us the privilege of having a grandchild. Em and Pete with Libby, Sophie and Leigh with Ben and now Oliver and Jude with Evie, as she was called. All of us, grandparents and parents, were incredibly fortunate. Would there possibly be any more in the future perhaps, or were we just being greedy?

Figure 469

A couple of weeks after that we spent a most enjoyable weekend in Clare, Suffolk with a group of friends from our MG club. This included a visit to a local brewery, a car rally through some very picturesque areas of the county and the opportunity to have supper with Gillian and Geoffrey, who lived just down the road from the hotel.

Given that we expected that the end of 2014 and the first few months of 2015 would be very busy with grandchildren, to ease the pressure on all of us we had temporarily taken 'The Barn' off the market. With Kate now in Welwyn Garden City helping Oliver and Jude look after Evie, I was on my own at the barn. Monday was spent hosting a Court Club luncheon and on the Friday I was volunteering at Blickling. In between times there was plenty to do to prepare 'The Barn', ready to possibly put it back on the market at the end of May. Kate having spent two weeks in Welwyn Garden City returned home on 24 April.

Later that month, we found a possible property in West Runton called The Lantern (Figs. 470 & 471). This was a 1920s Art Deco house which needed complete restoration, as it looked as though it hadn't been updated since being built. It was in a great position, overlooking the sea and had a reasonably large garden. We spoke to a local firm of architects, SMG in Sheringham, who we

Figure 470

Figure 471

discovered already knew the property well, and after our initial viewing we were certainly given plenty to think about. We kept this in mind and decided that perhaps it was not the right time to go back to living in a caravan, so we didn't pursue this opportunity!

I recall in one of my conversations with Kate, whilst she was in Welwyn Garden City, that I mentioned a property that I had seen for sale in Holt, that looked as if it would be suitable for us. However, I was aware that the 'For Sale' sign had gone, so assumed that it had been sold.

With Kate now back home I showed her the property, called Hanworth House, and she agreed that it would have been a good possibility (Fig. 472). So, at the weekend I decided to just check with the local Estate Agents to see if any of them recalled the property and what was its current status. After being sent to various agents I finally found that Arnolds were the last to have it on their books, but it had currently been withdrawn – no explanation as to why.

Figure 472

Having chatted to Kate again, we agreed on the Monday that we would ask Arnolds if they could check with the owners, to see if they would allow us to view the property, assuming that they were still of a mind to sell. As Kate was off on 10 May to help Em with Libby and prepare for the twins, a viewing was swiftly arranged for Tuesday 5 May. We both attended, and very much liked what we saw.

Chapter 7 Life in Retirement 2014 – 2025

During the viewing it transpired that the owners were about to sell two-thirds of the back garden to a builder. He had built the adjacent Caston Close and their garden would then enable him to add two or three more properties onto this cul-de-sac. Following the construction of these properties, the house would then be re-listed.

Despite the house requiring an extension, some updating, total re-decoration, along with having some minor subsidence rectified which could easily be sorted, we were still very interested. The next day we asked SMG architects to give us some ideas as to how the house could be modernised and enlarged, all within a set budget.

On 9 May, Evie had her first full day out with us, as we again joined Oliver and Jude at 'The Grand Designs Exhibition', with Evie all snug and warm in her pram. We all returned to Oliver's, laden with lots of innovative ideas as to how to improve, enhance and renovate our respective houses. As it later turned out, this was to be very fortuitous for us! Kate then set off to stay with Em and Pete, to help look after Libby until the twins were born, which meant she and I could only talk over the telephone.

With some ideas and rough costings from the architect which fitted our budget, coupled with ideas we had seen at the Grand Designs Exhibition, we contacted the estate agent again and explained that we were very interested in the house, but if the garden was sold, we would simply walk away. A very bold statement but we wanted to appear nonchalant and slightly ambivalent, when privately both of us were very keen indeed!

For some time, I had been endeavouring to find a book published in 1906, entitled *An English XIX Century Sportsman Bibliopole and Binder of Angling Books*, written by an American, William Loring Andrews (Fig. 473). This chronicled the work of my five times great-uncle, Thomas Gosden (see the family tree in the appendices).

Then, on 21 May, whilst searching the internet, I came across a copy in the USA. This was a particularly rare book with only 125 copies printed on Van Gelder handmade paper, with just a further 32 on Imperial Japan paper.

Having spoken to the seller and negotiated the price, I secured the purchase which was duly sent to me.

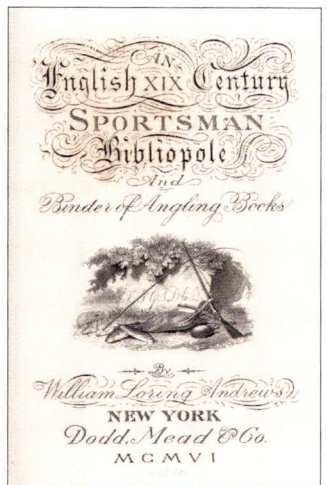

Figure 473

This spurred me on and in June, I found three other books, closer to home this time in Newmarket, that were actually bound by Thomas Gosden.

'The Barn' sale was still foremost in our minds, as we needed a quick sale, if we were to secure Hanworth House. On Monday, I spoke to Strutt & Parker, who put the barn back on the market and it was re-advertised on 22 May, with the first viewing booked for 10.30 on 30 May.

Arnolds spoke at length to the seller of Hanworth House, and eventually a couple of weeks later, having originally offered £474,000 which was not accepted, we increased it to £478,000, and on 27 May a deal was struck for us to purchase the house, with the whole garden intact. All we had to do now, was to sell 'The Barn'.

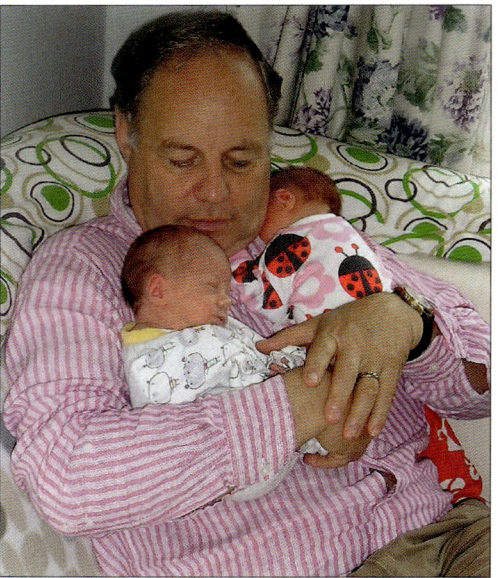
Figure 474

Kate was still staying with Em, Pete and Libby for eight weeks which had all been planned in advance. It was so fortuitous that she was there looking after Libby, as Leo and Francesca decided to arrive six weeks early on 27 May, in the 34th week of Em's pregnancy. I drove down to the hospital, to see them both when they were only just one day old, and again once they had come home eight days later (Fig. 474). Due to not only arriving early but being twins, I remember both of them being tiny. Leo (right) was born first at 16.09, weighing 5lbs 3oz and Francesca (left) followed at 16.30, weighing 4lbs 11oz.

Although Kate was still away at the time, after many telephone calls between the two of us, I was at last able to say that the first viewing resulted in us receiving an offer on 'The Barn', at the asking price of £685,000. We were both obviously very excited and it was also great news, as it demonstrated our ability to purchase Hanworth House.

No problems, we thought! So, with Kate now back in Norfolk and whilst all the paperwork was being undertaken in the background, we had another weekend away on 15 July, this time just outside Cheltenham. There we had terrific fun, racing Gertie, against ourselves, up and round the Bugatti Speed Hill Climb

Chapter 7 Life in Retirement 2014 – 2025

at Prescott. An amazing challenge both for us and for her, as we had never participated in anything like this before. It was also, an ideal opportunity to test out her new Blower (a Supercharger, in modern language). None of us disgraced ourselves and Gertie not only reached the phenomenal speed of 40 mph but also broke her own record with a winning time of 1 minute 50 seconds! On the day we were also 'entertained' by a 15-minute flying display by a Hurricane, exactly 75 years to the day since she took to the skies for her maiden flight. It was wonderful to see and very nostalgic.

Once all the excitement over the past few weeks had slightly died down, we discovered that the sellers of Hanworth House were not as 'open' as they had originally made out. It became clear that the sale was dependent upon the sellers being able to purchase a certain bungalow, and that the deal needed to be completed by the end of July.

If this was to be met, we needed to take action to secure our purchase. The barn sale already had had two exchange and completion dates agreed by the solicitors on both sides, but neither of them had materialised. So, an ultimatum was given by us, that if our purchasers did not exchange by 13 July, Walnut Barn would be put back on the market. They didn't! So 'The Barn' was back up for sale with Strutt & Parker!

On 4 August another couple came to view the barn, with their son who was living and working in the USA. The three of them had a good look around, asked lots of genuine questions and joined us for a cup of tea. They said that they were interested and would contact us again in a couple of days, when they returned from Europe. Apparently, the son was taking his family away to celebrate a special family occasion. They kept their word and on 8 August, over another cup of tea, they made an incredible cash offer of the full asking price. We accepted this, without hesitation. Their only stipulation was that we had to move quickly, possibly within weeks rather than months which whilst it surprised us, it also suited us perfectly. Later, on the very same day, a surveyor arrived to survey the barn. Clearly 'moving quickly' was very important and was seriously meant. I remember talking to Kate's brother Peter, who had recently retired as a solicitor, and knew about conveyancing, to check if it really was possible to conclude the purchase of a house in a matter of a few weeks. When I told him the name of their solicitors, Macfarlanes, he assured me that as one of the top firms in London, he wasn't surprised by the speed. Apparently, instead of searches etc., they simply insure against the risks. Given this we started to pack as quickly as we could.

Following the survey, the offer was officially confirmed between solicitors on 13 August and on 24 August, just sixteen days after the offer, we exchanged contracts, much to the surprise of Strutt & Parker who were endeavouring to

Figure 475

keep the original couple on board. They too were ready to exchange but we stuck to our instincts, and much to the dismay of Strutt & Parker went with our American family.

Exactly ten days later, on 3 September we had completed on the sale of the barn, and moved into Hanworth House, 23 Cromer Road, Holt! The entire sale had taken just under one month, from the first viewing on 4 August to moving in on 3 September. Kate and I were handed the keys to our front door (Fig. 475) and let ourselves in to our new home. The door was to be one of the first early changes to be made to Hanworth House!

The actual move was a mammoth undertaking, with six hired vehicles, two trailers, a large Luton removal van plus nine adults. I now totally agree with Kate that if you're thinking of moving yourselves, think twice, then don't do it!

During all this upheaval, we had Ben to stay on his own for 11 days, as Sophie and Leigh were off to Tenerife. He arrived on the day of the move and thoroughly enjoyed himself, as he was allowed to help us to unpack the vans and best of all to sit up in the cabs and pretend to drive them.

Whilst he was with us, we took him to The North Norfolk Railway, which he absolutely loved. We not only had a ride on two steam engines but also had a special guided tour around the workshops and yards with one of the members of our MG Club. He was an experienced engineer and oversaw the workshops that undertook the restoration and repairs to all the rolling stock. He also presented Ben with a picture of one of the steam trains, which we had framed for him, and he had it hung in his bedroom. Ben was in his element (Fig. 476).

Figure 476

Chapter 7 Life in Retirement 2014 – 2025

Whilst Ben enjoyed the railway, back in Surrey, Libby had her own 'grown up excitement' when she started full time school, with some of her friends from nursery.

A very proud day to see her wearing her uniform for the first time. Shown here in the traditional obligatory 'doorstep' photograph (Fig. 477).

Work started on the alterations for Hanworth House that didn't require planning consent and for the next three months we were unpacking boxes and making umpteen cups of coffee or tea for a crew of fantastic men. They were either down holes having first dug them out ready to lay new drains, up ladders and scaffolding to repair and repoint chimney pots, working on the first and ground floor exterior walls, replacing fascias, soffits or guttering, and finally installing all the front windows.

It was back to the reality of a house being upgraded, very similar to that at 'The Barn'! Once Ben had gone home we then stripped down the front porch to the bare wood and re-painted it in readiness for the final upheaval, as Anglian Windows were coming on 10 November to fit our new windows and front door. With a redesigned flower bed, driveway and all the exterior work finished, all the front was completed by Christmas.

Figure 477

As I said, none of this required planning consent and it totally transformed the front exterior of the house. To the extent that whenever we were working in the front garden, complete strangers walking past would often stop to chat and compliment us on how great it all looked. It was amazing that so many people approved, and much to our delight we also knew that we had passed the scrutiny of The Holt Society, as we had the secretary and his wife living opposite, who had had no objections. In fact, to the contrary for they and their fellow committee members were all in favour of the alterations that we were planning to carry out.

Our neighbours either side were also very supportive, in fact I had worked with one of them when we were both employed by Norwich Union, not that I knew that at the time when we purchased the house.

Having agreed the plans with our architect, for the back extension and the internal alterations, we submitted these at the end of September, to the council planning department. A site visit by them was then carried out on 2 November.

As a result, an Arboriculture Impact Assessment was required, and prior to the relocation of the garage this was agreed by the council. This assessment had to be carried out due to the close proximity of the proposed new garage, to an old apple tree, which we too wanted to preserve. So, we were delighted when it was all approved.

As agreed, on 10 November, Anglian Windows began fitting the new front windows and front door as well as some of the side windows, all of which made a huge difference especially when the scaffolding eventually came down. I added the number '23' to the door and fitted the doorbell pull which had originally come from Kate's home at the Vicarage, when she lived in Barton Turf. We had also used it at 'The Barn', so it was a small but tangible connection to her past.

Now that the scaffolding had been dismantled at the front, we decided that the name of the house should be carved into the front porch. Having found Luke Chapman, an excellent local wood sculptor, who would carve the letters into the wooden beam, we commissioned him to carry out the work. Since this was completed, we have received numerous comments on how good it looks, especially the way his lettering follows the curvature of the beam. The photographs are of Luke commencing the carving, having first attached a paper template (Fig. 478). Along with his finished work in figure 479.

Figure 478

Figure 479

Back in May, as a precaution we had commissioned a structural report which recommended a design and specification for dealing with the underpinning requirements. Then, in November we asked for a trial investigation which confirmed these requirements, and a local builder agreed to undertake the work. The excavations commenced on 30 November and four days later the work was passed both by our structural engineer and the building inspector. That was such a big relief and a giant step forward, and later the drains that had caused the subsidence were replaced, leaving us feeling very positive.

In early December, we needed to have a weekend in Middleham as there were Christmas bookings, so the cottage had to be 'dressed' accordingly. It was a welcome relief if truth be known, to see rooms without dust and no workmen wherever you turned and looked. But it didn't last long as we were back in Holt on the 14th. Good news was to come in the next post though – Planning Consent had been granted for our extension. Now work could start in earnest, in the early part of 2016.

With this wonderful outcome at the end of 2015, we took Christmas off and had a short respite from the renovations and mess. All our family came home for Christmas which was great, and we knew that in the New Year we would be selecting builders and constructing our new enlarged abode. In some respects that filled us with dread, but it was also exciting and would eventually provide us with another fabulous family home.

2016

As you may have already predicted, this year was dominated with updating and extending our new home, Hanworth House and it was in January that the 'real' work commenced. We were determined to have it all finished before Christmas!

Having watched numerous BBC *Grand Design* programmes, with Kevin McCloud, I am convinced that everyone says, *'we will be in by Christmas'*. What very few couples actually say, is which Christmas! Suffice to say, that we were determined by December 2016 to be joined by our contractors, friends and neighbours at an 'Open House Thank You' celebration, to toast the completion of our project. Well, that was the goal to which we aimed.

During the alterations, we enlarged and converted the house to create four en suite double bedrooms, an extended new kitchen/family room, a scullery, a completely new heating system, brand new electrics and redecoration throughout, with new floor coverings up and downstairs. We also removed four chimneys, one coal shed, a large garage, a washhouse-*cum*-pantry, a conservatory and many tonnes of soil and rubble. Believe it or not, this mayhem all took place whilst we still actually lived in the property! Following our barn conversion and whilst we had lived in a caravan, I seem to recall Kate saying, 'Never again!'

Throughout these major alterations there were so many incidents and stories that I could relate, both good and challenging, that I think the best way to record these is through an album of photographs, with suitable captions or a short narrative. So, I will briefly outline the year and add the album of the building works at the end of this section.

Right through the project, we had several tradesmen, but there were three that were the bedrock of the team. They were Norman, with his colleague Liam, and Gary. Norman and Liam were qualified builders and worked full time with us, building the house and then the garage. Gary too was a builder, and sometimes would need to return to finish off another job, which we were happy for him to do. He was a 'jack of all trades' and able to turn his hand to many building tasks, as well as laying slabs and carpentry etc. He was a very useful man to know. He and Liam were also volunteer firefighters, so were frequently seen running to their cars, when they were called out on a 'shout'.

The new extension was built using a timber frame construction and was produced by a local company who, at the time, was new to this scale of work. With all extensions of our size, they had to seek building regulations approval, and with their lack of experience it meant that Andy, the council's Building Inspector kept a very close eye on its erection and assembly. Without fail he would arrive unannounced, to check the standard of workmanship and their adherence to the regulations. He always wore a cowboy hat and steel capped boots, with his long hair tied in a ponytail, and dressed in jeans! Despite his somewhat outlandish appearance though, there was nothing that escaped his critical eye, which for us was most comforting. He really was a great asset to the project and certainly wouldn't have looked out of place at a Dolly Parton concert!

On the page opposite is a chronological summary of the key stages which gives a good overview of the progress made during the year. This is followed by a montage of photographs.

Building timetable

January
: Demolished wash house and coal store.
Footings dug and concreted.
Walls built up to damp proof course ready for timber frame.
Gable wall taken down.

February
: Stack of four scullery chimneys demolished.
Upstairs back ceilings demolished.
Timber structure built to roof level.
Trusses delivered, manhandled onto roof and fitted.

March
: All trusses finished, roof felted and battened. Roof watertight.
Water supply and drainage in place.
Steel work fitted in kitchen to support upstairs original wall.
Interior timber walls fitted both upstairs and in kitchen.
Survey by Wren Kitchens.
Old kitchen units dismantled and installed in the pantry.
Old outside kitchen wall demolished – now we could see the size of the extension.

April
: First fixing of electrics and plumbing.
Insulation fitted in walls and roof.
Plaster boarding finished.
Plastering.
External wall cladding brickwork finished.
Aga installed.
Kitchen painted.
Window openings measured and windows fitted inc. french doors.
Downstairs floor coverings laid.
Kitchen units delivered.

May
: Kitchen units fitted.
Roof tiling finished.
Second fixings of electrics and plumbing.
Pad for new garage laid.
Aga commissioned.

June
: Skirtings and architrave fitted.
Decorating continued.
Landscaping outside, Russell moved twenty tonnes of soil with JCB.
Internal doors hung.

July
: Carpets fitted.
We moved into our new bedroom on 9 July.

Figure 480

Figure 481

Living conditions during the build were somewhat shambolic, to say the least (Figs. 480 & 481). Downstairs we just had the original kitchen for a few weeks and the rest of the essentials were in the dining room.

The drawing room and one bedroom were our only sanctuary and as such were untouched, apart from re-decoration at a later date.

When the time came for the workmen to depart, the house at last became recognisable as a home. There was still a myriad of jobs though, some large, some small, to finish over the next two or three months. However, we had fulfilled our promise to be 'in by Christmas' so we were very happy indeed.

Unfortunately, we hadn't been able to take out Gertie (our 1934 MG) during all the building work, as she was being stored in the old garage, with a huge volume of packing boxes and builders' equipment carefully stacked around her. With the new garage now built, we were able to move her into this, and it now became her new abode, whilst we prepared to level the area around her old home.

We asked Russell, our friend and JCB owner, to see if he would come and undertake this. He agreed and having surveyed the entrance was convinced that his JCB would go between us and our neighbour (Fig. 482). With literally an inch each side, we dared not watch his unbelievable manoeuvres, and he admitted afterwards that he too was rather concerned! Over the next few

Chapter 7 Life in Retirement 2014 – 2025

Figure 482 (far left)
Figure 483 (above)
Figure 484 (left)

days, he had levelled the area leading to the old garage, in preparation for Gary to lay the initial slabs in front of the kitchen. My role, and that of Kate was to transfer the surplus soil to the front garden for removal (Figs. 483 & 484) and also to the back garden, where we were to make a wild area.

The old garage had a large concrete base, so we talked to Gary who suggested that this was turned into a raised arbour, with a step down to a second seating patio area, and he would easily be able to lay paving slabs on top of the concrete. This sounded a good idea, and we agreed that once we had removed the old garage, he would come back to lay the remaining slabs. First though, we wanted to finish off the garden around the back of the house, and we had both already made a really good start but there was much more landscaping to do, later in the year,

Whilst we were working hard, life outside of Hanworth House continued. Here I would like to mention just two key events that occurred during the year. Firstly, to celebrate Queen Elizabeth II's 90th birthday, on 12 June 2016, Holt held a

Figure 485

street party (Fig. 485). Kate is halfway down, on the righthand side, in a red jumper, next to our future MP Duncan Baker. These and other royal celebrations were held throughout the UK and secondly, they were followed on 23 June, when the UK voted to leave the European Union.

During the spring and summer months, Kate and I concentrated our efforts on the garden, for I, in particular, wanted to plant some trees before the planting season ended. Regrettably, during February Kate was unable to assist me in the garden, for she had had an emergency visit to the A&E with a possible dislocated hip. Fortunately, after many x-rays and blood tests, she was discharged and told to rest for six weeks.

So, whilst she had to stay indoors, I dug six huge holes, as we never seemed to purchase small trees, and subsequently planted one field maple, one rowan and four silver birch trees, which produced an instant upgrading of the area.

However, there was the matter of removing a long leylandii hedge. Which was a huge job requiring our tree surgeon to cut it down, chop the trunks for firewood (Fig. 486), and remove as much of the root plate as possible. My part was to help load his lorry with as much brush wood as we could.

For quite a long time we had dips in the grass where the roots were rotting down. But over several years, this has now rectified itself. This was only one side of the garden though, and the other side (Fig. 487) had a long laurel hedge.

Figure 486

Figure 487

Chapter 7 Life in Retirement 2014 – 2025

This was left for me to cut down and burn, and now that Kate was back on her feet, we erected along both sides of the garden, a 6' wooden fence, with concrete posts and gravel boards. This ensured that the whole garden was dog proof and ready for landscaping.

Both Kate and I wanted to become 'involved' with activities within the town, and one way to achieve this was to join the Holt Society. Our neighbour was the Membership Secretary, so we contacted him and paid our subscriptions. The Society not only produced some very useful booklets, but also held speaker events and visits throughout the year, all of which helped us to integrate into the town. Through joining we also managed to meet several of our other close neighbours, who have since become good friends.

Throughout the year, our close family were all nurturing their young children. Unfortunately, since her birth, Evie had been experiencing difficulties in regulating her body temperature, which sometimes resulted in febrile seizures, which as a family were most distressing and concerning. This was still the case in early October, which resulted, not for the first time, in her being admitted into hospital. This again was very disconcerting for both Oliver and Jude, but in time these seizures were to become less frequent and would cease altogether.

Time off, as you can imagine, was very limited for us, but we managed a most welcome week's holiday in our Yorkshire cottage. Just prior to our visit, Sophie, Leigh, Ben and Barney had stayed there again, during which time at her Employer's UK Congress in Harrogate, Sophie was presented with her latest veterinary qualification, a professional Certificate in Veterinary Nursing in Emergency and Critical Care along with the 2016 'Make a Difference' (MAD) award for Responsibility within a clinical setting. Both were well deserved and capped a brilliant year for her.

Following the arrival of Evie, Jude returned to her legal degree which she had been studying but had had a break due to her pregnancy. After successfully completing her final examinations, she graduated in November. Having returned to The Metropolitan Police (The Met), she was now using her new expertise to write a company Blog, hopefully for a firm of Intellectual Property Solicitors, an area in which she was keen to specialise.

Oliver was to follow in our footsteps and completed his 'Phase 2' of the extension to their bungalow. Although, it was not so much of an extension, rather a rebuild, for when it was all finished there was only one original wall left! In September, Kate and I, along with my mother were invited to a barbecue, so we were all able to see the completed works and it was very impressive.

437

REFLECTIONS UPON A FAMILY

On 10 September my cousins Christine, and her sister Rosemary hosted a gathering of the Gosden clan at Chris's house, in Culpho, Suffolk. It was always fun to meet up with long lost family and this was no exception. This time though, there was an obvious omission as my father wasn't there. So Mum, as the most senior Gosden cut the cake with David, my other cousin (Fig. 488). Amongst many other skills he was a keen genealogist and the family tree section in this memoir is mainly his work.

A family photograph was taken on the day (Fig. 489) to record the gathering. This updated the photograph earlier in the book, and as can be seen the whole family has extended.

Regrettably, as the image had to be taken from a distance, due to the expansion of the family, it is not so easy to identify everybody.

Figure 488

Figure 489

Chapter 7 Life in Retirement 2014 – 2025

Unlike Kate and I, and of course Oliver and Jude, Em and Pete had no time to indulge in building works, as Libby, Leo and Francesca took up all their time and more! In October though, it was Em's 40th birthday and all our family gathered together for a celebratory meal, in a lovely pub in East Molesey. Life in Chessington gradually settled down though for Em, Pete and family, and with both twins now walking, pre-school places looked a very attractive option!

Mid-October saw Oliver, Jude and Evie come to stay for a weekend. We all had a good walk around Weybourne Station, where we watched three steam trains on the heritage line, making their way from Sheringham to Holt and back, and in a field close by, admired some friendly horses, and stroked and fed them with some grass. It was a lovely weekend, concluding with Evie being measured on our kitchen door frame.

This was to become a regular occurrence every time any of the grandchildren came to see us. Sometimes, even the teddy bears needed measuring and that was a special job just for the grandchildren!

The first week in December we had the pleasure of Oliver, Jude and Evie to stay again. This time we walked the dogs around Pretty Corner, and then along Sheringham promenade with chips in hand. Once it was dark we then all walked into town to see Holt all lit up, with sparkling Christmas lights. A great introduction to what was to be a very happy Christmas.

However, before the year was to end, we owed our neighbours and friends a huge 'thank you', for tolerating all the disruption we had caused during our building works. Not forgetting our fantastic workmen, who had made our house a home again. So, on 15 December we hosted our promised 'At Home, Open House Thank You'. Forty-eight invitations were sent out, with thirty three people able to join us throughout that afternoon and well into the evening. With suitable drinks and plenty to eat, it was a lovely way to express our gratitude, and equally interesting for them to wander around the house and see what we had been doing.

For Christmas lunch, we treated ourselves to another Byfords meal which was superb. It was just what we both needed, quiet and relaxed, cooked and washed up by someone else and followed by Christmas pudding!

On Boxing Day, my sister Judy and her husband David came to see us, along with their children and grandchildren, some of whom had just partaken in the traditional Boxing Day Sea swim at Sheringham. Needless to say, after that test of endurance they most definitely needed a warm-up beside a log fire, hot drinks and cake – which was where we came in!

The New Year found us with all our family together again, in Hanworth

House, ready to celebrate our annual festive gathering. On New Year's Day, we all went to Sheringham beach, but not to swim I hasten to add. It was incredibly cold though, so instead, bags of hot chips were the order of the day!

An absolutely perfect conclusion to a very frenetic and at times a really stressful year. So, that was 2016 in a nutshell. To say it was hard work for all of us was a gross understatement. It was, nevertheless, again most enjoyable, rewarding and well worth the upheaval.

2017

Our second year in Holt was to be one of those years where the 'highs and lows' were certainly from one extreme to the other! All started well, as it was to be the first full year when we were not 'invaded' by builders and other tradespeople. However, this soon changed when we decided to continue landscaping the back garden.

In front of my fence that I had erected last year and following the clearance of the previous hedges, we decided to plant a new 'traditional' hedge on both sides of the garden. This would, we hoped, become a sanctuary for nesting birds which, after a few years proved to be very successful. But first it had to be planted, so with 160 young tree whips in hand, Kate and I took on the challenge, which took a whole day to complete. My previous work at Blickling though, came in handy and by the autumn all the whips had taken and were looking very healthy.

Next, we wanted to segment the garden with a wildlife section at the far end, in which we already had four large silver birch trees, that I had planted last year. Then from this wild part to the house, we wanted this to be more formal and to incorporate a children's climbing frame of some sort. The only issue here was that this necessitated the moving of a greenhouse, but actually, to our surprise, this was relatively easy to dismantle and re-assemble in its new location. The final section, closest to the house was to be a seating area with an arbour, created by the wisteria that had grown over the old garage.

Figure 490

Each area was sectioned off by a low picket fence and in the case of the wildlife area, a large eight-foot metal arch (Fig. 490), was positioned in the

Chapter 7 Life in Retirement 2014 – 2025

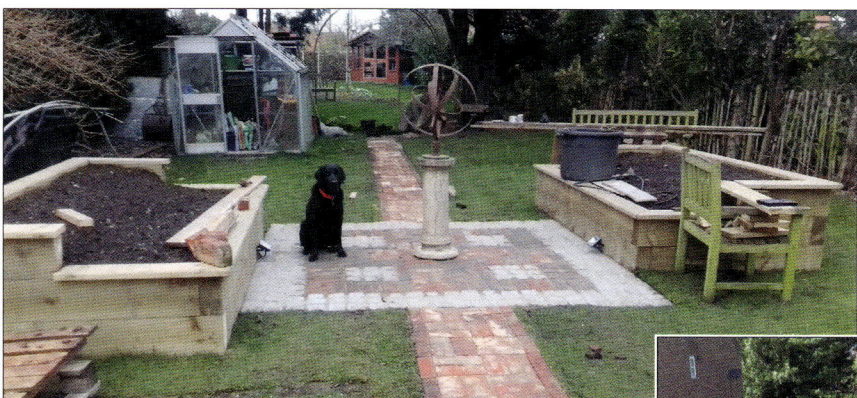

Figure 491

Figure 492

centre of the fence, to denote the change in the design of the garden. Throughout the wild section we created a meandering grass path, which was cut through the meadow, and gave us full access to the summer house, which was right at the end.

Within the formal side of the garden, I laid a brick path that concluded at the steps leading up to the arbour. Halfway along this brick weave path was located an armillary, positioned in the centre of a formal square made up of bricks and granite setts (Fig. 491). On either side of which, were raised beds made from railway sleepers. All of this 'hard landscaping' took the best part of January and February to complete, but it was well worth the hard work. As you can see, Dan was never one to miss a photographic opportunity!

Figure 493

However, the 'elephant in the room' was the old concrete and wooden double garage, which had to be demolished and cleared away (Figs. 492 & 493). So having removed the wooden and felted roof, Kate and I turned our attention to the concrete walls.

With sledgehammers at the ready we both 'knocked hell' out of the structure! At the conclusion, Ben, our grandson, who was staying with us at the time, made the best comment when he stood looking at the result and said *all this mess needs to be cleared up* – out of the mouth of babes.[37]

Anyway, it was all tidied up, and we carted umpteen barrow loads of rubble up the drive and into a skip. As agreed, Gary returned to lay the final part of the arbour, on top of the old garage base and this was to match up with his previous laying of slabs outside the scullery and kitchen doors. So now where the garage once stood, we had a lovely space in which to put a large table and eight chairs.

Towards the end of February, Archie suddenly became lame in one of his legs. Having had numerous tests at the vets, he was prescribed painkillers to help him, which thankfully they did. However, the consequence was that he couldn't partake in shoots or go on long walks, at least not for a while. So, this was compensated by having fun in the garden with both Kate and I, and the grandchildren when they came home. With all this attention, which both he and his brother Dan relished, his health improved and by April he was happy with a half hour walk, albeit on a lead.

Throughout the move and all the building works, I continued with my sittings as a magistrate and had joined the training committee for the Norfolk Bench. This was a new requirement, in that each English and Welsh Bench now had to have its own Justices' Training Approvals Authorisations and Appraisals Committee (JTAAAC), that supported its magistrates. In addition to sitting in the Adult Courts, I was also working to extend my expertise by training to become a Family Magistrate or as we were officially known, a Lay Judge. This training took place over two full days in March, and on 5 April 2017, I had my first Family Court sitting.

These family sittings were very different to crime sittings, as the former were civil rather than criminal cases. As such, the Lay Judges, who were due to sit on the bench, were presented in advance with confidential papers, to pre-read before the sitting. These gave details of families who were often going through a breakup, which in some incidences had resulted in the parents losing their focus on their own children. In all these cases it was the children who were our

---

37 This expression is a shortening and revision of expressions in the Old Testament of the Bible. Psalm 8:2

priority, so as a bench we had to agree and draft orders, that gave a framework to families and their support workers, in order that they could concentrate on the wellbeing of the child or children. Also, whilst drafting the order we had to give thought as to how the family would function, on a day-to-day basis with childcare and access, which was included in the Facts and Reasons that supported the order.

Some cases came under the title of Public Law, which could and frequently required thought to relocating the child or children, to a new foster home or permanent adoption. Some of this work could be very stressful but also really pleasing when you were able to secure a loving home for a child or siblings. The other cases were Private Law and involved families that were in dispute with each other, over where a child or children should reside and what access should be given to the other parent. Again, our duty was to ensure the safe wellbeing of the child or children. As I have said, this was very different to criminal work. Both are worthwhile though, and very rewarding.

Early in May we both attended a really interesting and, as it turned out, an expensive painting demonstration by Ian McMannus, in Picturecraft of Holt. The speed at which he painted was most impressive and wonderful to watch (Fig. 494), which prompted us to purchase the end result, and it was hung in our kitchen.

Back home, our next challenge was to spend some considerable time, laying out numerous parts of a new children's Climbing Fort. We read and re-read the instructions, repeatedly. Just how difficult could building a children's climbing fort be? It appeared that the answer was, very difficult, if not impossible! Then, after much head scratching and comments like '*I'm not going to be beaten*', we discovered that the wrong fixing pack had been delivered and consequently it was not compatible with the instructions. So, not totally our fault and we had never really doubted our DIY skills – well not for long, anyway!

Figure 494

The correct pack was duly delivered, and just after Easter the finished fort was proudly standing, ready for the grandchildren's approval. However, it did still take us a full day to erect! I am pleased to say that it has been in use nearly every day whenever the grandchildren come to stay and having seen their enjoyment as they played on it, it made all the hassle worthwhile.

As they grew up, different games would be invented ranging from pirates, having timed races running up the slide, not down, using it as a stage for theatre and shows, to seeing whilst they were still in motion on the swings if I, Grandpa, could pull off their boots and socks! All great fun and we just hoped that these joyous times of fun and laughter that they had had with Grannie and Grandpa in Holt, would help to build some lovely memories for each of them to recall, later on in life. Along with, of course, all the other activities that we had done with them over the years!

With spring just arriving, the four additional raised flower beds, in the centre of the garden, were prepared for planting. The larger two, adjacent to the armillary, were for my dahlias and the other ones, adjacent to two new rose arches, were for Kate's alstroemerias. Throughout that summer and subsequent ones, the blooms were glorious and provided many vases of flowers for the house.

That has set out most of the 'highs' but now, the 'lows' were to hit us!

All the heavy lifting, especially when erecting the fences, had caused me to attend the doctors regarding a lump in my groin. As both Kate and I suspected this was diagnosed as a hernia, which resulted in my first visit to the Norfolk and Norwich University Hospital (NNUH). After surgery and a period of recovery, I was back home just thankful that my operation had been both quick and successful.

However, Kate found that she was Vitamin D deficient and started a nine-month course of tablets. Whilst this helped to lessen her fatigue, it was to be a recurring issue, and she still takes Vitamin D on a daily basis. In addition, whilst exerting a lot of energy she found that she was becoming extremely breathless. Numerous tests were carried out at the NNUH, but none of them showed any abnormalities as they all came back normal, so we still didn't know what was causing it. Meantime, she had pains in her legs and feet which resulted in her seeing a biomechanic specialist and was given inserts for her shoes and leg exercises, which she has done daily. Not a good time, especially for Kate.

Throughout the summer I gave guided walks around Blickling Park, as well as giving access to The Mausoleum to those who dared to venture inside, and those

Chapter 7 Life in Retirement 2014 – 2025

who did were certainly impressed with the structure.

Lady Caroline Suffield commissioned the Mausoleum in 1793, as a resting place for her father and his two wives. She was the daughter of John Hobart who owned Blickling Hall, and was the second Earl of Buckinghamshire and former Lord Lieutenant of Ireland. I must admit that I was surprised that very few of the visitors, whom I showed around inside, noticed that there were no religious insignia or artefacts, either inside or out, despite having learnt of its use and that it had been consecrated by the Bishop of Norfolk. To my knowledge there was and still remains no plausible explanation as to why these have never been found.

Mid-June saw Gary laying the final slabs onto the base of the old garage, thus completing the patio/arbour which now looked really good. This was just in time for another drinks party, this time a small one just for our friends and neighbours.

Having previously resigned from the Met on 28 April, Jude commenced her new role as an ombudsman, on 5 June. This role gave her more opportunity as a budding solicitor to enhance and use her skills. Something that she had wanted to do for some time.

In court, my own legal work, using my previous knowledge of the Licensing Law, was coming to an end, as the Licensing work had been transferred from the magistrates to the local authorities. Magistrates were to adjudicate only on appeals and one of my last appeals was on 4 July.

However, another 'low' was brewing, for on 24 July 2017, following one of my regular prostate-specific-antigen (PSA) tests, I was diagnosed with possible prostate cancer. I was quickly referred to Mr Mills, a Urologist Consultant at the hospital, which resulted in a swift diagnosis on 1 August, with the first definitive signs of prostate cancer. I found this devastating and very difficult to deal with and this was certainly the lowest of the lows. The support I was to receive from the medical clinicians was wonderful and that coupled with the love and support of Kate, really helped me deal with what was to come.

After an MRI, a biopsy, numerous blood tests, *Tony Hancock's Half Hour* sketch, on BBC1, in 1961, entitled *The Blood Donor* came to mind, and after many sleepless nights, the consultant confirmed that there were traces of cancer and his advice was '*Nothing to worry about but we will keep a regular check on this.*' This was on 20 August and after a few stressful days I called on the Monday and asked if I could have surgery, to remove the prostate. To my surprise and utter relief this was undertaken on 3 October, just three months after the

PSA test! The National Health Service (NHS) had pulled out all the stops and the important 'all clear' followed in November.

I was relieved, to say the least, and agreed to take part in an 'Add-Aspirin' trial for the next five years. This trial was to establish whether a regular dosage of aspirin tablets would stop or delay various cancers returning.[38] Not only was I more than happy to be part of this research but there was also a definite positive for me, as it enabled me to have regular and frequent full blood tests, and should the cancer return, it would be detected very early on. Given my experiences of injections as a young boy, this was something of a test of faith, and on 6 September 2023, having finished the Add-Aspirin trial, I was discharged back to my GP, for normal annual tests.

Having outlined the 'lows' of the year I can now happily return to some more enjoyable 'highs'. Despite her breathlessness, Kate had also been active walking 4–6 miles regularly, with a group of like-minded lady friends, which she thoroughly enjoyed and kept her fit.

I followed up my membership of the Holt Society and took on the role of Membership Secretary. Our neighbour who was the previous membership secretary had resigned, due to him and his wife moving to be closer to their children in Lincolnshire. This was a role I was to hold for the next four years, before taking on the role of Chairman of the Society.

We did, however, during the first week of September manage to have a well deserved break in Middleham. Whilst we and our family had all enjoyed many memorable visits, we had decided that the time was right for us to sell Vale Cottage. It had provided us, our children and some of our grandchildren the opportunity to enjoy time away from home. With only two bedrooms though, their families were fast outgrowing the space available, hence our decision. So, once we had completed all the essential chores and prepared the cottage to go on the market, we then had time to walk in the Dales, visit the glorious Thorp Perrow Arboretum, and the Muker Show, which was really good and a very traditional local agricultural show. As always, our time at the cottage was really relaxing.

Vale Cottage went live on 'Rightmove' on Friday 22 September and on the following day the first viewing was booked. Later we accepted an offer on 5 November, which was conducted through Purple Bricks, and we were delighted that we achieved the full asking price of £179,995. This included any contents that we wished to leave there, as the cottage was to continue to be used as holiday accommodation. This was brilliant for us as it meant we didn't have to empty it all before the completion date! The purchasers, who lived in Colchester, didn't

---

38 Add-Aspirin, MRC CTU at UCL / www.addaspirintrial.org

Chapter 7 Life in Retirement 2014 – 2025

even view the property, they simply conducted all the transactions over the internet, which we found somewhat strange. Still, completion of the sale took place on 15 December in good time for Christmas, when from these funds we gave a further advance, to Em, Oliver and Sophie.

The next week was Ben's first day at school (Fig. 495), so we stayed with Sophie and Leigh for the weekend, and all went round The Vine, where the National Trust was restoring the roof. As this was a huge project, special access had been created for visitors to go and view the work being carried out. There was a lift that took you to the roof, which had been completely stripped of any tiles and covered with scaffolding and waterproof coverings. It was fascinating to see the work up close and be able to look at it from above!

Around the roof, for example on the rafters or at the base of a chimney, there were lots of Lego figures that children and adults could search for. Ben, who was a Lego fanatic, found this great fun and an exciting story that he could relate to his new school friends. We were delighted to hear that his first day went really well. My understanding is that following the conclusion of the work, these Lego figures have remained in situ. No doubt when the next restoration takes place in the future, a new generation of young children will have the same opportunity to search for them.

Figure 495

Figure 496

Later in November, along with twenty four other previous Chairman from Norwich No.1 Round Table, I joined the current Chairman to attend the 90th anniversary of its foundation in Norwich. The dinner was held in the Strangers Club, with the oldest guest being Stuart Bowen, who was chairman in 1958. The photograph (Fig. 496), taken by John Ragan who also attended

447

the dinner, shows me in the centre wearing a red bow tie, with Ian Malton my best man, standing beside me on my right.

Following Christmas drinks at Blickling Hall we prepared for our own Christmas but this time the tables were turned, and we were hosted in Welwyn Garden City by Oliver and Jude (Fig. 497).

Figure 497

All our family arrived there for Boxing Day lunch, and a delicious homemade beef wellington, with all the trimmings was cooked by Oliver, followed by trifle and profiteroles, all thoroughly enjoyed by us all. This certainly set a very high standard to uphold in the future! Kate and I stayed the night and drove home the next morning in thick snow, thankfully arriving back safe and sound!

One of my last acts for 2017 was to put my name forward to be a Deputy Bench Chair of the Norfolk Magistrates. I was to await the result to be announced in 2018!

As I said previously, a year of 'highs and lows' but upon reflection, the highs seem to have outnumbered the lows. So overall a good year leaving us with just Kate's breathlessness to be resolved.

Chapter 7 Life in Retirement 2014 – 2025

2018

January 2018 seemed to promise a more relaxing and a less stressful year than its predecessors. How wrong could we be!

All started well, as on 31 January I was informed that I had been successful in my application to become one of four, Deputy Bench Chairs of the Norfolk Magistrates Bench. This was not expected, as I really didn't think I had any real prospect of being elected, but I was pleased and humbled. So, we set about finishing our garden with some new flowerbeds, two rose arches and two ponds, one for fish, the other for wildlife. As you do!

Kate was still struggling with her breathing issues and attended the NNUH again for a further respiratory test. This involved a static cycling test which measured her breathing whilst undertaking some very strenuous exercise. As with all her other tests she passed with flying colours, so we were still no nearer knowing the root cause of her problem. So, at this point as there were no further tests that could be carried out, she was discharged by her consultant.

On 7 February, Kate and I along with a host of other people, were invited to a surprise 70th birthday celebration for Dick Meadows, a fellow magistrate. His wife, Sally, had booked the Cinema City auditorium for a private showing of Dick's favourite film *The Graduate*, which was followed by a luncheon in the pub opposite. Dick was most surprised, and a great time was had by all of us. I had great respect for Dick, who had been instrumental in persuading me to stand as a Deputy Chair, so I was very pleased to be included in his birthday celebrations. As it turned out he was to support me with even more advice and guidance in the future. But more on that later.

At the end of February, the UK was hit by severe weather conditions, when heavy snow fell over vast areas of the UK, including Norfolk. The conditions were very treacherous with 17 deaths recorded in the UK. Temperatures fell to -11 in places, schools closed, and businesses were severely impacted. The extreme weather lasted from 22 February through to around 4 March, following which the thaw caused severe flooding around the area. In Holt, whilst we had a good covering of snow, coupled with bitterly cold weather, we were spared the worst. We were also really fortunate, as from home we could easily walk into town for supplies, assuming the shops were open. So overall, if circumstances allowed, life was able to continue as near to normal as possible.

During the school half terms we often had Ben to stay on his own, and despite the snow the February holiday was no exception. He and I would often undertake gardening tasks together and this time there were some final fencing panels to be replaced. This occupied us both for a couple of days, interspersed with playing on the climbing frame, numerous ball games that he had 'invented' in the snow, and of course, eating Grannie's delicious meals. Ben was really helpful, and it was lovely to have him with us. As a thank you for his work, we all went to see the Cromer lifeboat, which was something that Ben was very keen to see.

Before he returned to Tadley though, we had the traditional visit to Starlings. This was a local newsagent and toy shop that most of our grandchildren visited on their final day, either with us or with their parents. Each had a set amount of money, and it was fascinating to watch and listen to their deliberations on why one item was better than the other. On this occasion, Ben made his decision and bought some Lego, and we returned home for Sophie and Leigh to take him back to Tadley.

Em and Pete, who had joined us for the weekend, had recently had some concerns about Libby, who seemed to be displaying some behavioural traits that needed some explanation. Following a visit to the doctors she was diagnosed as having high functioning autism. This was difficult for me to comprehend as, at the time, it was something that I knew very little about and we were very grateful that both Em and Pete felt able to share the diagnosis with us at this very early stage. It transpired that Pete recognised some of the traits in Libby, as being very similar to feelings that he had encountered when he was younger and at school. He was later to establish that he too had autism but not as severe or on the same spectrum as Libby.

The following weekend we had Oliver, Jude and Evie to stay, and a visit to the Sea Life Centre in Hunstanton proved to be the best thing since sliced bread! Whilst the adults found it fascinating, the lunch at the Kings Head in Letheringsett was perhaps more to our liking.

March commenced with Kate and I taking photographs of some of our paintings as we had decided, quite why I can't recall, to apply to be on *The Antiques Roadshow*. As such we had to submit some photographs to the BBC, along with any information and stories we knew about our paintings. We sent them various photographs of our collection, but in particular our David

Figure 498

Hodgson (Fig. 498), and then waited in hope for a positive response.

Kate's birthday followed in March and was celebrated with a most delicious 'Gentleman's Tea' in Folly's Tea Rooms in Holt – what 'Gentleman' neither of us knew. It was followed in the evening by a talk, about Sir John Gresham, who in 1555 founded Gresham's school in Holt. The talk was held in the Britten Building in the existing Gresham's School and was equally enjoyable, as well as absolutely fascinating.

Then the 'fun' really started! For at the end of March, Kate was asked to become Administrator for Holt and District Dementia Support. So far so good and totally manageable. However, shortly after this, Holt Dementia was to become a charity, which brought Kate enough work that it almost became a full-time job! The 'fun' was to continue, as the Chair of the Magistrates Bench had to stand down after only a few months into his three-year term, through ill health.

So, I along with the other deputies had to stand in until a new Bench Chairman was appointed.

After a lengthy election process, during which despite not having been Bench Chair himself, Dick Meadows was once again a great source of advice for me. I was duly elected as Chairman of the Norfolk Magistrates Bench, as per the email (Fig. 499), sent by Suzanne, our Court Administrator.

Like Kate, I found that I had taken on a full-time role, with three courts and approximately 200 magistrates, which was to become an even harder role when the whole world was to be hit by a devastating virus.

Kate knuckled down over the next few months, during which time she was to help prepare the group to obtain charitable status. As can be seen above, the outcome of my appointment wasn't known until mid October. So, I could and did, focus on supporting both Kate and working in the garden.

From: Clarke1, Suzanne (HMCS-Mag Court, Norwich)
Sent: 15 October 2018 10:02
To: Gosden JP, Keith; Archer JP, Sophie; Agnew JP, Jim;
Subject: Bench and Panel Chairmen 2019/2020

Dear Mr Gosden, Mrs Archer and Mr Agnew

Following my earlier phone calls, I write to confirm that you have each been elected as follows for the period 1st April 2019 to 31st March 2020:

Norfolk Bench Chairman – Mr Keith Gosden
Norfolk Family Panel Chairman – Mrs Sophie Archer
Norfolk Youth Panel Chairman – Mr Jim Agnew

May I offer my congratulations to you all; I look forward to working with you.

Kind regards

Suzanne Clarke
Legal Support Team Administrator
HMCTS | Norwich Magistrates' Court | Bishopsgate | Norwich | NR3 1UP
Phone: 01603 679579

Figure 499

Life over the summer became very busy for Kate, for not only did she redesign all the Holt Dementia literature, drew up several new documents, helped to proof-read numerous policies that had had to be re-written and approved for submission to the Charity Commission and then adopted by the committee, she finally helped a friend update the entire website. It was extremely onerous, but I believe that it was also enjoyable, as it was a totally new experience for Kate. Plus, she has an artistic eye and is extremely efficient and very diligent!

For Court I was also really busy, as I was sitting in both Crime and Family hearings, and on some evenings, I was Duty Magistrate on a rota, for 'Out of Hours' Search Warrants. In addition, prior to the commencement of their training, two or three times a year I was taking Attestations from prospective Police Officers and then approving and signing their appointment. Once their training ended, I then attended their passing-out ceremony. This was something that I hadn't been involved with previously and I found really satisfying, and it was lovely that on one occasion Kate was able to come to watch one of their passing-out ceremonies.

During May and June, I was experiencing issues with erections which resulted in consultations with both my GP and Mr Mills, my prostate consultant. It transpired that this was not uncommon following prostate surgery, and to correct this I was put on a waiting list for a Nesbit procedure. The actual operation wasn't to take place until December 2020, and as I wasn't in pain I didn't have any concerns about the wait.

During this time and much to our surprise, following a telephone call from the BBC, we had a visit from Marc Allum and his colleague Dan, who wanted to see the David Hodgson painting. They spent a long time with us looking at various other items, with a view to their inclusion in an upcoming recording of *The Antiques Roadshow*. The conclusion was that they would like to feature the Hodgson painting and to that end we were given a priority ticket, and asked to attend the recording at 08.30, on Cromer Pier, two days later!

We arrived with our picture well wrapped up and were asked to take a seat and await instructions. As we sat there patiently waiting, quite a few other people arrived, carrying their antiques and joined the queue. After a while our painting was taken and viewed by the experts, whilst we were ushered into the 'make up' room. Kate was told that her personal makeup was perfect so didn't need anything done. I though, had the works, powder on the face, hair coiffured and generally made to look presentable for the cameras. During this time and prior to filming, Philip Mould, an art expert presenter on the programme, had

Chapter 7 Life in Retirement 2014 – 2025

been looking at our painting, along with the information that we had supplied.

Once 'made up', we were ushered over to the filming area where we met Philip and a technician, who both explained what would happen. Following this, the filming commenced with the general introduction from Philip, followed by questions to both me and Kate. Regrettably, I had to ask for a pause in the filming, as I was aware that the description given by Philip included a reference to the Cathedral in the background. Tactfully, I hoped, I pointed out that this was in fact Norwich Castle, not the Cathedral. He was obviously a little embarrassed but grateful and the revised filming commenced. It concluded after about half an hour with a valuation of between £2,000 – £3,000, which was very much what we had expected, and it was good to have this professionally confirmed. To say nothing of having it filmed by the BBC!

Kate had this knack of going to places and seeing someone she knows, be it for example in a Swiss airport, on the beach or at a train station. It never ceased to amaze me just how many people she seemed to know. That day was no different, for just before we started filming, lo and behold she knew and chatted to one of the local television cameramen! I really shouldn't have been surprised, but I was!

Once our session had finished, we stayed on the Pier and watched several other items being filmed. It was then that I decided that we both needed an ice-cream. Our two dogs were now with us and if you are familiar with the programme, you will know there are 'fillers' in between the valuations, and that dogs are frequently filmed with their owners. This was to happen to us. So, with ice cream in hand and totally oblivious to a cameraman in the distance, I gave our dogs some ice cream, much to the annoyance of Kate, who suspected we would be on camera. Following a short nudge and comment from her we both looked over to the cameraman, who gave us a smile and a thumbs up. So, were we to be on the programme twice?

The BBC advised us that there would be two editions televised and the final 'edited' versions of these programmes would be screened later next year – but would my exploits of feeding ice-creams to our dogs be included? We awaited with bated breath, at least on my part!

On 18 June, we had a surprise and a most welcome invitation from our friends, Eleanor and David, who lived close by and along with Kate were trustees and members of the Holt Dementia Committee. They were staying and had asked us to join them for tea and supper, at the Watch House, also known as the

Figure 500

Figure 501

Halfway House, which was situated on Blakeney Point (Fig. 500).[39] In the 1800s, the building had been previously used as a lookout for ships in distress and/or to find smugglers.

When we visited, the house was extremely quiet, remote and very basic indeed, consisting of three rooms upstairs with camp beds, one room downstairs and nothing else! No electricity, water, bedding or food, that all had to be provided by those who were staying overnight. Cooking was outside, as was the loo! So, for all these reasons, coupled with its location, it was incredibly popular with maximum three-day visits being booked well in advance. We ate and sat outside for most of the time (Fig. 501), and arrived home late that evening, leaving Eleanor and David to stay there for the night. It was absolute bliss, so peaceful and most relaxing, with only the sound of the sea in the background and birds soaring in the sky. No wonder that it was so sought after and in constant demand.

In July, we both thought it would be lovely to celebrate our anniversary by having a holiday. We hastily made bookings for hotels in Cornwall and with Dan and Archie we set off to the 'Norway Inn' in Falmouth, that was to be our base for the first few days. With the benefit of some glorious weather, we had a very relaxing time and visited the Trelissick Gardens, the Lost Gardens of Heligan, walked the dogs along some lovely woodland trails and went to the East Pool Mine, an old tin mine that still had its beam engines in operation. On Saturday 21 July, we travelled to stay in Rick Stein's Sea Food Restaurant Hotel in Padstow, where we celebrated our 25th wedding anniversary in style and luxury. I can certainly confirm that we were well and truly spoilt.

---

39 Photograph Credit: Julian Douse cc-by-sa/2.0

Chapter 7 Life in Retirement 2014 – 2025

Whilst we were there, we made a point of visiting the grave of Sir John Betjeman at St. Endoc Church (Fig. 502). As there was no vehicular access to the church, the only way for us to reach it was from the village of Rock, from where we followed a 4.6-mile footpath through the sand dunes and across part of a recently built golf course. It was hard work but worth it, as it was certainly a very thought-provoking visit. When Sir John was laid to rest there, in 1984, the pallbearers had to carry his coffin in the pouring rain, across the same route bar the golf course, that we had just taken. Not an easy route for them to have to take and quite extraordinary!

Back at our hotel, which was perfect, all the staff treated us so well, especially when they recognised our anniversary with a beautiful platter (Fig. 503). A few days away was just what we needed, but for longer perhaps next time. We left on the Wednesday and drove back to Holt via Stourhead, a beautiful estate in Wiltshire, owned by the National Trust.

Figure 502

Figure 503

We arrived back in Holt for the last few days of the Holt Festival. Which was well timed as I and a local friend, Phil Barrett, had tickets to see Jasper Carrot on the Saturday, at an outside theatre at Gresham's school. It was well worth going to and thankfully wasn't interrupted by any rain. Kate met up with Polly, Phil's wife, and they both had a great evening out as well, treating themselves to a meal at a local restaurant.

Having now returned home and to our normal routine, I knuckled down to my new role, whilst Kate continued her work with Holt Dementia and what was really good was that we managed a few weekends away, staying with the children. Whilst we were with them, I remember one comment that they made, quite independent of each other, which we hadn't expected. Which was that they were all pleased that we hadn't moved away from Norfolk, as they and the grandchildren all liked coming to stay in Holt and being able to go to the seaside and other exciting places etc. Firstly, we didn't expect this at all, secondly, why didn't they say this a year or so back and thirdly, had we known this it would have saved us hours of time looking for places to live? But thankfully, it seems that in the end, Holt is 'home sweet home', which is fantastic as we love living here.

455

REFLECTIONS UPON A FAMILY

In September, I set up a small committee, consisting of the current town mayor, two previous mayors and an ex-town councillor. The North Norfolk District Council was offering a grant to five different Norfolk market towns, one of which was Holt and each town that was successful would receive £100,000. Bids had to be made by any local organisation, so long as it had the backing of the local inhabitants. So, our committee decided to see if we could bid for some money to upgrade an area in Holt called Fish Hill, to make it for pedestrians only.

We found that we were bidding against Holt Town Council, who also wanted to upgrade Fish Hill and whilst we came close, we weren't successful and lost out to them. However, it has taken them more than five years to get their scheme off the drawing board, so in that respect I was pleased we didn't have to take on such a long-term project.

Being Chairman of the Norfolk Magistrates Bench, meant that October was a very busy month for me. I attended numerous meetings with all manner of people and at my own expense I even had to purchase a new laptop!

My first official duty was to represent the Bench at the Justices' Service in Norwich Cathedral, where I joined the formal procession along with the Judges and other city dignitaries. This was followed in November by a similar event for Remembrance Sunday which always commenced with a wreath being laid at the City's War Memorial. I had had the privilege the previous year, of laying the wreath on behalf of the Norfolk Magistrates. For this year, I chose to ask our newest and youngest magistrate, Chloe Dannatt, to undertake this honour. She was incredibly pleased and proud to be asked to participate in this important ceremony.

Here I would point out that, on every Remembrance Sunday, I always had in my pocket my dad's war medals, along with a pocket Bible that my paternal grandfather had had rebound for my father, so that he could take it with him during WWII. Originally, it had been given to my grandfather by his father, for him to carry through WWI. So, it was very special. They just gave me a private reminder of my father's life.

Ben came to stay again during the Autumn Half Term, but this time I didn't ask him to help with the fencing. Instead, we went out for coastal walks with the dogs, had art and craft activities inside with Grannie, went to the Pumpkin House and when we were back home carved two faces on the pumpkin that we had bought. It looked brilliant all lit up. Finally, as school was coming up soon, he had a haircut!

We all had a wonderful time and were sad to see him being collected by his parents in preparation for Christmas school activities. In the following years though, he was to return many times.

We started to celebrate Christmas early by visiting the illuminations in Sheringham Park (Fig. 504) with Oliver, Jude, Evie and our friends Polly and Phil. The event was set up to celebrate through numerous illuminations Humphrey Repton's vision, and the work and structures of the park that he had designed in 1812. The whole event was really good and very well run, as you would expect from the National Trust. Evie, in particular, along with all the adults, were fascinated and thoroughly enjoyed all the changing lights and displays.

Figure 504

On 14 December, we dressed the house ready for Christmas and generally prepared for the arrival of our family. As usual, one morning before they all arrived, I commandeered the kitchen to make mince pies. Something that I have done for many years and as our family continue to grow, so does the number of mince pies required!

The first to come home were Em, Pete and family, who arrived on the 23rd, in time for Christmas Eve and Christmas Day. Oliver, Jude and Evie followed a few days afterwards to join us all for New Year. Unfortunately, due to career and work constraints Sophie, Leigh and Ben stayed in Tadley so were not able to join us. But the rest of us all had a wonderful Christmas together which rounded off what was certainly an interesting and eventful year.

2019

The New Year started with a very Christmassy theme, as we ventured out after dark to see the fabulous North Norfolk Railway Starlight Express, as it travelled between Sheringham and Holt. We stood and watched it at Kelling Halt on a crisp, starlit night. It was absolutely magical, as it slowly appeared in the distance, through the dark night air and chugged passed us within only a few feet. The photograph (Fig. 505) was taken whilst it was in Weybourne Station en route to Holt.

Figure 505

For a while the Christmas spirit lived on, certainly in Blakeney with their Christmas amateur dramatics production entitled *Sally Potter and the Trousers Evil*. As with all their productions this play was written by a member of the cast. It was all very light-hearted and as always produced and acted to a very high standard. Most of the players were local, so it was always very strange and a little disconcerting to see, for example, your own doctor in a very different guise, especially if the character being portrayed happened to be a rather voluptuous female!

Like last year, we had both continued with our services to the community, Kate with Holt Dementia, whilst I carried on working as Bench Chair for Norfolk. One fringe benefit of my work was meeting some really lovely and interesting people. On 3 January I drove to Euston Hall and met up with and had lunch with The Lord Lieutenants of Suffolk and Norfolk, Countess Euston and Lady Dannett, along with the Suffolk Bench Chairman. We had a delicious lunch and sorted out several activities and responsibilities for the year ahead.

One of the highlights for Kate took place on 1 February. Again, she had been one of the organisers, this time for the re-launch of Holt Dementia officially becoming a charity. She is seen here with their new Patron, Sir Norman Lamb, standing to her right (Fig. 506). He was the former Health

Figure 506

Secretary and North Norfolk MP. The launch with more than 70 guests was a resounding success.

Like Blakeney with its thespians, Holt too has had its fair share of very active residents. One of these being our friend Phil Barrett who organised a vast array of talks, writing courses, art appreciation classes and music concerts, to name but a few. I mentioned this to Charles Watt, the High Sheriff of Norfolk, as I was aware that he could give a High Sheriff award, to people who have contributed extensively to their local community. He was so impressed that in due course at one of Phil's music events he presented Phil with his award, or that was the plan!

Come the day, Phil was totally taken aback as I 'took over' the introduction of the evening concert and he saw an unfamiliar gentleman walking towards him dressed in all his formal regalia. Albeit known to Kate, it was unbeknown to me, as she had been unable to forewarn me that the High Sheriff had inadvertently forgotten the certificate! So, he congratulated Phil, explained the rationale for the award, and to the amusement of the audience the reason for his lack of the certificate! All ended well though, and Phil finally received his award a week later in his home, with the Sheriff again in his splendid robes (Fig. 507).

On the cultural front, the *Antiques Roadshow* was a huge highlight when it was first transmitted on 3 February 2019. As we had been advised, the filming had been edited into two episodes, each one to be shown on separate occasions, and to our surprise we were included in both programmes. On the first, my ice-cream exploits were exposed to the audience, whilst the second one had the more serious element of the valuation of our Hodgson painting and our unscripted response. We were mini 'celebrities' for a week or so, and as I wrote earlier were amazed at how

Figure 507

many people, as far afield as Northamptonshire, said '*I saw you on television…*' It was such an exciting and 'different' experience, with having the opportunity to chat to Philip Mould, being filmed and then to watch the programmes a few months later. Something that we thoroughly enjoyed, and still do when we watch the repeats!

Finally, in February Kate was diagnosed with a prolapse and referred to Mr. Gray, a gynaecological consultant, for further investigation and treatment, if necessary.

On 3 March, Kate and I along with Polly and Phil, attended the Justices' Service in King's Lynn, followed by a lovely meal at The Bank restaurant. We had invited them because Phil was brought up in King's Lynn and his father had been a magistrate.

This photograph was taken in the King's Lynn Guildhall, which is the largest surviving medieval Guildhall in the country. I am fourth from left on the back row (Fig. 508).

Figure 508

Whilst I refreshed my memory, looking through Kate's calendar, it was abundantly clear that both my work as a magistrate and Kate's for the Holt Dementia took up an inordinate amount of our time. It wasn't surprising therefore, that in April we booked a September holiday in Castle Combe.

Kate's birthday was spent in Tadley with myself, Sophie, Leigh and Ben. The surprise element came when we all went for a walk in Alice Holt's Timberline Trail in Farnham, where who should we meet, none other than Em, Pete and family. All planned and a lovely surprise for Kate. After a great day out, it was time for a 'grandchildren style' birthday meal (Fig. 509).

Figure 509

Chapter 7 Life in Retirement 2014 – 2025

Returning to Holt, we were to celebrate our wedding anniversary by attending a live interview, at Gresham's school, with Sir Tim Waterstone. As we had expected he was very eloquent and most interesting. He talked about his vision to establish a new style of bookshop and how in 1982 he had opened his first branch of Waterstones, in Old Brompton Road. He took the audience right through when he was operating over one hundred branches, up to when he sold the business in 1993 to WHSmith. Our celebrations continued that evening, and we finished with a delicious supper at the Anchor Pub in Morston.

Family and grandchildren came to stay at various times during the year, so there were days out, walks and visits to the beach, all of which went down well.

One of the best excursions was probably during the Jones's August summer holiday with us, when we all went to the Norfolk Broads, for a fabulous trip on the *Mississippi Steamboat*. A great day out with four-year-old Frankie, taking the helm on a straight stretch of the river! Her concentration on the job in hand, (Fig. 510) ensured no problems were encountered. We weren't sure if the other passengers were aware of the change in crew, as the swap over of 'skippers' was so smooth and professional! All done without a 'hitch'! Well done, Frankie!

Figure 510

Back on dry land we visited the Priory Maze in Sheringham. Whilst I had the excuse of looking after the dogs, everyone else navigated the maze, and thankfully all made it back to me.

September was the month that three grandchildren started 'proper' school for the first time. Evie was first, on 3 September, in Welwyn Garden City, closely followed by Leo and Frankie on the 12th, in Chessington. Again, (Figs. 511 & 512) are the obligatory first day photographs.

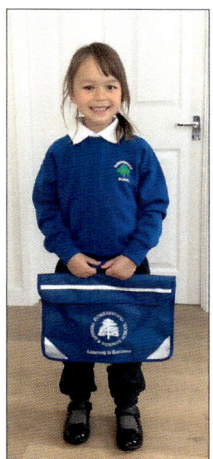

Figure 511

Figure 512

461

Then, once all the schools had started their Autumn Terms, we had our holiday in Castle Combe, where we stayed in Castle Combe Cottage, a delightful, historic property situated in a private gated close. We had a lovely relaxing time, ate out each day, visited Prince Charles's, now King Charles III, amazing Highgrove gardens in Doughton, wandered around the National Trust village of Lacock and its Abbey, found lots of picturesque country walks and just enjoyed each other's company and, of course, that of Dan and Archie as well. So much so that we booked a more extravagant holiday for 2020 to celebrate Kate's 70th birthday! More explanation of this will be outlined in the following 2020 section.

Figure 513

A visit to the Munnings exhibition at the end of October was another highlight. This was not only due to his wonderful paintings, of which 40 plus were from Canada, but also because after much investigation, Jenny Hand the Director of the Munnings Museum, confirmed that our little painting (Fig. 513), was indeed painted by Sir Alfred Munnings when he was very young. We were delighted to have this confirmation, for when we bought it, we had been told it was painted by him, although it doesn't have his signature on it, just his initials which was unusual.

Our final visit to a major exhibition took place when we visited Houghton Hall, where on display outside in the gardens there was a large collection of enormous Henry Moore sculptures and they looked really dramatic against the Norfolk sky! In the Hall itself there was also a selection of some of his hand-size sculptures, that were equally impressive.

Ben continued the 'new starts' of his three cousins and joined the Tadley Cub Pack. He looked both smart and proud in his new uniform (Fig. 514). It was so pleasing for me, to see the scouting tradition being kept alive and continued in the family.

Figure 514

Chapter 7 Life in Retirement 2014 – 2025

Many people, adults and children alike, consider places of worship to be very serious and certainly not much fun. So, Jane Hedges the Dean of Norwich Cathedral set out to challenge this view, and in September a local fairground installed a full-size helter-skelter, in the Nave (Fig. 515). This was greeted with equal amounts of consternation and bewilderment by the Cathedral community. However, it was a huge hit with all age groups of the public and being positioned in such a way it allowed those with a keen eye and head for heights, to see close up some of the world's largest collection of amazing, medieval roof bosses.

As I have just said, it was a huge success with so many people, including Ben our grandson. In subsequent years, it was followed by other, out of the ordinary exhibits including 'Dippy' the Diplodocus Dinosaur. Hopefully, these exhibitions 'opened' the cathedral to many people who would not have ordinarily visited a religious building.

Figure 515

Later that year, having previously watched many enjoyable hours of Agatha Christie's *Miss Marple*, we decided to try our luck on the Holt Heritage Line, at a 'Murder Mystery Steam Train' evening, with a full supper included. We were a little sceptical as the theme was 'Steam Punk' and many passengers had come appropriately dressed. Halfway through the evening we both guessed the murderer, but then for some reason we changed our minds, which was a mistake as we had been correct the first time! It was very apparent that like us, everyone in our carriage had thoroughly enjoyed themselves and the meal was fantastic. Needless to say, we were and still are no threat to Miss Marple!

At the Holt Christmas Lights switch-on, I watched Kate singing carols with the Holt Community Choir, and afterwards for a second time we saw the train covered in lights. So, we were now in Christmas mode. In the coming days we decided to see what it was actually like to travel inside the Starlight Express, which in our opinion was good, but certainly not as exciting as seeing it from the outside. However, no journey for me on a steam train can ever be a total disappointment, so all was well.

Kate was to publicly sing again with the Holt choir, this time joining forces with several other amateur choirs, as well as a number of professional soloists and all participating in Handel's *Messiah* in Holt Church, which was packed full with nearly 300 people! It was an incredibly moving performance, particularly when the Hallelujah chorus was sung.

Following this, just before the year ended, we watched the musical *Cats* with Phil and Polly, on the Cromer Cinema Live Theatre link, and afterwards had a scrumptious meal at The Red Lion Pub.

All these events rounded off a perfect year and one, for a change, that didn't involve any building works. Now, we were set up for a lovely Christmas in Welwyn Garden City again, with Oliver, Jude, Evie and all our family, which certainly didn't disappoint any of us.

2020

'Lock-up' 2020 from March onwards and consign it to history! Well, what else can I say about 2020 – which hasn't already been thought or spoken about, in the last few years!

For those of you who are reading this in the future, 2020 was the start of the global Covid-19 pandemic. By its very nature it caused death and misery worldwide. As at May 2023, the statistics provided grim reading.[40] There had been 687,225,609 cases worldwide with 6,866,773 deaths. In the UK there were 24,569,895 cases (which was the world's ninth highest by country) leading to 223,396 deaths (which was the world's sixth highest by country).

At the time of writing in 2024, it is considered that the high numbers of people who had now been vaccinated and/or had some immunity through being infected, meant that the disease now does not pose the same threat that it had between 2020/21. However, annual booster vaccinations will probably have to continue.

So, both 2020 and 2021 had been memorable years and mostly for all the wrong reasons. Still, having now outlined and given some context around this period, I will continue with my reflections.

---

40 Coronavirus – statista.com report published by John Elflein Aug 31, 2023

During this year, there were certainly some wonderful and poignant highlights, which for the right reasons kept us going and created some lovely and long-lasting memories.

In the February, before any Covid restrictions took their grip on society we had Evie to stay with us for a week, on her own. She really enjoyed seeing flour being made at Letheringsett Mill, and on hindsight whilst we were there, we should have bought more bags of it, given the future shortages of any kind of flour, throughout Covid! She also spent an enjoyable evening with Polly, whilst Phil, Polly's husband, took Kate to Norwich. I had been in London on court business and returned by train and as scheduled met Kate at the Spire hospital, where she had two skin tags removed, one from her face, the other from her back. All went well and upon our return home having had a story read to her, Evie was happily tucked up in bed.

At the end of February, we had a visit from John Hunter, who was in scouts with me, and his wife Karen. Since leaving university John had worked for Rolls Royce in Derby and, at the time, appeared to me to be a committed bachelor. So, it was somewhat of a surprise to learn that now he had retired, he had recently met and married Karen. This was wonderful news, as was their visit. They seemed very happy and comfortable together and all four of us had a great weekend, before they returned home on the Monday.

Due to schooling and lockdowns when we had needed to keep ourselves, our children and grandchildren safe from Covid, we had only been able to meet up for short walks, and due to the current restrictions to avoid spreading this terrifying virus we had to have two metres between each person. Enjoyable as these walks were, it was not the same as a summer seaside holiday. That was to be our priority in 2021.

For our major highlight though, we were to have a fabulous holiday in Thailand on the peninsula of Phuket, where in superb style we celebrated Kate's 70th birthday!

Having taken Dan and Archie the previous evening to their regular kennels, we flew on 12 March on an 11-hour flight from Heathrow to Bangkok. From there we had an hour's flight to Phuket, followed by a chauffeur driven car ride to where we were staying at Cape Panwa Hotel. Our first impressions of Phuket were that it was hot at 34°, there were very few underground electricity and telephone cables as they all seemed to be hung haphazardly on poles, there were acres of rubber tree plantations, palm trees in abundance and scooters everywhere. Most important of all though, everyone we met was friendly and very welcoming.

REFLECTIONS UPON A FAMILY

Figure 516 (right)
Figure 517 (below)
Figure 518 (below right)

Our hotel was superb with wonderful sea views, a private sandy beach (Fig. 516) which was interspersed with tall, statuesque palm trees. There was clearly a love of fish, as sculptures, ornaments, mobiles etc. were found everywhere around the hotel reception (Fig. 517).

We had just settled into our room E301 when there was a knock on the door, and room service presented Kate with a birthday cake (Fig. 518) which had lit sparklers and candles on top. What a great start! As it turned out and unbeknown to Kate, this would be the first of many cakes.

During our stay we spent many hours on the beach just soaking up the experience. I was interrupted though, several times with calls from magistrates wanting advice on what to do about Covid. A pandemic of this magnitude was completely new to all of us, and decisions on what to do were being made 'on the hoof', which as Chairman was difficult for me, as well as confusing, given that not all the UK Benches were being given the same advice.

The calls were to continue for many months, and it seemed even in Thailand thousands of miles away from home, there was no escape from being a Bench Chairman!

Chapter 7 Life in Retirement 2014 – 2025

On Kate's actual birthday we left the hotel early in the morning to be taken to an Elephant Sanctuary, where we were able to hand-feed and wash these beautiful and oh so gentle and docile animals.

Kate and I were really comfortable in their company, and they too appeared to feel the same with us. We fed them first with melons and then walked with them to a different area, where we spread mud all over their bodies (Fig. 519) which was then washed off by their own mahout (handler).

Figure 519

This wonderful interaction was then followed with all the elephants and visitors being taken for a bath. In Fig. 520, Kate can be seen in the centre, with her back to the camera, fifth from the left.

After we had all had showers, we watched a traditional Thai meal being cooked which then turned out to be our lunch. It was delicious as was the melon that followed. Then much to everyone's surprise, including mine and Kate's, she was suddenly presented with birthday cake number two. This time made out of melon, plus she was given a rendition of 'Happy Birthday'! Before we reluctantly left and whilst we were waiting in the back of a parked truck, one of the elephants came right up to me with its trunk extended and when I stroked it, he came even closer, as if to say, 'don't go'. It was truly magical and something I shall always remember.

Figure 520 (Kate)

467

Figure 521   *Figure 522*

Arriving back at our hotel room we found that Patcharin our chambermaid had left our towels in the shape of an elephant – she was so thoughtful!

Kate's birthday supper was taken on the terrace of Panwa House, part of the hotel complex but separated by a short walk along the private seashore.

Here Kate was presented with cake number three, smuggled from the UK by me. Then at the conclusion of the meal, to both our surprise cake number four arrived, (Fig. 521) which came from all the restaurant staff.

My birthday present to Kate was a set of gold bespoke earrings, made to match a necklace I had given her last year when we visited Lacock. I was able to film Kate opening her present and caught her reaction on my mobile phone. The still shot from the video confirms Kate's delight (Fig. 522).

The following day was lazy, with a visit to the Phuket Aquarium, followed by a promenade walk along Kantary Bay, before another delicious fish supper.

On the Tuesday morning, we had a crash course on how to snorkel, before we were taken by speed boat to a beautiful coral island. Where we landed beside a perilous looking floating pontoon, which in order not to fall off into the sea, we had to negotiate by running along it incredibly fast! We both succeeded and once on dry land we made ourselves comfortable on the beach.

This beach would normally have been full of tourists, but due to Covid-19 it was virtually empty and a pure delight, bordered by a beautiful deep blue sea that was incredibly inviting. These warm, azure, sky blue waters were home to a wonderful array of multi-coloured fish, which we were to discover whilst snorkelling. With such clear waters and the fish so close to the beach as well, we easily and excitedly swam amongst shoals of both large, small and unusual tropical fish, many species of which we had never seen before.

It certainly made yet another perfect day, especially as neither of us had ever been snorkelling before. It was an experience that is almost impossible

Chapter 7 Life in Retirement 2014 – 2025

to describe and one that we would certainly like to repeat, somewhere else. So, it was a definite thumbs up from both of us (Fig. 523).

Wednesday was spent cruising around the islands in *June Bahtra*, a fabulous, traditional Chinese Junk-rigged schooner (Fig. 524). Whilst on the boat we were treated to a superb meal and were given time to dive off the deck and swim in the sea, alongside some of the same fish species that we had swum with previously. There were only about a dozen of us on board, so we had plenty of time and space (Fig. 525) to enjoy the voyage.

At one point, we were taken by a traditional Longtail boat to Khao Phing Kan Island which had been used as a location in the 1974, James Bond film *The Man with the Golden Gun*. With so much interest in the '007' films the island was incredibly busy, but this did not spoil our visit.

Figure 524

Figure 523 (top left), Figure 525 (above)

Figure 526

We also had the opportunity to disembark and wander around Koh Panyee (Fig. 526), a floating village which was built on stilts in the eighteenth century, by Javanese fishermen. In 2020 it was inhabited solely by Muslim fishermen, whose standard of living was in sharp contrast to the modern 'tourist' restaurant, on the far side of the island. It was hard to comprehend how some of the population were begging whilst others who were equally poor, served tourists in an air-conditioned restaurant. Or indeed the contrast between their shacks that were their homes and the magnificent and opulent Darussalam Mosque, with its five golden domes, four of which can be seen in the background, on the left of the photograph (Fig. 526). This beautiful structure certainly stood out against the ramshackle houses and our brief stop was certainly thought provoking. It brought back memories to me of my time in India, with my impressions of the diverse variations of living conditions for the locals, again being reflected here on this floating village.

On our return to the *June Bahtra* we continued our journey through the Ao Phang-Nga marine National Park and were taken through a mangrove forest. Unfortunately, we didn't see any rare birds, but it was still really interesting to see how the mangroves were grown.

Our final couple of days were spent relaxing, swimming, reading and having some superb Thai massages, something Kate appreciated receiving, rather than giving to someone else. Our last day Saturday 21 was a little fraught, to say the least, due to the potential of Covid lockdowns locally and back in the UK. Thankfully, we managed to fly home on our scheduled flight, little realising at the time, that it was actually the last Thai Airline flight back to the UK. Phew!

Apart from our individual memories, Kate's presents and all our photographs, we also purchased a small memento of Kate's birthday treat, a mini model of an elephant (Fig. 527), which will always be a gentle reminder to us both, of a superb 70th birthday adventure.

Figure 527

Our drive home in the dark, from Heathrow around the M25, was nothing but surreal, in that for the entire journey there were literally no other vehicles on the road. The only logical reason we could put this down to, was possible travel restrictions due to the pandemic and we were very pleased to exit the M25 and continue our way home to Holt. It was a holiday of a lifetime and one that both Kate and I will remember with much happiness. Would we return? Probably not. For from our perspective the one good thing about the pandemic was that it reduced the tourists to just a trickle, and restaurants and beaches etc. were free of people, thus there was no queuing for tables or when trying to find a quiet spot on the sand. We both felt a return would not grant us that luxury and possibly spoil our idyllic memories.

Upon our arrival home we were greeted with a letter from Boris Johnson, that he had sent to every UK household. He was our Prime Minister at the time and his letter gave everyone an explanation about the Covid pandemic and in order to protect our health, the restrictions that were to be implemented. Following this on 23 March the government announced the first full lockdown, with the strict instructions that said, *'you must stay at home'*. This continued for three months through to June, with a second lockdown announced on 5 November that lasted for four weeks. The third lockdown commenced on 5 January 2021, and these measures were gradually lifted following the publication on 19 July of the government's 4-step plan. Known as the 'Roadmap Out of Lockdown', it gradually eased the restrictions through to later in the year 2021.

However, at the time of writing this memoir, it was slightly ironic that an inquiry into the handling of Covid by the government of the day, had revealed that much of the advice in the letter we had all received was, at the time, ignored or breached by a number of MPs and civil servants!

Overall, the general public were predominately compliant with all the different regulations, but they had changed people's interactions with each other and the way in which we lived our lives. I suspect and fear that some of these changes, such as shopping habits with more frequent use of home deliveries, the conduct of meetings through using internet-based video calls etc, may be with us on a permanent basis. In my humble opinion, these examples of change, whilst they protected us all at the time, in the longer term they removed much of the very necessary and natural face-to-face communication that we as a species rely upon. As humans we need this interaction and for me, in particular, this change in the society's continued method of contact through social media, is both unnatural and unwarranted.

There were high spots during the lockdowns though. One such case was that of a 99-year-old ex-soldier, Captain Tom Moore. As instructed, he remained in his own home environment, and set an example by attempting to walk, with the aid of a frame, one hundred times around his back garden. His challenge was to complete this before his one hundredth birthday, on 30 April 2020. In so doing he wanted to raise £1,000 for the NHS. He magnificently achieved the one hundred circuits, along with the respect of people worldwide, who had followed him in the news and on social media. This amazing support boosted his fundraising to a staggering £32.79 million.

This extraordinary feat really caught the imagination of the public and was a 'good news' item in the media for a number of weeks. For his endeavours and following the easing of restrictions, a month after his hundredth birthday, he was knighted on 17 July by Queen Elizabeth II, at Windsor Castle. For the rest of us he certainly helped to raise our spirits and distract us from the news about the dire consequences of Covid-19.

Figure 528

On 24 July 2020, Holt hit the headlines, when the local Budgens store caught fire and was razed to the ground (Fig. 528).[41] Much to the annoyance of the local residents, it took more than two years to have it rebuilt. But a few weeks after the fire, a temporary, upmarket 'pop up' shop was erected in the shop's car park, and bearing in mind the size of the structure, it catered well for all the locals and those who visited Holt, as it had all the required basics in the way of food, household goods and everyday necessities etc. So, we were fortunate and didn't have to travel far for our everyday bits and pieces.

Evie came for another holiday, this time with Oliver and Jude. She and Oliver arrived on 27 July, whilst Jude, due to work commitments, joined us all for the second week. Visits to the beach, playgrounds, rides in Gertie, all interspersed by walks, were the order of the week.

With Covid restrictions still lifted, in mid-August we then had Em, Pete and family home for their holiday. It was lovely to see them all and to enjoy their company with Libby, Leo and Frankie, who like all our grandchildren, lifted our spirits. For this holiday we managed to fit in a wildlife river trip from How Hill and a trip on the Holt steam railway – but not on the same day. This was in addition to the walks and ubiquitous days building sandcastles on the beach.

---

41 Photograph credit – Lee Smith and BBC

Chapter 7 Life in Retirement 2014 – 2025

Shortly after their departure, Ben came to stay whilst Sophie and Leigh had a mini break themselves. Again, we were able to continue the 'holiday' mode with him and one of his highlights was a visit to the local Military Museum at Muckleburgh. To add authenticity, we had all travelled in 'vintage' style in Gertie, which all three of us thoroughly enjoyed. Whether it was the fact that he was learning about WWII at school, and/or his great-grandfather had driven one of the tanks he saw in the museum, we didn't know. What we did notice and was crystal clear to us, was that he simply soaked up all the information like a sponge and asked for a second visit on a future stay with us! This was to be granted at a later date.

During the pandemic restrictions we had, like so many others, become familiar with communicating using TEAMS and ZOOM. More than we would have liked, if the truth be told. They had enabled us both to keep abreast of our work though, particularly for me in the courts and for Kate with her work with Holt and District Dementia Support.

More importantly though, via the ZOOM technology, Grannie was able to read simultaneously, Sunday bedtime stories to all our grandchildren (Fig. 529). In time this new medium was to enable significant changes as to how people, especially whilst at work, were able to conduct meetings etc. For us and the grandchildren it was used both to keep in contact with our families and for this special, bedtime story telling which was great fun and enjoyed by all of them.

In between lockdowns, we also managed to arrange a few meals out with friends, and these evenings were most pleasurable and definitely helped

Figure 529

everyone to relax. It was also great to catch up with everyone's news and make sure that they were still safe and well. Dan and Archie were oblivious to the world-wide changes and so long as they had regular walks, human company, two meals a day and a comfy bed, then life for them carried on being perfect!

What hadn't been perfect was Sophie's health over the past couple of years. In 2018 I had noticed that a longstanding mole on her forehead had changed and suggested that she had this checked out. This she did and in the spring of that year it was successfully removed and we all awaited the biopsy result which was malignant melanoma. However, on 25 May our diary records, Sophie was given the all-clear which was excellent news.

However, over time her cancer was discovered to have spread to a lymph node, reclassing her diagnosis to stage 3. After this was removed on 3 November 2020, she initially received the all-clear but after testing the sample again, regrettably, cancer cells were found. In December 2020 following several meetings between hospital staff, Sophie was offered and agreed to a course of immunotherapy treatment, to be given every 3 weeks over the course of a year. She also went on to have a PICC line inserted for 6 months, allowing her to have regular blood samples etc. taken, without the need for injections. With ongoing checks and scans Sophie has remained clear and she hopes the checks will decrease in regularity, as she draws closer to being cancer free for five years.

Following that very concerning news, three days later on 15 October, we were delighted to learn from Jude that she was pregnant. What fantastic and surprising news.

The penultimate health issue in that year related to me and was sorted out when I received a call from the Spire Hospital, to say that I could have the Nesbit procedure undertaken, on 1 December. All went well on the day, with the operation being carried out early in the morning, and later in the afternoon I was discharged home.

The final issue in the health list was just before Christmas when Kate had positive confirmation from her consultant gynaecologist that her prolapse didn't require immediate surgery. So, that was a bonus Christmas present for both of us and enabled us to look forward to 2021.

However, due to the Covid restrictions, our family and like hundreds of other families were not able to meet up and celebrate, so instead had to resort to telephone calls or Christmas messages via WhatsApp or text. For our family though, our non-Christmas was to be rectified in due course, with an 'Australasian' flavour.

Chapter 7 Life in Retirement 2014 – 2025

2021

In regard to Covid-19, despite all the measures put in place by the government, we commenced the new year very much in the same place as we had ended last year.

However, we did have other concerns, in that Dan was now feeling very stiff and having trouble in walking. After a veterinary consultation he was prescribed a larger dose of Previcox, his pain relief medication. This appeared to assist him, so we resumed our walks only for Kate to fall over a concealed tree root and badly hurt herself. She had aches and severe bruising all over, especially in her left arm, wrist, hip and knee. Having had an x-ray for her wrist which fortunately did not show any fractures, we felt that rest was the antidote, so over the next few days she took things easy and didn't join the dog walks. In fact, her first walk was not until 23 January, some 12 days after the fall and even this was a very short walk that lasted no more than 10 minutes. We were, however, hopeful that improvements would continue apace, but her foot didn't improve as fast as we thought, so the surgery was contacted, and she was referred for an x-ray.

On the Sunday, following the snowfall which we had all witnessed over the last few days, Kate and I had organised a snow competition for our grandchildren and now had certificates to award for the best snowman. In order to do this, at a full Zoom meeting with all our family we virtually presented them with their awards. First Prize, for the Tallest Snowman went to Evie. Libby, Leo and Frankie were awarded First Prize for the Cutest Snowman and finally, First Prize for the Most Original Snowman went to Ben. Everyone was congratulated and delighted when we sent them all their certificates.
Diplomatic as ever!

Since the Covid pandemic commenced, UK scientists had been working 24/7 to find a vaccine. One had now been approved and a mass vaccination programme was launched by the NHS to vaccinate those who fitted the criteria, which included both Kate and myself. We both had the AstraZeneca vaccination on 30 January and then spent all the next day in bed feeling very cold and extremely tired. Luckily this passed quickly, and thereafter all was well. We did feel safer though, so it was worth the discomfort. In case anyone wanted to check our proof of vaccination we had to always carry our certificates with us (Fig. 530). In fact, nobody ever asked to see these.

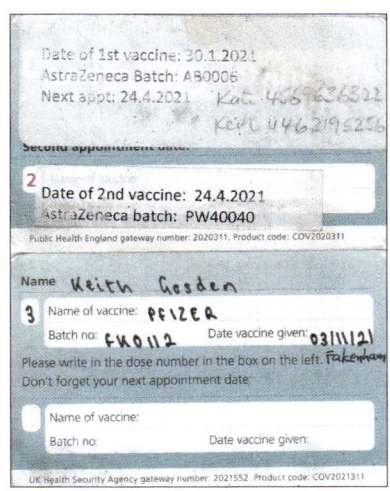

Figure 530

475

Kate's foot X-ray was taken on 1 February, followed by her first 20-minute walk, which was not a good idea as the walk ended up giving Kate additional pain!

My court work was still in full flow, with the courts now open but as a result of Covid many JPs had to take sick leave. I arranged a Zoom meeting with the Lord Lieutenant Lady Dannatt, as one of her roles was to support the Magistracy and I was able to bring her up to speed on the situation. She was very supportive and offered to help boost morale in any way I thought appropriate. I thanked her and said I would think about what could be undertaken.

Kate had sought help from Nick, an NHS physiotherapist, for in spite of a clear x-ray her leg and foot were not progressing, and he had suggested some exercises. But after a while, if anything, the pains now down either side of her tibia were worse and new bruising had appeared. Nick was advised of this current situation and Kate's exercises were amended accordingly which seemed to help relieve the pain.

On the morning of 2 February, the UK and many other countries were very upset to hear that Captain Sir Tom Moore had died in hospital from Covid-19, the very condition for which he had raised so much money and his family received hundreds of tributes.

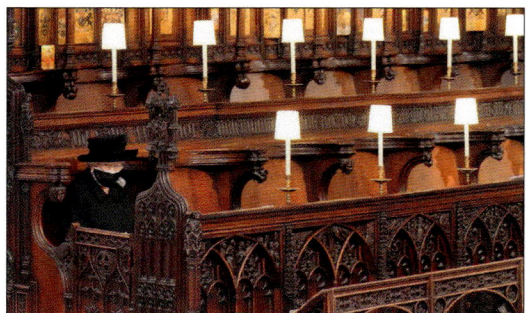

Figure 531

Then on 16 February, HRH Prince Phillip at the age of 99, was admitted to hospital, no reason was given though, other than it was believed not to be Covid related. He died at Windsor Castle, of 'old age', on 9 April with the Queen at his bedside. He was given a state funeral followed by a private ceremony on 17 April, in St. George's Chapel in Windsor Castle. It was significant that in the chapel, due to Covid restrictions his wife, Queen Elizabeth II, sat on her own (Fig. 531)[42] and apart from the rest of the royal family. Many commentators picked up on this and commented positively that even the Royal Family, like so many of her subjects, had had to adhere to the strict Covid regulations.

---

42 https://people.com/royals/queen-elizabeth-aide-shares-behind-scenes-prince-philip-funeral/

Chapter 7 Life in Retirement 2014 – 2025

Kate's health was now improving, to an extent that 18 February was a 'red letter' day, as not only was she able to complete a 25-minute walk with the dogs but was also able to walk downstairs properly. A great improvement from several weeks ago, which was most welcome.

An odd comparison, I know, but 18 February, was also a great day for NASA, as its Perseverance Rover landed on Mars, after having been launched in July 2020. At the time of writing, the Rover and its mini helicopter had spent over three years on the surface of Mars, actively exploring this planet and sending data back to NASA.[43]

So, both Kate and NASA had accomplished significant achievements which were to continue over the coming months. This was certainly the case for Kate, and for over three years in the case of NASA. Unfortunately, on 18 January 2024, after its 72nd flight the helicopter damaged its rotor blades on landing, and so NASA had to retire it on that date.

Sophie too was making good progress and commenced a series of PET scans every three months, these were to check on her progress at eradicating her cancer. Her fifth session of immunotherapy was successfully completed on 10 March, and by all accounts the treatment was working well with a very positive outcome anticipated.

I also had very positive results with my own cancer checks and every six months still endured the regular blood tests, I also continued to support the 5 year Add-Aspirin trial. Although by now, I was more convinced that my part in this was to take a regular placebo. I say this, for when I asked my NHS administrator about the three different levels which were, a placebo, 100mg or 300mg of aspirin, he was convinced that I wasn't on the highest dosage. Those particular patients apparently, had been showing clear signs of bruising, and that did not apply to me. Like me he had no confirmation, so it appeared that it was a choice between either a placebo or 100mg of aspirin. This was pleasing to hear, as I was a little concerned that when I stopped the trial my cancer could return from being in remission, because of not taking the aspirin. Whilst I had no verification of which level I was actually taking, the fact that I had had no side effects at all, gave me hope that I was taking a placebo. If correct, this would clearly indicate that my cancer operation had been successful.

To celebrate both our birthdays we went for two super walks. For mine we had a sunny and brisk cold walk from Blakeney to Morston and back, and for Kate's a lovely sunny, circular walk through Blickling woods. Both were followed by

---

43 Wikipedia – Timeline of Mars 2020

a typical National Trust tea, which were always excellent. Two days later on 17 March both Dan and Archie were seriously ill, to the point where we thought that neither of them would pull through. We and the vet suspected that they may have eaten something that clearly did not agree with them. Kate was brilliant and not only nursed them both, but also administered numerous different pills and encouraged them to drink water and eat tiny morsels of chicken. So, by the weekend they were, at least, able to stand up. Then, having both had their portions of chicken increased, coupled with a small amount of fish, by the Monday when the medication from the vet ran out, they were making very slow but steady progress. Their medication was extended through to the Friday and that certainly seemed to do the trick – our normal Dan and Archie were both back with us, thank goodness!

After two and a half years of being Bench Chairman, my term was to officially end on 31 March. However, I would continue with the duties until the Annual General Meeting (AGM) which took place on 27 April. Whilst I was honoured to have been chairman, it had certainly been an exhausting time, mainly due to Covid-19. Hardly a day went by, when I hadn't received either telephone calls or emails, from concerned JPs either seeking information or submitting requests to stand down for a while, due to either having contracted Covid or for protection as they were vulnerable and were already living with a weakened immune system.

Life in the courts had changed dramatically over the past two years. We had appearances over the internet rather than in person; we sat behind transparent screens so couldn't easily converse with our colleagues, and gatherings to say farewell to those who were leaving due to retirement or for other reasons, couldn't happen. It was a very different Bench to the one I joined back in 1999.

Strangely, we all seemed to accept the changes and whilst morale was low it wasn't as low as I had expected. In advance of my retirement, whilst in London attending

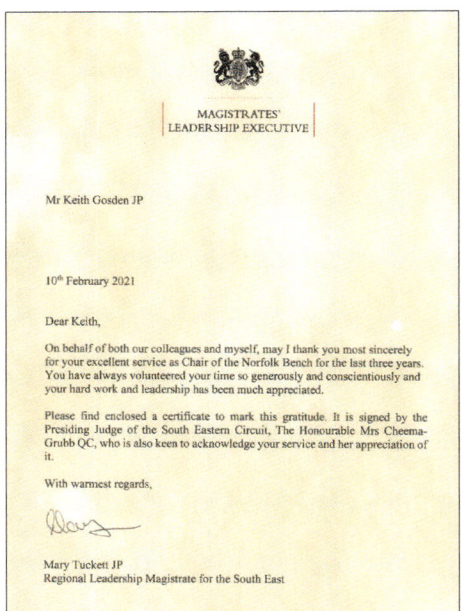

Figure 532

Chapter 7 Life in Retirement 2014 – 2025

my final Regional Leadership meeting on 10 February, I was presented with a certificate and letter (Figs. 532 & 533). Then before I officially stood down, one of my last duties was to swear in Michael Gurney as the next High Sheriff of Norfolk. As with the previous two High Sheriffs, whom I had sworn in and worked with, Michael was an excellent choice and was to be very successful in his role.

Figure 533

Having previously taken early retirement from paid employment with Aviva, when I was 59, according to the Government I was officially to become an old age pensioner (OAP) on 13 April 2021. As such, I received my first monthly instalment of the State Pension and £878.52 was paid into our bank! It was good to receive this, even though I didn't feel like an OAP, not that I knew how a senior citizen should feel. My paid employment had ceased years ago, and that 'void' had been easily filled with voluntary activities, hobbies and community projects within Holt. So, I hadn't ever considered myself either retired or a pensioner. I was still grateful though, to receive the state pension.

On Saturday 24 April, both Kate and I received our second Covid vaccination. This was a gentle reminder that whilst Covid wasn't causing the mayhem it once had, it also had not gone away. Our arms ached but again we were able to feel a little safer and more protected. The next day to celebrate a belated birthday for Ben, we met up with him, Sophie and Leigh in Wandlebury Country Park, just outside Cambridge. The sun shone, as we walked through the 110 acres of parkland, during which we came across some highland cattle, and with their enormous horns and long fringes they simply carried on munching their grass, completely oblivious to our presence. They were a lovely sight, and with them along with the sunshine and good company, it made the day most enjoyable.

On 27 April, the Bench AGM took place which was the formal conclusion to my chairmanship. As a reminder of the Covid restrictions, as if we all needed a reminder, the meeting was carried out over the internet, rather than face-to-face in County Hall. As tradition demanded, I opened the meeting, said a few heartfelt and sincere words of thanks to my deputies, and other panel chairmen for Youth and Family etc., then handed over to Nick, who had been elected as the next Bench Chairman.

Nick kindly thanked me and with the help of Kate, who was in the kitchen with me and acting on Nick's behalf, she presented me with not only the usual certificate, but also one of Annie Tempest's books (Fig. 534) and a brilliant print of a cartoon, painted and signed by her as well. I suspected that these had been selected with the help of Kate, as she was very much aware that I really liked Annie's work.

In fact, at one of the Court Club luncheons, at my invitation Annie had given a talk about her life and work producing cartoons for *Country Life* Magazine.

My cartoon gift (Fig. 535) was so appropriate, with its caption, 'Guilty as charged' and it was proudly hung in our kitchen.

Figure 534

Figure 535

Despite not being Bench Chairman, I was still very active as a magistrate, sitting in both the Family and Crime courts. So that side of the work continued unabated.

Just before I left my role as Bench Chairman, I had received the sad news that Jim Agnew, one of our longest serving magistrates, had died of cancer. At the time he was still an active JP, so this came as a huge shock to so many of us.

I was acutely aware that when a magistrate had reached the compulsory retirement age, which at that time was their 70th birthday, due to the Covid restrictions it had not been possible to continue the tradition of giving them a farewell presentation or gathering. This meant that there were many magistrates who collectively, had given many years of service, and instead of a presentation with colleagues, were simply posted their retirement certificate. So, now that

Chapter 7 Life in Retirement 2014 – 2025

the restrictions had been relaxed and we were able to meet up, it occurred to me that to thank them for their dedicated service, a garden party would be appropriate for all of them and their partners.

I mentioned earlier that following the impact of Covid, both I and the Lord Lieutenant, Lady Pippa Dannatt, were very keen to build up the morale of the Bench. So, with the new Chair's blessing I arranged to meet up with her again, this time primarily to ask if she, as Lord Lieutenant, would give a short speech at such an occasion, if I was able to find a venue and could organise the event. Pippa then completely bowled me over, by not only agreeing to speak but also insisted that the occasion should be held in her garden, and at her expense she would provide a marquee. On hearing my plans, she immediately had a date in mind, as she was already hosting an event for the retirement of Simon Bailey, the Chief Constable of Norfolk Constabulary. Thus, my garden party was scheduled to take place on the day prior to the Chief Constable's event, and again much to my amazement she offered me the use of all the facilities that were associated with Simon's occasion.

Given that all the costs, apart from the catering, would be met by Pippa, this meant that the surplus from the sale of tickets could be donated to a charity that was being set up by Jim Agnew's family, in memory of him. The invitation (Fig. 536) was duly sent out and acceptances poured in.

Figure 536

In May, I decided that I would make an application to join the regional Advisory Committee. The principal role of this committee was to interview and recommend the appointment of potential magistrates, to The Lord Chief Justice. I was successful with my application and following the appropriate training joined the interview panel. At the time, the process for selecting magistrates was under review and after a few months a completely new procedure was introduced.

Bizarrely, this meant that firstly, we had no information about the candidate, other than their name, and secondly, due to the adoption of a set script we were restricted as to the questions we could ask. The rationale for these changes was given as being an attempt to ensure that all applicants, across England and Wales were treated the same way, thus ensuring bias was removed. Whilst we understood the rationale which would improve the service and eliminate bias,

481

it omitted to take account of the fact that we had all been trained on how to understand and eradicate our own prejudices, and as such we had no evidence that this change would be effective or necessary.

This concerned us greatly, but we had to abide by the rules that had been laid down and regrettably, this radical change in the way the interviews were to be conducted, resulted in several resignations. I could understand that all candidates needed to be treated equally, but this new process gave little or no room for the interviewer to both establish and understand the personal details of the candidate, e.g. whether they were in employment, in what capacity and where they lived etc. That kind of information would have been really useful, in order that any recommendation for appointments would support the benches need to reflect a cross section of candidates and avoid bias towards any one element of society! Whilst I was concerned, going forward I persevered with the interviews.

On 8 June our family was increased again, this time by the arrival of Zoey Mei-Cee Gosden. She was an early bird, arriving at 03.18, at a good weight of just over 7lb 10½oz (3.47kg). A beautiful granddaughter indeed, snuggled up to her Grannie (Fig. 537) and cuddles were not restricted, for once she and Jude were home from hospital, Grandpa had his turn as well (Fig. 538).

Figure 537

Figure 538

Chapter 7 Life in Retirement 2014 – 2025

At the end of June, we caused some raised eyebrows when we asked a local cake shop, if they would kindly bake, ice and decorate a Christmas cake for us. *'You're very early'* was the retort, and our explanation was to create even more amusement. Through Covid restrictions last year, all our family had missed a Holt Christmas luncheon together. So, we had decided to have a 'Summer' Christmas instead on 21 August, and we wanted a traditional cake to have after our meal. This was greeted with much merriment by the bakers and a couple of days later the conversation was repeated with the butcher, when we ordered and arranged a delivery of several hot joints of roast pork, with all the trimmings. Both suppliers came up trumps, as I will describe in due course.

For a while, I had been thinking about the Holt Society possibly making a film about our Georgian town. This was to be aimed at an audience who, like my father when he was alive, due to his age and mental capacity was unable to visit the town or read books about it. Despite these limitations, he still liked to see and enjoy the town's historical buildings, hear about their history and relevance to the townscape. So, my thoughts were that a film may be of help to other people in similar circumstances.

I envisaged it taking the viewer along the route of the walks which were already well documented by the Society, during which an explanation would be given of the various architectural and social historic features of our town. I thought a commentary to the film could be given by Steve Benson, as he had led many walks through Holt in recent years, was an excellent raconteur, a retired teacher of History at Gresham's and a previous Chairman of the Society. Following a short conversation with him, during which he was very supportive of the concept, I decided to develop the idea further.

I spoke to our neighbour Joe, who I knew was a professional television cameraman, to see if he could recommend someone locally who might be able to help us. To my surprise, given the film's potential use he offered free of charge to carry out the filming himself. He also put me in touch with Scott his film editor who, for a modest charge, offered to edit it all.

With this 'in the bag', as Chairman of the Society I tabled the idea at our next committee meeting, to seek their agreement. They were totally supportive, so it was all systems go. I particularly wanted to include some old, black and white images of Holt, and compare these to the contemporary townscape, so the observer could see the 'then and now' views. To this end, I spent the next few weeks sorting photographs and a filming schedule. As Steve had led these walks many times and given his previous profession, he was a master at outlining history, so the narration would be in his own words and style.

When the day came for filming on 9 July, Steve, Kate and I met Joe at 05.00, outside our house, on a beautiful, sunny summer's day. We had to commence our walk early to avoid the noise and the hustle and bustle of Holt coming alive. We did not want delivery vans in the film, nor did we want lots of loud sounds from people going about their normal daily life.

The filming which took around four hours was great fun, with both Steve and I just walking and chatting in between stops, where Steve would deliver a commentary on a particular aspect of Holt. What we were totally unaware of was that Joe was not only filming us but that he wanted to include our informal conversations into the film, so whilst we walked from one location to another, he was also recording these friendly dialogues.

With the main filming completed, and without the need for us to be involved, Joe created some 'filler' sequences. These were activities that included the Holt Sunday Market, the Holt Heritage Steam Railway and its 1940's weekend. He also took some aerial drone shots of the town, to give the audience an impression of the size of Holt and its layout. Once I had sent the old photographs to Joe and Scott, they worked through the process of cutting and splicing all the filming and created it into a superb 30-minute film. At this stage, I then had to add a narration to the old, black and white photographs that appeared alongside the contemporary images.

The finished film, which everyone was thrilled to see, was so much better than I had imagined. It was sent free of charge, to all the Holt Society members, and has been shown numerous times to other organisations in and around Holt. It certainly helped to increase the awareness of not only Holt as a town, but also The Holt Society itself.

As a result of its professionalism and content, coupled with the fact that it had been so well received by those who had viewed it, the film had now been included in the University of East Anglia Film Archive, where it will be held for posterity.

In figure 539, Steve is seen explaining how the Great Fire of Holt in 1708, changed the town's future characteristics. In figure 540 he is outside the old White Horse pub, now an off licence. In figure 541, Joe is seen filming in Bull Street with Steve in the centre and me. Figure 542 is Joe filming outside the Blue Stone row of flint cottages.

Chapter 7 Life in Retirement 2014 – 2025

Figure 539 (top left), Figure 540 (top right), Figure 541 (above left), Figure 542 (above right)

Figure 543

Figure 544

In early August, I had booked myself on to a five-day residential art course, at Flatford Mill, which focused on drawing and painting in Gouache. My quest was to find a medium that I was happy with and to fulfil my ambition to paint more regularly. The course was very good, and my aim was to produce some half decent drawings (Figs. 543 & 544) and paintings in the style of the 1930's railway posters (Fig. 545).

I enjoyed the course very much but alas the future frequency of painting remained unaltered. One day, I will make the breakthrough, paint and be happy with my results enough to want to undertake another subject. Though, for now my efforts remain as they were prior to the course. I drew the sketches whilst staying at Flatford Mill, as was the picture of the fields, painted on the farm, next to the mill. The beehive (Fig. 546) was painted in our back garden following my return home.

Figure 545

Figure 546

Chapter 7 Life in Retirement 2014 – 2025

This just preceded the Joneses arriving for their holiday with us. During this, we managed to fit in a few walks around Blakeney, which included some crabbing along with a very successful picnic. On the Thursday, Oliver, Jude and their family all arrived and together we all had a brilliant visit to see Dippy, in Norwich Cathedral (Fig. 547). Dippy was the follow up to the earlier Helter Skelter and was equally well received.

Figure 547

The week concluded on Saturday 21 August, when Sophie, Leigh and Ben joined us all for our family 'Summer Australasian' Christmas. The cake had been collected, the pork delivered, the house was decorated and from the grandchildren's perspective, Santa had even left some presents under the tree!

The weather was predicted as light showers, so our Christmas lunch was held inside (Fig. 548), which as it turned out was just as well, as the heavens opened whilst we were eating. After lunch though, the sun came out, so we all returned to the garden to open all the exciting gifts (Fig. 549) and cut the cake (Fig. 550). It was a great fun day and certainly made up for the lack of a proper Christmas last year.

Figure 548

Figure 549 (top), Figure 550 (above)

487

Ben stayed with us for a further week, during which time we visited my mother, had lovely walks along the beach, searched and found some of the 'Go-Go' models of dinosaurs strategically place around Norwich, and we had our second visit to Dippy, this time with Ben. All of which kept both him and us very happy and busy.

When all the grandchildren and parents had returned to their respective homes, we were able to have some time to ourselves, which we spent visiting an exhibition of Crome paintings in the Castle Museum, along with a day in Burnham Overy, where we walked along the coastal path followed by a lovely pub lunch.

With the arrival of September, the Magistrates Garden Party was upon us. Images of the event are included (Figs. 551-555). The evening was a resounding

Figure 551

Figure 552

Figure 553

Figure 554

Figure 555

success and thoroughly enjoyed and appreciated by all who attended, both past and present magistrates and their partners. I welcomed everyone and thanked both Pippa and Lord Dannatt for their generosity and presented her, on behalf of the Bench, with a bouquet of flowers. She responded and extended her heartfelt thanks to all the Norfolk Magistrates for keeping the wheels of Justice turning, throughout the challenging times we had just lived through. I also gave Lord Dannett an unexpected gift. I had recently read an article about him in the *Norfolk Magazine*, where he was asked what his favourite tipple was. In response he had said Bells whisky, Schweppes soda and a packet of Hula Hoops. So, as you have probably guessed, this was my gift to him. Just as I had hoped, it came as a complete surprise and was very well received. We all enjoyed a lovely social evening, and afterwards I received many letters of thanks, including one from Jim's family, following our donation to their charity that had been set up in his honour.

In September we also enjoyed a holiday, which could not have come too soon! We travelled to the Riverside Inn in Aymestrey in Herefordshire, where we stayed for four nights. En route we called into David Austin Roses, not necessarily to purchase anything, but more to just have a look around and pick up some ideas for our garden.

We continued our journey and visited Much Wenlock where we had a walk along the old packhorse trail. This certainly wasn't as easy as we expected, due to the cobbles and loose stones, but the views were breathtaking. We arrived at the inn, which was very comfortable, and we and the dogs were made to feel very welcome. So much so that we booked an additional night's stop, to break our return journey home.

Our first full day in Herefordshire was spent at Croft Castle where we had a wonderful walk around the grounds, during which we saw an oak tree (Fig. 556) that was said to be 1,000 years old, along with others purporting to be a mere 500 years old.

Returning to the hotel we sat outside in our own private garden, with a glass of wine and listened to the river rippling by, whilst the birds sang in the overhanging trees. It was really glorious and so relaxing.

Figure 556

Our next day was a visit abroad, well into Wales actually, where we found a wonderful Wildlife Trust location 'Withybeds', an island of wet willow woodland, alongside the River Lugg. Here Dan and Archie had a swim whilst we just sat and admired the views and sounds. We were incredibly conscious though, that at the time there was a severe shortage of petrol, so at the tiny, local garage located in the village, we managed to fill up. This was very comforting, as we seriously did not want to become stranded, in the middle of nowhere!

From there we visited Berrington Hall, which was in the process of being restored by the National Trust. Our claim to fame here was that we saw and held the gate open for Kevin McCloud, and his partner. At the time, Kevin was the television presenter of *Grand Designs*. One of the garden's interesting features amongst others, was the lovely original kitchen garden with its curved wall designed by Capability Brown. This was unknown to most of the public, for until recently this location had been used by a local business, which had inflicted some serious damage to the fabric of the area, and it was this that was now under restoration.

Figure 557

Then on Sunday 26 September, after a three-and-a-half-hour journey, only broken by a stop at Clovelly (Fig. 557) for a walk around and a cream tea, we arrived in Padstow, our final location at Rick Stein's Seafood Restaurant hotel.

This was our second visit, and it was as good as the first, which was excellent. Whilst there were a lot of tourists again in Padstow, it didn't seem to be overwhelmingly crowded which was most encouraging, as parking in the town was very restricted. We were so fortunate in that again we had our own parking slot that was provided by the hotel.

Due to the fuel shortages, we stayed close to Padstow which wasn't an issue, as there was plenty to see and places to visit on foot.

One of the days, whilst walking around the shops in town, we visited a small gallery displaying some very attractive artworks. This visit was to cost us dear, as we both fell in love with a beautiful bronze figurine of a lady, sitting on a stool.

Chapter 7 Life in Retirement 2014 – 2025

It had originally attracted our attention as it was sculpted by Sheree Valentine Daines, an artist we both liked, and as I have mentioned previously, we have a few of her painted works. So, it was no surprise that this figurine came back to Norfolk with us! We both have almost 'zero' willpower, on occasions such as this!

Unlike our previous stay, this time we were to have the pleasure of meeting Rick Stein at a signing of his new book, just a few minutes' walk from the hotel. Having had her book duly signed by him, Kate managed to have a conversation with him about a shop in the town where, whilst on holiday many years ago, she had purchased her breakfasts and groceries and first sampled clotted cream. She had forgotten its name though, and sure enough Rick fondly remembered the shop and reminded Kate that it was called Hamiltons.

On our last day we walked along the Camel Trail, which had been a train line linking Padstow to Wadebridge. Since the removal of the lines, it had been transformed into a beautiful flat cycle and walking route, which was most enjoyable. It also had a lovely mobile drink and cake van, so on our return we just felt obliged to give them some custom!

En route home the next day, we stopped off at Port Isaac (Fig. 558), for a look around, as this was the village used for the location of one of our favourite television series *Doc Martin*.

Figure 558

It was very picturesque, and we had great fun picking out the various buildings that featured so prominently in the television production.

Regrettably, due to the continued shortage of petrol we had to cancel our stopover in Aymestrey. Then, safely back home again and thankfully without running out of petrol on the way, we unpacked, sorted out the washing etc. and a few days later treated ourselves to a visit to the cinema, to see the latest James Bond film *No Time to Die*. Another great film but as with everyone who saw it, we wondered if that really was the end of the franchise. We hoped not.

REFLECTIONS UPON A FAMILY

In early October, having just experienced a lovely holiday, we both thought it would be a good time to seek the views from the rest of our family on a possible UK holiday altogether. Having spoken to all three families, it was agreed that the idea was good and with that Kate commenced a search for a venue. After a long trawl through sites on the internet, she found an ideal location in Doughton in Gloucestershire. This was agreed by everyone, and a deposit was sent to confirm our booking for August 2023.

Later in October, Sophie and Leigh went up to Scotland for a break and Ben stayed with Leigh's parents. We messaged Sophie to check all was ok on 31 October, and at 19.00 that day received the following reply:

> [31/10/2021, 19:00] Sophie: *Yes, arrived back this afternoon, just in time to put Halloween decorations up. We had a good time, and the weather was kinder than it was in other places! Was just me and Leigh as had some things to sort out that we couldn't do with Ben around, so he had a holiday with Leigh's parents. No major news to discuss just back to work next week! X*
>
> [31/10/2021, 19:57] Keith Gosden: *Sounds good, always good to chat. Glad you can chat together but if you need a conversation we are here if it would help. Good luck on Wednesday at the hospital. Take care love Dad and Kate xx*
>
> [31/10/2021, 19:59] Sophie: *Thank you, yes had bloods done in Scotland so hopefully they get results OK. Will confirm with them tomorrow. Thanks x*

That was to be the last direct communication we were to have with Sophie until 12 February 2023, some 16 months later. Apart from one email on 7 January 2022 which Leigh had insisted Sophie wrote and shared with our family, and which is recorded in the 2022 section (see page 496).

At the time of writing this in 2024, we now know that Sophie had been sectioned in November 2021 and had been admitted into hospital, for a period of six weeks. Our family were not advised of this which obviously caused great concern and heightened our anxieties even more. We were all very concerned about her health and whereabouts, hence Leigh's insistence for the email, the contents of which were distressing for us all at the time.

Following the last text that I had received from Sophie on 31 October, in spite of asking Leigh whether anything had happened to her, he categorically would not say, so we simply did not know if she was alive or dead. It was very worrying. On 8 November Kate tried four times to contact her but had no reply, so instead she sent a text to Leigh. The next day he responded, saying that things were not good at home, but he was in contact with her through her friend. So, at least we now knew she was still alive.

We finally spoke to Leigh on Saturday 13th and we agreed to have Ben to stay with us over the next weekend.

Figure 559

On the following Friday we went to Tadley to collect him, and we met him out of school. He seemed well but we purposely kept well away from any conversation regarding his mum. Instead, when we arrived home, we took him on the Saturday to Gresham's Open Day. He thoroughly enjoyed himself, as we also did. He played on the drums in the music suite (Fig. 559), showed us in the science block how a 3D printer worked and seemed very calm and interested in all the displays. We did assure him though, that it was only a look around and not leading to a change of schools. On the Sunday we met Leigh at Wandlebury, and he and Ben made their way home.

We were very concerned about Ben, as the whole saga around Sophie must have been so confusing for him. Leigh too was concerned but was unable to relay any positive update on what was happening between him and Sophie. Whilst we obviously respected this, it didn't allay our anxieties.

By mid-October I was able to share the first cut of our film with Steve Benson which we both thought was very impressive. However, both Joe and Scott had ideas of how to further improve it, so we awaited the final version. A few days later having recorded the voice-overs for the photographs, I passed these on to Joe. I have to admit that I found this voice-over process not at all easy, for each time I listened to the playback it didn't sound like me and rather unnatural. So now, I am in awe of the actors who voice-over on films etc. They seem to make their voice sound so spontaneous and certainly not scripted, like mine!

In November I met up with a local estate agent, as I was endeavouring to set up a project within the Holt Society, to record as many of the cellars that we could find in Holt, for the Society's understanding was that none of them had been previously documented. As such our aim was to document with plans and photographs, a full record of as many as possible. The estate agent was able to help and gave me some excellent advice on how to move the project forward. I took all this on board and fed it back to the committee, who endorsed the idea.

November was always a month of celebration in Holt. Firstly, we celebrated Armistice Day with a war memorial service. This was followed, a week or so later by the traditional Christmas lights switch-on, coupled with a really good fireworks display. These always attracted a large crowd from both Holt residents and further afield and this year was no exception. The latter turned out to be highly successful and admired by everyone, especially the children.

For the last few months, I had become a little concerned about my ability to recall matters and feared that, perhaps, I could possibly have the onset of Alzheimer's. I talked this through with Kate who was a little surprised but very supportive and suggested that I contacted the doctors to obtain their views. I took this advice and on the 21st we both had a consultation with Dr Clarke. After a few questions followed by a test of my memory which entailed asking me various general knowledge questions, like who was the Prime Minister, what was the current date etc. I then had a short test of my cognitive functions, and for this I had to start from 100 and subtract a certain number, that Dr Clarke gave me. I continued these subtractions until told that I could stop. Whilst I didn't find this easy, I was very happy to hear that Dr Clarke didn't think I had the onset of Alzheimer's. We both left the surgery much relieved by this confirmation, but I was advised to take things a little easier.

With having two 'Hanworth House' Christmases in the same year, our second one was rapidly approaching. So, I made four dozen mince pies (Fig. 560) whilst Kate finished the last preparations in the bedrooms for our family. But we still knew nothing about Sophie, other than Leigh was in contact

Figure 560

Chapter 7 Life in Retirement 2014 – 2025

with her. Ben and Leigh spent Christmas in Tadley with Leigh's parents, so that was a good distraction from them all worrying about her. On the other hand, we had Christmas Day and Boxing Day to ourselves, with the Joneses arriving on the 29th, followed by the Gosdens the next day.

We had a good New Year with presents opened and enjoyed by all the grandchildren (Fig. 561). There was an enduring undercurrent concerning Sophie, but this didn't spoil our celebrations, which were to conclude with a lovely walk through Sheringham Park. The Joneses left on 1 January and following a much requested visit to the beach, the Gosdens made their way home the following day.

Figure 561

The year had been filled with numerous events, some within our own control and great fun, whilst others were very much outside our control. In the case of Covid it appeared that it was outside even the government's control, but I guess that was to be expected with a pandemic.

Anyway, to our knowledge all our family were still in good health, despite most of us having had mild attacks of covid, so we had to be grateful for this which we all were. However, the concerns around Sophie still niggled and were of great concern.

2022

We started the year with a clear up in the garden. Both hedges were trimmed and cleared away, including the yew tree where we found evidence of previous birds' nests.

Leigh, who liked to spend Christmas at home, came to ours afterwards with Ben, to stay for the weekend. We presumed that as Sophie was not with them, she was not around at that time. We didn't ask too many questions and just let Leigh say what he could or what he wanted to let us know. Regrettably they couldn't stay longer as Ben had school on the Monday.

What little Leigh knew of Sophie's condition etc. he shared with us, but it was very scant and to be honest we were none the wiser. However, he clearly knew more but, as I have previously mentioned, was hesitant to convey this, and upon returning home he insisted that Sophie shared with the family her current situation, which she did, via the email below.

> **From:** Sophie Bedford
> **Sent:** Friday, January 7, 2022 5:58:07 PM
> **To:** Keith Gosden; Oliver Gosden; Jude Gosden; Jeannette Crowe; Emily and Pete Jones
> **Cc:** Leigh Bedford
> **Subject:** Support for Leigh
>
> *Hi,*
>
> *As you all know, I've been off the grid for a while and there is probably speculation over what has happened and whether we're OK.*
>
> *Leigh has mentioned that he's seeing some of you soon so I thought I'd take this opportunity now to explain some of what's been going on.*
>
> *Back in October I suffered a severe mental breakdown to the point that the GP asked me to be assessed and I was then offered some hospitalised care while I got better. I took this opportunity.*
>
> *During this time I realised I had to step back from my current life in order to address some of my needs. I was able to see Ben before Christmas and speak to him on Christmas Day but at the moment he is just aware that I'm staying with a friend to get myself better.*
>
> *The truth of the matter as it stands right now, is that Leigh and I are separated, we are working with a professional to help us deal with our individual requirements but at this stage the future is uncertain.*

We will be explaining this to Ben in more detail on Monday, so he understands that I won't be coming home for a while.

Leigh has told me he would appreciate your support so this is why I'm emailing, you now [so you] have a better picture of the situation and he can use your support.

I am physically fine. I know some of you may want to contact me to say that you're thinking of me and there if I need anything. I know that already.

I am learning to listen to myself and what I need, and right now that is working through this with my close friends and the professionals, I have in place so would appreciate you not contacting me further.

Thanks Sophie

We didn't respond to this email, as we respected Sophie's final comment '…*so would appreciate you not contacting me further.*' Whilst we were relieved that she was alive it was distressing to feel that she could not or would not communicate with any of us. Instead, only confiding in friends who had only known her for a few years. There was more to this, as I will explain in February.

On Sunday 16 January, I had an unexpected call from Duncan Baker, our Westminster MP, at the time, to ask if I would consider standing as a Conservative District Councillor for North Norfolk. Whilst I was humbled to be asked, I declined as the position was not only too much of a commitment, but was also too political, something I have always tried to avoid. It was very gratifying to be asked though.

On 6 February, HRH Queen Elizabeth II became the UK's longest reigning monarch. Also, despite the covid vaccinations, Pete, Libby and Leo contracted covid again and had to isolate at home. It was now becoming clear that like other diseases, this one was here to stay and that regular vaccinations would be required.

The next day, we came across a post which Sophie had written on Facebook, in response to two memes (Figs. 562 & 563) that she found on the internet which she identified with and shared.

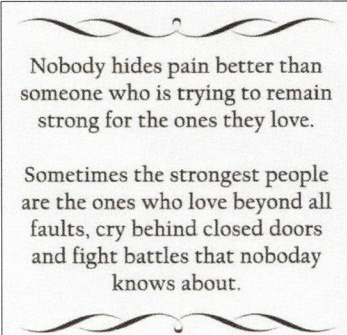

Figure 562

Figure 563

Sophie added the following comment:

> [Sophie] *This is very true one thing I am having to focus some time on is learning new habits and trying to resolve past issues that are still contributing to my behaviour patterns today. We can't fix what we were never taught. There are some things you can't just "sort out" for yourself. Team that with dealing with a child with their own emotions, how do you teach emotional regulation to a child when you never learnt it yourself.*
>
> *I'm very grateful that the school system now allows for Ben to have time dedicated to emotional coping skills. Something that will hopefully help him develop his own more healthy skills into adult life.*

Given that this criticism of her upbringing was now on a public forum, Kate and I in particular, were extremely annoyed and upset, to say the least. We had no way of contacting her, as we had discovered that she had 'blocked' all her family on all of her social media platforms. So consequently, on 9 February, we sent the following to Leigh in the hope that he would pass it on to Sophie.

> *Upon reading these* [correspondences] *both of us are deeply hurt and cross by the actual reference to a lack of teaching when you were a minor, regarding emotional regulation. Plus, the fact that you continue to express adverse comments on your upbringing, on a public arena but refuse to even talk to us, let alone give us a right of reply in privacy. Hence this email.*
>
> *Can we please remind you of a few facts that seem to have vacated your memory.*
>
> 1 *Whilst our two families were coming together, we had regular, indeed weekly, 'round table' conversations about how we all felt, what issues we had and how we could all help each other to deal with the changes in our lives. You were there and regularly taking part in these discussions both voicing your worries and putting forward suggestions.*
>
> 2 *We, as a family also sought professional help from a counsellor/therapist to help us all resolve any emotional issues that had been identified. We not only met as a family but also as individuals. Strategies were discussed and it was the responsibility of the individual to put these into operation.*
>
> *We would suggest that this was, at the time, the best way to deal with any emotional turmoil that any one of us was wrestling with. As we have said, you were part of this learning experience, and we totally reject the inference that we did not 'teach' you how to regulate emotions.*

To teach anyone successfully is a two-way process – a teacher, in this case your father and stepmother, along with a professional counsellor/therapist, outline a way forward and encourage the 'pupil' to engage. The 'pupil' has to take the advice on board, engage, put into practice the strategies and learn from the experience. It is very much down to the pupil to either accept this learning experience or ignore it.

We suggest, whilst you consider your upbringing, that you also reflect on just how much support you were given both during your time before and in the early years of your marriage;

- *You were supported through Bankruptcy.*
- *You came home and lived with us, as you had nowhere else to go.*
- *You were assisted by us financially, which also included the purchase of a wonderful dog to keep you company.*
- *You were assisted in finding a career in the veterinary profession, through the enrolment on appropriate courses and encouraged and applauded for the fantastic progress you have and continue to make as a veterinary nurse.*
- *You had substantial financial help in purchasing your own home, following your marriage.*
- *You had help from a Harley Street consultant, who identified and taught you both how to deal with Ben's dietary issues, that were causing you so much distress.*
- *We also strongly suggested that you had your mole checked out, which in the end was very sound advice.*

These are just a few examples of the love and care that has been freely given to you by us. We asked and expected nothing in return. We helped you willingly, because that's what parents do! Although we were unable to give you support during the years that you were living with your mum and Dale, as it was then that you chose to not communicate with us, in any way for a number of years. If the circumstances you experienced during this period have affected your current mental health issues, it would be very unfair to lay these at our door!

Your response to our continuous love, support and care, as we have said was to cut us both off from your life for a number of years, without any explanation. Now, some 20 years later you seek to do the same again, not only to us but also the rest of the family. Making it quite clear that friends are far more important. This, we would suggest is NOT THE WAY TO DEAL WITH 'EMOTIONAL REGULATION'. It may be 'satisfying' for you but is in fact causing huge emotional issues for others.

Think hard before you criticise those who seek to help you and just remember that, in the last few decades, the wider understanding of emotional issues has moved on leaps and bounds. So, don't judge others by the levels of today's knowledge.

We are just about here for you, but you are certainly making it extremely difficult both for yourself and for your wider family should you wish to return and rekindle the family bond. But that may well take time and patience.

Dad and Kate

As expected, no response was ever received.

We were delighted when Leigh advised us that Ben would like to come and stay for the half term, so we met up on 20 February, just outside Cambridge, to pick him up at a place that was well known to him. It was a sunny but blustery day, so we all had a hot drink in the local service station, whilst Ben thoroughly enjoyed his burger and chips. His stay meant that he was with us for my birthday which was lovely, and Kate prepared a birthday tea on the following Saturday. The most popular activity during the week seemed to be walking and playing on the beach whilst splashing in the bitterly cold sea. Which then developed into crabbing on an even colder day and even the crabs thought it was too inclement to come out!

Leading up to June, through the leadership of the Town Council, the town was actively preparing for the Queen's Platinum Jubilee celebrations. I had tentatively agreed with the Holt Society that we would work towards producing a Jubilee Slate to help mark this significant occasion, and this was an idea that I had been thinking about for a few weeks. I had envisaged, engraved on the left-hand side the key events from the monarch's reign, coupled on the right-hand side with contemporary events that had occurred in Holt. Much to my delight the committee thought it was worth pursuing.

My idea, along with a couple of others from different organisations in the town, was accepted by the Town Council, so the Holt Society opened talks with a local engraver. Regrettably, one of the suggestions didn't fully materialise, which resulted in just the Jubilee Slates and a Fairy Doors trail, both being managed and created by independent bodies and being the only long-term commemorations of the Jubilee. This meant that the Town Council did not

Chapter 7 Life in Retirement 2014 – 2025

actually have any installation themselves, which was a shame given the previous work in 1887, to acknowledge Queen Victoria's Jubilee, when the council of the day installed the Blind Sam gas light, on behalf of the town's residents. An image of Blind Sam is the current emblem of The Holt Society, so it was important to this association that in some way the current Monarch's Jubilee was acknowledged. However, that said the town now had two projects, both of which came to fruition.

After conversations with the engraver and given the number of possible events, he suggested that in order to keep the engraving font size large enough to read, that two slates should be used instead, which together would increase the cost by a couple of thousand pounds. Each of the slates would be six-foot-high, both inscribed with key events (Fig. 564). This concept was accepted, and The Holt Society moved forward with the design and fundraising.

Figure 564

501

To kick off fundraising, I drafted a letter to all the Holt Society members, that outlined the project along with the costs. Most of these were circulated by email but if a member didn't have an email address, then I and Ben, as he was staying with us, posted them. Where they resided locally, he and I delivered them by hand or if they were further afield, we took the letters to the post office. I think Ben enjoyed being a 'postman' for the day and thoroughly loved his time in Norfolk. He returned home, content and ready for school. We now waited to see how much would be raised by our members.

To celebrate Kate's birthday in March, we went with Dan and Archie to the Suffolk coast. It was a lovely, warm sunny day and perfect for walking around. First, we visited Southwold and meandered along the beach where the sea was so calm it was like a mill pond, we then followed this with a delicious cup of coffee on the pier. We had a lovely lunch in Walberswick, where I gave Kate a silver bracelet that matched a necklace that I had given her on another occasion, it was much appreciated, and she wore it straight away. Afterwards, we drove to Aldeburgh to admire the Maggie Hambling shell sculpture, that was located on the beach (Fig. 565). I wasn't aware of this installation and the size and detail took me by surprise. It was certainly impressive, very evocative with the sun shining down and reflecting off it, and with the waves behind it also appeared to be resting on the shoreline. The rest of the month was spent working in the garden preparing it for the summer.

Figure 565

Then, for some reason we decided to have a chat with our local vicar, Father Howard, about the possibility of us reserving a double burial site, in the churchyard.

Having walked around and spoken with him at great length, it was obvious that there simply was not room. So, we concluded that our wish to be buried together there, was not practical, and that we would have to reconsider the location for our resting place. This, at the time of writing is still outstanding and hopefully not a priority!

Chapter 7 Life in Retirement 2014 – 2025

Over the next few weeks, I was to sit on various interview panels, for potential magistrates both in Norfolk and elsewhere. Some were successful and were appointed, unfortunately, others did not make the grade. I and most of my colleagues were still struggling with the new regime and process, but we persevered.

For Leigh and Ben, 27 March was a significant day, as Sophie decided to return to Tadley. She had been staying with a friend, whilst also receiving professional hospital care for depression and anxiety. We have never fully understood why none of our family, especially Leigh, were not advised as to where she had gone in 2021. This was, and I regret to say, will likely to be a huge issue within the wider family for the foreseeable future. Whilst we all appreciated the mental welfare issues that Sophie has had and was still contending with, we simply could not understand her actions. Acts which had caused great anxiety to all of us and had led to some of our family suffering from thoughts that either she had left Leigh and Ben, or even died. Regrettably, Sophie simply does not appear to understand this, despite what she has been through herself, including being sectioned, which I assumed was voluntarily under the Mental Health Act. I fear it will take many years to heal the rifts, if they can ever be healed.

On a positive note, Zoey decided to start crawling on 4 April, so that meant stair gates and other safety measures needed to be put in place here, at home. We suspected that this would be for the final time, as all our three children now seemed contented with the size of their respective families.

In April, I took on more responsibility by being elected as Chairman of The Holt Society, which filled all my spare time and more! Not that it wasn't worthwhile, as I liked to support the town and to give something back to society. We were already working on the cellar survey and, of course, now had to organise the fundraising and installation of the Jubilee Slates. There was plenty of work to do and it certainly kept me occupied! I also wanted to record the numerous artefacts and documents that the Society had built up over the years. That was, however, a very large commitment, so would need to wait a while.

Eve's maternal aunts, cousins and uncle all lived close to London and a number of them supported Tottenham Hotspur Football Club that was colloquially known as 'Spurs'. As a consequence, she had shown an interest in the team, to the point where I thought she might like to see them play against Norwich in the final match of the season. To this end, as I had been given two tickets for the game in a private box, she and Oliver came for the day during the last weekend of May.

On the day of the match, Evie and I, or Eve as we now called her since Zoey was born, negotiated the crowds and found our way to the Executive Box. This was located in a really good position, high up at the corner of the pitch, enabling

REFLECTIONS UPON A FAMILY

Figure 566

Eve to have a good view of the game. We were introduced to the other guests and took our seats (Fig. 566). I knew very little about football, and even less about Spurs, so I was pleased that sitting beside us were two avid Spurs supporters, who were able to give Eve plenty of details. They pointed out who were the key players, what was happening during the game and why certain actions and decisions were important.

However, with Norwich being thrashed 5 – 0 it was a very one-sided commentary! Norwich had already been relegated and as this was the final match, it was probably the last time for quite a few seasons, before a re-match would take place. Eve enjoyed the game though, but I was unsure just how much she actually understood. However, the upside to this visit was that she took up playing football with a local club near to where she lived, and really enjoyed her matches.

Putting behind us the disappointment of the Spurs thrashing, Kate and I on 24 May, made our way to London, as we had been invited (Fig. 567) to a Buckingham Palace Garden Party.

The Lord Chamberlain is commanded by Her Majesty to invite

Mr. Keith Gosden
and Mrs. Katharine Sambrooke-Gosden

*to a Garden Party
at Buckingham Palace
on Wednesday, 25th May, 2022 from 4 to 6 p.m.*

This card does not admit

Figure 567

Chapter 7 Life in Retirement 2014 – 2025

We stayed overnight in the Blakemore Hotel, in Leinster Gardens and the next day, after breakfast and a change of clothes, ordered a taxi and proceeded to Constitution Hill, where we joined a throng of other invited guests. There was, as you might expect, lively banter and excitement amongst the queue, with photographs being taken by fellow guests to record the day (Fig. 568).

At 15.00 precisely, the palace gates were opened, and we made our way into the grounds, showing our yellow passes along with all the necessary photographic ID.

The event was held in the gardens which are not usually seen by the general public. They are actually laid out at the front of the Palace, but when looking from Pall Mall towards the building and its famous balcony, they appear to be at the rear. There were seats either arranged in small groups or in rows and to the left was a long range of marquees that housed the servery for our tea.

Figure 568

Figure 569

We were asked to stay on this beautifully manicured lawn, in front of the palace (Fig. 569) to await the arrival of the Royal Party. This was led by Prince William and his wife Catherine, and supported by the Earl and Countess of Wessex, Princess Beatrice and the Duke and Duchess of Gloucester. During their 'walkabout', they greeted, had conversations and shook hands with some of the guests, prior to them making their way to the far side of the lawn and into the Royal Marquee for their tea (Fig. 570).

REFLECTIONS UPON A FAMILY

Figure 570

This was the cue that we could collect our own tea from the guests' marquee. Unfortunately, at this point the heavens opened and all we could see were hundreds of multicoloured umbrellas!

However, undaunted by this sudden cloudburst, I collected some mini sandwiches, sausage rolls, vol-au-vents, quiche and cakes, as well as two cups of tea, all from a beautifully laid out servery and returned to join Kate. Although we were now very wet, we had in fact rather fortuitously just before the downpour, managed to secure seats in a really good position, which allowed us an excellent view of the Royal Marquee. So, whilst sitting under our umbrella we not only enjoyed our superb afternoon tea but also had a wonderful panorama of all the Royal Party and invited dignitaries having their tea as well!

Whilst the rain dampened the excitement and atmosphere for a while, the experience was one never to be forgotten (Fig. 571). Following the exit of the

Figure 571

Figure 572

506

Chapter 7 Life in Retirement 2014 – 2025

Royal Party, we were allowed at our leisure to walk through the superb gardens, on our way out of the palace grounds. Given that the sun was now shining, like many of the other guests, we took our time to stroll and view the horticulture along with the various sculptures and monuments, some of which were huge (Fig. 572)!

As you can only attend one Garden Party, unless you are awarded an honour in a subsequent year, visiting the Palace on an occasion like this was a once in a lifetime event, not only for us but for many of the other estimated 8,000 guests in attendance that day. So, we wanted to make sure we savoured the time we had had at this truly, unbelievable experience.

Once outside, we made our way back to the hotel, via Hyde Park and Kensington Gardens, which were equally impressive. Whilst we walked through the gardens, I felt slightly conspicuous in top hat and tails, for one or two people raised their eyebrows when seeing us both dressed in our finery. We could only presume that this was not a normal occurrence, during the evening on a Wednesday! Back at the hotel we changed and went out for a delicious Italian meal at Taomina restaurant in Ambassador Court.

Figure 573

The following day, we had arranged to meet up with Duncan Baker, our MP, for a private visit around Westminster Palace and the Houses of Parliament (Fig. 573). For a short while, we also had the opportunity to sit in both the Commons and the Lords and listened to some of the debates. After which we had lunch with Duncan in the Commons dining room. This entire visit was absolutely fascinating and really interesting. Then, after an amazing couple of days, we caught our train back to Norwich at 15.00 and were able to collect Dan and Archie from the kennels on our way home.

On the Friday, we returned Kate's hired fascinator, and my morning suit, including the top hat and resumed our normal life, but with the savoured memory that we had been to a Buckingham Palace Garden Party, which was very special indeed.

507

Figure 574

On 30 May, our Holt Society Slates were erected in Fish Hill (Fig. 574), ready for the grand unveiling on 2 June, by the Lord Lieutenant of Norfolk, Lady Pippa Dannatt. I had previously asked if she would kindly unveil the slates, which she was very happy to do, and to assist her she parked in our front driveway, as this was really close by. There was a full ceremony arranged by the Town Council which included a bagpiper and town crier.

I made a short speech to explain what the slates represented and why Fish Hill had been selected for their location, after which the official unveiling took place. The council had also arranged a community cake which Pippa cut before leaving. The whole event was very successful, and afterwards I received a charming message from Pippa thanking me for the day.

Later in June, we managed to both please our neighbours and saved ourselves an enormous amount of time clearing up leaves every autumn. This was achieved by having seven sycamore trees cut down, four of which were fully grown (Fig. 575). As can be seen by the size of these trees their removal made a significant difference to the airiness and space in our garden. Our neighbours were also very pleased, for it let more light into a conservatory and it had also enabled access to an overgrown part of another garden! In due course, the removal of these trees allowed us to erect a proper boundary fence between us and our immediate neighbour. This was not only a great improvement for us both, but also prompted her to landscape her newly exposed garden. Apparently, this area due to the lack of access and sunlight because of the dense canopies, had been totally neglected by her. So, a positive win for all of us.

Figure 575

Chapter 7 Life in Retirement 2014 – 2025

The summer sun set us up for the wider family to join us at home for some 'holiday' times by the sea. Whilst they weren't all able to meet up together, it was nevertheless lovely to see them in family groups, where we could go out on short visits, feed the ducks, go to the sea, climb on adventure playgrounds, or in the case of Ben, to drive a full-size diesel train (Fig. 576)!

It was then in July that Kate badly hurt her toe and elbow, which resulted in her suffering from a restless leg and shoulder. Despite MRI and CT scans, along with numerous blood tests the issue persisted. However, with some daily medication to relax the muscles, it became less irksome. The prognosis was that it should correct

Figure 576

itself in a few months – so fingers crossed! This was followed by both of us succumbing again to the dreaded covid but luckily this time it didn't persist for too long.

In September, we both enjoyed a short and well deserved break in Eastham, near Tenbury Wells in Worcestershire. We stayed in 'The Pig Sty' which was nothing like a sty at all and we thoroughly enjoyed our time there. One of the 'revisits' we made was to Elgar's birthplace, which as I have already alluded to, was now under the care of the National Trust, and in my opinion with its new buildings etc, it had lost some of its previous charm. Which was both regrettable and very disappointing. However, there was a new, beautiful life size sculpture of the Great Man, sitting on his bench and admiring his garden that was a delight to see (Fig. 577). So not a total disappointment after all.

Figure 577

We also had a fascinating visit around some Rock Houses in Kinver Edge. These homes had been created out of the soft red sandstone cliffs. The earliest record of their habitation was in 1777 and ended in the 1960s, when they were deemed unfit for habitation, due to there being no water supply or sanitary facilities. Some were restored by the National Trust in 1993 and 1996 which enabled us to understand the living conditions and just how 'homely' such houses could be made. (Fig. 578). The walks and visits were just what we needed and as a result we came home thoroughly rested.

Figure 578

The end of the year saw Dan's age catching up with him, as he had been suffering with arthritis in his front leg, which then became infected. Sadly, this meant much shorter walks, which his brother Archie found a little annoying. Whilst Dan was to make a slow but incomplete recovery, it was clear that this was to be a long-term condition. We were assured by the vet, that given his ongoing medication he wasn't experiencing any pain, which was reassuring.

Whilst the Holt Society had produced numerous books about Holt's Georgian architecture, it had none that outlined the life and work of its inhabitants, during this period in history. So, towards the end of the summer, The Society sponsored some excellent Georgian walks around the town, led and narrated by Margaret Bird. Margaret through her comprehensive and detailed work on the Georgian diaries of Mary Hardy, who had lived nearby in Letheringsett, most certainly had this knowledge, which was clearly of interest to many people who joined her walks.

I had asked Margaret if she would be willing to write a booklet about this particular walk, using elements of her previous text on Mary Hardy and her in-depth knowledge of the life and times of Georgian Holt. This booklet would then add to our repertoire of publications and would focus on the viewpoint of the inhabitants' working environment. She was delighted to be asked and within a matter of a month or two, The Holt Society had a very professional booklet, which was published in 2023. The cover of this was shown previously in figure 313 on page 296.

The UK, along with many countries throughout the world, were stunned and

Chapter 7 Life in Retirement 2014 – 2025

saddened on 8 September 2022, when they learnt that Queen Elizabeth II had died peacefully aged 96, at 15.10, whilst at Balmoral her Scottish home. This was such sad news for most of the nation, as she was well respected for her service and leadership, even by those who were not royalists. Her reign as our Queen for 70 years was the longest of any British monarch, and for 24 hours her coffin lay at rest in St. Giles' Cathedral in Edinburgh. It was then flown to London where she lay in state for four days whilst more than 250,000 people filed past, to pay their respects. There was a very moving state funeral on 19 September in Westminster Abbey, following which she was laid to rest at St. George's Chapel in Windsor, alongside her husband Prince Philip. A truly sad loss. She was succeeded by her eldest son King Charles III, whose coronation was held on 6 May 2023 at Westminster Abbey, along with his wife Camilla, who received the title of Queen Camilla and is styled 'Her Majesty The Queen'.

Figure 579

In October, Ben came and spent his half term with us in Holt. We had a great time and once again he was able to demonstrate his building skills, by helping myself and Gary our builder put up a new run of fencing. This secured our boundary following the removal of the sycamore trees. However, Ben's skills had developed further, and he was now able to teach his Grannie how to play Minecraft (Fig. 579). As he and his cousins grew up, they were slowly but surely turning the balance, from us teaching them, to us learning from them! It was just as it should be, but a sobering thought for us both.

Unfortunately, the year was to end with my mother having a very nasty fall outside her bungalow in Necton. It happened late one evening, so regrettably she was not found for a number of hours. She was immediately taken to hospital, where Kate and I met the ambulance and shortly afterwards we were joined by Sarah and Roger.

Mum was not in a good state and was formally admitted into hospital on 18 November. Here she stayed, whilst health and wellbeing checks were carried out and suitable home care arrangements were put in place by me and my sisters.

The photograph (Fig. 580) was taken in the hospital and shows a bright and contented Mum with book in hand. This conveyed a status that wasn't entirely correct, as behind this appearance she was suffering with confusion and anxiety. Over the next year or so, she was to regress further as I have outlined in the next sections.

Mum finally went home to Necton, on 6 December and we all visited her regularly as did her local friends who ensured she was both up, dressed and fed. It was clear to all of us, except Mum, that some difficult decisions would have to be made. As it was now close to Christmas, Kate and I were able to take her to her regular luncheon club, where she thoroughly enjoyed both the company and the festive lunch.

Figure 580

On Christmas Day, I took Mum to Necton Church for the morning service, after which she joined Kate and me in Holt for lunch at home. She obviously enjoyed herself but as I have indicated, she was not always aware of her surroundings or what she was capable of doing.

The Gosdens and Joneses came and spent New Year with us, which was lovely and a really good way to see out what had been a sometimes difficult and an extraordinary year.

2023

The year commenced with my sisters and me, along with Kate, David and Roger all endeavouring to ensure that Mum was comfortable and received the correct medication and support. It appeared that the medical staff, whether they were in the hospital or at her local practice, all seemed to have slightly differing views, on her state of health, the medication required and her ability to look after herself. Which was very confusing for all of us.

Once we had sorted this and her Lasting Power of Attorney had been enacted, we met up on 4 January with Laura and Dannie, who were two carers who had

Chapter 7 Life in Retirement 2014 – 2025

been recommended to us, by some of Mum's local friends. Mum seemed to get on well with them and was happy for them both to take it in turns in supporting her at home. This meant that there was less reliance on her local friends, who could now visit for a social chat, rather than a 'caring' call.

Towards the end of January, Kate and I attended a very interesting talk in Binham, where the speaker was Lord Butler who lived locally. His talk entitled 'Life with Five Prime Ministers', focused on his time from 1961 through to 1998 when he retired from his position as the Cabinet Secretary, and Head of the Civil Service. During which time he had worked with the Prime Ministers Edward Heath, Harold Wilson, Margaret Thatcher which included the period when the IRA bombed the Tory Conference Hotel in Brighton, John Major and finally Tony Blair. As you can imagine his repartee was excellent, his stories both witty and interesting but also discreet. A really good evening's entertainment.

On 17 February, Leigh sent the following WhatsApp message which came as a great disappointment, as we read this as saying that he and Sophie would not be joining us at Doughton in the summer, and therefore we presumed it also meant that Ben wouldn't come as well. The full transcript is below:

> *Evening Keith (and Kate). I'm really pleased that you and Sophie are building bridges and communicating more. This may appear in contrary to that but we, as a family, are going to pull out of the August family holiday. It is mainly my decision for various reasons including an unnecessary family pressure/expectation of developments targets with Sophie but also that I can't do it. Mentally I just can't. Last year really stressed me out with family visits and the holiday would be worse if the situation between Sophie hasn't improved. I have lost sleep over this. Plus, selfish reasons of a week in a house full of kids and babies, cooking, etc is the complete opposite of what a holiday is to us. Want to be honest. However, I did agree, and I accept full responsibility for the financial side of things as the rest of the family shouldn't suffer in that way because of me. I hope you both understand (though will be disappointed). This has been on my mind for a while and Sophie agrees after talking with her at some length.*

During February there was a concerted effort by both Sophie and me to repair the relationship between us. Sophie, through Leigh, suggested that I met up with her and her psychotherapist, which I did. At the consultation though, it transpired that Sophie felt that I had not defended her sufficiently when she was young, and that this had caused her issues with her self-confidence. She also maintained that her problems hadn't stemmed from her mother leaving or my marriage to Kate. At the time, I was not at all sure what focus or direction the meeting would take. As such, I was totally ill-prepared for Sophie's comments and couldn't counter this with my own views. So, if progress was to be made, I felt compelled to accept her rationale at the time. However, since then and having reflected on the circumstances whilst writing this memoir, I do feel that this simply was not the issue. I came to this conclusion having looked again at all the past photographs and documents that I have read for this book. I concluded that this evidence simply did not support her rationale. In the photographs when she was young, especially the ones before her mother left, she appears happy and very content. I do have an inkling though, that the issue stems from her time when she lived with her mother and stepfather, Dale. I believe this because, she has admitted that she had issues with her stepfather who, as I have previously outlined, was at the time effectively grooming her and was very coercive and controlling.

Whilst Sophie was permanently living with her mother and Dale, this behaviour by him was not fully understood by her, for when she visited us, we noticed that almost every hour she received a mobile call from Dale, asking what she was doing, where she was and who she was with. When we tactfully asked her for an explanation, as to the volume of calls, she just said that he was just showing concern for her. To us, this was more of a controlling influence and this, in my opinion, was evidenced by the fact that he was able to convince Sophie to allow him to use her income for paying household bills etc. Which over time, left Sophie short of funds, and ultimately with debts to the extent that she had to declare herself bankrupt. Those are not the actions of a stepfather who was 'showing concern'. Rather the opposite, in my opinion.

Looking afresh at my relationship with Sophie, I personally feel that either, she could be displaying a kind of avoidance syndrome, in that she is in some respects, 'passing' the blame for her mental state onto others, in this case, me. Or is it a case that she is simply not able to accept that, at the time, she had been subjected to the controlling influence of her stepfather? I cannot fully accept that I was the root cause and so have not taken this any further, as I would prefer to look forward, rather than try to rectify something that, in her opinion, happened some 24+ years ago. In any case, if my view is correct then it has nothing to do with me. It is sad that this has severely influenced and dare I say possibly permanently impaired, the father-daughter relationship that we once enjoyed. I hope that my fear is proved to be incorrect but only time will tell.

Chapter 7 Life in Retirement 2014 – 2025

Returning to my mother and her status, my sisters and I organised for her to have a couple of week's respite care in a home that was near to my sister Sarah. The home was very new and met all Mum's needs. When she initially visited, she was pleased with the 'hotel style' accommodation, and whilst there she was able to frequently spend both quality and just as importantly some safe time, with her children, grandchildren and great grandchildren, as seen in figure 581, with Jude, Zoey, Oliver and Eve. She also enjoyed social visits from her friends from Necton.

Figure 581

Her respite stay commenced on 6 February and Mum was very happy and thoroughly enjoyed her time there, and she soon made some new friends. So much so that we all thought it may well provide a longer-term solution.

After extending her respite visit, we all concluded that she was receiving much better care in the home, had people who she could talk to, all day long if she wanted, plus she was receiving good meals cooked for her, coupled with professional staff and help with any medical issues. As such, the decision was made to fund her for a permanent stay in the home, and to sell her bungalow in Necton to help defray the costs. It was a difficult decision, as for a while Mum kept thinking that she would be going home. However, what she was referring to was her childhood home called 'The Croft', not her bungalow in Necton. These were the signs of the advancement of her dementia which within a few months would become even more apparent.

Over the next three or four months, my sisters and their husbands along with Kate and myself were to spend what seemed like endless days, going through the contents of Mum's bungalow, throwing away unwanted items, distributing individual articles in accordance with her will, and then cleaning the bungalow.

Back in Holt and with Kate's birthday approaching in a couple of weeks, I had booked a short stay in London with a trip round the Tower of London. This was also to include a visit to the workings of Tower Bridge, and all revolved around a stay at a local hotel, concluding with a celebratory meal at The Ivy Tower Bridge restaurant.

REFLECTIONS UPON A FAMILY

Kate was aware of this, as it was a joint Christmas and birthday present, and the 'present' itself, in the form of an invitation (Fig. 582), she had received on Christmas Day last year.

A small selection of some of the photographs (Figs. 583 – 587) which we took during our time in London, are included in this memoir. These give a 'flavour' of two brilliant days. Many more were compiled into a separate 'Photo Book', as a reminder of this memorable visit. It was such a lovely occasion and given the family circumstances which made it a very stressful period at the time, we both thoroughly enjoyed ourselves.

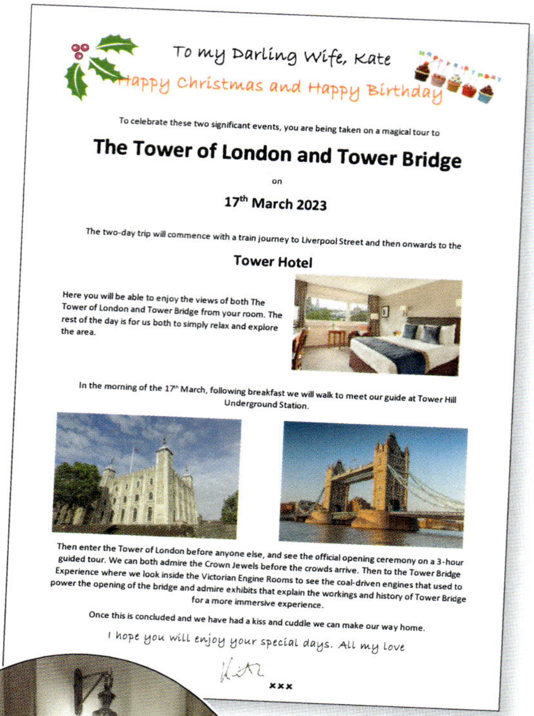

Figure 582 (above)
Figure 583 (far left)
Figure 584 (left)
Figure 585 (below far left)
Figure 586 (below centre)
Figure 587 (below)

Chapter 7 Life in Retirement 2014 – 2025

By the end of March, Kate and I found ourselves back at school, not in lessons but participating in Eve's school 'Grandparents Day'. Making Easter hats and pictures was the order of the day, and we all had great fun. As I was due to sit in court the next day, we had a lovely supper with Eve and all the family, before we left Welwyn Garden City to drive home.

The 3 April was not only Oliver's and my mother's birthday but also the Holt Society's AGM. As chairman, I obviously had to attend, and it all went very smoothly. Michael Gurney, the previous High Sheriff of Norfolk, whom I had sworn into office, gave a very thought-provoking talk, not only about his time whilst he was in this prestigious role but also the importance of the Judicial system. He was, as always, a very eloquent and articulate speaker.

All the Gosdens and Joneses came home for Easter and spent a very energetic time having fun on an Easter Egg hunt, then a day out at the Horse Sanctuary, several visits to the beach and finally a trip to our local swimming pool where we had hired, for all 11 of us, the entire children's area for an hour's session! I hasten to add that these were not all on the same day, and none of the activities seemed to tire them out! Oliver and I, along with 'the boys' also managed to find some time to ourselves, in order to visit Gramborough Hill in Salthouse where some of my father's ashes were scattered. This was just what I needed at the time – a father and son moment, plus two dogs, who inevitably brought me back to earth and reality! Still, between us, Oliver and I put the world to rights, chatted about the separation of his mother and me, and then made our way home. I have to admit that it was very tempting whilst we were together, to reveal to him that I was writing this memoir, and that in time he would be able to read all the details of that period in our lives, and much more besides. At the book's conception though, I had already agreed with Kate that it should be kept under wraps. So, I resisted the temptation, as I knew that if I told him it would spoil the surprise when the book was finally published, just after my 70th birthday. It was certainly the correct decision.

On 30 March, Holt saw the opening of a newly built Budgens supermarket on the same site of the previous shop, which had been destroyed some three years earlier, by a fire caused by an electrical fault. The new updated shop was officially opened by a local lady, Veronica Pearson, who as a ten your old schoolgirl had won a competition back in 1985, to open the previous store. This time around she was accompanied by her mother and daughter. After three years of shopping, in what was a temporary but swish looking tent like store, Holt now had a new modern and large supermarket again. Much to the delight of many of the local residents.

Good news was shared when on 14 April, Willian H. Brown, who was selling my mother's bungalow, confirmed that an offer had been made that matched the asking price of £270,000. After checking with my sisters, I confirmed that the offer was acceptable, and although there was some delay further down the chain, it eventually all went through, with the completion being confirmed on 29 August.

At the end of April, we had a day out with Sophie, Leigh and Ben, ostensibly to celebrate Ben's birthday and we all met up at Duxford for a visit to the Imperial War Museum. It had been years since I was last there, so it was really interesting to see how it had developed over the years. Ben was in his element, as whilst he doesn't like flying – to my knowledge he has never been on a proper flight – he was clambering around the planes and the static displays without any concerns. We had lunch together and then a short walk around the outside exhibits, before we made our way back home. Whilst we were all having lunch, Kate and I mentioned the family holiday and we checked to see if our assumption was correct that Ben was not going to join us. However, Ben indicated that he was very keen and was really excited at the prospect of having a holiday with his wider family. Both Sophie and Leigh, whilst being a little reticent at first, agreed it was a good idea, and they were happy for him to join us. This was very pleasing for all of us, as we didn't see as much of Ben as we had done in the past, mainly due to his school and cub scout activities, so it was good to hear that he was looking forward to our family holiday.

One interesting 'event', nothing to do with our visit, happened whilst we were there. The UK population had been advised that via our mobile phones, at a specific time a new National UK Emergency Test would be conducted. There was to be a warning signal at 15.00, in the form of a short but loud siren-like sound, a message 'Armageddon' would be displayed on our screen, our mobile would vibrate, and the whole test would last for 10 seconds. It was the very first time that such a UK wide warning like this had been tested, and it certainly worked for us and for most of the population. In future, when operational, this warning would sound where there was a local risk to life, e.g. severe flooding, fires or extreme weather etc. Just prior to the alarm, it was so interesting to see people checking their watches and then immediately look at their mobiles.

May was a relatively quiet month with gardening the main occupation by day and preparing for our holiday in the evenings. Except for one historic event and one very tragic time.

The historic event was, of course, the Coronation of King Charles III and his wife Queen Camilla on 6 May 2023. As is the custom now, the whole day's events were televised and minutely scrutinised by the press and others. For me, being a royalist, it was just good to see that sense had prevailed and Camilla, who was a divorcee and historically would not have normally been accepted as Queen, had been welcomed as such, not only by the Royal Family but by the general public as well. Just as it should be, in my opinion. It was also a time to show the world just how to deliver a day of ceremony and pageantry, to a standard that only the UK can deliver. Not that I am biased, of course!

The very tragic time was to happen on 9 May. I came downstairs to feed both Dan and Archie, but tragically Dan didn't seem keen to get off his bed to greet me, as one of his legs wasn't working. When I encouraged him, it was clear that he very much wanted to stand up but was physically unable to do so.

Kate came down and we both tried to establish what the problem was. We checked his paws in case he had stood on something, ran our hands over his pads to check for cuts etc, and Kate massaged his limb in case he had strained a muscle, but nothing came to light. We telephoned the vet, who asked to see him, so I carried him to the car and we set off leaving Archie at home. All this time, Dan was wagging his tail enjoying the attention, but the vet was not so happy. After a long consultation, we were advised to leave him for half an hour so he could be kept under observation. This we duly did and went into Sheringham to have a cup of coffee. We had just finished when the vet rang and asked us to return to the practice, where she told us that he had probably had a stroke during the night, and whilst he was with them, he had had another one which had affected two more of his legs. Clearly this was not good for him, and the only kind thing to do was to put him out of his misery.

The vet, who knew both Dan and Archie well, agreed that we should go home to fetch Archie, in order that he could say goodbye to his lifelong companion. Whilst we were away, they prepared Dan and it was to be just one single injection.

We returned and it was clear that Archie was very aware that things were not right. He sniffed around Dan and was also very concerned that both his Master and Mistress were obviously distressed. We reassured him and whilst one of the nurses took him away with a treat, we gave Dan a hug, stroked and talked to him whilst he went quietly to sleep. Archie was then brought back, and he seemed to understand that Dan was no longer with us, and incredibly, as before, he was more concerned about Kate and I being deeply upset. After reassuring him again, and before we made our way home, we chose a casket for Dan and completed all the necessary paperwork. We felt very lost with bringing only one dog back with us.

Following Dan's cremation, we were able to collect his ashes a few days later, and we buried him in one of his favourite locations in our garden. The photograph was taken in happier times on Rock beach, Dan with a red collar and Archie wearing a blue one, at a time when they had both enjoyed our 2021 holiday in Cornwall (Fig. 588).

It took Archie a good couple of months to become used to Dan not being around, for out of the two, Dan was very much the leader, so that made things difficult for Archie to understand. By the end of the summer though, he had come to terms with the change and was content to be a single dog. However, we had noticed that at night he very rarely slept on his bed, which they had both shared, preferring to sleep in the drawing room.

That was the end of a wonderful and loving relationship between us humans and Dan and Archie. But in time a new and just as tender relationship was to be built between Archie, a new friend and ourselves. I will elaborate more on that later. For now though, life proceeded in a new way for all of us. RIP Dan.

Figure 588

Later in the month, something that Kate had always desired came to fruition in the garden, when we added two olive trees to our paved area, outside the kitchen. Being around eight foot tall and in matching terracotta pots they certainly enhanced the garden and along with the herbs and geraniums that Kate and I had planted, the area had quite a mediterranean feel about it. So, Kate's wishes had been fulfilled.

At the end of May, Em, Pete *et al* came to stay for a short break, along with Oliver, Jude and their two children. Despite it being windy and cold, we all had a lovely walk from Blakeney, through the grounds of Wiveton Hall and back. Whilst the weather was inclement and a little breezy, the children seemed very happy on the play equipment, and we all had a good lunch in one of the Wiveton café outdoor huts, that overlooked the marshes and out to the sea.

On 24 July it was our Pearl Wedding Anniversary. I have to confess that as I had misunderstood the dates, I had bought Kate's present, a pearl pendant necklace and matching earrings, a year prior to this date. Luckily, I knew where I had hidden them, so I wrapped them up and gave them to Kate over dinner. She also presented me with my present which was a lovely personalised, embossed 30th wedding anniversary plaque. We were both delighted with our gifts, so all was well. We had a delicious, celebratory dinner at The Lodge at Salhouse, a restaurant which we had not been to before and it was well worth the visit.

Something that both Kate and I really enjoy seeing, both in our garden and when we are out on walks, are birds, butterflies and bees etc. We aren't avid naturalists but seeing nature as it should be, free and in abundance does give us much pleasure. So, when in early June, an opportunity came along to visit Wheatfen nature reserve, to see the swallowtail butterflies, which are relatively rare, we could not resist going. Whilst we wandered around we came across a group of 'mini experts', with their binoculars and cameras at the ready and listening to the reserve wardens, who told them where and when the butterflies had been visible. Alas, there were none to be seen, so we walked on alone for a while and then stopped beside a bunch of sweet williams. We thought it rather odd, to find a spray of cut flowers tied to a post, until one of the other rangers arrived

Figure 589

and told us that the swallowtail butterflies really like these flowers. So, these had been put out to attract them which made total sense and worked, as within a few minutes, Kate and I saw a swallowtail land a few feet away from us. Word soon spread, and it wasn't long before other people arrived to view and photograph it. This was a very special sighting, especially for me as I had never seen one before. The photograph (Fig. 589) was taken in 2022, by one of the rangers.

The following week, Kate and I visited an 'open garden' at The Old Rectory in Syderstone (Fig. 590). It was stunning with beautiful roses and wildlife areas full of white camassia, and the latter inspired Kate to plant some in our own wild garden.

Figure 590

Having lived in Holt for several years, and now having had the desire to write my memoir, I decided that the first task was to sort out all the storage boxes of 'treasures', that had not been unpacked since our move. What I didn't realise though, was that the boxes which were distributed around the house, plus in the loft, and in the garage, extended back to a time when both Kate and I were single, and leaving home for the first time. As a consequence, the 'treasures' which were to be included in this memoir not only had to be sorted and shared, but also the relevant stories chronologically organised. This was, for both of us not only very cathartic, revealing and interesting but also took an incredibly long time!

Figure 591

Still, we both agreed that the task should be tackled head on. Suffice to say that our exploits certainly took ages, and even as I write this, in November 2023, Kate (Fig. 591) was still updating and adding a narrative to her photographs, as well as cross checking her diaries that dated back to 1973! Without this research this memoir would have been almost impossible to write and illustrate. So again, as I have in my acknowledgements, I thank Kate for her patience and diligence. All this preparation enabled me to commence writing on 5 July 2023. At the end of November, some five months later, the first draft of Part One was almost ready for reading and editing. Then, following a full review, I anticipated being able to complete the writing by February 2025, which would then take me through to my 70th year, which was when I intended to conclude my narrative.

Unfortunately, whilst Mum had been very happy in her new home, her overall health had reflected her age of 92, and she had had another fall that again required a visit to hospital. Luckily, it wasn't as bad as her previous falls, that she had now forgotten all about, and after a thorough check-up she returned to her care home.

The staff were very concerned about her, so my sisters and I, as her next of kin, had a conversation with the manager about her wellbeing, and what might be the outcome in the next few months. Whilst this was difficult, it was necessary and professional. I don't recall similar conversations with Dad's care home which looking back is regrettable.

In early July, Kate and I had the opportunity to have a sail on the *Albion*, one of the few Norfolk Wherries that are still on the broads. This was organised by our court social club, so all the sailors and crew were well known to us all. It was a lovely, sunny day and the sailing was fantastic. Commencing after lunch, we sailed for around an hour and a half down the river Thurne and then returned to Womack Water where she was permanently berthed. This took slightly longer as during the return we were sailing windward which meant we were 'beating against the wind'.

Figure 592

Both Kate and I each took a turn at the helm, which was not as easy as the more experienced skipper made it look. *Albion* is a large craft, and you really had 'to put your back into it', as seen in the photograph of Kate (Fig. 592). The other passengers were not so keen, preferring to simply enjoy the sail and sunshine (Fig. 593) which for them was just as enjoyable.

Figure 593

On the last day of July, we and my immediate family collected the final items from Necton that needed to be sorted at home. This was followed on 3 August, with the arrival at Mum's bungalow of the clearance company, who removed all the large pieces of furniture along with the other smaller bits and pieces that were no longer required. Then once empty the property was thoroughly cleaned, ready for its new occupants, and as I have said the exchange and completion were finalised at the end of August. It was the end of an era, with the last home of our parents having now been sold.

As the saying goes 'when one door closes another opens', and our other door was our family holiday. This was to be a 'first', because we were not going to be in Norfolk, instead we were in Gloucestershire. This Cotswold holiday had been organised for over two years, mainly by Kate, and it resulted in us staying in two enormous adjoining barns, in the village of Doughton which had been made famous through King Charles III, having his private residence, Highgrove, on the edge of the village.

As I mentioned earlier, regrettably Sophie and Leigh decided that it would be wiser for them not to join us, as Leigh's WhatsApp message in February had outlined. So, after attending his grandmother's 70th birthday celebration, Sophie and Leigh brought Ben over to Doughton and they then returned back to Tadley.

Regrettably, it was only for a week, but what a week! We had a wonderful time, and the grandchildren loved all being together. In some cases, they shared bedrooms and on the last night the largest bedroom was made into a dormitory, with some of them sleeping in beds, whilst others were on the floor! Whilst the holiday was great it was also exhausting for the adults but the bonds and memories that the children now share made it all so worthwhile.

During that week we visited the Cotswold Country Park and beach where the youngsters and some of their parents went paddling (Fig. 594). Left to right are Oliver, Em, Pete and Kate all obscuring various grandchildren! A visit to Tetbury Police Station Museum which whilst small, was very good and thoroughly enjoyed by the children and adults alike. A walk through Westonbirt Arboretum, was a hit with its many trees available for climbing, as were the outdoor games at Tinkley Gate. Blackberry picking in the countryside around the barns where we were staying seemed to be a definite favourite, especially with the children as they were able to eat the berries straight off the bush. Afterwards some of them helped Grannie to make

Figure 594

blackberry and apple crumble for supper, so they were lucky enough to eat more blackberries, again!

In the main barn there was a balcony which overlooked the kitchen and the adjoining drawing room. This became a favourite place for the grandchildren where they made umpteen paper aeroplanes, and then had a great game to see whose plane would either fly the furthest or land on top of an adult. Naturally, the grown-ups had to fly them back and scored a 'hit' if theirs landed on one of the children.

All the rafters over both these rooms were 'decorated' with long balloons, which Eve had brought with her and blown up. She made quite a few balloon characters, mainly sausage dogs, but to have the balloons all the way around the two rooms seemed to take preference. The art of balancing a table mat on your head (Fig. 595) was also a great game! It was obviously important that even the youngest should be allowed to join in (Fig. 596)!

Figure 595

Figure 596

In order that the cooking of supper was shared, the grown-ups had all agreed that each couple would provide and cook two meals, and everyone would help with the washing up, which worked really well. However, there was one 'special' meal that was to be a surprise. Pete was due to celebrate his 60th birthday later in the year, and as we were all together Em decided that a special lunch for him would be rather good. Kate found a pub just outside Tetbury, with a private room which was ideal for our family celebration. The meal was really good, and Pete had no idea what was happening until a traditional birthday cake with candles was presented to him, at the end of the meal!

REFLECTIONS UPON A FAMILY

Figure 597 *Figure 598*

One slightly quieter activity was painting outside in the garden (Fig. 597). This gave time for some of the adults to start packing for the return home. However, there was one promise that had to be fulfilled. All the children had been promised a 'sleepover' in one bedroom on the final night. The promise was kept, as I have said and to our surprise, whilst it started rowdy it wasn't long before the bedroom floor was strewn with various sleeping children. A sign of a good and most enjoyable holiday!

Our final breakfast was served, enjoyed and cleared away (Fig. 598). This time without the head gear. All in all, the holiday was a great success, and the view was that the concept of a family holiday should be repeated, if finances allowed, in a couple of years' time.

I am not sure what state the other grown-ups were in, but certainly Kate and I were delighted that it had all gone well but we were certainly worn out. Having anticipated this, I had booked a five-day break in Bourton-on-the-Water, in a hotel where we could relax and recover.

We had already agreed to meet Sophie and Leigh at our hotel, so that Ben could go home with them. So, once we had all departed the barns, we drove from Doughton to Bourton, stopping en route in Painswick to visit a Rococo Garden which was full of tree sculptures that Ben thoroughly enjoyed exploring. On reaching the hotel we parked the car and in fact didn't use it for an entire week, such was the 'entertainment' in the town.

Chapter 7 Life in Retirement 2014 – 2025

Whilst we awaited the arrival of Sophie and Leigh, Ben, Kate and I went for a walk around, over the bridges and beside its famous river, the Windrush. Despite the cold water, children of all ages were playing in the river, but for short periods only! Having suggested that Ben also went in, he was not so sure. That view suddenly changed though, when I threw a pound coin into the water for him to collect and keep. It was most certainly cold, but he was a pound better off (Fig. 599)!

Figure 599

That was soon spent on an ice cream, of all things, which then required a further financial contribution from Grandpa! Having dried off, warmed up and then consumed his ice cream he was united with his family and Barney their dog, and made his way home in the comfort of his parents' car.

The following day, with just Kate and I, there was to be a very different river experience. Unbeknown to us, it was the annual water football match. Now with my limited understanding of football, I had always thought that it was played on grass and the objective was to score a goal by kicking the ball into the opponent's goal. This certainly didn't correlate with the rules that were in operation on that day.

Firstly, it was played in the river, and secondly, the objective seemed to be to make as many of the spectators, that included us, as wet as possible! If any of the team happened to kick the ball in a goal at either end that was a happy coincidence. On a serious note though, it did raise a good sum of money for several local charities. Plus, it was great entertainment, as can be seen in the photographs (Figs. 600 & 601). We never did find out the actual score as this

Figure 600

Figure 601

527

seemed to differ depending on who you asked! But it was great fun and most entertaining whilst it also, of course, supported several local charities.

The following days were certainly restful and most enjoyable. We had meals out each day with all but one of the venues being superb. The disaster was a local pub which was holding a pub quiz on the night. Would that interfere with our meal we asked, '*oh no sir, it's in the other bar*', was the response. Whilst the actual quiz and the contestants were indeed in the other bar, the quizmaster and his microphone were next to us! A lesson learnt – check all the arrangements before booking!

Back in my childhood, I recall a family holiday with my parents in Bourton-on-the-Water and we wandered around the model village, which is a one-ninth scaled replica of the centre of the actual village itself. Kate and I renewed my visit (Fig. 602) and most of it was just as I had recalled. What I didn't realise though, was that it was updated every so often, with new houses that had been built or new frontages that had been added (Fig. 603), in the actual centre of the village. So, with these additions the replica truly reflected the area as it currently stood. The ongoing management really was a remarkable undertaking.

Figure 602

Figure 603

We had a visit around the town's Motor Museum which included not only cars and bicycles, but also numerous items all connected to the transport theme. It was fascinating but a little disconcerting seeing many exhibits in a museum that we both recalled from our childhood. On another day, we spent a relaxing time at the Birdland Park and Gardens and our final walk with Archie was to Greystones Nature Reserve. This was wonderfully peaceful whilst we meandered through the wildflower meadows and listened to all the birdsongs.

Chapter 7 Life in Retirement 2014 – 2025

Following the conclusion of our holidays, back in Norfolk on 3 September, we joined Oliver to go and see Mum, who was very pleased to see us and appeared to be well. Following a good chat, we left and the three of us had a lovely pub lunch. Whilst there wasn't a specific reason for this, there were in fact two events that called for a celebration. Firstly, it was eight years to the day that we had moved into Hanworth House and secondly, after five years of my participation in the Add-Aspirin trial, it was the last day for me to take a tablet! Both of these occasions, from my perspective, had been a success.

Figure 604

Later that month, we both enjoyed a lovely day out on a guided tour of St. Benet's Abbey (Fig. 604).[44] We had often seen this in the distance or from the river but had never actually been to the site. It was a protected site managed by the Norfolk Archaeological Trust who described it as:

'The Abbey of St. Benet at Holme lies deep in the Broads, close to the meeting place of the rivers Bure and Ant. This was the only Norfolk monastery founded in the Anglo-Saxon period which continued in use throughout the Middle Ages and is the only monastery in England which was not closed down by Henry VIII – the Bishop of Norwich is still the Abbot.'

Our visit was really interesting and gave both of us the opportunity to see the ruins, close up and with an expert guide.

On 25 September, we learnt the tragic news that Jude's father, after a long battle with Parkinson's and other related conditions, had passed away in hospital. We obviously sent our sympathies and asked if we could attend his funeral.

This was gratefully accepted but what we didn't understand was that his funeral, on 18 October, was a Buddhist and Taoist ceremony. This was not something that either of us had experienced before and we found it very moving and were very pleased to be able to attend and support Jude and her family. At the end of the year, Jude and Eve flew over to Hong Kong with her wider family, to lay her father's ashes in the family village.

After the distress of Jude's loss, she and Oliver took a short break at a country club, just outside Norwich, whilst we looked after Eve and Zoey. Whilst the circumstances weren't ideal, we did enjoy having both the grandchildren to

---

[44] https://images.app.goo.gl/WGaNJHBhmssfx9bU7

stay on their own, for the very first time. On the 28th, they certainly enjoyed the Halloween Spider Trail through Sheringham Park, and a different Halloween Trail in our local garden centre. After which we all met up with Oliver and Jude for a lovely lunch at the country club.

Towards the end of October, we had a long chat with Em on the telephone, regarding Libby and her current status pertaining to her autism and other ongoing concerns. We were aware that she had not been happy at all at her special school, and as agreed by the teaching staff, she had had a number of weeks when she had not attended. But as she knew that she would have to return to the school at some time or other, she had now started to behave in a detrimental way to herself whilst at home. At the time, this behaviour gave everyone serious concerns and it would continue to do so. So, from a practical and welfare context, Em said that reluctantly they did not think it would be wise for them to come to Holt for Christmas, which is what they usually did. We totally understood this and assured her that we would find a different way of seeing them all, where Libby would be comfortable in her own surroundings.

On 11 November, Kate and I had agreed to join a guided tour around the Guildhall in Norwich which at one time was the main centre for justice in Norfolk. This again had been organised by our court social club and it started at 11.15, which gave us time beforehand, to attend the Remembrance Ceremony for Armistice Day, which was always held outside the City Hall. As I have written previously, on these occasions I always had in my pocket, my dad's war medals and his father's small bible, so that I felt that they were part of the day, and that day I had privately repeated this tradition.

The visit to the Guildhall was very good and most informative, made even more interesting by the extensive, historical and encyclopaedic knowledge of our guide, and we heard facts about Norwich that none of our group knew. For instance, that in 1404, when Norwich was the second largest city in England, Henry IV endowed the city of Norwich with a civic charter and proclaimed it to be a county in its own right, inside the wider county of Norfolk. This 15th century status remained in place until 1 April 1974 when it was changed under The Local Government Act of 1972. This revelation was a complete surprise to all of us.

A view of the Guildhall, as it looked in 2023, is shown in figure 605.[45] Our very knowledgeable guide took us to the Undercroft, where prisoners had been held

---

45 Picture credit – Norwich360.com

Chapter 7 Life in Retirement 2014 – 2025

Figure 605

prior to execution. The cellars (Fig. 606) actually pre-date the Guildhall and were thought to be part of the original Toll House which stood on the site, prior to the Guildhall being built.

The door (Fig. 607) was thought to be the original one from when the Guildhall cellars were used as prison cells and was thought to have been crafted between 1407 and 1413. It looked most intimidating, which was probably just to remind the prisoners of the severity of their crimes and the harshness of their sentence.

We also viewed the various court rooms, including Court number 1 (Fig. 608), which was also known as the Sword Room, where our guide explained the layout and how the courts were conducted. However, some traditions haven't changed in 500+ years, for at the time of writing this text, in the Great Yarmouth Court, which is a new modern building, the magistrates are still proceeded by one of the ushers, who carries a sword which is then placed under the royal crest behind the Bench!

Figure 606

Figure 607

Figure 608

I have to say that this Magistrates' Court in the Guildhall gave a much more serious impression than Norfolk's modern-day replacement. The style of this court of justice must have certainly helped to confirm the seriousness of being taken to court. Something that some of the present-day criminals just seem to accept as part of life, which does not help their rehabilitation.

In mid-November we both had the opportunity to listen to the author Elly Griffiths being interviewed (Fig. 609) about her recent books. She had written numerous murder mysteries and was a favourite author of Kate's. Whilst I had not read any of her books and was unfamiliar with the characters and plots, like Kate I was fascinated to hear how the stories developed and why particular Norfolk locations were chosen. It was a great evening and afterwards I purchased as Christmas presents for Kate, Elly's two latest books which she personally signed for me.

Figure 609

As I have previously explained, whilst I was writing this memoir Kate had been sorting hundreds of photographs into years and then wrote the dates and locations on the back of each one. At the end of 2023, she was at a point where the most difficult images needed to be identified. This was to involve her checking her previous diary entries, contained within her own collection that extended back 50+ years to 1973, along with those of her mother's which went back to 1955 – now that is a date I recognise, is that a coincidence or not? Having ascertained the possible locality of each of these unidentified images, she then had to either carry out a search on Google or where necessary on Google Earth, and check alongside each photograph to confirm its location. It was both methodical and exhausting work but so rewarding, knowing that most of the photographs had finally been dated and their identity determined. Kate's diligence and tenacity is so commendable and much appreciated by me and hopefully will be by future generations!

The end of 2023 was fast approaching and on 14 November, with our friends Polly and Phil, we watched the Holt Christmas lights being switched on. It always made me feel very Christmasy seeing the High Street, the Market Place and many of the yards all illuminated with lovely twinkly and shimmering decorations.

As you would expect, the shop windows were always full of Christmas wares, which no doubt would soon be replaced with merchandise, ready for the Boxing Day/January sales.

Chapter 7 Life in Retirement 2014 – 2025

The switch-on was always followed with a superb display of fireworks (Fig. 610).[46]

On 12 December we received photographic confirmation that Jude and Eve (Fig. 611) had arrived safely in Hong Kong, after a 15-hour flight via Helsinki.

So, Christmas 2023 and the New Year for 2024 was very different for our family. Jude and Eve were in Hong Kong, laying Jude's father to rest with his family ancestors. Oliver and Zoey came to us at Hanworth House, which was a lovely surprise, whilst Em and her family stayed in Chessington, as this was a known familiar and 'safe' environment for Libby. Sophie, Leigh and Ben had already been to see us for a weekend in November, so they remained in Tadley.

Figure 610

We managed to chat to all three families on Christmas Day and then on 31 December to surprise three of our grandchildren we drove down to see the Joneses, to celebrate the New Year with them which was lovely. All of which concluded another super year.

Figure 611

---

46 Picture credit – Love Holt

533

2024

On 1 January, we started the year with Em, Pete, Libby, Leo and Frankie. We had all seen the New Year in and watched the television coverage of the London fireworks display, which was really most impressive. After which Kate and I returned to our hotel, for what was left of the night! In the morning, we all met up again and visited the RHS gardens at Wisley. The weather was kind, and the visit was a great success (Fig. 612).

Figure 612

Upon our return to Holt, we booked up a Valentine Day stay at the Dial House B&B in Reepham, using our gift voucher that Em and Pete had kindly given to us as a Christmas present. During our stay we treated ourselves to a massage and in the evening a meal at the local Kings Arms restaurant. All most enjoyable and a lovely, unexpected gift.

In addition to this 'luxury', we had been invited to join Oliver, Jude and family on a summer holiday. So, Kate did a lot of research and found an ideal location not far from Perugia in Umbria, central Italy and the holiday was booked for August. It was something to look forward to, during the cold winter days.

Despite having taken all the decorations down, for Kate and me Christmas finally concluded on 11 January, as that was the evening we attended the last night's performance of *It's Christmas, Carol* by the Blakeney Players (Fig. 613). As always, it was written by one of their own troupe and performed by the amateur dramatic group. It was really very good, as all their previous plays had been, and at times they had the audience in absolute fits of laughter. It certainly finished one year nicely and set us up for the start of 2024, perfectly.

Figure 613

Chapter 7 Life in Retirement 2014 – 2025

Just over a week later, I sat at my computer, on the corner of the kitchen table, and felt very smug. It was 22 January, and not only had we survived the overnight battering from storm Isha, that had lashed the UK with rain and 99 mph winds (69 mph in North Norfolk) but I had finally finished reading and editing my first draft of this memoir up to the end of 2023. On 2 February, with the text having been drafted through to the end of last year, we made an appointment to meet both my potential printer and our graphic designer. It was really interesting to hear their comments and see examples of some of the books that they had previously produced. I very much hoped in the months leading up to my 70th birthday in 2025, that I would have concluded all my alterations and commissioned them to print a hardback book for my family and friends to read at their leisure. The meeting was very successful, and we came away feeling very positive.

Since my father died having lived with dementia, for some time I had been very concerned about my own health as I seemed to be losing my memory. As I approached 70, this simply could have been a natural progression, but by comparison to Kate, who was five years older than me, my loss seemed to be more intense. Despite having seen my doctor in 2021, who carried out a very simple memory test and referred me for a head scan, the result of which was 'normal', none of these actions reassured me at all. So, at the end of January 2024, I spoke to a different doctor, who this time recommended that I undertook a Memory Assessment, that I will explain in more detail later on. However, whilst I awaited that test, my doctor prescribed 20mg of Citalopram. This was an antidepressant which I was to take daily and would help reduce my levels of anxiety, which proved to be very helpful. I had been informed that a full assessment could last around two hours. Having agreed to this, I hoped that the appointment of a consultant would materialise in the next few months and that the results would prove to be negative.

Regrettably, February was a very difficult month for the family. Just over a year ago, Mum had moved permanently into the local care home, where previously she had had a respite stay. Both my sisters, their families, Kate and I and friends from Necton had been visiting regularly, and for the first few months Mum was very comfortable, mobile and lucid. It was clear though, that her loss of memory was now causing her and her loved ones concern and during the last six months her health had also declined which was an additional cause for concern. She then was to take a turn for the worst.

Kate and I received a call from the care home on 21 February to say that Mum was close to leaving us and it would be wise to come and say our last goodbyes. With that I telephoned Sarah and Judy to advise them both of the situation. Judy, who had just returned from a birthday visit to Edinburgh, packed a bag for her and David, and they set off from their home in Lesbury, Northumberland, to join us at the care home.

Over the next day Mum slept for most of the time and her breathing was very laboured. During the next 24 hours, most of her grandchildren were able to visit her and Mum was able to give the occasional facial indication of recognition, so I was sure that she knew that her family were close by.

On the 24th, Judy, David, Sarah, Roger and I, along with Kate, stayed with her through to the late evening, at which time she appeared very stable, so we all agreed that we would leave, and would return the next day. We discussed this with the night staff who agreed that they would call me should her condition deteriorate. We all left and made our way home, except Judy and David who went back to where they were staying locally. En route home, I had a message from David to say that Judy had left her mobile phone behind at the care home, so would I call him should they need to return before the morning.

At 02.30 the next morning on the 25th, I had a call from Stuart, a member of the night staff, to say that Mum's breathing had changed, and it would be wise for us all to return. Whilst on this call which had lasted only a couple of minutes, Stuart had gone into Mum's room to check something with a member of staff, who was quietly sitting with her. It was at that point that he uttered the words *'she's passed, I'm so sorry'*. There was nothing I or anyone else could do. The last of her generation of Gosdens had left us.

I telephoned Roger and Sarah who, after knocking over a glass of water in the process of answering the telephone, made their way to the care home and were the first to arrive. I called David several times, but there was no answer, so we left home to join Sarah and Roger. Sarah had also called David quite a few times as well, equally without success. As protocol dictated, the home had called a doctor, and I was pleased to hear that Roger and Sarah had been present when she had arrived. The doctor signed the Death Certificate that recorded Mum's death at 04.30. Kate and I arrived just after she had left, and the four of us spoke to the staff. We were all really upset, of course, but given the previous breathing concerns we were not surprised. We all left Mum in the care of the night staff and drove home to have some breakfast, exhausted and very emotional having been up since 02.30 that morning.

Later, Judy telephoned and to me sounded bright and breezy, to find out how we all were, which at the time was appreciated. However, she was clearly totally oblivious to the fact Mum had died and that both I and Sarah via David's mobile, had been endeavouring to contact her. Needless to say, she was very distressed and annoyed that she and David had not been advised. I attempted to explain the steps which both Sarah and I had taken to avoid this happening but given Judy's state of despair she just put the telephone down on me. I was, and still am, annoyed by her response. But this is something that I have had to come to terms with, as neither Judy nor David have ever accepted any responsibility for not having answered our mobile calls. I appreciated that the night before, Judy had left her telephone behind at the care home, but why she didn't undertake the short journey back to retrieve it and why David's mobile was not accepting early morning calls, we shall never know. For not having their mobiles available no apology has ever been offered by either of them, which was and still is so unfortunate. In fact, the opposite occurred when later I was reprimanded by David for the content of the call. This didn't help the situation and was unwarranted, but history is history.

Anyway, Mum died peacefully having spent a wonderful life on this earth, which lasted 92 years and 320+ days. During which she enjoyed 62 years of marriage to my father and brought up three children. As she often used to say to me, during her time at the care home, it's been good, but I am now ready to go.

Her obituary (Fig. 614) followed the release of her death certificate. It was written by me, Judy and Sarah and placed in *The Eastern Daily Press*, our regional newspaper.

DAPHNE GOSDEN

Published on 09/03/2024

GOSDEN DAPHNE Passed away peacefully on Sunday, February 25th, 2024, aged 92 years. Wife of Len (deceased), Mum to Judy, Keith and Sarah, Mum-in-law to David, Kate and Roger, Grandmother and Great-Grandmother. Private family cremation followed by Thanksgiving Service at All Saints' Church, Necton on Wednesday, March 20th at 2.30 p.m., all welcome. Family flowers only. Donations to Alzheimer's Society or Necton Church.

Figure 614

My birthday was the following day on 26 February, and I was pleased that this was not going to be forever linked to my mother's death. As it was, I was joined on the day by David, the friend who I regularly walked with and we both had a lovely ramble with Archie, my and Kate's old and faithful dog. Firstly, we drove a few miles just outside Holt and then we walked through the fields which led us down to the Dun Cow pub in Salthouse. Here, we were joined by our wives, Kate and Eleanor, and we all had a splendid lunch together, after which the ladies returned home and David, Archie and I retraced our steps back to our car, where we concluded our walk.

The next few weeks were a whirlwind of telephone calls, text messages and meetings to sort out the arrangements for Mum's cremation and Service of Thanksgiving. She had meticulously drafted all the details for both these services, so on that front there wasn't a lot of work for us to do. We had a constructive meeting though, with Mum's local vicar who, having checked through her drafts, compiled a formal order of service for the thanksgiving. Given that my two sisters were more knowledgeable on religious matters than me, I passed Mum's cremation draft to them and suggested that they might like to arrange this part of the day. Once everything was organised, the three of us chose a photograph of Mum to go on the front of each service sheet. The order of services were then printed by the funeral directors and with the flowers agreed and ordered, we were well prepared for Mum's cremation which was immediately followed by the Thanksgiving Service. I have to say that Mum, my two sisters and the vicar did a wonderful job and produced two very moving services.

On 4 March 2024, I had a telephone call from Sophie to say, after a long discussion with Leigh, that she had decided to take a full break from employment, in the hope that this would help her mental health. Whilst this may have seemed extreme to us, we all felt that it was a wise decision. I just hoped that at some point, when she was fully recovered, she would be able to return to a career that she clearly both enjoyed and in which she was extremely competent.

On 15 March, Kate's birthday was celebrated with me and Archie when we had a most relaxing walk around Holkham Hall estate. The sun shone, the birds were singing and luckily the deer, who normally graze on the grass around the trees, were well away next to the lake. So, this meant that Archie could roam off his lead, at his own pace. Following the walk, we had a lovely lunch in the Victoria hotel, prior to strolling down Queen Anne's Drive to the seashore. Here we sat quietly just soaking up the sea air and observing nature welcoming the arrival of spring. A wonderful day!

Later that week, we had a guided tour around one of the 'hidden' streets under Castle Meadow in Norwich. The street, which ran along the course of the old castle moat, was built in the late 1400s and had a number of tenements which were occupied by families of weavers who worked in this industry. Some of whom were really young children from just five years of age upwards!

The conditions were appalling with no evidence of a fresh water supply or drainage. Water was fetched from wells, dotted around the city, whilst sewage was dumped close to the tenements, in the ditch around the castle. The picture

Figure 615

Chapter 7 Life in Retirement 2014 – 2025

(Fig. 615)[47] shows one of the houses hidden under Castle Meadow, which in 2024 was the main road next to Norwich Castle.

Sometimes you can have a 'wonderful' day, not because it's a birthday or a celebration but simply because the day is thought provoking, well organised and gives you a sense of pride. This was the case on 20 March when Kate and I, along with other family members attended Mum's cremation. After which in her local church in Necton, the thanksgiving service (Fig. 616) took place with both her family and friends in attendance.

At the second service Oliver gave a beautiful eulogy that was both humorous and thoughtful. He was very nervous, but the delivery was excellent and Kate and I were very proud of him. Mum now rests with Dad in Necton churchyard and some of her ashes have been united with his, on Grambrough Hill in Salthouse. This was a favourite place for both of them to bird watch and as such had allowed us to fulfil their wishes.

Figure 616

I have included a photograph, taken by Jude in Necton Church on the day of the thanksgiving. Left to right are Judy, myself and Sarah standing behind our mother's floral tribute (Fig. 617).

Despite the sobering last few days, the month concluded with some very positive news.

Ben had been working very hard in Cubs, in order to achieve his Silver Award, the highest one he could gain, prior his moving up into the Scout Troop. He accomplished this and on Monday 25 March, was presented by the local Mayor with his badge and

Figure 617

---

47 Photo credit, Daniel Tink. Shoebox Enterprises.

certificate (Fig. 618), at a formal ceremony in the local Council Chamber, near his home.

He was, quite rightly so, very proud as were both his parents and his Grannie and Grandpa. Scouting now beckoned for Ben, with more opportunities to develop additional skills, and for him to build his self-confidence whilst also having great fun.

Figure 618

Regrettably, the good news didn't last for as long as I had hoped. For as I have mentioned previously, for a couple of years I had been concerned about my own health. In December 2021, I had seen Dr Clarke, as I thought I was demonstrating symptoms of dementia /Alzheimer's. My father had died of this condition, and it had also been considered a contributary complication to my mother's recent death. Thankfully, in 2021 I had been assured that I didn't have the early stages of dementia or any of the other neurological conditions. However, over two years later the symptoms still persisted, in addition I was having nightly hallucinations and during the day was short-tempered and was demonstrating forgetfulness and irritability.

As a result, on 26 January 2024, as I have already alluded to, I attended the surgery again for some further guidance on how I could overcome the three key symptoms, and return to my previous demeanour, which was not being forgetful etc., or indeed anxious and snappy. Kate accompanied me again, as she too was concerned about my apparent changes of mood. This time I had asked to see Dr Kopelman, whom we both liked and were always very assured by her expertise.

I explained to her the most recent symptoms, and I felt that my possible dementia had, in my view, most definitely become more acute. I described to her how this had manifested itself in that I often couldn't recall simple facts, like the day of the week, people's names and what I was doing in a particular activity. Frequently I was unable to recall the word(s) that I wanted to say, that meant conversations had to be abandoned, which on many occasions was really embarrassing. Recently, I had also found that when I was using a computer, which I spent years doing whilst working, I was forgetting how to do simple tasks that previously were undertaken without a second thought. I appreciated that this could have been related to an update in software, but whilst I was in employment when upgrades were previously carried out, this particular symptom was not prevalent. Sometimes I would start something and then halfway through couldn't recall what I should be doing – like getting ready to go out and knowing I needed gloves but then not remembering what I needed to find. Lastly, I certainly didn't seem to have the patience that I had had previously, and thought perhaps this was simply a sign of old age. I was not sure. So, all these symptoms were explained in great detail to Dr Kopelman, who was incredibly understanding.

Back in 2021, Kate had thought like Dr Clarke that I was simply doing too much, and consequently my brain was overloaded. However, in 2024 I found this explanation hard to accept, for since 2021 as suggested by Dr Clarke, I had gradually taken steps to lessen my workload. I had retired from my highly stressful role in Aviva, cut down my court sittings from Crime and Family to just Family and in April stood down as Chair of the Holt Society. I didn't think there was anything else that I could have 'given up'!

I outlined all this to Dr Kopelman who then undertook a short test which was different to the one Dr Clarke had undertaken. After a discussion about my current circumstances and feelings, I was finally offered the opportunity to have an in-depth consultation with Dr Neil Ashford a Consultant Psychiatrist, from the Norfolk and Suffolk NHS Foundation Trust. I accepted this without hesitation as both Kate and I thought this was an excellent opportunity to establish if there was anything at all that we needed to be concerned about. The downside was that there would probably be a six-month waiting list. During this time, I continued to take my 20mg of Citalopram each day, which was certainly helping with my anxiety.

We thanked Dr Kopelman and returned to our everyday lives. However, out of the blue on 2 April, only a matter of a few weeks after my appointment with Dr Kopelman, I received a personal telephone call from Neil Ashford. He asked if he could come on 4 April to see me at home, we agreed a time and he explained what he was intending to talk to me about.

The day arrived and I was very nervous, especially when he stood on our front doorstep. Now, my expectation was to meet a well-presented consultant who looked professional and filled his patients with confidence. However, upon opening the door, I was greeted by a mature gentleman, dressed in jeans, with long white hair who looked for all the world like Professor Einstein, as can be seen here (Fig. 619).[48]

Figure 619

---

48 Photo credit, West Norfolk Dementia Network – Contented Dementia Trust

Having sat down and given him a pen, as he had lost his, we chatted for about 25 minutes with regards to my concerns and life history. During this time my first impressions were to be totally dismissed as he was extremely professional and knowledgeable. Both Kate and I felt very confident and relaxed, as he went on to outline what he proposed to undertake which would take a couple of hours. For me, that meant I had to undergo the dreaded memory test. Unlike my previous ones, this one was much longer, far more in-depth and comprehensive. It went by the snappy title of the Addenbrooke's Cognitive Examination-ACE-III. It was designed to test my attention, orientation, memory, language, visual perceptual and visuospatial skills.

At the conclusion of this test, I had the agonising wait whilst Neil immediately assessed and marked my results. There were a couple of answers that he needed me to clarify by simply answering these questions again. One was the counting of various dots displayed randomly over a sheet of paper. I carefully counted these twice and confirmed my answers. Kate was then asked to count them, and her answer was one more than mine. Neil re-checked my results with me, and I again confirmed that I was happy with my answers. It was a very minor difference but who was correct?

Having had a chat, completed the test, had my re-test confirmed, the whole session took about 90 minutes overall. He then re-evaluated the results which he gave to me, and it was not good news. He confirmed, once and for all, that I was living with the very early stages of Alzheimer's. He was very quick to assure me that this could be treated, and whilst the medication he was going to ask Dr. Kopelman to prescribe, would not offer a cure but it would slow down its progress. He also said that he would write a full report that would be sent to the practice and a copy would be sent to me. This was to contain his email, in order that at any time I could contact him if I had concerns or didn't understand something. It was then that he advised me that his diagnosis was very marginal, hence his double checking of a couple of answers. He would explain all this later in his confirmation letter.

This seemed an odd thing to admit, but I was grateful to now know for certain what was wrong with me and that my suspicions, in 2021, were indeed correct. It was not good news and now I had the awful task of telling my family and our close friends. We both thought this was important as I was, as I have outlined, already having to abandon some conversations due to forgetfulness, which if picked up by them would have been of upmost concern. The opportunity to advise our family presented itself earlier than expected, as Oliver telephoned the next day and wanted to meet up to 'have a chat'. Kate and I thought that this was a little ominous but willingly agreed to meet, a couple of days later for lunch in Newmarket.

Oliver in fact just wanted to 'bounce off' us both some concerns and possible solutions, to ascertain if we thought they were sensible. This was certainly just what I did when I was in business with my father, and we were pleased to assist Oliver. So, having heard his thoughts we certainly concurred with his ideas and strategies. Oliver was always very supportive of his staff and strived to give them the opportunities that would progress their skills. On this occasion though, he was seeking our support in his desire to become more involved, as a Council Member, within his own professional body the Recruitment & Employment Confederation (REC). Kate and I fully supported and encouraged him to pursue this ambition. After this long chat over lunch, I then had the opportunity to outline my health issues and the consultation with Neil Ashford which, given that this was totally unexpected by Oliver, I thought he took it very well. He was not only grateful for being told but was most encouraging in his outlook for what would eventually be the outcome.

I was now faced with the task of talking to both Em and Sophie. Ideally, I wanted to tell them face to face but having just told Oliver I didn't want to delay in telling them as well, as I felt that that was unfair. It was absolutely necessary that this conversation took place straight away, as they would have over time realised something was wrong and would then be faced with an awkward dilemma as to what to do or say. So, I telephoned both of them over the next couple of days. They too were surprised but accepted the situation and were very supportive. I had said to all of them that when I received the official confirmation letter, I would willingly share this information, so they knew as much detail as we did. To put our children into this position was not what Kate and I wanted, and these three conversations were, without doubt, the hardest I have had to carry out since having to support Kate, whilst I told each of them that Angus had died.

A few days later, Neil's letter duly arrived and with some trepidation I began to read its contents. Whilst the outcome was no different to the diagnosis that he had given us, whilst he was with us at home, in that I had the early stages of Alzheimer's, which was a form of dementia. It wasn't quite as bad as I had thought. His letter contained the full results of all the tests that I had carried out during the dreaded consultation. I was to learn that the scoring was out of 100. Working backwards from 100 down to 88 was considered to be normal, whilst between 87 down to 83 was considered to be inconclusive. A score of 82 or below though, was a conclusive dementia result, and I scored 81 which was just into the confirmed dementia range by 1 point. Which was nowhere as bad as I had anticipated.

This was encouraging and I was a little more reassured having read the following words in his letter '*As for the diagnosis I have given you, it is as early in the illness as could possibly be diagnosed which is absolutely* [the] *right time to start treatment for maximum benefit in slowing progression and preserving skills*'. Encouraging indeed, and I was to be prescribed both Donepezil and Mirtazapine, the latter for my sleep problems.

Whilst this was all very frightening and concerning, both Kate and I along with the children were all looking on the positive side. With the certain hope that having had an early diagnosis, and now being prescribed modern drugs that these would slow down the symptoms, as well as the progression of the disease. We knew there was no cure, but to be given longer time to enjoy life with my family was very positive and treasured.

For me, the consequences of Alzheimer's are manifold, as it appears not to be the same each day, which is a little perplexing. One day I am not able to finish sentences and will forget words, which lead to conversations being discontinued. On another day if I think hard before I start to talk, I can revert to a more normal conversation. This dichotomy then leads to frustration and self-consciousness. I guess though, over time, I will come to terms with this, just as family and friends will as well.

Throughout the consultation and whilst I read Neil's letter, I have to admit that I had several constant thoughts. What will happen to Kate and the wider family, when I am gone? How uncomfortable and possibly distressing my journey was going to be to this end? Will I end up in a care home not knowing who I am or to whom I am talking? Will I become marginalised and talked about rather than talked to? I'm sure that these are very similar thoughts that other people have when they have just been diagnosed with an incurable disease, so I don't really want to dwell on this, and will move on and instead consider the issues that probably are going through the minds of my family and friends.

Clearly, they are shocked by the diagnosis but also, I suspect, they are wondering if they should finish my sentences when I can't remember a word, or would that be rude? The answer is that it very much depends on how I am feeling at the time which, of course, is about as much help as an ashtray on a motorbike! It's true though, I never know how I will react – will I be grateful, frustrated, embarrassed or thankful? I regret I simply don't know. What I do know, is that if there are several conversations going on around the table, i.e. during a meal, I find it incredibly difficult to focus on one particular dialogue, in order that I can join in with their discussion. It seems to be easier for me to understand what people are saying if they look at me before they start chatting and make a point of including me in their conflab. Also, if the conversation is a little slower, but not so slow that it's obvious, then when I am thinking of

Chapter 7 Life in Retirement 2014 – 2025

a response my brain seems to be able to support me more actively. Luckily, I don't seem to have lost my sharp, quick sense of humour, which seems to be something that comes naturally, much to the pleasure, I hope, of all my family and friends.

Only the other day whilst sitting in Court, and I hasten to add here not with any of the public present in the courtroom, one of my fellow magistrates commented to a recently appointed one, who was not sure how to react to my repartee, that '*it's always fun when you sit with Keith*'. The provider of this remark was totally unaware of my recent diagnosis, so it was a really good feeling to know that I appeared my normal self!

The reality of life however, hits home every so often – we had an appointment to see our solicitors, to make sure that both our wills still reflected our wishes. Then, once back home, Kate tactfully suggested that we sat down and chatted about any arrangements that I may have thought about for my funeral, so they could be included with all our legal documents! Both these occurrences were very practical and necessary, but they certainly did hit home!

Without a fanfare, spring arrived in early May. The sun began to apply its warmth to the ground, which resulted in trees and flowers waking up, bursting into bloom and dressing for the season. Whilst this was wonderful and for most of the time very welcome, it did result in each week, the lawnmower having to be pressed into action. Regrettably, my little 'grass cutting' helper from 2014, had grown up and was now not available to assist in this sometimes irksome task. The lawn though, did look good each time it had had a haircut.

Another garden that looked very pleasing in the spring sun was that of Oxburgh Hall. Kate and I along with Archie spent a very relaxing day there, at the commencement of the early May Bank Holiday. The views across the meadows, looking towards the Hall were very scenic (Fig. 620). So, it was at this spot that Kate and I sat, relaxed and admired this view, whilst we listened to the cuckoo call in the woods behind us.

Figure 620

It was all quite moving, especially as it was the first cuckoo that we had heard for a number of years. Archie was content with a rest, lying down next to us, followed by a cooling off dip in a large, muddy puddle, as most labradors do!

We spent a lovely day out on 11 May, at Wimpole Hall in Cambridgeshire, where we had met up with Oliver, Jude, Eve, Zoey and for a short while Gillian, Kate's sister, who joined us all for 'elevenses'. The sun came out which made the day even better than expected. Having wandered through the estate we visited the farm, which coincided with feeding time for the pigs! What a cacophony of noise they made! It sounded just like a packed tube station with the hubbub of the heaving passengers trying to board the trains. Only this was pigs and piglets trying to find the food that was being thrown into their pens. Afterwards, much to the delight of Eve and Zoey, we arrived at the adventure playground where they had great fun and then we all sat under a tree and ate ice creams.

Figure 621

A further walk around the estate revealed a perfect little seat for Zoey (Fig. 621), the youngest of our three generations, and for us adults there were impeccable gardens galore that filled us all with envy.

By mid-May, pursuant to my confirmation that no adverse side effects had been experienced from taking the 5mg of Donepezil, my prescription in line with Neil's recommendation was updated by the doctors. As a result, this dosage was increased to the full 10mg and if this too gave no adverse effects, then for maximum benefit the final addition of some Memantine tablets would be prescribed. Hopefully, this would then continue to slow the progress of my Alzheimer's, and I would be able to return to a more normal routine. Time would tell!

Given that May is very much the commencement of the St. John's Ambulance and the National Open Garden Scheme, as in preceding years, we visited several gardens previously unknown to us. Our criteria for selection was very simple, firstly, they should be reasonably local and look inviting, secondly, dogs must be welcomed and finally, they must have homemade cakes and tea! The latter was very much my requirement. All these criteria were met by Blickling Lodge which we visited on 19 May. What a fabulous garden it was too, with its beautiful and very tranquil riverside walks, an enclosed wall garden in which there was a swimming pool, coupled with a full-size cricket pitch in the front garden! It also had some very handsome, centrally heated dog kennels, located on the boundary of the cricket square, shown here on a misty morning (Fig. 622).[49] I suspected these would have impressed Archie, if only he could have understood what they were used for. I recall we spent nearly two hours wandering around the grounds, after which as it was incredibly hot, we sat under a huge parasol whilst we enjoyed the views, and to end a lovely afternoon we simply had to sample the cakes which were definitely most delicious.

Figure 622

The 22 May started damp and became worse as the day progressed. However, there was a dramatic surprise at 18.00 as the Prime Minister, Rishi Sunak, ventured out of Number 10 Downing Street, into torrential rain, to announce that there would be a UK election on 4 July. He appeared with no umbrella and in a suit that obviously became incredibly wet (Fig. 623).[50]

Listening to the radio the next day one MP's comment was *'The image of a man, who says I'm the only one with a plan, standing in the rain without an umbrella is, to put it politely, pretty farcical.'*[51]

Figure 623

---

49 Blickling Lodge, image courtesy of National Open Garden Scheme.org.uk
50 Photo credit – Reuters/MAJA SMIEJKOWSKA
51 Sir Keir Starmer on BBC Radio 4's Today programme (24.05.2024)

That said, the announcement certainly put 'the cat amongst the pigeons,' and whilst an election was legally required by early 2025, it was not expected on 4 July 2024. We were, of course, to await the sabre rattling between the various parties, followed by the outpouring of literature from constituent Members of Parliament, which would inevitably commence in earnest, with visitations from our own local prospective MPs. We were mindful though, at the time, that the opinion polls gave the opposition Labour Party a very healthy lead.

The Conservative Party had been in power for the last fourteen years, which was longer than any of our grandchildren had been on this earth. According to the BBC, during those fourteen years, the country had had five different prime ministers, seven chancellors, eight foreign secretaries and no fewer than sixteen housing ministers! At the time I wondered what my grandchildren's young impressions would be of a General Election?

So, just what did we both do on this momentous day of his announcement? We went to the dentist! Still, pulling teeth is a fair comparison to political broadcasts. We awaited with some trepidation to hear the election results when we awoke on the morning of 5 July.

Our six-monthly checkups with the dentist were more than compensated the following day, by a wonderful walk around the National Trust Sheringham Park, where we were joined by our friend Phil Barrett. At that time of year, the rhododendrons and azaleas were spectacular, their blooms cascading from the bushes into a riot of colours, were just wonderful to see, especially from above whilst standing in the viewing tower. So, all this with convivial company, a cup of tea with a National Trust panini and a piece of cake, was a delight!

Figure 624

Bank Holiday Monday continued the theme of visiting gardens, with a gentle meander around the grounds surrounding the Grade II listed Lexham Hall, situated just outside Swaffham. So, not far away from home, thankfully. I say thankfully for whilst we were enjoying both the gardens and the tea, we also had to dodge the thunderous downpours of rain. The gardens, as you would expect, were beautifully manicured and exhibited many plants in bloom, some known to Kate, others were very new to both of us. The property afforded us the opportunity to meander around the lake and along a three-acre

Chapter 7 Life in Retirement 2014 – 2025

Figure 625 *Figure 626*

woodland path (Figs. 624 and 625). Some of the plants were set out in front of the superb crinkle-crankle wall (Fig. 626) along with many other equally endearing locations. Through the woodland we picked our way around muddy and waterlogged areas and, fortunately, as we were wearing very suitable footwear were able to observe newly hatched ducklings at the water's edge. They appeared to be rather scared at the expanse of water lying between them and the ultimate safety of their mum. We stood to watch, and they all managed to reach her without any mishaps. Plus, we could see that in the adjacent field there was a small flock of newborn lambs and two beautiful swans that were obviously protecting their nest. It was whilst traversing this terrain that we both had to suddenly seek shelter from the torrential rain, and whilst waiting for it to cease we had another unexpected bonus of seeing a young stoat, with its telltale black tip to its tail, also scampering for cover.

The June sun was to confirm that summer was definitely just around the corner, as did the continuing proliferation of gardens that were open to the public. Kate and I continued to take full advantage of these opportunities, so long as they met our criteria and, luckily, all the ones we wanted to visit permitted 'four legged friends'.

During this month, we were also finalising arrangements for our Italian summer holiday in mid-August. With the final balances paid, Kate turned her attention to learning some Italian phrases. A friend of ours who also lives in Holt, not only spoke fluent Italian but also taught the language at the University of the Third Age (U3A), and he kindly offered to help Kate. After just her first lesson, Kate was rehearsing key phrases daily. I had been warned that to assist her memory there would be numerous 'post-it-notes' (Fig. 627) going up around the house, on which would be written these prime phrases. I wasn't sure if I too was supposed to learn these, but having not yet mastered my own native language to the same degree as Kate, learning an additional one would have been a very tall order, indeed!

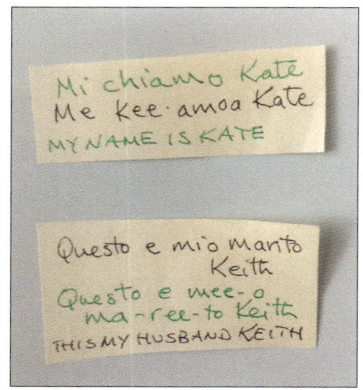

Figure 627

However, quite rightly, Kate was determined to be able to greet people, undertake basic shopping and generally converse in Italian. This would show that she was endeavouring to be polite and had made a concerted effort to communicate in their own language. I was certain that it would work, for when Kate puts her mind to something she is relentless in her endeavours to achieve the required result.

Post-it-notes in Italian were not the only signs of the Mediterranean around our house. Outside our French doors our two olive trees appeared to be either showing signs of having small fruits, or were they possibly new leaf buds? Having not had olive trees previously we had no idea but nonetheless we were very excited. Time would tell if our expectations and hopes were to be realised.

In some respects, June 6 was an ordinary summer's day, except that one significant event took place when Judy, Sarah and I along with our partners David, Roger and Kate, attended a very short interment service in Necton churchyard, where we buried some of our mother's ashes, alongside those of our father. Her remaining ashes, as per her wishes and like those of our father, were then duly scattered, on the same day, by us all at the top of Gramborough Hill, in Salthouse. For me, whilst this was a moving moment of 'closure', somehow it wasn't a sad one at all. They had both lived a wonderful life together, although like all couples they had endured low points, but these were overwhelmed by the far more memorable highs. I would like to think that they were content with their time on this earth and were proud of their many achievements. We, as their children, were certainly immensely proud of them both. Whilst not being as religious as they were, I hoped they had found peace together (Fig. 628).

Figure 628

Chapter 7 Life in Retirement 2014 – 2025

After returning home from Salthouse, Sarah, Roger, Kate and I all enjoyed afternoon tea, in the summer sun, in our garden at Hanworth House. Then, later that evening the four of us returned to Salthouse where we had a superb meal at the Dun Cow pub. Regrettably, Judy and David were not able to join us, and I just wondered if the brother / sister relationship I had with Judy would endure. Unlike my relationship with Sarah, which has always been good, with Judy it is very strained on both sides, and now that our parents have died we simply don't seem to have anything in common – I do hope I am wrong. From my perspective I will continue to keep communications open but the ball is now in Judy's court.

In early June, I contacted Neil my consultant, to arrange a prescription for my next course of medication. This was agreed and I duly collected it from the pharmacist. The pack consisted of four weeks of a daily Memantine tablet and the first week commenced with a 5mg dosage. Thereafter, this was increased by 5mg each week and concluded on the fourth week with a daily 20mg tablet. Subsequently, as I had had no side effects, I would continue to take this for the foreseeable future, along with my Donepezil.

I had now settled into this routine of medication quite well and seemed to have also 'rationalised' myself to living with my condition. This process had not been easy, for at first I instantly thought I had the prospect of exiting this world within the next two or three years. Which to me meant having little or no time to fulfil my ambitions and watch my grandchildren develop into adulthood. A very sobering situation which didn't appeal to me at all. I realised though, by listening to others, especially Kate who was and continues to be a tower of strength, that this was simply not necessarily the case. In fact, I recall whilst out walking with David, the friend with whom I regularly walk, that during a conversation he told me of someone he knew well and who also lived with Alzheimer's. He had had the condition for around 15 years and during that time had also been taking medication. More importantly though, David hadn't noticed any appreciable deterioration in this person's manner or memory. Which I found very encouraging and certainly gave me hope. I have to say that it was something that Kate had consistently said but I clearly needed someone else to tell me, which was where David came in – my belated apologies to Kate!

The conversation with David continued when he enquired about how I was feeling generally about my diagnosis. I tried to explain that I really wasn't able to give a definitive answer, as I couldn't actually see or feel an appreciative improvement since starting all my medication. I told him that I knew Alzheimer's couldn't be cured, like a headache could be by taking a tablet after which you felt much better. Therefore, it was virtually impossible to judge if my memory was stable, or deteriorating and if the latter, was it at the same rate it was prior to my medication?

I explained to David that sometimes I am 'pricked' by my mental ability to recall something that I thought I simply could not remember. I told him that this was an odd feeling and always came as a positive surprise, so much so it made me think that as a result of taking the medication, the degeneration of my memory could be slowing down. David endorsed my belief, and we hoped that my memory loss was indeed going to stabilize. So, after that beneficial chat, we finished our very enjoyable countryside walk and went to the local pub for a drink and a light lunch – which was most pleasurable and far less taxing than the previous conversation!

I would add here that this recall situation still occurs, which is most encouraging for everyone, especially me!

By the middle of June, I was in a much more positive frame of mind than when I awoke on the first day of that month which started as an obvious 'Alzheimer's Day'. For me, the sun now shone both literally and metaphorically and I really felt that life was good and more importantly I definitely had something to offer.

On 25 June, I was sitting in Court, along with two other magistrates, listening and endeavouring to offer solutions to a number of different families, who had issues and personal conflicts that I too had experienced. Thankfully though, not as severe as theirs. Unlike them, I had the excitement of going home to a wonderful wife, a leisurely meal with some friends and then a short walk to watch 'The Pantaloons', in an outdoor performance of Shakespeare's *A Midsummer Night's Dream* (Fig. 629). This might sound rather heavy but as described by the actors, it was delivered as a '*hilarious version of Shakespeare's timeless comedy*' – told as ever in their own distinctive and anarchic style.

Figure 629

We had seen this particular company on several occasions and yet again it was a most welcome and thoroughly amusing experience, in good company, with sunshine and a bottle of wine!

Earlier in the day, whilst having a break from court, I had had lunch in the Cathedral Close, where I reflected upon my first and probably the start of many more embarrassing incidents which I now refer to as being an 'Alzheimer's moment'.

Whilst standing in the queue at the delicatessen, deciding what bap and filling I would like to have prepared for me, the young assistant dutifully asked what I had chosen. That was easy, *'a brown bap with butter and brie and some….'.* then came the embarrassing moment. I knew what I wanted but could not remember what it was called, despite having previously ordered the same lunch, many times, from the same shop. Could I remember, no, I couldn't! I tried to guess and looked around for clues, perhaps the word was on the menu board, but it wasn't, so my stumbling continued. By now the assistant was looking expectantly at me and I was becoming more and more tongue-tied and embarrassed. I endeavoured to describe what I wanted to accompany my brie – *'it's a red sauce with small berries in it',* I said in the vein hope that I would receive the reply *'oh you mean…'* But a blank face persisted before me, from the young lady who was patiently waiting with an open bap in front of her, knife ready for action. Fortunately, her colleague had overheard my dilemma and said, *'cranberry sauce'.* Yes! I excitedly agreed and thanked them both profusely whilst explaining that it was an unexpected Alzheimer's moment! They were both very kind and sympathetic, but I found the entire episode highly embarrassing and frustrating. Luckily, the duly prepared bap was excellent and just what I needed! But, going forward, was this the kind of scenario I was going to have to learn to live with? I feared that this could be the case.

The glorious hot summer weather continued throughout June allowing Kate, I and Archie to enjoy a late afternoon walk across Wells beach (Fig. 630). This was then followed by the ubiquitous ice-cream!

Old age and senility caught up with me again on 1 July 2024 as I posted my first application for a government Attendance Allowance. Sobering thoughts, but these were soon dismissed as Kate and I collected some brochures for a possible holiday in St. Lucia, evidence that in our minds we were not as old as we sometimes felt!

Figure 630

But as always, we couldn't avoid reality, for over the next two or three days my cognitive responses took a downward spiral. Temporarily I hoped. But it was a clear reminder from my brain that I shouldn't get carried away with ideas beyond my mental capabilities. This 'prick' of my conscience made me seriously think hard about my writing and the desire to have this memoir completed by the time I reached 70 in 2025. Was that too much I asked myself, was I doing justice to the text and when matters did not go as planned, was that fair on both my own ability and more importantly on that of my loved ones, who have to bear the strain of me? So, after a long night thinking about these questions – why do I always think about complex issues just at the time I should be relaxing and going to sleep – I reached a decision with which I was happy. I would move my 'goal posts' and set my sights on having the text of my book ending in October 2024, rather than February 2025 as previously planned. This would then allow for it to be ready for distribution by my birthday, rather than finishing the drafting in February 2025 and having it ready for editing, printing and distributing later in the year. I sought the opinion of Kate, which was paramount in all I do, and an agreement was reached.

Given my condition, without the unending love and support of Kate I really do not know how I could have functioned over the last few months. Kate is a tower of strength and so positive. Life with me is not easy, as my mood moves to and fro more times than our grandchildren do when playing on the garden swing, but through all of these moods Kate remains calm, supportive and loving – she is simply remarkable and a joy to love.

Anyway, back to my memoir, I had explained my current situation to my three key external 'suppliers', Ruth my professional proofreader, Kaarin the graphic designer and Kevin the printer, and sought their thoughts on a possible change to the timetable. They were all sympathetic and very accommodating, so my new target date was confirmed for the end of October, with distribution to the family on my birthday.

Despite my deterioration, I honestly still believed that I was neither knocking on death's door, nor even walking down the corridor towards it. I was easily confused and muddled though, so a postponement really was the correct way forward. It was a shame, but then life doesn't always go according to plan, and looking to the future I simply needed to be even more mindful of my abilities.

To add to an already complex array of emotions, in early July I received a note from David Riddington, in his capacity as my mother's executor, saying that the Probate Office had approved all the paperwork, and that the inheritance could now be paid to all the beneficiaries. Em, Oliver and Sophie, along with my parents' other five grandchildren, were duly contacted and asked to submit their bank details to David, in order that he could transfer the funds of

£1,958.16 to each of them. Judy, Sarah and I were each to receive an equal share of the remaining funds that amounted to £46,995.90 each. Whilst the financial settlement was nice to receive, I would obviously have preferred to have had both my parents alive and well, but as I was realising life doesn't play by those rules. This truly was the end of an era, a sobering thought, in amongst many others at that time.

In endeavouring to finish the month on a positive and more upbeat note I paid the final balance for our Italian holiday, with Oliver, Jude and their children. We were all, for a variety of reasons, really looking forward to our time away.

Following the General Election the previous day, we awoke on the morning of 5 July to a new government. As predicted by all the pundits, Labour came out on top with a whopping majority in the new Parliament of 412 MPs, out of the 650. So, after 14 years of a Tory government, we now had a huge change.

Some said that this was not unexpected, due to the joint debacles of both Liz Truss and Boris Johnson. Liz Truss was Prime Minister in 2022 for just 49 days, making her the shortest-serving prime minister in British history. She presided over a financial crisis after her mini budget caused mayhem for the economy. Boris Johnson, on the other hand, who was Prime Minister from 2019-2022 also had his crisis following the Covid pandemic. Plus, his 'Partygate' scandal occurred when several members of his government held parties in 10 Downing Street, which were in direct contravention to his own Covid restrictions. Consequently, this led to his eventual resignation and a loss of confidence in the overall government. These two major incidents were seen by political correspondents and the public, as having had a significant impact on the voting choices in this current election. It was also thought that these events possibly reduced the number of people who actually bothered to vote. In fact, it was only

Figure 631

Figure 632

just a fraction higher at 59.7%, than the lowest ever previously recorded in 1918 at 57.3%.

Liz Truss who lost her seat, and Boris who subsequently resigned as Prime Minister in 2022 were both no longer MPs. With some trepidation we awaited the running of our country by Sir Keir Starmer our new Labour Prime Minister.

Figure 633

As he said in his victorious speech: '*We did it. You campaigned for it, you fought for it, you voted for it, and now it has arrived – change begins now*'. So, just what would be these changes, and would they unite the country? I hoped so for all our sakes and whilst it was not my choice of party, we all had to wait and see. The images shown here are the 'Ins' and 'Outs', along with King Charles III's invitation to Sir Keir Starmer to form a new government (Figs. 631 – 633).[52]

July 6 was yet another momentous day as there was a new addition to the Gosden family. But this time our new member was Max, a 13-week-old, black pedigree Labrador puppy! Born on 3 April, the same birthday as both my mother and Oliver. Max was collected from Lincolnshire and came home in the car with us and Archie. Both seemed very happy in each other's company and slept most of the journey home. Once back and fed, they then spent much of the evening lying on the drawing room floor at our feet, being stroked whilst we watched television.

Like both Archie and Dan, Max seemed to be very gentle, calm and incredibly alert, hence our selection on the day. So, hopefully with Kate's training, now that Dan was no longer with us, he would prove to be a perfect partner for Archie. Figures 634 – 636 are Max asleep under the kitchen table with his toy pheasant, along with a couple of other photographs taken the day we brought him home. By sheer coincidence, Kate noticed that our calendar entries show that thirteen years ago we collected Dan and Archie as 8-week-old puppies, a month and a day before, on 5 June 2011!

---

52 Credits to Reuters, Getty Images, left & right (previous page) and Buckingham Palace, above

Figure 634   *Figure 635*   *Figure 636*

It was fascinating to see how Max dealt with so many of his new learning experiences. One weekend, Kate and I went to the shops in Holt and had to walk through the regular Sunday Market with its stalls and numerous people. Some were local, others were visitors, there were lots of dogs and one or two people were on mobility scooters, all incidences that Max had never encountered before. Therefore, everything and everybody had to be sniffed, watched and in some cases well and truly avoided. The latter was most definitely indicated to us, when his tail went between his legs, and he sought reassurance from us that he was ok. He most certainly received our praise and throughout his walk he also received countless admiring looks and strokes from the many shoppers and visitors.

Back home, Kate decided to vacuum the carpet. Again, for Max hearing and seeing a Dyson cleaner being used, warranted yet another cautious sniff and then to sit down and with his head on one side, study it from a safe distance! Clearly his memory bank was being filled and his confidence levels were gradually being increased.

Figure 637

To cap off the weekend, Sir Lewis Hamilton, joint seven times Formula One World Drivers' Championship winner, won the British Grand Prix for a record ninth time. To add to his vast collection of accolades, he had set another new record for achieving the most wins at a single circuit. But this time I suspected that it was even sweeter for Lewis as he had reduced his most recent arch-rival, Max Verstappen to second place. Lewis is seen here with his well-earned trophy (Fig. 637).[53] Perfect!

---

53 Image credit – Reuters

Not that we knew it at the time, when I arose from my slumbers at 05.30 in the morning, that 11 July was to have three watershed moments in the production of my memoir. Having awoken and made my way downstairs, I left Kate to catch up on the sleep that she had lost overnight, by having to deal with Max who, bless him, needed to go out three times during the night. I partially prepared our own breakfast as normal and then sometime later took Kate a cup of tea. Back downstairs, to their delight, I fed both Archie and Max. They were now able to not only wait patiently, although rather excitedly in the case of Max, but they were able to eat together in the same room without Max interfering with Archie's food. This was, in our opinion, a great step forward! Food is a very 'protected' commodity for dogs, particularly Archie, and one where additional help with its consumption from a new arrival is normally met with a cautionary growl. Not today though! Whilst I finished preparing both Kate's and my own breakfast, they enjoyed theirs without any incidents at all. A great start to the day after what had been a very interrupted night.

Later that morning, Kate and I were off to have a meeting with Kaarin, our graphic designer and typesetter and I wanted to take with me the most up-to-date version of my book. So, whilst both Archie and Max relaxed and having digested their breakfast, I then took to writing within this memoir my page of acknowledgements. All went well and by 09.00, Kate had had her breakfast and had found time to read my words of acknowledgement, and with some minor corrections we both agreed on my wording. Over breakfast we had chatted about the 'disrupted' night and both felt that it was probably a one-off, as normally Max was good and usually only woke us up once during the night. Later in the morning we were ready to go off for our meeting.

This was to be our first 'formal' progress review with Kaarin and the day before I had written some notes and prepared an agenda. Given my Alzheimer's, this process was now very necessary for me, as I was having some embarrassing pregnant pauses, whilst my brain caught up with my hopes and aspirations. Then and subsequently these occurrences would frequently lead me to forget where my train of thought was heading and exactly where I was on that journey. So, extensive notes were now important and were particularly significant on the day we met Kaarin, as I wanted to float a suggestion to her that may not have been to her liking.

Previously, as I have already explained, Kaarin and I had agreed via emails and telephone calls that a new timetable would be devised, and I would conclude my writing at the end of October 2024. This would then be passed to Kaarin for setting etc. and the book would be printed by my birthday. This schedule was not what I originally desired, as I really wanted to conclude the text on my 70th birthday, but I felt that would possibly put too much pressure on me. However, having given this more thought I was hoping that at our meeting I could convince Kaarin to allow me to give her the text in early October, as planned. Then submit month by month, additional supplementary text right through to my birthday. If accepted and assuming I was able to manage this, the original plan to conclude the book on my birthday in 2025 could be met. I was very aware that this was probably not an ideal position for her, who I appreciated would most likely prefer to have the whole text in one single delivery.

We had had to take Max with us and once having successfully introduced him to both her and her partner, we kept our fingers crossed that he would be happy to stay close by to us, in his secure crate. He was so good, and we didn't hear a peep from him throughout the time we were there. Knowing I knew that Max was settled, and with the support of Kate I set out my ideas to Kaarin and outlined the items on my agenda. Then the watershed moment arrived, as I explained the rationale for my new staggered delivery and to the complete surprise of both Kate and me, she readily agreed without issue. Whilst being totally unexpected and a relief, it meant that it would enable me to meet my ambitious target, at a pace I could accommodate. In addition, it confirmed to me that simply by being open and honest about how my condition can impair my brain's functionality, with suitable adaptations implemented, my Alzheimer's could be easily accommodated. People are both willing and able to accept change. Kaarin and her partner, who was to assist during the design and layout work by editing and preparing the images, were both extremely understanding and adaptable, which for me was just perfect.

The rest of the meeting was spent agreeing details of the proposed design and layout which was equally successful. The result was a total meeting of minds on both sides, which left both Kate and I with a feeling of confidence, excitement and total justification that the choice of Kaarin, to undertake this work, was a very wise one. As such, we knew that my manuscript would be in very safe hands. The icing on the cake was that throughout the entire two-hour meeting, Max had been the most well-behaved puppy, anyone could have wanted!

That night the final watershed came about, because for the first time Max didn't wake up or whine during the night. In fact, at 06.00 the next morning all I heard was a small whimper that indicated not only was he alive but also ready to start the day!

Funnily enough, over breakfast we both commented that Max's 'sleep in' had reminded us both of our experiences of being new parents with a newborn baby, who for the first time had just slept through the night, and how reassured we were that all was well, having double checked that he or she was still breathing!

It was now 08.00, the dogs and fish had been fed, I had written my daily update to this memoir and was ready for the day ahead, which was to include yet another new sound and experience for Max – meeting the lawnmower! Like the previous 'meetings', after a few sniffs and long stares, he was very happy to simply follow me up and down the lawn!

Figure 638

Following our meeting with Kaarin, she kindly sent me a draft layout just so I could see what it looked like. She had used a previous version of Chapter 1, which included all our agreed changes. This helped Kate and me to fully understand the pagination, especially after we had printed the document out, cut the pages to size along with the proposed cover, and created a mini book (Fig. 638). This may sound a little daft, but just seeing a draft version, for the first time was very exciting and more importantly it allowed us to understand just what the final printed book could possibly look like. I have to say in my own very biased opinion, of course, that it did look really professional, and I was incredibly pleased!

I did have to accept, however, that this was as the youngsters would say, '*sad*' but it still represented a tangible version of what was to be my first and probably only book. So, I was very proud and exhilarated by my achievements thus far. In looking through the pages we could both see that all the changes were now in place and, as such, we were able to consider a few tweaks to the design for the final version which might or might not be agreed.

Later in the day, we were fortunate enough to be able to visit an exhibition of recent paintings by Kieron Williamson, a young and extremely talented, local artist. He had held his first exhibition in Holt, at the age of just six, and at that time astounded by his competence and skill, buyers from around the world queued up to pay huge sums of money for his paintings. As a result, the media nicknamed him 'Mini Monet'. Now, at the age of 21 his talents had developed even further and were reflected in the price of his works which sold for between £295.00 and £21,000! Unlike at his first exhibition, this time we didn't purchase any of his paintings, but it was wonderful to see how he had developed his obvious skills. He certainly had the prospect of a superb and, probably, very lucrative and long-lasting career ahead of him.

Our evening was spent at yet another exhibition. This time it was a private preview award ceremony for ceramics and art. It heralded the opening of the annual Holt Festival programme of events, which were to commence the next day.

Chapter 7 Life in Retirement 2014 – 2025

On 20 July, I was again feeling rather 'smug' with myself, as well as excited, for I had just finished, after three long days of reading, editing and generally tweaking my text thus far. This was my most recent complete read through and to my overwhelming delight, I found it to be quite good! Although, I suspected that inevitably there would be many more alterations and additions to follow. But so far, I was pleased and enthusiastic at the prospect of its forthcoming conclusion and publication.

My feeling of excitement was further heightened, as I was also looking forward to our much earnt and awaited Italian holiday, which was only just under three weeks away. I appreciated that it was only for a week, but hopefully it would be a wonderful seven days, and I was certain that with Kate, Oliver, Jude, Eve, and Zoey all there as well, that was to be the case. I couldn't wait!

The weekend of July 20 and 21 brought home to us all just how reliant society is upon technology. This manifested itself when a worldwide 'outage' of the Microsoft platform created havoc for a multitude of businesses. It affected an estimated 8.5m devices worldwide and resulted in an approximate value of £4.1billion in financial losses. It was calamitous! In the UK alone, airline flight information, travel bookings, NHS data, doctors' practice data and prescriptions, along with many other essential services were all seriously affected.

It transpired that all this was simply caused by a single defect or 'bug' in a cybersecurity update, from CrowdStrike Holdings Inc., based in the United States. This had been sent around the world to many of the Microsoft systems.[54] These were networks that very clearly we all relied upon, and which as a result subsequently crashed. We all just hoped that 'normal service' was to resume as soon as possible, which eventually it did.

On a much closer and happier note, Kate and I were sent this wonderful photograph of Zoey (Fig. 639) on 21 July, having a fabulous time in

Figure 639

---

54 Paraphrased from a Quote by USA insurance company Parametrix and reported by the BBC on 27 July 2024

561

the sun, picking strawberries and raspberries – not sure though, how many made their way to the punnet, let alone home, but a great day out was had by all. What a lovely picture, thanks Jude!

Later that day, we both had a fascinating walk around the other various art exhibitions that formed part of the Holt Festival. One exhibit, in the exhibition entitled 'German Expressionists and the Third Reich' was not only very pleasing but also had a very disturbing history and relevance, to the exhibition's title. The extract from the catalogue (Fig. 640) outlined the story and the painting's significance[55] and it is accompanied here by my own photograph of the painting (Fig. 641).

For both of us the exhibit was most thought provoking, and a clear reminder of just how precarious life was for some during WWII.

Figure 640

Figure 641

Celebration of our 31st wedding anniversary on 24 July was split into two parts. On the day we both had an enjoyable evening meal at Sculthorpe Mill, which was just outside Fakenham, whilst two days later for the final event of the 2024 Holt Festival, on one of Gresham's playing fields we joined an enthusiastic throng, many of whom were locals, to hear the 'Bootleg Beatles' perform on stage.

An excited audience of about 300 attended, along with some 20-30 who 'gate crashed', and stood to watch the show from outside the boundary wall. The concert comprised music and popular Beatles hits from the 1960s and 70s. Most of the audience had probably grown up with the Beatles music, but there was a sizeable number of the younger generation, some from Gresham's school, who also thoroughly enjoyed the various renditions of the Beatles classics.

---

55 Courtesy of Holt Festival 2024 Art-Zine catalogue

Chapter 7 Life in Retirement 2014 – 2025

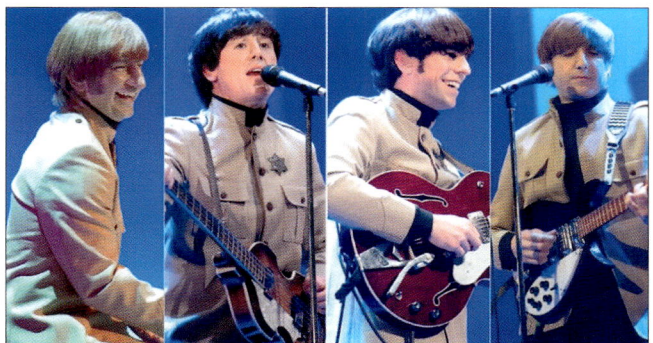

Figure 642

Figure 643

Figure 644

Figure 645

On the way in, we had joined our friends Polly and Phil, and were making our way to the seating area on the field when we met up with some old friends from my Round Table days, who included our best man Ian Malton and his wife Lin. This chance encounter made an already perfect day even better! We enjoyed a fun and nostalgic packed evening and by the end of the three-and-a-half-hour concert very few of the audience were sitting. Those who were still seated in the comfort of their picnic chairs, were now endeavouring to watch the performance through the throng of dancers that included Kate and me, along with our various friends. These photographs perfectly tell the story (Figs. 642[56] – 645).

---

56 Image 642 credit – bootlegbeatles.com.

563

We had the opportunity to chat again with Ian and Lin during the interval and much to our delight discovered that they were staying overnight in their palatial motorhome, just down the road from us on a very secluded caravan site. So, we arranged to meet up with them the next morning at 10.30. When we arrived, we were greeted with tables and chairs all set outside in the sunshine and Ian was just about to start cooking breakfast. Whilst we all sat and reminisced, the smell of eggs, bacon, mushrooms and fried potatoes pervaded around the site and was mouthwatering, so by the time it was ready to be served we were all very hungry. It was absolutely delicious. I wondered why food was always so much tastier when it was cooked out in the open and eaten amongst convivial company? Anyway, we had a great morning having spent a couple of hours with them, before leaving to take Archie and Max on a walk.

Now having lived at Hanworth House for several years, Kate and I decided that the time was right to upgrade our arbour, which we had created when the garage was demolished. This was prompted by the fact that given its age and the weight of the ever-growing wisteria that was clambering across it, some of the original woodwork had now become unsafe. To that end, we had organised a site visit by a local engineering company, during which we agreed a design for a metal structure that they would construct, deliver and erect later in the year. So, we awaited its arrival, hopefully after our Italian holiday.

Figure 646

The expression 'A baptism of fire' sprang to mind when I was reviewing the first few weeks of our new UK Government. Thus far, there had been numerous riots across England, as shown (Fig. 646),[57] all of which had been attributed to far-right activists, who claimed to be protesting at the murder of three young girls in Southport, who whilst attending their regular

---

57 Courtesy of Getty Images and BBC

Chapter 7 Life in Retirement 2014 – 2025

dance class had been brutally stabbed. In Rotherham alone this had resulted in more than 400 arrests and around 100 people being charged. At the time, it was suggested that some of this disorder stemmed from the circulation on various social media platforms, of alleged 'misinformation' that related to the Southport stabbing. It was all very disconcerting for the general UK population, and we all wondered just where this would end up and how the new government would deal with the situation. Thankfully, they effectively dealt with the riots and the disturbance subsided. Over the next few months, numerous prosecutions followed, which resulted in custodial sentences being handed down to both adults and a 15-year-old boy!

The allegations pertaining to the possible uses of social media had drawn further comments from Elon Musk, who was one of the world's richest men at the time, and owner of 'X', one of the main social media sites. He already had had a public 'spat' with the new UK Prime Minister over the rights or wrongs of how social media worked and its role in disseminating information. He also allegedly had suggested that 'civil war was inevitable' in the UK, which resulted in a sharp rebuff from the PM's spokesman and followed up by further comments from both sides. As I said, it was indeed a baptism of fire. Only time would tell the outcome, which we all hoped would result in calm and sense prevailing.

Our August family holiday with Oliver, Jude, Eve and Zoey was on an olive grove farm, close to Casacastalda in Umbria, Italy. It commenced with an interesting landing by British Airways upon arrival at San Francesco d'Assisi Airport in Perugia. As the plane descended, the rear wheels touched the runway then to our surprise and also our fellow passengers, the pilot flew up into a steep climb away from the runway and undertook a half hour flight around the area, in order to try a second approach. This time he made a successful landing. Apparently, the first attempt had to be aborted as the cross winds were too great, so he had to allow the winds to subside, before he could try again!

Once out of the plane, the temperature was hot, which was to prove to be a hallmark for the entire week, apart from one hour, which you can read about further on. The accommodation was perfect, with fabulous views from our veranda, which overlooked the Umbrian hills, with the Apennine mountains on the horizon (Fig. 647). As was the inviting pool which was soon in daily use giving much fun and a very welcome cooling down, to all of us.

We had unanimously agreed that alternate days would be a 'chill out' day on the farm, so our first full day was just relaxing. After a good night's sleep,

REFLECTIONS UPON A FAMILY

a croissant breakfast, a quick shopping spree for supplies, we had nothing else planned, so it just had to be a lovely, long play in the pool! At supper we perused Kate's research on possible locations to visit, explored those areas on Google and decided on a few 'must visits' for the week ahead. We had hired a car at the airport, so on 10 August our first journey was to the ancient town of Assisi, with its beautiful Basilica of San Franscesco d'Assisi, (Fig. 648) paved streets and wide piazzas (Fig. 649). First though, we had to find our way around the

Figure 647

Figure 648

Figure 649

Figure 650

town, so as was the order of the day, via the adult mobiles, Google Maps was consulted. My own mobile was to capture that moment (Fig. 650)!

Sadly, with technology taking the upper hand, the days of unfolding and reading paper maps that blow about in the wind, combined with paper guidebooks to find interesting places, seemed to be coming to an end. We eventually found our route and our meander round the town was really interesting, the frescoes in the Basilica were magnificent and the lunch that commenced our visit was most enjoyable.

On Monday 12 August, we decided to avoid the heat and ventured underground to visit the Frasassi caves in Genga. These caves, one of Italy's greatest caverns, are home to an impressive array of stalactites and stalagmites (Fig. 651). Some of the caves were tall enough to house a cathedral. And 'yes' they were vast! Our tour guide took us along the route entering various caverns where we were able to see and touch the numerous natural limestone sculptures. All these created over 190 million years by the combined effect of water and rock. During our tour we could feel the stalactites dripping down from the ceiling of the cave and splash onto the growing stalagmites. Apparently, if they did this for long enough, they could join to become a column, as seen in figure 651, and according to our guide that could take 70,000 years! It was truly fascinating and totally awe inspiring when you considered how long these particular structures had taken to be created, and they were still forming droplet by droplet.

Figure 651

Back at the farm, we all had our daily visit to the pool, with its slide and various floats etc. and then we all changed and joined the other guests who were also staying there, for a traditional pizza evening. Once a week our host would always ask a local mobile pizzeria to come to cook for everyone. She and her granddaughter provided us all with copious and endless varieties of delicious pizza, which we as guests could serve ourselves, as often and as much as we wished. These were all totally authentic and completely different to the ones we buy at home from the supermarkets. With wine, sun and great company, the evening was a huge success and perfectly set us up for the next day. We even had

Figure 652

a family photograph of us all (Fig. 652), taken by Paul, the owner of the olive grove.

During our stay and quite by coincidence, Jude who had a love of using a particular make of handmade paper had found that this was actually manufactured in Fabriano, by a company, who in the 12th century had been instrumental in its original production and the subsequent addition of watermarks. Fortunately, to drive there was only a short distance away, so we agreed that our next visit would be to their museum. As we wandered around, one of the Italian guides suddenly arranged for just the six of us to have our own private guide in English which was located in part of one the displays. We all felt rather privileged, Jude was in her element and with me having been in the printing business it was an absolutely fascinating tour.

The next section of the museum was equally interesting and something that appealed to all of us, including the children, who in the case of Eve (Fig. 653) was able to make in the traditional handmade way, her own sheet of paper with a special watermark. The sheet was then dried, sized and was ready for her to take home at the end of the visit. It was a wonderful hands-on experience for her, and we all left far more knowledgeable as to how paper was made traditionally in medieval Italy. Given the history of our family's involvement in bookbinding and printing, this all made the trip really special.

Looking around the rest of the museum we discovered a wonderful

Figure 653

display of contemporary paintings which formed part of an exhibition. The quality of the artwork by the obviously very talented artists was most impressive. As were the frescos, painted 800 years earlier by the medieval monks, on the walls of the monastery, now the museum. It was certainly well worth the visit, extremely rewarding and thoroughly enjoyed by everyone. We just had to follow it up with ice creams all round. Even the prospect of a swim in the pool, when we returned to the farm, did not stop Eve and Zoey sleeping all the way back.

The following day Jude and Oliver returned, this time to the Fabriano shop, where significant purchases were made to ensure that stocks of various notebooks for both of them, and paper for Eve and Zoey, were taken back to the UK!

Back at the farm our swim, in temperatures of 35 degrees, was 'interrupted' by a very sudden hailstorm which according to the locals was very unusual. It lasted for almost an hour and not only caused significant damage to all the surrounding trees but also severe bruising to Kate and me, as we had had to shelter by the pool, still in our swimming costumes! Eventually we managed to return to our house, having run up the now incredibly slippery steps, which were covered in flowing ice, at the same time trying to dodge the hailstones which were at least 3cm in size! They certainly hurt when they hit you! Oliver and Jude who had returned to the house just as the storm commenced, were really concerned about us, and totally surprised when we looked like 'drowned rats' as we rushed in through the door, covered with very red marks visible on our arms and legs, which the next day turned into very large bruises. Luckily, we had no other physical damage and over time our wounds healed – it was an experience that will be remembered, for a long time by us all! We retired after supper to the noise of the generator that had kicked in due to the ensuing power cut, and the next morning we awoke to the sound of leaves and melted ice being swept away by Paul and his colleagues.

We spoke to him later and he told us that he had owned the farm for 20 years and a storm of that intensity and ferocity was something he had never ever experienced before and that it was an extremely rare occurrence. To our astonishment, he also told us that due to all the hail, the water level in the pool had risen by 10 cm! Which was a huge volume of water!

For the rest of the day the sun shone, and a glorious day beckoned.

It was Wednesday and the next day, was to be our last day in Italy so there were things that we all wanted to do or see before we left for the return flight. I set out to capture the view from our terrace, in a quick coloured pen and ink drawing which once back home I could work into a painting. This went well and I was pleased with the outcome. Oliver and the children played in the pool whilst Jude and Kate started to gather together all our belongings, to ensure that nothing

Figure 654

was left behind. Later in the day, we all went to Gubbio and as we walked around the town, we saw groups of men all dressed in mediaeval costume. They were flag throwers, known as sbandieratori, and were accompanied by marching drummers and trumpeters. They were rehearsing and preparing for Ferragosto, a public holiday in Italy, to commemorate the start of the festival of The Feast of the Assumption of the Virgin Mary. We had been advised that the town 'came alive' in the evening and we certainly weren't disappointed, with tourists and locals all enjoying an evening meal just as the sun was setting (Fig. 654). We too had a lovely traditional supper in an outdoor restaurant called Orto.

Figure 655

Our final full day started with a swim and concluded with a visit to Perugia. Here we found, almost by accident, the Porta Marzia. This was an ancient, Etruscan gateway inserted as a blind arch (Fig. 655)[58] into the masonry of the Rocca Paolina, which was a 16th century architectural structure that extended over the wide surroundings of the Landone Hill, on which Perugia stood. Rocca Paolina or Paolino Fortress was the monumental gateway located at the southern end of the Etruscan city wall, where it entered the Via Amerina, which in the middle of the third century B.C. had been extended toward Perugia, in order to strengthen relations between the city and Rome.

---

58 Credit – Adobe Stock

Chapter 7 Life in Retirement 2014 – 2025

Figure 656

Figure 657

Inside we found a wonderful labyrinth of cobbled streets and rooms, one of which contained a vast oven, others were used for exhibitions, a museum and one was a fascinating leather workshop, where Kate bought a beautiful, multicoloured handbag. The whole place was spectacular, and I wondered just how the builders, at that time, knew how to create such a magnificent and substantial structure. Could we today, build something like this using the same tools and to a standard that would endure for centuries? I would like to think so but I'm not that certain. My photograph (Fig. 656) is the inside whilst standing on one of the main streets which gives an indication of the vast building and its complexity. Whilst inside I could not resist the image (Fig. 657) of Eve and Zoey patiently sitting together,

Figure 658

Figure 659

571

whilst we adults admired the breathtaking construction surrounding us. Our final group photograph, whilst still in the Rocca Paolina (Fig. 658), was taken by Jude, just prior to our flight home (Fig. 659), which this time was smooth and without incident. All together a wonderful and memorable holiday.

Upon our return home, in the early hours of 16 August, life resumed very much where we had left it, just a week before. The next day I was sitting in court and at the weekend I was cutting the grass and tidying the garden, whilst Kate finished unpacking, washed clothes and prepared for Ben, who was our next long-awaited guest. Having not seen him since our family gathering last year, we both eagerly awaited his arrival on the Sunday, for him to start his week's holiday with us.

I am sure it's a comment that all grandparents make, but when he arrived, we were very aware that he had matured from a young boy into a tall and confident 11-year-old young man. Like all our grandchildren, he was a pleasure to be with and we were very proud and acutely aware of just how lucky we are to be able to say this, as not all grandchildren want to stay with their grandparents and vice versa.

Sophie and Leigh had brought Ben to Holt, so as the sun was shining, we all sat in the garden for a long chat and a cup of tea. Their two dogs, Blade a golden labrador and Oslo a two-year-old golden retriever, were introduced to Max. Whilst Archie the most senior of the pack, just looked on, or perhaps given his advanced years was he just keeping out of the way? Anyway, they all made friends especially Oslo and Max who as youngsters played really well together. Much to my relief, I had also noticed whilst we were all talking, a much-improved relationship between myself and Sophie. Had we turned a corner? I sincerely hoped so.

After tea we bade them farewell and proceeded to take Ben with his football to the local playground to have a kickabout, where he was to convincingly prove that his football skills were considerably better than either of mine or Kate's. That's another story though. We were just on our way there, when we became aware that Leigh and Sophie's car was suddenly approaching us. They had hastily returned, because whilst they were at ours, they had forgotten to give me a book. It was a small journal entitled '*Dad, I want to hear your story*' into which I could record various memories, thoughts and anecdotes about my life, that Sophie could share with Ben and Leigh. I was taken aback by this lovely gesture, as it was certainly not expected, but was given with such thought and love. Clearly at long last our father and daughter relationship was beginning to be rekindled.

Chapter 7 Life in Retirement 2014 – 2025

As I didn't want to spoil the moment I resisted the temptation, as I had already done with Oliver, to mention that I was already writing this memoir, which of course would fulfil those same objectives and more, and would be given next year to both Sophie and Ben, along with the wider family. I was really touched and pleased to receive this gesture, as I saw it as a positive step forward to how our relationship should be.

The football game was very one-sided with Ben in total control! This positive advance in his maturity and confidence was a pleasure to behold.

The following day was dull and occasionally damp, so indoor entertainment was the order of the day. So, Ben's long awaited return visit to the local Muckleburgh Military Collection in Weybourne came to fruition, and we all had a most enjoyable time. Especially as we were all able to re-acquaint ourselves with the full-size Sherman Tank as driven by my father in WWII. As well as many other exhibits, some of which were familiar, others were new. Following the purchase of souvenirs, it was back home and as the weather had improved another football kickabout at the local playground was a welcome pastime, before supper and bed.

Throughout the week, Ben created some wonderful electronic images on his tablet. The main one being a train station, through which you could enter and look around at all the features that he had included e.g. a signal box, offices, waiting room, café and loo etc. It never ceased to amaze me how adept the younger generation were and how quickly they learnt new technological skills on their computers, in order for them to build those types of entertainment. In my day Meccano and Airfix models were the main toys that allowed us to build models. These are still available but nowadays the draw of handheld technology is the younger generation's main amusement. Oh, how times have changed as, of course, they always will.

On the Wednesday, we drove the short distance to Holkham Hall, where the huge adventure playground was again the main attraction for Ben. This woodland play area with its extensive apparatus, many treehouses, ladders, bridges, climbing frames, along with a long zipwire was always a draw for children, and Ben was certainly in his element. After a full day of fun, we returned home where Ben and Grannie made some lovely flapjacks. Ben's culinary prowess was also demonstrated when he made some garlic bread to accompany our supper. Apparently, the recipe for this was learnt whilst on a recent scout camp, and clearly well remembered as the result was excellent. Following another now mandatory kickabout at the recreation ground, we all had supper together. Kate then made sure Ben was all settled and comfy in bed, before we relaxed in the drawing room and when the time came, bedtime for us was a most welcome rest.

Walking around Blickling Hall park, with refreshments at the end was the main event on Thursday, whilst on Friday Ben's request to visit Holt Country Park with Max and Archie was to be that day's highlight.

Having the grandchildren to stay, especially on their own, had always been a privilege for Kate and me, and our time spent with Ben was no exception. However, towards the end of the week we were both aware that whilst he was very much enjoying his time with us, he seemed to have something on his mind, which was clearly giving him some private concerns. We both quietly chatted to him about this but were assured that all was well. In our opinion though, it didn't seem to be totally correct. We had hoped that he would be able to confide in us, in order that we could help him put his mind at rest but we both agreed not to pursue the matter any further. We did think that perhaps he was concerned about the upcoming move to senior school, just over a week after his return home. Time would tell.

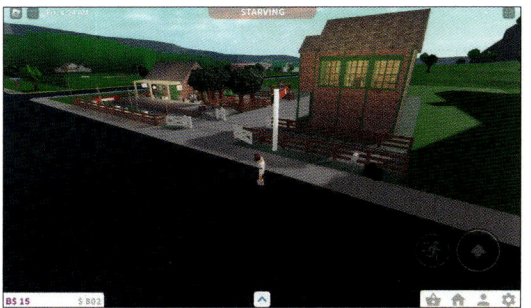
Figure 660

In the meantime, his creative and computer skills using his Bloxburg software, were very much in evidence with further enhancements to his model train station, as can be seen in the screen shot (Fig. 660).

Friday saw Ben striking out on a new venture when we attended a demonstration of glass blowing and the creation of some miniature glass animals. To his credit Ben participated in a one-to-one tutorial where he was able to produce a tea-light holder from molten glass (Fig. 661) through to the point where it entered the kiln to cool overnight.

Saturday morning, the last full day of Ben's stay, commenced with a return visit to Langham Glass in Fakenham, to collect his work of art, which was amazing. After lunch another of Ben's requests was realised, which was to spend time at his beloved North Norfolk Railway stations in both Holt and Sheringham. This was to provide a totally unexpected and memorable moment for him, just as we were leaving Sheringham station to take a last quick look at one of

Figure 661

Chapter 7 Life in Retirement 2014 – 2025

the guest engines that was all fired up and waiting at the end of the platform. Whilst admiring, the 1954 built National Coal Boards No 18 engine, named 'Austerity', Ben was invited to board the footplate by an obviously very knowledgeable and proud driver, where he was given a full 15-minute lesson, on how a steam engine worked. Ben was in his element, learning about how the steam was produced, how it was measured and controlled, what the functions were of all the various levers and controls and when and how to add the fuel. The latter just had to be experienced by the now apprentice fireman (Fig. 662).

Figure 662

On our way home, we asked what he had enjoyed most over his week with us and as quick as a flash the answer was being on the train! Clearly a moment with Grannie and Grandpa that will be remembered and savoured – Perfect!

On Sunday we all met up with Sophie and Leigh at Oxburgh Hall, and after a cup of coffee we bade farewell to Ben and returned home to prepare for the arrival of Em, Pete, Libby, Frankie and Leo, who were to stay for a few days before returning to Chessington and their school studies in their new academic year.

Despite August being the main holiday season and schools being closed, a major step forward was agreed for Holt when North Norfolk District Council approved the plans by Gresham's School, for the conversion of Holt Hall. The proposal was to convert the Victorian Hall into a new school for the junior scholars, giving them modern classrooms and up to date music and sports facilities. Whilst there had been some local concerns, regarding the proposed work, the ambitious £25m plans were now approved and work was planned to commence in 2025, with completion projected to be in 2026/27. This would ensure the long-term future of the Grade II listed building which was in a very run-down state when Gresham's purchased it in 2023 for £4.25m from Norfolk County Council. Today, I hope that all works progress well, and that

Figure 663

Holt gains yet another wonderful facility (Fig. 663),[59] for both the town and the school children. It promises to both regenerate a long-lost historic asset to the townscape whilst creating an exciting and innovative schooling environment, in which future generations of children will flourish. All of which, in my opinion, are aspirations to be applauded. Much of the cost of these works was generously gifted by Gresham's alumni, Sir James Dyson.

Having returned Ben to his parents at Oxburgh Hall on 25 August, whilst on our way home Kate told me about an unexpected message she had recently received from Em. Apparently Libby, now aged 13, had been exploring and endeavouring to understand gender identity. As a result of her quest for knowledge, she had asked that in the future, people called her Kenny. Whilst neither I nor Kate had any issues with this, we did ask Em to point out to her that due to my Alzheimer's, my memory was not as good as it had been and, as such, I might slip back to using her birth name. Not through any malice or objection but simply due to my own condition. Both Em and Kenny understood and I hoped that this wouldn't happen, but if it did, I equally hoped that Kenny wouldn't mind.

As they were all to arrive on the Wednesday, we busily prepared the house, ingredients were purchased, and Kate cooked several meals in advance. Having now prepared all the rooms and filled the food cupboards, we turned our attention to the garden.

On the Bank Holiday Monday 26 August, I toiled all day and managed to not only cut the grass but at the top of the garden also trimmed the sides and tops of the two hedges. By supper time I was left with just the task of raking up the hedge clippings and taking them next morning, in three one-tonne builders' bags, to the local recycling centre. By chance, the next day we had a visit from our Lawn Care company who both scarified the entire lawn and reseeded elements of it that had worn a little thin. Whilst in time the result would look really good but I had lost all my nice stripes in the lawn, created the previous day by my careful mowing! Still, I was sure the Joneses wouldn't mind.

---

59 Image Gresham's School / North Norfolk District Council / EDP

Whilst taking a short but well-deserved respite from our gardening chores, to enjoy an afternoon cuppa in the summer sun, Kate and I chatted about our times with the grandchildren and when these might be repeated. It was then, all of a sudden, Kate recalled that a week or so prior to going to Italy we had booked up to have a Christmas break, at the Westleton Crown pub in Suffolk. Both of us had completely forgotten this, so it was a very welcome surprise, especially as when we checked the details, we found that we had already prepaid in full. Thank goodness Kate had suddenly remembered. We wouldn't have missed it though, as it was already in our diaries!

Em, Pete, Kenny, Leo and Frankie all arrived safe and sound late on Wednesday 28 August. Unfortunately, due to traffic delays and the need to have more frequent breaks to alleviate the stress for Kenny, the journey was considerably longer than normal. They eventually arrived at 23.45, much later than expected but they were home in Holt, exhausted and very happy.

After a good night's sleep and breakfast, we all set off to Blakeney in the summer sun to try and catch some crabs, or as they call it in Norfolk, to go gillying. This was a favourite fun time of our family and one that was requested by them all. En route we had to purchase some bait in the form of a packet of bacon and with breakfasts in hand for the crabs, we made our way to our first location, on the harbour quayside. This was however, already full of other families all seeking to catch the elusive crabs, so we ventured further along the estuary to try our luck. Fortune was not on our side as no catches were made, nor were any crabs seen! So, we walked to a small bridge where success had been achieved in the past and we weren't disappointed. With four lines being baited and lowered into the small creek, we were soon pulling up crabs, which clung to their breakfast of bacon, and were then placed carefully into the awaiting buckets already full of water. The crabs came singly, in pairs and in some cases three or four, but due to their young age, they had little ability to hold on to their food, so skill was required to raise them without dropping them back into the estuary. As time progressed, the expertise improved of both the children and the adults, and after about an hour we had 15 small crabs, all scampering around in our large buckets of water. It was time then to release them back out to the freedom of the estuary (Fig. 664).

Figure 664

Back at home, we all enjoyed a visit to the park and played with the dogs in the garden. Not forgetting the swings on our climbing frame, of course. Kate's home-cooked supper was enjoyed by us all, and this particular meal had an unexpected twist. Frankie decided to not only try a little Colman's English mustard, but to everyone's surprise, including hers I suspected, she decided that the taste was not only palatable but also really good! So, during her stay this additional relish was added to several other meals! By the latter part of the evening, it was time to rest and think about the next day's adventures.

Given that some grandchildren and indeed parents slept longer than others, breakfast the next morning was staggered. Kate and I though, had been up and about from 06.30 as both dogs, Max in particular, needed to go into the garden and they also needed to have breakfast at their normal time of 07.00. No problem at all, but quite what we do when the clocks change next month, we weren't sure!

With glorious weather again forecast, we all decided that a day by the sea was in order. This time our destination was to be Holkham beach, where none of the Joneses had been before and with the tide out the huge expanse of sand would enable buckets and spades to be employed (Fig. 665). After a light lunch at the Lookout, a small restaurant on the Holkham Estate, we made our way down to the beach where we found a small rivulet, which was an ideal safe place for our

Figure 665

Chapter 7 Life in Retirement 2014 – 2025

grandchildren and both Max and Archie to rest and play. Suncream was duly applied, and it was time to have fun, make sandcastles and splash around! After a couple of hours on the sand, which included exploratory walks over the dunes for Leo and Frankie with Mummy and Daddy, it was time to pack and return home. Such a shame, as Max in particular, was very comfortable asleep in the warm sunshine (Fig. 666).

Once all three grandchildren were snuggled down in bed, but not quite asleep as there was clearly too much chatting to be done, we adults thought about what new and different activities we could enjoy the next day. Em found a new

Figure 666

place to visit that was to be a challenge to all of us. She proceeded to book us all in for a visit the next morning which was to include a 'handling' experience. Handling what and where, we were to find out later?

The next day after breakfast we made our way to the Bug Park in Lenwade. A new attraction and one that was unknown to either Kate or me. Here, we were to be 'challenged' to hold and be informed about various creepy crawly bugs but not, thankfully, any spiders, which both I and certainly Frankie, were very pleased about. That said, without cause for concern, large and giant millipedes, cockroaches and snails were one at a time placed on outstretched hands to admire and touch. All the children and adults did very well, but unfortunately there wasn't enough space for me to be able to join the handling session, so my role was to be our 'official photographer' which I was more than happy with! Here are some of our photographs, one taken by Em as proof that we attended (Fig. 667), a very brave Frankie with her millipede (Fig. 668) and finally the

Figure 667

Figure 668

579

tarantula (Fig. 669) that no-one was allowed to hold!

All three grandchildren participated and were really good, so the visit to the outside play area and souvenir shop were both welcomed treats. Mementoes in hand, we returned home for more playing, supper and bed.

During their stay, the traditional visit to Starlings took place – this was a newsagent come toy shop on the High Street in Holt.

Figure 669

Whenever some of our grandchildren came to stay, these trips to the shops had become a regular treat and it was fascinating to see how their choice of toys had changed over the years. Purchases were made from a combination of pocket money and some 'top up' finances from parents and grandparents. They all chose several different 'treasures' except, in amongst Frankie and Leo's purchases, an everlasting pencil seemed to appeal to both of them.

Over the last few months Leo had been saving his pocket money in order that he could, with a small amount of assistance from Mum and Dad, purchase a much-desired Nintendo Switch console. This was to cost over £150, and to his credit Leo had scrimped, saved and undertaken extra tasks at home to earn some additional cash, and was very close to having sufficient funds to fulfil his dream. Kate and I also threw down some challenges for him e.g. helping with the washing up, hanging out the laundry, tidying away the garden chairs, and when completed each job would add to his savings, enabling him to reach his target prior to returning home. Needless to say, he accepted these challenges, fulfilled each with gusto and payment was delivered to a very happy and proud grandson. In order that all three of them had some extra pocket money, we also gave each of them a five pound note to spend as they wished.

Sunday was their final day with us, so having checked that no clothes were left behind, the suitcases were packed, and the car was loaded. We all had a final stroll to the playground (Fig. 670), and then after a delicious

Figure 670

lunch the journey home commenced. It was sad to see them go and as had happened before, Frankie was very upset and tried to hide in the library in the vain hope that she could stay longer. Only the promise that they would all return in the next school holiday placated the situation and made the drive home less tearful than on previous visits. Having returned home safely and with Leo's console purchased (Fig. 671), a few days later we received two lovely thank you letters from both Leo and Frankie.

Figure 671

So, the night of 1 September, an early bedtime for us was the order of the day. But only once a couple of loads of washing were finished and hung out to dry, the house tidied, the dogs walked and fed, the catchup of 'The Archers' had been listened to and supper was prepared and eaten. Oh yes, not forgetting the pruning of the wisteria over the arbour, in preparation for the delivery of the replacement new metal structure, had all been completed! We did live a very full and busy life!

Kate and I had now been able to spend time with all our family. Firstly, in Italy with Oliver, Jude, Eve and Zoey, then Sophie and Leigh before Ben stayed on his own in Holt, and now with Em, Pete, Kenny, Leo and Frankie. It was a little exhausting, as all these occasions were in succession, but they were so enjoyable we couldn't have wished for a better summer with them all.

The next morning was to remind both of us of our ages, as aches and pains in our joints were quite noticeable. At 06.00 I had been woken by Max and Archie, who both needed to go into the garden for their morning ablutions. After I had fed the dogs Kate joined me, and over breakfast we both enjoyed a reflective chat about our weeks with the family. I cleared and washed up the breakfast things and then commenced writing these memoirs. I found it quite relaxing and therapeutic, so it was good relaxation for me. Kate, on the other hand, finished washing the bed linen, did a whole lot of ironing, made the beds and spring cleaned and then after lunch, happily spent an hour or so doing some pilates. Pilates was something which she thoroughly enjoyed, and it was clearly very beneficial for her. For obvious reasons though, she had been unable to do these exercises over the past few weeks.

August was also the month that Jude left full-time employment, to concentrate on her final Legal Master's degree and we all hoped that her desire would be fulfilled to become a lawyer, specialising in Intellectual Property. The answer to this would not be known until a few months after my 70th birthday, so regrettably out of scope for this memoir.

Anyway, the early autumn weather gave Kate and I the opportunity to continue to further cut back the wisteria over the pergola. This wasn't as easy as we had expected, but eventually after much tracing of branches, we succeeded in bringing it to what we thought, was a condition that would allow the new framework to be installed. The conclusion of this work then led me to think about re-landscaping the area just behind the arbour, where we had a small wildlife pond that provided a habitat for a wide variety of creatures. This was just what we had planned when we first created it, and we had thoroughly enjoyed watching all the wildlife. The trouble was that in the adjacent shrubbery, an enormous and out of control forsythia, along with an equally large rosemary bush, both required continuous maintenance by us. So, I began to think that if these were removed it would allow us to expand the pond and reduce the ongoing upkeep. I mentioned this to Kate, who to my surprise agreed and having checked the costs and work involved we concluded that this would be our next challenge.

To that end a few days later, in preparation for excavating the area to enlarge the pond, I set about completely removing the forsythia and some of the surrounding vegetation. This, as I suspected, was no easy task but following two days of cutting, clearing and digging out of roots etc., all of which became a huge playground for Max, the task was almost achieved. Just the rosemary and the preparation for the new pond were left to tackle and that was to be undertaken later on in the year, perhaps over the winter. For now, we had an area that could be measured and planned ready for the redesigned installation.

Through his games and obvious love for us and life in general, the arrival of Max was a positive joy in so many respects, other than when he 'assisted' with the gardening! There was one drawback though, which he had in common with all labradors, which was the moulting of his hair. It could be found all around the house and clearing it up proved too much for our very mature Dyson vacuum cleaner. So, at great expense a new one was purchased which proved far more effective at picking up the never-ending quantities of dog hairs from both him and Archie. A positive win for modern technology, if only we could find someone who could utilise mountains of dog hair, we would become very rich. Alas, it was only the birds at nesting time and the dustmen who benefitted!

The week commencing 9 September was to be more like a 'normal' one for us both. On the Tuesday, I attended a Holt Society committee meeting, the next day

Chapter 7 Life in Retirement 2014 – 2025

I had another leisurely walk with David, this time around the Holkham estate, on the Friday I sat in the Family Court and on the Saturday, we watched the *Last Night of the Proms* on television. As always this was such a joyous occasion, with both tremendous music and very talented soloists, plus it was an annual event that we definitely endeavoured to watch.

Having taken the boys for a lovely walk on the Sunday we followed this with a trip into Norwich to the Theatre Royal. Here we listened to Michael Palin giving a most enjoyable and jocose talk, as he related certain events that he had been involved in and people he had met throughout his career. All of which he had written about in his fourth and latest autobiography *There and Back* (Fig. 672).[60]

Figure 672

Over the last 50 years, given Michael's professional television background of satire and travel programmes, the book was a combination of his thoughts and personal diary entries between 1999 and 2009. He read extracts from it, revisited some of his fondest memories, interspersed his talk with what appeared to be off-the-cuff views and comments and with the help of rarely seen photographs and video, he brought those momentous times to life. At the conclusion he read a couple of short stories from Enid Blyton's book *The Faraway Tree*, one I certainly recalled as I had had it read to me as a child. However, his adaptation was somewhat different and a little 'near the knuckle'. He had the audience in absolute stitches and as I suspected, like me, most of them had probably grown up with her book. Apparently, her original publication was currently being made into a film to be entitled *The Magic Faraway Tree*, which featured Michael, along with other well-known actors and was due to be released in 2025 – so, one to look out for! If the extracts he read were from an actual book, and not simply a monologue written for the show, I would love to find a copy – this conundrum I was to investigate further. At the end of the evening, the packed theatre was rapturous in their applause having just sat and listened to a very honest and highly amusing hour and a half talk from Michael. The whole performance was so professional, illuminating and very funny indeed. A wonderful evening.

All those aforementioned activities reflected a lovely relaxing week which also witnessed both Kate and I conclude our reading of most of this draft text,

---

60 Copyright © 2024 Prominent Palin Productions Ltd acknowledged · A Rokka Design Website

583

to date. As such, we were well on our way to meeting our commitment, to send the text to Ruth again for her final read through, at the end of the month. Although, I regret that it would not be to the same professional standard as Michael's!

The following week Kate's brother Peter and Jane his wife came to stay. Peter had booked tickets for us all to see the *Cromer End of the Pier Show*, and before I explain about this, I thought I should put some context around the pier itself.

Cromer has had a pier from as far back as 1391. The current version in 2025 is made of iron and is about 500 feet long (151 metres). This was built in 1902 after a succession of previous wooden structures had succumbed to the ravages of the sea and winds and had been swept away. This possible catastrophe rose its head again during the storm surge in December 2013, but due to the recent £1.2m refurbishment which had been concluded in October of that year, by the owners North Norfolk District Council, the only damage inflicted was that the box office and parts of the theatre were destroyed, along with sections of the wooden walkway. Since then, in 2015 and again in 2024 the pier had been voted 'Pier of The Year' by the National Piers Society, as well as being granted Grade II Heritage status. In July 2015, it was reported that Cromer was now the only *End of the Pier Variety Show* remaining in Europe.

Figure 673 is the Pier taken in 2024, in the early evening with a high tide. In the foreground can be seen the granite boulder sea defences which helped to protect the promenade wall from collapsing again, as it had during the sea surge in 2013. This was where I stood to take the photograph.

Figure 673

Now returning to our visit to the Cromer Pier, these variety shows were always worthwhile and once again a most enjoyable evening's performance of harmless comedy and variety entertainment was had by us all. The pre-publicity said, '*Expect all the glitz and glamour worthy of the only full season end of pier show in the world*' and we were certainly not disappointed. Both the Summer and Christmas seasons lasted for two months with 116 shows each season! Given it was almost the conclusion of the Summer one, in his introductory banter the comedian and compere

Chapter 7 Life in Retirement 2014 – 2025

host deliberately pointed out that the audience was not very large at all! However, we were still treated to numerous costume and scene changes, acrobats, dance and song routines and a very talented comedian from Armenia. The whole evening was of a very high standard, and we all returned home feeling much better for having gone to watch it. The pier (Fig. 674) is seen later that evening, with the photograph being taken on our way out after the performance.

Figure 674

The whole show was very worthwhile and thoroughly enjoyed, even by the audience members who just happened to be picked on to join the artiste up on the stage, as part of their act! It was not just those in the front row who were chosen either. Wherever you sat – and we were in the fifth row from the front – you were not safe, not even up in the circle! We had preceded the show with a delicious pre-theatre meal, in their restaurant which was also on the pier. It was a thoroughly typical evening at a seaside holiday show, just as all four of us recalled from our youth, and long may it continue for the current youngsters.

As families do, during Peter and Jane's short stay we had some lovely conversations, full of memories and catch ups, coupled with a particularly good walk over Kelling Heath with the dogs. All in all, a lovely time which we hoped would be repeated soon.

After the success of the Summer Pier Show, Kate and I booked tickets to go on 29 December to see their Christmas Special production. This would be great fun again, particularly as it was on the last night. We had invited Phil and Polly to join us, as we thought that they had never been to see a Christmas Pier show. So, it was something to look forward to after our Christmas away.

For whatever reason, 6 September started as one of my 'bad' days because I awoke in a very sombre mood and my Alzheimer's seemed to be worse. It may have been I was subconsciously aware that on that day I was to attend a Thanksgiving Service for a JP colleague, whom I had known all the time I had been a magistrate.

Ski Cator, as she was known, had joined the bench in 1986 and had held many roles as a magistrate, including being the last Bench Chairman, before all the Norfolk-based benches merged in 2011, to become the Norfolk Bench. Ski had sat on the Criminal Bench, as I also had at the time, and in addition she sat and indeed chaired for a while the Youth Bench. She was very popular and held in high regard by all who knew her, so there was considerable shock when we were all advised in June that having been diagnosed with pancreatic cancer, she had resigned from the bench. Sadly, she passed away on 5 August and the Thanksgiving Service was held in Norwich Cathedral. So, understandably, on that day I was in a reflective mood.

At home, I changed into my suit and made my way to the Norwich Court where I parked my car, as this was adjacent to the Cathedral. Previously Kate and I had chatted as to whether she would come with me, but we were both very aware that this text had to be sent to the professional reader, by the end of the month and time was at a premium. So, Kate stayed at home to continue the mammoth task of reading and editing my manuscript. Once in Norwich, I walked in the sunshine to the service and sat in the nave with Andrea Middleton the current Bench Chairman and my predecessor Eamonn Lambert. The congregation was huge and there were only a few places available and by the commencement of the service all the seats in the nave, those behind the font and all those in the side aisles had been taken. This was confirmation of just how incredibly popular she was and such a very active person in the wider community.

We all stood whilst the Lord-Lieutenant of Norfolk took her seat, followed by the three presiding Bishops, which gave an indication of the high esteem in which Ski was held throughout Norfolk and beyond. The service was wonderful and very moving. It had been meticulously planned and arranged by Ski, which to many of us in the congregation was of no surprise. It truly reflected her admirable character of 'no nonsense or questions' and this was confirmed when the eulogy was given by a close friend, of some 50 years standing. He stated that he had been asked by Ski to '*say a few words*' and when he politely suggested that perhaps a close family member might be a wiser choice, Ski had been adamant that he was the right person and proceeded to hand him a sheaf of papers saying, '*and this is what I want you to say*'! To his credit, having outlined the conversation to an enthralled and amused congregation, he proceeded to read verbatim, the text he had been given. This outlined Ski's life and her achievements, and it was then embellished with his own perspective on her lifetime, since he had known her. It was well received, as were the other elements of the service and we all left much the wiser, reflective and honoured that we had played a part, be it large or small, in her wonderful life.

Summer was now giving way to Autumn as we approached the end of September. As such, the grass didn't require weekly trims, but the autumn

Chapter 7 Life in Retirement 2014 – 2025

Figure 675

winds were shaking their leaves off the trees. I quite liked autumn, so I had no problems with this.

Kate and I took time out from reading, to go on a lovely morning nature walk through Cley Nature Reserve (Fig. 675), led by their expert ranger. This was really interesting, relaxing and informative, especially as we saw many birds including a gannet that had come inland for food, a number of ruffs, and a spoonbill, something that neither of us had ever seen before. We heard a Cetti's warbler, followed by the star of the day which was a single osprey gliding overhead. A wonderful morning all round. The day was topped off with supper hosted by Eleanor and David where we were introduced to a couple, Jane and Duncan who had recently moved to Holt and had previously lived in various places around the world. In fact, Jane had been brought up in Gozo, and they still had frequent visits there, staying in her family home. After our holiday in Italy, Oliver and Jude had suggested having another one together and after much searching, we all agreed that Gozo sounded ideal. So, Jane and Duncan were able to give us some really useful information and tips on the best places to visit and the areas to avoid. This was incredibly helpful and all this along with great company, delicious food and drink, made for a great evening.

Work was progressing at pace on the memoir, as several final deadlines were fast approaching. I was due to send the text back to Ruth for a final read through and I had also asked Polly to read it as well. I had now received some suggested alterations from Polly, which I amended in the text. Polly not being a family member was unbiased and with her previous profession being a University Professor, she was used to reading and marking theses, so was able to provide some very helpful and insightful advice. I had also decided to make things easier for Kaarin the graphic designer and, of course, you the readers, by changing the way the images were referenced. All these alterations were duly undertaken whilst the text was still being compiled daily! Kate was also editing elements of the text and reading out her suggestions, so it was very 'full on'. As such, we both had to work sat opposite each other at our computers in the kitchen whilst much to Archie and Max's consternation they had to wait patiently for their walk. It was hard work, but the end was in sight, and I was very pleased with all the positive feedback that I had received.

Archie was certainly feeling his age and during the day slept more, compared to Max who in a good way was very active with short bursts of sleep! He was indeed proving to be a very intelligent dog and one that enjoyed and learnt from Kate's training. We just needed to stop him pulling on his lead when out walking, but that would come, I was sure.

Our next challenge was to definitely book our 2025 holiday in Gozo with Oliver, Jude and family. This wasn't easy as Oliver had found accommodation that we all liked but we had to navigate and book it through Airbnb, that was a new site for us. We eventually succeeded and having let Oliver and Jude know the good news, we were all now looking forward to two weeks in Gozo, in August next year. During our stay, it will be great for Kate and me to have a few nostalgic return excursions to Malta.

The 26 September 2024 was a key milestone in the progress of this memoir, in that I and Kate had completed all the major updates, which we needed to undertake prior to sending the text to Ruth for her final proof reading. It wasn't, however, the conclusion of the narrative, for once Ruth had returned her alterations, Kate wanted to check some other areas, and I needed to draft the future text through to my birthday. But it was certainly a major achievement.

One thing I had learnt over the years was that I needed to allow the professionals, and in this case, they were Ruth, Kaarin and Polly, to administer their expertise, whilst I focused on the job in hand of writing my memoir and present it to Kaarin in a coherent fashion. So, with this in mind, I concentrated my attention on re-numbering all my separate images, to correspond with the ones in the text, and as I have already mentioned, this would provide Kaarin with a comprehensive and logical file of photographs and images of documents. This took much longer than expected, as my Alzheimer's impacted upon my ability to sequentially number the photographs, and then enter that number into the correct part of the text. After four attempts on my own, I became so frustrated and annoyed, that I then tried it with Kate's and my computer side by side, and with her help it was all satisfactorily achieved.

The next day was one of relaxation and a well deserved change! Max was given some more training, to which he was responding positively, and I continued with my writing. In the evening, we attended a talk given by Dr James Thompson, about the history of eight, significant stain glass windows, in Holt church. Over many years these were commissioned by successive generations of the local Hales family. Dr Thomson, a retired NHS consultant surgeon and a Holt resident, had developed during his retirement and throughout the pandemic lockdowns, a keen interest in recording all these, plus the other stained-glass windows that are all in our church. We had previously been to his first talk, which was really good, so we were keen to attend this one, which focused on the Hales family. Amazingly, the current generation still lived in Holt, and in the same residence that their family had lived in for well over one hundred years. Kate knew one of the family members and she came and sat next to her, which was rather good, as she gave Kate a book about the Hales family which had been written by her grandmother, at the grand old age of 90! James delivered a very interesting talk, and took the audience through the history and the influence the Hales family had had, and indeed still has on the fabric of the town's church. He meticulously explained the meaning and significance of many of the images contained within each window, and his talk was beautifully illustrated by some excellent photographs by James Sidgwick, one of the son's of our friends Eleanor and David. A truly wonderful talk.

October was designated as the final month for reading, checking facts and amending the text of this memoir, before it was sent to Kaarin. To conclude this work, we eagerly awaited the response from Ruth's read through, which was due on 4 October. All this was to take place whilst we endeavoured to live our lives, as two retired senior citizens!

We had recently noticed in the local newspaper that my old secondary school, The Hewett School in Norwich, was to undergo a major rebuilding programme. Apparently, plans had been approved by Norwich City Council and the school was to be redeveloped. The architect's drawing shows its proposed new look

Figure 676

(Fig. 676).[61] Whilst this was great news for the city it did remind me that many of the key buildings of my past, were either going to be changed or be demolished. The Hewett School was going to be redesigned, Colemans Wines had gone, Colmans Foods had partly been converted into flats, whilst the factory and the rest of the offices were still vacant and finally, the Norwich Aviva offices from which I had worked, had now been sold and converted into a school! How times had changed!

At home, thanks to Kate's dedicated training, there were some very positive improvements in Max's behaviour. He was still only six months old and now he was just about walking to heal, certainly sitting on command, his recall was 99% and he had virtually stopped jumping up. I too had been taking him out on a lead, to try to stop him pulling, for at times he was too strong for Kate, and she feared that he would pull her over. Kate had found the gundog training CD, which was invaluable when she trained Archie and Dan, so we re-watched it and applied the suggested correction methods to Max. These certainly seemed to work, and we kept our fingers crossed that this would continue and enable Kate to go out on her own, with Max on a lead. He was now certainly looking more like a dog rather than a puppy.

Kate also decided to telephone our previous gundog trainer, who had been excellent when he had helped us to train both Dan and Archie, in the etiquette of 'picking up', at our local shoot. Since then, he had unfortunately moved to Suffolk, but he was really pleased to hear from us again, and confirmed our approach in training Max. During the telephone call he was also more than happy to give us some additional advice, along with some really helpful tips. So, that was all very reassuring.

On Friday 4 October we took some time out to join Sophie, Leigh and Ben for supper at the Dun Cow in Salthouse. Leigh had texted Kate a few days earlier and asked if we were around, as they were in the area and would we like to meet up for a meal. So at first, we weren't at all sure what this was going to be and wondered did they have some vital news to tell us, be it good or not so good? We needn't have worried though, as it was simply a friendly meal. They were staying

---

61 Image by LSI Architects, The Inspiration Trust and courtesy of the EDP.

Chapter 7 Life in Retirement 2014 – 2025

near Norwich as the next day Sophie was undertaking a cancer night-time charity walk with a friend, around the centre of the city. We relaxed and enjoyed the company and the meal. Having been sent details of the walk the next morning, we sponsored her. Her walk was a huge success (Fig. 677) and her group raised just over three thousand pounds.

Figure 677

During our meal, Sophie also shared some of the results of a new painting hobby that she had just taken up. They were excellent and had been undertaken whilst at a 'Brush Party', not something that either Kate or I had come across before. However, it gave Sophie pleasure, was relaxing and her achievements were certainly to be commended, so that was all good news.

She also told us that she had entered a photographic competition, run by *Vet Times* magazine which, amongst other publications and general support to the veterinary profession, produced calendars with images of pets, which had been submitted by the public. For the 2025 edition the theme was 'Rescue and Rehab'. As Sophie and Leigh's latest addition to their family was a rescued cat, which they with the help of their local vet, had nurtured back to good health, she decided to enter her photograph of KitKat (Fig. 678). This had now been included in the final 30 images and these were to be put forward for a public vote.

Figure 678

We obviously supported this and placed our vote the following day. With her new hobby of painting, and the move away from veterinary nursing, with full-time night shifts, it seemed that Sophie was mentally in a much more positive place. As such, the father and daughter relationship that I had missed for so long, was slowly returning, thank goodness.

Also on 4 October, Ruth kept her word and forwarded her suggested minor amendments, which were mainly grammatical, and I was able to incorporate these into the text. For the remainder of that week, Kate and I had spent a long and productive time re-reading and checking the contents of this text. I had found this extremely hard due to my condition, coupled with the pressures of needing to have the work finished by the end of the month, and the fact that deep down, I was very concerned that Kate was due to have an operation, in a week's time.

The operation was to rectify a prolapse and whilst having spoken at length with the surgeon, Kate was very content with the situation, but I was still very worried. As a result, I had become very distressed which had impacted upon my mood and the control of my feelings. This was not a good position for me to be in, and initially I thought I would simply abandon and stop the book altogether. This was a knee jerk decision which, in my heart, I knew was wrong, but I just could not see a way forward.

I argued with Kate which was most unusual for us, and she endeavoured to talk some sense into me, but I would have nothing to do with it. Was this me responding or was it my Alzheimer's, I didn't know. What I did know was that I felt lost, suicidal and very scared of the immediate future, but logic told me to move away from what lies ahead and to stop writing this memoir. So, I went out for a short walk with Max, had a complete rest from compiling this book, had supper with Kate and a relatively restful night's sleep.

The next day, what was left of my brain seemed to have rationalised the situation and whilst I seemed only a little better, my thoughts were, at least, more coherent. I had now decided that I would complete my memoir, through to the end of October and then see how I felt. I had contacted Neil, my consultant, but to no avail, so I thought I might talk to Kate and see if she thought a visit to my own GP, might be useful.

In my own mind, I was so clear about what I considered to be the rapid development of my Alzheimer's, and having seen both my parents live and die with this condition, I knew that my future was to be horrendous, bleak, and very upsetting for my loved ones. Hence my suicidal thoughts. But with careful consideration to the words and thoughts of Kate, coupled with the excitement of Oliver, who had sought my advice on a possible purchase of a new car, my thoughts slowly changed. If both these people had faith in my opinions

Chapter 7 Life in Retirement 2014 – 2025

and judgement, then why didn't I? I needed to move on and as our children's generation would have said, 'get a grip'! So, I decided to stick with my plan, visit the doctors, support Kate and endeavour to calm down. There was nothing that could be done about my condition, so I just needed to come to terms that this was something I had to accept, however unpalatable. Kate had reminded me that I had some Mirtazapine tablets, which I had forgotten about, which would not only help with my anxiety but would also make me sleep more soundly. I took these and over the next few days, to the delight of Kate and me, my mood returned to a more even keel.

The morning of 9 October started with a new outlook. Oliver had purchased his new car, Kate was relaxed, or as relaxed as anyone could be about an operation and I was still alive. It was to be a good day with great progress being made on reading the memoir text. The following day, Kate and I along with Max and Archie, joined Sarah and Roger for a lovely walk through Blickling Hall parkland, followed by a traditional National Trust coffee and a piece of cake. Once rested, fed and watered we took the opportunity to view the very recently restored James Corbridge's estate map, dated 1729 (Fig. 679).

It was fascinating to see how the park had been changed in the early 1700s,

Figure 679

by the Hobart family, who owned Blickling Hall at the time. We were able to see the route that we had just walked, which included elements of one of the three avenues, which once formed a goose-foot feature of trees through the park. It is not known if Corbridge, at the time, was either drawing what was visible in the park or offering a possible new design, as the evidence of a fourth avenue as shown on his map, has never been identified on the estate. For whichever reason he drew the map there are indications today of at least one avenue remaining which extends out from the west side of the Hall, and we had walked along part of this.

Within this memoir, I have previously mentioned the severe storms in the late 1980s which had hit the UK and caused much damage through winds gusting up to 100 mph. Well, on the evening of 9 October, we heard that a hurricane, named Milton, was expected to cause havoc over Florida, with winds up to 120 mph, and this was very concerning. Considerable damage was caused that day, with some 3 million homes without power, extensive flooding and regrettably at least 16 lives were lost.

Following this the next morning, our own BBC weather forecast for 10 October, informed us that winds of 14,408 mph, and overnight temperatures of 404° were to prevail in the UK. This was, apparently, the remnants of hurricane Milton which had hit Florida the night before and had now been downgraded to a tornado. We were very worried, to say the least, until the BBC weather channel issued a statement an hour or so later saying: '*We have an issue with some of the weather data from our forecast provider which is generating incorrect numbers and text on our BBC Weather app and website. We are really, really sorry about this and are working very hard to fix the problem*'. That was such a relief, but it just showed that modern technology was not infallible. I wondered what might have happened if the technology of Artificial Intelligence (AI) had activated protection measures that were automatically linked to the weather forecast – I didn't like to consider the consequences, but it made one think. Anyway, be that as it may, the correct forecast was in fact for 43 mph winds, which were the remains of hurricane Milton, and we all hoped that it wouldn't bring too much damage.

The week concluded with Kate having her pre operation assessment before her actual operation the next week. All was well so we both hoped that her operation on the 15th would go ahead as planned and be successful. Having already taken Max and Archie to the home of their dog minder, the evening before on the 14th, we rose early on the Tuesday to ensure that Kate arrived at

Chapter 7 Life in Retirement 2014 – 2025

the hospital for her 07.00 appointment. Having wished her well and given her a kiss and hug, I returned home, collected the dogs and awaited the call to say that the operation had been a success.

As it turned out, this was to be a longer wait than I expected. Kate's procedure was the second on the list and was expected to take place at around 11.00, lasting about two and a half hours. However, by mid-afternoon I hadn't received a call and was becoming rather anxious. So just after 16.00 I telephoned the hospital to enquire what the position was but without success. Then at 16.32, to my relief I received a call from Kate to say that having had the operation, spent time in the recovery ward she was now on the Cley ward, and all was well. A speedy, but safe drive to the hospital and we were reunited.

Apparently, Kate's surgeon had needed to undertake a full hysterectomy, which we had been warned might be required. Still the important thing though, was that Kate was well, the operation was a success and whilst a full recovery would entail six weeks of rest, she was to be discharged the next day. I returned home and called all the children to let them know the good news, followed by a WhatsApp message to my sisters. Kate would speak to her brother and sisters later on.

Whilst all this was happening, Oliver and Jude had been up to Leeds to collect their new car, a shiny black Mercedes-Benz S20 (Fig. 680). Whilst they were driving home, a very happy Oliver gave me a call, to wish Kate well and to tell me all about his new purchase. We were to see this when he came up to Holt the following weekend. During our conversations he outlined the progress that his business had made. Sales had continued to rise, and he had now decided to expand his operation by creating a holding company, Teachers Holdings Group, with four subsidiaries – Teachers Together, Tutors Together, Support Together and Together Group Investments. All of which would be developed over the next few years. Oliver and Jude had built up from nothing, an impressive business and

Figure 680

I along with Kate were very pleased for them both. In addition, like his sisters Em and Sophie, he has forged a loving relationship with his children, who along with our other grandchildren are a credit to their parents. As most grandparents are, Kate and I are very proud of our children's and grandchildren's achievements,

REFLECTIONS UPON A FAMILY

but sometimes this just needs to be said out loud, hence this comment!

By the weekend, Kate was settled in at home resting and by the Sunday was even back reading and checking this memoir. On the other hand, I was undertaking all the cooking and cleaning, because Kate was not allowed to do any heavy lifting! By the end of October, Kate was feeling much better but still had to be very careful to not lift heavy items and to continue to take things easy.

The 27 October was the day of putting the clocks back by one hour, as British Summer Time had officially ended. Our fear that Max would be very confused by this change did not materialise as after a couple of days he had acclimatised to the new mealtimes. That was very pleasing for both Kate and me.

On the 31st, I sat in the Family court, and for me it was a sad and emotional Public Law case, where the local authority was requesting an order, to allow a three-month-old baby to be placed for adoption. The details were difficult to read but in summary both parents had no interest in caring for their child, they weren't married, and the mother's other children had already been adopted. As a bench, we considered the case very carefully which lasted for 4 hours, after which we consented to the order. I just hoped that the young baby would be brought up in a loving and caring family. Regrettably, of course, I will never know the outcome.

Court sittings in Norwich were to continue to dominate the first couple of weeks of November. One in particular extended to two days, so this was very 'full on'. It was so very satisfying though, knowing that when I left the court the children were going to receive the care and love that they both craved, and should, of course have already been receiving.

However, the main event, from the global news outlets perspective, was the USA presidential elections. On 4 November, the Republican Donald Trump was the victor. He beat his Democratic rival Kamala Harris, by a considerable margin (Fig. 681).[62] As we all expected, this was to dominate the news over the

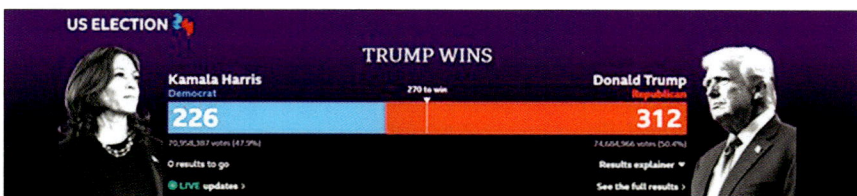

Figure 681

---

62 Image courtesy of BBC/News

Chapter 7 Life in Retirement 2014 – 2025

coming weeks, and I expected this to continue through to handover of power on 20 January 2025. We will await the outcome and then see what stance our new government takes.

I was very pleased to learn from Sophie that her photographic entry (see page 591) for the *Vet Times* calendar, 'KitKat' had been selected as one of the images in their 2025 calendar. In my, totally biased opinion, I thought the photograph entry, coupled with the sub-story of the care and attention that Sophie and her colleagues had lavished on this poor neglected feline, thoroughly deserved to be recognised in this way. So, an excellent outcome and I look forward to seeing the calendar if I can find a copy.

Mid November we needed a top up of dog food supplies so, early on Saturday morning we drove to Fakenham to our usual Animal Food warehouse to replenish our stock. Whilst driving along an almost empty road, we couldn't help but notice that autumn had dressed the countryside. With a low blanket of mist across the fields we proceeded to drive through the cathedral-like canopy of beech trees with their yellow and golden leaves, all about to be abandoned in the light wind. Their summer clothing of green leaves was now a distant memory, but their replacement was truly beautiful and very picturesque. Autumn was certainly making itself at home which also led Kate and I to conclude that as no fruits had manifest themselves on our olive trees, the buds that we had seen earlier in the year must have been leaf buds after all. Perhaps fruits will come next year.

A very well attended and organised Service of Remembrance was conducted on Sunday 10 November at the Holt War Memorial. The general public, including Kate and I, lined the pavement whilst the service was led by Father Howard Stoker, our local vicar, along with representatives from other denominations, as well as scouts, guides, youth groups, army, royal navy, police and fire services to name but a few. This was a regular event and was always extremely well supported. At the Cenotaph, in Whitehall London, the King attended a similar service on behalf of the nation (Fig. 682).[63]

Figure 682

---

63 Image courtesy of BBC/News/Reuters

597

At 18.00, also on the 10th, Kate and I had finally concluded our read-through of all my text to date, which meant that it was now ready to send to Kaarin to have the images prepared by her partner, whilst she undertook the task of creating the final layout. I would then continue to send her the last of my text through to the end of February next year and hopefully this would be a small task by comparison to theirs.

With the text and all the images now on a data stick ready for Kaarin, who was spending a week in Devon with her mother, I took Kate out for a lovely, celebratory evening meal, at the Victoria Hotel in Holkham. This was to thank her for all the support she had given me throughout the last eighteen months whilst I had been compiling this memoir, and also to assist in her recovery from her hysterectomy. We both had a wonderful meal and the following morning we were able to start the day without thinking about 'the book'! In fact, I returned to undertaking some garden improvements that were long overdue, following which we both went to Wells in Norfolk to an exhibition of some of Sir Alfred Munnings original literary art works. They were absolutely stunning as can be seen in these two simple pencil sketches. (Figs. 683 & 684).

Figure 683

Figure 684

With his head turned, you could almost hear the horse saying, 'are you drawing me?' Munnings was clearly a master of the arts if ever there was one.

The very next day I noticed that the town's christmas tree had been erected by the war memorial and the festive lights were being hung throughout the town. It seemed that time waited for no man. There didn't appear to be as many going up this year though, which may have been a reflection on the hard economic environment that the shops had been enduring, and still were in 2024. I was sure that the town would look wonderful again and be ready for the 'switch on', which took place on the 15th,

Chapter 7 Life in Retirement 2014 – 2025

Figure 685

and leading up to Christmas would bring joy to all who visited the high street and yards. Looking very festive in figure 685 is Byfords in Shirehall Plain, just off Holt High Street.

If ever I sought confirmation that Labradors were intelligent, I did not need to look any further than at Max. After six warm months since his birth, come the autumn he had found the warmest place to sleep in the kitchen – in front of the Aga! How did he know, it must just be dog brainpower! Mind you, he was incredibly tired having enjoyed a really good walk around Alderfen Broad, with his mistress and master so I could well understand his desire to pick the best place to relax.

The 20 November was a momentous day, as Kate and I finally handed over the text and images of this memoir, to Kaarin and Kev in order for them to commence the graphic design and layout process. Then, as agreed, I would supply monthly updates to them, through to my birthday in February 2025.

November concluded with a day of hard work erecting our new arbour that we had designed and was made by our local engineering company. However, Kate and I had previously complicated the design, by asking if it could be erected in such a way that allowed the wisteria to lie on top of the new structure, instead of underneath as it had with the previous framework. This had been agreed with Ken, who owned the company and when the individual components were delivered, earlier in the week, we both agreed a method of achieving our aim. Saturday 30 November was the day set for the assembly, so the day before I removed some of the existing wooden structure, in order that access would be easier whilst also leaving sufficient framework ensuring the wisteria stayed in place.

When Ken had delivered all the components, he then set them all out methodically in order of erection, so they were now all in readiness for the Saturday. Ken arrived just before 08.00 and with our friend Phil, and Oliver, who had driven up the night before, we were all assembled and ready to tackle the assembly process.

It all seemed to work really well on the day and the four of us spent four hours putting up the support legs, positioning the top struts making sure that the vegetation was well supported and then Ken bolted it all together. Once this was completed, Oliver, Ken and Bernie, Kens brother, who had arrived with drills and a chain saw, bolted the foot plates to the paving slabs, and then with me cut down the remains of the previous wooden structure. Throughout all this activity Kate kept us all fed and watered with tea, coffee and chocolate biscuits! It was a magnificent achievement on a glorious, dry autumn day and we were delighted with our new arbour!

Figures 686 – 689 show the progress made, commencing with an image of the previous pergola, followed by us putting up the corner posts, then the cross members and concluding with the finished article.

Figure 686

Figure 687

Chapter 7 Life in Retirement 2014 – 2025

Figure 688

Figure 689

December greeted us with a very special and exciting delivery, for on Monday 2nd, we received the first two chapters of this memoir, all beautifully typeset and laid out for us to approve. Also, within this final draft all the relevant photographs had been strategically and artistically positioned and, in some cases, they had been beautifully enhanced, way beyond our expectations. Although there were some very minor changes, approve we certainly did! To say we were impressed was an understatement, just seeing the very professional layout made all the hard work over the past 18 months, worth every moment. Having confirmed our alterations and agreed the layout, we left Kaarin and Kev to continue working their magic on the rest of the draft.

Back in April 2023, whilst we had been at Duxford, I mentioned that there had been a Government National Test for its Emergency Alert Services. Since that date, this emergency warning system has now been activated in various small, concentrated parts of the UK. For the first time though, on 6 December it was activated in reality on a much wider scale throughout parts of Wales and south-west England. This was to warn the population of possible life-threatening dangers from the impending arrival of Storm Darragh, with winds of 90 mph forecast throughout the area, along with very heavy rain. In fact, the authorities were correct in their warning, as overnight and throughout the following days, Wales, Western England and parts of Scotland were hit with winds gusting up to 93 mph, along with severe flooding. This caused over 945,000 homes to lose their electricity supply, trains and flights to be cancelled, roads closed due to fallen trees and tragically some deaths. The power and severity of our climate change which we are all currently experiencing is devastating and makes me wonder just where it will all end! However, on a positive note it seems that we do now have an effective warning system for storms, so lessons have certainly been learnt and implemented since the storm of 1987.

A few days later, whilst sitting comfortably with Kate and eating my lunch, I suddenly noticed without any warning that a heron had landed in the garden and was clearly eyeing up our goldfish as a possible snack. I pointed this out to Kate by which time Max had also spied it. When we opened the patio door the interloper took absolutely no notice, until Max arrived on the scene and as they stood staring at each other we wondered who would back off first. Max was certainly curious but given that this was his first encounter with a bird that was probably twice his height, it was quite understandable as to why he had been hesitant in approaching it. However, with one loud bark which was pretty impressive, given that he was only eight months old, then followed by a short run towards the visitor, he saw off the heron which gracefully flew away. Which I suspect was much to Max's relief. So, another conquest for him, and confirmation for us that our life size, metal heron sculpture was neither a deterrent nor effective in any way at all! I was sure though, that the pond netting had certainly saved our fish from being a lunchtime snack!

Christmas was now rapidly approaching, so with cards and newsletters written and circulated, presents wrapped and delivered and the house decorated, we were almost ready for our Christmas break in Westleton. Before that treat though, we had to take Max to the vet as he needed to be neutered. Not something that we particularly wanted to have done but given his temperament the vet thought that it would be advisable. The night after the operation, whilst the anaesthetic was leaving his body, was somewhat of a nightmare not only for him but also for Kate and me. Suffice to say that his howling gradually morphed into full time whining and total disorientation, which resulted in me having to stay downstairs to reassure him, through to 02.00 when both he and I finally had some sleep. Kate was then up with him around 06.30 until such time as I arose a few hours later. He rapidly improved over the next few days and thankfully was almost back to his normal self again. So, we hoped that he would be well on the way to a complete recovery in time for some Christmas walks. Our hopes were fulfilled for just seven days after his operation he was 'discharged' by the vet on 23 December.

As I outlined previously, Christmas was to be enjoyed in The Crown at Westleton in Suffolk. Now, I have to say here that Kate is incredibly organised

Chapter 7 Life in Retirement 2014 – 2025

and has pre-typed lists of everything that needs to be taken on a holiday. There is a column for each trip which is cross checked, ticked or striked through accordingly. This list runs to six sides of A4 paper and ensures that all eventualities are covered. Once Kate is content with the packing, then my role is to pack the car, secure the house and make our way to our destination. Kate's 'process' has never failed us and works beautifully and, of course, I am in awe of this foolproof system that is very much to my benefit! It seems that 'ticking off' lists is something of a family tradition which has now also been carried on by Em. Judy, Kate's eldest sister once sent her a most appropriate birthday card (Fig. 690) that now has pride of place at home!

Figure 690

Anyway, on Christmas Eve we set off on our way south, with Max and Archie settled in the back of the car. En route we stopped off to admire Blythburgh Church which given that the village is quite small, its church was enormous. At some point in its history the community must have been both very important and home to some very wealthy church benefactors. This manifested itself in the church having a number of huge stunning arches on both sides of the nave, and in the roof some remarkable bosses, carved angels and painted ceiling joists (Fig. 691). We only stayed for a while to admire the architecture, as we needed to make our way. So, we continued our journey, albeit a short one for by now we were only eight minutes from our destination.

Figure 691

Having arrived safely we checked into The Crown and found our accommodation. It was 'compact', to say the least but it was acceptable given that we were only sleeping in the room, and the boys soon made themselves at home on the two fluffy dog beds that had been provided for them! Supper and sleep were the order of the day and with a very comfortable king-size bed we awaited Christmas Day.

After opening our gifts and enjoying a scrumptious breakfast we went for a short walk with the boys to explore the area. After which we returned to The

Figure 692

Crown, where we changed and were then ready for our festive Christmas lunch.

A quick look at the menu (Fig. 692) and we knew we were in for a treat, and we certainly weren't disappointed. It was a real treat, as were the entire three days. It was just perfect to not have to worry about purchasing and preparing the food, cooking it and finally washing up afterwards!

Once we had digested and relaxed for a while we decided to take a short drive to Dunwich. Here we all enjoyed a lovely walk along the almost deserted seashore. Whilst this wasn't the first seaside paddle that Max had experienced but given that it was his first real walk, since being signed off by the vet, he was determined to enjoy the experience. So, despite the cold air and sea mist, he was constantly in and out of the sea. He obviously had great fun even though he discovered that he couldn't actually catch the waves! Archie, on the other hand, was far more sedate in his old age and just mooched along the sand, hoping to find some delectable morsel to sniff!

Boxing Day we spent visiting the local towns of Leiston, where we visited the ruined Abbey, Thorpeness with its famous 'Head in the Clouds' house and finally Aldeburgh where we had a lovely coffee and mince pies! Supper was again enjoyed in the restaurant before relaxing and bed. In the morning it was reality time, for following our breakfast we had to gather our belongings and pack the car, ready for the journey home. A very successful Christmas that was relaxing, stress free and certainly the right decision we had made way back in July, when we booked it. Once home it was time to prepare to host Oliver, Jude, Eve and Zoey, who arrived two days later to celebrate the New Year with us. Just what would that bring I wondered, apart from the obvious family celebrations?

Prior to the New Year though, we treated and took Phil and Polly to the last night of the Cromer *End of the Pier Christmas Show*. This was to thank them for all their help throughout the year. As we expected the performance was very professional, highly entertaining and a wonderful way to conclude what, at times, had been a very difficult year for both Kate and me.

Chapter 7 Life in Retirement 2014 – 2025

2025

We both saw the New Year in, at home in Holt, with Oliver, Jude, Eve and Zoey. We all watched in comfort the spectacular London Fireworks which were superb – and even better when seen on the television, whilst sitting beside a lit and cosy, gas coal fire and with a glass of port in hand. The television pictures of London looked very cold indeed!

After a good night's sleep, Eve and Zoey decided to play shops at the bottom of the stairs and used as their counter the low wall, where the treads turned a corner. This was definitely a favourite game for all our grandchildren and could last for as long as they and the adults were interested! Normally, it would keep them all amused for an hour or so, and this was the case on New Year's Day. I just wonder if when they are older and possibly have their own children, they will remember the games they played at Grannie and Grandpa's and create similar situations for their family. I do hope so, as they have all certainly enjoyed the 'shopping' experience in Holt and it is good that their 'role playing' teaches them about life skills. However, later in the afternoon, the previous late night began to catch up with Zoey. Despite the attraction of Daffel, the favourite rocking horse (Fig. 693) and later the reclining chair in the library all snuggled up to her 'big sister' (Fig. 694), in the evening her proper bed won the day. Figure 693 was actually taken by Eve, aged just nine, who clearly has an 'eye' for a good picture – a budding 'David Bailey' in the making?

Figure 693

Figure 694

Sadly, 2 January was the day for Oliver and family to return home. So, after packing and stowing everything safely into their car, we all then had a great lunch at the King's Head in Letheringsett.

605

After which, each of us returned to our respective abodes, which left Kate and I in a very quiet home, but looking forward to the next time we could all be together again. This would probably be in April at the draft launch of this memoir which I hope will be a huge surprise to everyone!

Twelfth night was upon us and the Christmas decorations were packed away for another year. Whilst doing so we had to remember where we had 'hidden' the twelve robins. Traditionally these are all hidden around the house (Fig. 695) for our grandchildren to find, just as their parents did when they were their age, which always gives our grandchildren something to look forward to and remember their Christmases with Grannie and Grandpa. It also meant that the next year we had to remember not to repeat the previous hiding places!

Figure 695

On 6 January many parts of the UK were experiencing either deep snow or severe flooding but thankfully in Holt we only had some light rain. I was really struck by this endearing image, which had appeared on the BBC news site, of some inquisitive sheep, caught in a snow covered field (Fig. 696)[64]. You can just imagine the sheep's thoughts when they realised that the farmer having just fed them was now on his way back to the farm – is there any pudding? They certainly look well nourished though, so I am sure that the farmer was caring for them really well and it appears that the three in the background are still eating their first course!

Figure 696

I guess that if I had followed through on my childhood vision of being a farmer, all those years ago, I could easily have been the tractor driver, having just fed my flock. Instead, I am the one sitting comfortably at my computer in a warm kitchen, ruminating on things that may had been, whilst Kate is cooking supper on the Aga and our two dogs are fast asleep by the drawing room fire. I think my choice was the right one, but it was a close call, at the time!

---

64 Image credit, BBC/Andy Artist

Chapter 7 Life in Retirement 2014 – 2025

Today, 12 January, I finished reading the proof of the first few chapters of this memoir, all beautifully typeset and laid out, accompanied by some very professionally enhanced photographs. Whilst I say it myself, it was really good reading those sections again and most enjoyable, as it was at a time when all around me there was sadness. This was due to the winter blues setting in and regrettably Kate and I had had to attend a number of funerals of both friends and JP colleagues. I guess that at our age this was to be expected but it was a sobering thought. Roll on the summer sun and our next holiday!

It has occurred to me that whilst the thought of creating a memoir was conceived months prior to my diagnosis of Alzheimer's, the very fact that I shall have this book to look at and read will most certainly assist my memory in the latter stages of my life. If I am unable to read it then Kate and other family members and friends can always read sections to me, instead! Regrettably, due to my condition, in the future I am quite likely to forget its contents soon after hearing them, but that's just part of the Alzheimer's journey which I am sure will be frustrating to those I love.

Back to reality and after lunch, to round off a very relaxing weekend, Kate and I with the dogs went for a lovely frosty walk, over Holt Lowes. I find it very relaxing walking either on my own or with Kate, the dogs, friends or a combination of all three. This is privately enhanced through being able to juggle between my fingers whilst I have my hand in my pocket, two small, smooth circular stones. I don't recall where I found them, probably either on a beach or on a path, but I have had them for a number of years now and hopefully will continue to do so for years to come. One is black with a small indentation, the other is brown and both being about the size of an old penny coin (Fig. 697). Little things that stick in my memory and help me to relax.

Figure 697

My mother often said to me that becoming older is not fun, and just now I have to agree with her, as I both look and feel like a 90-year-old man! For currently when I take Archie and Max for a walk I am walking very slowly with the aid of a stick. Like many 90-year-olds are prone to do I, at only 69, fell over on one particular walk across Salthouse Heath and whilst the only thing I hurt was my pride, I felt very ancient indeed lying on the ground looking up to the sky. Even the dogs were surprised to see me down at their level and luckily no one else was around to witness my fall! The cause of all this had, just a few hours earlier, been diagnosed by the doctor as trochanteric bursitis. Apparently, this is a common condition which is caused by a painful swelling of the bursa, the fluid-filled sac that acts as a cushion between the hip bone and tendon. By backtracking on what I had been doing over the past few days, Kate and I with the doctor concluded that this had been caused when repotting our two olive trees which had been incredibly heavy. I certainly won't repot them again! But the good news was that a) I didn't need a hip replacement, which was my main concern and b) if I took the doctor's advice and the prescribed tablets all should be well in about six weeks. In the meantime, my 70th birthday in February feels like it will be a 90th celebration! Happy(ish) days!

By mid January, Kate and I had received Chapters 5 and 6 which took us up to 2012. As previously, this was all beautifully illustrated and typeset, ready for us to carefully read through, amend as necessary and return to Kaarin. This took us three full days and late on the Sunday we sent back our suggested changes, along with a number of questions relating to typography protocol, e.g. if any words, names or titles etc. should be in italics, as these were somewhat confusing to us. Luckily, we had an expert in Kaarin to help us. Even with this careful editing we were sure that like many of the books in our library, this memoir would contain the odd one or two errors, which unfortunately will be inevitable.

The 23 January was definitely a major milestone, for Kaarin and Kev had sent me to approve the completed work up to the end of 2024. This meant that now I just had to record January and February 2025 which hopefully wouldn't take too much effort. Throughout this time, whilst I have been checking through this memoir I have been extremely impressed not only with the typesetting and layout but also the quality of the images and I went to bed that night very proud that I had written a book! Over the next few days Kate and I read the

Chapter 7 Life in Retirement 2014 – 2025

final elements of the text, fortunately there were not very many alterations and these changes were agreed with Kaarin.

During the last week of January, the UK was hit by two horrendous storms. The first, Storm Éowyn, was not as serious in Norfolk as it had been in the West and North of the UK. Here it had been recorded as being the most powerful and severe storm since WWII. It caused havoc with winds up to 135 mph, recorded on 24 January in Cairnwell, Scotland.[65] Immense damage was caused to the road and rail networks, trees and buildings, regrettably leaving thousands of homes without power for several days and loss of life. If that wasn't bad enough this was followed, a few days later, by the second one, Storm Herminia which arrived from Spain through France and hit much of Wales and southern England. Again, bringing chaos, power outages and damage to many properties with wind speeds up to 83 mph in Berry Head, Devon.[66] If anyone needed evidence of climate change then these dramatic and extreme swings in the weather should prove the point, but there are people, some in very high positions and with enormous influence, who simply won't accept this.

The next couple of days found me being very emotional and upset, to the point that Kate had to wake me up very early one morning, as I was in tears whilst still being asleep! The situation had arisen, for in my thoughts I had been forcibly reminded, like a train hitting the buffers, about my Alzheimer's and the reality of its consequences.

The day before, I had decided to surprise Kate with a holiday, as I had successfully done many times before in our marriage. This time it was to visit Sorrento and to see the recently revealed treasures in Pompeii which we had seen on a recent television programme. I went to our normal travel agent in Holt and spoke to Joan, who again was both very knowledgeable and helpful, as she had been when we went to Thailand. I came away with some wonderful ideas which she would develop into a proposal and send to me later that day. All was fine and I awaited her email. When it arrived she had kindly outlined three options, all of which looked really good but I was faced with having to make a decision, as to which one to choose! Something I found that I simply didn't

---

65 Wikepedia – Storm Éowyn
66 BBC – 27 January 2025

have the cognitive ability to do. So, I simply had to ask Kate for help which, of course, ruined the surprise element and really upset me. I was so distressed because what would, a few years ago, have been a very simple decision was now beyond me. Couple this, with the knowledge that knowing that my cognitive powers were only going to become worse and that there was nothing I could do to correct this, made the scenario more unbearable. It is as if a part of my brain, which gives me understanding and logic is totally intact and functioning normally, whilst the other part that gives me the ability to remember and reason is quickly deteriorating. I appreciate that my diagnosis, of which I am on the cusp, outlined this scenario but it is so cruel that my brain allows me to understand this, but regrettably science is currently unable to rectify the situation. As a result, I simply had to spoil the surprise element, tell Kate all about my plans and let her guide me to a joint decision. Not what I wanted at all!

Later that evening I was washing up, after we had had friends round for a supper party, which was highly successful and most enjoyable, when I found that again my memory failed me, as I was unable to recall where certain crockery and utensils lived. It was not as if I didn't know, because I did, but I had to stop and think very hard about every action. So, once again, I was reminded of my deterioration and the speed at which this was happening. Naturally, I was terribly upset but did not want to burden Kate with my thoughts, so kept these to myself, despite her asking me what was wrong and endeavouring to help.

Consequently, all of this boiled up to my emotional upset during the night. Kate had been wonderful, we had had a hug in bed, and I had poured my thoughts out to her whilst I dried my eyes. We talked for ages and both agreed that once I had written those episodes into this memoir that it would be a good idea to send that extract to Neil, my consultant, to see if he could offer any medication enhancement to my prescription, that might help to alleviate some of those issues. I have done this and await the outcome.

The month concluded on a very positive note with firstly, the festoon lights being installed around the arbour (Fig. 698). Insert taken in May with the wisteria in bloom. They looked fantastic and have finished it all off perfectly. We were now looking forward to dining al fresco during the summer evenings, assuming that the weather will allow us to do so.

Then secondly, I was sent the final text through to the end of the book, for Kate and I to carefully read, amend and return to Kaarin. This was a huge task, which took us a week of reading, making notes and double checking the accuracy of the text, before we were both happy to feedback our thoughts to her.

Chapter 7 Life in Retirement 2014 – 2025

Figure 698

We achieved this on 31 January and as we had agreed I was also able to include the penultimate month's text. The final section will be returned to Kaarin in February and will include my 70th birthday which will be the conclusion to this memoir.

Over the last few months, I have been very conscious that my time on this earth is limited. This is not a morbid thought but simply one of reality. However, like many people, including both my parents and as I have previously explained my fellow magistrate Ski Cator, all of whom spent their last few cognitive months sorting out their funeral arrangements etc. I have had a desire to finish many outstanding matters in order to avoid, when I am gone, those whom I love being left with having to undertake these tasks on their own. However, I must say that I really don't consider myself to be 'in my last few cognitive months' but I do have to accept that I am probably approaching my final decade.

The most important matters to which I have referred to are replacing the arbour, which has now recently been superbly undertaken, followed by stripping, repairing and retiling the front porch roof and the rooves over the two bay windows, decorating the porch itself and finally securing the garden so that Max is safe. Having decided to use the inheritance from my mother, I spent January and early February working with Kate to find competent tradesmen who could undertake these tasks. This was successfully achieved and now over the next few months all the outstanding works will be carried out. These will leave us both with a tidier, more solid, water resistant home, an arbour which now will not fall over and is most attractive at night when all lit up and, of course, a dog proof garden!

So, as my grand age of 70 rapidly approaches later this month I have been able to chronicle the many and very happy times I have enjoyed, plus the odd one or two that perhaps were not so good. However, whilst recently in bed thinking about the title, and mulling over these final few paragraphs, it struck me at 03.00am, did I actually have the correct title! Should it perhaps have been *Reflections upon a wonderful Family*, as it surely has been and unequivocally continues to be? Anyway, I am past the point of changing the title now, so I trust that my reflections have revealed what a remarkable family I have had and still have today.

I have to admit that compiling this memoir has been a labour of love for both of us. It commenced in the spring of 2023, when Kate and I sorted out most of our photographs and documents, some of which are included within these pages. This was all prior to 5 July 2023 which was when the first lines of text were tentatively written onto a page. So, from conception through to its draft release this April, it has taken around 21 months in total. I expect that after my birthday there will be further changes before its final release sometime later in the year.

The last couple of days had been warm and sunny, so on 5 February I spent some time tidying areas of the back garden. Winter leaves were collected and dead plants trimmed to enable the spring weather to bring them back to their summer beauty. Kate and I ordered some new plants and shrubs to re-stock the areas that now needed filling.

Once again, Kate and I were to attend another Thanksgiving Service at our local church. This time it was more sobering as it was in memory of a lovely couple, who we knew well and who had retired to live in Holt. It wasn't through old age that they left us so unexpectantly, but regrettably it was due to a tragic road accident, when they were crossing the main road, in High Kelling to go home from church. This occurred just before Christmas, on 22 December. They were both holding hands and whilst carefully walking across they were hit by

Chapter 7 Life in Retirement 2014 – 2025

an oncoming car. It was not speeding but the driver simply didn't see them, and he was ultimately charged with driving without due care and attention. It was a huge tragedy for all concerned and their very moving service attracted a full church of around 200 people, which evidenced their esteemed profile in Holt. A very sad loss of two people who gave so much to our community.

Figure 699

On Friday 8 February, we went off to the Holt Community Centre to watch the film *The Rocky Horror Picture Show* (Fig. 699).[67] This was released back in 1975, the same year as the Holt Community Centre was opened and was all part of their 50th anniversary celebrations. One of these celebratory events included a film festival, partly organised by our friend Phil Barrett and it had run throughout the weekend, showing seven films all released in 1975. This was the only one that we attended, as some of the others we had seen numerous times in our youth, e.g. *Jaws*, *Three Days of the Condor* and *Monty Python and the Holy Grail*. Kate had already seen and enjoyed the Rocky Horror film when it first came out and gently persuaded me to go with her. Was it a good choice? Well, I think the description of 'weird' summed up my impression. The soundtrack, whilst not being composed by either the 'Beatles' or the 'Rolling Stones', in my opinion it was heavily influenced by both groups and was brilliant. The film's story line, as I said was bizarre but certainly not something that made me think of leaving. Still, it was a lovely evening and concluded, much to the enjoyment of some of the audience, with Kate demonstrating how to do the '*Time Warp*' dance!

In complete contrast, the next day I awoke and undertook my regular Sunday routine of winding up our collection of timepieces. With five longcase clocks, one carriage, two station clocks, a wall and a couple of mantle clocks, I find this weekly tradition always very satisfying, especially as they all keep very good time. I am very much aware that the actual sound of our clocks ticking and striking are all really relaxing for me. Later in the day, we drove into Norwich and we both thoroughly enjoyed a visit to see the J. M. W. Turner exhibition (Fig. 700) in the now upgraded Castle Museum. This was, of course, totally and utterly different to *The Rocky Horror Picture Show*, both of which were most enjoyable in their own way.

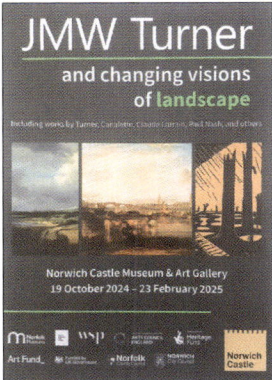

Figure 700

---

67 Image credit – IMDb

613

Today, 12 February we were supposed to have been switched over to Digital Voice which was a new digital service to replace the outdated landline throughout the UK. Not an easy move and even the BT telephone helpline operator, who was calling my mobile via a video link, was somewhat confused when looking at our connections! Apparently, because our line goes through an interior wall it raised all sorts of issues. So much so that a British Telecom (BT) home tech expert would now have to come round to sort out all the problems! Fortunately, we still had some connectivity but not any of our BT services, so mobile calls were the order of the day, until such time as we could be connected to our BT line, once again.

To the great delight of the children in Norfolk and I suspect a number of mums and dads, including Kate and me, Paddington Bear was unveiled in Norwich and officially welcomed as its newest resident. He now sits proudly in the Cathedral Close where he sits to eat his lunch of marmalade sandwiches. He can be seen here (Fig. 701)[68] accompanied by some of the Norwich Cathedral choristers, sitting with him for company, whilst all eating their own sandwiches.

Figure 701

Paddington had arrived in Norwich as the city had been triumphant over 90 other towns and cities to win a competition, to find an exceptional home for this marmalade-loving bear. He is now the 24th specially commissioned statue and it is so good to know companies are still prepared to spend money creating such models, simply in order that both children and adults alike can enjoy their fictional characters. I appreciate that it's all part of the advertising for the films and books but there are much cheaper advertising mediums that could have been used. So, hats off to the advertising agency and company for their work, and as can be seen in the photograph it is much appreciated and will continue to be so for a long time!

Whilst Paddington eats his sandwiches, here in Holt we had the final run of fencing erected, thus ensuring the entire garden was 'dog proof'. However,

---

68 Image credit – Denise Bradley / EDP

Chapter 7 Life in Retirement 2014 – 2025

if Ben was here, he would say, *'all this mess needs to be cleared up!'* (page 442). Which of course it was, over the next three days. With the garden now fully secure we could happily let both Max and Archie out without the fear that Max, in particular, would again escape to explore the town!

Over recent weeks, we have been both invited to and hosted a number of supper parties, some with close friends others with a mix of friends and people who were new to us and had only recently moved into Holt. It is always good to meet new faces and in our case we have met and enjoyed the company of a couple who had previously lived in Gozo for many years. So, in advance of our holiday there this summer, when they came for supper they were definitely able to recommend places to visit, the best restaurants to frequent and shops where we can buy local produce to cook and eat. Whilst the world appears very big, it is strange how often you can meet people close by, who either have knowledge or have been to the same places as yourself. So, perhaps the world isn't that large after all! Anyway, thanks mainly to Kate our supper parties were excellent, and I am sure the Gozo recommendations will be fantastic, as well.

The conclusion of February 2025 was full of not only surprises, adventures and romance but also fun and exploration. As you may have already worked out it was all because I celebrated my 70th birthday. Kate had been planning this surprise celebration since last year and it worked superbly, as I had no idea at all as to what she had up her sleeve and what I was about to experience alongside her!

It all began on Monday 24 February when Kate commenced packing. I had previously been told that I wasn't to arrange anything for the week of my birthday, which I dutifully abided by. On previous holidays I am normally 'involved' in the packing, but not this time. I wasn't allowed to know what was needed in the way of clothes etc. for fear that I would guess or at the very least surmise what was to follow. I was though, allowed to go and purchase some dog food and other pet necessities beforehand, so I could safely assume that wherever we were going we would be accompanied by our two faithful friends, Archie and Max.

The next morning, I loaded up the back seat of the car with numerous pieces of luggage etc., put the dogs in the back, so they had their own area to sit in and with Kate as master navigator, we set off. Turn right, keep going, take the second exit off the roundabout … were the key orders of the day from Kate and these instructions were then replicated by the dulcet tones of the satnav. Thankfully it was also giving me the same directions, so it enabled Kate and I to have a more relaxed journey with lots of interesting conversations – but still no clues!

REFLECTIONS UPON A FAMILY

Figure 702

At around 13.00 I was guided to Kyson Hill, owned by the National Trust where we parked and took 'the boys' for a lovely walk beside the estuary of the river Deben, towards Woodbridge. Whilst this was lovely with panoramic views, regrettably the tide was out so the estuary mud was in abundance, and Max took full advantage of this! Not a great start to our time away and Kate was not impressed, particularly as she had to rub Max down before he was allowed back into the car! Once he was sorted out though, we were on our way again and seven minutes later we arrived at our ultimate destination Seckford Hall (Fig. 702),[69] just a few miles from Woodbridge in Suffolk.

This was no ordinary hotel, it was a luxurious Tudor Manor built in the 1530s, extended over the years and was now run as a hotel and spa complex. Later I was to discover that one claim to its fame was that Enid Blyton, when she was nineteen, had stayed there in 1916, as her friends lived in part of the hall. So, this made me wonder, could the manor have had some influence on her inspiration for her *Faraway Tree* collection of stories, some of which were read to me by my mother, all those years ago? The hotel now had its own golf course, not that that facility interested either of us, unlike its Spa where we both had really relaxing massages.

It was a total surprise and one that I won't forget for years to come and the realisation that this was to be our home for the next few days began to sink in, as Kate booked us in at the reception, whilst 'the boys' stayed in the car. Her meticulous attention to detail began to reveal itself when we were shown to our suite of rooms. First, I was greeted with a 'Happy Birthday' banner on the door. Then inside, the rooms were all decked out with birthday balloons and on the

Figure 703

---

69 Image credit – *East Anglian Daily Times*

table (Fig. 703) was a box of chocolates, two glasses, an ice bucket that contained a bottle of 'fizz', on top of which was a postcard. This read '*Love you forever and a day, always by your side. All my love Kate xxx*'. All topped off with a birthday cake! What more could anyone want? Well, the answer was clear as Max needed to be hosed down and washed before he was allowed anywhere near us, let alone into our palatial accommodation! Having undertaken this task myself, which Max thought was great fun, he was duly dried and allowed to join us inside. Once settled into our suite we began to relax and albeit a day early I lit and blew out the candles on my cake, so we each could have a slice, before we made our way to the Maybush Inn in Waldringfield, where we had a delicious meal.

On the 26 February 2025 at precisely 07.45 I turned 70! To mark the day Kate gave me her card, along with some others that she had brought from home and we had our photograph (Fig. 704) kindly taken of us by the hotel receptionist. What a day it was, bitterly cold, probably colder than the actual day I was born in 1955. I was, as can be seen, of course now somewhat heavier than all those years ago and certainly much taller than my 20 inches recorded in Figure 4 on page 19. Here I was once again ready for the world in front of me! This time though, I could have my own choice of breakfast before we all left to explore Sutton Hoo, another National Trust property and somewhere that neither of us had visited before.

As I have said it was bitterly cold. This didn't spoil our walk though, around the sites of the ancient Anglo-Saxon burial mounds.

Figure 704

617

These were within the Royal Burial Ground of possibly King Rædwald, his wife and some pagan warriors. Here we climbed to the top of the viewing tower where we could see the layout of the site, along with visiting the exhibition hall, both of which were very thought provoking. Afterwards we sat and enjoyed a hot cup of National Trust coffee and some of their cakes, and we planned the rest of our day. Well, as much as I was allowed to plan as there were still surprises to come! First we made our way over the Orwell Bridge to Pin Mill, famous for the Thames Sailing Barge race that takes place annually in July. Here we took the boys on a brief meander around the estuary as the cold weather and rain prevented further exploration. Returning to the warmth and comfort of Seckford Hall, we were able to relax prior to making our way to the restaurant for a lovely birthday supper. As anticipated, this was delicious and exceeded our expectations. Yet again the forensic thought and detail that Kate had put into my birthday week was evident, for suddenly during the meal yet another surprise came about, as I was handed my presents from Kate. After carefully unwrapping the first one a beautiful model of a reclining hare was revealed. I had seen and commented upon this many months previously and it now resides in our drawing room back in Holt. (Fig. 705).

When I opened my second present from Kate (Fig. 706), I found an original 1976 copy of *Dr. Fegg's NASTY Book of Knowledge,* written by Terry Jones and Michael Palin. This included extracts from Enid Blyton's *Famous Five* books which were read out by Michael, when we both saw him at the Norwich Theatre Royal, back in September 2024. Also included in this present was an updated version, of the same book, now entitled *Dr. Fegg's Encyclopaedia of All World Knowledge,* published in 1984, with a handwritten dedication to me, from Michael Palin. These are both collectable books and must have taken considerable time to find and in the case of the 1984 version, have it personally signed as well. They also both linked into where we were staying in that, as I have mentioned before, Enid Blyton the author of the *Famous Five* books and my own childhood favourite *The Magic Faraway Tree,* had also stayed there.

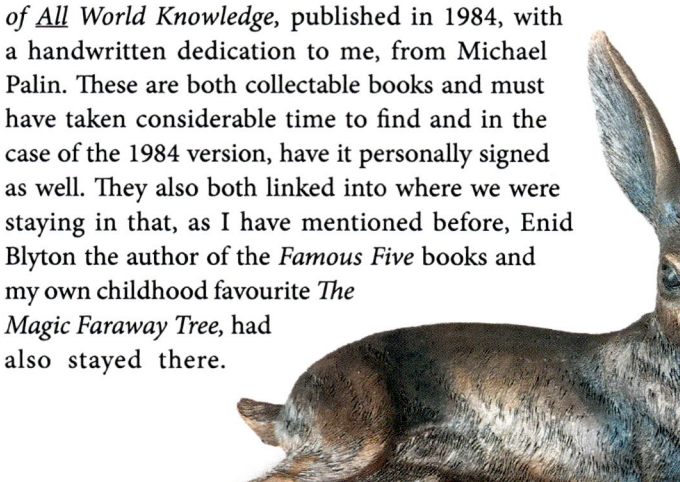

Figure 705

Chapter 7 Life in Retirement 2014 – 2025

Figure 706

These ingenious links to my childhood when I had had her books read to me, also last year when we saw Michael at the theatre and now when we stayed at Seckford Hall, were very clever indeed. Of course, none of that happened by accident so I cannot thank Kate enough. Before we retired to the comfort of our room, I looked through the books which are gloriously Michael Palin in every respect, and I reflected on just how much time, effort and love Kate had put into my 70th birthday. A perfect end to a wonderful day.

The next day was to include yet another surprise. I was advised that after breakfast we were going for a short drive. Nothing else, not our destination, why we were going there or what we were intending to do when we arrived!

Sure enough, at 10.30 we duly pulled into a small hamlet five minutes drive from the hall. Having been advised to park in the drive of a house we alighted the car and Kate proceeded to ring the doorbell – what on earth were we doing! To my utter astonishment the door opened, and my cousin Chris Pearce appeared and greeted us both. Yet again I was speechless! It had never occurred to me that we may have been close to Chris's new abode! We were ushered in and after a long and convivial chat over a cup of coffee, followed by a guided tour around the house and garden, we all left for lunch at the Riverside restaurant in Woodbridge. It was so lovely to meet up with Chris and hear all about her move, the planned alterations she wanted to make to her new home and, of course, her choral engagements both past and future, which she and her friends from the Ipswich Choral Society had undertaken and were now planning. Once again, the surprise was perfect and kept a total secret, for goodness only knows how many months. Perfect!

Following this and having said goodbye to Chris, we took the dogs for a walk along the estuary, this time towards Kyson Hill. The weather was much kinder and the views over the water were beautiful. However, it was now my opportunity to give Kate a treat, so when we returned to the hotel, we both enjoyed a lovely, long professional massage in their Spa. I had hoped this would be even more relaxing for Kate, if that was possible, as now she was to receive a massage, rather than having to give one in her professional capacity. Apparently it was, so that was a success, as was my slightly longer 'Inner Calm' massage which I thoroughly enjoyed. After which we topped the day off with yet another delicious supper, this time in the hotel's bar.

Friday 28 was not only the conclusion of my birthday celebrations but time to pack up and return home. It had been a very relaxing few days, so having enjoyed another wonderful breakfast we bade farewell to Suffolk and welcomed Norfolk and home.

That evening I drafted my penultimate thoughts for this memoir. Whilst doing so I reflected not only on my life in Kent and Norfolk but also on the love and support that all my family and friends have shown to me over the years.

Now, I would like to take this opportunity to say that writing down all my memories etc. has been a very cathartic experience and I am very proud to have been able to recount, to you the reader, my many life journeys and events. I am equally delighted that I have concluded in the manner and timescale that I had originally conceived which, of course, is due in the main to Kate's encouragement and her constant and loving support and who amongst others I acknowledge later.

The first draft of the book was launched on 26 March 2025, when Kate and I hosted 42 family members and close friends at Hanworth House, during which I 'introduced' this memoir. For the day we had had a small number of draft books printed and bound which our guests could peruse during the afternoon. Afterwards close family were given a draft book to take away and asked to feed back any observations and corrections they had and these, where agreed, were then included. I have to admit I waited in trepidation, coupled with much excitement as to how the memoir would be received. In fact, the feedback was positive and with some minor corrections and clarifications I was pleased that the family were happy with my narrative.

So, now I conclude this chapter with the most recent family photograph (Fig. 707) taken at the conclusion of the day, by my brother-in-law, David Riddington. I can be seen proudly holding a draft copy. With glorious weather along with some excellent canapés the day was fantastic and enjoyed by us all.

Chapter 7 Life in Retirement 2014 – 2025

Figure 707

Standing left to right – Kenny Jones, Ben Bedford, Leigh Bedford, Sophie Bedford, Em Jones, Peter Jones, Oliver Gosden, Jude Gosden
Seated middle left to right – Myself, holding my memoir, with Kate my wife, our two dogs, 13-year-old Archie next to Kate and one-year-old Max looking at the camera
Seated front row left to right – Zoey Gosden, Eve Gosden, Leo Jones, Frankie Jones

That momentous occasion was then to be followed later in the year by not one but two holidays abroad. The first in May to Sorrento and Pompeii with Kate, where we hoped to view the recently uncovered parts of the Roman city of Pompeii, destroyed in 79 AD by the eruption of Mount Vesuvius. Then in the summer to Gozo and Malta, again with Kate but also Oliver, Jude, Eve and Zoey. I was sure that both of these holidays would be great fun, relaxing and a total change for both Kate and me from our normal daily activities.

Upon our return we will have the final version of Reflections Upon a Family professionally printed and bound and I will look forward to seeing this followed by its distribution to my family and friends.

A perfect way to conclude my 70th year.

CHAPTER 8

The Gosden Mystery

Whilst this final chapter is not totally related to my own memories, I feel it is still interesting and worth recording. The mystery is historic, played out before I was born, or my parents were even married, and it has rumbled on for many years. I had hoped that the research that had been undertaken by both David Gosden and me would solve the mystery. But, of course, we will never know for sure.

Whilst I was working on our family tree with David, he mentioned that he had discovered an interesting and somewhat controversial issue within the family. When encouraged by me, and others who he had also spoken to about this revelation, he said that he would only reveal the details once the last of that generation had died. Regrettably, for us all and in particular his wife Raquel and son Christopher, David predeceased my mother who was the last of that generation. Thus, this resulted in the knowledge of his 'discovery' being taken to his grave.

However, being intrigued by his comments, I endeavoured to ascertain the 'interesting and controversial' issue. As part of my research, Christopher kindly gave me copies of David's papers. Whilst I cannot say for certain that I have found the answer, I can say that I think it possibly had something to do with Cyril Gosden, his sister Win Horton née Gosden and Len Gosden my father, and the inheritance which they each received in 1952 following the death of their mother, coupled with the demise of E. C. Porter. It was interesting to note that, for whatever reason, it appeared Cyril, David's father, was the only one who had kept these documents. My father retained and gave me many of his own contemporary papers, but the ones pertaining to his inheritance were notable by their absence.

In short, it appeared that the estate left by my grandfather and grandmother who died in 1951 and 1952 respectively, was valued at £2,853.10s.1d (Fig. 708) which at the time, was a reasonably large sum of money. To put this into context, some eight years later in 1960, my father was earning £1,000 per annum.

Chapter 8 The Gosden Mystery

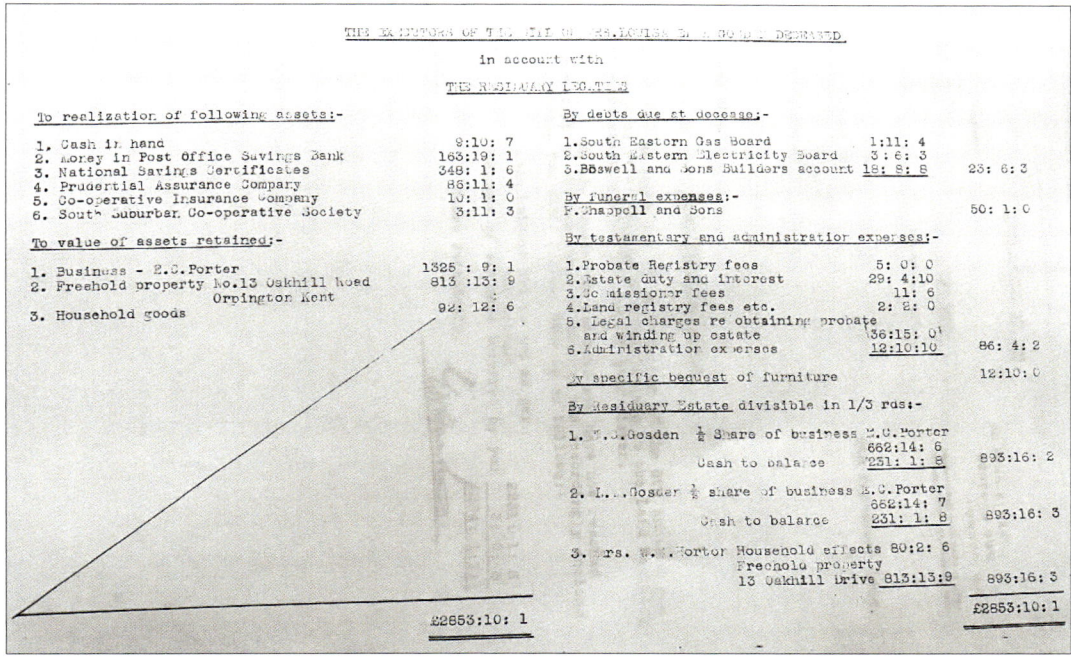

Figure 708

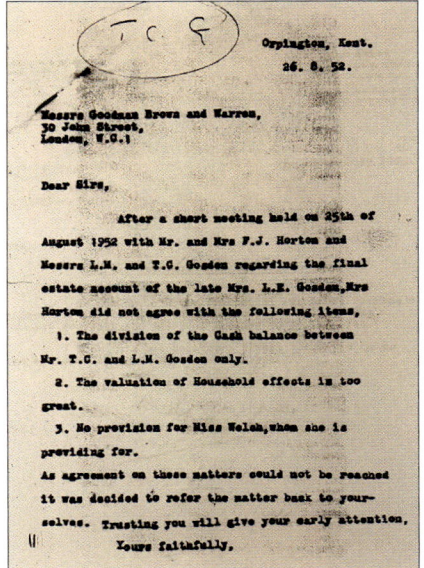

Figure 709

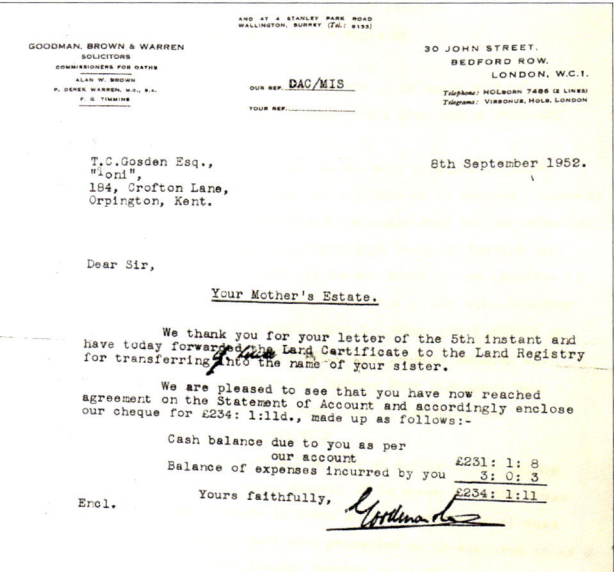

Figure 710

REFLECTIONS UPON A FAMILY

As set out in a letter dated 26 August 1952 (Fig. 709) and taken from the supporting papers, it was clear that my Auntie Win and Frank Horton her husband, were unhappy with the proposed division of the cash, of which she received none. Along with the inflated valuation of the household effects and the absence of any provision for Miss Welsh, Cyril's, my father's, and Win's aunt, who was living with her and Frank. Clearly from the letter that was sent to the executors, this issue was not resolved and required the intervention and mediation services from solicitors. A couple of weeks later though, the matter was resolved, as can be seen in the letter, dated 8 September 1952 (Fig. 710).

However, whilst that is a mystery in itself, I suspected that the larger mystery was to follow regarding the bulk of the inheritance that Cyril and my father received, and then lost through the collapse of their business E. C. Porter. They were each given shares worth £662.14s and a few pence which equated to the valuation of the business at the time. We know the company was wound up on 4 March 1955, as set out in the synopsis of recent relatives, under Leonard Gosden (see page 640). However, during the period of the settlement and inheritance it was very likely that the business was in some difficulty at that time. This thought is supported by a letter to my father dated 11 September 1953 that stated the business was in a 'difficult financial position'. This was sent just a year after the concerns that Win and Frank had raised which I have outlined previously. The letter (Fig. 711) from Cyril and my father's accountants states

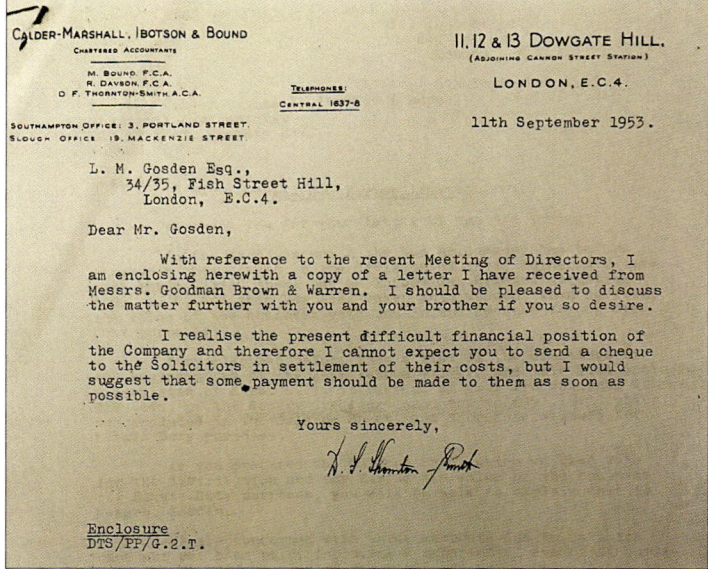

Figure 711

that this financial position was well understood, from which I can only assume that it wasn't a recent phenomenon and may have been accumulating over the previous months. Given this, it was very possible that both my father and his brother Cyril would have been aware that their half shares in the business which had been valued at £622/14/6, a year earlier for the inheritance, were highly unlikely to deliver this amount. As such, they may well have been concerned about agreeing to their sister's view that her share of the inheritance was inequitable. So, one just wonders why and how such a swift negotiation was accomplished, to resolve her concerns.

My suspicions are that given the financial position of the business it was very probable that both my father and Cyril stood to lose a substantial part of their inheritance, being the value of the business. The mystery for me was firstly, what had caused the financial demise of the business secondly, why was the business allowed to be wound up and liquidated on 22 February 1955, rather than either being sold as a going concern or even at a knock down price and thirdly, did either of them seek any recompense from their sister Win, as and when she sold her parents' property? Unfortunately, as all the beneficiaries have now passed away, we shall never know!

It was interesting to note that at the time of the winding up, my father was not employed at E. C. Porter because from December 1954 through to June 1955, he was working for Hogben and Perrett. I am not aware as to where Cyril was working when the company was wound up. Equally, I am unaware of any payment to my father or his brother relating to any residual proceeds from the winding up of the business.

Whilst I cannot say categorically that my suspicions are correct and, of course, they have been made with hindsight, which is a huge advantage, but even so it leaves some curious unanswered questions. However, it was obviously settled amicably as the letter (Fig. 710), not only confirms that the cash inheritance paid to Cyril was for £231/1/8 plus expenses, but also the transfer of their parents' property went to Win, which obviously concluded the matter. What I can say, is my father and Win held no lasting animosity between each other, as Win, Frank and their two children, Rosemary and Christine, all moved up to Norfolk to be near to us in Norwich. Indeed, one of my Uncle Frank's dying wishes before he died of cancer, on 20 April 1972, was that he wanted in his absence my dad to support Win and her children. A commitment that dad willingly undertook.

My take on all this is that 'all is well that ends well' which is precisely how this concluded.

Endnote

Thank you for reading this memoir on a family, of which I am very proud to have been a small part. I sincerely hope that you have enjoyed reading it as much as I have had the pleasure and enjoyment in researching and drafting its contents. Early in the summer of 2023 when I commenced its compilation, I had no idea that my research and planning would take the length of time it took to actually conclude, and that it would reveal such a vast number of forgotten and in some cases previously unidentified interesting facts that I have now been able to include. As a result, what I had envisaged being a relatively quick task has in fact taken considerably longer.

In my opinion, my life thus far has been well lived and thoroughly enjoyed. The saying goes that *'you reap what you sow'*. I must say that the seeds I was given in 1955 were some of the best, apart from perhaps the odd one or two questionable ones. But even these gave me renewed confidence and the opportunity to learn, grow and move forward again. Since joining the scouting movement right through to my 70th birthday and beyond, I have aspired to both support and lead work which would enrich and add value to the community around me, whether that was in the Scouts, Rotaract, Round Table, the Holt Society and lastly being a Magistrate. As such, I feel I have given back a little of the goodwill and support that has been granted to me and I hope that this has given pleasure to others, as it certainly has to me.

I have thoroughly enjoyed reminiscing over the past, and I am happy to say that now is not the end of my time on this earth. I am looking forward to many more happy years ahead. However though, it is unlikely that there will be a sequel to this book, for now anyway!

Here I have decided to include a quote from one of my and my father's favourite authors, A.G. Street. It was extracted from his 1929 book *A Year in my Life*, when talking about a conversation he had with a New Zealander in 1927, and it very much reflects my own views:

> *'It seems queer that the cleverer man becomes, the less respect he seems to pay to Mother Earth'.*

Oh, how true this saying was back then, and more worryingly how true it is today, almost 100 years later. If man continues at his current destructive pace, with war mongering between nations, the development of more destructive weapons, unrelenting damage to the climate and the wildlife which share our environment, I fear the outlook for future generations of my beloved family, and the society as a whole will not be as welcoming as they would wish. I just hope that this is not the reality.

As outlined in this memoir, my memories are mainly positive and have reflected a life that has brought me much happiness, love and contentment but also much concern for society in general. I sincerely hope that the succeeding world's inhabitants consider their approach, as to how they live and therefore what they leave to their future generations. My hope is that this will be a civilisation that is more content and thoughtful, than the one that I fear they will have probably inherited from my own generation.

Regrettably, I have to own up to not being well read, but I have often found a nugget of wisdom when I have become engrossed in literature. This particular one is credited to Rabbi Hyman Schachtel, in his 1954 book entitled *The Real Enjoyment of Living*, where he professes that:

'Happiness is not having what you want but wanting what you have'.

This is probably paraphrased from the words of St. Augustine (354 – 430 AD), the theologian, philosopher and Bishop of Hippo Regius. Wherever it came from or by whom it was written, it is a sentiment that I fully endorse and will continue to do so.

With that final thought, I wish you all much love, fulfilment and happiness and leave you with an actual image (Fig. 712) of two very happy teddy bears. Boston is on the left and belongs to Kate, Teddy on the right belongs to me. Both of which very much reflect the impression of two extremely happy and contented humans, they being myself and Kate.

REFLECTIONS UPON A FAMILY

Figure 712

Boston Sturgess and Teddy Gosden, both a little 'life worn' but together for ever and a day!

Acknowledgements

As so many authors will testify, especially laymen such as myself, writing a book is an extremely daunting task. In my case, I started with a vague course of action and a head full of ideas and quotes, but nevertheless I was still faced with a blank computer screen, onto which I had to translate and type all these thoughts into coherent words and sentences. This I found was my biggest challenge and whilst I hope it has indeed been achieved, I trust that for you it has been an entertaining and enlightening read, which is probably down to the enormous help that others over the past years have given me.

This work would not have been possible had it not been for the extraordinary patience and support of Kate my wife, along with our family both close and distant, coupled with the papers and memories of my mother and father. In addition, I am indebted to my work colleagues, school and social friends. Every one of you have helped to weave this tapestry, which has enabled me to write my own *Reflections upon a Family*.

I would like to offer here my sincere thanks to all members of my family that have quite possibly without their knowledge, guided me and provided me with information, documents and photographs which have all been so helpful in my quest to record this memoir.

I am indebted to both my late parents without whom I would not have been born, and this work would clearly not have been possible. Also, my sisters Judy Riddington and Sarah Wiltshire for their unknowing input over the years, through comments and conversations that I have been able to recall and weave into this text. Wider family members including my cousins Chris Pearce and Rosemary Tidaldi have also been of enormous help, along with Christopher Gosden who was able to provide historic documents pertaining to my paternal grandfather. Thanks also to the numerous other people, known and unknown, who have either consciously or unconsciously shaped my life over the years.

My motivation and guiding thoughts throughout this memoir have been to record my family history, in order that all those family members mentioned, and their current and future families can read this book at their leisure. For this I am totally indebted to our children Emily Jones, Angus Hutchison-Brown,

Oliver Gosden, Sophie Bedford and their respective spouses and children. I thank you all. I am also most grateful to my close family who, following the launch of the draft on 26 April 2025, kindly undertook a final overview of the text. Their comments and suggested corrections were much appreciated and where appropriate were included in this, the final version, which was distributed later in the Autumn of 2025.

As I have described, our life has had its ups and downs, as all families do, but we are still and will always be a loving and close family.

I must also offer my sincere thanks to some 'professionals' whose help, advice and expertise has been of great value. Ruth Lunn, Lead Editor of UK Book Publishing, and Leaf Arbuthnot, Assistant Editor of *The Week* and book reviewer for various newspapers and publications. Both have provided some helpful corrections and suggestions. Finally, to Kaarin Wall and her partner Kevin Parker at Wiz Graphics for the overall design and layout that has been so important. Given that many of my ancestors worked within the associated industries, it was paramount to me to have a 'professional' hardback book. So, my thanks also go to Kevin Ames and his employers at both Swallowtail Print and Page Bros (Norwich) Ltd, for the superb final product. I am sure that my forebears would approve of the quality and appearance of the final article. I certainly do!

Whilst writing this book I also found it enormously helpful to have feedback from a trusted source who was 'outside' the scenarios being written. This unenviable task was readily accepted by Polly Binns and her husband Phil Barrett. For friends to undertake such an arduous task is a sign of real friendship, and I acknowledge this and thank them both most sincerely for their support, diligence and politeness. I am pleased to say that we all still remain good friends!

I reserve my final thanks to my long suffering, very talented, much loved and adored wife, Kate.

'Kate, without your love, guidance, forbearance, support and enduring encouragement, this memoir would not have been at all possible. I cannot thank you enough. Your patience in editing my grammar, spelling and overall syntax has been extraordinary and so much appreciated by me. You have been an inspiration to me in so many ways, both throughout our marriage and before. Thank you, darling.'

Kate I just hope that now you have finished reading and amending this tome, you are as pleased as I am with the result of OUR combined work!

Thank you one and all.

APPENDICES

ADVERTISEMENT.

The former Impressions of a Series of Game, &c. having met with a distinguished reception, the present re-arranged form is submitted at the suggestion of several Gentlemen, Sportsmen, and Admirers of the Graphic Art; who have signified a desire of obtaining them in the form of a Book. To obtain impressions from an engraved button, however anxiously it might have been sought, has never succeeded till the present moment, and here it has been admirably performed. The Animals and Birds were drawn on the surface of the buttons by A. COOPER, Esq. R. A. and the engraving, in the most masterly manner, by Mr. JOHN SCOTT, whose celebrity in this line of art is sufficiently well known. The accompanying notices attached to each subject, are extracted from Bewick and Daniel.

October 1, 1821.

THOMAS GOSDEN.

Appendices

Keith, meaning: OUTDOORSY!

To conclude these memories, I would like to say that my approach to life has been beautifully summed up by, of all things, some words on a mug as shown in figure AP1. This was given to me years ago and purports to give the meaning of the name 'Keith'.

With a little 'personalisation' and minor changes by me, I believe that these words truly align with my thoughts and aspirations. So, with my apologies to the original author, whoever you are, I leave you to ponder our words.

> I'm a lover of forests,
> The sea and the land.
> Respect for nature
> Is one thing I demand.
>
> When my work is complete
> And I've finished my chores,
> I like to spend time
> In the spacious outdoors.
>
> With my love of Kate
> And family ambitions fulfilled,
> My life's work is nearly complete.
> So, I am more than thrilled.
>
> My visions are becoming true,
> My dreams taking shape.
> I am so proud of all the lives
> That I have helped to create.
>
> *Cheers!*

Figure AP1

REFLECTIONS UPON A FAMILY

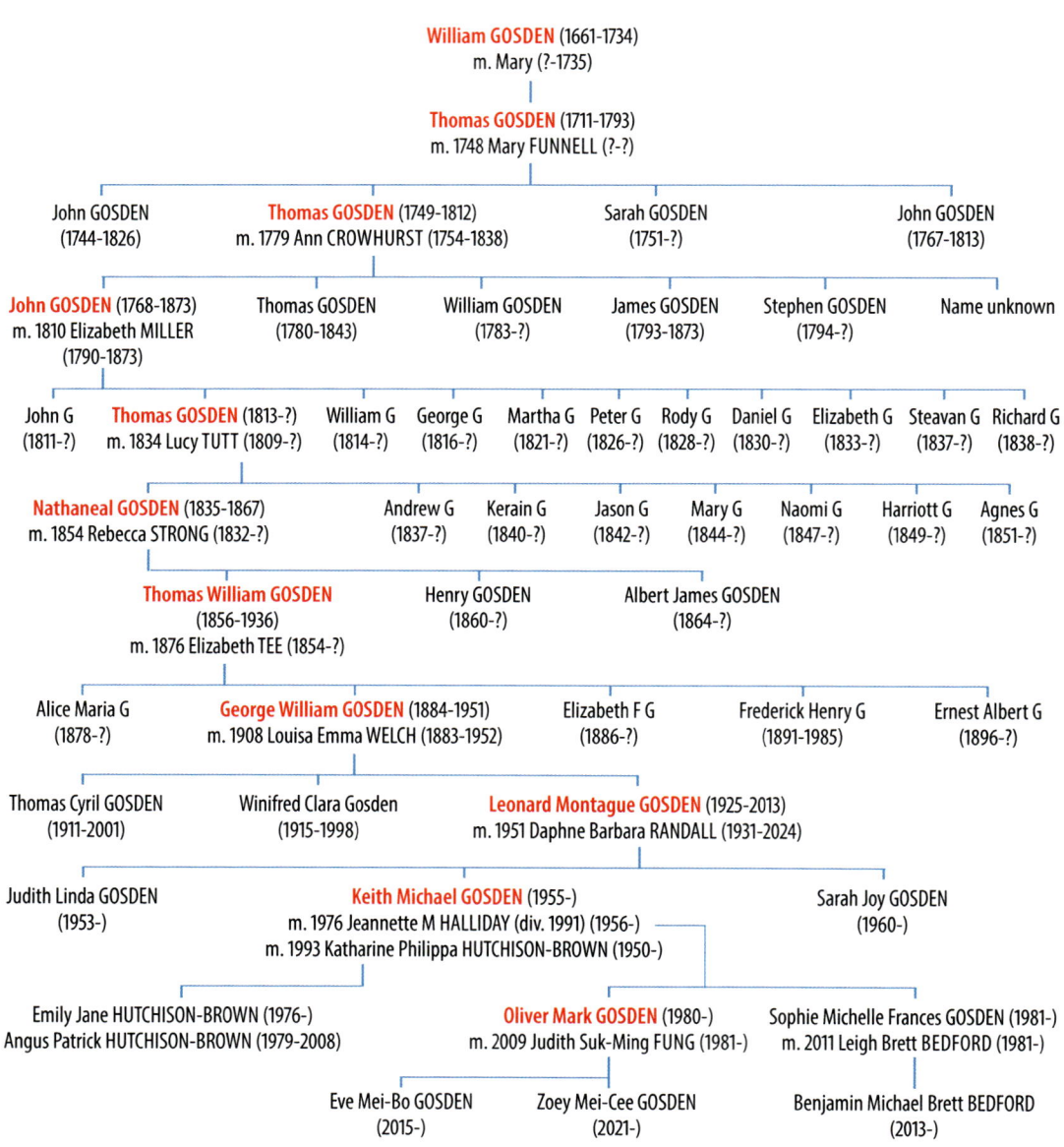

Figure AP2

Supplemental note regarding the Family Tree

Since the drafting of this Family Tree and just prior to its printing, my sister Sarah forwarded to me, the document (Fig. AP3) that she had received from the church wardens in Arlington, where a number of our ancestors are buried. Whilst this information does seem to support the family tree, I have not had time to validate and cross reference all the details. There is concern though, regarding Thomas Gosden's birth which was either in 1748 or 1749, and also doubt as to Martha's parentage (Figs. AP2 and AP3). However, I have included it for completeness.

Plot No: Sector H 107 – 110

Thomas Gosden
1748 – 24th December 1812
Ann Gosden
1761 – 24th February 1838

Thomas and his brother John (b.1744) were both born in Rye but moved to Arlington where they had family connections.

Thomas married Ann Crowhurst of Hellingly in 1779 and they had six children. Only their son James and his family are buried in Arlington.

James b. 1793 married Mary White of Hellingly in 1820 and they had four children, two of whom are buried in this churchyard.

Martha Anna born 1821 died 10th January 1822 age 3 months.

James Henry born 1822 died 22nd December 1834 age 12 years. James was their only son.

The Gosdens were a family of farmers and landowners with a long association with Arlington and the neighbouring villages. With the death of their son James, and their daughters having no children, this line of the Gosden family also ends.

| To the memory of **THOMAS GOSDEN** Late of this parish, Who died Dec: 24th 1812, Aged 63 years. Also of ANN his wife Who died Febry 24th 1838 Aged 84 years | To the memory of **JAMES GOSDEN** son of Thomas and Ann Gosden Who died at Hellingly In this county July 11: 1873 Aged 80 years Also of MARY his wife Who died May 5:1867 Aged 75 years | In memory of **JAMES HENRY** only son of James & Mary Gosden of Wilmington who died Dec 22nd 1834, Aged 12 years Also of **MARTHA ANNA** their daughter who died Jan 10th 1822 Aged 3 months |

Figure AP3

Synopsis of Recent Relatives

From the findings of both David Gosden and myself the first known occurrence of the surname GOSEDENN was believed to be in 1296 at Slaugham. A small Sussex village which in 2025 lies between Crawley and Brighton, and its notable landmarks are its Norman Church and the ruin of Slaugham Place which was built around 1579. This was the former home of Sir Walter Covert, part of which is now a fashionable wedding venue. This surname GOSEDENN was consequently modified over the years to GOSDEN and this current spelling was first identified in use during 1364. They are both listed in the Oxford Dictionary of English Surnames.

Slaugham is only a few miles from the next known family location which is the village of Arlington. Before the coming of the railways in the early 1800s there was little movement of the population, and it was usual to marry someone from a nearby village. Finding a partner further afield was rare, until public transport became available. It is therefore reasonable to assume that this is why the name is found mainly around Arlington until the mid-1800s. The earliest record is William Gosden as set out below.

The following synopsis supports the family tree (1661 – 2025) as can be seen in figure AP2. I hope it will add some additional narrative and understanding to the schematic tree. These details have been compiled by me, following some more detective work by myself and David Gosden.

William GOSDEN (1661 – 1734)

Little is known of his family other than they were involved in farming (yeomen), supplying beer and brick making.

The family were to develop further and move into other professions including printing and bookbinding as will be outlined further. As with William, little is known of the next three generations, but my research will continue.

Thomas GOSDEN (1711 – 1793)
Thomas GOSDEN (1749 – 1812) } No more definitive information is known
John GOSDEN (1768 – 1873)

As a consequence of this lack of clarity this next section has concentrated on the details of generations from the late eighteenth century onwards.

Thomas GOSDEN (1780 – 1843)

Thomas, my five times great-uncle, whilst I am not a direct descendant of him, he is included here as he was a bibliopole and a specialist in sport and angling. He was also an accomplished artist, a publisher, a seller of prints and books and a bookbinder. He compiled several albums of his watercolours portraying monuments and tombs and was an ardent book collector.

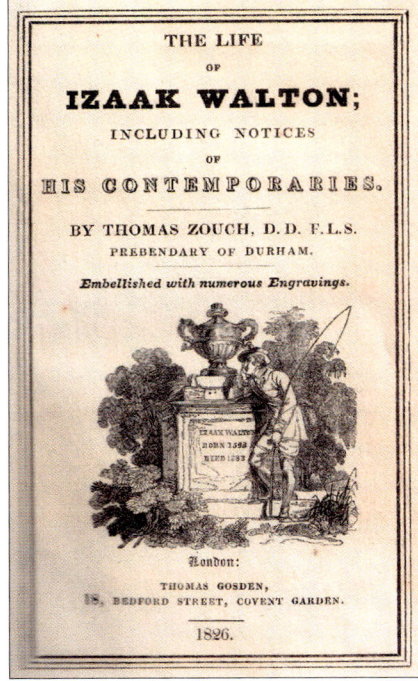
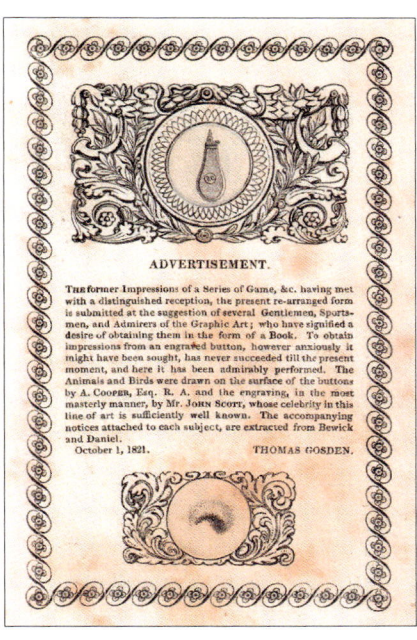

Figure AP4 (left)
Figure AP5 (above)

Trade cards and advertisements indicate he worked from 18 Bedford Street, Covent Garden where he had his 'Sportsman's Repository', as shown on the book plate (Fig. AP4), and at various times he was based at 107 St. Martin's Lane, Charing Cross. In 1821, learning that Bonaparte had engraved silver buttons on his sporting jacket, he met up with his friend Mr Scott who offered to engrave a set for him if Thomas first supplied the buttons. Thomas then produced a book cover using the impressions of Scott's work. Additional paper copies of these engravings were bound either on large paper which cost seven shillings or on small paper for five shillings. The advertisement (Fig. AP5) is to be found in the small paper edition, a copy of which is in my collection. In Jacksons Oxford Journal, Thomas was found to have been declared bankrupt in June 1826. He died suddenly in 1843.

Thomas GOSDEN (1813 – ?)

Thomas was born in Arlington in 1813 and had eight children, the eldest of whom was Nathaneal (or Nathaniel which is a modern spelling). Little more is known to me, of Thomas's life.

Nathaneal GOSDEN (1835 – 1867)

Nathaneal is recorded as being a 'carman' or 'carter', someone who delivered goods by cart and horse. He married Rebecca Strong from St. Pancras, Middlesex in 1854, and at some point they lived in Southwark, Surrey. After Nathaneal's death and following the boundary changes of 1889, Southwark was to become part of London. He died young, possibly of 'town' disease (Townes-Brocks syndrome, a rare genetic disease). How Nathaneal and Rebecca met is unknown and as to why and how they ended up in Southwark, at present there are no known details.

Thomas William GOSDEN (1856 – 1936)

Thomas William was Nathaneal's first son. In 1876 he married Elizabeth Tee, who was the daughter of the owner of the firm in which he worked. This was called Tee and Whiting Stationers, which were possibly printers as well. Thomas and Elizabeth lived at 53 Trinity Street, Newington and following on from Thomas (1780 – 1843) he continued the family involvement in the printing and publishing industry. When his daughter Alice was 22, it is understood that she was working in her father's business as a vellum sewer. At the time, vellum was produced from calfskin rather than the current cotton and wood pulp and as it was an expensive product it required careful and expert handling. Thomas died on 11 November 1936 and left an estate of £1,329 /14s /3d, which was a considerable sum of money.

George William GOSDEN (15.04.1884 – 20.02.1951)

George William (Fig. AP6) was the first son of Thomas William. He married Louisa Emma Welch, the daughter of the caretaker at the local church school. Their marriage in 1909 was recorded in the St. Saviour District of Southwark. His occupation was documented in 1911 as being a 'Foreman, Book Finisher'.

During the First World War he served in the Royal Flying Corps which was the forerunner of the RAF. He was a member of the 60 Squadron, and his skills in civilian life of working with leather and canvas were clearly an asset during the war, as he became a rigger, and it is believed a mechanic as well. When the

Figure AP6

aeroplanes returned after the raids and aerial 'dog fights', the canvas which covered the aeroplane would require much attention, and it was the riggers job to look after and repair this canvas rigging.

In 1917 George was based in Arras, France with the 60 Squadron, and for some time he maintained Billy Bishop's aircraft. For his extraordinary wartime exploits, Bishop was awarded a VC, CB, DSO + Bar, MC, DFC, ED and the Victoria Cross. He was promoted in 1939 to Air Marshal, shortly after the start of WWII and died in September 1956. There were other pilots flying from French airfields who were also awarded various gallantry medals, but none as distinguished as the Canadian born Willian Avery Bishop, colloquially known as 'Billy'.

Having survived WWI, George returned to his trade as a bookbinder and gold leaf lettering expert, in his own business E. C. Porter. His business card is seen in (Fig. AP7).

Regrettably, his brother-in-law, Henry Thomas Welch, died 1 October 1916, as a result of his injuries sustained at the Battle of the Somme.

Just before my grandfather died, one of his last requests made to my mother and father was that they had an extra tier made for their wedding cake, in order that he could have it all to himself.

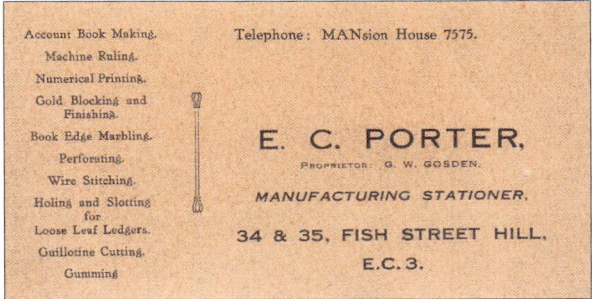

Figure AP7

Sadly, he died suddenly whilst in Farnborough Hospital just four months prior to their wedding on 20 February 1951. His death certificate records the cause of his demise as being coronary thrombosis, femoral artery thrombosis and arteriosclerosis (generalised). He was aged just 66. The certificate also describes him as a Master Book-binder, which in 1951 was a significant step up from being a Foreman Book Finisher in 1911.

His wife Emma (born 27 June 1883) died the following year from what the family believed to be a 'broken heart'.

Leonard Montague GOSDEN (6.10.1925 – 14.04.2013)

Leonard was the third child of George William, the first being Thomas Cyril (known as Cyril) and the second was Winifred Clara. He was born at home, 90 Ederline Avenue, Norbury, Kent and the family then moved to 13 Oakhill Road, Orpington. As a child he attended the local school, where he sat next to Ron Sewell, who was to be a lifelong friend and best man at his wedding.

On 10 February 1943, Leonard enlisted for WWII and joined the Royal Armoured Corps and in Bovington he was trained as a Sherman Tank driver and saw active service in Northern Europe and Italy (Fig. AP8 and AP9). He served with the 4th/7th Dragoon Guards from 10 November 1943 to 27 July 1945, followed by 4th Royal Tank Regiment from 28 June 1945 to 28 September 1947. After which on 29 September he was discharged and transferred to the reserves. His final military service was to undertake training in Thetford from 14 July 1951 through to 28 July. But post training there is no further military service recorded. Len, as he was known was fully discharged on 10 February 1954.

Prior to the war and following being demobilised, he had worked as a book binding apprentice in his father's business, E. C. Porter, at 34 and 35 Fish Street Hill, EC3. His profession is confirmed on his army application papers. In the early 1950s he was still at E. C. Porter, as there is a letter dated 26 February 1951 addressed to L. Gosden Esq. from Dixon and Co, offering him sincere

Figure AP8

Figure AP9

condolences on the death of his father, and this was sent to Messrs E. C. Porter, 34 and 35 Fish Street Hill.

A further letter dated 2 March 1952 from Super Write Services Ltd was sent to Mr Gosden (which could have been either my dad or his brother Cyril) offering condolences on the death of their mother. It is assumed that Len was working for E. C. Porter in 1952 as this particular letter was amongst his papers.

It was around that time that E. C. Porter became a limited company. Then, for whatever reason, it sadly subsequently ceased trading, and this was recorded in the London Gazette on 4 March 1955 (Fig. AP10).

Len was employed by Hogben and Perrett, certainly from December 1954 through to 10 June 1955. A third party 'reference letter' confirms that he was made redundant on 10 June of that year. However, between June 1955 to April 1958 his employment is unclear.

Figure AP10

Dad, as he now was to me, joined on 23 April 1958 a company called The Solicitors' Law Stationery Society Ltd (trading as Oyez Stationery). This is confirmed by a letter dated 21 April of the same year. Then, following his promotion to a Sales Representative for the Eastern Area, our family moved to Norfolk in 1960. Having reached the position of Field Sales Manager (Northern) Dad was made redundant by Robert Maxwell, who had purchased Oyez, and his employment ceased in 1973. At the time the circumstances of his leaving were never recounted to me and I only found this out many years later.

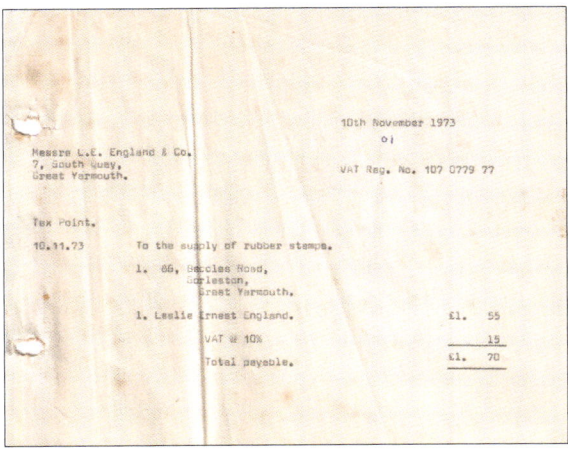

Figure AP11

In October 1973 he started L. M. Gosden Management Services Ltd. which traded very successfully for a number of years. The first invoice is dated 10 November 1973 (Fig. AP11). In conjunction with the Head Office in Norwich he also opened branches in Northampton and Colchester. As I have outlined in this memoir, the company was eventually wound up and sold to Shaw and Sons in 1992 and having previously reduced his hours, Dad fully retired at this point.

He was a devout Christian, a Gideon, a sailor of dinghy boats, a keen amateur watercolour painter and, with my mother, a voluntary prison visitor. Later in retirement he was to live with dementia and his last months were spent in a care home in Swaffham. With his family by his side, he died peacefully on 14 April 2013.

Keith Michael GOSDEN JP DMS (26.02.1955 –)

See the contents of this memoir.

Oliver Mark GOSDEN (3.04.1980 –)

Oliver (AP12) was born in Hingham, Norfolk, on his paternal grandmother's 49th birthday. He was educated at Cringleford School and Taverham High School. Further details of his life, of course, can be found within the text of this memoir.

On 15 May 2020 he set up his own business, 'Teachers Together' which in 2025 is a private Limited Company. Jude his wife became a director on 18 March 2022 and at the time of writing there is a team of six people. The business is trading profitably, it has a very positive reputation, and they have recently moved to larger offices in Welwyn Garden City.

Figure AP12